South Carolina
Master Gardener Training Manual

South Carolina Master Gardener Training Manual

Edited by Terasa Lott & Cory Tanner

©2025 Clemson University

ISBN 978-1-63804-168-9
LCCN 2025942677

Published by Clemson Extension Publishing an imprint of Clemson University Press
Interior design by Andrea Rieder
Cover design by Brittany Becker
Cover images provided by Barbara Smith, Cory Tanner, and Zachary Snipes
Original illustrations by Emily Martin, Lindsay Scott, and Abby Rehard

For ordering information, please visit our website www.clemson.edu/press.

Contents

Introduction	1
Chapter 1. Soils and Plant Nutrition	3
Chapter 2. Understanding Plants	15
Chapter 3. Plant Propagation	55
Chapter 4. Growing Healthy Lawns	77
Chapter 5. Trees and Shrubs	139
Chapter 6. Herbaceous Plants	179
Chapter 7. Home Vegetable and Herb Gardening	195
Chapter 8. Fruit Gardening	231
Chapter 9. Watering Plants and Landscapes	301
Chapter 10. Understanding Insects	329
Chapter 11. Plant Diseases and Disorders	347
Chapter 12. Dealing with Weeds	365
Chapter 13. Pest Management	383
Chapter 14. Diagnosing and Managing Plant Problems	403
Glossary	451

Introduction

Gardening can be one of the most challenging endeavors—and one of the most rewarding. This handbook provides a comprehensive overview of horticulture-related topics, from soils and plant nutrition to plant pathology and everything in between. Although this handbook is designed as a text for the South Carolina Master Gardener Program, anyone who wishes to grow plants or improve their garden may find value in its contents.

HISTORY OF THE MASTER GARDENER PROGRAM

2023 marked the 50th anniversary of the Master Gardener Program. Faced with an overwhelming public demand for home gardening information, area Extension Agents David Gibby and Bill Sheer proposed a train-the-trainer model in which experts would train volunteers in the science of gardening; in turn, these volunteers would share that information with the public. Although initially met with skepticism from the administration at Washington State Extension, the concept was embraced by the public. Approximately 200 people participated in the first Master Gardener training classes offered in King and Pierce counties in 1973.

Today, there are Master Gardener programs in most U.S. states and the District of Columbia. These programs are primarily carried out by Cooperative Extension Services based in various land-grant institutions. Massachusetts and some Canadian provinces, however, are home to affiliate programs. These programs are not run through Extension but do participate in the bi-annual International Master Gardener Conference (IMGC). According to the 2020 National Extension Master Gardener Survey, at least 84,700 Extension Master Gardener volunteers contributed 3.1 million hours of service valued at 76.4 million dollars.

The South Carolina Master Gardener Program trains, selects, and utilizes knowledgeable volunteers to facilitate the work of the local Consumer Horticulture Agents by delivering research-based information. First offered in Charleston County in 1981, it is now offered in more than half of the state's 46 counties. South Carolina Master Gardeners are a part of Clemson Cooperative Extension.

Becoming a South Carolina Master Gardener is a two-part process that begins with completion of the Master Gardener Volunteer Training Class. During this class, participants receive at least 40 hours of intensive, practical horticultural training. After the instructional requirements are met, participants complete 40 hours of educational service through various avenues such as assisting clients at an Extension office, speaking to garden clubs or civic groups, and conducting Ask A Master Gardener clinics. The title South Carolina Master Gardener is awarded upon completion of both the instructional and service components. Following initial certification, Master Gardeners meet annual requirements of 20 hours of volunteer work in their communities and 10 hours of continuing education.

From July 1, 2022, through June 30, 2023, South Carolina Master Gardeners helped fulfill Clemson Cooperative Extension's mission by reaching 184,210 adults and 24,256 youth during 66,219 hours of volunteer service. Based on a 230-day work year (a total of 1725 hours) per Extension Agent, the hours of service provided by Master Gardeners are equivalent to 38.4 full-time Extension Agents. Using the April 2023 Independent Sector Value of $31.80, this service has a value of $2,105,764.20

Welcome to the South Carolina Master Gardener Program. We hope your training provides you with knowledge, skills, and experience that help you provide accurate gardening advice and solutions.

Chapter 1
Soils and Plant Nutrition

Authors: Joey Williamson, Ph.D. and Robert F. Polomski, Ph.D.

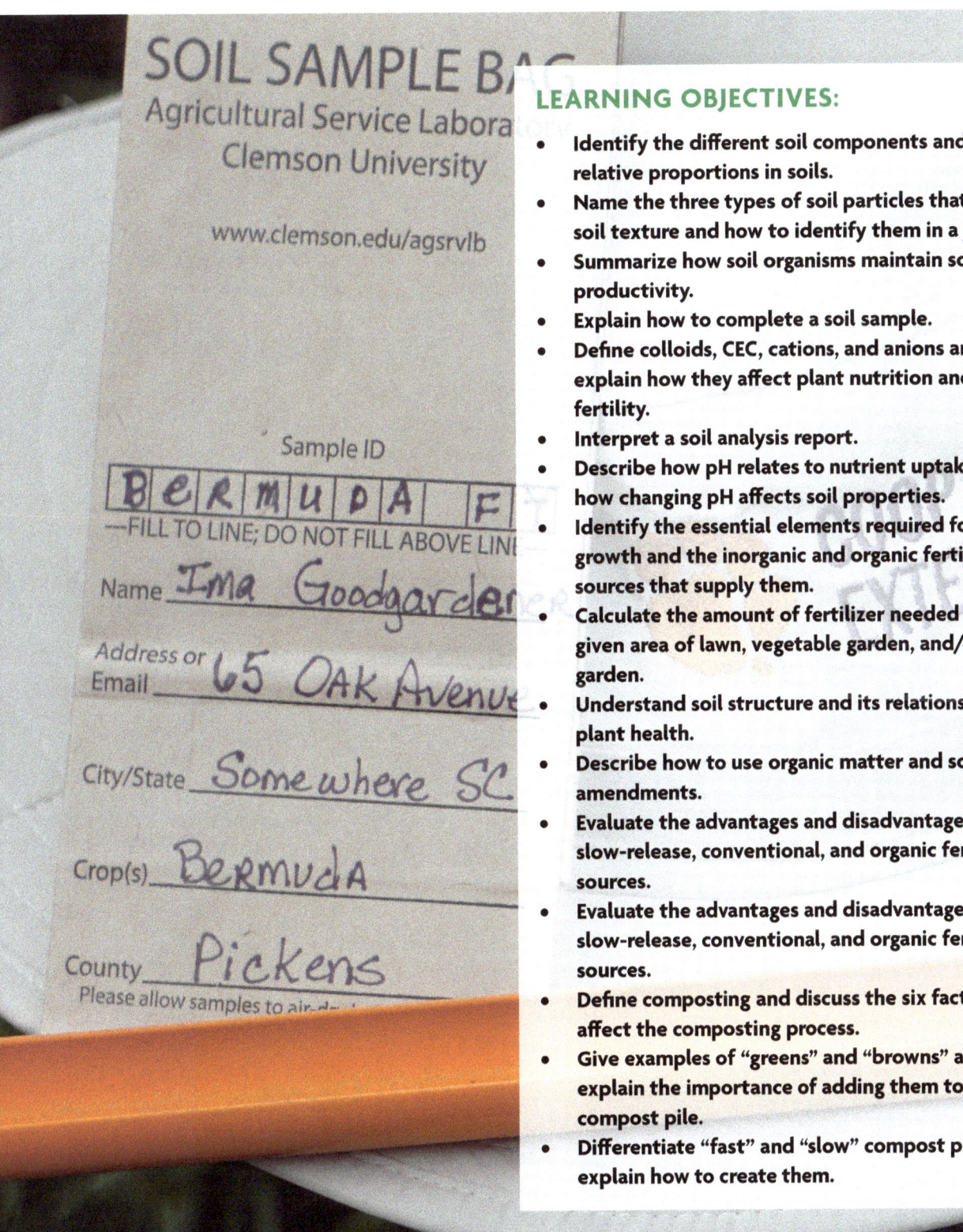

LEARNING OBJECTIVES:

- Identify the different soil components and their relative proportions in soils.
- Name the three types of soil particles that affect soil texture and how to identify them in a jar test.
- Summarize how soil organisms maintain soil productivity.
- Explain how to complete a soil sample.
- Define colloids, CEC, cations, and anions and explain how they affect plant nutrition and soil fertility.
- Interpret a soil analysis report.
- Describe how pH relates to nutrient uptake and how changing pH affects soil properties.
- Identify the essential elements required for plant growth and the inorganic and organic fertilizer sources that supply them.
- Calculate the amount of fertilizer needed for a given area of lawn, vegetable garden, and/or flower garden.
- Understand soil structure and its relationship to plant health.
- Describe how to use organic matter and soil amendments.
- Evaluate the advantages and disadvantages of slow-release, conventional, and organic fertilizer sources.
- Evaluate the advantages and disadvantages of slow-release, conventional, and organic fertilizer sources.
- Define composting and discuss the six factors that affect the composting process.
- Give examples of "greens" and "browns" and explain the importance of adding them to a compost pile.
- Differentiate "fast" and "slow" compost piles and explain how to create them.

INTRODUCTION

Soil is the foundation of any garden or landscape. In fact, soil is one of the three primary environmental factors involved in plant growth; the other two are sunlight (both heat and light) and air (carbon dioxide and oxygen). This chapter will introduce you to the wonders and complexity of soil and, hopefully, give you an appreciation for the many dynamic processes that occur right beneath our feet.

FIGURE 1.1 The ideal soil texture is a loamy soil that is a balanced mixture of sand, silt, and clay particles.
Image Credit: Andrew Jeffers, Clemson University

SOIL COMPONENTS

Some folks pick up a handful of soil and call it "dirt"—a term that over-simplifies its importance and complexity. Examine soil closely and you'll find that it's comprised of minerals from weathered rocks, air, water, and decaying organic matter. A healthy soil harbors a treasure trove of living organisms, such as earthworms, fungi, and bacteria. These various components of soil supply our plants with minerals and nutrients, air, moisture, and support. Soil in different places may have more or less of any component, so soil can be fertile and productive or inhospitable for plant growth.

The ideal soil for plant growth is made up of near-equal parts solid materials and pore spaces (by volume). In this ideal soil, the solid material is about 45% mineral matter and 5% organic matter; half of the pore space is filled with water and the other half with air.

The amount of pore spaces occupied by air and water changes from time to time and from place to place. As water moves in the soil, it pushes out air as it fills the pores. When water drains from the soil, evaporates, or is absorbed by plant roots, air fills these empty spaces.

Physical and Chemical Properties

A soil's physical and chemical properties affect plant growth and soil management. Some important physical and chemical properties of soil are mineral content, texture, structure, porosity, cation exchange capacity, and organic matter content.

Minerals

Soils consist of particles of varying sizes and shapes. There are three categories of soil based on the size of the particles: sand, silt, and clay (Figure 1.1). Sand grains can be seen with the naked eye, silt can only be seen with a 10x magnifying hand lens, and clay particles can only be seen with an electron microscope.

Texture

The relative proportions of sand, silt, and clay minerals in soil is called soil texture. It is one of the most important physical properties for plant growth. Soil texture determines tilth—the physical condition of soil and its nutrient- and water-holding capacities (Figure 1.2).

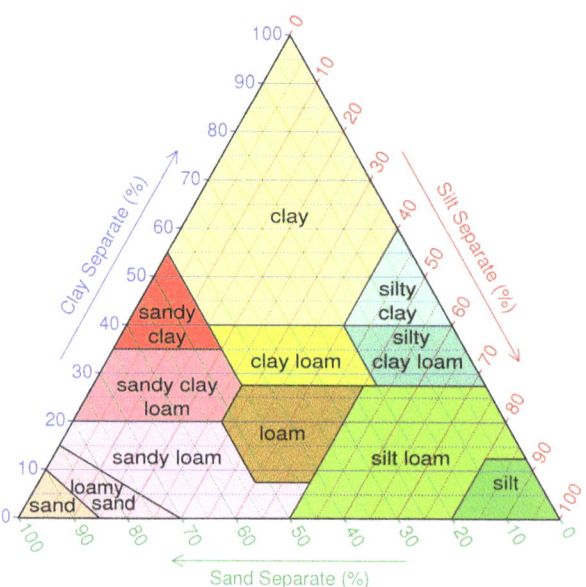

FIGURE 1.2 Soil textural triangle
Image Credit: cmglee, Mikenorton, United States Department of Agriculture, CC BY-SA 4.0, via Wikimedia Commons

Structure

In silt and clay soils, the particles do not occur individually; instead, they clump together. The arrangement and organization of these clumps, or aggregates, is referred to as soil structure. A soil with good structure has good water infiltration and drainage and allows for the movement of air and water.

The easiest way to improve soil structure is to regularly add organic matter, which binds the soil particles together. Coarse-textured sandy soils greatly benefit from the addition of organic matter that aids in increasing water retention and improving fertility.

To avoid damaging soil structure, never dig or cultivate when the soil is too wet or too dry. When soil sticks to a shovel, the soil is too wet. Postpone digging until it dries (Figure 1.3).

FIGURE 1.3 If soil sticks to a shovel, the soil is too wet to be worked.
Image Credit: Robert Polomski, Clemson University

Fertility and Cation Exchange Capacity

Nutrients or minerals occur in the soil as elements or groups of elements with electrical charges, called ions. Ions with negative charges, such as nitrate (NO_3^-) and sulfate (SO_4^{2-}), are called anions. Positively charged ions, such as potassium (K^+) and magnesium (Mg^{+2}) are called cations. Like tiny magnets attracted to metal, ions are attracted to the outside of soil particles. Clay particles have negative charges that attract positively charged cations. These cations are then adsorbed onto the outer surface layer of the clay particles. The clay minerals eventually release or exchange the cations into soil water, making them available for uptake by plant roots. These hold-and-release events happen as the soil maintains a chemical balance between the ions clinging onto soil surfaces and the ones present in the water-containing soil pores. Since the negatively charged clay particles repel anions such as nitrate-nitrogen (NO_3^-), they move freely with water. Because of this, nitrate-nitrogen stays in the soil solution and can either be absorbed by plant roots or leached from the soil (Figure 1.4).

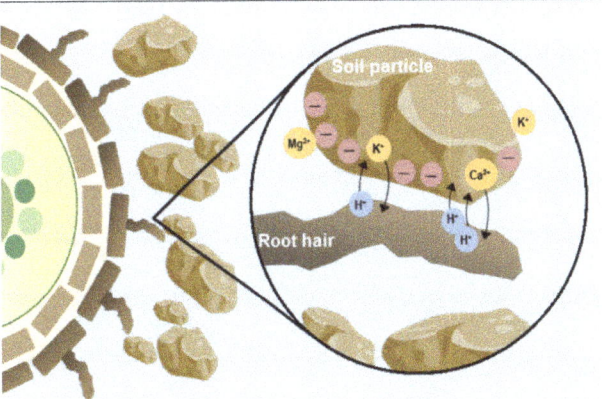

FIGURE 1.4 Negatively charged clay particles behave like magnets. Positively charged ions (cations) in the soil solution are attracted to the negatively charged clay particle. Negatively charged ions (anions) are repelled and move with water.
Image Credit: LSU AgCenter: Cation Exchange Capacity

Soil scientists determine the cation exchange capacity (CEC) of a soil, which measures the amount or quantity of cations held in the soil, as a measure of fertility or productivity. These cations move between clay minerals and the soil solution and between the soil solution and plant roots. The CEC depends on the amounts and kinds of clay and organic matter present. Clay and humus hold more exchangeable cations than a soil with a low clay content and little organic matter.

The highly weathered soils of the southern United States have low levels of organic matter and therefore a very low CEC. Sandy soils inherently have a low CEC; they retain only small quantities of cations, so they have low fertility levels. Since the CEC of organic matter far exceed the CEC of clay minerals, organic matter can be added to raise the overall CEC of a soil.

Organic Matter

The mineral component of soil comes from rocks; the organic component comes from living organisms. There are two types of organic matter in soil: humus, a stable material that resists further rapid decay; and organic materials, which range from decomposing plant and animal material to relatively stable compost.

Composting is the biological decomposition of organic materials—such as leaves, grass, manure, and food wastes—into a dark, crumbly form of organic matter that bears no resemblance to the organic source. Composting is the same process that decays leaves and other organic remains in nature, except that composting controls the conditions so the materials decompose faster (Figure 1.5).

FIGURE 1.5 Composting accelerates the natural decomposition process by managing the organic materials, volume, aeration, moisture, surface area/particle size, and the temperatures reached during the composting process
Image Credit: Robert Polomski, Clemson University

Organic matter offers a variety of benefits to soil:

- The improvement of physical structure or tilth;
- Improved drainage in clay soils due to particles of organic matter separating the clay particles to improve air and water movement in the soil, allowing for deeper and more extensive root development;
- Improved fertility and water retention in coarse-textured sandy soils that otherwise hold little water; and
- The release of nutrients to plants as beneficial microorganisms (bacteria and fungi) break down the organic matter, convert it to humus, and release minerals.

Some soils naturally contain very little organic matter. In our region, most soils are low in organic soil matter because warm temperatures and high rainfall speed up decomposition. The annual application of organic matter is necessary in maintaining reasonable levels in garden soils. Commonly available sources of organic matter include compost, manures, leaf mold, rotten saw dust, and cover crops. Microorganisms decompose organic matter and use the resulting material as a carbon and energy source. As this occurs, they release nutrients for absorption by plant roots.

Sand is often touted as the perfect fix for improving drainage in clay soils. You can improve drainage in 8-inch-deep clay soil by removing 6 inches of clay and replacing it with 6 inches of sand; otherwise, the soil will be better suited for making bricks than growing plants.

Adding Organic Matter with Compost. Compost is used as an organic soil amendment to improve physical, chemical, and biological properties of soil. Adding compost will increase the moisture-holding capacity of sandy soils, thereby reducing drought damage to plants. When added to heavy clay soils, compost improves drainage and aeration and reduces waterlogging damage to plants. Compost increases the ability of the soil to hold and release essential nutrients and promotes the activity of earthworms and beneficial microorganisms. Other benefits of compost include improved seedling emergence and water infiltration via reduced soil crusting.

Yearly additions of compost create a desirable soil structure, making the soil much easier to work. To improve a soil's physical properties, you can add and incorporate 1-2 inches of well-decomposed compost in the top 6-8 inches of soil. Sandy soils require less compost than clay soils, so adjust accordingly.

To a limited extent, compost is a source of nutrients. However, the release of nutrients from compost is slow, and the nutrient content is too low to supply all the nutrients necessary for plant growth. Differences in nutrient content are probably caused by several factors, including the age of the compost, amount of water added, plant species, and amount of soil mixed into the pile during turning.

Adding Organic Matter with Cover Crops. A cover crop is a crop planted in a garden to protect the soil from erosion and improve soil quality. Cover crops can be divided into two groups: legumes and non-legumes. Legumes are associated with "nitrogen-fixing" bacteria. These rhizobia bacteria reside in the plants' roots and capture, or "fix", nitrogen from the air, making this nitrogen available to the legume. Non-legume cover crops provide less nitrogen but more organic matter.

Both legume and non-legume cover crops can be categorized as either warm- or cool-season species. Cool-season legumes include clovers, Austrian winter peas, and vetch. Warm-season legumes include all the southern peas and the common beans. Cool-season non-legumes include the cereals oats, wheat, rye, and barley. Warm-season non-legumes include buckwheat, Sudan grass, and Sudan-sorghum hybrids.

When a cover crop is tilled into the soil, the additional organic matter improves soil structure, increases water- and nutrient-holding capacity, and supplies nutrients to future crops. The type of cover crop and the length of time it grows determines how much organic matter and nutrients will be returned to the soil. A legume may provide more nitrogen but less total organic matter than a vigorously growing non-legume, such as a grain crop.

Regular use of cover crops over a period of years slowly raises the organic matter content of the soil, increasing the activity of soil organisms such as earthworms, beneficial bacteria, and fungi. As these organisms break down the organic materials, they help improve soil structure and tilth, which makes the soil a more favorable place for root development.

For more information on Cover Crops in SC, see HGIC 1252.

SOIL TESTING

Ideally, soil testing should take place before fertilization to determine the soil pH and nutrient levels. It can be done at any time of year, but only on soil that has not recently had fertilizer or lime applied. Soil testing helps customize fertilizer and lime application to suit the needs of specific plants. It also helps prevent over-fertilization, which can cause excessive vegetative growth, delayed maturity, and salt burn, or under-fertilization, which can cause nutrient deficiencies. In addition, testing the soil in advance can protect against environmental hazards like leaching and runoff, which can result from excessive fertilizer application.

FIGURE 1.7 Core samples should be mixed thoroughly before transferring to a soil bag.
Image Credit: Joey Williamson, Clemson Univeristy

For an accurate soil test, collect a representative sample. This means collecting at least 8-10 separate cores and combining them into one composite sample. The samples should include soil from the surface to a depth of 4-6 inches in all areas except for lawns (where cores should be taken from a depth of 2-4 inches). You can use a garden trowel, spade, shovel, or soil probe to collect samples (Figure 1.6). Place the samples in a clean plastic bucket and mix them thoroughly (Figure 1.7). Since individual lawns, gardens, and landscape beds have likely been fertilized and limed differently in the past, they should be submitted separately rather than combined into a single sample. Each composite sample must include a minimum of 2 cups of soil. You can bring these samples to your county Extension office in a clean jar or zip-lock bag and then transfer them to a soil sample bag (Figure 1.8).

Soil samples are sent to Clemson's Agricultural Service Lab for analysis. The results will be mailed or emailed along with recommendations for lime and fertilizer (per 1000 square feet). For more information on soil sampling, see HGIC 1652.

FIGURE 1.6 Lawn, garden, and landscape bed samples may be dug with a trowel.
Image Credit: Joey Williamson, Clemson University

FIGURE 1.8 Be sure to fill only to the fill line.
Image Credit: Joey Williamson, Clemson University

The major impact of extreme pH levels on plant growth relates to the availability of plant nutrients and the soil concentration of plant-toxic minerals (Figure 1.9). In highly acid soils (pH<5.5), aluminum and manganese become highly available at toxic levels. At low pH levels, nitrogen, phosphorus, potassium, calcium, and magnesium become unavailable; at high pH values (pH≥7), phosphorus, iron, copper, zinc, boron, and manganese become less available.

Adding more fertilizer to soil with a particularly low or high pH will not help. Soil requires the addition of ground agricultural limestone to raise pH or elemental sulfur or aluminum sulfate to lower pH. Soil test results provide the information needed to adjust pH for the crop(s) in question.

pH

pH refers to the relative acidity or alkalinity (basicity) of a substance. The pH scale contains 14 divisions, known as pH units. pH values range from 0 to 14; a value of 7 is neutral. Values below 7 are acidic, and values above 7 are alkaline.

The pH of soil is one of several environmental conditions that affect plant growth. A near neutral or slightly acidic soil with a pH between 6 and 7 is considered ideal for most plants. However, some plants prefer acidic conditions. Some plants, such as Irish potatoes, are intentionally grown at a pH of 5-5.5 to prevent damage from potato scab disease. This disease becomes more severe when the pH levels increase.

Plant Nutrients

Plants need 17 mineral elements (nutrients) for their growth and development. Plants obtain the three most abundant elements—carbon, hydrogen, and oxygen—from water and the air. The other 14 elements come from the soil.

The 14 elements are divided into three groups. The first group, often referred to as primary nutrients, is composed of nitrogen, phosphorus, and potassium. The second group contains sulfur, calcium, and magnesium. Collectively, the primary and secondary nutrients are known as macronutrients. The third group, known as micronutrients, because they are needed only in small amounts, is composed of iron, copper, manganese, molybdenum, zinc, boron, chlorine, and nickel. All 17 nutrients are important, because a deficiency or excess of one or more nutrients affects plant growth and development.

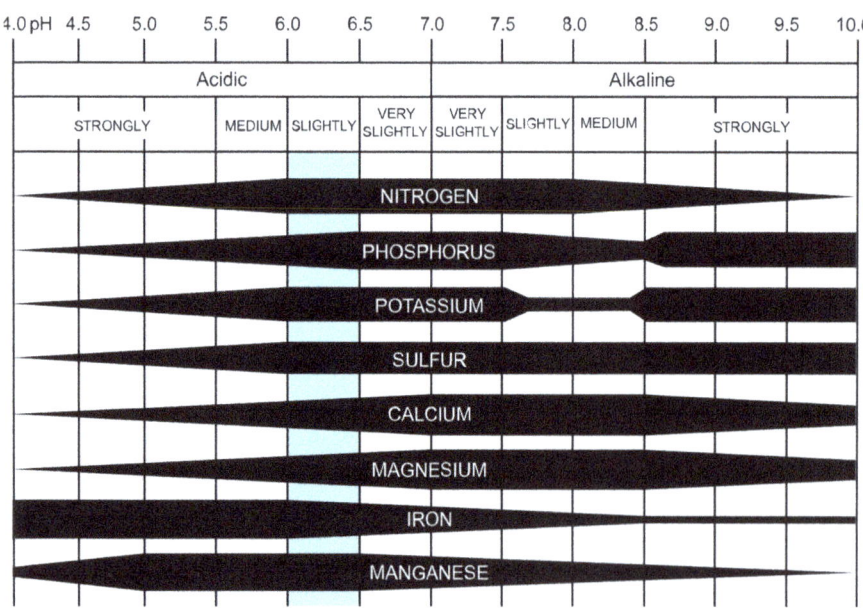

Figure 1.9 Effect of soil pH on nutrient availability
Image Credit: CoolKoon [CC BY 4.0 (https://creativecommons.org/licenses/by/4.0)]

TABLE 1.1 ESSENTIAL NUTRIENTS FOR PLANT GROWTH

MACRONUTRIENTS

Nutrient	Function	Deficiency Symptoms	Toxicity Symptoms	Comments
Nitrogen (N)	• Responsible for rapid foliage growth and green color • Easily leaches from soil • Mobile in plant, moving to new growth	• Reduced growth • Light-green to yellow foliage (chlorosis) • Reds and purples may intensify in some plants • Reduced lateral breaks • Symptoms appear first on older growth	• Succulent growth; leaves are dark green, thick, and brittle • Poor fruit set • Excess ammonia can induce calcium deficiency	• High N under low light can cause leaf curl • Uptake inhibited by high P levels
Phosphorus (P)	• Promotes root formation and growth • Affects quality of seed, fruit, and flower production • Increases disease resistance • Does not leach from soil readily • Mobile in plant, moving to new growth	• Reduced growth • Leaves dark green; purple or red color in older leaves, especially on the underside along veins • Leaf shape may be distorted • Thin stems • Limited root growth	• Appears as micronutrient deficiency of Zn, Fe, or Co	• Rapidly fixed on soil particles • When applied under acid conditions, fixes with Fe, Mn, and Al • High P interferes with absorption of N and micronutrients • Used in relatively small amounts compared to N and K • Availability is lowest in cold soils
Potassium (K)	• Helps plants overcome drought stress • Improves winter hardiness • Increases disease resistance • Improves rigidity of stalks • Leaches from soil • Mobile in plant	• Reduced growth • Shortened internodes • Chlorotic/burned margins of older leaves • Necrotic (dead) spots on older leaves • Reduction of lateral breaks and tendency to wilt readily • Poorly developed root systems • Weak stalks	• Causes N deficiency and may affect the uptake of other nutrients	• High N/low K favors vegetative growth • Low N/high K promotes reproductive growth (flower, fruit) • Excess calcium impedes uptake of K

continued

MACRONUTRIENTS CONTINUED

Nutrient	Function	Deficiency Symptoms	Toxicity Symptoms	Comments
Magnesium (Mg)	• Leaches from sandy soil • Mobile in plant	• Reduced growth • Yellowish, bronze, or reddish color of older leaves, while veins stay green • Leaf margins may curl upward or downward	• Interferes with Ca uptake • Small necrotic spots on older leaves • Smaller veins in older leaves amy turn brown • In advanced stage, young leaves may be spotted	• Commonly deficient in foliage plants because it is leached and not replaced • Epsom salt at a rate of 1 tsp/gal may be used two times a year • Can be absorbed by leaves if sprayed in a weak solution • Dolomitic lime can be applied in outdoor situations to treat a deficiency
Calcium (Ca)	• Moderately leachable • Limited mobility in plant • Essential for growth of shoot and root tips	• Inhibition of bud growth • Roots turn black and rot • Young leaves scalloped and abnormally green • Leaf tips may stick together • Cupping of mature leaves • Blossom end rot of many fruits • Pits on root vegetables; stem structure is weak • Premature shedding of fruit and buds	• Interferes with Mg absorption • High Ca usually causes high pH	• Ca is rarely deficient if the correct pH is maintained
Sulfur (S)	• Leachable • Not mobile • Contributes to odor and taste in some vegetables	• Rarely deficient • General yellowing of the young leaves, then entire plan • Veins lighter in color than adjoining interveinal area • Roots and stems are small, hard, and woody	• Sulfur excess is usually in the form of air pollution	• Sulfur excess is difficult to control, but rarely a problem

MICRONUTRIENTS

Nutrient	Function	Deficiency Symptoms	Toxicity Symptoms	Comments
Iron (Fe)	• Accumulates in oldest leaves and is relatively mobile • Necessary for maintenance of chlorophyll	• Interveinal chlorosis primarily on young tissue, which may become white • Fe deficiency may occur even if Fe is in soil when: soil is high in Ca; soil is poorly drained; soil is oxygen deficient; nematodes attack roots; or soil is high in Mn, pH, or P • Fe should be added in the chelated form; the type of chelate needed depends on soil pH • Foliar fertilization will temporarily correct the deficiency • May be deficient in centipede grass where pH and P are high	• Rare except in flooded soils	
Boron (B)	• Important in enabling photosynthetic transfer • Very immobile in plants	• Failure to set seed • Internal breakdown of fruit or vegetable • Death of apical buds, giving rise to witches' broom • Failure of root tip to elongate normally • Young leaves become thick, leathery, and chlorotic • Rust-colored cracks and corking on young stems, petioles, and flower stalks (such as heart rot of beets and stem crack of celery) • Breakdown occurs at the base of the youngest shoots	• Tips and edges of leaves exhibit necrotic spots coalescing into a marginal scorch similar to high-soluble salts • Oldest leaves affected first • Can occur in low pH soils • Plants are easily damaged by excess application • Looks like MG deficiency (green veins on a yellow leaf)	

continued

MICRONUTRIENTS CONTINUED

Nutrient	Function	Deficiency Symptoms	Toxicity Symptoms	Comments
Zinc (Zn)	• Needed for enzyme activity	• Young leaves small, sometimes missing leaf blades • Short internodes • Distorted/puckered leaf margins • Interveinal chlorosis	• Severe stunting/reddening • Poor germination • Wilting of older leaves • Chlorosis of entire leaves; edges and main vein often maintain more color • Can be caused by galvanized metal	
Copper (Cu)	• Needed for enzyme activity	• New growth small, misshapen, wilted • In some species, young leaves may show interveinal chlorosis while tips of older leaves remain green	• Can occur at low pH • Shows up as Fe deficiency	
Manganese (Mn)	• Needed for enzyme activity	• Interveinal chlorosis with smallest leaves remaining green, producing a checkered effect • Grey or tan spots usually develop in chlorotic areas • Dead spots may drop out of the leaf • Poor bloom size and color • Induced by excessively high pH	• Reduction in growth/brown spotting on leaves • Shows us as Fe deficiency • Found under strongly acidic conditions	
Molybdenum (Mo)	• Needed for enzyme activity	• Interveinal chlorosis on older or midstem leaves • Twisted leaves whiptail • Nitrogen deficiency symptoms may develop • Marginal scorching and rolling/cupping of leaves	• Intense yellow or purple color • Rarely observed	

MICRONUTRIENTS CONTINUED

Nutrient	Function	Deficiency Symptoms	Toxicity Symptoms	Comments
Chlorine (Cl)	• Needed for enzyme activity	• Wilted leaves which become bronze, then chlorotic, then die • Club roots	• Salt injury • Leaf burn • May increase succulence	
Cobalt (Co)	• Needed by plants recently established • Essential for nitrogen fixation	• Little is known about its deficiency symptoms	• Little is known about its toxicity symptoms	
Nickel (Ni)	• Needed for enzyme activity • Essential for seed development	• Little is known about its deficiency symptoms	• Little is known about its toxicity symptoms	

FERTILIZERS

When the soil does not supply enough nutrients, we apply fertilizers to make up for the deficit. The recommended fertilizer differs based on soil test results, the appearance of the plants, and the purpose of fertilization.

Fertilizer grade, or guaranteed analysis, refers to how much of a specific element is present in a specific formulation of fertilizer (based on percentage by weight). All fertilizers are labeled with three numbers that indicate the guaranteed analysis. These three numbers give the percentage, by weight, of nitrogen (N), phosphate (phosphoric pentoxide, P_2O_5), and potash (potassium oxide, K_2O) contained in that specific mixture of fertilizer (Figure 1.10).

State regulations require that actual analysis values be within certain limits of the labeled fertilizer grade. Often, to simplify these labels, these numbers are said to represent nitrogen, phosphorus, and potassium, (N-P-K). In reality, the numbers represent nitrogen, phosphate, and potash (N-P_2O_5-K_2O). For example, in a 100 lb. bag of fertilizer labeled 10-10-10, there are 10 lbs. of N, 10 lbs. of P_2O_5, and 10 lbs. of K_2O. The remaining weight, in this case 70 lb., is comprised of a nutrient carrier.

FIGURE 1.10 Fertilizer ratios printed on the label indicate the amounts of N-P-K unless otherwise noted

Image Credit: LayLa Burgess, Clemson University

A fertilizer containing all three nutrients, such as one labeled 16-4-8, is referred to as a complete fertilizer. If soil tests indicate high levels of phosphorus and potassium, then only an incomplete fertilizer is necessary—one that supplies only nitrogen, such as one labeled 21-0-0.

In addition to the nitrogen, phosphate, and potash, a fertilizer may contain nutrients such as calcium, magnesium, and sulfur. While plants do need and use these nutrients in fairly large quantities, they are often unnecessary because of the high calcium and magnesium contents of most SC soils. Many soils along the SC coastline are particularly high in calcium due to the pulverized seashells in the soil. Large quantities of calcium and magnesium are also present when acidic soil is limed with dolomitic limestone. The slow decomposition of organic matter in soil usually provides sufficient sulfur, which is why it's important to leave grass clippings on the lawn and compost leaves.

Some fertilizers contain micronutrients such as zinc, copper, and iron. While there are instances of deficiencies of one or more micronutrients in specific plant-growth settings, most micronutrients in fertilizer are included as a preventative measure and may not cause a response in plant growth. However, many micronutrients are present at lower levels in sandy soils. Buy and apply only those nutrients that the soil test results indicate are necessary. If one plant species has a micronutrient deficiency, apply the recommended rate of the deficient nutrient. Leaving grass clippings on the lawn, mulching with leaves, and applying compost are usually sufficient approaches to providing micronutrients (and macronutrients) to growing plants.

Types of Fertilizers

Inorganic manufactured fertilizers contain a variety of salts and minerals. They're typically fast-acting, but some contain water-insoluble nitrogen (W.I.N.), meaning some or all of the inorganic nitrogen is coated to slow down its release into the soil. Soil temperature and moisture affects the release of the nitrogen into the soil. Fertilizers containing coated nitrogen include ammonium sulfate, calcium nitrate, superphosphate, and potassium sulfate.

Synthetic organic fertilizers are human-made carbon-based fertilizers, such as urea formaldehyde, isobutylidene diurea (IBDU), and sulfur-coated urea. In addition to sufficient temperature and moisture, sulfur-coated urea requires microbes to consume the sulfur coating to release the nitrogen.

Natural organic fertilizers are derived from naturally occurring, once-living sources such as composted animal manure, cottonseed meal, and bloodmeal. Although they contain relatively low concentrations of actual nutrients compared to inorganic or synthetic organic fertilizers, they increase the organic matter content of the soil and improve soil structure.

Because organic fertilizers depend on organisms in the soil to break them down and release nutrients, most are effective only when soil is moist and the soil temperature is warm enough for organisms to be active. Microbial activity is also influenced by soil pH and aeration. Microbial activity decreases significantly below a pH of 6, so soils may need to be limed; if so, soil test recommendations will report this. When packaged as fertilizers, these products show the fertilizer grades on the label. Some organic materials, particularly composted manures, are sold as soil conditioners and do not have a nutrient guarantee, although small amounts of nutrients are present. Most natural organics contain primarily one of the three major nutrients, and little or none of the other two. However, there are many complete, blended organic fertilizers that contain nitrogen, phosphorus, and potash. Others have only low levels of all three (1-5% each).

In general, organic fertilizers release nutrients over a long period of time. One potential drawback is that they may not release enough of their primary nutrient quickly enough to give the plant what it needs for best growth.

Compared to synthetic fertilizer formulations, organic fertilizers contain relatively low concentrations of actual nutrients but perform some important functions that synthetic formulations do not. Some of these functions include increasing the soil's organic matter content, improving the soil's physical structure, and increasing beneficial bacterial and fungal activity—particularly the mycorrhizal fungi that make other nutrients more available to plants.

Chapter 2
Understanding Plants

Revised and updated by Cory Tanner and Paul Thompson

Previous version prepared by Bob Polomski, Ph.D., Vance Baird, Ph.D., Patrick D. McMillan, Ph.D., Gary Forrester and Milton D. Taylor, Ph.D.

LEARNING OBJECTIVES

- Describe early divisions within the plant kingdom, including the distinction between vascular and non-vascular plants, gymnosperms and angiosperms, and the difference between monocots and dicots.
- Describe the structure and function of basic plant parts such as roots, stems, leaves, flowers, fruits, and seeds.
- Understand the roles of plant tissues, including apical meristems, the cambium, vascular tissues, and leaf tissues, and their function in plant growth and development.
- Identify the parts of a scientific plant name, including genus, species, variety, and cultivar.
- Explain the usefulness of binomial nomenclature and scientific classification.
- Describe the classification of plants based on their use (ornamental/edible), form (tree, shrub, vine, groundcover), leaf retention (evergreen/deciduous), climatic adaptation/hardiness, or life cycle (perennial, biennial, or annual).
- Understand the processes, including the roles of inputs and outputs, of photosynthesis, respiration, and transpiration.
- Understand the function of stomata and turgor pressure in photosynthesis, respiration, and transpiration.
- Understand the wavelengths of light and how plant pigments use specific wavelengths during photosynthesis.
- Understand how light, temperature, water, humidity, and nutrition affect photosynthesis, respiration, transpiration, and plant growth.
- Understand the concept of photoperiod and how it relates to short-day, long-day, and day-neutral plants.
- Understand the concept of thermoperiod and how it relates to hardy plants, non-hardy plants, and chilling units.

INTRODUCTION

Basic knowledge of botany and plant physiology is essential to successful gardening. In this chapter, you will learn about plant parts and their functions, how plants are classified and identified, and how primary physiological processes impact plant growth and development. This information will prepare you to understand how environmental stresses, pests, and diseases interact with plants and how to address those challenges.

BASIC BOTANY

Botany is the study of plants. Several centuries ago, botany dealt primarily with plants used for medicinal purposes, typically by physicians who also studied the similarities between plants and animals. Today, it has become a foundational scientific discipline that encompasses several fields of study, including:

- **physiology**, the study of plant growth and development;
- **morphology** and **anatomy**, the study of plant form and structures;
- **taxonomy** and systematics, the study of the naming and systematic classification of plants and their relationships to one another;
- **genetics** and breeding, the study of genes and their expression and inheritance; and
- **ecology**, the study of the relationships between plants and their environments.

Another branch of botany is **horticulture**, which means "garden cultivation" (from the Latin *hortus* and *cultura*, which mean garden and cultivation, respectively). Horticulture is the art and science of the intensive cultivation and use of fruits, vegetables, ornamentals, herbs, and other high-value—often perishable—specialty crops. It also includes landscape installation and design.

The basic principles addressed in this chapter, along with some intuition and experience, will help you identify plants, diagnose plant problems, and get excited about learning more about plants.

This manual focuses on two groups of vascular plants. The first group is flowering plants, or **angiosperms**, of which there are about 260,000 species. We cultivate angiosperms in our vegetable gardens, orchards, homes, lawns, and landscapes.

The second major group is **gymnosperms**, of which there are about 760 species. These plants lack flowers and produce "naked," or exposed, seeds that are not completely enclosed within a fruit. From an evolutionary standpoint, gymnosperms are more primitive than angiosperms. Gymnosperms include conifers such as cedar, juniper, cypress, and pine, as well as cycads and ginkgo.

Flowering plants are called angiosperms because their seeds are typically enclosed in a dry or fleshy fruit that develops from the ovary of the flower. Gymnosperms like conifers, cycads, and ginkgo have seeds that lie exposed at the base of scales, usually in a cone. Mosses and ferns belong to other divisions that we don't cover in depth within this book.

Angiosperms have traditionally been divided into two groups based on the number of seed leaves, or **cotyledons**, they possess. **Dicots** have a pair of cotyledons; there are about 200,000 species of dicotyledons, including asters, rhododendrons, tomatoes, oaks, and apples. **Monocots** have a single cotyledon. There are about 70,000 species of monocots, including bamboos; grasses; cereal grains like wheat, oats, barley, rice, and rye; palms; lilies; irises; and orchids. The unique characteristics of monocots and dicots are discussed in more detail throughout this chapter.

"Dicot" was an artificial classification term that emphasized the difference between monocots and other angiosperms. Technically, they are called eudicots, from the scientific class Eudicotyledone. However, for simplicity, we use the term dicot throughout this manual. Roughly 72% of angiosperms are dicots and 25% are monocots. The remaining 3% are **magnoliids**, angiosperms with primitive features and the ancestors of monocots and dicots.

PLANT PARTS AND THEIR FUNCTION

A typical plant has roots that anchor it into the soil and absorb water and dissolved minerals (Figure 2.1). The stem supports the **photosynthesizing**—or food-producing—leaves. Water is absorbed by the roots, flows through the stem, and escapes from the leaves. These vegetative plant parts, as well as shoots and buds, are used to propagate plants asexually, often as cuttings. The sexual reproductive parts of plants include floral **buds**, **flowers**, **fruits**, and **seeds**.

These various plant parts, or organs, are derived from different tissues. Tissues are formed from cells, which are the basic structural and physiological building blocks of living things. As plant cells divide and change

CHAPTER 2 - BOTANY AND PLANT PHYSIOLOGY

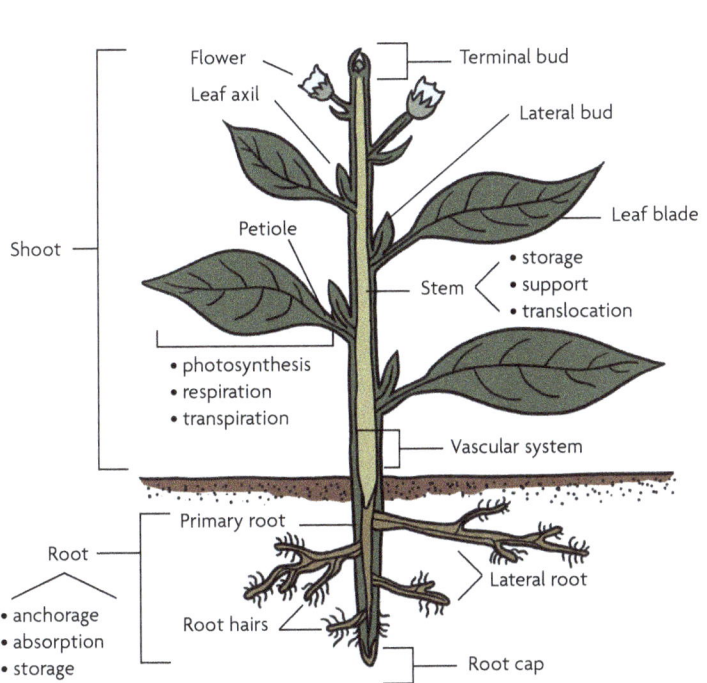

Figure 2.1 Principal parts of a vascular plant

in an orderly process, they produce different types of tissues that combine to form complex organs such as leaves, flowers, fruits, stems, and roots.

Plant Tissues

There are two major kinds of tissues: **meristematic** and **permanent**. Meristematic tissue is comprised of dividing cells, while permanent tissue is made up of cells that have already completed growth and differentiation. Differentiation is a process whereby identical cells become distinct from one another and from the meristematic cells from which they originated. Meristematic tissues, or meristems, have cells that actively divide, develop, and grow into differentiated cells, tissues, and organs.

The tips of shoots and roots have **apical meristems**, which allow these organs to elongate. This **primary growth** process results in an increase in stem and root length, which enables the plant to quickly raise its leaves to sunlight or spread its roots to mine the soil for mineral nutrients. Apical meristems produce new leaves, lateral buds, or roots. In annuals, they eventually produce flowers, as is the case for chrysanthemums, corn, poinsettias, and sunflowers.

Lateral meristems are located throughout the length of the stem and extend into the roots of plants, typically perennials. Lateral meristems produce secondary growth in stems and roots, causing them to thicken or increase in girth; this provides stability and support.

Grasses have an additional meristem, called an **intercalary meristem**, located at the base of each leaf. It produces new cells that regenerate new leafy growth, which explains why grasses can be mowed or grazed repeatedly without negative effects.

Permanent tissue also develops from meristems; it is fully differentiated. Permanent tissue is classified as simple or complex. Simple tissues are comprised of one type of cell, such as the epidermis, parenchyma, sclerenchyma, collenchyma, and cork tissues. Complex tissues, such as the **vascular tissues—xylem** and **phloem—**, contain two or more cell types within one tissue.

Roots

The structure and growth habits of roots have a pronounced effect on the size and vigor of the plant, its ability to adapt to certain soil types, and its response to cultural practices and irrigation.

The first root that emerges from a germinating seed is the **radicle**, or embryonic root. It anchors the seedling into the soil and absorbs water and minerals—two important functions of roots. A **primary root** develops from the radicle and branches to produce secondary, or lateral, roots, which are side or branch roots that arise from within the parent root.

If the primary root elongates downward into the soil with a limited amount of secondary branching, it becomes a **taproot system** (Figure 2.2). Alfalfa, cotton, parsley, ginkgo, pawpaw, and pecan produce long, deep-rooted taproots with few lateral or fibrous roots. Severing the apical root meristem at an early age causes the taproot to branch and become more fibrous; this is a commercial nursery practice on young taprooted trees that encourages the development of a compact, **fibrous root system** that improves the success of transplanting into the landscape or orchard.

In fibrous root systems, the primary root branches early and repeatedly. These multibranched roots grow close to the soil surface, such as the roots of grasses, which makes them well suited for controlling soil erosion. To appreciate the extent of a fibrous root system, researchers calculated the total surface area of a four-month-old rye

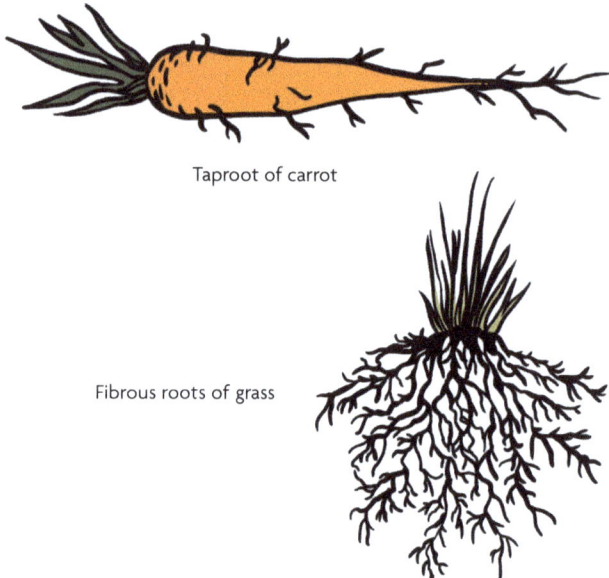

Figure 2.2 Two kinds of root structures

plant (*Secale cereale*). In a 6 qt. container of soil, the rye plant's entire root system measured 6,879 sq. ft.

Some plant species have both fibrous and taproot systems, while others adopt one or the other based on the availability of water. For example, when the soil surface is moist, the plant produces fibrous roots. During dry periods, a taproot forms to enable the plant to probe deeper in search of water.

Another important function of roots is food storage. Perennial plants, such as herbaceous perennials and many **trees** and **shrubs**, rely on carbohydrates stored in their roots to support new spring growth. In some cases, the roots become specialized to the sole purpose of storing food. For example, carrot, parsnip, radish, salsify, and turnip have fleshy taproots specifically suited to storing food. Dahlia and sweet potato produce secondary roots that develop into fleshy storage structures called tuberous roots.

An Inside Look at Roots

There are two important exterior parts of the root: the root cap and root hairs. The root cap, located at the tip of the root, protects the meristem, which is directly behind it. The root cap is thought to be the organ that perceives gravity and "communicates" which way is down to the root's apical meristem. Root hairs extend from epidermal cells behind the root tip. They increase the surface area of the root system, allowing for increased intake of water and minerals in the soil. As the root grows, old root hairs die, and new ones replace them on the younger portion of the growing tip.

There are three major internal parts of a root (Figure 2.3). The meristem at the tip of the root manufactures new cells; this is where the cells divide. Behind it is where cells elongate, or lengthen, to push the root through the soil.

Following this area where the cells elongate is the area where they mature. Here, cells differentiate into specific tissues, such as **epidermis**, **cortex** (Latin for "shell"), or vascular tissues. The epidermis, comprised of the outermost layer of cells surrounding the root, develops root hairs in this region, which is also called the root-hair zone. Cortex (cortical) cells allow oxygen and water to move between the cells and store food. A column of vascular tissues comprised of primary xylem and primary phloem in the center of the root is called the **stele** or vascular cylinder, which transports food and water. The stele is surrounded by a single layer of cells called the **endodermis**, which regulates the flow of water and nutrients entering the root from the soil and into the xylem. Just inside the endodermis is the **pericycle**, a meristematic region which gives rise to lateral roots in the region of maturation. They grow outwards through the surrounding endodermis, cortex, and epidermis.

Stems and Shoots

Often, the most prominent aboveground features of plants are the **shoots**, a collective term for the stems and their leaves. The shoots support the leaves, the photosynthetic organs, buds, flowers, and fruits. Shoots also serve as pipelines for water, minerals, and sugars. Leafy shoots are comprised of developing stems and leaves, while flowering shoots have stems and flowers.

Shoots have a more complex structure than roots. Unlike a root, a shoot has **nodes** where one or more leaves and buds are attached (Figure 2.4). The shoot also has **internodes**, the sections between nodes. The apical meristem, or tip, of the shoot produces leaves and buds, whereas the root tip does not produce lateral organs. (Recall that the lateral roots emerge behind the root tip in the region of maturation.)

Stems can be nonwoody (**herbaceous**) or **woody**. The stem develops from the **epicotyl**, or embryonic shoot, of a seed or from the apical meristem of a bud on an existing stem. The early stem growth of both woody and nonwoody stems produces primary tissues.

Woody plants experience a **secondary growth** which results in the production of wood and bark, called secondary tissues. Secondary growth is important in woody dicots and gymnosperms because it increases

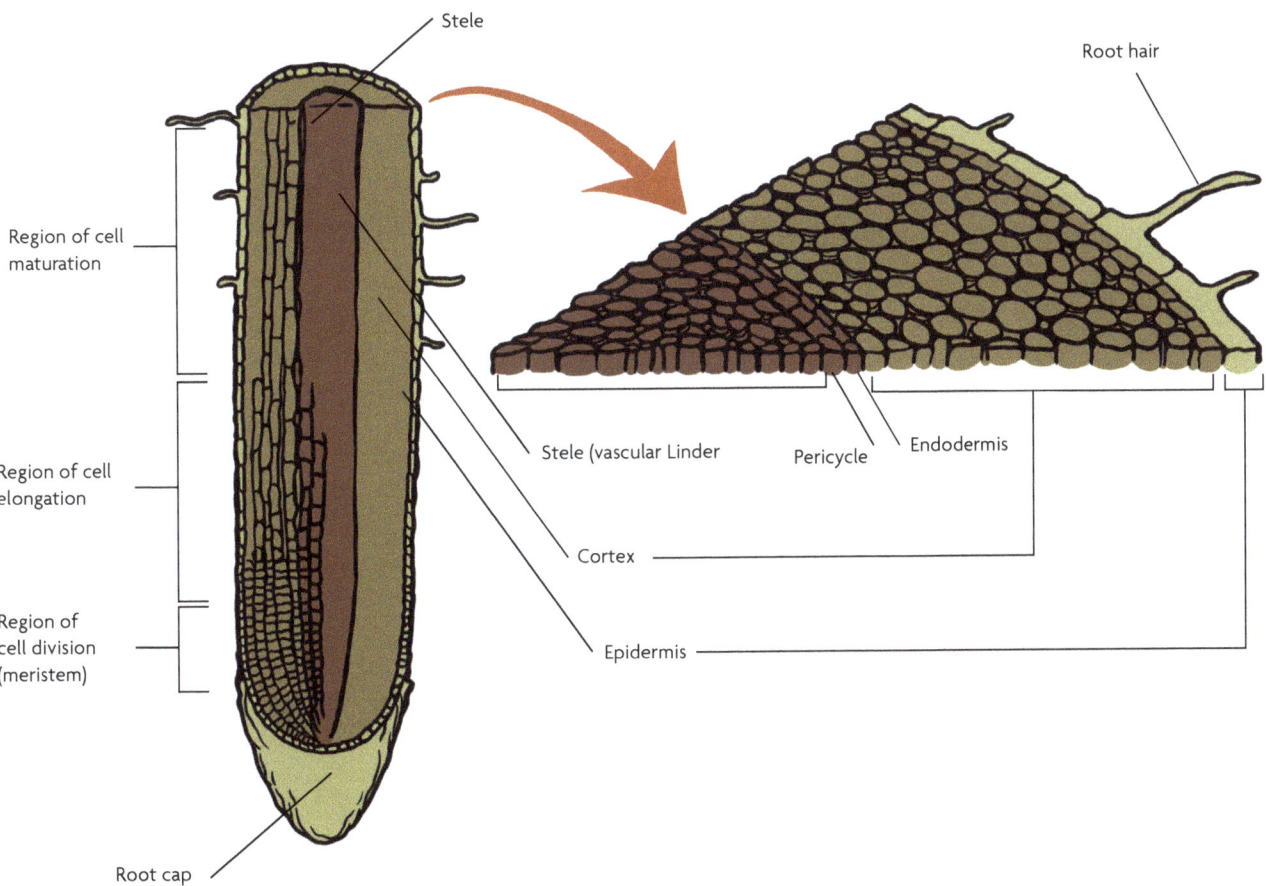

Figure 2.3 Internal root structure

the girth of roots and stems. The secondary growth, comprised mostly of xylem tissue, is important for moving water and minerals to the outermost reaches of the stem; it also strengthens the roots and stems.

The two major functions of stems are support and transport. The stem supports the leaves, which are the principal photosynthesizing organs, and orients them towards light. Substances produced in the leaves are transported through the stem to developing plant parts and storage tissues. Water and minerals are carried upward from the roots and into the leaves via the stem.

A **twig** is a woody stem in the current or previous year's growth. A **branch** is a stem that is more than one year of age; branches may have lateral stems. A **trunk** is the main stem of a woody plant.

Stem Forms

Stems occur in a diverse array of forms (Figure 2.5). Modified stems—those that differ significantly from the typical stem morphology—can be found both above and below ground. Above-ground modified stems are called crowns, stolons, or spurs.

A **crown** is a collection of short stems having leaves and flowers on short internodes. Strawberries, dandelions, African violets, and many ferns have crowns; the leaves occur in a rosette-type pattern.

A **stolon** is a fleshy or semiwoody horizontal stem that grows on the surface of the soil. It forms a new plant at one or more nodes. The runners on strawberries and centipedegrass are stolons. Like all stems, stolons have nodes and buds or leaves. The nodes on the stolon are locations where lateral buds and adventitious roots will emerge, creating new plantlets. Other plants with stolons that produce plantlets along their length include ajuga and strawberry begonia.

Spurs are short, stubby stems, such as the branches of some fruit trees—including apples, pears, cherries, and plums—and ginkgo. These compressed fruiting branches bear flowers, leaves, and eventually fruits (or as is the case with gingko, naked ovules).

Belowground stems include **bulbs**, **corms**, **rhizomes**, and **tubers**. Tulips, lilies, daffodils, and onions produce bulbs. A true bulb is a highly compressed stem surrounded

Figure 2.4 Structural parts of a stem

by fleshy storage leaves called scales. The scales surround a central bud located at the tip of the stem. In the spring, the stem elongates and grows leaves and flowers. The carbohydrates produced by the leaves are channeled into the bulb and stored for the following year.

Gladiolus, crocus, and freesia have a solid, thickened, compressed stem called a corm. Buds on the corm sprout to produce upright stems of leaves and flowers. Unlike bulbs, corms do not have fleshy scales.

Rhizomes, like stolons, are specialized stems that grow horizontally. They grow at or just below the soil surface. In some plants, rhizomes act as a storage organ and can be used in propagation. Some rhizomes are compressed and fleshy, like those of bearded iris and canna. They can also be slender and wiry, as those of bermudagrass. Johnsongrass is a particularly troublesome weed due primarily to its spreading rhizomes.

A tuber is an enlarged portion of an underground stem. While the aboveground stem bears leaves and flowers, the underground terminal portion of the stem swells into a tuber and accumulates starches and sugars. In Irish potato, each bud (or eye) on the tuber represents a node and contains a cluster of buds that sprout when planted to form new aboveground stems.

Some plants, such as dahlia and sweet potato, produce underground storage organs called tuberous roots. While often confused with bulbs and tubers, these are roots—not stems—because they lack nodes, buds, or internodes.

Inside Stems

Herbaceous Stems. The stems of herbaceous or nonwoody plants have a thin outer protective tissue called the epidermis. The epidermis is covered by the **cuticle**, which protects against water loss. Inside the epidermis is the cortex; in some herbaceous plants, the cortex is green due to the presence of **chloroplasts**.

Bundles of vascular tissues are located inside the stem and held in place by the pith and cortex. The straw-like vascular bundles transport water, minerals, and food throughout the plants. The half of the vascular bundle facing the inside of the stem is xylem tissue. Water and dissolved minerals are transported from the roots via the xylem tissue and deposited into the stems and leaves.

The outer half of the vascular bundle contains phloem tissue. It carries **photosynthates**—the sugars or "food" manufactured during photosynthesis—and other compounds from the leaves to other parts of the plant. Products carried in the phloem can move up or down within the plant. Together, these vascular bundles form an intricate network of tubes that extend from the tips of every root, shoot, and leaf (Figure 2.6).

The vascular bundles of monocots and dicots are arranged differently. In monocots, the vascular bundles are scattered throughout the stem and surrounded by a soft tissue of thin-walled cells (Figure 2.7). In dicots, the vascular bundles occur in a distinct ring in the stem, called a continuous vascular system. In herbaceous dicot stems, cortex and pith surround the vascular bundles. The vascular bundles provide rigid support, but the soft pith and cortex offer flexibility. The vascular bundles act like steel rods used to reinforce a concrete pillar.

Hardwoods (Angiosperms) and Softwoods (Conifers). The vascular bundles of woody dicots differ from herbaceous dicots. Each vascular bundle has a single row of cells between the xylem and phloem called the **vascular cambium**. The vascular cambium is meristematic tissue, so it is a site of cell division and active growth. The cells in the vascular cambium divide laterally and longitudinally, which increases the diameter of stems and roots during secondary growth and causes herbaceous stems and roots to become woody. Stems that remain herbaceous either do not have a vascular cambium or have one that is active for a single season.

Stems and roots of woody plants have two lateral meristems that produce secondary growth: the vascular cambium, which increases the girth of the stem or trunk, and the cork cambium, which produces cork (the outer protective tissue of tree bark). The inner side of the vascular cambium produces new cells with

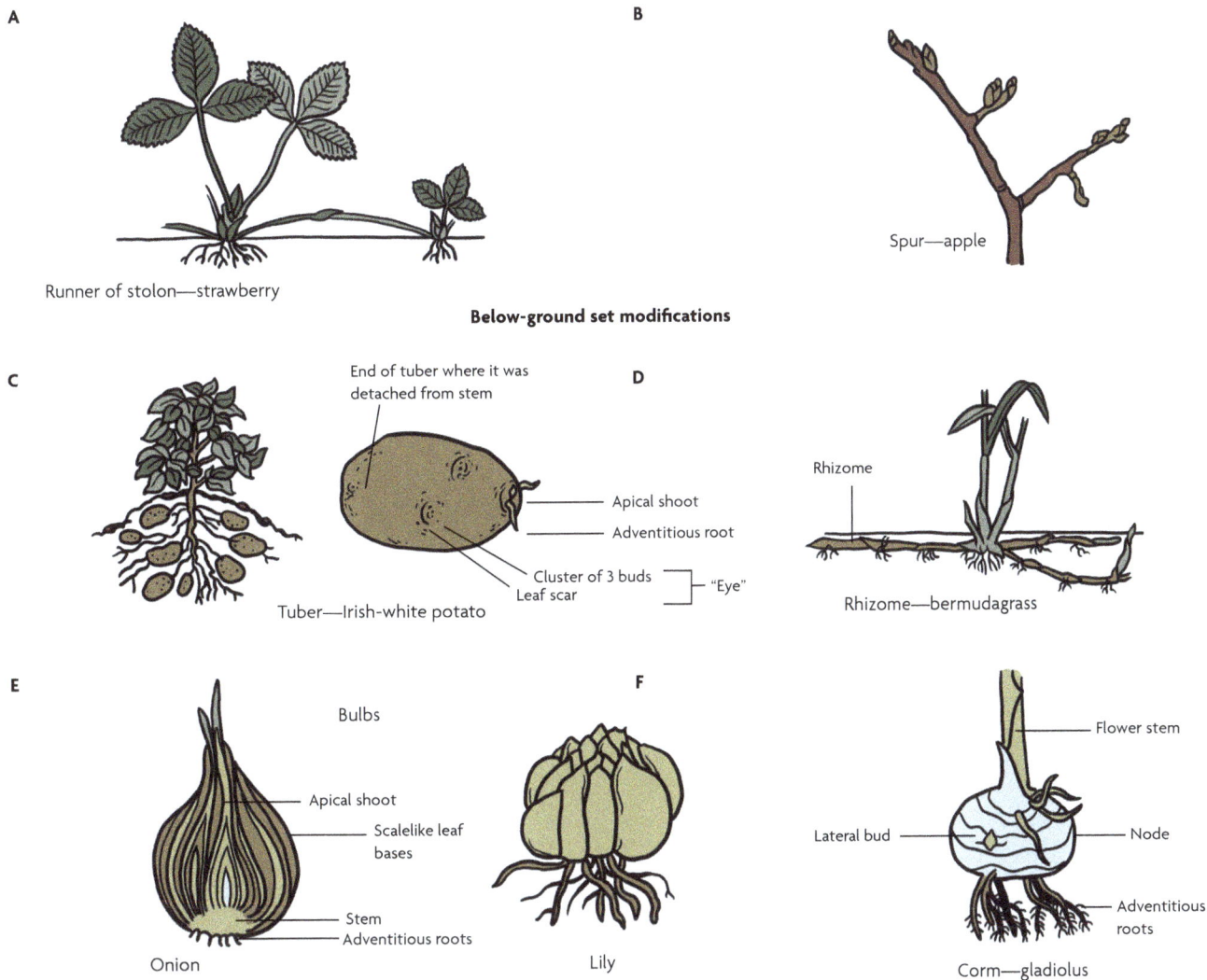

Figure 2.5 Types of modified stem structures of selected horticultural plants

thick, woody walls. This secondary xylem, or wood, conducts water and minerals. The newly formed wood near the cambium is called active xylem, or sapwood (Figure 2.8). In the inner area is inactive xylem, or heartwood. A majority of the wood we harvest from trees is heartwood. The trunk and the central portion of large tree limbs are made of heartwood. Although this inactive xylem cannot transport water and minerals, it provides structural strength and serves as a deposit for waste products and other cellular debris. The perimeter of the trunk is comprised of active xylem, which explain why "hollow" trees can remain alive—the living and active xylem, cambium, and phloem resides in the outer perimeter of the trunk.

Growth rings are produced in the xylem as new xylem develops. An annual ring represents one year of growth and reveals a tree's age. Most, but not all, woody dicots have growth rings.

Woody stems called **canes** contain relatively large amounts of **pith**, a soft, spongy tissue whose chief function is food storage. Blackberries, grapes, raspberries, and roses have canes.

The vascular cambium also divides outwardly to produce secondary phloem. These living cells conduct carbohydrates and other products of photosynthesis. As the new secondary phloem forms on the outer face of the vascular cambium, it crushes the older phloem tissue. Then, cambium cells divide laterally to increase the circumference of this meristematic region.

Cambium is most active in spring and early summer. Collectively, all the tissues produced on the outside of the vascular cambium are called **bark**. During this time of active cell division, the bark "slips" easily so it can be separated from the xylem. This is an important period for grafting and "budding" plants (see Chapter 3, Plant Propagation).

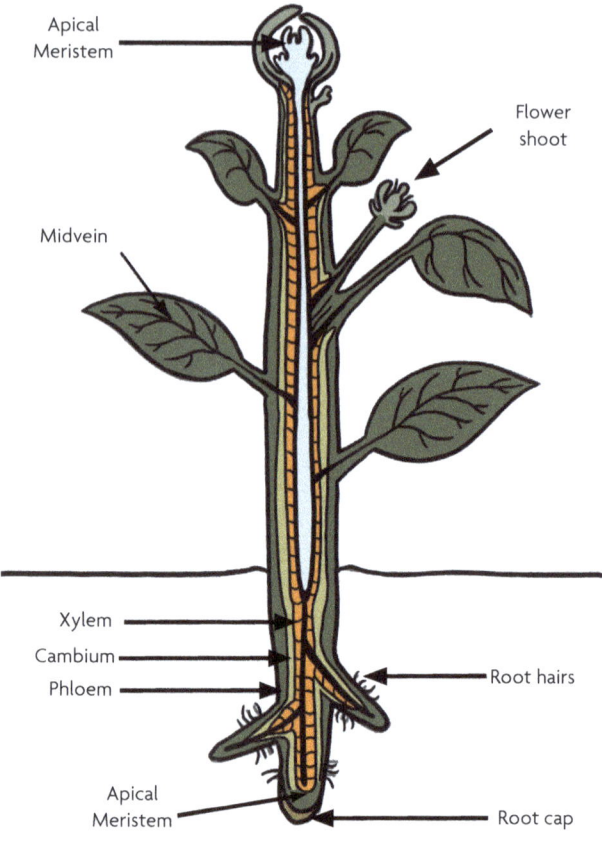

Figure 2.6 A plant's vascular system is a continuous connection between the root tips, leaves, and shoot tips

On a woody dicot stem, the epidermis is replaced by cork produced by the cork cambium. This meristematic tissue creates many cells that grow outwardly and fewer that grow inwardly. The cells growing outwardly become cork cells; those produced inwardly become phelloderm, a living parenchyma tissue. Cork cells deposit suberin, a waxy waterproofing substance, on their outer walls to make them resistant to water penetration or loss and gas exchange. The cork cells die but retain their ability to resist dehydration, diseases, insects, and extreme temperatures.

Woody monocots, such as palms, develop a thick trunk by primary growth alone. Below the terminal growing point (apical meristem) in the trunk, cells divide and enlarge, causing the stem to grow in circumference. This is called diffuse secondary growth, because no actual lateral meristem is involved. The lack of secondary growth in palms is readily apparent; their stems are essentially the same diameter along their entire length and lack growth rings in their cross-sections. The outermost cells form a hard crust when they are crushed and dried out; this crust differs structurally from the cork created by other kinds of trees but has the same function. Palms don't have rigid cores, so the trunks are flexible. This trait helps palms cope with hurricane-force winds.

The stems of other monocots, like bamboos and many grasses, have hollow centers. Their stem tissues and vascular bundles are fortified with long, thick-walled cells called fibers. The nodes inside their tube-like stems have reinforcing plates that prevent the stems from collapsing.

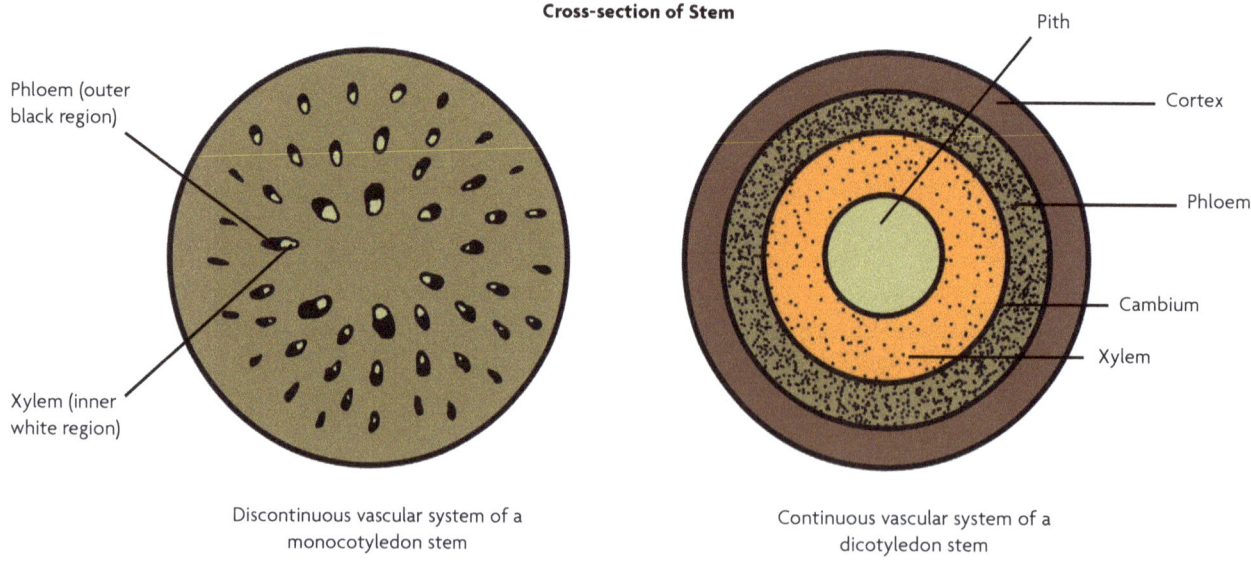

Figure 2.7 Primary components of the vascular system differ in monocots and dicots

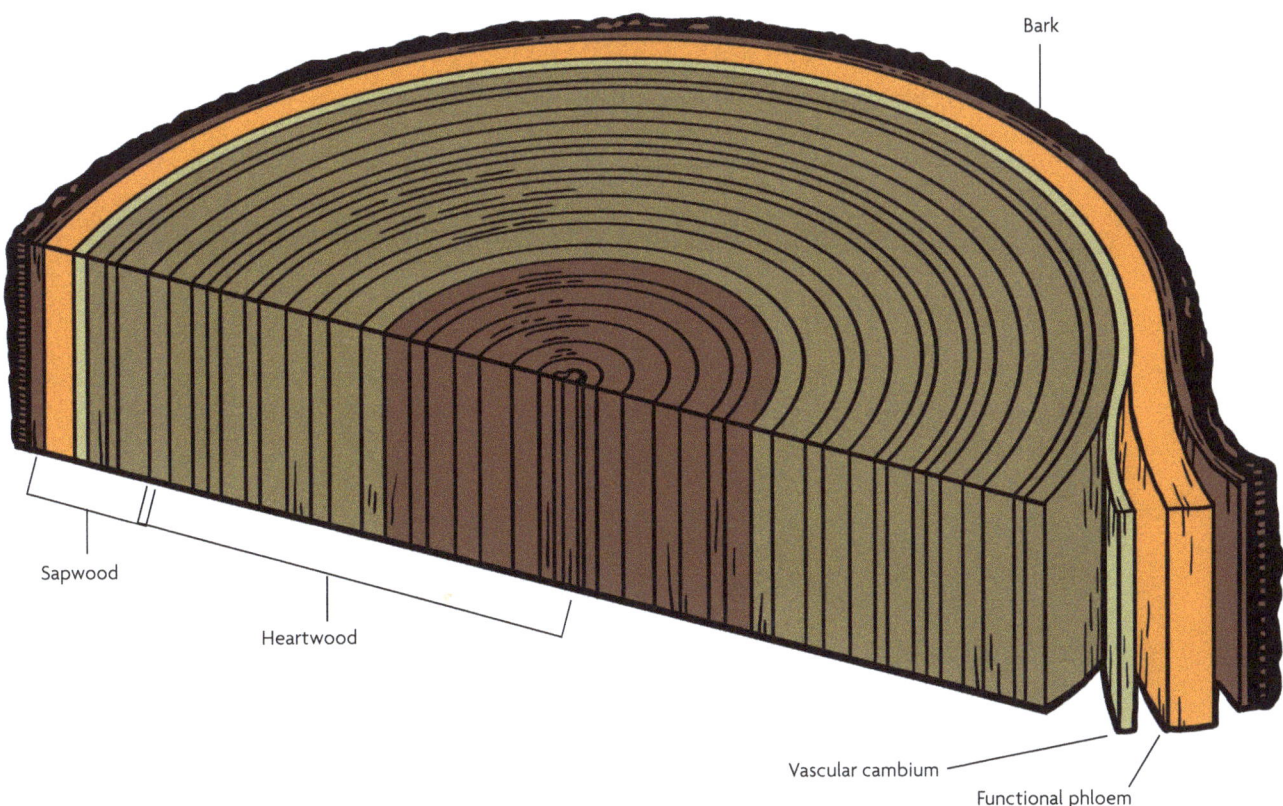

Figure 2.8 Cross-section of a hardwood dicot tree trunk.

Buds

A bud is an undeveloped collection of shoot or flower parts comprised of meristematic tissue. Buds form in the **axils** of leaves at nodes, or on the ends of branches. They usually do not form on roots, though they can. Vegetative buds produce leaves and shoots. Flower buds open and produce flowers. Mixed buds produce both shoots and flowers.

Buds are most noticeable on deciduous plants after the leaves fall. A leaf scar remains where the leaf petiole was attached, below the bud.

Buds are named according to their position on the stem (Figure 2.9). Terminal (or apical) buds are on the tips of stems or shoots. Those found along the sides of stems are called **lateral buds**. Most lateral buds are located on leaf axils—the point where the leaf attaches to the stem and creates an angle—and called **axillary buds**. Buds that occur at the base of terminal buds and at the sides of axillary buds are called **accessory buds**.

Latent buds occur on the internodes of stems, most often on broadleaf evergreens and some deciduous plants (such as crape myrtle). Latent buds remain dormant and unseen for long periods of time until pruning or injury to the stem generates growth.

Adventitious buds form in positions that are neither terminal nor axillary. They may develop at the edge of a leaf blade or from callus tissue at the cut end of a stem or root. One example of an adventitious bud is a **sucker**, an upright shoot that arises from a horizontal root.

The buds of trees and shrubs in temperate regions typically develop a protective outer layer of small, leathery scales or modified leaves. Annual plants and herbaceous perennials have naked buds whose outer leaves are green and somewhat succulent.

Buds on many woody and perennial plants require exposure to a certain number of days below a critical temperature before resuming growth in the spring; we cover this idea more thoroughly later on in this chapter.

After shedding their leaves in the fall, deciduous twigs reveal leaf scars below their axillary buds. Sometimes, small dots are visible inside the leaf scars. These leaf traces, or vascular bundle scars, are remnants of the vascular bundles that transported food and water between the stem and the leaf petiole. When the leaf is shed, the remaining leaf scar gets covered with a thin layer of cork to prevent fungal invasions and reduce water loss. In winter, leaf scar characteristics can help identify plants.

Terminal bud scars occur when the overlapping

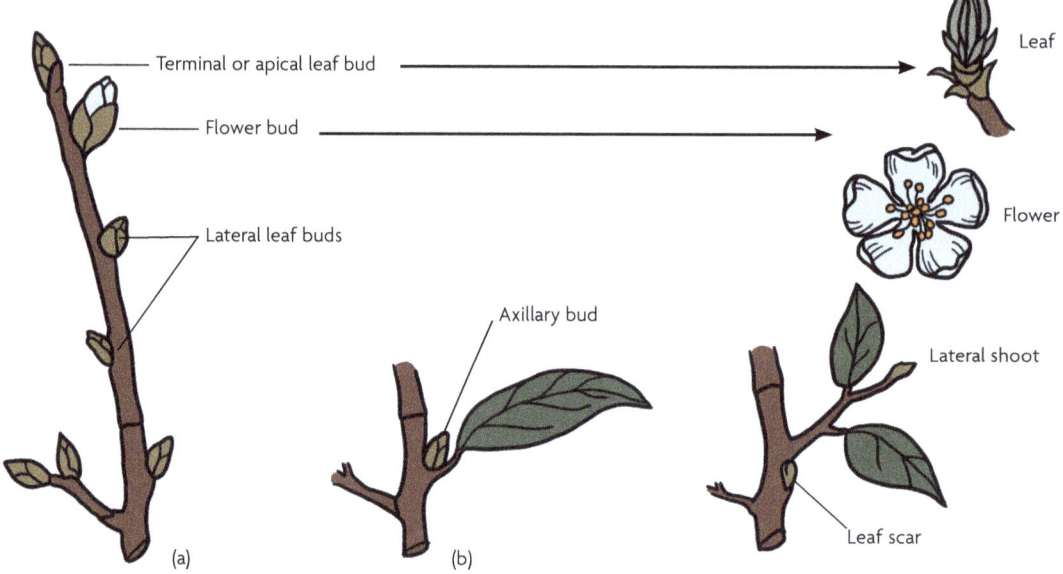

Figure 2.9 Types of buds on woody twigs.

bud scales that protect the terminal buds during winter are shed as the bud "breaks" or starts growing. The bud scales leave behind concentric rings of scars. Each spring, one set of terminal bud scars is created on the stem. By counting the terminal bud scars on a stem or branch, you can determine its age (Figure 2.10). Also, you can evaluate the annual growth rate by measuring the length of the twig from the terminal bud back to the first set of terminal bud scars. This measurement is a good indicator of plant vigor.

Evergreen trees and shrubs do not go dormant, so their leaf bud scars will not help determine their age. However, evergreen stems usually have leaf scars farther back, on older growth, due to normal aging and leaf drop; this occurs every 3-4 years as opposed to the annual leaf drop of deciduous plants.

Edible Buds

The eyes of Irish potato tubers are leaf scars, or nodes, that contain three buds; the center bud normally breaks dormancy and produces new leafy shoots. Brussels sprouts are large vegetative lateral or axillary buds that arise on the main stem of the plant. Cabbage and head lettuce have unusually large terminal buds. In the case of globe artichoke, we eat both the fleshy basal portions of the **bracts** of the flower bud and the solid stem portion of the bud. We eat the edible flower buds, small leaves associated with buds, and some portions of the stems of both broccoli and cauliflower.

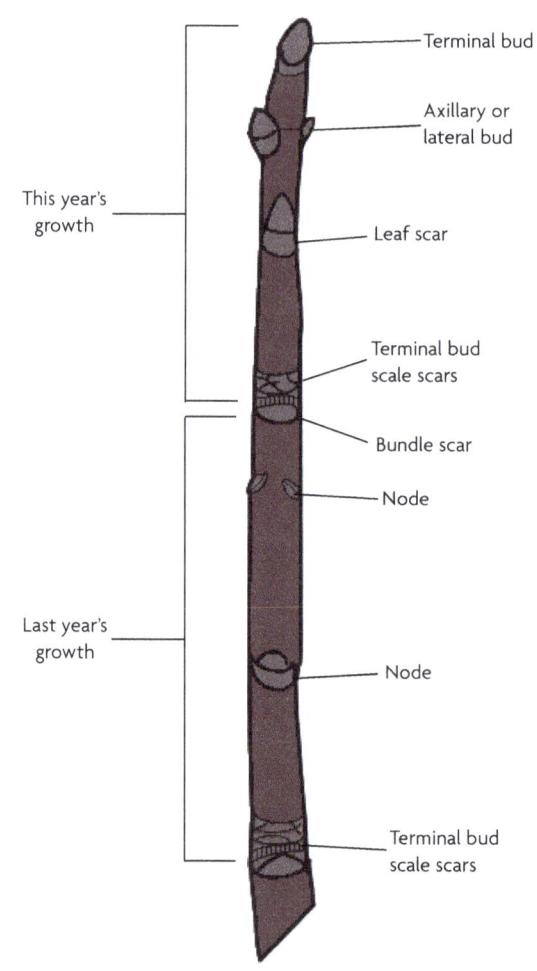

Figure 2.10 Woody twig or stem with oppositely arranged buds. The distance between the terminal bud scale scar and the current terminal bud is a measure of annual growth.

Leaves

The primary purpose of leaves is to capture light energy and manufacture food through photosynthesis. The products of photosynthesis, such as carbohydrates, are called photosynthates; photosynthates are transported via the phloem through the stem and throughout the plant. The broad, sheet-like blades of leaves present a large area for light energy to be intercepted and absorbed.

Some leaves are attached to the stem by a **petiole** (Figure 2.11), which extends the leaf away from the stem and allows the leaf to track the sun and rotate during the day. The petiole has conducting tissues that allow water, nutrients, and photosynthates to move between the stem and leaf blade. It also provides flexibility to the leaf during heavy winds or rains. In some plants, such as celery and rhubarb, the petiole becomes thick and fleshy and contains a large amount of storage tissue.

The leaves of other plants attach directly to the stem without a petiole. These are called sessile, or stalkless, leaves. Grasses, wheat, and rice all have sessile leaves.

Stipules are leaflike organs usually found at the base of a petiole or on the node of a stem; willows, strawberries, and geraniums all have stipules. Occasionally, stipules are fused to the petiole; this is seen in roses, crabapples, and callery pears. Stipules often drop as leaves mature, but those that persist or enlarge are helpful in identifying plants.

Inside a Leaf

The blade of a leaf resembles a sandwich (Figure 2.12). On the top and bottom of the blade are thin protective layers of cells, called the epidermis; the primary functions of the epidermis are to protect the inner leaf tissue and reduce and regulate water loss. The arrangement of epidermal cells determines the texture of the leaf surface.

The epidermis may be covered by a cuticle layer on both the upper and lower surfaces of the epidermis. The cuticle, which is comprised of a waxy, paraffin-like compound called cutin, restricts water loss from the leaves. An ancillary benefit of the cuticle is that it gives an attractive sheen to the leaves of some houseplants. Cuticle thickness influences foliar uptake of fertilizers and pesticides. Plants with thin leaf cuticles, like tomato plants, will readily absorb foliar applications; thick, waxy leaves, like those of evergreen magnolias and hollies, tend to shed liquids rather than absorb them through the leaf cuticle.

Between the upper and lower epidermis is the **mesophyll**, where photosynthesis occurs. The mesophyll contains numerous chloroplasts. In **mesophytes**—plants that require conditions that are neither too wet nor too dry—the mesophyll is divided into two layers. The upper layer is made of dense, closely packed palisade parenchyma cells; the lower layer contains loosely packed spongy parenchyma cells with lots of air spaces in between. The looseness and air spaces allow carbon dioxide, water vapor, and oxygen to move freely between them.

Weaving through the mesophyll is a network of vascular bundles, or veins, that attach to the vascular system of the stem. The veins contain xylem—usually on top—and phloem—usually below. These cells supply the leaf with water and collect and transport photosynthates.

The chloroplasts inside this region of the leaf need carbon dioxide, light, and water. Gas enters the leaf through microscopic pores called **stomata** (singular: stoma). Stomata are predominantly located on the underside of the leaf. Water lilies and other aquatic plants are an exception; most of their stomata are on the

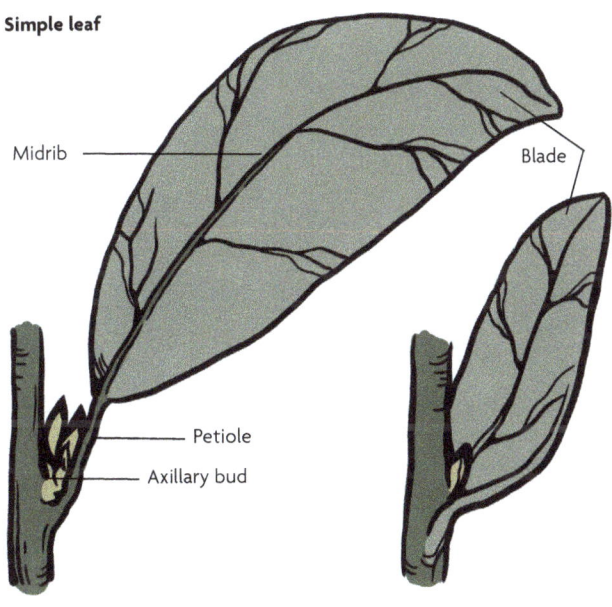

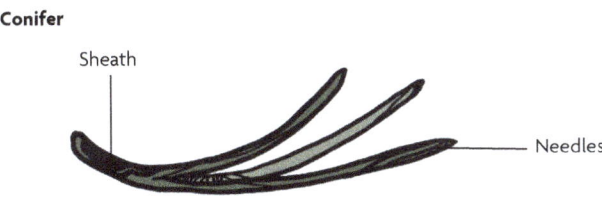

Figure 2.11 Botanical terms used to describe a simple leaf.

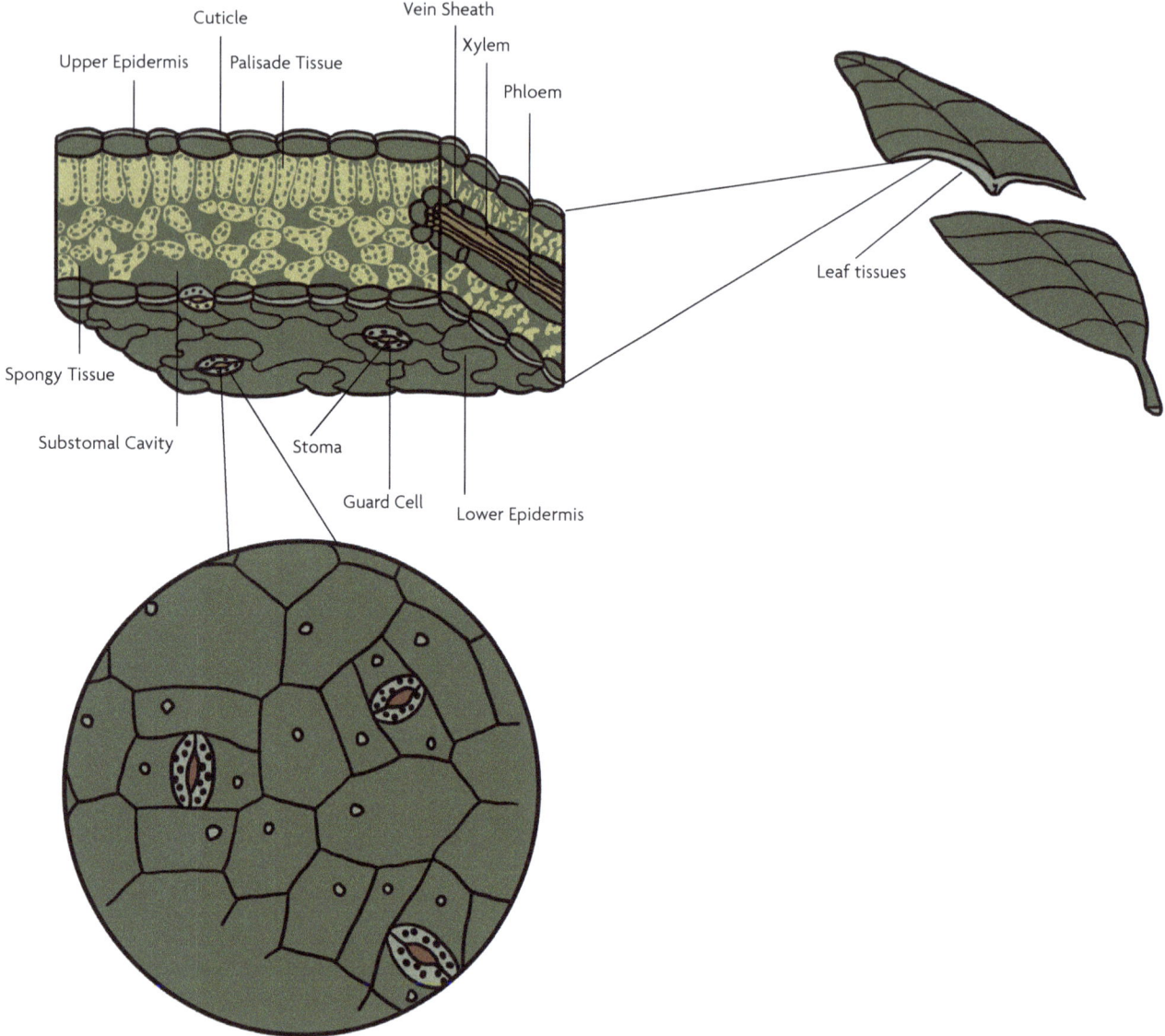

Figure 2.12 An inside look at leaf structure.

upper leaf surface because the lower side is underwater.

The number and size of stomata vary widely among species. Bordering each stoma is a pair of specialized **guard cells** that control the opening and closing of each stoma. These cells allow carbon dioxide—one of the raw materials of photosynthesis—to enter the leaf while water vapor and oxygen—the product of photosynthesis—escape. Water can also enter through the stomata.

When water is lost by the leaves, the process is called **transpiration**. Transpiration is important for regulating temperature in the leaf, but the process also provides the force that drives water from the roots, through the stem, and out through the leaves.

Stomata close at night, because photosynthesis doesn't occur without sunlight. They also close during the day if water loss from the leaves exceeds the amount absorbed by roots. This survival mechanism conserves water at the expense of shutting down the production of food, of which there is often enough stored to maintain plant life.

Although needlelike leaves look different from broadleaf leaves, their internal structures are very much the same. For example, a Virginia pine needle contains mesophyll, guard cells, stomata, an epidermis, and a cuticle. It also has a vascular bundle comprised of xylem and phloem. Many needled conifers also have vein-like resin ducts, which are not found in angiosperms. A resin duct carries resin, the sticky substance created by pines and other conifers.

Leaf Type

A simple leaf has a blade that is a single continuous unit. A **compound leaf** is made of several separate leaflets that grow from the same petiole. A deeply lobed leaf may look like a compound leaf, but if the leaflets are connected by narrow bands of blade tissue, the leaf may be classified as a simple leaf. If the leaflets have separate stalks—especially if these stalks are jointed at the point of union with the main leafstalk—the leaf is considered compound. Some leaves may be doubly compound, such as Kentucky coffeetree (*Gymnocladus dioicus*); doubly-compound leaves have two divisions of leaflets. Heavenly bamboo (*Nandina domestica*) has tripinnately compound leaves with three divisions of leaflets.

A pinnately compound leaf has leaves arranged along a central axis (Figure 2.13), while a palmately compound leaf arises from a single point at the tip of a petiole, like the fingers of your hand or the leaves from buckeye trees (*Aesculus spp.*). Plants with compound leaves consisting of three leaflets—such as clover, poison ivy, and strawberry—are said to have **trifoliate** leaves.

Figure 2.13 Leaf types.

Leaf Blade and Leaf Margin. Other leaf characteristics that help in plant identification include the type of leaf margin—including lobed, wavy, and toothed—and the shape of the leaf tip (or **apex**) and its base.

There are an almost overwhelming number of terms used to describe the overall shape of the leaf, the shape of the leaf apex and base, and the leaf margin. See Figures 2.14-2.16 for examples.

Venation of Leaves. Venation refers to the patterns in which veins are distributed in a leaf blade. There are two principal types of venation in leaves: parallel veining and net veining. (Figure 2.17).

Parallel-veined leaves have veins that run parallel to each other and are connected laterally by tiny, straight veinlets. Most monocots show parallel venation. The most common type of parallel veining is found in grasses, in which the veins run from the base of the blade to the apex of the leaf. Another type of parallel venation is seen in banana, canna, and cast-iron plant; in these plants, the

Figure 2.14 Leaf bases (top) and leaf tips or apices (bottom)

parallel veins run laterally from the midrib.

Net-veined or reticulate-veined leaves have veins that branch from the main rib or ribs and then subdivide into finer veinlets. These veinlets then unite to create a complicated-looking network. This system of enmeshed veins provides more resistance to tearing than most parallel-veined leaves. Dicots usually have net-veined leaves.

Net venation may be either pinnate or palmate. In pinnate venation, the veins extend laterally from the midrib to the edge; apple, cherry, peach, beech, and elm trees all show pinnate net venation. Palmate venation occurs in grape and maple leaves, where the principal veins extend outward—like the ribs of a fan—from the petiole apex or insertion point near the base of the leaf blade.

Leaf Textures. The texture of leaves is helpful in identification. Some of the many leaf textures that can be helpful include:

- Coriaceous (tough and leathery),
- Downy (covered with short, soft hairs),
- Hirsute (pubescent with coarse, stiff hairs),
- Hispid (rough with bristles, stiff hairs, or minute prickles),
- Pubescent (hairy),
- Scabrous (rough to the touch, like sandpaper),
- Smooth (shiny, hairless surface),
- Succulent (juicy, fleshy, soft, and thick), and
- Tomentose (covered with matted, wooly hairs).

Figure 2.15 Examples of leaf shapes.

Figure 2.16 **Examples of leaf margins.**

Leaf Arrangement. The way that leaves are arranged along a stem can also be used to identify plants (Figure 2.18). Alternate leaves have one leaf per node, with each leaf located on the opposite side of the stem from the leaves directly above or below it; this arrangement is often referred to as spiral. Opposite leaves grow across the stem from each other, though the two opposite leaves occur at the same node. Whorled leaves create a circle around the stem when three or more equally spaced leaves grow from the same node. In a rosulate arrangement, the basal leaves form a rosette around stem with extremely short nodes; this is often called a **basal rosette**.

Modified Leaves and Stems

Sometimes, the leaves and stems of a plant are nontypical in that they do not fit the identification patterns most commonly used to classify them. For example, grape tendrils are modified stems that coil around structures. Boston ivy and Virginia creeper have tendrils with adhesive disks at their tips. Most tendrils, however, are modifications of leaves—as with garden pea.

Spines, thorns, and prickles are modified appendages that defend plants from herbivores or other plant-eating animals. Spines are modified leaves that are hard and dry and cannot photosynthesize. Thorns are modified branches that occur in the leaf axils. The prickles on roses are mistakenly called thorns, but a prickle is a sharp outgrowth of the cortex and epidermis in the

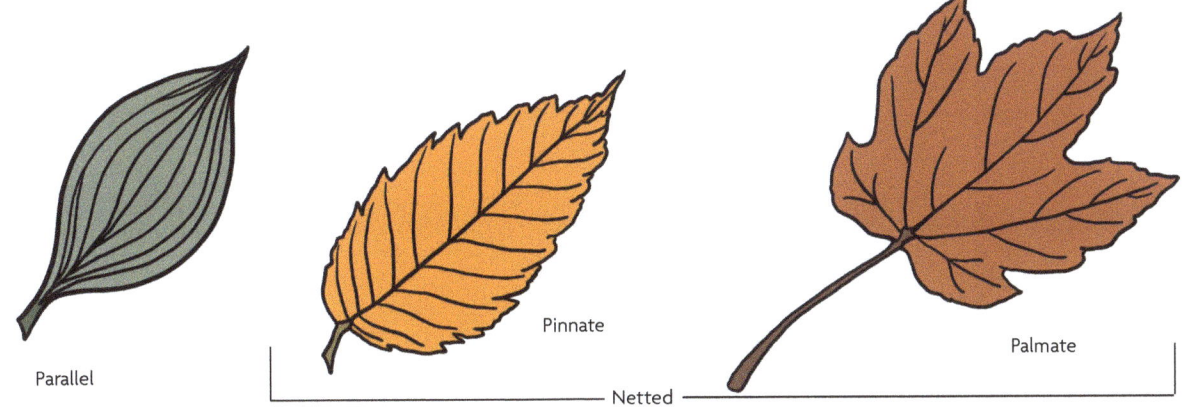

Figure 2.17 Types of leaf venation

Figure 2.18 Different types of leaf arrangement

stem. So the "thorns" on rose stems are actually prickles.

Bracts are also modified leaves. These showy structures in dogwoods and poinsettias look like brightly colored flower petals, but they are actually leafy bracts that surround minute flowers.

Flowers

Seed-producing plants have both vegetative and reproductive phases. During the sexual reproductive phase, gymnosperms produce seeds; angiosperms produce flowers that develop into fruits with seeds.

Flowers come in a variety of shapes, forms, and sizes. Taxonomists use flowers extensively to identify and classify plants. Like stems and leaves, flowers have their own morphological features, and knowing the appropriate terms to identify these features is important when identifying plants.

The stalk of a flower is called a **peduncle**. The stalk of an individual flower in an **inflorescence**, or flower cluster, is called a **pedicel**. The **receptacle** is the enlarged tip of the pedicel where the floral structures are attached. Receptacles can bear up to four structures: sepals, petals, stamens, and carpels. At the tip of the pedicel is the apical meristem, or flower bud, that gives rise to floral tissues. In sunflowers, roses, and poinsettias, the apical meristem is at the tip of the pedicel; tomato and temperate zone fruit trees present the apical meristem in the axils of leaves on the lower end of the stem.

Flower Structure

A typical flower has four major parts: **sepals**, **petals**, **stamens**, and **carpels** (Figure 2.19). The petals and sepals are sterile floral parts not directly involved in sexual reproduction, but they do use color to attract pollinators.

Sepals are small, green, leaf-like structures on the base of the flower to protect the other floral parts. They are the "caps" on tomatoes and strawberries. Collectively, the sepals are called the **calyx**.

Petals are the colorful parts of flowers. Collectively, they are called the **corolla**. The number of petals on a

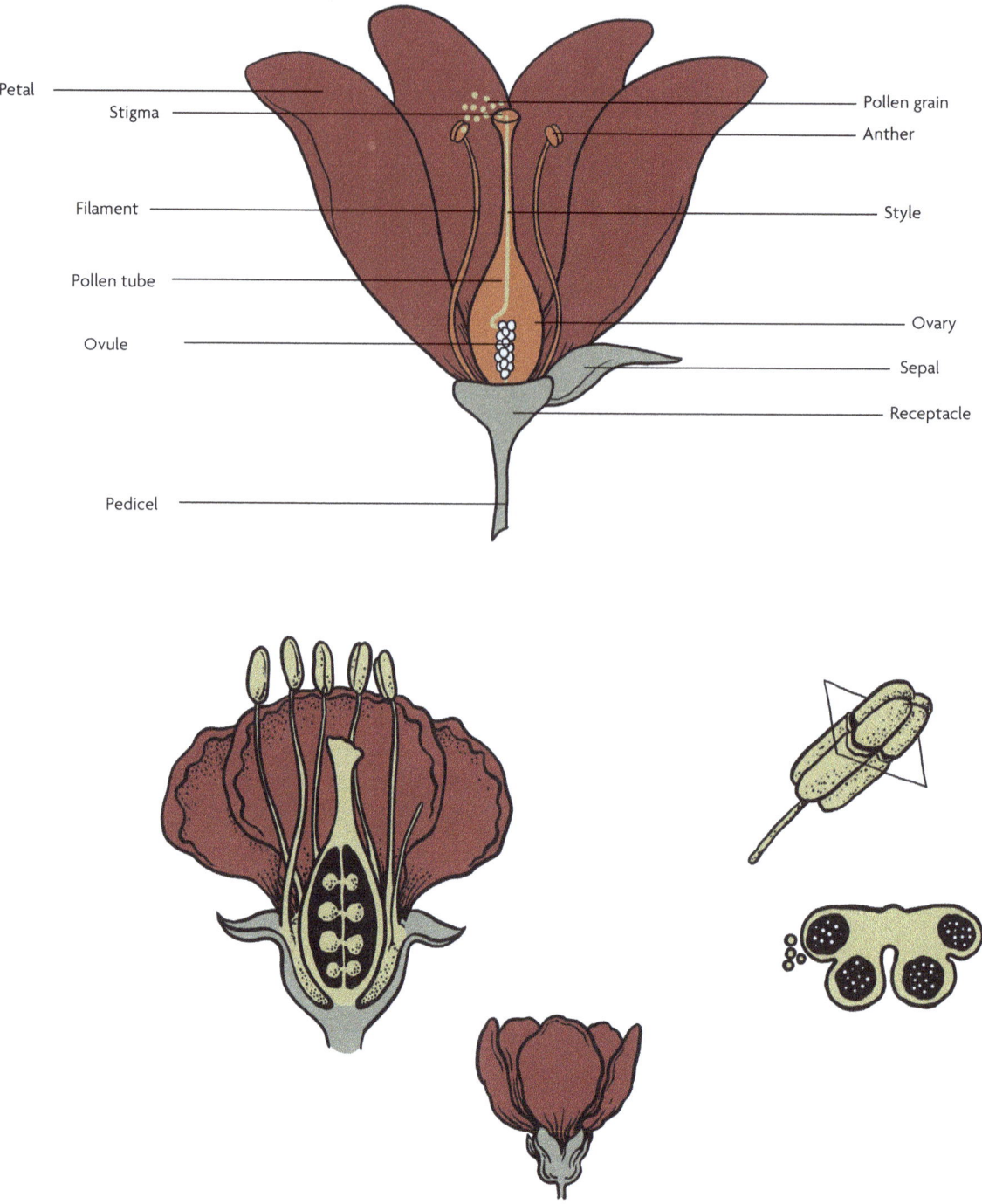

Figure 2.19 Parts of a typical angiosperm flower

flower is often used in the identification of plant families and genera. In some plants, such as lilies, sepals and petals are indistinguishable; these sepals and petals together are called **tepals**.

Flowers are often brightly colored or patterned and contain a fragrance or nectar to attract insects, birds, and other animals. In the process of searching for nectar, these pollinators transfer pollen from flower to flower.

Flowers of dicots typically have sepals and/or petals in multiples of four or five. In monocots, these floral parts typically occur in multiples of three. Sepals and petals form the outermost whorls of a flower and are collectively called the **perianth**.

The fertile parts of a flower are the stamens and carpels. The stamen is the male reproductive organ and consists of a pollen sac, called the **anther**, and a long supporting **filament** that holds the anther in position; from this position, the pollen can be dispersed by wind or carried to the stigma by pollinators.

The carpel contains **ovules** that develop into seeds after being fertilized. A flower may have one or more carpels. An individual carpel or a group of fused carpels are called a **pistil**. The pistil is the female reproductive structure of the plant; it is generally shaped like a bowling pin and located in the center of the flower. The pistil includes the **stigma**, **style**, and **ovary**. The stigma is located at the top and connected to the ovary by the style. The ovary contains the eggs, which reside in the ovules. After the egg is fertilized, the ovule develops into a seed.

A complete flower has all four floral parts: sepals, petals, stamens, and pistils (carpels). Tomatoes, peas, apples, and strawberries have complete flowers. If any one of these essential parts is absent, the flower is said to be incomplete.

Flowers that contain both stamens and pistils are said to be perfect, while imperfect flowers are missing either stamens or pistils. Imperfect flowers are termed **staminate** (male) when they contain only stamens and lack pistils, or **pistillate** (female) when they only possess pistils and no stamens. The catkins in alder, pecans, poplars, oaks, and willows only produce staminate flowers; the seeds of these species are produced in smaller, pistillate flowers. A sterile flower typically lacks stamens and pistils and is not involved in sexual reproduction.

Plants with perfect flowers or separate staminate and pistillate flowers on the same plant are called **monoecious** (Greek for "one house"). Most flowering plants are monoecious. Monoecious plants include alder, pecan, and oak. Some plants bear only male flowers at the beginning of the growing season but later develop both sexes, as is the case with corn, cucumbers, melons, pumpkin, and squash.

Dioecious (Greek for "two houses") plants have staminate and pistillate flowers on separate plants; asparagus, spinach, muscadine, persimmon, poplar, and willow are all dioecious plants. Most holly plants are either male or female plants. Both male and female plants must be nearby for pollination and fruit set, and therefore fruit or berry production, of dioecious plants. In holly, for instance, a male plant should be within 30-40 ft. of a female holly plant. Only female plants will bear fruit, but only pollination from a male plant will start that process.

The attractiveness and fragrance of flowers have not evolved for our pleasure, but to ensure the continued survival of the species. Flowers that rely on pollinators, such as insects and birds, rely on fragrance and color to attract them. Moth- and bat-pollinated flowers open at night and are often white, which makes them visible in dim light. Some night-blooming plants release their strongest fragrance at night.

Wind-pollinated flowers lack the need to attract pollinators and are often not very showy. They are designed to be pollinated by the movement of the wind. These flowers are often located in the upper reaches of the plant so that plenty of dry, powdery pollen can be carried for long distances. Wind-pollinated dicots include beech, oak, pecan, birch, and elm. The primitive gymnosperms also rely on wind for pollination. Each spring, their male cones produce copious amounts of yellow pollen grains that look like yellow dust.

In grasses, the anthers hang from long filaments to catch breezes, and the tiny, inconspicuous flowers have featherlike stigmas that move in the air to capture pollen.

Types of Inflorescences

Some plants, called solitary flowers, bear only one flower per stem. Others produce clusters of flowers, called an inflorescence. There are various kinds of branched inflorescences (Figure 2.20). A **spike** is an inflorescence in which many individual flowers or stemless florets are attached to an elongated flower stem or peduncle, as in gladiolus and tuberose. A **raceme** is similar to a spike, but the florets have short stalks attached to the main stem, as in hyacinth, snapdragon, and radish.

The flowers in grasses occur in a **panicle**, which is an indeterminate branching raceme.

A **corymb** is an inflorescence of individual florets whose stalks, or pedicels, are arranged at random along the peduncle; the florets create a rounded top, such as those in yarrow, candytuft, and hydrangea. A corymb is an indeterminate inflorescence, because the peduncles can continue to elongate further as the flowers continue to open.

An **umbel** is similar to a corymb except the pedicels all arise from one point at the tip of a stem on the peduncle and are about the same length. Carrot, dill, lily-of-the-Nile, and onion produce umbels.

A **composite inflorescence**, also called a head inflorescence, is made up of many stemless florets (primarily of plants in the sunflower family (Asteraceae)). A typical composite head has a central region of **disc flowers** surrounded by a ring of ray flowers. Often, the ray flowers are sterile and have a single purpose: attracting pollinators. We can see this type of feature in sunflowers, black-eyed Susans, coneflowers, and asters. With some sunflower relatives, such as chrysanthemums and dahlias, the two flower types in the inflorescences are

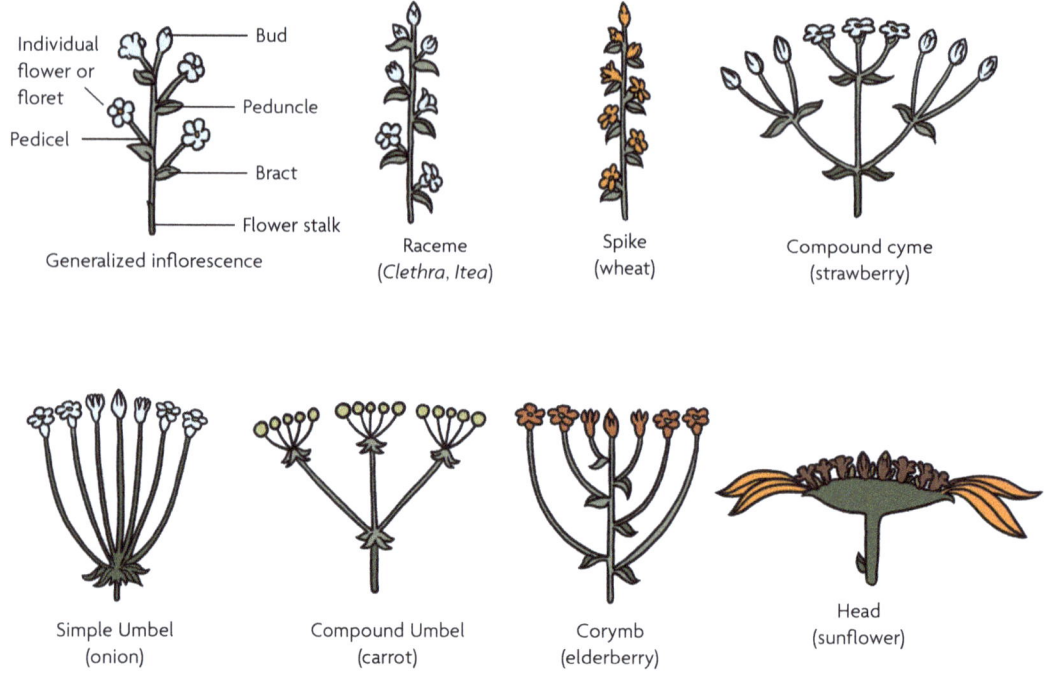

Figure 2.20 Types of inflorescences

indistinguishable from one another.

A **cyme** is a broad, flat-topped inflorescence. The top floret opens first and blooms downward along the peduncle, as in dogwood. A cyme is a determinate inflorescence, because the flower is produced at the terminal end and is the first part to form, preventing any further elongation of the inflorescence.

A **spadix** is a densely flowered structure surrounded by a spathe, like those of calla lilies, peace lilies, and jack-in-the-pulpit.

Flower Induction

The juvenile period of a plant begins at the seedling stage and lasts until the mature stage, when it flowers. Juvenility can last for a few weeks or a few months in annuals, and a few years (like in apples) to many years (like in olives) in woody perennials. Seed-propagated ornamentals, such as southern magnolia, may remain juvenile for eight or more years before their first flowers form.

During the juvenile period, plants may exhibit unique morphological traits. Pear trees, for example, can have thorns as juveniles that they lose when they mature. English ivy leaves are lobed on juvenile plants and entire on mature plants. Also, mature English ivy becomes shrub-like and produces upright growth instead of trailing branches.

As a general rule, juvenile plants or plant parts more readily produce adventitious roots than mature plants or mature plant parts, which means that they will root more easily. It is also easier to graft juvenile plant parts than older plant sections.

A plant is mature when it is capable of initiating flowers. The reproductive phase in flowering plants begins when the meristems in the growing shoot tips, or buds, are induced to produce reproductive organs (flowers).

The time of year when flowers are initiated, and the time required from initiation to flowering, depends on the species. Many perennial plants initiate cells of flower tissue in their meristems months before the flowers develop. Spring-flowering woody plants initiate flower buds on the previous summer's shoots and are said to flower on "old wood." Pruning these plants in winter will remove their flower buds and reduce the number of flowers produced in the spring. Annuals can reach maturity and bloom just weeks after germinating.

Some plant species will flower regardless of environmental conditions. In other plant species, several factors influence the induction and development of flowers. Daylength, or **photoperiod** (number of daylight hours, see p. 51), light intensity, soil moisture content, temperature, and the nutrient status of the plant influence the development of flowers and fruits.

Reproductive Development

Once a flower develops and opens, the stage is set for reproduction. **Pollination** occurs when compatible pollen from the anther comes into contact with the stigma. When this pollen transfer occurs within the same flower, on the same plant, or between plants of the same cultivar, it's called self-pollination. When the transfer occurs on different flowers on different cultivars, it's called cross-pollination. Cross-pollination often results in increased fruit size and fruit set.

When pollination is unsuccessful, it could be the result of incompatibility between cultivars or species. Incompatibility results from factors that inhibit the germination of the pollen grain or growth of the pollen tube, either of which prevents fertilization.

Fruit plants are often described as self-fruitful or self-unfruitful. A self-fruitful plant will reproduce sexually by itself, meaning that a single plant is sufficient to product fruit. Examples include blackberries, figs, peaches, and strawberries. Flowers of self-unfruitful plants are incompatible with their own pollen and require pollen from a different cultivar for best pollination and fruit set. Apples, blueberries, and plums are generally self-unfruitful.

Fertilization in angiosperms occurs when sperm nuclei from the pollen tube enters the ovule. One sperm nucleus unites with the egg to form a **zygote**, which will become an embryo (and eventually a new plant). The other sperm nucleus unites with two polar nuclei in the embryo sac to form the **endosperm**, which develops into food tissue. In most angiosperms, the time between pollination and fertilization is between 24-48 hours.

In cone-bearing gymnosperms, the male pollen-producing cones are produced separately from the female ovule-containing cones. There are no walls around the ovaries like there are in angiosperms, so naked seeds develop on the cone scales.

Fruits

Structure

When fertilization is successful, angiosperms produce seeds and fruits; gymnosperms produce only seeds. Some gymnosperms bear seeds in cones, while others, such as gingko, bear seeds surrounded by a fleshy structure called an aril. The fleshy, berry-like cones of juniper have fused, fleshy scales. Mosses and ferns reproduce by spores rather than seeds.

In a botanical sense, fruits only arise from flowering plants because floral organs become fruit tissue. Botanical fruits are different from the popular horticultural use of the terms fruits and vegetables. Some botanical fruits are called vegetables, such as corn, cucumber, eggplant, squash, and tomato. Botanically, tomatoes are a fruit because they develop from a flower—as do squash, cucumbers, and eggplants.

Botanically, a fruit is the mature ovary and other flower parts that have fused together. The fruit may include the receptacle along with floral parts such as petals, sepals, stamens, and the stylar portions of the pistil. The fruit also includes any seeds contained in the ovary.

Fruits are classified according to the number of ovaries that comprise the structure. Fruits may be simple, aggregate, or multiple (Figure 2.21).

Fruits are also classified by the nature and structure of their ovary wall, or pericarp. In mature fruit, those in which the enclosed seed is fully developed, the ovary wall may be fleshy or dry.

Simple Fruits

There are five types of simple, fleshy fruits: berry, pepo, hesperidium, drupe, and pome (Figure 2.21).

- When the entire pericarp of simple fruits is fleshy, the fruit is a **berry**; botanical berries include eggplant, grape, blueberry, and tomato. In horticulture, the term "berry" refers to the edible portion of some "small fruits".
- A **pepo** is a berry with a hard rind—like cucumber, pumpkin, and squash—that consists of exocarp and receptacle tissue.
- Citrus fruits are a kind of berry called a **hesperidium**; the leathery rinds of hesperidiums are made up of exocarp and mesocarp, and the edible, juicy portion of the fruit is endocarp.
- Simple fleshy fruits with a stony endocarp—such as almond, apricot, cherry, olive, peach, and plum—are called **drupes**, or stone fruits. The skin is exocarp, and the fleshy, edible portion is the mesocarp.
- When the inner portion of the fruit's pericarp forms a dry, paper-like "core," it is called a **pome**; pomes include apple, pear, and quince.

Other types of simple fruits are dry. Instead of becoming fleshy, the fruit wall becomes papery or leathery and hard. Simple fruits with dry ovary walls are classified into two categories by their ability to **dehisce**, or split apart when ripe: **dehiscent** or **indehiscent** (Figure 2.22).

- Dry dehiscent fruits split open along a defined suture or seam at maturity and release many seeds while still attached to the plant. Capsules

Figure 2.21 Examples of fleshy fruits

(as in poppies), follicles (as in larkspur), pods (as in peas) and siliques (as in crucifer) are all dehiscent structures.
- Dry simple fruits that do not dehisce or split open when ripe are called indehiscent fruits. They produce pulpy or nutlike fruits with a fruit wall that does not split at a seam. The achenes of strawberry, caryopses of corn, nuts of acorn, schizocarps of maple, and samaras of elm are all indehiscent forms.

Aggregate Fruits

An **aggregate fruit** consists of clusters of individual fruits that develop from a single flower with many pistils on a common receptacle. The ovaries are fertilized separately and independently. If the ovules are not pollinated successfully, fruits are misshapen. The individual fruits may be:

- **drupelets** (stony), as in blackberries and raspberries, which develop from separate ovaries

Figure 2.22 Examples of dry fruits

formed within a single flower and attached to the fleshy receptacle; or
- **achenes**, as in strawberry. When the strawberry fruit matures, the red, fleshy receptacle grows and enlarges to many times its original size before it softens and turns red. The true fruits, called achenes, are dry, ripened ovaries on the surface of the receptacle; each achene contains a single seed.

Multiple Fruits

Multiple fruits come from a tight cluster of many separate, independent flowers in a single inflorescence, borne on a single structure. Each flower has its own calyx, corolla, and ovary (only one), which results in the development of a pericarp. When the fruit matures, the pericarps fuse into a solid edible mass like pineapple. A fig is a multiple fruit made of many small drupes contained *inside* a fleshy receptacle, while a mulberry fruit is comprised of many drupelets borne *on* a fleshy receptacle.

Seeds

A seed, or mature ovule, is made up of three parts (Figure 2.23).

The dry and sometimes hard outer covering, or skin, is called a **seed coat** (testa); it protects the seed from disease and insects and prevents water from entering the seed and initiating the germination process before the proper time. Some thick seed coats need to be scarified or etched for water to reach the inside.

Inside the seed is the embryo, which looks like a miniature plant. It has a seedling root called a **radicle**, a short stem or embryonic shoot called a **plumule**, and leaves. When germination occurs, the embryo grows into a seedling. The root and stem tips of the embryo have apical meristems that begin primary growth.

Cotyledons, or seed leaves, are also present. In flowering plants, there may be one or two cotyledons; this distinction divides angiosperms into dicots (two cotyledons) and monocots (one cotyledon). The cotyledons are a part of the embryo. They expand after they emerge from the soil and then gradually shrink in size and shrivel as they transfer their stored foods to the seedling.

In addition to the cotyledon, the embryo relies on the endosperm, a built-in food supply of proteins, carbohydrates, or fats sustain the seedling during germination.

Seeds vary in shape, size, structure, and dissemination method. Some seeds, like those of milkweed and dandelion, have downy tufts that allow them to travel great distances on the air. Other seeds, such as maple and ash, have wings called samaras that help them fly. Orchids produce fine, dust-like seeds that can be carried by the wind.

Some fruits, like cockleburs and beggarticks, have hooks or barbs that catch on clothing or animal fur and help them hitchhike for great distances. Other fruit is enticing to animals that digest the fruit and distribute the seeds in their feces. Other seeds are eaten by animals but have tough seed coats that allow them to pass through the digestive tract unharmed.

Seed Germination

Seeds that are capable of germinating are said to be viable. **Germination** begins when the seed absorbs water through the seed coat (Figure 2.24). Water, oxygen, light, and temperature all affect germination. All plants require a continuous supply of oxygen and water to germinate, but they vary in their requirement for temperature and light. Each species often germinates best within an optimal range of temperatures rather than at one specific temperature. For more information about seed germination, refer to "Plant Propagation" in Chapter 3 and "Home Vegetable and Herb Gardening" in Chapter 8.

Water jumpstarts the process of converting the large food molecules of starch, protein, and fats in cotyledons

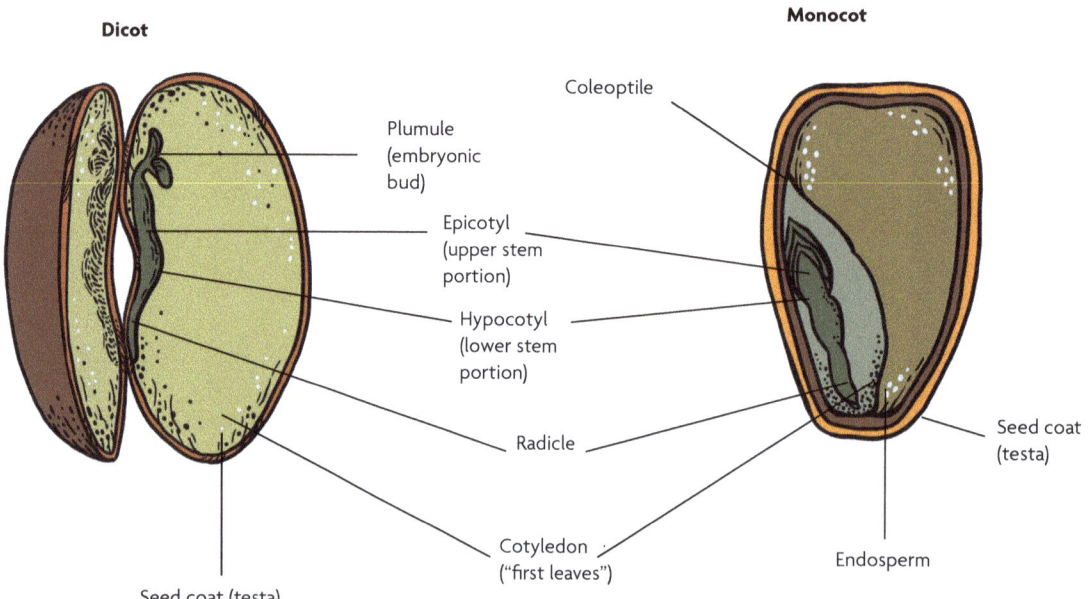

Figure 2.23 Parts of a dicot and monocot seed.

Germination of a monocot—Onion (*Allium cepa*)

Germination fo a dicot—Bean (*Phaseolus vulgaris*)

Figure 2.24 Germination of a monocot and dicot

or endosperm into sugars and amino acids, which can be transported and used by the embryo to create and grow new cells in the meristem. The radicle is the first part of the seedling to emerge from the seed. This embryonic root develops into a primary root that gives rise to root hairs and lateral roots.

Then the embryonic shoot, or **hypocotyl**, emerges and grows. The tip of the hypocotyl curves downward to pull the young seed leaves through the soil and protect the apical meristem contained between them. The cotyledons that encase the embryo are usually different in shape from the leaves produced by the mature plant, and the number of cotyledons identifies the plant as a monocot or dicot.

Germination ends when the shoot emerges from the soil. After the first leaves emerge from the soil and unfold, the plant no longer depends on stored food reserves from the cotyledons and endosperm. It begins to photosynthesize and produce its own food resources. The next chapter covers the physiological process of photosynthesis.

Classification of Horticultural Plants

To study and understand plants, they must be classified in an understandable way. Horticulturists and gardeners organize plants based on the length and season of their growth cycle, form or morphological habit, leaf retention, hardiness, and end use.

Growth Cycles

Plants are classified by the number of growing seasons required to complete their life cycle.

From a botanist's standpoint, **annuals** are plants that complete their entire life cycle in less than one calendar year; they grow, flower, produce seed, and then die without regard to temperature or other environmental conditions. Horticulturists define them differently, since annuals also include tropicals and other tender perennials that thrive for years in frost-free climates. Annuals are considered seasonal plants that occupy certain seasonal niches in the landscape before winter's cold or summer's heat causes them to decline or die.

Biennials start from seed and produce vegetative structures and food-storage organs the first season. During the first winter, a hardy evergreen rosette of basal leaves persists. During the second season, the plant bolts—a flower stalk emerges from the vegetative plant, produces flowers and seeds, and completes its life cycle. Then the plant dies. Carrots, beets, cabbage, celery, and onions are biennials whose flowers produce seeds that develop during the second year of growth. Hollyhock, foxglove, and sweet William are biennials commonly grown for their attractive flowers.

Perennial plants live for many years. After reaching maturity, they typically produce flowers and seeds annually. Perennials are classified as herbaceous (the botanical term for nonwoody plants) if the fleshy, soft tissue top dies back to the ground each winter and new stems grow from the crown each spring. They are classified as woody if the hard, fibrous top-growth persists, as it does in shrubs or trees.

Form or Structure

Grouped according to form, woody plants fall into the categories of vines, ground cover, shrubs, and trees.

A vine is a plant that develops long, trailing stems that grow along the ground or are supported by another plant or structure. Some twining vines, like hops or honeysuckle, circle a support clockwise; others, like pole beans and Dutchman's pipe vine, circle counterclockwise. Climbing vines can be supported by aerial roots like those in English ivy and poison ivy; slender tendrils

  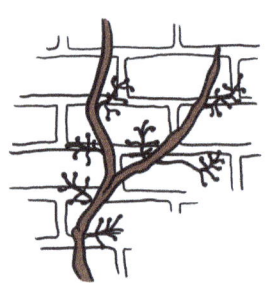 

Some vines have tendrils that wrap around any type of support.

The twining vines climb by winding their stems around any available support.

Some clinging vines climb by means of tendrils with disk-like adhesive tips that attach to any surface.

Other clinging vines attach themselves with small aerial rootlets along the stem.

Figure 2.25 Types of vines.

that encircle the supporting object, such as those in cucumber, gourds, grapes, and passionflowers; or tendrils with adhesive tips, such as Virginia creeper and Boston ivy (Figure 2.25).

Ground covers are vigorous, low-growing, ground-hugging herbaceous and woody plants that act as "living mulches" with their dense mat of stems and leaves. They range in height from a few inches to a couple feet. This catchall category of landscape plants includes shrubs, vines, perennials, ferns, ornamental grasses and sedges, and bamboos.

Shrubs and trees are self-supporting plants. A shrub has many stems that emerge from a single point or crown. A tree is characterized by a main trunk (and usually a distinct crown). Trees can be further classified by the general shape of their crowns, for which there are several descriptive terms.

Leaf and Needle Retention

Perennial plants generally fall into one of three categories: **deciduous**, **semievergreen**, or **evergreen**.

- Deciduous plants lose all of their leaves at some time during the fall and winter months.
- Semievergreen plants carry leaves for most of the year.
- Evergreen plants do not lose all of their leaves at once; the oldest leaves are shed periodically. At any time of year, evergreen plants have leaves. Evergreen plants are further divided into broad-leaved (such as boxwood, yaupon holly, and southern magnolia) or needle-leaved (such as cypress, juniper, and pine).

Climatic Adaptation

Perennial plants are classified by their ability to tolerate low temperatures. Tropical plants that originate in warm, frost-free regions between the tropics of Cancer and Capricorn are severely damaged or killed when temperatures fall to or below freezing (32°F). Subtropical plants tolerate brief exposures to temperatures near or slightly below freezing, usually overnight before and after slightly warmer days.

On the other hand, hardy temperate plants can survive in the prolonged below-freezing temperatures that occur in cold winter climates, and some can endure extreme low temperatures (depending on the hardiness of the plant). Hardy plants are classified based on cold hardiness zones. You can determine local hardiness zones on the USDA's plant hardiness zone map (planthardiness.ars.usda.gov/).

Most annual vegetables, flowers, and lawn and ornamental grasses are also classified by their temperature tolerances. Plants that tolerate a short-term period of freezing temperatures are known as hardy crops. Those that are killed or injured by freezing temperatures are nonhardy or tender crops. Plants are sometimes classified according to their temperature requirements during the growing season. Cool-season crops such as broccoli, cabbage, and garden peas grow best during the cooler months of the year; warm-season plants such as corn, tomatoes, and watermelons produce the highest-quality produce during the warmer summer months.

Uses

One ancient classification system categorized plants according to their uses. They were separated into those that were edible, those that provided fibers that could be spun into thread, those used as sources of drugs or spices, and those with ornamental value. Ornamentals are plants cultivated primarily for aesthetic beauty or to enhance the environment. Edible plants include those we think of as fruits, nuts, herbs, and vegetables.

There are problems with this classification system. Many edible crops, including tomato, pepper and cucumbers, are commonly classified as vegetables even though the edible portions are, botanically speaking, fruits. Some ornamental plants are edible as well as ornamental, such as serviceberry, blueberry, and pawpaw.

The horticultural classification system, which groups plants according to their economic importance, cultural requirements, and use and marketing, is an arbitrary system that changes as new plants are discovered and old ones are abandoned.

Scientific Plant Classification

The most precise method for classifying or categorizing all plants is a hierarchical system that accounts for the evolutionary associations between plants. This system of groups within groups is organized into categories. The broadest category is the plant kingdom (Plantae), which is divided into phyla (singular phylum), classes, orders, families, **genera** (singular genus), and **species** (singular species).

Many of the plants that are familiar to gardeners belong to two phyla of seed-bearing plants: the cone-bearing plants, or conifers (*Coniferophyta*), such as pines, firs, and spruces, and the true flowering plants, or angiosperms (*Anthophyta*).

Flowering plants, the most diverse group, are further divided into two classes: monocotyledons (grasses, palms, lilies, orchids) and dicotyledons (all other flowering plants). The term monocotyledon, or monocot, means "one seed leaf"; dicotyledon, or dicot, means "two seed leaves." So, a single leaf emerges from a germinating monocot seed while a pair of leaves emerge from a dicot seed.

Monocots and dicots have different morphological features. Typically, monocots have one seed leaf, flower parts multiples of three, vascular tissues arranged in scattered bundles, and leaves with parallel veins. Their primary vascular bundles in the stem are scattered, and there is no true secondary growth (Figure 2.26).

Dicots have two seed leaves, flowers parts in fours, fives, or multiples of these, vascular tissues arranged in concentric circles, and a netted pattern of leaf veins. Their primary vascular bundles are arranged in a ring in the stem. Many have vascular cambium and undergo secondary growth. In addition, monocots and dicots have physiological processes that differ from one another.

At the family level of classification, which is of interest to gardeners, plants share a number of structural and cultural similarities. For example, one well-known family of monocots are the grasses (*Poaceae*), and a well-known family of dicots includes roses, apples, pears, and firethorn (*Rosaceae*). Scientific family names always end with the suffix –aceae. Although these two families are very different, the individuals within them have many similar structural features, cultural requirements, and pest problems.

The scientific system of plant classification can be a useful tool for horticulturists when identifying unknown plants and developing or understanding cultural practices and problems associated with a given plant. Plants in the same species, and often those in the same genus, can be grafted to one another. Moreover, plants in a species and among species within a genus are often sexually compatible. However, among horticultural crops, there are several exceptions to this general rule.

Scientific Naming of Plants

The numerous attempts throughout history to identify and name plants in an orderly fashion gave birth to the internationally recognized botanical or scientific method of naming plants. Early attempts at identification relied on Latin words to describe various aspects of a plant. As botanists identified and classified more and more plants, the length of individual names increased. It was not uncommon for plant names or descriptions to have eight or more words.

In the mid-1750s, a Swedish botanist named Carolus Linnaeus (1707-1778) published Species Plantarum (which means "The Kinds of Plants") and changed the way plants are named.

Linnaeus, known as the father of taxonomy, shortened plant names to two words apiece, like how many people have one first name and one last name. Our last name identifies us as a member of a particular group, such as the Smith family or the Martinez family. In plant names, this group identifier is called the genus. Our first name specifically identifies which member of our surname group we are; John Smith and Paul Smith are identified as two distinct individuals within the Smith family. In plant identification, this more direct

Monocot

- Vascular tissues scattered in stem
- Flower parts in 3s or multiples
- Leaf venation parallel
- Seedlings with one seed leaf

Dicot

- Vascular tissues in a circular pattern or joined into a ring
- Flower parts in 4s or 5s or multiples
- Leaf venation branched
- Seedlings with two seed leaves

Figure 2.26 Comparison of monocot and dicot structures

identifier is called a **specific epithet**. When naming plants, we put the genus first and the specific epithet name next. For example, a man named John Smith would be referred to as Smith John—a member of the Smith family known individually as John. The cabbage palmetto, the state tree of South Carolina, is officially called a *Sabal palmetto*. Sabal is the genus; palmetto is the specific epithet. The two words together, or binomial, reference a species.

This naming format is known as the Latin system of **binomial nomenclature**. It's based on the principle that plants can be grouped according to similarities in morphological structures that are a result of their common ancestral history.

Sometimes a genus name is followed by "sp." The "sp." refers to a singular species or a plant whose specific epithet is not known; for example, "*Acer sp.*" can refer to any one plant in the genus Acer. "spp." is the plural form of "sp."; "*Acer spp.*" refers to all the species in the maple genus.

Plant nomenclature is written in Latin. In the 18th century, Latin was the language of science, and scientists carefully chose Latin plant names that provided information about the plant. Over the years, the system has been modified and expanded—but it is still the foundation of the modern system.

There is a specific way to write or type scientific names. Genus names are proper nouns and should always be capitalized; specific epithets are usually adjectives and always lower case.

The names of plants and other organisms follow the rules and recommendations of the International Code of Nomenclature for Algae, Fungi, and Plants. Before 2011, this was called the International Code of Botanical Nomenclature (ICBN). The current classification of the South Carolina state flower, Carolina jessamine (*Gelsemium sempervirens*), according to the Global Biodiversity Information Facility website, is:

Kingdom: Plantae
Phylum: Tracheophyta
Class: Magnoliopsida
Order: Gentianales
Family: Gelsemiaceae
Genus: *Gelsemium*
Specific epithet: *sempervirens*

Some plants may have a third Latin name after the genus and species; this third name refers to a subdivision of the species. These subdivisions are called varieties or subspecies; the two are essentially interchangeable terms. The differences between a true species and a **variety** of that species are inheritable and should show in succeeding generations. Variety is indicated in the plant name by "var." preceding the variety name. Subspecies is indicated by "subsp." in the same position. *Cercis canadensis* var. *alba*, for example, is an example of a variety of eastern redbud (*Cercis canadensis*) which has white flowers instead of the normal pink. *Hydrangea arborescens* subsp. *radiata* is a subspecies of smooth hydrangea that has silvery-white backing to the leaves and more showy sepals than the species. These true botanical subspecies and varieties may occur in natural plant populations.

Occasionally a plant name may have the letter "x" between the genus and species. This represents an interspecific hybrid resulting from a cross between two species within the genus. For example, *Viburnum* x *burkwoodii* (Burkwood viburnum) resulted from a cross between *V. carlesii* and *V. utile*.

When a plant name has the letter "x" before the genus name, then it is an intergeneric hybrid (a hybrid between two different genera). These are rare, but x*Fatshedera lizei*, for example, resulted from a cross between *Fatsia japonica* and *Hedera helix*.

Horticultural plants often have an additional name that follows the species name: the **cultivar** (a conjunction of the term "cultivated variety"). When a plant has a unique characteristic that differs from its species—such as different-colored flowers, shorter stature, or colorful leaves—it may be selected and maintained as a cultivar. Future generations of cultivars retain their distinguishing characteristics. Cultivars typically do not occur in nature and must be cultivated. Cultivar names are capitalized and either written with single quotes or followed by "cv." 'Gold Rush' dawn redwood (*Metasequoia glyptostroboides* 'Gold Rush') and Cherokee Chief dogwood (*Cornus florida* var. *rubra* cv. Cherokee Chief) are both cultivars. 'Gold Rush' has gold-colored leaves instead of the species' usually green; 'Cherokee Chief' dogwood has bracts of a deeper red than that of other plants of the rubra variety. Gardeners and horticulturists often refer to cultivars as varieties, but this is not the botanically correct term.

If the person who discovers a unique cultivar thinks it has considerable economic value, they may file for a plant patent. Plant patents have become a profitable component of the nursery industry, and patented plants are now common in the trade. The patent holder controls the propagation and distribution of patented plants and collects royalties on the plants produced. Only licensed nurseries are approved to propagate and sell patented plants; it is illegal to propagate them at home without permission. Patent status is usually printed on tags, labels, and literature distributed with plants, identified by a plant patent number (PP). For instance, *Magnolia grandiflora* 'Southern Charm' is PP 13,049. United States plant patents expire after 20 years. Once a patent expires, anyone can propagate and sell the plant.

Since plant patents expire, it is increasingly common to find trademarked names associated with plants. Officially registered trademarks expire after 10 years. However, the trademarks can be renewed perpetually in 10-year increments. This marketing name is not a part of the scientific name; however, it is easy to confuse some plants' trademarked names with their cultivar names, especially when the cultivar is a nonsensical word, but the trademark name is descriptive and/or appealing. For example, the scientific name of QVTIA live oak is *Quercus virginiana* 'QVTIA' (PP 11219). The official cultivar name is QVTIA, but its marketing name is Highrise®. The patented *Magnolia grandiflora* 'Southern Charm' is sold under the trademark of Teddy Bear® magnolia. Other trademarks may apply to a group of plants. One example is the popular line of Knock Out® roses. In this case, the trademark Knock Out® applies to a line or brand of roses, not a specific cultivar. Knock Out® roses include *Rosa* 'Radrazz' PP 11836 CPBR 0993 [The Knock Out® Rose], *Rosa* 'Radtko' PP 16202 CPBR 3104 [The Double Knock Out® Rose], and *Rosa* 'Radcon' PP 15070 CPBR 2044 [The Pink Knock Out® Rose].

In each of the examples above, the trademark name may be retained by the business or individual long after the patent expires. This means that while other nurseries will be able to propagate and sell the plant, they won't be able to sell it under the well-known trademark name without the permission of the brand.

For more detailed information on the legal implications of patented and trademarked plants, refer to the section on Copyrights, Trademarks, and Patents: Propagation Concerns in Chapter 3: Plant Propagation.

Although Latin names may be difficult to pronounce, they can also convey a lot of valuable and interesting information.

A species names may give you a clue as to the geographic origin of the plant, such as live oak (*Quercus virginiana*), American elm (*Ulmus americana*), Japanese andromeda (*Pieris japonica*), and Carolina buckthorn (*Rhamnus caroliniana*). Of course, these species names can also be misleading. For example, eastern red bud (*Cercis canadensis*) suggests that the plant is from Canada, but the vast majority of its native range is south of the Canadian border.

Other times, a botanical name honors the contributions of early botanists and plant explorers or commemorates a famous individual. For example, black-eyed Susan (*Rudbeckia hirta*) is named for Olaf Rudbeck, Carolus Linnaeus's mentor, who is known as the "father of modern botany." Magnolia was named after Pierre Magnol, a French botany professor. Wisteria (*Wisteria spp.*) was named after Caspar Wistar, a professor of anatomy at the University of Pennsylvania. Swedish botanist Karl Thunberg is referenced in several plant names, including Japanese black pine (*Pinus thunbergiana*) and blackeyed susan vine (*Thunbergia alata*). The botanist John Bartram named the Franklin tree (*Franklinia alatamaha*) to honor his friend Benjamin Franklin.

Often, scientific names are based in Latin. These Latin roots can give hints to a plant's size, form, growth style, color, or smell. Some names even identify a plant as deciduous or evergreen. See table 2.1 for some of the more common plants with helpful Latin names.

One complication of modern plant taxonomy is that scientific names are not permanent. They can and often do change as we learn more about plants and how they are related. Historically, plants were classified based on morphological features like flowers, leaves, and fruit, but modern molecular genetics have revolutionized our

TABLE 2.1 LATIN ROOTS IN BOTANICAL PLANT NAMES

Latin Root	Meaning	Example
Minor	Small	Periwinkle (*Vinca minor*)
Ovata	Oval- or egg-shaped	Mountain camellia (*Stewartia ovata*)
Macro	Large	Dutchman's pipe (*Aristolochia macrophylla*)
Erectus	Upright	Stinking Benjamin (*Trillium erectum*)
Scandens	Climbing	Bleeding heart (*Dicentra scandens*)
Repens	Creeping	Trailing arbutus (*Epigaea repens*)
Alba	White	White oak (*Quercus alba*)
Nigra	Black	River birch (*Betula nigra*)
Roseus	Rose-colored	Rose coreopsis (*Coreopsis rosea*)
Fulvus	Orange-gray-yellow	Orange daylily (*Hemerocallis fulva*)
Fragrans	Odor or fragrance	Fragrant tea-olive (*Osmanthus fragrans*)
Odoratus	Fragrant or perfumed	Sweet pea (*Lathyrus odoratus*)
Foetidus	Fetid, stinking, or evil-smelling	Bear's-foot hellebore (*Helleborus foetidus*)
Decidua	Deciduous	Possumhaw holly (*Ilex decidua*)
Semper virens	Always green	Yellow jessamin (*Gelsemium sempervirens*)

understanding of evolutionary relationships. As a result, many plants have been assigned new species names or genus names over the past 20-30 years. For example, muscadine grapes were traditionally classified in the grape genus, *Vitis*. Recent genetic evidence, along with morphological features, have convinced most botanists that muscadines are different enough from *Vitis* grape species to deserve their own genus. They have since been awarded the genus name of *Muscadinia*. These changes can be frustrating for the gardener or horticulturist, but they are important to organization, clarity, and the overall science of botany.

Although scientific names may be intimidating, they establish a plant's identity, remember:

- A plant may have several common names that differ between geographic regions.
- Sometimes, two unrelated plants share a common name. For example, the common name quince may refer to both the edible fruit tree, *Cydonia oblonga*, and multiple species of ornamental flowering shrubs in the genus *Chaenomeles*.
- A plant can only have one scientific name.

Understanding the plant classification system can help you discover the similarities and differences between plants.

While it's important to understand the scientific names of plants, it's not important to know how to pronounce them. Often, others aren't sure of how to say them either. As long as both parties know the scientific names of the plants about which they're talking, communication will be clear.

PLANT PHYSIOLOGY

Photosynthesis, respiration, and transpiration are the three basic functions of plants.

Photosynthesis

One of the major differences between plants and animals is that most plants can make their own food. To do so, a plant requires energy from sunlight to react with **chlorophyll**—the green pigment in plants—carbon dioxide from the air, and water from the soil. If any of these ingredients is lacking, food production from photosynthesis will stop. If any ingredient is removed for too long, the plant will die.

Photosynthes literally means "to put together with light." In plants, light is absorbed by photosynthetic pigments in the chloroplasts of cells and used as energy to chemically convert carbon dioxide to sugar and gaseous oxygen. The photosynthetic process releases oxygen and produces sugar (Figure 2.27). Sugar molecules formed during photosynthesis serve as a plant's primary source of food. Photosynthesis in its simplest form is represented by this equation:

$$\text{Carbon Dioxide} + \text{Water} \xrightarrow[\text{Chlorophyll}]{\text{Sunlight}} \text{Sugar} + \text{Oxygen}$$

The most abundant pigment in plants is chlorophyll, found in the membrane of chloroplasts. Chlorophyll A is involved directly in the light reactions of photosynthesis, but plant cells also contain pigments such as chlorophyll B, carotenoids, and anthocyanins. The color of the pigment is produced by the **wavelengths** of reflected light, or the light wavelengths not absorbed by the leaf. The action spectrum of photosynthesis is the relative effectiveness of different wavelengths of light at generating the electrons needed for photosynthesis (Figure 2.28). The absorption spectrum of chlorophyll B peaks at wavelengths where the absorption of chlorophyll A begins to dip. The chlorophylls have minimum absorption in the range of green light, so they reflect it and appear green in color. However, there is some photosynthetic activity even at green wavelengths, because **accessory pigments**, such as carotenoids, are still present.

Each pigment reacts with only a narrow range of the light spectrum, so usually, plants need to produce several kinds of pigments—each of a different color—to capture more of the sun's energy. Carotenoids are usually red, orange, or yellow pigments; these pigments include the carotene compound, which gives carrots their color. Carotenoids cannot transfer energy from the sun directly to the photosynthetic pathway; instead, they pass their absorbed energy to chlorophyll pigments. Because of this, they are called accessory pigments. The relative abundance of pigments in leaves gives them their color.

Plants store the energy from light in carbohydrates such as sugars and starches; they can use the stored energy when light is limited. Plants can also move these chemicals to their roots. Throughout the plant, sugars and starches are converted back to water and carbon dioxide, and the stored energy is released to perform activities necessary for growth. This process is called respiration.

Only cells that have chlorophyll can produce energy. Most of these cells are in the mesophyll layer of a plant's leaves—between the upper and lower epidermis of the leaf—but any plant part that is green contains chlorophyll

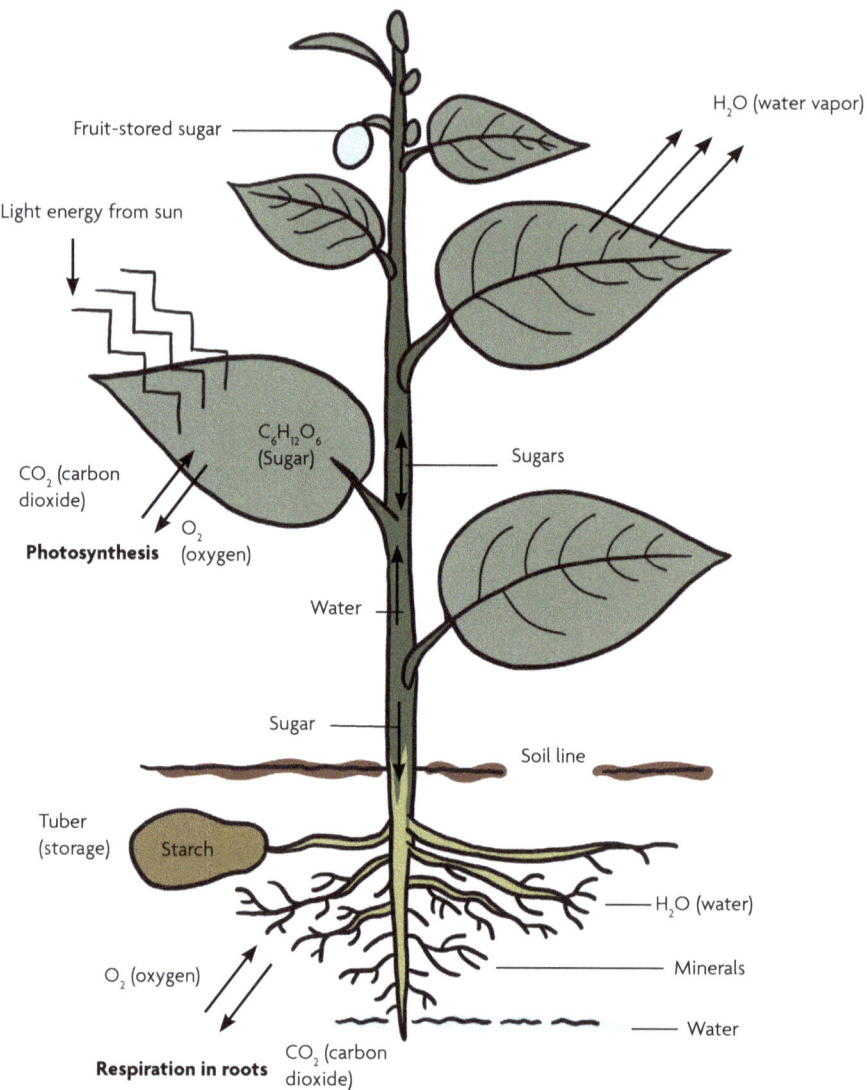

Figure 2.27 Illustration of photosynthesis and respiration. Photosynthesis and respiration are complementary processes. Photosynthesis, which takes place in the chloroplasts of leaves, uses sunlight, carbon dioxide, and water to produce glucose and oxygen. Respiration, which takes place in the mitochondria of all plant cells, uses glucose and oxygen to produce energy and release carbon dioxide and water.

activity increases as the intensity of the sunlight increases. This increase leads to greater food production. Many garden crops, such as tomatoes, respond best to maximum sunlight. When light intensity drops, tomato production decreases drastically. Only a small number of tomato varieties will produce any fruit in greenhouses from late fall to early spring months, when sunlight is minimal, without artificial lighting. Other plants, such as dogwoods, azaleas, hostas, and ferns, can produce sufficient food for optimal growth at lower light levels. In fact, excessive light levels may harm some shade-loving plants, often indicated by bleaching of the chlorophyll, increased production of other pigments (the red color of anthocyanins), leaf scorching, leaf edge burn, or bark or stem damage.

Water is also a vital component of photosynthesis. To begin with, hydration maintains a plant's turgor—the firmness or fullness of plant tissue. Turgor pressure in a cell is like air pressure in an inflated tire. Turgor maintains the plant's shape and ensures cell growth. Then, chlorophyll splits water into separate hydrogen and oxygen molecules as it absorbs the sun's energy. The cells release oxygen into the atmosphere and use hydrogen to make carbohydrates and other energy-storing compounds. Additionally, water dissolves minerals from the soil and transports them from the roots to the rest of the plant. Some minerals are required for efficient photosynthesis; they are components of the chlorophyll molecules, catalysts of the process, and raw materials used to grow tissue.

For photosynthesis to occur, the stomata must be open to allow carbon dioxide (CO_2) to enter the leaf. CO_2 in the air is usually plentiful enough that it is not a limiting factor in plant growth. However, since

(even stems, roots, and fruits). The chlorophyll pigment traps light energy within a specific wavelength for use in manufacturing the sugar and starches that serve as the plant's food supply. Plants are the primary source of food for all other living things, so chlorophyll is at least indirectly responsible for supplying food to all living things on Earth; coupled with its role in the release of the oxygen that all animals depend on to breathe, it is hard to overstate the importance of this pigment.

Photosynthesis depends on the availability of light. Plant species vary somewhat in the light levels needed for optimal photosynthesis, but usually, photosynthetic

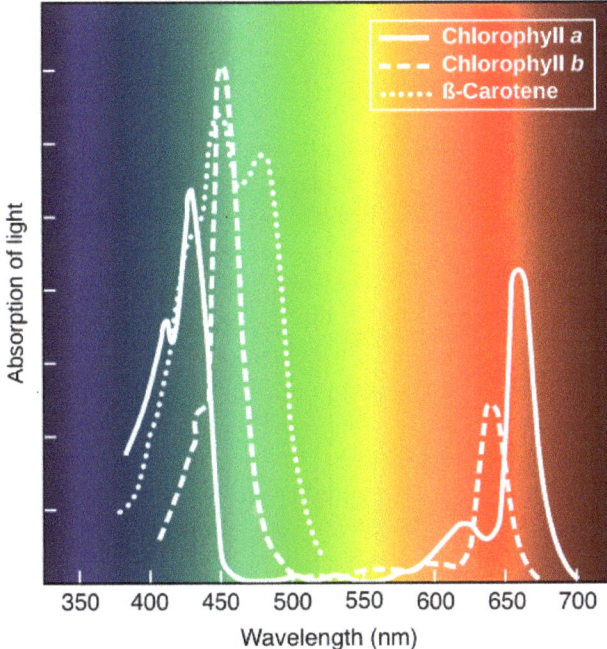

Figure 2.28 In the electromagnetic spectrum of energy, only a small portion is visible light. Plants primarily absorb light from the red and blue regions of the visible spectrum.
Image Credit: *Biology* by OpenStax. CC BY 4.0

the superior heat and drought tolerance of warm-season grasses.

Although temperature is not a leading factor in photosynthesis, it is still important. Photosynthesis occurs at its highest rate from 65-85°F and decreases with temperatures outside of this range.

Respiration

Carbohydrates made during photosynthesis are valuable when they become energy. The plant uses this energy to build new tissues or to keep the plant growing. The chemical process by which the sugars and starches produced in photosynthesis are converted into energy is called **oxidation**. Oxidation is similar to the burning of wood or coal to produce heat. Controlled oxidation in a living cell, known as **respiration**, is shown in its simplest form by this equation:

Sugar + Oxygen → Carbon dioxide + Water + Heat

This equation is just the opposite of that used to illustrate photosynthesis. However, respiration is accomplished through a complicated series of reactions regulated by enzymes. Complex carbohydrates break down and become simple carbohydrates, carbon dioxide, and water; the plant can use the energy released by this reaction in many other cell processes and functions. We can think of photosynthesis as a building process and respiration as a break-down process.

A plant's rate of respiration depends primarily on the temperature and nearly doubles for every 18°F rise between 40 and 96°F; additionally, the availability of oxygen and carbohydrates impact the respiration rate. At any given temperature, young, rapidly growing tissues have the highest rate of respiration while dormant tissues have the lowest. Respiration always occurs in living tissues, even in plant parts removed during harvest. Thus, storage conditions for harvested fruits and vegetables are very important.

The respiration process is the reverse of photosynthesis. But unlike photosynthesis, respiration takes place at night as well as during the day. Respiration occurs in all life forms and in all cells. The release of accumulated carbon dioxide and the uptake of oxygen occurs at the cellular level. In animals, blood carries both carbon dioxide and oxygen to and from the atmosphere by means of lungs or gills. In plants, oxygen and carbon dioxide move within the plant from a region of higher concentration of those molecules to a region of lower concentration. This movement

CO_2 is consumed when making sugars, a well-sealed greenhouse may not allow enough outside air to enter during the winter to maintain adequate levels. In these conditions, roses, carnations, tomatoes, and other plants improve if CO_2 levels increase due to adequate venting or the use of carbon dioxide generators; in small greenhouses, dry ice can also increase CO_2 levels.

There are certain types of plants that vary in basic morphology, allowing some to be more efficient in certain environments. One good example of this difference in efficiency is the difference between cool season grasses and warm season grasses. Physiologically, cool-season turfgrasses are called C3 (Calvin cycle) grasses; that is, their photosynthetic pathway involves using carbon dioxide linked to form a series of three-carbon molecules that are directly transformed into glucose, a six-carbon sugar. Warm-season grasses use the more photosynthetically efficient C4 (Hatch and Stack) pathway in which carbon is first fixed in a four-carbon intermediary compound before being transformed into glucose in the Calvin cycle. Thus, warm-season plants are more photosynthetically efficient than cool season plants. This is especially true as temperatures rise during the summer. This helps explain the lack of heat and drought tolerance of cool-season grasses and

Transpiration

Transpiration is the loss of water vapor from leaves through the stomata via evaporation. The process is directly responsible for the movement of water from the soil and into the leaves; this water carries nutrients from dissolved minerals. Transpiration also aids a plant's temperature regulation, cooling the plant as it becomes too warm.

Plants regulate transpiration by opening and closing their stomata. Stomata are small openings bordered by guard cells in the epidermis of leaves and stems (Figure 2.29). Stomata open when the guard cells take up water and swell, allowing carbon dioxide to enter the leaf for photosynthesis and water vapor to escape. They typically close at night or when the roots sense a deficit of water in the soil, as during a drought.

Water moves along a force/concentration gradient, which is relatively high in the soil and root zone area and relatively low in the air and leaf area (Figure 2.30). As water evaporates from the leaves, a tension develops between the leaves and the roots. The unique properties of water allow it to flow in a long column that acts like a bungee cord to "pull" itself up through the plant with its own tension. There is a continuous column of water in the xylem as long as the stomata are open and water is available in the soil. The upward movement of water from the roots through the xylem to the uppermost leaves is caused primarily by transpiration. Water loss from the stomates creates a diffusion gradient from the soil, through the plant, and into the atmosphere that is sufficient to pull the water through the plant.

Most plant species adapted to temperate climates close their stomata at night, and transpiration ceases. Transpiration helps to cool plants on hot days through the cooling effect of evaporation and serves to transport minerals from the soil, organic compounds from the roots, and sugars and plant chemicals to plant cells.

The amount of water lost from the plant through transpiration depends on environmental factors such as temperature, relative humidity, and wind or air movement. As temperature or air movement increases, transpiration increases. As humidity decreases, transpiration increases.

Environmental Factors That Affect Plant Growth

A plant's environment determines how well a plant grows and how widely its seeds are distributed. If any environmental condition is less than ideal, it can stunt plant growth and limit the plant's geographic reach for distribution. For example, cacti and succulents are adapted to thrive with very little water; this is how they can survive in deserts. However, they can receive too

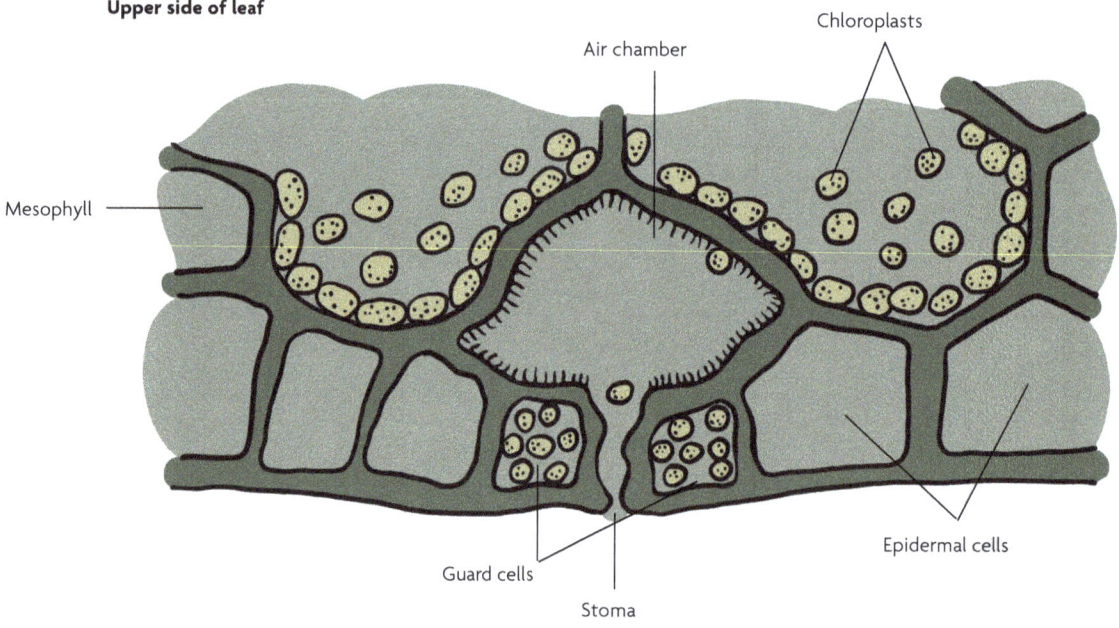

Figure 2.29 Cross-section of a leaf showing the location of the stoma and guard cells

Figure 2.30 Transpiration and water movement occurs as a result of a water potential gradient. The water vapor pressure deficit of the air must be lower than the water potential of the leaves for transpiration to occur.

are caused either directly or indirectly by environmental stressors. Therefore, it is important to understand the environmental factors that affect plant growth: light, temperature, water, humidity, and nutrition.

Light

Three principal characteristics of light affect plant growth: quantity, quality, and duration.

Light quantity refers to the intensity or concentration of sunlight and varies with the season. Maximum light quantity occurs in the summer and minimum light quantity occurs in winter. Up to a point, the more sunlight a plant receives, the better it can produce food via photosynthesis. As the quantity of sunlight decreases, so does the efficiency of the photosynthetic process. Sometimes, however, a particularly high quantity of light can overheat or dehydrate a plant. You can decrease light quantity in a garden by using overstory trees or shade cloth above the plants; in a greenhouse, you can cover the structure with a woven shade cloth. You can increase light quantity by surrounding plants with reflective material, white backgrounds, or supplemental lights.

Light quality refers to the color or wavelength of light that reaches the plant. Plants are sensitive to almost the same range of light energy as is the human eye; however, human vision and plant light usage are very different. The natural daylight we see is the visible portion of the light spectrum emitted by the sun. When white light passes through a prism, it separates into the colors of

much moisture in other environments, which limits their growth. One critical consideration in making plant recommendations for a given landscape is the cold or heat tolerance of the plant species. Tropical flowers accustomed to warm, moist environments are unlikely to thrive in a cool, dry climate, for example.

Most problems with a plant's growth or appearance

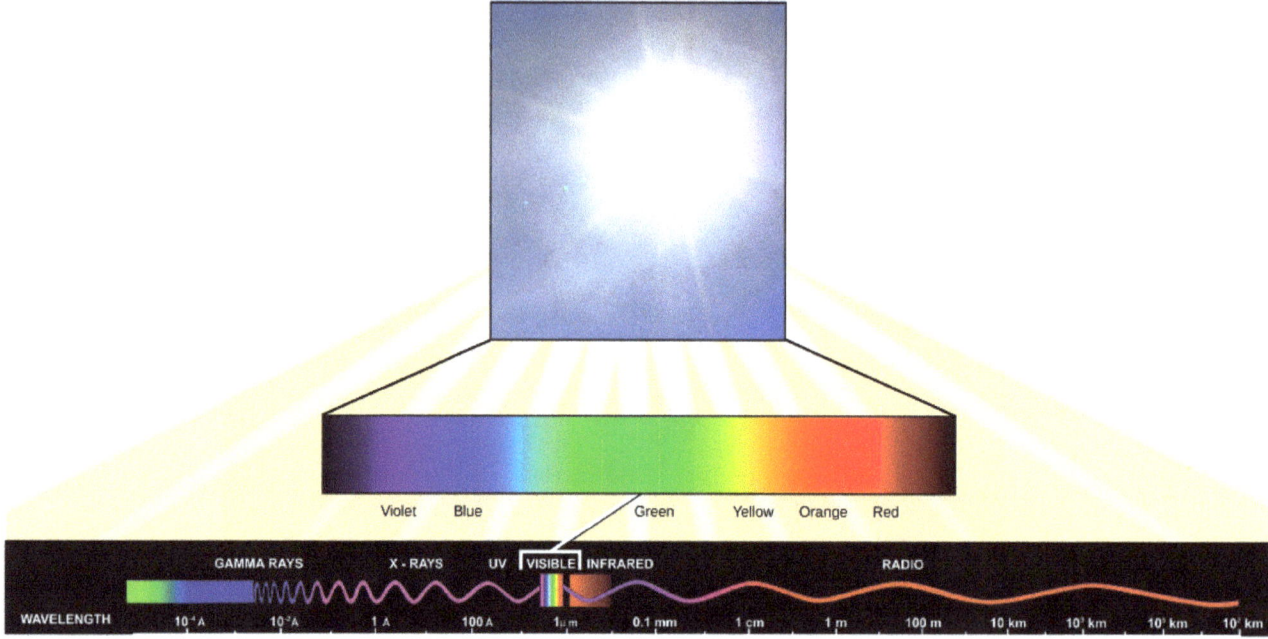

Figure 2.31 The visible light spectrum within the electomagnetic spectrum.
Image Credit: *Biology* by OpenStax. CC BY 4.0

differing wavelengths, called a spectrum: red, orange, yellow, green, blue, indigo, and violet (Figure 2.31). The shorter the wavelength, the greater the energy. Visible wavelengths range from about 400 nm (violet/blue) to 700 nm (red); nm stands for nanometer, a unit of length that is one billionth of a meter. Ultraviolet (UV) light is shorter than the blue range, and far-red, infrared, and heat are longer than red. The sun emits all of these wavelengths, and all of the wavelengths have some effect on plant growth.

Humans see best in the yellow/green region, while red and blue are the most effective wavelengths for photosynthesis. The yellow/green region is photosynthetically inefficient. It takes a much greater amount of energy from yellow/green light to drive photosynthesis than it does with either blue or red light.

Changes in light quality can induce physiological, biochemical, and morphological changes in the plant, which allow it to adapt to changes in the environment. The process by which light influences the form of plants is called **photomorphogenesis**. Studies at Clemson University and other institutions have found that far-red light—which is invisible to us but useful to plants—affects plant structure. For example, plants shaded by taller neighboring plants often develop elongated stems and/or larger leaves. The plants adapt to the lack of light by growing taller and producing larger leaves that can capture more sunlight for photosynthesis.

These morphological changes are caused not only by a reduction in light quantity but also by the kind of light reaching the plant. Ordinarily, there is less far-red than red in sunlight. However, when red light is absorbed or "filtered out" by higher leaves, the relative amount of far-red light increases in the lower, shaded leaves—which results in a change in plant form.

No artificial light can duplicate the light quality produced by the sun. However, modern LED technology is getting closer. Incandescent light has a broad range of wavelengths but lacks blue light and emits more heat; incandescent lights also emit a higher percentage of far-red than red light, which can cause plants to "stretch." You can increase the intensity of an incandescent light to drive photosynthesis, but at a certain level, heat becomes a problem.

Fluorescent light contains blue and red light but no far-red. The intensity of fluorescent lights is very low, so it is not photosynthetically effective except when the lights can be placed very close to the plants, as with African violets. Fluorescent lights are well-suited to seed germination, because red light promotes the germination of many seeds while far-red inhibits germination. Cool white, warm white, and expensive grow-light bulbs are all commercially available as fluorescent tubes. Of the three, cool white tubes are the best value for seed starting. Grow lights produce a spectrum that attempts to mimic sunlight as closely as possible. They have more red light than cool white bulbs. Grow lights are well-suited for growing flowering plants but are costly, and some researchers consider them of equal or lesser value than regular cool white, fluorescent lights.

Within the last decade, the use of light emitting diode (LED) technology has become more common in horticultural crop production. LED grow lights offer many benefits over other light sources, including reduced energy use, longer lifespan, more compact device size, and greater design flexibility. Additionally, LED grow lights produce much less heat than incandescent lighting—permitting closer proximity to plants—, and their wavelengths are customized for optimal plant growth. While LED grow lights are more expensive than incandescent and fluorescent bulbs, they may have value for the home gardener—particularly for indoor seed starting.

Light duration refers to the amount of time that a plant is exposed to or deprived of sunlight and is called photoperiod. In a natural environment, light duration is equal to the day length (the proportion of light and dark in a 24-hour period). Photoperiodism refers to the effects of day length on plant development. When scientists began to study photoperiods, they thought that flowering was triggered by the length of the light periods. However, they soon discovered it is not the length of the light period, but the length of uninterrupted dark periods, that is critical to flower development. Many plants' photoperiods control their ability to flower.

Depending on their flowering response to the duration of light or darkness, plants can be classified into three categories: short-day, long-day, or day-neutral plants.

Short-day or long-night plants require a critical period of uninterrupted darkness to flower (Figure 2.32). Chrysanthemum, Poinsettia, and Thanksgiving cactus are all short-day plants.

Long-day or short-night plants only form flowers when they experience long periods of light and short periods of darkness. Almost all summer flowering plants, such as Black-eyed Susan, Shasta daisy, and Purple Coneflower, are long-day plants.

Day-neutral plants form flowers regardless of day length. Many of the day-neutral plants originated in the equatorial tropics, where day length remains near 12 hours year-round. Day-neutral plants include geraniums and begonias.

Some plants do not fit neatly into any one category but are responsive to combinations of day lengths. For example, petunias will flower regardless of day length, but they flower earlier and more profusely with long days.

You can also manipulate plants into experiencing a different day length than what is occurring naturally. Since chrysanthemums flower during the short days of spring or fall, they can suffer during winter, when the days are longer. To trick them into flowering despite the time of year, you can draw a black cloth over the plant for 13 hours each day to keep out all light and simulate darkness; this should continue until flower buds initiate and develop to the point where first color begins to show. To bring a long-day plant into flower when sunlight is no longer than 12 hours, you can add artificial light to extend day length until flower buds are formed and first color shows.

Temperature

Temperature affects a plant's productivity and growth; there are both warm- and cool-season crops. If temperatures are high and day length is long, cool-season crops such as spinach will "**bolt**"—that is, initiate flower development. Temperatures that are too low for warm-season crops, such as tomato or eggplant, will prevent

Figure 2.32 A short-day plant flowers when the period of darkness exceeds the critical minimum. A long-day plant flowers when the night length is less than the critical minimum.

fruit set. Adverse temperatures also cause stunted growth and poor-quality vegetables. For example, high growing temperatures cause bitterness in lettuce.

Sometimes, it is possible to manipulate flowering with a combination of both temperatures and day length. Chrysanthemums will flower for longer if daytime temperatures are at least 59°F. Christmas cactus flower with short days or low temperatures. Temperature alone also influences flowering. You can force daffodil flowering, for example, by putting the bulbs in cold storage in October at 35-40°F. Besides encouraging rooting, the cold temperatures cause the stems to elongate. Then, you can transfer the bulbs to a warm greenhouse in midwinter, where rapid growth begins. In 3-4 weeks, the flowers are ready to be cut.

Thermoperiod refers to a daily temperature change. Plants respond to and produce maximum growth when exposed to a daytime temperature that is about 10-15 degrees higher than the night temperature. This allows the plant to photosynthesize and respire during an optimum daytime temperature and to reduce the rate of respiration during the cooler night. Higher temperatures increase respiration—sometimes above the rate of photosynthesis. This means that the products of photosynthesis are used more rapidly than they are produced. For growth to occur, photosynthesis must be greater than respiration.

Temperatures that are too low can result in poor growth. Photosynthesis slows down, and as a result, growth slows—producing lower yields. Not all plants grow best within the same temperature range. For example, snapdragons grow best at nighttime temperatures of 55°F, while poinsettias grow best at nighttime temperatures of 62°F. Cyclamen does well under very cool conditions, whereas many bedding plants prefer higher temperatures.

In some cases, however, plants require a certain number of days with low temperatures to grow properly. This is usually true of crops that grow best in colder regions. Peaches are a prime example of this: most varieties require 700 to 1,000 hours between 32°F-45°F before they break their rest period and begin growth. Most lilies require six weeks of temperatures near 33°F before they will bloom.

Plants are classified as either **hardy** or **nonhardy** depending on their ability to withstand cold temperatures. Winter injury can occur to nonhardy plants if temperatures are too low or if unseasonably low temperatures occur earlier or later than usual. Winter injury may also occur due to desiccation or drying out. Plants need water during the winter, but when the soil is frozen, the movement of water into the plant is severely restricted. On a windy winter day, evergreens like hollies, magnolias, and many conifers can become water-deficient in just a few minutes, and their leaves or needles turn brown. On the other hand, periods of above-average temperatures during the winter—coupled with rain showers and followed by temperatures falling rapidly to below freezing—can result in bark-splitting in azaleas, rhododendrons, and *Pieris japonica*.

Wide variations in winter temperatures can cause premature bud-break in some plants and consequent freeze damage to fruit buds. Late spring frosts can ruin entire peach crops. If temperatures drop too low during the winter, entire trees of some species can be killed by the freezing and splitting of plant cells and tissue. The roots of many plants are less temperature-hardy than their stems and buds.

Water

Water is a primary component of photosynthesis, respiration, and transpiration. It maintains the turgor of tissues and transports nutrients throughout the plant. Water is the major constituent of cell protoplasm. Through turgor pressure and other changes in the cell, water regulates the opening and closing of the stomates, which regulate transpiration. The gradual evaporation of water from the leaf surface near the stomates helps regulate overall plant temperature. Water also provides the pressure to move a root through the soil. Among the most critical roles of water is that of a solvent for minerals moving into the plant and for carbohydrates moving to their site of use or storage.

Relative humidity is the ratio of water vapor in the air at a given temperature and pressure to the amount of water the air can hold at that temperature and pressure, expressed as a percentage. For example, if a pound of air at 75°F can hold 4 grams of water vapor, and there are only 3 grams of water in the air, then the relative humidity (RH) is calculated as follows:

RH = water in air/water that air can hold (at constant temperature and pressure)

Example: $3g\ H_2O / 4g\ H_2O \times 100 = 75\%$ relative humidity.

Warm air can hold more water vapor than cold air. Therefore, if the amount of water in the air stays the same and the temperature increases, the relative humidity decreases.

Water vapor will move from an area of high relative humidity to one of low relative humidity. The greater the difference in humidity, the faster the water will move.

When the relative humidity in the air space between

leaf cells approaches 100% and the stomates open, water vapor rushes out. As water moves out, a bubble of high humidity forms around the stomate. This bubble of humidity helps slow down transpiration and cool the leaf. If winds blow the humidity bubble away, transpiration increases.

Nutrient Uptake

Plant growth and development both depend on the availability of water and several essential mineral nutrients (see Chapter 1, "Soils and Plant Nutrition.") Photosynthesis, respiration, and other processes require these nutrients, which unite with carbohydrates to form important compounds.

Plants obtain all water and most of their mineral nutrients from the soil. Most water and mineral uptake occurs along the very small, fibrous portions of a plant's root system through a combination of chemical and physical processes. Some of these processes require root cells to expend chemical energy through respiration.

Water from soil is mostly pulled from the soil up through the plant and out of the stomata by transpiration. Some of the plant-essential nutrients dissolve in the soil water and are transported to the root surface during the process. As discussed in Chapter 1, most nutrient elements are absorbed as charged ions, which may be positively charged cations or negatively charged anions. Nutrients also move to the root surface by diffusing along a concentration gradient or by physically intercepting growing root tips. Once nutrients are near the root surface, their uptake by the roots often involves the expenditure of chemical energy.

Plants absorb nutrients from minerals both passively and actively. Passive nutrient uptake requires no energy output by the plant. Nutrients flow through the plant because of the different concentrations of the nutrient between the soil solution and the liquid within the cell. Nutrients that are actively absorbed require energy from the plant. If no oxygen is available to a plant's roots, the plant cannot metabolize the sugar to produce energy; therefore, the plant can't absorb the nutrients.

Anything that slows or prevents the production of sugars in the leaves can slow nutrient absorption. If the plant is under stress because of low light or extreme temperatures, it may develop nutrient deficiencies. The stage of growth or how actively the plant is growing may also affect uptake. Many plants go into a rest state, or dormancy, for part of the year. During this period, they absorb very few nutrients.

Nutrients transported from the roots to living cells by the vascular system move into the cells through the cell membranes. Cells absorb nutrients in three different ways.

First, an entire molecule or ion pair may move through the membrane. If the cell is using energy or active transport to absorb the ions, then only one ion of the pair is pulled into the cell. The other will follow to keep the number of positive and negative charges even. Most anions are absorbed actively.

The second way of keeping the charges inside the cell balanced while absorbing a new ion is to exchange one charged ion for another one of the same charge. The cells will often release a hydrogen ion (H+) so that it can absorb another positive ion, such as potassium (K+). Since this is a simple, or passive, absorption, it may not require energy. In this way, the cell can passively absorb cations.

Both of the above absorption methods can be passive or active. However, the third method, the carrier system, always involves active absorption—which requires energy. Scientists have discovered specialized chemicals within the cell membrane that act as carriers. A carrier attracts an ion outside the cell membrane and releases it inside the cell, all via chemical changes. Once the ion is inside the cell, it attaches to other ions so that it does not move out of the cell. Complex chemical reactions are involved in the entire process.

Although cells can absorb nutrients passively, research shows that plants do require some active absorption to grow and be healthy. The same factors that affect root absorption—discussed earlier in this chapter—also affect absorption by the cell.

Chapter 3
Plant Propagation

*Revised and updated by Bob Polomski,
Jeanne Briggs, and Jeff Adelberg
Previous version prepared by: Bob Polomski*

LEARNING OBJECTIVES
- Understand the basic principles of starting plants from seed.
- Know how to propagate plants from leaf, stem, and root cuttings.
- Be familiar with layering, grafting, and budding as methods of plant propagation.

INTRODUCTION

Plant propagation is the process of making new plants from existing ones. Propagation can increase the numbers of species, perpetuate an existing species, or maintain the vigor of a species. You can propagate plants using seeds (sexual propagation) or vegetative plant parts (asexual propagation). In this chapter, we discuss the advantages and disadvantages of sexual and vegetative propagation as well as several methods of asexual propagation: cuttings, layers, divisions of subterranean stems, and grafting.

SEXUAL OR SEED PROPAGATION

Sexual propagation follows the union of pollen and egg, creating a new plant using the genetic material of two parent plants. This third plant will not be an exact copy of either parent. Sexual propagation involves the floral parts of a plant; pollen from the male anthers unites with the egg in the female ovule to produce a seed. The seed is made up of three parts: the outer protective seed coat; the endosperm, which is a food reserve; and the **embryo**, which is the young plant itself. When a seed is mature and placed in a favorable environment, it will germinate and begin to grow.

There are several advantages of sexual propagation. First and foremost, it may be a cheaper and faster method than asexual propagation. Second, it is the only way to obtain new varieties and hybrid vigor. Third, it is the only viable method of propagation for some plant species. Fourth, it is a way to avoid transmitting many diseases.

Although most plants produce seeds, seed propagation is most common for grains, vegetables, annual flowers, and easy-to-grow perennials. It is less common to use seed propagation to grow woody fruit plants, woody ornamentals, and some of the more difficult-to-germinate perennials. It is even more rare to propagate hybrid or highly-selected plants from seeds, as these new plants grown from seed rarely resemble the parents.

Although seed-propagated perennials take several years to flower and fruit, sexual propagation is often the preferred method. For example, nurseries raise rootstocks for grafting from seeds, because seed propagation can give rise to seedlings that may be superior to their parents. Many native plant nurseries propagate from seeds to enhance diversity in gardens and stagger the timing of fruit production—which helps sustain wildlife.

Seeds

To obtain quality plants, sexual propagation must begin with quality seeds from a reliable source. Many newer vegetable and flower varieties are hybrids and may cost more than open-pollinated plants. However, hybrid plants are usually more vigorous, have greater uniformity, and produce more fruit or flowers than non-hybrids. They may also be resistant to specific diseases or have unique cultural characteristics.

Some seeds will keep for several years if stored properly, but it is best to purchase only enough seeds for the year in which you'll plant them. Quality seed does not include seeds from other crops or weeds and has little debris. The seed packet provides essential information about the variety, the year the seeds were packaged, percent germination, and notes about any chemical treatment of the seeds. Always store seeds in a cool, dry place. Laminated foil packets help ensure dry storage, but paper packets should be stored in tightly-closed jars or containers kept in a low-humidity environment around 40°F.

Many gardeners harvest and save seed from their own gardens. It's important to know that many varieties of plants will cross pollinate, which results in diversity among the offspring. This may be desirable, or you may want to take precautions to avoid unexpected characteristics in future plants. Seed produced from hybrid plants do not reliably produce consistent results.

Factors Affecting Germination

Seed germination is affected by four environmental factors: water, oxygen, light, and temperature.

Water

Seed germination begins with the absorption of water. Seeds readily absorb water due to the nature of the seed coat, and successful germination requires a continuous supply of adequate water. Once the imbibition process has begun, a dry period will kill the embryo. Professional growers often germinate seeds under a mist irrigation system, which keeps the growing medium uniformly moist and maintains high humidity levels.

Light

Light can stimulate or inhibit the germination of seeds. Crops that need light for seeds to germinate include ageratum, begonia, browallia, impatiens, lettuce, and petunia. Conversely, seeds of calendula, centaurea, annual phlox, verbena, and vinca germinate best in the dark. Many plants have no specific light or dark requirements. Seed catalogs and seed packets often list germination or cultural tips for individual varieties.

When sowing light-requiring seeds, do as nature does: place them directly on the soil surface. If necessary, you can apply a light covering of fine peat moss or fine vermiculite. If applied in moderation, these two materials will permit some light to reach the seeds and will not limit germination. When starting seeds in the home, you can provide supplemental lighting with fluorescent lights suspended 2-4 in. above the seeds for 16-18 hours a day.

Oxygen

In all viable (living) seed, respiration takes place. The respiration rate in **quiescent** ("sleeping") seed is low, but they still require some oxygen. During the germination process, the respiration rate increases; the medium in which the seeds are planted should be loose and well-aerated. If the oxygen supply is limited or reduced, it can retard or inhibit germination.

Temperature

The temperature of the planting medium not only affects the number of seeds that germinate but also the rate of germination. Some seeds will germinate over a wide range of temperatures, whereas others require temperatures within a narrow range. Many seeds have minimum, maximum, and optimum germination temperatures.

For example, tomato seed has a minimum germination temperature of 50°F and a maximum temperature of 95°F, but an optimum germination temperature of about 80°F. Where germination temperatures are listed, they are usually the optimum temperatures unless otherwise specified. Generally, plants germinate best between 65-75°F. It's important to know that these growing temperatures refer to the temperature of the growing medium, not the air temperature; seeds are in contact with the medium. Germination flats may have to be placed in special chambers or on radiators, heating cables, or heating mats to maintain the ideal temperature and achieve maximum germination percentages.

Germination begins when certain internal requirements have been met. A seed must have a mature embryo; contain a large enough food supply, either in the endosperm or cotyledons, to sustain the embryo during germination; and contain enough hormones to start the

TABLE 3.1

Plant	Approximate time to Seed before Last Frost	Approximate Germination Time (Days)	Germination Temperature (F°)	Germination in Light (L) or Dark (D)
Begonia	≥ 12 weeks	10-15	70	L
Geranium	≥ 12 weeks	10-20	70	L
Pansy (Viola)	≥ 12 weeks	5-10	65	D
Dianthus	10 weeks	5-10	70	--
Impatiens	10 weeks	15-20	70	L
Verbena	10 weeks	15-20	65	D
Ageratum	8 weeks	5-10	70	L
Alyssum	8 weeks	5-10	70	--
Phlox	8 weeks	5-10	65	D
Aster	6 weeks	5-10	70	--
Centurea	6 weeks	5-10	65	D
Zinnia	6 weeks	5-10	70	--
Cucumber	≤ 4 weeks	5-10	85	--
Cosmos	≤ 4 weeks	5-10	70	--
Squash	≤ 4 weeks	5-10	85	--

germination process. Seedlings emerge when the young plant breaks through the surface of the medium.

Refer to table 3.1 for the requirements of seed germination in selected crops.

Breaking Dormancy

Many domesticated crops, such as vegetables and annual flowers, have no dormancy; when quiescent, they will germinate without any special treatment. For many trees, shrubs, and non-domesticated species, it is difficult to break dormancy under ideal environmental conditions. However, there are various treatments that can break dormancy and begin germination. These treatments include seed scarification, seed stratification, and the use of sphagnum peat moss.

Seed scarification involves breaking, scratching, or softening the seed coat so that water can enter and germination can begin. There are several methods of scarifying seeds. Mechanical methods of scarification include filing seeds with a metal file, rubbing them with sandpaper, or cracking them with a hammer to weaken the seed coat. Hot water scarification involves putting the seeds in hot water (170-212°F) and allowing them to soak for 12-24 hours before planting. In another method—called warm-moist scarification—seeds are stored in warm, damp, nonsterile containers where seed coats decay and break down over several months.

Seed stratification is a procedure used on the seeds of some fall-ripening trees and shrubs of the temperate zone that will not germinate unless chilled underground as they overwinter. Stratification can satisfy this so-called "after ripening" requirement. To stratify seeds, fill a clay pot or flat with sand or vermiculite, leaving about 1 in. of space between the level of the medium and the top of the container. Place the seeds on top of the medium and cover them with another ½ in. of sand or vermiculite. Water thoroughly and allow the excess water to drain through the bottom. Place the whole container, with the moist medium and seeds, in a plastic bag, and seal the bag using a twist tie or rubber band. Place the bag in a refrigerator, and check periodically that the medium is moist but not wet. Additional water is usually not necessary. After 10-12 weeks, remove the bag from the refrigerator, take the container out, set it in a warm place, and water it often enough to keep the medium moist. Soon, the seedlings should emerge. When the young plants are about 3 in. tall, transplant them into pots to grow until time for setting outside.

Another procedure for breaking dormancy uses sphagnum peat moss. Wet the moss thoroughly, then squeeze out the excess water with your hands. Mix the seeds with the moss and place the material in a plastic bag. Use a twist tie or rubber band to secure the top of the bag and put the bag in a refrigerator. Check it periodically. If there is condensation on the inside of the bag, the process will probably be successful. The process is effective in temperatures between 35-45°F; most refrigerators operate in this range. After 10-12 weeks, remove the bag from the refrigerator and plant the seeds in pots to germinate and grow. Handle the seeds carefully; often, small roots and shoots are emerging at the end of the stratification period. Take care to avoid breaking these off.

These procedures successfully germinate the seeds of most fruit and nut trees.

STARTING SEEDLINGS

Media

Seeds can be "started," or sown, in many kinds of materials: vermiculite, perlite, sand, mixtures of other soilless or artificial media, and various amended soil mixes are all appropriate. Ideally, the germinating medium should be uniform, fine, well-aerated, loose, and free of insects, pathogens, and weed seeds. A good seed-starting medium should also be low in fertility or total soluble salts and capable of holding and moving moisture by capillary action.

An artificial, soilless mix is a good germination medium. This mix is primarily sphagnum peat moss and vermiculite, both of which are generally free of diseases, weed seeds, and insects. The ingredients are readily available, easy to handle, and lightweight; additionally, they produce uniform plant growth. Ready-made "peat-lite" mixes or similar products are commercially available, but you can also make them at home by combining:

- 4 quarts shredded sphagnum peat moss,
- 4 quarts fine-grade vermiculite,
- 1 tbsp. superphosphate, and
- 2 tbsp. of ground limestone.

Another mix simply includes equal parts of vermiculite, perlite, and milled sphagnum moss. These are both low-fertility mixes, so it's important to water seedlings with a diluted fertilizer solution soon after they emerge.

Do not use garden soil by itself to start seedlings. It

is not sterile, does not drain well, and will shrink from the sides of the containers if allowed to dry.

Containers

A wide variety of containers, available at retail outlets or recycled from other uses, can serve as containers for seed germination. Always use clean containers; if the containers have previously held soil, they should be sterilized by rinsing in a solution of 1 part chlorine bleach to 9 parts water. Used plastic garden pots work well, but only if they are sterilized.

You can recycle plastic household containers, milk cartons, aluminum foil pans, and paper or plastic cups as seed germination containers, but always punch small holes in the bottom to provide drainage. You can also purchase wooden or plastic flats from garden stores or make them from scrap lumber; two-inch-high 12x12 in. containers are often easiest to handle, but be sure to leave about 1/8-3/16-in. gaps between the boards in the bottom. Clay or plastic flower-type pots are available at many garden, hardware, and variety stores.

Pots and strips made of compressed peat, as well as plastic cell packs, are commercially available for starting seeds. Each cell or small pot holds a single plant, which reduces the risk of root injury when transplanting. Peat pellets, peat or fiber-based blocks, and expanded plastic-foam cubes are growing media that form their own containers.

Seeding

The proper time to sow seeds indoors for transplants depends on when the plants can safely be moved outdoors. Seeding date ranges from 4-12 weeks prior to the last spring freeze, depending on the speed of germination, rate of growth, and cultural conditions. One common mistake is to sow seeds too early and, consequentially, having to hold them under low light or improper temperature conditions. This usually results in tall, weak, spindly plants that do not perform well in the garden.

After selecting a container, fill it to within ¾ in. from the top with moistened medium. For very small seeds, at least the top ¼ in. should be a finely screened mix or a layer of vermiculite. Lightly firm the medium at the corners and edges with your fingers or a block of wood to provide a uniform, flat surface. For medium to large seeds, make furrows about 1-2 in. apart and ½-in. deep across the surface of the growing medium using a narrow board, pot label, or pencil. Sowing in rows allows for sufficient light and air movement and hinders the spread of damping-off fungus. Seedlings in rows are also easier to label and to handle at transplanting time than those sown by broadcasting. Sow the seeds sparingly and uniformly by gently tapping the seed packet as you move along the row. Lightly cover the seeds with dry vermiculite or sifted medium if they require darkness for germination. A suitable planting depth is usually about twice the diameter of the seed.

Do not plant seeds too far beneath the surface. Extremely fine seeds—such as petunia, begonia, and snapdragon—are not covered, but instead lightly pressed into the medium or watered-in with a fine spray-mist. If you broadcast these seeds, strive for a uniform stand of seedlings by sowing half the seeds in one direction and the other half in the perpendicular direction.

Frequently, it's best to sow large seeds in small containers or cell-packs that eliminate the need for early transplanting. Usually, you'll want to sow 2-3 seeds per unit and thin them later to allow the strongest seedling to grow.

Seed Tape

Most garden stores and seed catalogs offer both indoor and outdoor seed tapes. Seed tape combines the seeds and the medium; it contains precisely spaced seeds enclosed in an organic, water-soluble material. When planted, the tape dissolves, and the seeds germinate normally. Seed tapes are especially convenient for tiny, hard-to-handle seeds, but are much more expensive per seed. Seed tapes allow uniform emergence of seedlings, eliminate overcrowding, and facilitate perfectly straight rows. The tape can be cut at any point to plant in multiple rows.

Pre-germination

Another method of starting plants involves sprouting the seeds before they are planted in pots or the garden. This method reduces the time to germinate, because it is easy to control temperature and moisture levels. It also guarantees a high percentage of seed germination since none are lost to environmental factors.

To pre-germinate seeds, lay seeds between folds of cotton cloth or paper towels on a layer of vermiculite (or a similar material) in a pan. Keep them moist and warm. When roots begin to emerge, place the seeds in containers or plant them directly in the garden. During transplanting, be careful to not break off tender roots.

When planting pre-germinated seeds in a container that will be set out in the garden, place one seed in each 2-3-in. container. Plant the seeds at only half their recommended depth. Gently press a little potting mix over the sprouted seed and add about 1/2 in. of vermiculite or milled sphagnum to the surface. These materials will keep the surface uniformly moist but are light enough for the shoot to push through. Keep the pots in a warm place and care for them just as you would any other newly transplanted seedlings.

One convenient way to plant small, delicate, pre-germinated seeds is to suspend them in a gel. You can make a gel by blending cornstarch with boiling water to a consistency thick enough to keep the seeds suspended. Be sure to cool thoroughly before use. Place the gel with seedlings in a plastic bag with a hole in it. Squeeze the gel through the hole along a pre-marked garden row. Spacing of seeds is determined by the number of seeds in the gel. If the spacing is too dense, add more gel; if too wide, add more seeds. The gel will keep the germinating seeds moist until they establish themselves in the garden soil.

Watering

After seed has been sown, thoroughly moisten the planting mix. Use a fine mist spray or place the container in a pan or tray that has about 1 in. of warm water in the bottom. Avoid splashing or excessive flooding that might displace small seeds. When the planting mix is saturated, set the container aside to drain.

Ideally, seed flats should remain moist during the germination period without having to add water. One way to maintain moisture is to slip the whole flat or pot into a clear plastic bag. The plastic should be at least 1 to 1½ in. above the soil. Keep the container out of direct sunlight to avoid overheating the seeds.

Many home gardeners cover their flats with panes of glass or plastic wrap instead of using a plastic bag. You can also use commercially available plastic domes that fit snugly over a standard flat. Be sure to remove the plastic bag or cover as soon as the first seedlings appear. Then, as the surface of the growing medium dries, water carefully to avoid washing the seedlings out of the medium. If possible, consider watering from the bottom of the container.

Temperature and Light

Since most seeds will germinate best at an optimum temperature—usually higher than most home night temperatures—you must provide special warm areas. The use of thermostatically controlled heating cables is an excellent way to supply constant heat.

After germination and seedling establishment, move the flats to a cool, bright location with good air circulation. Ideally, the night temperature should be 55-60°F, and daytime temperatures should be between 65-70°F. These ranges will prevent soft, leggy growth and minimize disease. Of course, some crops germinate or grow best at a different or constant temperature; these must be handled separately from the rest of the plants.

Seedlings must receive bright sunlight immediately after emergence. If possible, place them in a south-facing window. If a large, bright window is unavailable, place the seedlings under a fluorescent light. Use two 40-watt, cool-white fluorescent tubes. Position the plants 2-4 in. from the tubes and keep the lights on for about 16-18 hours each day. Periodically raise the lights as the seedlings grow. Alternatively, use LED grow lights designed for seed germination.

TRANSPLANTING AND HANDLING SEEDLINGS

If plants were not seeded in separate containers or cells, they must be transplanted to give them proper growing space. One common mistake made by gardeners is to leave the seedlings in the seed flat for too long. The ideal time to transplant young seedlings is when they are small enough that there is little danger of transplant shock or slowing of seedling growth. This is usually about the time the first true leaves appear above or between the cotyledons (seed leaves).

You can purchase or prepare seedling growing mixes and containers that are similar to those used for germinating seed. However, the medium should contain more plant nutrients than a germination mix, and some commercial soilless mixes contain fertilizer. When fertilizing, use a soluble houseplant fertilizer at the dilution rate recommended by the manufacturer about every 2 weeks after the seedlings are established. Remember that young seedlings are easily damaged by too much fertilizer, especially if under any moisture stress.

To transplant seedlings, carefully dig out the small plants with a knife or wooden plant label. Let the group of seedlings fall apart and pick out individual plants. Avoid tearing roots in the process. Handle small seedlings by the leaves and not by the delicate stems. Punch a hole in the medium into which the seedling will be planted, deep enough so the seedling can be placed at the same depth it was growing in the seed flat. Gently water after planting and place in the shade or under fluorescent lights for a few days. Avoid direct heat sources, and continue watering and fertilizing as you did for the seed flats.

Most plants transplant well and can be started indoors, but a few—including zinnias and cucurbits such as melons and squash—can be difficult. These are generally seeded outdoors at the outset or sown directly into individual containers indoors.

Containers for Transplanting

To transplant seedlings, you can choose from a wide variety of containers. The ideal container type will depend on the type of plant to be transplanted and its individual growing conditions. Use containers that are inexpensive, durable, and appropriate for the space. It's fine to use standard pots, but they tend to waste space and take too long to dry out—limiting the amount of oxygen available to the seedling.

Many types of containers are available commercially. Individual pots or strips of connected pots fit close together, are inexpensive, and can be planted directly in the garden. There are also various sizes of containers made of pressed peat. When setting out plants grown in peat pots, be careful to cover the pot completely. If the top edge of the peat pot extends above the soil level, it may act as a wick and draw water away from the soil in the pot. To avoid this, tear off the top lip of the pot and plant it flush with the soil level.

Compressed peat pellets, when soaked in water, expand to form compact individual pots. They waste no space, do not fall apart as easily as peat pots, and can be set directly in the garden. If you wish to avoid transplanting seedlings altogether, compressed peat pellets are a good choice for direct sowing.

Commercial bedding plant owners often use plastic cell packs, which are strips of connected individual pots, because they can withstand frequent handling.

Hardening-Off Seedlings

Plants grown indoors have no resistance to UV radiation and need to acclimate slowly to sunlight to avoid getting "burned" upon exposure. Hardening-off is the process of altering the quality of plant growth to withstand the change in environmental conditions the plants face when transferred from a greenhouse or home to the garden. If plants produced in a greenhouse or indoors are planted outside without a conditioning period between the two environments, they may experience a severe reduction in growth.

Hardening-off can be accomplished by gradually lowering temperatures and reducing water and fertilization. This procedure results in an accumulation of carbohydrates and a thickening of cell walls. A change from a soft, succulent growth to a firmer, harder growth is desired.

The process should be started at least 2 weeks before planting in the garden. If possible, move plants to a shady spot outdoors where the temperature is between 45-50°F and the plants are protected from wind. A cold frame is an excellent tool for this purpose. When you move the plants outdoors, ensure they are shaded; then, gradually move them into more sunlight. Each day, gradually increase the length of exposure. Do not put tender seedlings outdoors on windy days or when temperatures are below 45°F. Reduce the frequency of watering to slow plant growth, but do not allow plants to wilt. Even cold-hardy plants will be damaged if exposed to freezing temperatures before they are hardened-off. After proper hardening-off, however, they can be planted outdoors and withstand light frosts without damage.

The hardening-off process is intended to slow plant growth. However, if the process is taken to the extreme, it can stop plant growth and do significant damage to certain crops. For example, a severe hardening-off process in cauliflower will produce thumb-sized heads that fail to develop further; cucumbers and melons will stop growing if hardened-off too severely.

ASEXUAL OR VEGETATIVE PROPAGATION

Vegetative or **asexual propagation** involves taking a vegetative part from one plant to regenerate a new one. Genetically, the new plant is identical to the plant from which the root, stem, or leaf was taken.

Asexual propagation is the best way to maintain some species, particularly if using an individual plant that best represents that species. Clones are groups of plants that are identical to their sole parent and can only be propagated asexually. The 'Bartlett' pear (1770) and the 'Delicious' apple (1870) are two examples of clones that have been asexually propagated for many years.

The most popular methods of asexual propagation are cuttings, layering, and grafting. Cuttings involve rooting a severed piece of the parent plant. Layering is rooting a part of the parent and then severing it. Grafting joins two plant parts together.

Asexual propagation has several advantages: it may be the easiest and fastest method to propagate certain species; it may be the only way to perpetuate some cultivars; it bypasses the juvenile characteristics of some species.

Cuttings

Many types of plants, both woody and herbaceous, are frequently propagated with cuttings. A cutting is a plant part (stem, root, or leaf) that is severed from the parent plant and will regenerate itself, forming a whole new plant.

Take cuttings with a sharp knife or razor blade to reduce injury to the parent plant. Dip the cutting tool in rubbing (isopropyl) alcohol or a mixture of 1 part bleach and 9 parts water to prevent transmitting diseases from infected plant parts to healthy ones. Remove flowers and flower buds from the cutting to allow it to use its energy and stored carbohydrates for root and shoot formation rather than fruit and seed production. To hasten rooting, to increase the number of roots, or to obtain more uniform rooting (except on soft, fleshy stems), use a **rooting hormone**, preferably one containing a fungicide. Prevent possible contamination of the entire supply of rooting hormone by putting some of it in a separate container and dipping the cuttings.

Typical rooting mediums include coarse sand, vermiculite, or a mixture of equal parts peat and perlite or vermiculite. The rooting medium should be sterile and low in fertility, drain well enough to provide oxygen, and retain enough moisture to prevent water stress. Moisten the medium before inserting cuttings and keep it evenly moist while cuttings are rooting and forming new shoots. Enclose the potted cuttings in a clear plastic bag sealed with a twist tie to maintain high humidity levels and reduce moisture stress.

Place stem and leaf cuttings in bright, indirect light. Root cuttings must be exposed to light to stimulate adventitious bud and shoot development. Adventitious buds originate in unexpected locations—locations other than the leaf axil, where they are expected to occur. The end of the root cutting that came from the stem side of the root should be exposed to light when planted.

Stem Cuttings

Many plant species are propagated by stem cuttings. For many plants, you can take these cuttings at any time of the year. Generally, however, you should take stem cuttings of woody evergreen plants in the fall or the dormant season and cuttings of deciduous plants in late spring and summer (Figure 3.1).

Tip Cuttings. Detach a 2-6-in. piece of stem that includes the terminal bud. Make the cut just below a node. Remove lower leaves that would touch or be covered by the medium. Dip the stem in rooting hormone, if desired, and gently tap the end of the cutting to remove any excess. Insert the cutting deeply enough into the medium to support itself. Usually, at least one node should be below the surface; this is not necessary on all plant species, but some species will only root except at leaf nodes.

Medial Cuttings. Make two cuts on the stem. The first cut should be just above a node, and the second cut just below a node 2-6 in. down the stem. Prepare and insert the cutting as you would a tip cutting. Be sure to position it right side up. To determine which end is up, look for axial buds, which are always oriented above the leaves on the stem in the leaf axils.

Cane Cutting. Cut cane-like stems into sections containing one or two "eyes," or nodes. Treat the ends

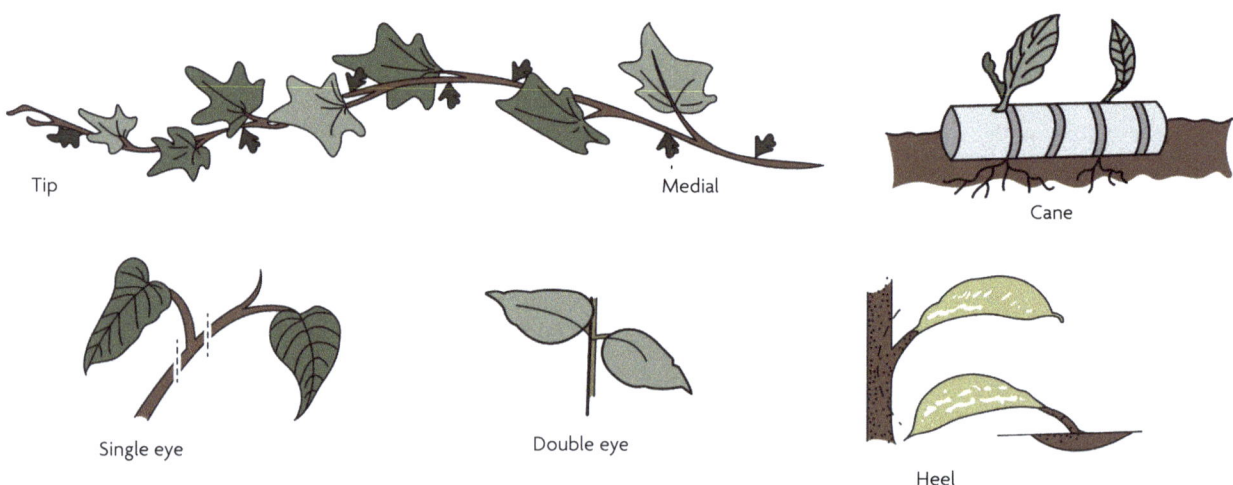

Figure 3.1 Examples of techniques for propagating plants by stem cuttings.

with a fungicide or dust with activated charcoal and allow to dry for several hours. Then, lay the section down horizontally with about half of the cutting below the medium surface and the eyes facing upward or to the side. Cane cuttings are usually potted when roots and new shoots appear; however, it's common to detach and re-root new shoots from dracaena and croton.

Single Eye. This cutting method is used for plants with alternate leaves when space or stock material is limited. Cut the stem about ½ in. above and ½ in. below a node. Place the cutting horizontally or vertically in the medium.

Double Eye. The double eye method is used for plants with opposite leaves when space or plant material is limited. Cut the stem about ½ in. above and ½ in. below the same node. Insert the cutting vertically in the medium with the node just touching the surface.

Heel Cuttings. This method makes efficient use of stock material with woody stems. Heel cuttings include the branch base, or heel, on the cutting. Make a shield-shaped cut about halfway through the wood around a leaf and axial bud. Insert the shield horizontally into the medium.

Leaf Cuttings

Leaf cuttings are used almost exclusively for a few indoor plants and succulents. Leaves of most plants will either produce a few roots but no plantlets or just decay. Figure 3.2 illustrates four types of leaf cuttings.

Whole Leaf With Petiole. Detach the leaf and ½-1½ in. of petiole. Insert the lower end of the petiole into the medium. One or more new plants will form at the base of the petiole. The plantlets may be severed from the leaf when they have their own roots. This method works well for African violets.

Whole Leaf Without Petiole. This method is used for plants with sessile leaves (leaves without petioles). Insert the cutting vertically into the medium. A new plant will form from the axillary bud. The leaf may be removed when the new plant has its own roots.

Split Vein. Detach a leaf from the stock plant. Slit its veins on the lower leaf surface. Lay the cutting, lower side down, on the medium. New plants will form at each cut. If the leaf tends to curl up, hold it in place by covering the margins with the rooting medium or pinning it down. Propagation via split vein cutting is effective for rex begonias.

Leaf Section. This method is frequently used to propagate snake plants and fibrous rooted begonias. Cut begonia leaves into wedges with at least one vein. Lay the leaves flat on the medium. A new plant will arise at the vein. Cut snake plant leaves into 2-in. sections. Consistently make the lower cut slanted and the upper cut straight to identify which end is the top. Insert the cutting vertically. Roots will form relatively quickly, and eventually, a new plant will appear at the base of the cutting. These and other succulent cuttings will rot if kept too moist. Leaf cuttings from succulents and fleshy-type plants should be allowed to dry for 12-24 hours before being stuck in the rooting medium to reduce the chances of rot.

Root Cuttings

Much less frequently, plants are propagated via root cuttings. Root cuttings are usually taken from 2- to 3-year-old plants during their dormant season, during which they have a large supply of carbohydrates. Root cuttings of some species produce new shoots that form their own root systems; other plants develop root systems from the cuttings before producing new shoots.

Plants With Large Roots. Make a straight top cut. Then, make a slanted cut 2-6 in. below the first cut. Store the cutting for about three weeks in moist sawdust, peat moss, or sand at 40°F. Remove from storage. Insert the cutting vertically, with its top about level with the surface of the rooting medium. Propagators often perform this method outdoors.

Plants With Small Roots. Take 1- to 2-in. sections of roots. Insert the cuttings horizontally about ½ in. below the surface of the medium. Propagators most often perform this method indoors or in a hotbed.

Layering

Stems still attached to their parent plant may form roots where they touch a rooting medium. Severed from the parent plant, the rooted stem becomes a new plant. This

Figure 3.2 Types of leaf cuttings

method of vegetative propagation, called **layering**, has a high success rate because it prevents the water stress and carbohydrate shortage that plague cuttings.

Some plants layer themselves naturally, but sometimes plant propagators assist the process. Layering is enhanced by girdling the stem where it is bent, by wounding one side of the stem, or by bending it very sharply. The rooting medium should be moist and well-aerated. Figure 3.3 illustrates four layering techniques, and table 3.2 provides examples of common plants suitable for layering.

Tip Layering

Dig a hole 3-4 in. deep. Insert the shoot tip and cover it with soil. The tip grows downward first, then bends sharply and grows upward. Roots form at the bend, and the recurved tip becomes a new plant. Remove the tip layer and plant it in early spring or fall. Plants that can be propagated with this technique include purple and black raspberries, trailing blackberries, and grapes.

Simple Layering

Bend the stem to the ground. Cover part of it with soil, leaving the last 6-12 in. exposed. Bend the tip into a vertical position and stake in place. The sharp bend will often induce rooting, but wounding the lower side of the branch or loosening the bark by twisting the stem may help. You can propagate plants such as rhododendron, forsythia, and honeysuckle in this way.

Compound or Serpentine Layering

This method works for plants with flexible stems. Bend the stem to the rooting medium as you would for simple layering but cover and expose alternating sections of the stem. Wound the lower side of the stem sections that will be covered. You can propagate both heart-leaf philodendron and pothos in this manner.

Mound or Stool Layering

During the dormant season, cut the plant back to 1 in. above the ground and mound soil over the shortened stem. In the spring, dormant buds will "break" (come out of dormancy and grow) and produce shoots that develop through the soil mound. Rooting will occur at the base of the young shoots. Once rooted, you can cut the shoots below the new root system and plant them in a new location. Propagators commonly use this method for apple, pear, and quince rootstocks.

Dropping is a mound layering technique used for dwarf shrubs such as rhododendrons and some dwarf conifers. For dropping, the propagator buries the whole plant and leaves only the tips of the shoots exposed aboveground.

Air Layering

Propagators use air layering to induce plant stems to form roots while still attached to the mother plant. After the rooted top is removed, the mother plant will produce leaves below the cut. Air layering is an effective method for propagating large plants with heavy stems or to rejuvenate tall, spindly plants like dumb cane and rubber tree (Figure 3.4).

Select a healthy, vigorously growing main stem or lateral branch. At a point 12-15 in. below the tip, make a 1- to 2-in. long slanting cut upward, about ¼- ½ the diameter of the stem. Insert a toothpick between the two surfaces to keep them apart and dust them with a

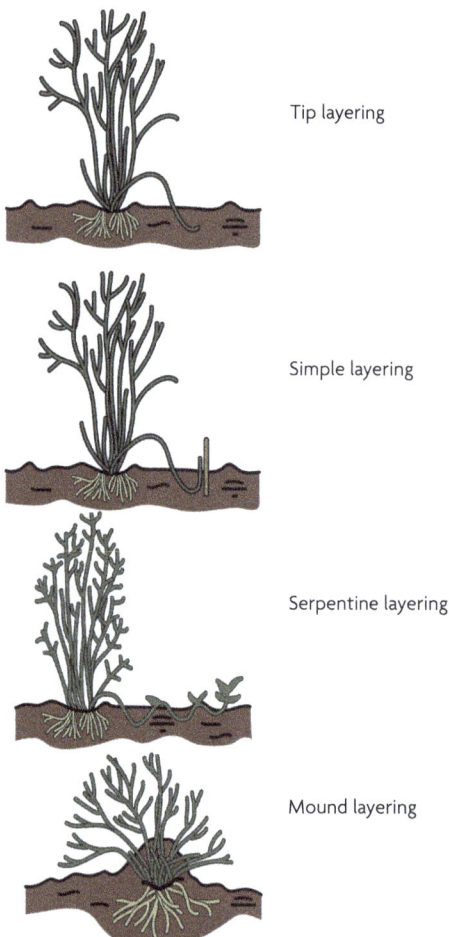

Figure 3.3 Producing new plants from layering

Tip layering

Simple layering

Serpentine layering

Mound layering

TABLE 3.2

Plant	Layering Time	Layering Method	Rooting Time
Akebia	Early Spring – Early Autumn	Serpentine	12-18 months
Azalea spp.	Early-Late Winter	Simple	9-12 months
Azalea spp.	Early-Mid Spring	Air	12-18 months
Camellia spp.	Late Winter – Early Spring	Simple	6-12 months
Campsis radicans	Mid-Late Autumn	Simple/Serpentine	9-12 months
Clematis spp.	Mid-Late Autumn	Simple/Serpentine	9-12 months
Daphne spp.	Early-Mid Summer	Simple	6-9 months
Forsythia spp.	Mid-Late Spring	Simple	6-9 months
Fothergilla spp.	Late Summer – Early Autumn	Simple	12-18 months
Hamamelis spp.	Early-Mid Spring	Air	12-18 months
Ilex spp.	Late Summer-Mid Autumn	Air	12-18 months
Ilex spp.	Early-Mid Spring	Simple	9-12 months
Jasminum spp.	Early-Mid Spring	Simple	6-9 months
Magnolia spp.	Early-Mid Spring	Simple	12-18 months
Magnolia spp.	Mid-Spring – Late Summer	Air	18-24 months
Rhododendron spp.	Early-Mid Spring	Simple	12-18 months
Viburnum spp.	Early-Mid Spring	Simple	9-12 months

rooting hormone. On large, thick stems, make slanting cuts on opposite sides of the stems and dust rooting hormone onto the cut surfaces. Take a handful or two of long-fibered sphagnum moss that has been soaked in water, squeeze out the excess water, and pack the wet moss around the cut, holding it in place with a plastic bag or aluminum foil. A good substitute for the moss is a peat pellet that has been soaked in water and formed a pot. Slice the peat pot vertically on one side and open it up so it will fit neatly over the stem.

Once you see a healthy ball of white roots beneath the plastic, sever the new plant just below the moss ball, remove the wrapping—being careful not to damage the roots—and pot it in a suitable medium.

Separation and Division

Separation and division are propagation techniques used for plants with multiple growing points at or just below the soil surface. Separation is used when a plant produces naturally detachable structures. This method is common for bulb- and corm-producing plants. These structures can be separated without cutting. Division is the term used when plant parts with individual growing points are cut into sections. This method is used for plants with stolons, rhizomes, runners, stem tubers, and herbaceous crowns.

Bulbs. When propagating bulb-producing plants, new bulbs form beside the original bulb. Separating bulb clumps every 3-5 years encourages the growth of large flowers and increases the bulb population. Dig up the clump after the leaves have withered and gently pull apart the bulbs; replant them immediately so roots can begin to develop. Small, separated bulbs may not flower for 2-3 years, but large ones should bloom the first year. Bulb-producing plants commonly propagated by separation include tulip and narcissus.

Corms. A corm is a swollen underground stem (Figure 3.5). Each year, a new corm forms on top of the old one, which shrivels and dies. Cormels (tiny corms) form between the old and the new corm. On the upper surface of the new corm, buds develop; these become from the new plant the following year. After the leaves wither, cut the tops to within ½ in. of the corm. Dig up the corms and gently separate the cormels, new corms, and old corms. Discard the old corms and replant the new corms and cormels. The cormels may take 2-3 years to produce a blooming-size corm. You can propagate crocus and gladiolus using this separation method.

Figure 3.4a Overall caption: Air layering camellia. This photo: A branch the size of a pencil or larger.
Image Credit: Jackie Jordan, Clemson University

Figure 3.4b Two cuts made 1.5 inches apart.
Image Credit: Jackie Jordan, Clemson University

Figure 3.4c A horizontal incision between the cuts.
Image Credit: Jackie Jordan, Clemson University

Figure 3.4d Showing bark removed.
Image Credit: Jackie Jordan, Clemson University

Figure 3.4e Wrapping wound with sphagnum moss.
Image Credit: Jackie Jordan, Clemson University

Figure 3.4f Polyethlene film to hold moss.
Image Credit: Jackie Jordan, Clemson University

Stolons and Runners. A stolon is a modified stem that grows horizontally above the soil surface; it produces new shoots where it touches the ground (Figure 3.6). A runner is a specialized stem that originates from a leaf axil at the crown and grows along the ground or downward from a hanging basket, producing new plants at the nodes. Plants that produce stolons or runners are propagated by severing the new plants from their parent stems. Propagators can root plantlets at the tips of runners while they're still attached to the parent plant or detach them and place them in a rooting medium. You can reproduce strawberry and spider plant in this manner.

Rhizomes. A rhizome is similar to a stolon but occurs just below, or partially below, the soil surface (Figure 3.7). Rhizomes range from thick, fleshy, and short, to slender and elongated. To propagate, rhizomes of both types are propagated are cut into sections. Each section must include at least one growing point, lateral bud or "eye," to be successful. Iris and ginger plants are reproduced with this method of division.

Offsets. Plants with a rosetted stem may reproduce by forming new shoots (often called pups) at their base or in the leaf axils. Sever the new shoots from the parent plant after they have developed their own root system. Unrooted offsets of some species may be removed and placed in a rooting medium. Some of these must be cut off, while others may be simply lifted off of the parent stem. Date palm, haworthia, bromeliads, daylilies, and many cacti and succulents can be propagated by offsets.

Crowns. Plants with more than one rooted crown may be divided and the crowns planted separately (Figure 3.8). If the stems are not joined, gently pull the plants apart. If the crowns are united by horizontal stems, cut the stems and roots with a sharp knife to minimize injury. Divisions of some outdoor plants should be dusted with a fungicide before they are replanted. Snake plant, hosta, and daylily are commonly propagated by division.

Refer to table 3.3 below for common perennials suitable for division.

GRAFTING

Grafting is the act, science, and art of joining two plants together so they will function as one compound plant. Grafting is not a means of developing new varieties, but rather getting two plants to work together as one. The upper part of the graft, called the **scion**, consists of a piece of shoot with wood, bark, and many dormant buds that will produce the stem and branches; this becomes the top of the plant. The lower portion, called the **rootstock** or understock, becomes the root system

CHAPTER 3 - PLANT PROPAGATION • 67

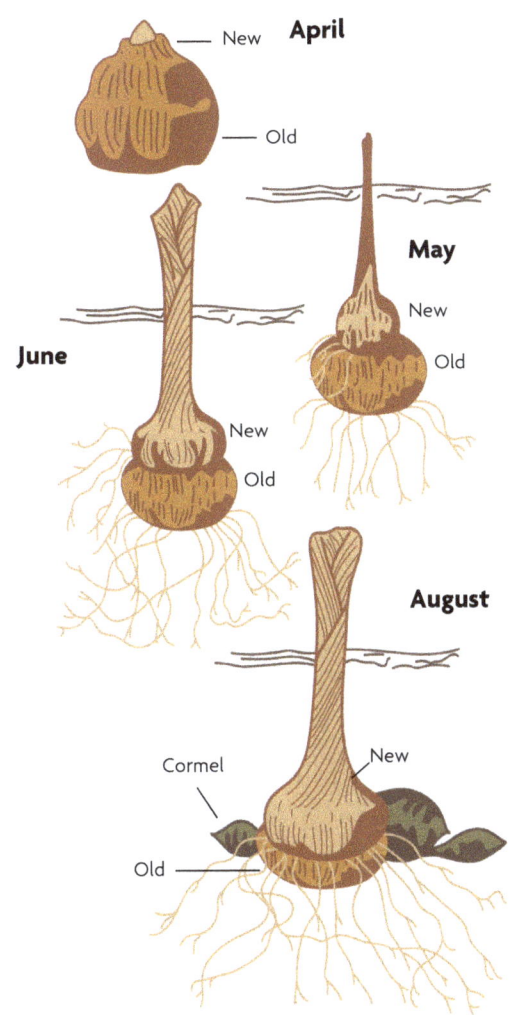

Figure 3.5 Development of a Gladiolus corm

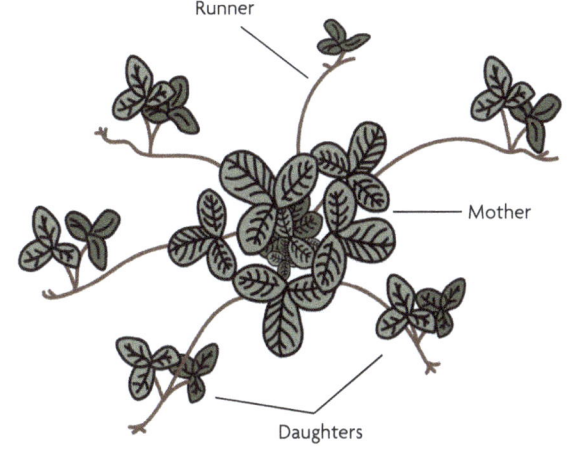

Figure 3.6 Vegetatively propagating plants by stolons and runners.

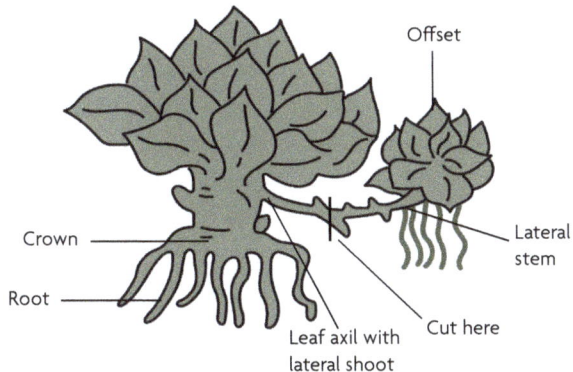

Figure 3.7 Dividing offsets from a succulent

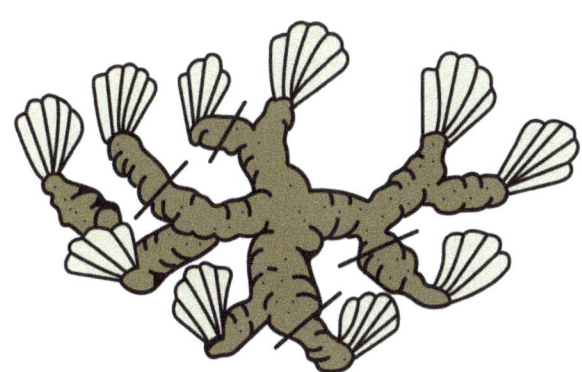

Figure 3.8 Crown division of Iris

TABLE 3.3

Plant	Division Time	Plant	Division Time	Plant	Division Time
Aster (hardy)	Spring	Ferns	Early Spring	Phlox	Spring
Baptisia (false indigo)	Spring or Autumn	Hosta (plantain lily)	Spring or Autumn	Primula	Summer
Chrysanthemum	Spring	Iris, bulbous (Dutch)	Late Summer or Autumn	Red-Hot Poker (kniphofia)	Spring
Columbine	Spring	Iris, rhizomatous (German)	Summer	Rudbeckia	Spring or Autumn
Coneflower (echinacea)	Spring or Autumn	Iris, fibrous (Japanese)	Summer	Shasta Daisy	Spring
Coreopsis	Spring	Lily	Fall	Yarrow (achillea)	Early Spring
Daylily	Spring or Late Summer	Oriental Poppy	Summer	Yucca	Spring or Autumn

and lower part of the trunk. When the scion is grafted onto the rootstock, the cambium of the two must touch. **Cambium** is a layer of cells located between the wood and bark of a stem from which new bark and wood cells originate.

Although grafting usually refers to joining only two plants, it is also possible to combine several. A third plant added between two others becomes the trunk (or at least a portion of it); This is called an **interstem**. Multiple grafts may produce an apple tree with several varieties or a rose-of-sharon with several different colors of flowers.

Grafting is used on some plants that are highly variable when grown from seeds. Others are difficult or impossible to reproduce from cuttings or using other propagation techniques. Grafting, or **topworking**, is a way to change the production of a large tree to a new variety. It is also a method of using a root system better adapted to a specific soil or climate than that produced naturally by a non-grafted plant. Grafting is also a way to produce dwarf plants using special understocks or interstems.

Not all plants can be grafted; it is impossible to graft monocots like grasses and palms. Also, only plants closely related botanically form a good graft union. The stock and scion must be compatible. Incompatible grafts may not form a union, or the union may be weak. A poor union results in plants that either grow poorly, break off, or die.

Grafters have determined the compatibility of plants through many years of trial and error. However, one rule of thumb is that the closer taxonomically related two plants are, the greater the chance of forming a successful union. Most varieties of a particular fruit or flowering species are interchangeable and can be grafted; because of differences in vigor, though, some are better able to support others as understocks. For example, although a union is possible, sour cherry is not a good understock for sweet cherry. It is more common to graft sweet cherry onto Mazzard (*Prunus avium*) or Mahaleb (*P. mahaleb*) seedlings.

Plants of the same botanical genus and specific epithet can usually be grafted even if they are of different varieties. Plants of the same genus but of a different specific epithet may often be grafted, but they are often weak or short-lived; it is also possible that they do not unite at all.

Plants of different genera are less successfully grafted, although there are some cases where this is possible. For example, quince (Cydonia) may be used as a dwarfing rootstock for pear (Pyrus). A number of Cotoneaster species have been grafted onto hawthorn (Crataegus).

Plants of different families cannot be grafted successfully. Although some grafters report relatively short-lived grafts of herbaceous plants of different families, there is no successful practice for commercial or home grafting of woody plants of different families.

Timing

The best time for successful grafting is after the chance of severe cold has passed but well before hot weather arrives. Therefore, most grafting is done in late winter or early spring before or just as new growth begins. It can continue a few weeks after growth has started if you have dormant scion wood in storage and the weather is not too warm.

Equipment

Knife. A sharp, high-quality knife is key to successful grafting. Although there are special grafting and budding knives available, you can also use almost any good pocketknife.

Grafting Wax. After you make a graft, you should cover it to help retain moisture. You can do this with either hand wax or brush wax; hand wax is most common for home grafting. You can soften hand wax with the heat of your hand and apply it easily. You can brush on other heated waxes, but if the wax gets too hot, it can damage the tender cambial tissue. You can also seal the graft with latex paint.

Grafting Tape. Grafting tape has a cloth backing that decomposes before girdling can occur. Grafting tape, electrical tape, and masking tape can all bind grafts for which there is not enough natural pressure. Masking tape is most suitable for grafts where little pressure is required, such as a whip graft.

Poly Tape. You can wrap clear, stretchable polyethylene tape around a graft to give mechanical support, prevent moisture loss, and keep out pests. One disadvantage of poly tape is that you must remove the tape after the graft heals.

Budding Strips. Budding strips are elastic bands that look like cut rubber bands. Budding strips secure several types of grafts. Rubber budding strips expand with growth and usually do not need to be cut—they deteriorate after a short time.

Grafting Tool. There are specially designed tools developed specifically for grafting. The most common one is used for cleft grafting; it has a blade used to split the stub and a wedge to hold the split open while you insert the scions. If this tool is unavailable, use a heavy knife and a fairly wide wedge—at least 2 in. long—for cleft grafting. Use a mallet or hammer to pound the grafting tool or heavy knife into the stub, split the stub, and insert the wedge to open the split.

Nails. Veneer, bridge, and inarching grafts require long, thin nails. Half-inch nails are long enough for most grafts; however, bridge grafting may require three-quarter-inch nails.

Types of Grafting Techniques

Grafting techniques can be divided into two basic types, largely determined by the size of the understock. In the first type, a graft joins a scion and understock of nearly equal sizes; in the second type, a graft joins a small scion to a much larger understock. In the case of a much larger understock, there may be several scions attached to the same understock; this happens in both cleft and bark grafting.

With either type of technique, four conditions must be met for successful grafts:

- the scion and rootstock must be compatible,
- the scion and rootstock must be at the proper physiological stage,
- the cambial layers of the scion and stock must meet, and
- the graft union must stay moist until the wound has healed.

Grafts with Similar Scion and Understock Sizes

Whip Grafting. Whip grafts are fairly easy to perform and heal rapidly (Figure 3.9). They are most successful when the stock and scion are of similar diameter, preferably between ¼ to ½ in. The stock for a whip graft can be a plant growing in either the field or a garden.

Bench or pot grafting is when a potted or dormant bare-root understock is grafted indoors. The stock should be smooth and straight grained. Do not attempt a graft near developed side twigs or branches.

The scion should be 1-year-old wood, preferably the same size as the stock. If the stock is larger than the scion, contact can be made on only one side. The scion should never be larger than the stock.

Preparing the Stock and Scion. It is essential to use a very sharp, high-quality knife when grafting and to make sure that your cuts in both the stock and the scion match. Your first cut should be a single, smooth action that doesn't cause waves or whittling; you can practice your cutting on extra twigs before cutting into the stock or scion.

Cutting the Stock. First, make a slanting cut about 10-12 in. above the roots on a clonal rootstock. Then, make a slanting cut about 1-2 in. above the roots on seedling understock. Although grafts can be a simple union of two slanting cuts, a whip-and-tongue system can result in a stronger graft. To form the "tongue," hold the slanted, one-sided cut facing you and support it with your finger. About one-third down from the tip of this cut, make a downward cut into the wood of about ½-in. long. This cut should be as close to parallel with the grain as possible.

Cutting the Scion. Cutting the scion is very similar to cutting the stock; the only difference is the location of the cut. Cuts should be on the bottom of the scion but the top of the stock. The more similar the cuts are on the scion and the stock, the greater the chances of a successful graft union.

Fitting the Stock and Scion. After cutting both parts of the graft, push them together tightly enough so that the cut surfaces match as closely as possible. The cambial areas—directly under the bark—must be aligned for the union to develop. If the scion and stock are not the same size, match the cambium on just one side. The lower tip of the scion should not hang over the stock.

Wrapping the Graft. In most cases, it is a good idea to wrap the graft; this keeps it tight and prevents it from drying out. Wrap the graft with a rubber budding strip, grafting tape, or a plastic tape such as electrical tape. If the wrapping material does not decay naturally, cut or remove it about a month after growth begins.

Waxing. To further prevent the graft union from drying out, wax the area. Cover the wrapped area with wax or special latex grafting paint as uniformly as possible. In wrapping and waxing, be careful not to dislodge the matching cambial areas.

Grafts with Small Scions and Large Understocks

Cleft Grafting. The cleft graft is most used to top-work a tree; top-work refers to changing a tree from one variety to another. It can be used on either young or mature trees. Young trees may be cleft-grafted on the trunk, while older trees are grafted on smaller branches—not more than 2½ in. in diameter. Branches fully exposed to sunlight and in the mainstream of sap flow host more successful grafts than those in shaded or inactive areas. Grafts on upright branches grow better than those on horizontal branches (Figure 3.10).

Preparing the Stock. The grafter saws off branches or the trunk of stock trees to provide access for the scions to be grafted in. It's important to leave a 'nurse-limb' to keep the tree alive until the grafted scions are growing well; if the scions grow well, you can remove this nurse limb in midsummer or top-work it the following winter. Select a section of the stock that is smooth, knot free, and straight grained. When removing a branch, be sure to saw at a right angle to the grain. Do not tear or split the bark; the bark must be tight to form a successful graft. Use a grafting tool or a heavy knife to split the stock through the center; you can use a mallet to tap the knife if necessary. The split should extend approximately 2 in. into the branch.

Preparing the Scion. For the scion, collect one-year-old wood when it is dormant in January or February. The piece should be about 3/8-5/8 in. in diameter. Cut a long section for the scion that has two or three buds—no more—and enough space below the lowest bud that you can insert it into the stock with that bud just above the insertion. Always note or mark the top and bottom of the scion when you cut it.

Store the dormant scion in a sealed plastic bag with a moist medium such as sphagnum moss, sawdust, or

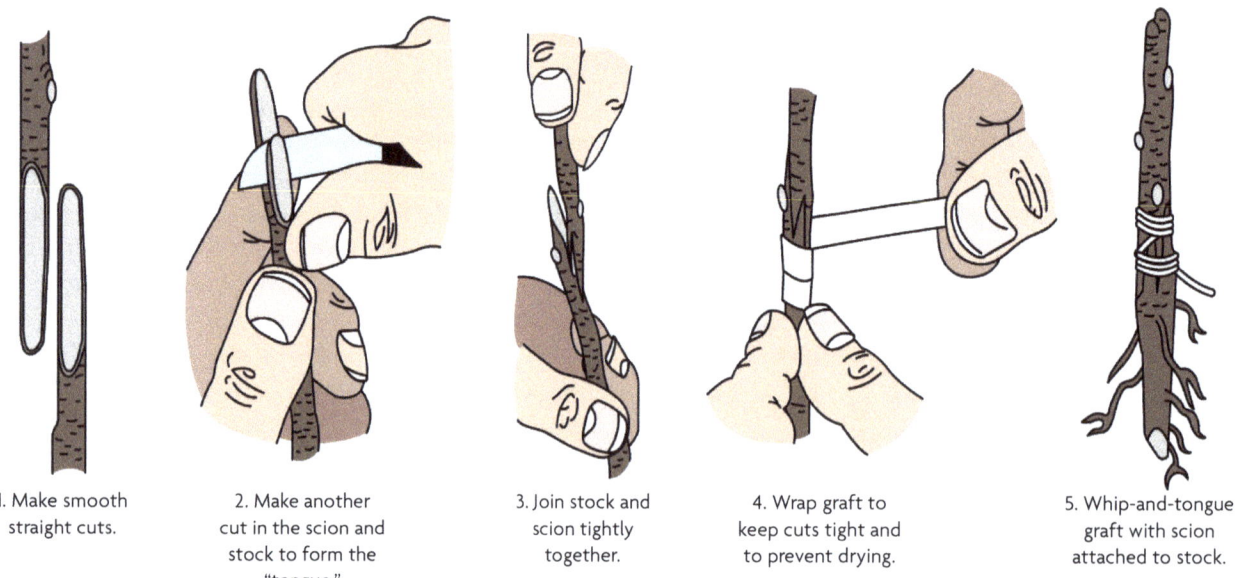

1. Make smooth straight cuts.
2. Make another cut in the scion and stock to form the "tongue."
3. Join stock and scion tightly together.
4. Wrap graft to keep cuts tight and to prevent drying.
5. Whip-and-tongue graft with scion attached to stock.

Figure 3.9 Whip grafting process

paper towels; do not let the wood dry out. Keep the sealed scion refrigerated between 34-40°F until the rootstock begins to grow in the spring.

To prepare the scion for grafting, make a long, smooth cut that begins below the lowest bud and extends towards the base of the scion, approximately 1-1½ in. long. Then turn the scion over and make a second cut on the opposite side, in the same location and of the same length. These two cuts create a wedge-shaped base to the scion that is slightly thicker on the side with the lowest bud than the other side. The wedge does not need to be sharp pointed; in fact, a blunt point is preferable.

Inserting the Scion. Using a grafting chisel or a small wedge, open the cut in the stock wide enough to insert the scion easily.

Place the thicker side of the scion, with the lowest bud, towards the outside of the stock. Ensure that the cambium of both the scion and stock are in contact. Maximum contact is obtained with straight positioning, but a slight slant helps ensure cambial contact. The best contact point is about ¼ in. below the shoulder of the stock.

Remove the wedge or chisel from the slit. The cut surface of the scion wedge should be almost entirely hidden, and the pressure between the stock and the scion should be greatest where the cambia touch. Usually, you will want to insert two scions—one on each side—for the greatest chance of at least one successful graft.

Waxing the Cleft Graft. Wax the cleft graft to cover all cut surfaces. Cracks sometimes develop as the wax sets; check the wax after a few days and again after several weeks to ensure that all surfaces are kept covered.

Caring for the Graft. During the first season, do not prune grafted branches; if the grafts grow vigorously, you may need to pinch out the tips to stimulate branching. Very long shoots may break loose during strong winds. Cleft grafts should grow vigorously. They need only light pruning to shape their development; never prune them heavily.

After the first year, some training and branch selection may be necessary. Do this at the usual pruning time, late winter or early spring. If both scions in a cleft grow, shorten one to allow the other to develop and become dominant. Do not remove the second graft until later, as it will help cover the wound more quickly.

In top-working large trees, it is best to graft about

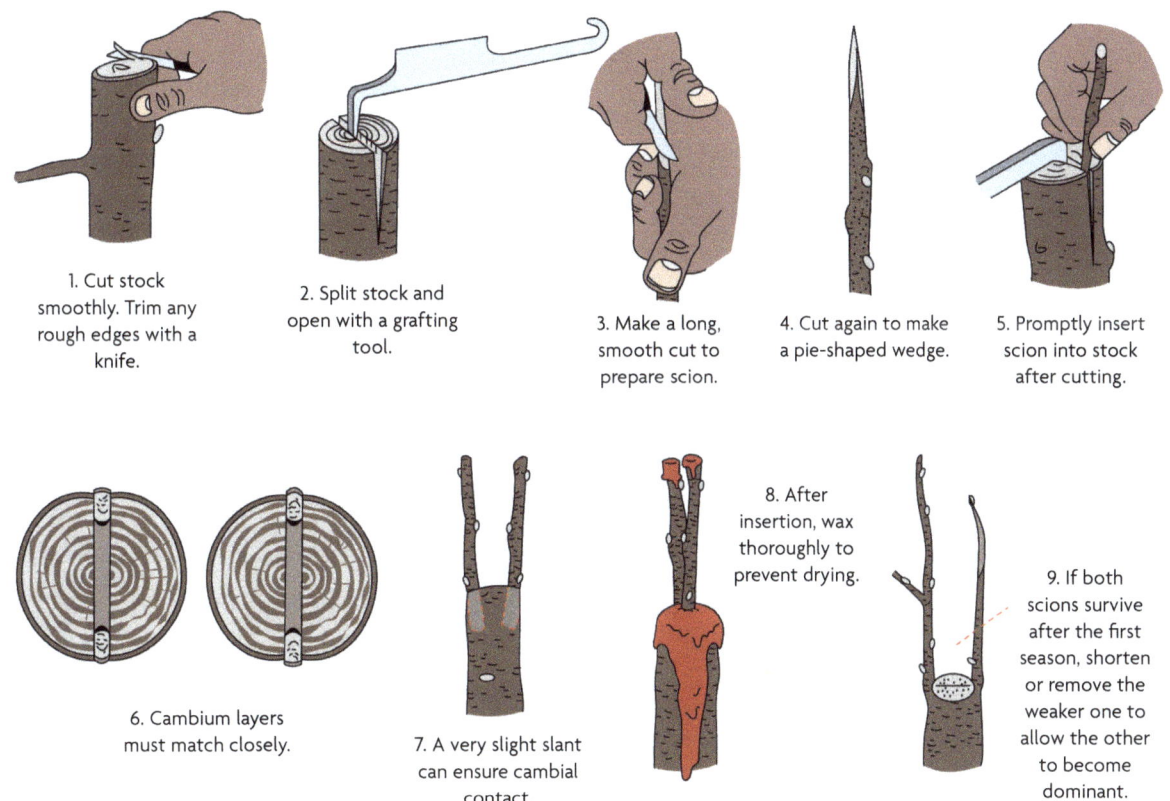

Figure 3.10 **Process for cleft grafting**

half the branches the first year and the second half the next. The best time to topwork is just before new growth begins in the spring. The first year, start with the upper center limbs.

Bark Grafting (Veneer Grafting). Bark grafting is relatively easy and requires no special tools. It is similar to cleft grafting and suitable for branches ranging from one to several inches in diameter (Figure 3.11).

Stock Preparation. Cut off the branch or trunk at a right angle as you would for a cleft graft. You can only make a bark graft when the bark "slips" and growth begins in mid- to late-spring.

There are two methods for cutting into the stock:

- Make a single ¾-in. slit in the bark, or
- Make two slits in the bark, with the space between them equal to width of the scion.

Scion Preparation. Scionwood should be from the previous season's growth and be ¼-½-in. in diameter. The wood should be dormant and from deciduous plants. Keep the scion refrigerated and wrapped in a moist paper towel—or stored in moist sphagnum moss in a cool place—in a plastic bag. The scions must be moist and cool until it is time to make the graft.

Before grafting, recut the base of the scion. Ideally, the scion should be 4-5 in. long and have two or three buds. Prepare the base of the scion by cutting 1½-2 in. from the base and then downward, forming a shoulder and one long, smooth cut. The long cut should extend about 1/3 of the way through the twig; the base should be strong enough to insert into the stock, but not too thick. On the opposite side of the scion, make a short cut to shape the base of the scion into a wedge. This wedge shape will make it easier to insert the scion into the stock.

Inserting the Scion. Usually, but not always, you will need to use a knife to lift the bark at the top of the slit. Then, push the scion down and center it in the slit (or between both slits if the double-slit method is used). Insert the scion until the shoulder rests on the stub. If the scion is particularly large, you can use one or two small nails to tighten the scion to the stock; electrical or masking tape may also do the trick.

Cover the graft completely with wax on all open surfaces. All cut surfaces should stay covered in wax until the graft has completely healed. After the graft union has taken and growth has started, cut off any side shoots or twigs that would shade or compete with the development of the new graft.

Budding

Budding is a simple method of grafting used to propagate many woody plants; budding grafts use a single bud as the scion rather than a length of stem. Budding requires many of the same conditions and materials used for other forms of grafting.

The most common use of budding is to multiply a variety that cannot be produced from seed. It is a common method for producing fruit trees, roses, and many varieties of ornamental trees and shrubs. It may also be used for top-working trees that cannot be easily grafted with cleft or whip grafts. Stone fruits like cherry, plum, and peach are often propagated using budding.

T-Budding. T-budding is faster than any other grafting technique. With a little practice, the right conditions, and compatible plants, t-budding can be a very successful grafting method. Beginning grafters usually have more success with t-budding than with other grafting methods. T-budding is also well-adapted to ¼ -1-in.-diameter plant shoots. In larger branches,

  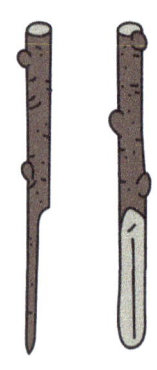  

1. Stock may be prepared with a single cut (left) or a double cut (right).

2. Cut the scion to form a pie-shaped wedge.

3. Insert scions into the prepared single-cut (left) or double-cut (right).

Figure 3.11 Bark grafting process

though, you can still insert buds in vigorously growing twigs near the upper part of the plant (Figure 3.12).

Besides being more successful, t-budding also forms a stronger union than do those made with other grafting techniques. Additionally, t-budding requires only a single bud as a scion; with several buds, you can produce several new plants even when scion wood is scarce.

Timing. A plant is ready for a t-bud graft almost any time that the bark of the stock "slips" or separates easily from the wood. Budding grafts in the fall or when the stock is dormant is easiest for beginners. Dormant budding can take place in late August or early September.

Bud Collection and Stock Selection. Usually, t-budding is used for fruit trees like citrus, peaches, and pears and ornamental trees like flowering cherry, flowering crabapple, and dogwood.

For the scion, collect a budstick (a terminal shoot) from the current season's growth; this should be free of insects and disease. Clip off the leaves, leaving about ¼-½ in. of the petiole as a handle. It's best to use budsticks as soon as you take them from the tree, but you can also store them in in cool, moist conditions for several days. Buds from the center of the twig tend to form more successful grafts than those near the tip or base.

For the understock, select a young stem between ½-1 in. in diameter. Younger plants selected as understock must have new, vigorous growth. Wipe any soil from the stock and remove any leaves that may interfere with budding. Cut the rootstock about ½ in. above the bud.

Preparing the Understock. A very sharp knife is important to preparing the stock for t-budding. Some are available commercially, but any knife that is sharp enough will do.

Start by selecting a smooth, branch-free part of the understock and making a vertical cut parallel with the grain of the wood by drawing the knife upwards. The cut should be about 1½ in. long. Position this cut so the bud will fall in the proper location; once inserted, the bud should be at about the center of this vertical slit. Then, make a cross cut at the top of the vertical cut to form a "T." This cross cut should cut through the bark but not the wood itself. Use a slight downward angle to make it easier to insert the bud. Then, gently lift the bark at the junction of the two cuts with the knife; if the bark is slipping properly, this step may not be necessary.

Creating the graft. Cut a bud from the middle of the budstick, placing the knife blade ½-¾ in. below the base of the selected bud before making a smooth, slicing cut upwards that extends to ½-¾ in. above the bud; this cut should remove only a slim sliver of the underlying wood. Then make a horizontal cut just above the bud, freeing it from the stick. You can use the petiole as a handle. As you finish the cut, bring the knife upward to release the bud. The wood attached to the bud (called a shield) must be cut straight; a curve in this wood will make poor contact with the rootstock and is not likely to form a successful graft. Immediately insert the cut bud into the understock before either can dry out.

To insert the bud, hold it by the petiole and gently raise the edges of the T incision. Slide the bud into the slit so it is covered by the two flaps. The top of the shield should be even with or slightly below the crosscut; you may need to trim the bud so it fits properly.

Finally, wrap a rubber budding strip three or four times above and below the bud to hold it tight to the stock. Start below the bud and wrap upward to keep from pushing the bud out of the cut and to force out any air pockets. Try to cover the horizontal cut of the T with a single loop of the wrap. Finish with a self-binding loop. Be careful not to cover the bud itself—only the area of the incision.

Caring for the Graft. Check the bud 7-10 days after insertion. If a union has taken place, the bud and shield will look fresh, not dry and shriveled. At this time, you can remove any non-elastic wrapping materials. If you used elastic wrapping bands, you can cut them at any time. Some will deteriorate naturally in a few weeks.

Dormant buds are not forced to grow until the following spring. After the bud starts swelling, cut off the stock about ½ in. above the cross of the "T." As the bud begins growing, buds from the rootstock may develop shoots. They should all be removed as soon as they appear.

Do not prune the new branch that develops from the bud during the first summer. If there is danger of it being broken by wind, tie it to a stake or otherwise support it; do not remove it.

Patch Budding. T-budding and patch budding are the most common of the several budding techniques. Patch budding is slower and more difficult than T-budding, but it is useful for thick-barked trees that cannot be T-budded. In South Carolina, patch budding is suitable for walnuts, pecans, and their relatives.

For successful patch budding, both the bark of the understock and the budstick must slip easily. You'll most likely want to perform your patch budding graft in late summer or early fall, but you can also do it in the spring as soon as the bark slips. It is best to have a budstick and understock of similar diameters, although it is possible to place a patch bud on stocks as large as 4 in. in diameter.

For a successful patch bud, it is essential that the size of the bud and its attached bark be the same size as the patch cut on the understock. For this reason, there are double-bladed knives or other special tools devised to make perfectly parallel horizontal cuts, usually about an inch apart.

Bud Preparation. For patch budding in late summer, select wood for budsticks two to three weeks in advance. Cut the leaf blades from the budsticks but leave the petioles. Do not cut the budsticks from the tree. By the time you do the budding, the petioles will have dropped or will be easy to remove; the leaf scar will have healed over. Cut the budsticks as needed and keep them moist and protected from direct sun or intense heat. Then remove the bud from the budstick.

Use the double knife to make parallel horizontal cuts equal distances above and below the bud. Then, make vertical cuts about 1 in. apart at each end of the horizontal cuts, forming a 1-in.-square patch.

Remove the patch from the budstick by pushing sideways. Be careful; pulling the patch from the stick may pull out the center of the bud. If the core of the bud stays on the budstick, the patchbud will not grow.

Preparation of the Understock. On the understock, you'll create patch similar to the one created for the bud; this patch must also be made in a clean, straight-grained portion of the understock. Cut the patch in the understock before the patchbud is removed from the budstick.

Remove the bark from the understock and quickly insert the patch containing the bud. Do this quickly so that neither the bud nor the understock dry out. Ideally, the inserted patch will fit snugly on all sides; however, it is more important that the patch is snug on the top and bottom than on all four sides.

Immediately after insertion, wrap the patch. Often, nursery adhesive tape or masking tape are suitable for patch buds. If the bark of the understock is thicker than that of the bud, pare it down so that the bud will not be loose once wrapped. Be careful not to wrap the bud itself but to cover all four cuts around it. Make sure the wrapping does not restrict the bud union.

About 10 days after budding, check the buds and release the wrapping by making a single vertical cut away from the bud on the back side of the understock. Do not try to pull off the wrapping if it sticks to the bud or understock—you only want to release tension.

As with other forms of budding, do not cut the stock back until the bud union is complete. When the budding is done in fall, do not cut the stock back until growth starts in the spring. If the budding is done in the spring, cut the stock back about 10 days after you inserted the bud, once it has formed a union.

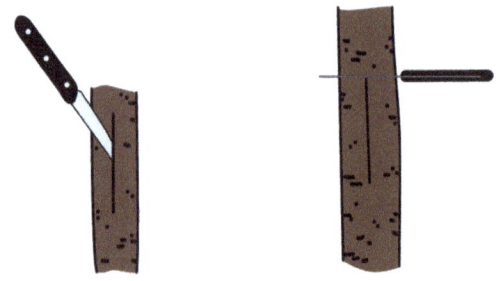

1. Prepare the understock by making a T-shaped cut with a sharp knife..

2. Slide the bud into the vertical slit until the top is even with or below the cross cut.

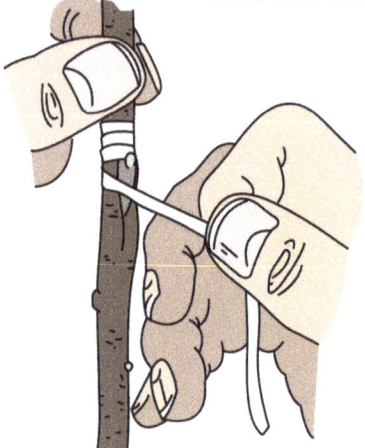

3. Wrap the bud tightly with a budding rubber.

Figure 3.12 T-budding process

PLANT TISSUE CULTURE AT HOME

Tissue culture is a process that involves exposing plant tissue to a specific regimen of nutrients, hormones, and light under sterile, *in vitro* conditions to produce many new plants, each a clone of the original mother plant, over a very short time. Tissue culture plants are advantageous in that they provide:

- disease free growth,
- a healthier and more fibrous root system,
- a bushier branching habit, and
- a higher survival rate.

One obstacle to at-home tissue culture is the necessity of maintaining hospital-sterile conditions and practicing exacting laboratory techniques. Also, tissue culture may take a couple of years to produce large numbers of one plant, so it is not suited to gardens or small nurseries. Many woody plant species and cultivars are difficult to produce in tissue culture, and the technical procedures for the aseptic or sterile culture of plant cells, tissues, and organs are as diverse as the plant material being "tissue cultured."

COPYRIGHTS, TRADEMARKS, AND PATENTS: PROPAGATION CONCERNS

Jeanne Hertzog, J.D., Lexington County Master Gardener.

Before you begin propagating plants, you should become familiar with copyrights, trademarks, and patents. There is a lot of confusion about these three terms; the common belief is that these legal protections only apply when you are selling the final product, but that is not how the law is written.

Copyrights protect the works of authors and creators, such as novels, poetry, movies, songs, and computer software. When something is copyrighted, you will usually see the symbol ©. The period of protection can vary, but it is likely to last for at least 70 years after the work is created. The good news is that copyrights do not apply to plants unless you are dealing with certain "works" such as photographs of plants or written material about them; when it comes to propagation, you're pretty much in the clear regarding copyrights.

Trademarks are names, phrases, symbols and the like that identify a business or product brand. Trademarking can be as simple as writing ™ after a name, which grants that business the rights to that name.

The second trademark type is a registered trademark, which is designated by the superscript ®; this trademark is registered by the U.S. Patent and Trademark Office. Once officially registered, a business or individual has exclusive rights to the trademarked name or phrase used in a commercial context for 10 years—and the trademark can be renewed in 10-year increments. Trademarks can be used with, but not ascribed to, an individual item produced by the owner of the trademark. A trademark name becomes invalid when the trademark name becomes a generic name identified with the product.

Patents are the biggest concern when it comes to propagation. Regardless of whether a plant name is trademarked, the plant may be patented. In 1930, federal law began offering legal protection to the person who invents or creates and asexually reproduces any new, distinct variety of plant; this change was an incentive for plant breeders to develop new varieties. Plants found in nature are specifically excluded from patents. The plant must have resulted from cultivation, and it may be the result of a sport, mutant, or hybrid. The plant must be stable through any of a number of means of asexual propagation, such as grafting, budding, cuttings, bulbs, rhizomes, tissue culture, etc. The owner of the plant must apply for a patent within one year; once they do, the law excludes anyone from asexually reproducing the plant for the duration of the patent—currently, 20 years. During that time, the "inventor" has exclusive rights to propagate the plant or to license others to do so. Propagation of a patented plant for any purpose without permission from the patent owner is illegal and an infringement of the plant patent owner's rights.

Licensed propagators typically tag the plant with a warning: "Asexual reproduction of this plant is prohibited." You will see the patent number prefixed with the letters "PP," which stand for "Plant Patent," or the letters "PPAF" if the plant patent has been "applied for," but not yet granted; plants awaiting pending patents are also protected by law.

As an example, Hydrangea macrophylla 'Bailmer' (PP#15,298) is a member of the Endless Summer® group, a protected trademark of a collection of four reblooming hydrangeas. 'Bailmer' (PP#15,298) was patented in the U.S. in 2001.

When is it permissible to propagate plants? The owner of a patented plant can give permission to someone to propagate the plant while the patent is in effect, although we might speculate that this is unlikely without payment. More useful is the knowledge that you can propagate plants when there is no patent on the plant (or once the patent has expired). After the patent has expired, the subject matter of the patent becomes public domain, meaning that the plant can be asexually reproduced, used, or sold without permission from the patent holder. If the plant has been on the market 20 years or less, you may have to do a bit of research to determine its status.

Noteworthy is the fact that if the plant name is trademarked, the name may still be protected even after 20 years, so you may need to call yoaur plant by a different name. Also, nothing in the patent law prohibits making use of pollen or seeds from a patented plant. The law only protects the owner of the patent from asexual reproduction (grafting, rooting cuttings, etc.) and there is no problem if you are gathering seeds or experimenting with sexual reproduction of your patented plants.

So, fellow Master Gardeners, have a great time in the garden and properly propagate our plants!

Reprinted with permission: The Green Sheet, vol. 113, March – April 2005. Revised by R. F. Polomski.

Ed. Note: Presently, trademarked plant names are becoming generic names in the marketplace, resulting in consumers identifying a particular plant by its trademarked name. A plant can only have one cultivar name, which is in the public domain. When a trademarked name becomes a pseudo-cultivar name or is used interchangeably with the cultivar name, it violates the legal use of trademarks and makes a mockery of the International Code of Nomenclature for Cultivated Plants. For more information on this topic, see "Name that plant - the misuse of trademarks in horticulture" by Tony Avent (https://www.plantdelights.com/blogs/articles/name-that-plant)

Chapter 4
Growing Healthy Lawns

Revised and updated by Adam Gore, Ph.D
Previous version prepared by Bob Polomski and Bert McCarty, Ph.D.

LEARNING OBJECTIVES
- Recognize the basic functions of turfgrass in the landscape.
- Know the names and important characteristics of recommended cool-season and warm-season turfgrasses.
- Identify turfgrasses common to South Carolina.
- Know how to select the most appropriate turfgrass for a home lawn based on growing conditions.
- Understand the basics of lawn establishment.
- Describe proper maintenance practices that include fertilizing, mowing, aerating, irrigating, and dethatching.
- Identify and manage common pest problems.
- Understand the importance of maintaining healthy turfgrass using IPM to avoid insect, weed, and disease issues.

INTRODUCTION

The idea of creating turfgrass lawns or managing pre-established turfgrass can cause conflict in many gardening circles. Sustainable gardeners often view turfgrass as a hindrance to conservative landscaping, deeming turf a high-maintenance plant requiring substantial inputs. Turfgrass, though, like any other plant, can be beneficial when you follow the same principles of plant selection and placement as you would with any woody ornamental or tree. When used appropriately, turfgrass adds beauty and value to property and is one of the most versatile and functional plants in the landscape. Turfgrass enhances the environment in many ways, which is particularly important in urban areas. Turf is one of the most effective plant covers in reducing soil erosion and surface runoff while recharging ground water—which results in more efficient use of rainfall. A turf area can reduce heat by as much as 30°F when replacing concrete or asphalt and as much as 14°F when replacing bare soil. The cooling effect of the average lawn is equal to over 8 tons of air conditioning, which is twice that of the average home's central air conditioning unit. Turf also absorbs dust and other air pollutants and produces oxygen. Turfgrasses provide the best surface for outdoor activities, including recreational and sporting activities. Although turfgrass management may seem a daunting task for many gardeners, it becomes more and more feasible with patience, persistence, and knowledge.

TURFGRASS IDENTIFICATION

Turfgrasses are divided into two basic categories based on their adaptation zones: cool-season turfgrasses thrive in northern climates or cooler areas and include ryegrasses, fescues and bluegrasses; warm-season turfgrasses grow best in warmer regions and include St. Augustinegrass, bermudagrass, centipedegrass, zoysiagrass, and some species of *Paspalum*.

Although many characteristics of turfgrasses are useful for identification (Table 4.1), it may be necessary to look at a grass's seedhead parts to identify the plant with certainty; other plant parts used for identification can be affected by environmental factors or management practices. Figure 4.1 illustrates these structures and provides some general characteristics useful for identifying common turfgrasses.

Stolons are above-ground stems, commonly referred to as "runners;" rhizomes are below-ground stems. Both are capable of producing a new plant and allow a grass to creep or grow laterally. Grasses consisting of rhizomes or stolons are effective in growing into or recovering areas damaged or thinned by traffic, compaction, insects, disease, or poor growing conditions.

There are several terms used in grass identification:

- Texture refers to leaf or blade width. Coarse texture grasses have wide leaf blades, whereas fine texture grasses have narrow or finer blade widths. Of the warm-season grasses, St. Augustinegrass is considered a coarse-textured species while hybrid bermudagrass is considered a fine-textured turf.
- The ligule is a structure found at the intersection of the blade and sheath. It can take various form but is common seen as a translucent membrane or fringe of hairs.
- The bud leaf is the arrangement of an emerging new leaf or leaves in the budshoot. In general, bud leaves are classified as rolled or folded. For example, the new shoots of tall fescue are rolled; the new shoots of centipedegrass are folded. Rolled means they are circular, like a rolled piece of paper. Folded means they are flat but doubled over, like a folded sheet of paper.

TURFGRASS SELECTION

Perhaps the most important factor in establishing and maintaining an attractive and manageable lawn is to choose a turfgrass that is adapted to your region and to your landscape or site. Be aware that there can be significant differences in soil type and growing conditions—especially if soil was brought to the site during construction—even locally or between distinct parts of a small site. It is important to consider these parameters when selecting a turfgrass.

The turfgrass should also be suited to your project. Trying to establish a turfgrass species in an area poorly suited to the species' growth requires special management techniques to produce and maintain a quality lawn. Since a lawn is intended to be a permanent planting, selecting the right turfgrass is an important first step. Selection should be based on:

- Region of adaptation,
- Tolerance to local environmental conditions (including any soil limitations),
- Desired turf quality,
- Expected maintenance levels, and
- Potential uses for the lawn.

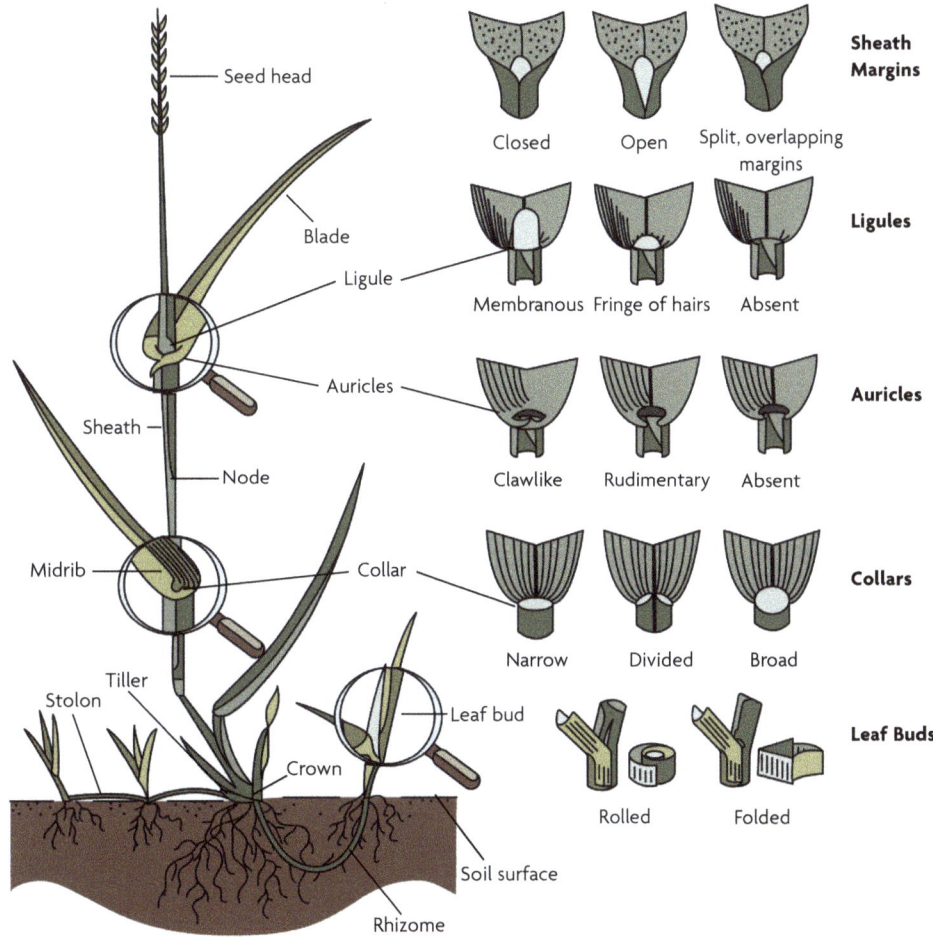

Figure 4.1 Illustration of the various parts of a grass plant. The primary leaf structures used to identify grasses are the ligule, auricle, collar, and sheath.

The right type of grass—one that suits your needs and is adapted to local conditions—will always give better results. Grasses vary in the type of climate they prefer, the amount of water and nutrients they need, their resistance to pests, their tolerance for shade and salt, and their hardiness.

If you are establishing a new lawn or renovating an old one, do some research to identify the best kind of grass for your site. If you are working with an established lawn that fails to thrive despite proper care, you should consider the possibility that the original lawn is made up of the wrong type of turfgrass for the site conditions. Consider replanting the suffering lawn with a different kind of grass that is better adapted to your site or evaluating the site to determine if turf is the appropriate plant to establish. There are many situations where turfgrass may not be the best choice.

Region of Adaptation

Turfgrasses belong to one of four climate categories based on the climate to which they are best suited: cool humid, warm humid, cool arid, and warm arid (Figure 4.2). More simply, turfgrasses are either warm-season turfgrass and cool-season turfgrass. Cool-season turfgrasses are adapted to the cool humid and irrigated cool arid climatic regions; they include bluegrasses, fescues, and ryegrasses (see Table 4.2). Warm-season turfgrasses are adapted to the warm humid and irrigated warm arid regions; they include bahiagrass, bermudagrass, carpetgrass, centipedegrass, St. Augustinegrass, seashore paspalum, and zoysiagrass (see Table 4.3).

South Carolina has a warm, humid climate that transitions to a cool, humid climate in the upper Piedmont. Cool-season turfgrasses are better suited to the upper Piedmont and Mountain regions. In the

TABLE 4.1 Identifying characteristics of common turfgrass species.

Common Name	Scientific Name	Stolons	Rhizomes	Texture[1]	Leaf Ligule[2]	Leaf Bud[3]	Other Characteristics
Cool Season Grasses							
Bluegrass, Annual	Poa annua	NO	NO	F	L	F	Boat shaped leaf tip, dual veins in middle; smooth leaf with occasional wave along margin
Bluegrass, Kentucky	Poa pratensis	NO	YES	M	S	F	Boat shaped leaf tip; dual veins in middle; smooth leaf
Fescue, Red	Festuca rubra	NO	FEW	F	S	F	Leaf very narrow, needlelike and usually folded
Fescue, Tall	Festuca arundinacea	NO	NO	C	S	R	Leaf margin rough to touch; red stem base; veins prominent; auricles small, hairy
Ryegrass, Annual	Lolium multiflorum	NO	NO	C	S	R	Underleaf shiny; red stem base; veins prominent
Ryegrass, Perennial	Lolium perenne	NO	NO	M	S	F	Underleaf shiny; red stem base; veins prominent; claw-like auricles
Warm Season Grasses							
Bahiagrass	Paspalum notatum	YES	YES	C	SH	R	Two to three spiked seedhead.
Bermudagrass	Cynodon dactylon	YES	YES	C-F	H	R-F	Tillers grow at 30-60° angle; some hairs on leaf surface; long stolons
Carpetgrass	Axonopus affinis	YES	NO	C	SH	F	Two to five spiked seedhead.
Centipedegrass	Eremochloa ophiuroides	YES	NO	C	SH	F	Single spike seedhead blades, hairy along edges; crabapple green color
Seashore Paspalum	Paspalum vaginatum	YES	YES	C-M	M	R-F	Blue-green color, seedhead with 2-3 spikes, popular for salt water areas
St. Augustinegrass	Stenotaphrum secundatum	YES	NO	C	SH	F	Boat-shaped leaf tip, single spike seedhead
Zoysiagrass	Zoysia spp.	YES	YES	C-F	H	R	Tillers grow at 90° angle; sheaths compressed; tuft of hairs at collar; hairy on leaf surface; very knotty nodes.

[1] C= coarse; M= medium; F= fine
[2] S= short; M= medium, L= Long, H= hairy
[3] R= rolled; F=folded

transition zone throughout the Piedmont, both cool- and warm-season grasses can grow. Warm-season grasses are well-suited to the Sandhills and the Coastal Plain. Tall fescue, a cool-season turfgrass, could be cultivated in the Sandhills but would require a high level of management and a gardener with a thorough knowledge of turfgrass culture.

Tolerance for Environmental Stressors

When selecting a turfgrass for your lawn, select one that tolerates your local environmental stressors. These stressors include seasonal temperature extremes, the availability of moisture, soil conditions, the possibility of salt problems, the amount of available sun or shade, and the amount of traffic the turf will have to tolerate.

Figure 4.2 **The four main climatic categories of the United States for turfgrasses.**

Quality and Required Maintenance

The quality of lawn you desire is important in the selection process; the quality will determine how much maintenance you need to provide for successful lawn upkeep. Determine if you want your lawn to be a showplace, an average lawn, or just a functional living cover that controls soil erosion. A decent, average-looking lawn will require less time and input than a superior, weed-free lawn. A living cover made up of various flowering and non-flowering plant species will require the least amount of maintenance but may be invaded by numerous off-species plants, including some that are considered weeds.

Lawn quality is directly related to lawn maintenance. Moreover, most turfgrasses have an optimum level of maintenance that includes fertilizing, mowing, watering, and pest management. In general, a low-maintenance approach entails minimal fertilizing, mowing as needed, and seldom using any type of irrigation or pesticide. A medium-maintenance approach requires more frequent fertilizing, mowing weekly or biweekly, and watering as needed; often, pesticides use will increase to control troublesome weeds, insects, or diseases. A high-maintenance lawn requires frequent fertilizing, weekly or twice-weekly mowing, regular watering during the growing season, routine dethatching and aerification, and consistent management of pests, weeds, insects, and disease. Providing inadequate or excessive care to certain turfgrass species will result in pest development and a decline in quality.

Intended Use

The final consideration in turfgrass selection should be how the lawn will be used. Certain species of turfgrass are more adapted to heavy traffic, while other species are more suited to lighter use. In high-traffic spaces, planting species that are slow-growing or only marginally adapted to the climate of the area will result in turf thinning or the need to reestablish annually. Most turfgrass species will thrive under light traffic—such as the occasional picnic or party—but only a few species will survive constant foot traffic from kids or animals. During the selection process, determine how much foot or vehicular traffic the turf will be subjected to and choose a turf hardy enough to withstand it.

COOL-SEASON TURFGRASSES

As one might guess, cool-season turfgrasses grow best during the cooler months of the year. The ideal air temperature for cool-season turfgrass growth is between 60-75°F. During hot summer months, these grasses may go dormant or be injured; they are better adapted to the upper Piedmont and Mountain regions than the warmer areas of South Carolina (Table 4.2). One advantage to planting cool-season grasses is that all the species that grow in South Carolina can be planted from seed, which is the most economical way of establishing or renovating a lawn. These grasses will remain green throughout the year and have the most attractive color during fall, winter, and spring.

One disadvantage to cool-season grasses is their high susceptibility to disease during the warm, humid summer months. Disease can result in complete loss of the turfgrass if the lawn is neglected or improperly managed. In areas where cool-season turfgrasses are limited due to environmental adaptation, they will thin and require reseeding annually during the fall months; cool-season grasses in warmer areas require an in-depth knowledge of turfgrass management to remain attractive.

Tall fescue is the most popular cool-season species for home lawns in South Carolina. The use of chewings fescue and red fescue is much more limited, and these grasses are more suited to shady areas; because of this, they are often included in seed blends for shaded areas. Kentucky bluegrass is adapted to the western-most mountainous regions of the state and is used much less frequently than tall fescue. Annual bluegrass can be found growing throughout the state during the cooler seasons and is usually considered a weed when growing in a stand of warm-season turf. Bentgrass is also adapted to the cooler regions of South Carolina, but usually, this grass is used for golf course putting greens. The ryegrasses are suitable only for temporary covers in areas where a permanent turf will be planted and for winter overseeding of dormant warm-season lawns.

Tall Fescue (*Lolium arundinacea*, formerly *Festuca arundinacea*)

Tall fescue is a popular grass in the Mountain and upper Piedmont regions of South Carolina. It is a perennial, bunch-type grass that is considered a good utility turfgrass. It establishes quickly from seed and grows well in full sun to partial shade. It is adapted to a wide range of soil conditions but prefers a fertile, moist, fine-textured soil high in organic matter. Tall fescue grows best in soils with a pH between 5.5-6.5, but it will tolerate a pH between 4.7-8.5. Tall fescue can tolerate wet soil conditions as well as periods of submersion, and it is often used in drainage areas.

Tall fescue grows rapidly during the spring and fall months, requiring frequent mowing. It shows good heat and drought tolerance for a cool-season turfgrass but not enough to thrive in the hotter Sandhills and Coastal regions of South Carolina. It will thin out if irrigation is unavailable and if rainfall is lacking under high temperatures. Tall fescue will remain green during most of the summer and winter but grows little during periods of extreme heat or cold. One drawback to planting tall fescue is that it tends to thin out and become clumpy, which allows weeds to establish themselves more easily if the grass is not properly managed or suited to the environment. Reseeding is required each fall to maintain an adequate stand of grass.

Kentucky-31 (K-31) is the old, common variety of tall fescue often used in pastures for livestock. Most of the new cultivars referred to as "turf-type" tall fescues have slightly narrower leaves, darker green color, slower vertical growth rates, greater density and better shade tolerance than K-31. Some varieties of turf-type tall fescue are better than others at resisting disease and tolerating drought. In general, most properly-managed turf-type tall fescues will produce a better-looking lawn than K-31. For updated tall fescue variety information, contact your local county Extension agent. Variety trials are performed annually at multiple land-grant institutions around the country.

Fine Fescue (*Festuca species*)

Fine fescue is the collective name for several fine-leaved species of grasses in the genus *Festuca*. Native to the cool, forested European Alps, fine fescues have delicate, wiry leaves that are usually less than ¼-in. wide and have a clumpy, bristle-like appearance. Red fescue (*Festuca rubra*) and spreading fescue (*F. pratensis*) have slow-spreading rhizomes, while chewings fescue (*F. rubra ssp. commutata*), sheep fescue (*F. ovina*), and hard fescue (*F. longifolia*) have a bunch-type growth habit. Hard fescue has a deep green color, whereas sheep fescue is bluish-green.

Red or creeping red fescue is adapted to shady locations in cool, moist, mountainous areas. Chewings, hard, and sheep fescues tolerate full sun or partial shade. They are often planted in shaded, low-traffic areas. If left unmowed, their leaves and seedheads provide a low maintenance, natural look.

As a group, the fine fescues are noted for shade tolerance, winter hardiness, and adaptability to infertile, dry soils. They do not tolerate wet, poorly-drained soils very well, but are well adapted to dry, shady conditions and low-maintenance situations. They do not tolerate extensive traffic or heat and do not persist below the upper Piedmont region (<1,000 ft. elevation) except as clumps in shaded areas.

Fine fescues are rarely used alone; instead, they are often mixed with other cool-season grasses—such as Kentucky bluegrass and perennial ryegrass—in seed blends. They are also used in blends for winter overseeding of warm-season turfgrasses.

Red fescue tolerates shady conditions better than any of the other cool-season grasses. It is often mixed with Kentucky bluegrass. Red fescue tends to prevail in the shade, while bluegrass dominates the stand in full sun.

Kentucky Bluegrass (*Poa pratensis*)

Kentucky bluegrass is adapted to the upper Piedmont and Mountain regions (elevation > 900 ft.) of South Carolina. Soils that are moist, well-drained, and fertile, with a pH between 6-7, are best suited to Kentucky bluegrass. This grass does best in full sun, but certain varieties tolerate partial shade. These shade-tolerant varieties are often mixed with red fescue to seed shady areas.

During dry periods in the summer, Kentucky bluegrass may turn brown and go dormant; however, it is capable of surviving an extended drought and can initiate new growth from underground stems (rhizomes) when moisture conditions are favorable. To maintain a green Kentucky bluegrass lawn in South Carolina in the summer, you will need irrigation during dry spells.

When planted on a suitable site and properly managed, Kentucky bluegrass provides a quality turf. However, it is a high-maintenance turfgrass. If managed poorly, thatch can become a serious problem, particularly with vigorous-growing varieties of Kentucky bluegrass that are particularly well maintained.

Annual Ryegrass (*Lolium multiflorum*)

Annual ryegrass is not a permanent lawn grass. As the name suggests, it is an annual species that dies out the following spring and summer after fall planting. It is used to establish a quick cover during the winter to control erosion on sites that cannot be planted with a permanent turfgrass due to cold temperatures.

Annual ryegrass is also used by itself or in a mixture with other cool-season grasses as an overseeded grass for green color during the winter on dormant, warm-seeded lawns. When used alone, annual ryegrass will provide a marginal overseeding cover, but it does not handle environmental stresses well. It often dies out before the winter is over.

Perennial Ryegrass (*Lolium perenne*)

Perennial ryegrass is similar to annual ryegrass in many ways, but under the right conditions, it can stay alive for an extra 2-4 weeks in the spring or early summer. As with annual ryegrass, perennial rye is used to cover bare areas in the fall and winter and to provide winter color to dormant, warm-season lawns.

Perennial ryegrass is superior to annual ryegrass due to its increased heat and disease resistance. However, perennial ryegrass is still unreliable as a permanent lawn due to susceptibility to certain diseases in the summer. There are other fine-textured varieties that have higher disease resistance and better mowing qualities. Perennial ryegrass may survive for several years in cooler environments, particularly in the absence of competition from other grasses, however in hot and humid climates, like that experienced in South Carolina use of ryegrasses should be limited to overseeding warm-season lawns.

WARM-SEASON TURFGRASSES

Warm-season turfgrasses grow best during the warmer months of spring, summer, and fall; they grow best between 80-95°F. Certain warm-season grasses will turn off-color during the driest periods of summer. All warm-season turfgrasses will become dormant during the winter but resume growth as the temperature warms in spring.

Seven warm-season turfgrasses are commonly grown in South Carolina: bahiagrass, bermudagrass, carpetgrass, centipedegrass, seashore paspalum, St. Augustinegrass, and zoysiagrass (Table 4.3). The two largest limiting factors for the potential use of individual warm-season species in some parts of the state are their limited tolerance to cold temperatures and the availability of light.

Bahiagrass (*Paspalum notatum*)

Common bahiagrass was introduced from Brazil in 1914 and used as a pasture grass on the poor-quality, sandy soils of the southeastern United States. The ability of bahiagrass to persist on infertile, dry soils and to resist most pests (especially nematodes) made it an increasingly popular lawn grass for use where function is more important than appearance.

TABLE 4.2 General comparisons of the major cool-season turfgrasses for South Carolina lawns.

	Chewings Fescue	Kentucky Bluegrass	Perennial Ryegrass	Red Fescue	Tall Fescue
Area Best Adapted	Mountains	Mountains/Upper Piedmont	Mountains	Mountains/Piedmont	Mountains/Piedmont
Growth Habit	Bunch	Rhizomes	Bunch	Rhizomes	Bunch
Establishment Rate	Very slow	Slow	Very fast	Medium	Medium
Mowing Height (inches)	1 ½ to 2 ½	1 ½ to 2 ½	1 ½ to 2 ½	1 ½ to 2 ½	2 ½ to 3 1/2
Mowing Frequency	Medium	Medium	Medium-High	Medium	High
Days to first mowing after seeding	14 to 21	30 to 35	7 to 14	12 to 17	14 to 21
Disease Tendency	Medium	Medium	Medium	Medium	Low
Drought Tolerance	Excellent	Good	Good	Very good	Excellent
Heat Tolerance	Fair	Fair	Poor to Fair	Fair	Good
Salt Tolerance	Good	Poor	Good	Good	Good
Shade Tolerance	Excellent	Poor to Fair	Fair	Excellent	Good
Thatch Tendency	Medium	Medium	Low	Medium	Low
Wear Tolerance	Fair	Good	Poor	Good	Good

Generally, bahiagrass will not provide as fine a lawn as the other warm-season turfgrasses described in this section; this lesser attractiveness is due to its relatively open growth habit and tall, unsightly seedheads produced from May through October. It is suitable for out-of-the-way areas that require a low-maintenance vegetative cover.

Bahiagrass can be inexpensively grown from seed. Once established, it develops an extensive root system that makes it highly resistant to drought. These qualities have made it a popular grass species for roadside erosion control.

The prolific seedheads and tough leaves and stems make it difficult to mow bahiagrass. For the best appearance, bahiagrass should be cut with a heavy-duty rotary mower or a flail mower. Bahiagrass is poorly adapted to alkaline or high-pH soils and will not thrive in areas subject to salt spray. Compared to other lawn grasses, bahiagrass has fewer pest problems, although mole crickets can cause severe damage.

There are three varieties of bahiagrass seed or sod sold for lawns:

- Common bahiagrass is the least attractive bahigrass because of its light green color, coarse texture, and prostrate, open-type growth habit. It has a low tolerance for cold temperatures and is not recommended for use in home lawns.
- Argentine bahiagrass is the best variety for lawns. It has wider leaves than Pensacola bahiagrass but longer and narrower leaves than Common bahiagrass. It forms a dense sod, has good color and cold hardiness, responds well to fertilization, and produces fewer seedheads. Argentine is least susceptible to dollar spot disease.
- Pensacola bahiagrass was selected from plantings found in Pensacola, Florida, in 1935, and it has become the most common variety of bahiagrass. Pensacola is used extensively along roadsides in the southern United States due to its deep, fibrous root system and readily available seed. Although Pensacola produces excessive amounts of seedheads, its long, narrow, blue-green leaves have made it a popular choice for homeowners.

Seashore Paspalum (*Paspalum vaginatum*)

Seashore paspalum is a relative of bahiagrass also known as sand knotgrass, siltgrass, and saltwater couch. Seashore paspalum grows along the coastal regions of North Carolina through Florida and west to Texas. Often growing in brackish water, it has the highest salt tolerance of any turfgrass. Seashore paspalum has dark blue-green leaves and spreads by rhizomes and stolons.

Several cultivars of seashore paspalum that either resemble coarse-leaved common bermudagrasses or fine-leaved hybrid bermudagrasses are available. It produces a fairly dense turf when mowed regularly at 1.5 in. or less.

Seashore paspalum does not tolerate prolonged freezing conditions as well as bermudagrass, so currently, there are limited varieties available for use in coastal areas. Seashore paspalum tolerates more shade than bermudagrass but less shade than other turfgrasses. Seashore paspalum can be difficult to maintain in a home lawn situation as it requires constant, specific care.

Bermudagrass (*Cynodon* species)

Native to eastern Africa, bermudagrass is a long-lived turfgrass adapted to succeed throughout South Carolina. It thrives in a wide variety of growing conditions and soil types and tolerates a wide range of soil pH. Bermudagrass is highly salt-tolerant, which makes it a good choice for coastal regions where salt sprays and flooding may occur.

Bermudagrass produces an aggressive, dark green, dense lawn which is adapted to the soil and climatic conditions in South Carolina. It has excellent wear and drought tolerance, which makes it ideal for home lawns, parks, golf courses, and athletic fields. Bermudagrass establishes rapidly and competes well against weeds. However, its aggressive nature can be troublesome due to its ability to spread by both above- and below-ground runners that are difficult to control in groundcovers, flower beds, and walkways. Bermudagrass will not tolerate shade; it will gradually thin out and disappear under trees or building overhangs.

Bermudagrass requires a high level of management to attain a showcase-quality lawn. Because of its rapid growth rate, mowing practices should include a reel-type mower. Rotary mowers will work fine only if the blades are sharp. Due to its rapid growth, thatch buildup can become a problem with bermudagrass. Common bermudagrass tends to accumulate less thatch than hybrid bermudagrass.

Bermudagrasses have very few serious pest problems but are subject to attack from sting-nematodes when grown in sandy soils. Nematode damage causes shallow-rooted plants that do not respond to water and fertilizer, resulting in thin, weak areas invaded by weeds. If you suspect nematodes, submit a nematode sample for analysis.

Common or hybrid bermudagrass varieties can be used in home lawns. Common bermudagrass (*Cynodon dactylon*) is a spindly grass considered a weed ("wiregrass") by many people, but managed well, it can become a quality lawn grass. Recent years have seen the release of improved types of common bermudagrass. Many of these "improved" grasses look similar to hybrid bermudagrass varieties but can be planted by seed. These newer types can cope with environmental conditions better than the older, common bermudagrass.

Hybrid bermudagrasses (*Cynodon dactylon x C. transvaalensis*) are superior to common bermudagrass. They produce no viable seed and must be sprigged, plugged, or sodded. Compared to common bermudagrass, hybrid bermudagrasses are more resistant to disease, grow more densely, are more resistant to weeds, produce fewer seedheads, have finer and softer texture, and have the most desirable color. The hybrids also demand the highest degree of maintenance for the best appearance of any of the warm-season grasses, such as frequent close mowing, regular fertilizing, edging, and dethatching.

Turfgrass breeding programs are steadily producing new varieties of both improved and hybrid bermudagrasses in order to meet new market demands such as increased drought resistance, decreased fertilization demands, and higher shade tolerance. Contact your local county Extension agent for up-to-date information on bermudagrass cultivars for your site.

Carpetgrass (*Axonopus affinis*)

Carpetgrass is a creeping warm-season grass native to the West Indies that closely resembles centipedegrass. Carpetgrass is not widely used as a lawn grass in South Carolina, but it is sometimes used on soils that are too infertile or too poorly drained for other grasses. It is also commonly mixed with centipedegrass. Carpetgrass is adapted to soils that stay wet for most of the year—making it a good choice for flood plain areas.

A carpetgrass lawn usually has a rough or ragged appearance because of seed stems that are hard to mow. It grows well in sun or partial shade if the soil is moist, but it tolerates less shade than St. Augustinegrass or centipedegrass.

Carpetgrass is very shallow-rooted. It has low tolerance for drought or cold; it turns brown with the first cold spell and slowly greens up in the spring. There are no improved varieties of carpetgrass on the market.

Centipedegrass (*Eremochloa ophiuroides*)

Centipedegrass was brought into the United States from southeast Asia. It is a slow-growing turfgrass that will grow best from the Coastal Plain to the Sandhills. It has a natural yellow-green color—described by some as "Granny Smith-green"—and spreads by centipede-like stolons that give it its name. It is adapted for use as a low maintenance, general-purpose turf. Centipedegrass requires less fertilizer or mowing than other warm-season grasses. Since it only produces surface runners, centipedegrass can be easily controlled around flower beds and along walkways. It is the ideal grass for anyone wanting a fairly attractive lawn that needs little care.

Common centipede can be established from seeds, sprigs, plugs, or sod. Since it is slow- growing, it takes longer than bermudagrass or St. Augustinegrass for centipedegrass to completely cover newly-planted areas.

Centipedegrass is more shade-tolerant than bermudagrass, but it cannot tolerate shade as well as St. Augustinegrass or zoysiagrass. There are some disadvantages to centipedegrass, including its susceptibility to winterkill—especially during the spring, when cold temperatures can be interrupted by warmer temperatures. Centipedegrass does not grow well when faced with:

- traffic,
- soil compaction,
- high-phosphorus soils,
- low-potassium soils,
- excessive nitrogen fertilization, or
- high pH soils.

Centipedegrass is also susceptible to several diseases. Brown patch and dollar spot can cause extensive damage under certain conditions. Centipedegrass is especially susceptible to ground pearls and plant parasitic nematodes; these two soil-inhabiting pests can be particularly destructive on centipedegrass because of the limited control measures suited for home lawns.

A disorder called "centipedegrass decline" usually occurs in the spring when parts of the lawn fail to come out of dormancy. Sometimes, parts of the lawn start to green up and grow, but then they die in late spring and summer. Several factors can contribute to centipedegrass decline, including a high soil pH, high amounts of nitrogen and phosphorus applied during the previous growing season, heavy thatch buildup, poor cultural practices, cold and dry winter dormancy periods, nematodes, or diseases that make the grass susceptible to injury.

Most of the centipedegrass that is available in the marketplace is of the common variety. It can be established by seed, but because the seed is expensive, it is usually planted by sodding or plugging.

There are improved varieties of centipedegrass available, including Centennial, Oklawn, Covington, Santee, TennTurf, and TifBlair. The improved cultivars have better cold tolerance than the common variety. However, some of these newer varieties—such as Covington—must be vegetatively propagated and are selected specifically for their improved cold tolerance. Currently, only TifBlair is available as seed. Centennial will perform a little better on alkaline soils than common centipedegrass. Santee is suited for the lower one-third of South Carolina, and Covington is suited for all areas except the Upstate.

St. Augustinegrass (*Stenotaphrum secundatum*)

St. Augustinegrass, or "Charleston grass," is adapted to the warm, humid southern regions of the United States, and historically, it has grown well along the South Carolina coast to the lower Midland regions. St. Augustinegrass has large, flat stems and broad, coarse leaves. It has an attractive blue-green color and forms a deep, dense turf. St. Augustinegrass spreads by stolons, so it is easily controlled around borders. It prefers well-drained, fertile soils. For an acceptable quality lawn, St. Augustinegrass requires supplemental irrigation and a moderate level of soil fertility and maintenance during the growing season.

St. Augustinegrass has high salt tolerance and will handle shade better than other warm-season turfgrasses. It is quick and easy to establish St. Augustinegrass from sod, and there is no seed available.

St. Augustinegrass has several characteristics that may limit its use in certain situations. The coarse leaf texture is objectionable to some people because it resembles crabgrass. During drought conditions, it will not remain green without supplemental irrigation. St. Augustinegrass can handle damp conditions for short periods of time, but damp soils will promote disease problems such as large patch and gray leaf spot. It has poor wear tolerance and can be damaged by cold temperatures. St. Augustinegrass is the least cold tolerant of any commercially used warm-season turfgrasses, however due to years of selective breeding, St. Augustinegrass is now able to be grown successfully in the lower Piedmont areas. Excessive thatch can become a problem under high fertilization scenarios and excessive irrigation. The major pest associated with St. Augustinegrass is the chinch bug; however, there are chinch-bug resistant cultivars. St. Augustine Decline Virus (SADV) is a major disease problem in some parts of the United States, but it has not been a problem yet in South Carolina.

There are numerous improved cultivars of St. Augustinegrass available in the marketplace. When selecting a variety of St. Augustinegrass, compare the different varieties available in your area to find one that will fit your needs. These improved varieties are designed to have different benefits, such as resistance to particular insect or disease problems or an improved tolerance for environmental stress.

Zoysiagrass (*Zoysia* spp.)

Zoysiagrass is adapted to a wide range of soils and tolerant to cold temperatures, shade, and salt spray. Zoysia is one of the most cold-tolerant of the warm-season turfgrasses. It performs well in full sun or partial shade but will thin out in dense shade—the most shade-tolerant varieties still require 4-5 hours of direct sunlight.

Zoysiagrass forms a low, slow-growing, very dense lawn that resists weed invasions. The slow growth is advantageous because it can be mowed less frequently than other grasses and is easier to keep out of flower beds than bermudagrass. However, zoysiagrass is tougher to mow than other warm-season turfgrasses due to its high silica concentration that creates a tougher, stiffer leaf blade. It is important to be able to maintain mower blade sharpness if managing zoysiagrass.

There are three types of zoysiagrasses: *Zoysia japonica*, *Z. matrella*, and *Z. tenuifolia*. The first two species are more commonly used as turf in South Carolina, whereas *Z. tenuifolia* is more often used as an ornamental plant. The fine-bladed varieties of *Z. matrella*, such as Diamond, are often seen on golf courses; the wide-bladed *Z. japonica* is more often used for lawns. The improved cultivars of zoysiagrass must be planted by vegetative means and can be extremely slow to establish. It may take two growing seasons to cover a lawn with zoysiagrass when planted by plugs or sprigs. You can start zoysiagrass from seed, but it will likely take two years to establish full coverage.

All zoysiagrasses form a heavy thatch layer, especially when mowed high, mowed infrequently, or fertilized excessively. Thatch needs to be removed periodically by dethatching. Be careful when dethatching zoysiagrass—because of its slow growth rate, you must dethatch early enough in the growing season to allow time for recovery before winter dormancy. If using a dethatching rake, spacing between tines should be at last 2 in. apart.

Zoysia recovers slowly from injury, grows poorly on compacted soils, has a high fertility requirement, and requires frequent watering during the summer months. It looks best when mowed with a reel-type mower, although you can maintain an attractive zoysia lawn using a rotary mower with sharp blades; be ready to sharpen mower blades every two to three weeks during weekly mowing cycles.

There are several species and varieties of zoysiagrass that vary widely in color, texture, and establishment rate, and more varieties are tested each year. Check with your local county Extension agent for updated information about zoysiagrass varieties.

LAWN ESTABLISHMENT

There are four steps to turfgrass establishment:

1. select a turfgrass that is adapted for the area in which it will be planted;
2. prepare the soil for planting;
3. plant by seed, sod, plugs, or sprigs; and
4. maintain the newly-planted lawn to ensure successful establishment and growth.

Turfgrass Selection

Proper turfgrass selection is one of the most important factors in the successful establishment, longevity, and ease of maintenance of a home lawn. The lawn grass you select should be adapted to your site, match the level of lawn quality you desire, and be suited to the level of management you are willing to provide.

Besides carefully choosing the right turfgrass species, you must select a specific cultivar of your determined species. Some turfgrass cultivars perform better than others in South Carolina. Therefore, deciding which cultivar to purchase is an important consideration. Also, be aware that cultivar availability may be limited in certain locations and that new cultivars appear in the marketplace from time to time. Your selection may be influenced by these factors.

Selecting an inappropriate species and variety of turfgrass will lead to a lawn of inferior quality and overall dissatisfaction.

TABLE 4.3 General comparisons of warm-season turfgrasses for South Carolina lawns.

	Bahiagrass	Bermu-dagrass	Carpetgrass	Centipe-degrass	Seashore paspalum	St. Augustine-grass	Zoysiagrass
Area Best Adapted	Statewide excluding Mountains	Statewide	Lower Piedmont to Coastal Plain	Statewide excluding Mountains	Coastal Plain	Lower Piedmont to Coastal Plain	Statewide
Establishment Method	Seed or sod	Seed[a], sod, plugs, or sprigs	Seed or sprigs	Seed, sod, plugs, or sprigs	Sod, plugs, or sprigs	Sod, plugs, or sprigs	Seed, sod, plugs, or sprigs
Maintenance Level	Low	Medium to High	Low	Low	Medium	Medium	Medium to High
Mowing Height (inches)	3 – 4	½ - 1½	1 - 2	1 - 2	1 – 1½	2½[b] - 4	½ - 2
Mowing Frequency	High	High	Low	Low	Medium	Medium	Medium
Mower Preference	Rotary	Reel	Rotary	Rotary	Rotary	Rotary	Reel
Cold Tolerance	Poor	Fair	Poor	Poor	Very Poor	Poor	Fair to Good
Disease Tendency	Low	Low	Low	Low	Low	Medium	Medium
Drought Tolerance	Excellent	Excellent	Poor	Fair	Fair to Good	Good	Excellent
Nematode Tolerance	Very good	Poor to Fair	Poor	Poor	Unknown	Fair to Good	Poor
Salt Tolerance	Very poor	Excellent	Poor	Poor	Excellent	Good	Good to Excellent
Shade Tolerance	Poor	Very poor	Fair	Fair	Poor to Fair	Good	Fair to Good
Thatch Tendency	Low	High	Low	Medium	Low	Medium	High
Wear Tolerance	Good	Excellent	Poor	Poor	Good	Fair	Excellent

[a]Common bermudagrass varieties only
[b]Dwarf St. Augustinegrass varieties only

Soil Preparation

As with any plant, the key to establishing and maintaining a lawn is proper soil preparation. Soil preparation will look the same whether you are planting by seed, sprigs, plugs, or sod.

A Note on Amending Heavy Clay Soils with Sand

There are areas of South Carolina, predominately the Piedmont and Mountain regions, that have a naturally heavy clay soil type. Modifying the soil with sand is only recommended in instances where drainage is poor or compaction is excessive. It is common to add sand to clay soils on golf course putting greens. However, due to the high cost of proper modification and the need for exact specifications, it is rare to use sand to modify soil in home lawns.

Any sand amendment must contain at least 75% medium-sized sand to provide improved aeration. Modification below this level will decrease pore space in the soil and overall turf quality. Turfgrasses grown in a soil that has been extensively modified with sand will likely require more frequent irrigation and fertilization. Clay soils may require some type of internal drainage system if they retain excessive moisture.

Soil Testing

Soil testing will determine whether a soil's pH and nutrient (phosphorus, potassium, calcium, and magnesium) levels are in a range that encourages turfgrass growth. The soil test report will indicate how much fertilizer or lime should be applied. Lime and fertilizer applications are most successful when they are mixed into the upper 4-6 in. of the soil, so having the soil tested early in the process is important. This will allow time to incorporate any amendments. Contact a local county Extension office for instructions on taking and submitting soil samples.

Clean and Rough Grade

Remove all debris from the location where you'll be establishing your turfgrass. This "debris" includes rocks, bottles, large roots, and old tree stumps. If the area needs extensive grading, remove the topsoil and stockpile it for replacement after the rough grade is established. The site should have a gentle slope of 1 - 2% (1 - 2 ft. of fall per 100 ft.) away from any structure. The rough grade should conform to the final grade after the topsoil is replaced. Slopes more than 10% should be sodded rather than seeded, due to the potential for erosion.

If you intend to install an irrigation system, make sure that it is properly designed and installed according to design specifications. Installation is easier before the turf has been planted. Be sure that underground components of the irrigation system are buried deeply enough to avoid problems with routine cultural practices that will be performed on the lawn, such as aerification, as well as below any frost line. For South Carolina, a depth of 12 in. is recommended for irrigation lines to avoid freezing.

A properly designed irrigation system should also separate turfed areas from ornamental planting beds. Trees, woody ornamentals, annual flowers, and perennial flowers will have different watering schedules than turf. An irrigation system's capacity to perform properly is limited by its design and construction. A poorly designed or improperly installed system will never operate satisfactorily.

Deep Tillage

Rototilling loosens compacted soil and improves the speed and depth of rooting. A tractor-mounted or self-propelled tiller will adequately till the soil. Till in two directions, as deeply as possible—preferably 6-8 in.— to ensure a thorough and uniform seedbed mixture.

The subsurface may become compacted during rough grading, especially if the ground is wet. This compacted layer must be broken up. A spring-tooth harrow works well on lightly compacted soils; a small rotovator may be needed for more heavily compacted sites.

Take care not to destroy the existing trees in the lawn. Cutting a large percentage of a tree's roots during soil tillage can severely damage or kill a tree. Do not cover trees' roots with soil. If additional soil is necessary at a tree base, construct a "tree well" (Figure 4.3).

Return the Topsoil

Once you have established the subsurface, spread the stockpiled topsoil. Allow for a final depth of at least 6 - 8 in. after the soil has settled. A 1-ft. root zone depth is ideal; this usually means spreading about 8 - 10 in. of topsoil over the subgrade. On steep slopes or where there are rock outcrops, proper maintenance requires at least 12 in. of topsoil.

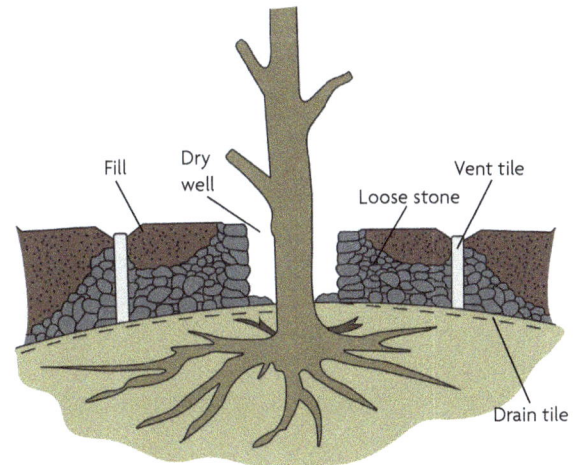

Figure 4.3 Tree well system installed before raising the surrounding soil level to prevent or reduce injury cause by soil fill

TABLE 4.4 Soil amendments and their rate of application for incorporating into top 6 to 8 inches of turfgrass soil.

Material	Volume Cubic yards per 1000 sq. ft.	Depth of amendment in inches before incorporation
Composted sludge[a]	3 to 6	1 to 2
Sawdust[b]	3 to 6	1 to 2
Composted yard trimmings	3 to 6	1 to 2
Sphagnum peat moss	3	1
Farm manure (rotted)[a]	3	1

[a]Do not apply additional nitrogen at establishment when using composted sludge or farm manure.
[b]Incorporate 40 lbs. of 10-10-10 per 1,000 sq. ft. with the sawdust *in lieu* of standard fertilization recommendation when using sawdust.

You can improve soil by adding organic matter (Table 4.4). Organic matter reduces fertilizer leaching as well as improves water retention in sandy soils and drainage in clay soils. Soils that are very poorly drained, such as muck soils, will need additional drainage methods to avoid soil saturation. To achieve a good growing condition for all turfgrass species, good drainage is essential.

Delay final grading and incorporation of the fertilizer until just prior to planting time. If this is done too far in advance, some fertilizer may leach out and the soil may become crusted.

Fertilization and Liming

Apply fertilizer and lime or sulfur (if needed), as recommended by the soil test, into the upper 6 - 8 in. of soil. In the absence of a soil test, contact a local county Extension office for recommendations.

Apply a "starter-type" fertilizer that contains a higher amount of phosphate, which turfgrass seedlings require. Apply 20-30 lbs. of a commercial grade fertilizer—such as 5-10- 15, 6-18-18, or 5-10-10—per 1,000 sq. ft. of lawn. If your fertilizer contains a water-soluble, quick-release source of nitrogen, do not apply more than 1.5 lbs. of actual nitrogen per 1,000 sq. ft. prior to planting. If your fertilizer contains a water-insoluble, slow-release source of nitrogen such as urea formaldehyde, you can apply 3-5 lbs. of actual nitrogen per 1,000 sq. ft. prior to planting.

After the fertilizer and lime are worked into the soil, the soil should be firmed by rolling with a water ballast roller before seeding, sodding, or plugging (Figure 4.4). Do not pulverize the soil. The best soil for seeding has a granular texture with small clods of soil varying from 0.125 – 0.75 in. in diameter.

Figure 4.4 Water ballast roller
Image Credit: Landzie.com

However, if the area is to be sprigged, the top 2 – 3 in. of the soil should remain loose so that a portion of each sprig can be "set" or pushed into the soil. On light, sandy soils, firm the seedbed before planting to help prevent the soil from drying out. Now it is time to plant.

Seeding

Successful turfgrass establishment from seed is heavily influenced by the procedures followed before, during, and after seeding. This process starts with selecting top quality seed.

Selecting Your Seed

South Carolina law requires that each container of seed have a tag that lists the turfgrass species and variety, purity, percent germination, and weed content. A typical seed label (Figure 4.5) contains information about the seed variety, germination, content of other crop seed, inert matter, weed seed, noxious weeds, and more.

Variety. Each species or variety of grass seed is listed by its purity ("Pure Seed"), which is the amount of desired seed expressed as a percentage of the total weight of the container. Ideally, you should look for a seed with a purity of 90% or higher. Look for the specific trade names for varieties of a species rather than the generic species or kind listing.

Germination. The germination figure on a seed label indicates how much of each variety of pure seed will "sprout" to produce a grass plant. In Figure 4.5, the germination rate of turf-type tall fescue is 80%. The higher the percentage, the better.

To compare different lots of seed, calculate the percentage of pure live seed. To do this, multiply the percentage of Pure Seed by the percentage of Germination. For example, the germination rate on our sample tag is 80% and the amount of pure seed is 47.2%, so 38% of the bag will produce normal plants. We know this because ([0.80 x 0.472] x 100 = 37.76%).

Other Crop Seed. If there are any kinds of lawn seed other than those listed under "Variety," they will be listed on the label by weight percentage. These "off types" of seed are not specifically named, but they can detract from the appearance of the lawn. On our example tag, "Other Crop Seed" is 2% by weight. This is a bit higher than desired, but not out of the ordinary. The lower the percentage of other crop seed, the better when evaluating or comparing labels.

Inert Matter. Inert matter is any substance in the box or bag that is not capable of growing; this could include broken seed that could not be cleaned out, sand, chaff, or a filler that's added to take up space. Many companies will also include or coat seed in mulch or something similar. This coating is sometimes listed as inert matter or on its own. In our example, the inert matter is listed at 0.75%—an acceptable level, and the coating material is 50%. The lower the percentage of inert matter, the better.

Weed Seed. If any weed seed is present, it is listed by percentage of weight. Although we don't want to buy any weed seeds with our lawn seeds, it is very difficult and expensive to catch all the weed seeds during the cleaning process. Acceptable limits range from 0.3-0.5%. In our example, 0.05% is well below the acceptable level. The higher the percentage of weed seed shown on the label, the poorer the quality of the box or bag you are buying.

Noxious Weeds. The South Carolina Department of Agriculture maintains a list of weeds that are so troublesome and undesirable that their presence must be stated on the seed label. For a quality lawn, avoid boxes, bags, or bins that indicate the presence of noxious weeds.

Other Information. The tags on seed should also include the name of the producer or distributor, the origin of the variety (where it was grown), lot number (used for tracing the container through

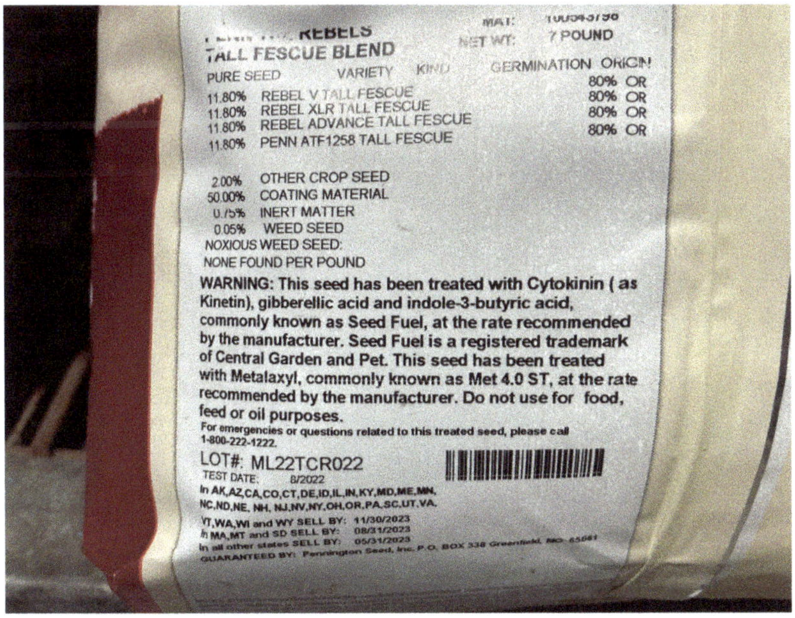

Figure 4.5 Seed label for average box store seed
Image Credit: Adam Gore, Clemson University

TABLE 4.5 Seeding rates for lawns.

Grass Species	Pounds per 1,000 sq. ft.	Planting Time	Days to Germinate
Cool-Season Grasses			
Kentucky Bluegrass[a]	2 to 3	September to October is best; early spring is second best	6 to 30
Red Fescue[a]	3 to 5	September to October is best; early spring is second best	14
Ryegrass[b], **Annual**	5 to 10	September to November	3 to 7
Ryegrass[b], **Perennial**	5 to 10	September to November	3 to 7
Tall Fescue / Turf Type[a]	5 to 8 / 4 to 6	September to October is best; early spring is second best	6 to 12
Warm-Season Grasses			
Bahiagrass (scarified)	7 to 10	April to July; May is best	7 to 21
Carpetgrass	3 to 5	April to July; May is best	10 to 20
Centipedegrass	¼ to ½	April to July; May is best	10 to 20
Common Bermudagrass			
Hulled	2	April to July; May is best	10 to 20
Unhulled	4	Fall	14 to 21
Zoysiagrass	½ to 2	April to July; May is best	10 to 14

[a]Late spring and early summer seedings of cool-season grasses usually result in failure. If spring or early summer seeding is necessary, as much as 50% of the grass may die during the heat of summer because of the lack of develop root system. Turfgrass can be replanted in the fall to improve the stand.
[b]Ryegrass is used as an overseeding on warm-season grass to produce green color during the winter.

marketing channels), and seed lot testing date. SC state law requires that a bag or box be retested and relabeled after nine months if it hasn't sold. Always check and consider the month and year the seed was tested.

In short, read the label and buy quality seed. Be aware of new and improved varieties of turfgrass that better resist insects, disease, and drought. Table 4.5 lists proper seeding rates and times for turfgrasses.

Best Practice for Seeding

There are many seeding methods, ranging from sowing by hand to sowing over large areas with mechanical equipment. Even seed distribution is important for overall uniformity. The seedbed should be well-prepared and leveled. Rake the entire area with a garden rake.

You should apply seed mechanically, either with a drop-type or rotary spreader. Mechanical seeders provide a more uniform distribution of seed than hand seeding. For best distribution, sow one-half the required

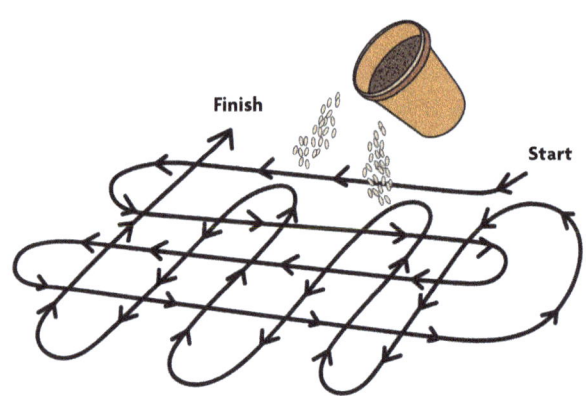

Figure 4.6 Divide the quantity of the seed intro two equal parts, and spread half the seed in one direction and the other half at a right angle to the first

amount in one direction and apply the remainder at right angles to the first seeding (Figure 4.6). For very small seed, like centipedegrass or bermudagrass, it may be helpful to mix the seed with a carrier such as corn meal, grits, or organic fertilizer to distribute the seed evenly. When mixing seed with a carrier, make sure that the seed and carrier remain thoroughly mixed during application.

After sowing the seed, use a rake to mix the grass seed into the top ½ in. of soil. Then roll the seedbed with a light or empty water-ballast roller to ensure sufficient seed-to-soil contact. Mulch the seedbed to prevent soil erosion, retain moisture, and prevent crusting of the soil surface.

The most common mulch is straw; this straw should always be free of weeds. One bale of straw (60-80 lbs.) will cover about 1,000 sq. ft. of turf. Use enough weed-free straw so that 50-75% of the bare ground is protected. You can remove the straw when the turf reaches a height of 1 – 1.5 in., or you can leave it to decompose if it is not spread too thickly. Peat moss or aged sawdust do not make good mulch for seeded lawns, as these materials compete with the seed for water and are slow to decay.

Water the lawn as soon as possible after seeding. Watering with a fine spray will help seed to germinate but be sure not to wash the seed away and avoid water puddling.

Caring for the Newly Seeded Lawn

The first 2-3 months after seeding a lawn are critical to its successful establishment. You should pay particular attention to watering, fertilization, mowing, and weed control.

Watering. Proper watering is the most critical part of establishing turfgrasses from seed. Failure to provide the newly-seeded lawn with enough moisture will result in poor establishment. Supply water frequently, as the quantity of water is less important than the frequency of the watering at this stage; the soil should be moist but not waterlogged. In general, water 2-3 times a day in small quantities for about 2-3 weeks or until you see small seedlings emerge.

The frequency of daily watering will vary from site to site depending on soil types and weather conditions. Establishing turf from seed on a sandy soil under hot, dry conditions will require more frequent watering than a grass that is being established on a heavier soil under cooler, wetter conditions. Watering is often more of a judgement call than a calculation. Just maintain a consistent watering program to ensure adequate moisture for germination.

If the surface of the soil is allowed to dry out at any time after the seeds have begun to swell and before roots have developed, many of the seedlings will die. Initial watering should be a fine spray or from sprinklers with a low precipitation rate. Coarse spray and high water pressure or high precipitation rates will erode the soil and wash away the seeds. Water lightly and frequently so the seedlings do not dry out. The goal is to provide water often enough to keep the seedbed moist but not saturated until the plants can develop sufficient root systems to take advantage of deeper but less-frequent watering. The soil should be approximately as moist as a wrung-out sponge. Soils that have not been mulched tend to dry out quickly. These conditions, require frequent irrigation under certain weather conditions. Less irrigation is necessary if the site is mulched. As the seedlings mature and their roots develop, reduce the number of waterings but increase the volume or duration of each irrigation to moisten the entire root zone, not just the soil surface.

Fertilization. A light application of nitrogen fertilizer when the seedlings are between 1.5 - 2 in. tall will substantially enhance the establishment rate.

Apply approximately 0.5 lb. of actual nitrogen per 1,000 sq. ft., such as 3 lbs. of 16-4-8 or any commercially available liquid fertilizers, and water it into the soil. Avoid applying excessively high levels of nitrogen, which will restrict root, rhizome, and stolon growth and encourage disease outbreaks.

Mowing. Begin normal mowing practices when the turfgrass seedlings reach a height that is one-third higher than the normal mowing height. Once you start mowing, mow routinely at a constant cutting height. Do not allow the seedlings to reach an excessively tall height before cutting them back. Never mow more than 1/3 of the leaf blade at a time.

Newly germinated turfgrass seedlings have a small, shallow root system that is easy to pull out of the ground when mowing. Maintain a sharp cutting blade to help prevent these seedlings from being removed from the soil, and do not use a bag to collect clippings as you could unintentionally remove new seedlings.

Weed Control. Timing of weed control practices is also critically important once seeds have germinated. Most herbicides are somewhat toxic to newly germinated turfgrass plants, so you should delay postemergence applications of herbicide as long as possible after seeding. Generally, you should wait until the lawn has been established and mowed at least three times before applying a postemergent herbicide; however, you should always refer to the pesticide label instructions for the appropriate application timing.

Vegetative Planting

Vegetative planting is the transplanting of pieces of grass. Solid sodding covers the entire seedbed with vegetation. Spot sodding, plugging, sprigging, and stolonizing refer to the planting of pieces of sod or individual stems or underground runners.

Most warm season turfgrasses are established by planting vegetative plant parts. Exceptions include carpetgrass, centipedegrass, common bermudagrass, and some Japanese lawngrass (*Zoysia japonica*) varieties, which can be established from seed as well as vegetatively propagated.

Sodding

Sodding is more expensive than sprigging or plugging but produces a so-called "instant" lawn. Sodding is useful for a quick, aesthetic fix or to prevent soil erosion. Sod is the fastest way to establish a high-quality turf. The process of establishing sod involves preparing the soil, obtaining high-quality sod, transplanting, and caring for the planted sod.

Soil Preparation. You should prepare soil for sodding identically to how you would for seeding (see above).

Sod Quality. Before buying sod, inspect it carefully for weeds, diseases, and insects. It is recommended to purchase sod that has been certified by South Carolina's Department of Plant Industry (DPI) Certified Grass certificate as it proves purity of grass as well as limits potential pest problems. Sod of warm-season grasses that is cut in late winter or early spring may be more prone to ripping or tearing if cut shallow due to the transfer of energy during Spring transition. Purchased sod should be stored in a cool, shady place until used, but do not store it for too long. Sod, particularly those pieces at top and edges of pallets, is prone to drying out so a light irrigation cycle may be necessary if installation is delayed.

Sodding. The primary objective in transplanting sod is to achieve quick rooting, or "knitting," into the existing soil. To speed up rooting, prepare the soil properly, keep the soil moist, and prevent the sod from drying out.

Sod of cool- and warm-season grasses can be installed at any time during the year. However, summer sodding of cool-season grasses is discouraged because of the stress caused by heat and the lack of moisture. When sodding in the summer, moisten the soil before laying the sod to avoid placing the turf roots in contact with excessively dry, hot soil. Additionally, be ready to irrigate.

Figure 4.7 Place sod pieces tightly together in a staggered, checkerboard pattern, similar to bricks in a wall.
Image Credit: Adam Gore, Clemson University

Winter or dormant sodding of warm-season grasses is a routine commercial practice even though the chances for survival are lower than they would be during the growing season. For best results, cool-season turfgrasses should be sodded in the fall or early spring, and warm-season turfgrass should be sodded during the late spring through early fall.

When installing sod, establish a straight line lengthwise through the lawn area. Lay the sod on either side of the line with the ends staggered in a checkerboard fashion (Figure 4.7). A sharpened concrete trowel is useful for cutting pieces, forcing the sod tight but not overlapping, and leveling small depressions.

Do not stretch the sod while laying. The sod will shrink when it dries and cause voids. Stagger the lateral joints to promote more uniform growth and strength. On steep slopes, lay the sod across the angle of the slope; it may be necessary to peg the sod to the soil with stakes to keep it from sliding. Immediately after the sod has been transplanted, roll or tamp it. This will eliminate any air spaces between the soil and the sod. Roots will not grow through an air space to reach the soil. Roll perpendicular to the direction the sod was laid.

Water newly transplanted sod immediately to wet the top 3 in. of the soil below and enhance rooting. Do not let the soil dry out until there is a good union between the sod and soil surface. To smooth out the surface of the lawn, apply light, frequent applications of soil or sand as a topdressing. Gaps between sod pieces should be minimal if the sod is placed properly; however, there may still be a few gaps that show up between the pieces. These gaps can be filled with sand or a sand/compost mixture to encourage the sod to knit together.

Post-Transplant Care. Irrigate newly transplanted sod as you would a newly seeded area. In the absence of adequate rainfall, water daily or as often as necessary to keep the soil moist. When the sod starts to root into the underlying soil, water more deeply and thoroughly but less frequently.

Do not mow sod until it is firmly and securely rooted in place. Mowing to a height, and with the same frequency, as you would an established turf. Fertilizer should be unnecessary, since the grass grows under optimum conditions at the sod farm and there is fertilizer incorporated into the soil before sodding. You can start a fertility program after the sod has established a good root system according to soil test results.

Plugging

Plugging is the planting of 2- to 4-in. diameter square, circular, or block-shaped pieces of sod at regular intervals. Three to ten times as much planting material is necessary for plugging as would be for sprigging (Table 4.6). This procedure can be used to repair damaged areas in a lawn or to fully establish a lawn. Establishing a lawn using turfgrass plugs can be successful and useful when the cost of solid sodding would be prohibitive. The most common turfgrasses started with plugs are the warm-season turfgrasses bermudagrass, centipedegrass, St. Augustinegrass, and zoysiagrass (Figure 4.8). Turf plugs are planted into prepared soil with approximately 6 - 12 in. between their centers. The closer the plugs are

Figure 4.8 Establishing a new area using plugs.
Image Credit: Adam Gore, Clemson University

planted together, the faster the sod will cover the area; however, the closer the plugs are planted together, the more plugs will be required to cover the lawn.

Prior to plugging, prepare as you would prior to seeding or sodding. There are special machines designed to plant plugs, but you can plug smaller areas by hand. Transplant warm-season turfgrasses in the late spring or early summer. This provides the turf with optimum growing conditions for successful establishment. After the plugs have been transplanted, roll the planting bed to ensure good plant-to-soil contact. Water following the same guidelines as you would when sodding. Post-plugging care involves mowing at the recommended height and frequency of your chosen turfgrass. Fertilize 3-4 weeks after plugging and water properly to enhance establishment.

TABLE 4.6 Plugging and sprigging rates for warm-season grasses.

Turfgrass		Spacing (inches)	Amount of sod (sq. ft.)/ 1,000 sq. ft.*
Bermudagrass	2-inch plugs	12	30 to 50
	Sprigs	12	2 to 5
Centipedegrass	2-inch plugs	6	100 to 150
	Sprigs	6	30 to 50
St. Augustinegrass	2-inch plugs	6 to 12	30 to 50
	Sprigs	6 to 12	10 to 15
Zoysiagrass	2-inch plugs	6	100 to 150
	Sprigs	6	8 to 15

*Based on estimates of 1 sw. ft. of sod = 80 linear ft. or sprigs; 1 sq. yd. of sod = 1 bushel of sprigs; and 1 sq. yd. of sod yields 324 two-inch plugs. Numbers in column refer to number of square feet of sod from which either two-inch plugs or sprigs can be obtained.

Sprigging and Stolonizing

The highest-quality varieties of bermudagrass, St. Augustinegrass, and zoysiagrass must be planted vegetatively—using sod, plugs, or sprigs—as no seed is available for hybrid cultivars. Sprigging is the planting of stolons or rhizomes in furrows or small holes.

Sprigging. A sprig is an individual stem or piece of stem of grass that does not have any adhering soil. As long as a sprig has at least one node or joint, it has the potential of developing into a grass plant. A suitable sprig should have two to four nodes from which roots can develop. The sprigs are prepared by mechanical shredding or hand-tearing of sod into individual pieces. Sprigs are usually purchased by the bushel and can be difficult to find in some regions. You can also harvest sprigs from ornamental beds in the landscape into which the turf has encroached. Simply pull the runners from the soil and replant them in thinned areas.

Sprigs have little or no soil from the area where they were harvested, so they are ideal for areas in which you want to avoid soil contamination. Prepare soil for sprigging as you would for other methods of planting.

To plant sprigs, dig furrows 8 - 12 in. apart and place the sprigs 1-2 in. into the soil—deeper if there is little moisture, shallower if adequate moisture is available—every 4-6 in. along the furrows; the closer the sprigs are, the faster the grass will cover the soil. After placing the sprigs in the furrows, cover a part of the sprig with soil and press it firm. Leave the leaves exposed at the soil surface (Figure 4.9). You can do this with a roller or by stepping on the soil around the sprig. Water as soon as possible after planting.

Another method of sprigging is to place the sprigs on the soil surface at the desired interval end-to-end, about 6 in. apart, and press one end of the sprig into the soil with a notched stick or blunt piece of metal (like a dull shovel). A portion of the sprig should be left above ground and exposed to light. Regardless of the planting method, each sprig should be tamped or rolled firmly into the soil. Since the sprigs are planted at a shallow depth, they are very prone to drying out. Light, frequent waterings are necessary until roots become well-established and will likely be required for several weeks after planting depending on rate of establishment. Mulching can also be used in vegetative planting to conserve moisture and control erosion.

Stolonizing. Stolonizing is the broadcasting of stolons on the soil surface, as with sprigging, and covering the stolons by topdressing or pressing them into the soil (Figure 4.10). Stolonizing requires more planting material but will produce a quicker cover than sprigs. It is extremely important to maintain a moist surface during the establishment period (Figure 4.11). The soil surface can dry out quickly, especially on sandy soils during hot, dry, windy weather. Allowing the soil surface to dry will cause the sprigs or stolons to dry out.

LAWN RENOVATION

Renovation is the improvement of a turfgrass stand without starting over from scratch. Re-establishment refers to completely replacing the old lawn with a new one. Turfgrass renovation is necessary when the existing turfgrass has declined to a point where cultural practices will not revive the turf, but complete reestablishment is

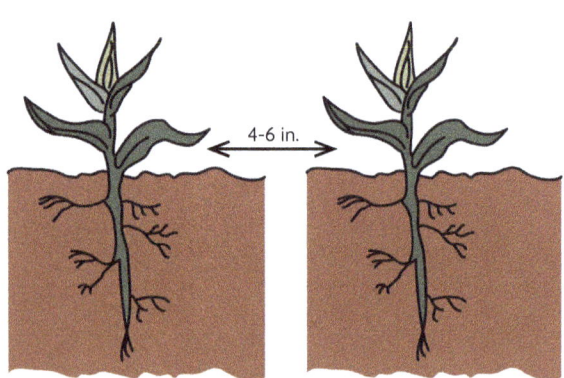

Figure 4.9 When sprigging, leave 1/3 to 1/4 of each sprig above ground and 4 to 6 inches between sprigs in the furrow

Figure 4.10 Fresh stolons are spread on a prepared soil surface.
Image Credit: Adam Gore, Clemson University

Figure 4.11 Soil during sprigging and stolonizing should remain damp until rooting has been established.
Image Credit: Adam Gore, Clemson University

Step-by-Step Lawn Renovation Process

Step 1 – Determine cause of lawn failure

Planting grass into a problem area without understanding the cause of its failure will likely result in another failed lawn. Examine the physical condition of the soil to determine if there are drainage issues. Research the management practices formerly used on the turf, including fertilizing, watering and pesticide applications, to determine if poor management of the preexisting turf species could be an issue. Check for soil-inhabiting pests such as nematodes or ground pearls. A hardier turf, able to withstand these pests or other difficulties, may be necessary. After you have identified all problems that could have led to the failure of the previous turf and have selected an appropriate replacement, it is time to prepare the site for a new lawn

unnecessary. Generally, if at least half the area comprises desirable turf, renovation will succeed.

Several factors can cause turfgrass to deteriorate, including:

- improper mowing, watering, and fertilizing;
- poor drainage;
- soil compaction;
- excessive thatch;
- incorrect pesticide usage;
- lawn pests such as insects or diseases;
- improperly-selected grass species;
- excessive shade;
- tree and shrub root competition; and
- winter injury.

In areas of areas of excessive shade and tree/shrub root problems it may be necessary to replace lawn grasses with mulch or a shade-tolerant groundcover or naturalizing the area.

Renovation Timing

Cool-season turfgrasses are best renovated in early fall (September to October), at the beginning of their growing season. Trying to reestablish a cool-season turfgrass in the spring does not allow the lawn to mature before the onset of summer stressors. Warm-season turfgrasses are best renovated in the spring or early summer (April to June). Renovating warm-season grasses in the fall often results in winter-damaged turf.

Step 2 – Test the soil

Soil testing provides base nutrient levels as well as the pH of the soil. Fertilizer and lime or sulfur applications should be based on these soil test results to achieve a better growing environment. Contact a county Extension agent for soil sampling information.

Step 3 – Eliminate all undesirable plants

Identify and eliminate any weeds or unwanted turf on the site. You can contact your local county Extension office for help in weed identification and recommendations for their control. Depending on the replanting method, you may want to eliminate all vegetative growth in the area using a nonselective herbicide. Be aware that some weed control products require a waiting period between the time of application and replanting. Follow the product label instructions for information about proper handling and application.

Step 4 – Mow and rake the area

If you plan to leave vegetative material on site, mow the area lower than normal and remove the clippings, leaves, and other debris by sweeping or raking. Do this if you plan to reseed or plug. Leaving some vegetative material will help hold your seed in place, but don't create a future weed problem by leaving unwanted plant material or other turf species. If you are sprigging or sodding the site, you must remove all vegetative material to assure good turf/soil contact.

Step 5 – Remove excessive thatch

Thatch is a layer of partially decomposed plant material that builds up on the surface of the soil. When leaving any type of turf, dethatching will open the turf to allow the seed to settle to the soil. Usually, any more than 0.5 in. of thatch on general turf areas decreases turf vigor by restricting the movement of air, water, fertilizer, and pesticides into the soil. Excessive thatch also restricts root development and harbors insects and diseases. Mechanically remove thatch with a vertical mower or a power rake. This equipment is often available for rent. Refer to the section titled "Thatch Development and Control" for more information.

Step 6 – Cultivate the soil

Cultivate the soil by tilling or coring—also called "aerifying"—to loosen compacted soil. A coring machine, which removes a soil core, is most effective. After coring, use a vertical mower to help break up the soil cores brought to the surface. Coring is most effective when the soil is moist, because the tines will penetrate more deeply.

Step 7 – Follow soil analysis recommendations

Add fertilizer and lime according to soil test recommendations. On bare soils, till these products into the top 4 - 6 in. of the seedbed. On sites with preexisting vegetative material, spread your products evenly over the site and water them in.

Step 8 – Disburse grass material

Seed, sod, plug, or sprig new grass into the area. You may want to adjust the planting rates to balance any turf already present. For example, if 50% of the area has good turf, reduce the recommended planting rate by half. Be sure to get good seed-to-soil contact when sowing seed. Rake the seed into the soil or cover it by topdressing with a thin layer (0.25 in.) of soil. When seeding into existing lawn grasses, an old rug or broom can help move seed under leaf material into underlying soil layer. Afterwards, firm the soil by lightly rolling. Where there is little existing grass or where erosion may be a problem, use a light mulch. Some available rental machines cultivate and plant simultaneously.

Vegetative materials need to be planted into the soil. In small areas, use an axe or trowel to make a small opening for your sprig or plug. Place sprigs or plugs 6 - 12 in. apart and firm the soil around them. Any technique that places part of the sprig or plug below the soil surface is suitable.

Step 9 - Water

Apply water immediately after planting and keep the soil moist—not wet—until the seedlings or sprigs are well established. This usually requires light watering multiple times per day for 2 - 3 weeks, depending on rainfall.

Step 10 - Mow

Mow the grass when it reaches 1.5 times its recommended height and start normal maintenance practices.

BASIC LAWN MANAGEMENT PRACTICES

Lawn quality can be described as "minimal maintenance," "average," or "above-average." A minimal-maintenance lawn is just what it sounds like: a lawn that requires practically no input from the turf manager other than a few basic acts such as infrequent mowing or some irrigation during particularly dry, hot weather. Management at this level will produce a low-quality turf that may thin over time, may contain multiple species of turf, and will have some weeds. Without control, insect and disease problems will further decrease turf quality.

An average-quality lawn requires basic maintenance such as mowing, lime application as necessary, and fertilization. This type of lawn may have several types of grasses and some weeds. An average-quality lawn can be obtained with minimal money, time, and effort.

An above-average or superior-quality lawn requires additional care—like weed, disease, and insect control—along with routine management practices such as watering, fertilizing and mowing. You can care for these lawns yourself or purchase these services from a lawn service company. Generally, lawns in the above-average quality range have a dense population of a single lawn grass species and minimal or no weeds.

The density and quality of a lawn should reflect the desire of the landscaper or landowner. A well-maintained lawn is beneficial in preventing soil erosion, enriching the soil's organic composition, and acting as a living filter for water as it passes through the soil. By correctly carrying out basic lawn maintenance practices, you may also reduce the need for supplementary practices like pest control.

Soil Testing

One of the first steps in producing and maintaining an attractive lawn is to get an analysis of a representative soil sample from the lawn site. The "Soils and Plant Nutrition" chapter in this book provides instructions for taking soil samples and submitting soil samples for analysis by the Agricultural Service Laboratory; you can also reach out to your local county Extension agent for more information.

Proper sampling is important to ensure representative test results and correct fertilizer recommendations. Once the soil is analyzed, you will receive a report with the plant nutrient levels and fertilizer and lime recommendations based on your soil pH and what you want to grow.

Soil test results supply a wealth of information concerning the nutritional status of a soil and may aid in the detection of problems that could limit turfgrass growth. Soil testing protects against the expense and environmental hazards that can result from excessive fertilizer applications. A typical soil test supplies information about soil pH, lime requirements, phosphorus, potassium, calcium, magnesium, zinc, and manganese. The nitrogen requirements of turfgrass cannot be evaluated reliably by a soil test, so the report will not contain a nitrogen recommendation.

Balancing Soil Acidity and Alkalinity

The acidity or alkalinity of a soil, expressed as pH, affects a plant's ability to absorb nutrients present in the soil. Most lawn grasses grow well when the soil pH is between 5.5-6.5, though individual grass species may tolerate pH levels outside of this range (Table 4.7). A pH either too low or too high will reduce the availability of plant nutrients; therefore, it is very important to maintain an adequate soil pH.

Typically, South Carolina soils are more highly weathered and oxidized, resulting in naturally occurring acidic pH levels. Normally, liming materials are used to increase soil pH and supply the essential nutrients of calcium and magnesium, while sulfur is used to lower soil pH. The two most commonly available liming materials are calcitic and dolomitic limestones. In instances where soil tests indicate low levels of magnesium or calcium and a low pH, use dolomitic limestone.

On rare occasions, normally occurring in coastal areas or areas using lower quality irrigation water, sulfur is used to decrease pH levels. The two common sulfur products are elemental sulfur and aluminum sulfate. The amount of lime or sulfur required to properly adjust soil pH depends on the species or variety of turfgrass, soil type, and soil pH. The greater the amount of organic matter or clay in the soil, the more lime or sulfur will be required to change the pH. Be sure to apply lime or sulfur in accordance with soil test results. If there is a question on the amount of lime or sulfur needed, contact your local Extension Office.

Generally, it takes about three to six months for lime and sulfur to have their maximum effect on soil acidity as liming requires the chemical reaction of hydrolysis to increase pH and sulfur requires microbial breakdown. If you can, plan ahead so that any necessary amendments can be tilled into the soil, where they will react more quickly.

Fertilizing

Understanding the nutritional requirements of your lawn and understanding soil nutrient levels are perhaps the most important aspects to producing a quality stand

TABLE 4.7 Lawn grasses best adapted for various soil pH levels.

pH			
5 to 5.4	5.5 to 5.9	6 to 6.4	6.5 to 6.9
Bermudagrass	Bermudagrass	Bermudagrass	Bermudagrass
Carpetgrass	Carpetgrass	Bluegrass	Bluegrass
Centipedegrass	Centipedegrass	Fescue	Fescue
Bahiagrass	Bahiagrass	Italian ryegrass	Perennial ryegrass
	Italian ryegrass	Perennial ryegrass	St. Augustinegrass
	Fine fescue	St. Augustinegrass	Zoysiagrass
		Zoysiagrass	

Credit: L. B. McCarty, 2003, Southern Lawns.

of turfgrass. However, exceeding recommended fertilizer application rates or applying fertilizer at the wrong time can be just as detrimental as providing insufficient nutrition.

Lawn fertilization is the application of elements in various formulations with the goal of producing optimum turf growth. Lawns require the greatest quantities of the macronutrients nitrogen, phosphorous, and potassium; these nutrients should be applied as recommended by soil test results. Calcium, magnesium, and sulfur are secondary nutrients that are sometimes needed in small quantities and less frequently. These secondary elements are usually present in a large enough quantity in the soil that they do not need to be added via fertilization unless soil pH inhibits their availability. Sometimes, very small quantities of micronutrients—in this case, iron, manganese, zinc, copper, molybdenum, chlorine, boron, and nickel—are required, but this isn't common or frequent. Micronutrients are as essential as the major elements but are required in such small amounts that most soils already contain sufficient levels. Usually, tissue testing is necessary to quantify minor elements and diagnose micronutrient deficiencies.

Reading Fertilizer Labels

Fertilizers are often described by their ratio composition, written as three numbers—for example, 10-10-10 or 16-4-8. These three numbers give the percent by weight of nitrogen (N), phosphate (P_2O_5), and potash (K_2O). For example, in a 16-4-8 fertilizer, nitrogen makes up 16% of the weight, phosphate—which supplies phosphorus—accounts for 4%, and potash—a source of potassium—makes up 8%. The remaining weight of the fertilizer comes from a nutrient carrier; you can calculate the percentage of this carrier by subtracting the combined nutrient percentage from 100%. A fertilizer containing all three macronutrients, such as a 16-4-8, is referred to as a "complete" fertilizer. If soil tests indicate high levels of phosphorus and potassium, then you can select a fertilizer that supplies only nitrogen, such as 16-0-0.

The fertilizer ratio of a 16-4-8 fertilizer is 4:1:2. Similarly, a 14-7-14 analysis has a 2:1:2 ratio. Generally, mature lawns require equivalent levels of nitrogen and potassium, especially on sandy soils; ratios of 4:1:2 or 4:1:3 are normally recommended for most home lawn situations.

If a soil test indicates the need for additional phosphate or potash, you can apply a complete fertilizer or separate fertilizers that provide only phosphate or potassium. Fertilizers normally used to correct severe phosphorus and/or potassium deficiencies are 0-15-30, 0-12-0, 0-0-53, or 0-0-60. Never apply more than 3 lbs. of 0-0-54 or 0-0-60 per 1,000 sq. ft. to an established turf without watering afterwards to prevent foliar burn.

Nitrogen

Nitrogen is probably the most important element you can apply to affect plant growth. Nitrogen will affect a turfgrass in several ways, including the grass's color, density, shoot and root growth, susceptibility to diseases and insects, environmental stress resistance, and ability to recover from damage. A nitrogen fertility program should allow for slow, steady growth. Applying excessive amounts of nitrogen will encourage shoot growth at the expense of root growth, increase the incidence of diseases and thatch accumulation, and make the turf more prone to winter damage.

Several factors influence the nitrogen requirements of your lawn, including the species of grass being grown, the soil type, and environmental conditions. The timing of a nitrogen application is also critical to the development of a lawn. Fertilizing warm-season turfgrasses too early in the spring with high levels of nitrogen can cause a reduction in root growth as the plants emerge from dormancy. Fertilizing these grasses too late in the fall may increase the chance of winter damage. Cool-season turfgrasses should be fertilized with nitrogen during the fall and early spring; fertilizing these grasses with nitrogen during the summer will increase the chances of disease.

Both primary and secondary elements, if present, are listed on the fertilizer label. The label also lists the materials from which the fertilizer is made. This information appears beside the "derived from" statement. Figure 4.12 presents an example of a mixed fertilizer containing several different sources of nitrogen.

In addition to complete fertilizers, some materials are used almost exclusively to supply nitrogen to the lawn for increased vegetative growth and dark green color. These materials include ammonium nitrate (33% N), ammonium sulfate (20% N), IBDU (31% N), urea (45% N), calcium nitrate (15.5% N), and urea-form (38% N). Be careful when using soluble N fertilizers, as the percentage of N is generally higher and there is an increased chance of fertilizer burn if it's applied improperly.

Nitrogen Availability. The source of the nitrogen in fertilizers influences nitrogen availability and turf response. There are two categories of nitrogen sources: quick-release and slow-release, though they may also be

TABLE 4.8 A guide to rate of fertilizer materials to use on lawns.

Nitrogen Fertilizer	% Nitrogen	Pounds needed to supply 1 pound of actual nitrogen per 1,000 sq. ft. of lawn
Quick-release N (inorganics)		
Nitrate of soda	16	6
Nitrate of soda-potash	15	7
Nitrate of potash	13	8
Calcium nitrate	15.5	7
Ammonium nitrate	33.5	3
Ammonium nitrate + lime	18	5
Ammonium sulfate	20.5	5
Mono-ammonium phosphate	11-48-0	9
Diammonium phospate	18-46-0	5.5
Quick-release N (organics)		
Urea	45-47	2
Cyanamid	21	5
Slow-release N (natural organics)		
Sewage sludge	6	16
Castor pomace	4-6	25-16
Cottonseed meal	7	15
Processed tankages	5-10	20-10
Garbage tankage	2-3	40-30
Slow-release N (synthetics)		
Ureaform (UF)	38	2.5
Nitroform	38	2
IBDU	31	3
Sulfur-coated urea	36	3
Polymer-/Plastic-/Resin-coated urea	varies	varies

CAUTION: *Practically all inorganic fertilizers can "burn" lawn grasses. These materials should be applied when temperatures are cool and watered into the lawn immediately after application. When using slow-release sources of nitrogen, 2 pounds of N can be safely applied per 1,000 sq. ft. per application.*

referred to as soluble and insoluble, respectively.

Quick-release materials are water soluble, are readily available to the plant, more susceptible to leaching, and have a relatively short response period. Quick-release nitrogen sources include ammonium nitrate, urea, ammonium sulfate, and calcium nitrate (Table 4.8).

Slow-release nitrogen sources release their nitrogen over extended periods of time and can be applied less frequently and at comparatively higher rates than the soluble nitrogen sources. When applied properly, they also reduce the chances of fertilizer "burn" that is common with ammonium nitrate and urea. Fertilizer burn is the brownish or straw-colored discoloration that occurs on grass blades as a result of excessive contact with a soluble fertilizer; it can be minimized by watering the lawn immediately after fertilizing. Slow-release sources are less susceptible to leaching and are preferable for sandy soils, which tend to leach more readily than soils containing a higher percentage of organic matter or clay. They are a good choice for areas where the potential of runoff is very high, such as slopes, compacted soil, or sparsely covered lawns; since the nutrients are released slowly, the potential for runoff and water contamination is less. Slow-release sources of nitrogen include urea

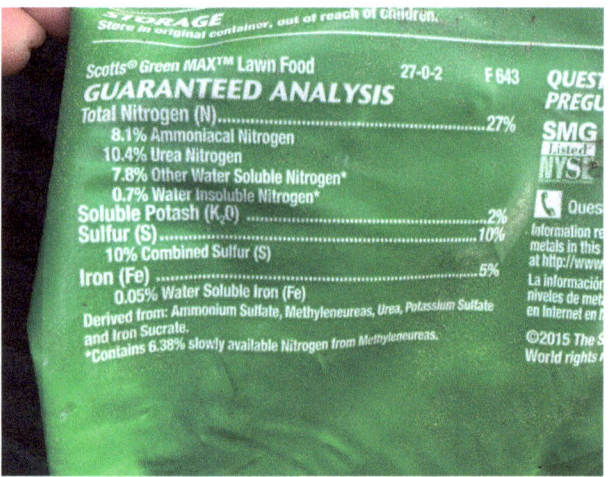

Figure 4.12 A fertilizer label is a guaranteed analysis of a containers components.
Adam Gore, Clemson Extension

formaldehyde (UF); UF-based products (methylene ureas); sulfur-coated urea (SCU); isobutylidene diurea (IBDU); natural organics such as bone meal, fish meal, dried blood, and animal manures; and activated sewage sludge.

If a fertilizer contains a slow-release nitrogen source, it will be listed on the label as Water Insoluble Nitrogen (W.I.N.) (Figure 4.12). If W.I.N. is not on the fertilizer label, assume that it is all water-soluble or quick-release nitrogen. The higher the amount of W.I.N., the more slowly the nitrogen will be released. Select a slow-release fertilizer that contains at least 50% water-insoluble nitrogen.

Products containing slow-release sources of nutrients usually have one or more of the following terms: "water-insoluble," "coated slow-release," "slow-release," "controlled release," "slowly available water soluble," or "occluded slow-release." Sulfur-coated urea is an example of a source of water-insoluble nitrogen for which a water-soluble source of nitrogen, such as urea, is treated with a polymer or element to slow its release.

Phosphorus

Phosphorus is another major element necessary for plant growth and is the second number presented in a fertilizer analysis. Phosphorus is primarily involved in transforming energy within the plant. Phosphorus is generally required in smaller amounts than either nitrogen or potassium, but it plays a critical role in the establishment of turfgrasses. On soils that are low in phosphorous, a light application of this element will increase the growth rate during establishment; however, high levels of phosphorous can cause problems with turfgrass growth. Centipedegrass is especially sensitive to high phosphorous levels, so it is important to submit soil samples for nutrient analysis on a regular basis if you are managing centipedegrass.

Potassium

Potassium is the third macronutrient number on a fertilizer analysis. This element is almost as important to turfgrass growth as nitrogen. Potassium is critical for plant growth from the establishment phase through complete coverage. Adequate levels of potassium in the soil will allow the plant to withstand environmental and mechanical stresses. In most turfgrasses, sufficient potassium levels improve tolerance to heat, cold, drought, and disease.

For lawns, the best yearly fertilization program usually includes applications of a complete fertilizer and of nitrogen-only fertilizer applications. The complete fertilizer supplies nitrogen, phosphorus, and potassium—along with some micronutrients—while the nitrogen material supplies mainly nitrogen. While nitrogen fertilization is based on the desired growth rate and type of turfgrass being grown, you should base phosphorus and potassium fertilization rates on the recommendations of a soil test.

Micronutrients

If there is a deficiency of micronutrients in your soil, you should apply fertilizers that contain micronutrients. Micronutrient deficiencies usually occur in soils that have an imbalanced pH or unhealthy content of organic matter. Look for possible micronutrient deficiencies in soils that are extremely acid or alkaline, soils that contain very little organic matter (if any), and muck soils. Micronutrient deficiencies are hard to diagnosis visually and are best determined through tissue testing.

Many times, warm-season grasses such as centipedegrass, St. Augustinegrass, and zoysiagrass may appear yellow in the early spring due to inconsistent nutrient uptake resulting from cold soil temperatures and a lack of root growth. Fertilizing with nitrogen during this transition period may not be best, as it often encourages disease and insect problems during wet springs. Often, the addition of iron to these grasses provides the desirable dark green color without stimulating excessive grass growth as often occurs when fertilizing with nitrogen. Usually, iron sulfate (2 oz. per

3-5 gallons of water per 1,000 sq. ft.) or a chelated iron source are used to provide this greening effect. The effect from supplemental iron application is only temporary (about 2-4 weeks); therefore, repeat applications are necessary for summer-long color, though it is best not to apply more than once per month during the growing season in most home lawn situations. Do not apply iron to wet grass or when the air temperature is above 80°F. Water-in immediately after application to minimize turf "burn" and to make the nutrients available to the grass plants.

Fertilizer Burn

All fertilizers can burn turf if applied incorrectly. Never exceed the recommended rate or you may damage the lawn. Always apply fertilizers when the grass leaves are dry. Granular fertilizers should be watered into the lawn thoroughly after application to wash the fertilizer into the soil (where the nutrients can be used by the grass plants). This will also reduce the potential for surface runoff—especially on slopes—and volatilization.

Avoid applying fertilizer to non-turfed or impervious areas like driveways, roads, or bare soil. Also avoid fertilizing close to the shoreline of streams, rivers, and lakes. Install a non-mowed, vegetated buffer strip along the edge of water sources to absorb any runoff nutrients and prevent them from contaminating the water.

Never leave unused fertilizer in a spreader. Fertilizer salts are corrosive and can ruin the spreader. Be sure to collect the unused fertilizer and pour it back into the bag, not on a driveway or road. Rinse the spreader thoroughly with water and allow it to dry. Lubricate the spreader with a light machine oil to prevent rusting and keep the working parts in good condition.

Fertilizer Application Rate and Timing

Fertilizer application rates are determined by the type and amount of nitrogen present in the fertilizer and the turfgrass species you are growing. Nitrogen is the nutrient most used by the turf, and often, it will burn the lawn if applied excessively. An almost universal recommendation for turfgrass fertilization is to apply no more than 1 lb. of actual nitrogen per 1,000 sq. ft. of lawn if more than one-half (50%) of the nitrogen comes from a water-soluble source. If all of the nitrogen in the fertilizer is slow-release organic nitrogen, increase this rate to 2 lbs. of actual nitrogen per 1,000 sq. ft. (Table 4.9).

To determine how much fertilizer to apply to deliver 1 lb. of actual nitrogen, use this equation:

100 ÷ % Nitrogen = amount of pounds of fertilizer required per 1,000 sq. ft. to apply 1 pound of actual nitrogen.

For example, assume you have a 20-5-10 fertilizer that contains a quick-release, water-soluble nitrogen source such as ammonium sulfate. By using the formula (100 ÷ 20), you need to apply 5 lbs. of 20-5-10 fertilizer per 1,000 sq. ft. of lawn to apply 1 lb. of actual nitrogen.

To apply 0.5 pound of nitrogen per 1,000 sq. ft., use this equation:

50 ÷ % Nitrogen = amount of pounds of fertilizer required per 1,000 square feet to apply ½ pound of actual nitrogen.

Table 4.8 lists a variety of fertilizers and their rate of application to apply 1 lb. of N per 1,000 sq. ft. of lawn.

Proper timing of nitrogen application varies for cool- and warm-season turfgrasses due to their different growth cycles. Excessive application of nitrogen to cool-season turfgrasses in spring is detrimental; it leads to excessive leaf growth at the expense of stored food reserves and root growth. This growth increases the potential injury to lawns from summer diseases and drought. Applications of nitrogen to warm-season lawns in the fall can predispose the grass to winter injury and encourage disease development.

When a soil test of the lawn is not available, use Table 4.9 as a guide for fertilizing your lawn. Note that one program offers a "low-maintenance" approach that will result in an average-quality lawn. The "high-maintenance" program is appropriate for those who seek an above-average lawn. The right schedule for you is the one that produces the quality of lawn you desire and that fits your management style. For example, to obtain an average-quality St. Augustinegrass lawn on the coast with a low-maintenance program, apply a complete fertilizer (C)—such as 16–4–8, 10–10–10, or 6–6–6—in April and August. Apply supplemental iron (Fe) in June to provide green color without resulting in excessively lush growth.

Once you choose the appropriate fertilization schedule for your lawn, determine how much fertilizer you want to apply and how often; there is a suggested range, but the amount and application frequency are influenced by the quality of turf you desire, your source of nitrogen, the soil type, the type and age of the turfgrass, the length of the growing season, the expected

TABLE 4.9 Suggested maintenance fertilization schedule for South Carolina lawns.

Lawn grass	Maintenance Level	Jan	Feb	Mar	Apr	May	June	July	Aug	Sept	Oct	Nov	Dec	Total Pounds N per 1,000 sq. ft.
Piedmont and Mountains														
Bermudagrass	High	-	-	N*	-	C	N	N	C	-	N*	-	N*	3–6
	Low	-	-	-	-	C	N	-	C	-	-	-	-	1–3
Carpetgrass	High	-	-	-	-	C	N	-	C	-	-	-	-	2–3
	Low	-	-	-	-	C	N	-	-	-	-	-	-	1–2
Centipedegrass	High	-	-	-	Fe	C	-	Fe	C	-	-	-	-	1–2
	Low	-	-	-	-	C	-	Fe	-	-	-	-	-	0–1
St. Augustinegrass	High	-	-	-	Fe	C	N⁺	-	C	Fe	-	-	-	1–2
	Low	-	-	-	-	-	Fe	-	-	-	-	-	-	0–1
Zoysiagrass	High	-	-	N*	-	C	N	N	C	-	-	N*	-	2–5
	Low	-	-	-	-	C	-	-	C	-	-	-	-	1–3
Tall Fescue	High	-	C	-	-	-	-	-	-	C	-	C	-	2–3
	Low	-	C	-	-	-	-	-	-	C	-	-	-	1–2
Sandhills and Coastal Plains														
Bahiagrass	High	-	-	Fe	C	Fe	N	-	C	-	-	-	-	2–4
	Low	-	-	-	C	-	Fe	-	C	-	-	-	-	1–2
Bermudagrass	High	-	N*	-	C	N	N	-	C	-	N*	-	N*	4–6
	Low	-	-	-	-	-	N	-	C	-	-	-	-	2–3
Carpetgrass	High	-	-	-	C	-	N	-	C	-	-	-	-	1–3
	Low	-	-	-	C	-	-	-	C	-	-	-	-	½–1
Centipedegrass	High	-	-	Fe	C	-	Fe	-	C	Fe	-	-	-	1–2
	Low	-	-	-	C	-	Fe	-	C	Fe	-	-	-	½–1
St. Augustinegrass	High	-	-	-	C	N⁺	N⁺	-	C	-	N*	-	-	2–4
	Low	-	-	-	C	-	Fe	-	C	-	-	-	-	1–2
Zoysiagrass	High	-	N*	-	C	-	N	-	C	-	N*	-	N*	3–5
	Low	-	-	-	C	-	-	-	C	-	-	-	-	1–3

C = Apply a complete fertilizer (such as 16-4-8 or 12-4-8) at 1 lb. N/1,000 sq. ft. for high maintenance lawns or ½ lb. N/1,000 sq. ft. for low maintenance lawns. An additional potassium application at 1 lb. K/1,000 sq. ft. in late August through mid-September may increase winter hardiness. Phosphorus is normally not needed on established centipedegrass lawns unless recommended by soil test results.
N = Water-soluble inorganic nitrogen source is applied at 1 lb. N/1,000 sq. ft. for high maintenance lawns or ½ lb. N/1,000 sq. ft. for low maintenance lawns.
Fe = apply iron to provide dark green color without stimulating excessive grass growth. Ferrous sulfate (2 oz. in 3 to 5 gal. water per 1,000 sq. ft.) or a cheleated iron source may be used when temperatures are above 80°F and good soil moisture is present.
N* = overseeded with ryegrass for winter color. Apply ½ lb. N per 1,000 sq. ft.
N⁺ = To reduce chinch bug problems, use a slow-release N source during the summer

Notes
(1) Yearly total nitrogen is suggested rate. Actual rates depend on location and aesthetic desired
(2) Fertilizing centipedegrass in excess of 2 lb. N/1,000 sq. ft. is not recommended and may encourage centipedegrass decline.

traffic, the amount of shade, and whether you recycle or return your clippings to the lawn.

Evaluate your lawn based on these factors; each one affects the amount and frequency of nitrogen application. Then, choose the amount and frequency that best suits your situation. Proper turfgrass fertilization programs should be tailored to specific turfgrasses and sites.

Desired Lawn Quality. Turfgrass quality is a measure of density, color, uniformity (how much of the lawn is covered with the desired turfgrass rather than weeds or other species of grasses), smoothness, growth habit, and texture. If you want an above-average lawn, you must make a commitment to selecting the right turfgrass species, mowing frequently, and more frequently applying slightly higher rates of nitrogen. In addition, you must commit to appropriate irrigation, aerification, and pesticide applications.

Soil Type. Sandy soils generally leach more nitrogen than silt loam and clay loam soils. Therefore, sandy soils often require more frequent nitrogen applications when using quick-release sources of nitrogen. You can minimize leaching by using slow-release nitrogen sources; in turn, this reduces the amount of nitrogen released into nearby streams and lakes.

To reduce the potential for runoff and allow water to penetrate soil that is compacted, on slopes, or in natural drainage areas, you may need to aerate the soil. Do this using an aerifier or core aerator, a machine which pulls small cores of soil from the lawn.

Type and Age of Turfgrass. It's best to apply nitrogen to cool-season grasses, such as tall fescue, in late summer and fall; warm-season grasses perform best when nitrogen is applied in mid-spring to midsummer. Newly-established lawns or lawns lacking density or ground cover benefit from properly-timed applications of nitrogen until ground cover and density have reached a desirable level. A mature centipedegrass and carpetgrass lawn requires lower levels of nitrogen than a lawn of other warm-season grasses.

Length of the Growing Season. Turfgrass growing in an area with a longer growing season, such as our Coastal region, requires more nitrogen.

Traffic. If you anticipate heavy traffic or use of the lawn, apply more nitrogen to help the grass recuperate and recover from injury.

Shade. Grasses growing in heavily-shaded areas require only 50-67% as much nitrogen as grasses growing in full sun. Reducing the amount of nitrogen to grasses growing in the shade reduces the incidence of disease. Since cool-season grass plants utilize nitrogen better when sunlight can reach the grass leaves, time your fertilizer application to any cool season grasses for after when most leaves have fallen from the trees in the fall.

Clipping Recycling. A lawn receives significant amounts of nitrogen and potassium when clippings are returned or left on the ground after mowing; returning clippings can provide up to 25% of a lawn's total fertility need. Recycling turfgrass clippings contributes very little to thatch and provides nutrients and organic matter. If you're recycling grass clippings, you can apply less external nitrogen. Do not allow excess clippings to lay on top of grass as this shading can cause discoloration. Clippings should fall into grass canopy.

Fertilizer Application Equipment

You can apply fertilizers in either a dry or a liquid formulation. When applying fertilizer, it is extremely important to apply it uniformly to the whole lawn. Uneven fertilizer applications will result in an uneven greening or streaking in the lawn. Additionally, fertilizer applied in excess may "burn" the turf, leaving brown or dead areas. Apply fertilizer uniformly, using appropriate equipment, at the correct rate, and with a properly calibrated spreader.

There are two basic types of dry fertilizer spreaders for use on home lawns. Each type of spreader has a dial to adjust the opening(s) or exit holes for the fertilizer. These openings should vary when using different kinds of fertilizers. Some companies list the settings of certain brand name spreaders on the fertilizer label. If your spreader is not listed, don't just guess the appropriate setting. Calibrate your spreader to determine the right setting that will dispense the correct amount of fertilizer. Calibration helps you avoid the mistake of applying too much—which can harm the lawn and the environment—or too little, which will stunt or damage lawn development.

Broadcast-Type Spreaders. Rotary or cyclone spreaders, referred to as broadcast-type spreaders, have a rotating disc that "throws out" fertilizer in a semi-circular pattern as it is pushed (Figure 4.13). These spreaders are best suited for covering large areas quickly. They do not naturally distribute the fertilizer uniformly, but you can achieve uniformity by controlling the overlap. Rotary spreaders usually provide better distribution when encountering sharp turns; they tend to cover a broader swath of the lawn and fan the fertilizer out at the edges.

Calibrating a Rotary Spreader. Follow these steps to calibrate a rotary or cyclone spreader.

Figure 4.13 The spinning disk on a rotary spreaders can cast a large semicircular pattern.
Image Credit: Adam Gore, Clemson University

1. Gather the following materials:
   a. Rotary spreader; check to see that the parts are in working order
   b. Bucket
   c. hand-held calculator
   d. tape measure, at least 50 ft. long
   e. scale
   f. fertilizer
2. A rotary spreader slings the fertilizer out in a wide, uneven pattern, and more fertilizer falls in the center than at the edges. About 2/3 of the entire application width—called the "effective width"—receives a uniform amount of fertilizer. Measure the effective width of your spreader by:
   a. Finding a hard surface on which you can see fallen fertilizer.
   b. Placing some fertilizer—but not much—into the spreader's hopper.
   c. Walking a short distance at a regular pace before stopping.
   d. Measuring the application width of the fertilizer band.
   e. Multiplying the application width by 2/3 or 0.66. For example, if the fertilizer is cast out in an 8-ft.-wide swath, the effective width is 5 ft. (0.66 x 8 ft.). This 5-ft.-wide band receives an even amount of fertilizer. A 1½-ft.-wide band on either side receives less fertilizer.
   f. Sweeping up the fertilizer and returning it to the bag.
   Knowing the effective width of your spreader makes the rest of the calibration process easier.
3. When you're ready to fertilize your lawn, find a flat portion in which you can calibrate the amount of fertilizer delivered by your spreader. Mark off an area of your lawn that measures 1,000 sq. ft. In our example, the effective width is 5 ft. So, the length must be 200 ft. to create a 1,000 sq. ft. test area (1,000 sq. ft. ÷ 5 ft.). It is best if this site is less visible so that potential damage isn't easily seen.
4. To apply 1 lb. of nitrogen per 1,000 sq. ft. with a 16-4-8 fertilizer, you need to spread 6 lbs. of fertilizer (100 ÷ 16). However, to deliver it uniformly and avoid gaps, make two passes. Apply one-half of the total amount in one direction and the other half perpendicularly to the first. When doing this, calibrate the spreader based on one-half the application rate, or 3 lbs. of 16-4-8 fertilizer.
5. Weigh some fertilizer (10 lbs. may be easiest) and put it in the hopper with the spreader in the "closed" position.
6. Set your spreader according to the fertilizer label, which may specify the setting for your spreader. If it's not listed, start at a low setting to avoid applying too much fertilizer.
7. Start walking from about 10 ft. behind the starting point you marked earlier. Open the spreader when you reach the starting line and are walking at a "normal" pace.
8. Maintain a normal pace and close the hopper when you cross the finish line.
9. Weigh the remaining fertilizer in the spreader and subtract the final weight from the starting weight to determine how much fertilizer you applied over the 1,000 ft. area. For example, if you poured in 10 lbs. of fertilizer at the start and ended with 8 lbs. in the hopper, then you spread 2 lbs. of fertilizer over the 1,000 sq. ft. area.
10. In the hypothetical example in step 9, you applied less nitrogen than you need. So, go back to step 5 and repeat the process with the spreader set at a higher setting. Move your calibration test site to another part of the lawn to avoid applying too much fertilizer to that area. Once you've found the correct setting to apply 3 lbs. of 16-4-8 per 1,000 sq. ft., record it for future reference.

Drop-Type Spreaders. Drop-type spreaders "drop" fertilizer through a series of openings at the base of the hopper (Figure 4.14). This type is best suited to fertilizing small areas or trying to prevent material from getting on sidewalks or paved surfaces. Drop-type spreaders are not as easy to maneuver around trees and shrubs as

CHAPTER 4 - TURFGRASS ESTABLISHMENT AND MANAGEMENT • 107

Figure 4.14 Drop-type spreader.
Image Credit: Michael Goatley, Virginia Tech

Figure 4.15 Drop-type spreader with calibration pan attached.
Image Credit: Michael Goatley, Virginia Tech

rotary spreaders. When using this kind of spreader, be sure to overlap the wheel tracks, because the fertilizer only falls between the wheels.

Calibrating a Drop-Type Spreader. You can calibrate drop-type spreaders following similar steps to those used to calibrate drop-type spreaders.

1. Check the spreader to make certain all parts are operating properly.
2. Create a "catch pan" for the fertilizer (Fig. 4.15) by making a V-shaped or box-shaped trough out of heavy cardboard (or use a piece of aluminum guttering).
3. Attach the trough securely beneath the spreader to catch the fertilizer.
4. Measure the width of the spreader.
5. Mark off an area that, when multiplied by the width of the spreader, will cover a 100 sq. ft. area. Divide 100 sq. ft. by the spreader width or use the following table to help you determine how far you should walk to cover a 100 sq. ft. area:

Spreader Width	Travelling Distance
1.5 ft.	66.6 ft. (66 ft. 7 in.)
2 ft.	50 ft.
3 ft.	33.3 ft. (33 ft. 4 in.)

6. Set the spreader on the opening number suggested by the manufacturer on the fertilizer bag. If there is no number, select the lowest setting and proceed at progressively higher settings (which denote larger openings).
7. Fill the spreader with fertilizer (but be sure you know how much you're starting with).
8. Determine the amount of fertilizer that should be applied to the calibration area. For example, to apply 1 lb. of actual nitrogen per 1,000 sq. ft. using a 10-10-10 fertilizer, 10 lbs. of fertilizer should be applied per 1,000 sq. ft. (100 ÷ 10). Since the calibration area is only 100 sq. ft., you will only need to apply 1 lb. of fertilizer (100 sq. ft. divided by 10).
9. Start walking. Open the spreader as you cross the starting line and walk the length of the calibration area. Close it as you cross the finish line.
10. Weigh the collected material and write it down next to the spreader settings. Take at least three trial runs for each setting. Then, find the average to determine an average application rate for each setting.
11. Select the right spreader setting. Assume you obtained the following results from your trials with your spreader:

Example of calibration trial results:

Setting	Average Output/100 sq. ft.
1	2 oz.
3	3 oz.
5	6 oz.
7	8 oz. (0.5 lb.)
9	10 oz.
11	16 oz. (1 lb.)

Use spreader setting 11 to apply 10 lbs. of 10-10-10 fertilizer per 1,000 sq. ft. (or 1 lb. of actual nitrogen per 1,000 sq. ft.). If you want to apply one-half of the total amount in one direction and the other half at 90 degrees to the first to obtain uniform coverage, use spreader setting 7 to apply 5 lbs. of fertilizer per 1,000 sq. ft.

Use the same calibration procedure for any product you want to apply. Since the quantity applied depends on the physical properties of the material, the same settings do not apply to different materials, even if the ratios are the same. Once the spreader is calibrated and set for the proper rate for a single material, you can accurately treat any size area.

Mowing

Mowing is one of the most essential management practices to producing a high-quality lawn. Mowing makes the difference between a lawn and a pasture or meadow. It directly affects the health and quality of a lawn. Proper mowing is important in creating a high-quality lawn, because it encourages a dense stand of grass plants. A dense turf keeps out weeds by providing competition for sunlight and nutrients. A weak, thin turf allows weed seeds to germinate and grow. When mowing a lawn, important factors to consider include height of cut, frequency of cut, and the type of mower used.

Height of Cut

For best appearance, mow turfgrasses to a height specific to the species. A grass that spreads horizontally can usually be mowed shorter than an upright-growing, bunch-type grass. Grasses with narrow blades can generally be mowed closer than grasses with wide blades. Turfgrasses under stress from heat, drought, or shade should be mowed at a higher height. Table 4.10 outlines suggested mowing height, frequency, and mower type for lawn turfgrasses in South Carolina.

Frequency of Cut

Mow your lawn regularly. A good rule of thumb is to remove no more than one-third of the grass height at any single mowing. For example, if you are maintaining your centipede lawn at 1.5 in., mow the lawn when it is approximately 2 in. high. Cutting off more than one-third of the blade at one time can stop the roots from growing as unnecessary energy is moved towards leaf growth which also results in requiring more frequent watering during dry summers to keep the plants alive. Also, following the one-third rule produces smaller

TABLE 4.10 Suggested mowing heights and frequencies for cool- and warm-season turfgrasses.

Turfgrass	Cutting Height (inches)	Frequency (days)	Best Mower Type
Cool-season Grasses			
Kentucky Bluegrass*	1½ to 2½	7 to 14	Rotary
Fine Fescue	2 to 2	10 to 14	Rotary
Tall Fescue*	2½ to 3½	7 to 14	Rotary
Ryegrass (overseeding)	1½ to 2½	7 to 14	Rotary
Warm-season Grasses			
Bahiagrass	3 to 4	7 to 17	Rotary
Bermudagrass			
-Common	1 to 2¼	3 to 5	Reel or Rotary
-Hybrid	½ to 1½	2 to 5	Reel
Carpetgrass	1 to 2	10 to 14	Rotary
Centipedegrass	1 to 2	10 to 14	Rotary
St. Augustinegrass	2½ to 4	7 to 14	Rotary
Zoysiagrass			
-Fine-blade	½ to 1½	4 to 7	Reel
-Wide-blade	1 to 2	5 to 14	Reel

*Only certain varieties will tolerate the lower mowing heights

Note

(1) Grass grown in shade should be mowed slightly higher.

clippings; in turn, these clippings disappear more quickly by filtering down to the soil surface. Leaving sufficient height when mowing avoids the possibility of scalping the turf, which could lead to turf death. If the grass becomes too tall between mowings, raise the mowing height and gradually reduce it until you reach your target lawn height.

Types of Mowers

Lawn mowers are available in a wide variety of sizes and styles and with a variety of features. Traditionally, homeowners use two basic types of mowers: rotary mowers (see Figure 4.16) and reel mowers (see Figure 4.17). More recently, mulching, flail, and string mowers have become available. Most mowers are available as push- or self-propelled models. There are front, side, and rear clipping discharge models. The choice of mower often depends on personal preference. When considering purchasing a mower, consider the size of the lawn, the species of turfgrass, and what level of lawn maintenance you plan to provide.

Rotary Mowers. Rotary mowers are the most popular mowers because they are less expensive, easy to maneuver, and simple to maintain. The mower blade cuts the grass blade on impact in a chopping or slicing action. Most rotary mowers cannot give a quality cut lower than one inch; however, they are versatile and can be used on taller grasses and weeds, for mulching grass clippings, and for general trimming.

Mulching Mowers. One modification of rotary mowers is mulching mowers. These are designed to cut leaf blades into very small pieces that can fall into the lawn rather than remain on top of the grass. Because the pieces are so small, they decompose more quickly than blades cut to traditional size. The mower blades of mulching mowers are designed to create a mild vacuum in the mower deck until the leaf blades are cut into small-enough pieces. Mulching mowers do not have the traditional discharge chutes that most rotary mowers do, and they are less effective when used in wet or tall grass.

String Mowers. String mowers are similar to rotary mowers but with monofilament lines rather than blades. String mowers require high-speed motors to spin the line fast enough to cut cleanly. String mowers are most often used for trimming, edging, and cutting hard-to-mow areas.

Reel Mowers. Reel mowers are used to mow highly maintained lawns for which appearance is very important. Reel mowers cut with a scissor-like action that produces a particularly clean, even cut. They are used at cutting heights of 2 in. or less. Bermudagrass and zoysiagrass are best cut with reel mowers. Reel-type mowers require a relatively smooth surface to obtain a high-quality cut. Using reel mowers on extremely uneven surfaces will result in scalped areas.

The number of blades needed to produce a smooth, uniform cut will depend on the mowing height; generally, as the height is lowered, the reel will require more blades (Table 4.11).

Maintaining sharp cutting blades allows the mower to cut the grass cleanly, ensuring rapid healing and regrowth. When dull blades tear and bruise the leaves, the wounded grass plants weaken and are less able to ward off invading weeds or recover from disease and

Figure 4.16 Rotary mowers are very common for home lawns, particularly with the introduction of zero-turn mowers.
Image Credit: Adam Gore, Clemson University

Figure 4.17 A reel mower is well-suited for mowing of higher quality grasses such as hybrid bermuda and zoysiagrass.
Image Credit: Adam Gore, Clemson University

TABLE 4.11 Number of blades needed on a reel mower for various cutting heights.

Cutting Height (inches)	Number of Blades
> 1	5
½ - 1	6
¼ - ½	7 – 9
< ¼	11 - 13

insect attacks. Dull blades result in streak, uneven grass that can temporarily yellow for 2-3 days following mowing.

Recycling Grass Clippings

Return or recycle your grass clippings to the lawn. Grass clippings contain about 4% nitrogen, 0.5-1% phosphorus, 2-3% potassium, and smaller amounts of other essential plant nutrients essentially serving as a 4-1-3 fertilizer. When left on the lawn, the nutrients from the clippings eventually return to the soil as the leaf blades decompose.

Irrigating

Turfgrasses, like all living plants, require water to survive and grow. Since rainfall patterns vary, seasonal droughts are common in South Carolina. During long, dry hot periods in the summer, you have two choices when it comes to lawn irrigation: (1) do not water and watch the lawn turn brown and go dormant or (2) water the grass to keep it green.

Unfortunately, each choice bears some consequences. Besides increasing mowing time, watering may encourage weed growth, stimulate disease outbreaks, and raise your water bill.

Some turfgrass species and cultivars can survive dry periods better than others. The most drought-resistant warm season grasses are bahiagrass, common and hybrid bermudagrass, and zoysiagrass. Under severe drought conditions with no supplemental irrigation, these turfgrass will go dormant and turn brown as growth ceases and the leaves die. When favorable moisture conditions return, new growth emerges from the crowns, rhizome, and stolons. Deep root systems also help turfgrasses withstand droughts and recuperate from dry spells.

Tall fescue will go dormant and turn brown during moderate summer drought periods but recovers quickly with adequate rainfall. On the other hand, severe summertime drought conditions with no water for three or more weeks result in thinned-out fescue lawns that require reseeding the next fall.

Deciding When to Water

The most efficient way to water a lawn is to apply water when the lawn begins to show signs of wilting- stress from a lack of water. You can use the following techniques to identify signs or indications of a lack of water:

- Color test: when water becomes unavailable for an extended period, a lawn will exhibit a bluish-gray cast.
- Footprinting: walk across your lawn late in the day and examine the lawn behind you to see if your steps left footprints. If you don't leave footprints, the tissues in the grass have enough water to reform once the weight is gone. If you do leave footprints, it is because there are insufficient water levels in the grass tissues. When the grass blades are compressed by your foot, the low water levels prevent the grass blades from springing back up. If your footprints remain for a long time, water the lawn to prevent the grass from turning brown and becoming dormant.
- Leaf check: grass leaves respond to dryness by visibly wilting, rolling, or folding.
- Screwdriver test: press a screwdriver or similar object into the lawn soil. If the soil is dry, it will be difficult to push the screwdriver into the ground. Use the screwdriver test to confirm the results of other visual methods to help you decide when to irrigate.

Deciding How Much to Water

The amount of water to apply at any one time varies with the amount of water present in the soil, the water-holding capacity of the soil, and the drainage characteristics of the soil. Efficient watering wets only the turfgrass rootzone, does not saturate the soil, and does not create runoff.

When the soil is dry, thoroughly wetting the area will require ¾-1 in. of water. This is equivalent to 465-620 gallons of water per 1,000 sq. ft. of lawn.

Generally, turfgrass requires no more than 0.3 in. of water per day (Table 4.12). Under extreme conditions, water use can be as high as 0.4 in. per day. During the winter, when grasses are not actively growing, water use can be as little as 0.05 in. per day. A simple watering schedule could include applying ¾ in. of water whenever the lawn shows water deficiency symptoms as described above. This amount of water, which will replace the water lost by the lawn grasses during summer dry spells, will moisten the root zone area. Once you apply this amount, do not apply more water until the stress symptoms reappear. In most situations, your entire lawn will not dry at once. There will be small areas, called 'localized dry spots' (LDS), that will appear first. If you have LDS, you only need to water those particular spots and can hold off on watering the entire lawn until the entire lawn is dry.

If you have a heavy clay soil and cannot apply ¾ in. of water in a single cycle without significant runoff, apply a little at a time and allow the water to soak in before you continue. Determine the depth of penetration using the screwdriver test. If you have a portable sprinkler, move it frequently to avoid surface runoff and excessive water use.

TABLE 4.12 General average summer turfgrass evapotranspiration (ET)* rates in humid regions. Generally, ET rates at other seasons are much lower.

Turfgrass	Summer ET Rates	
	Inches/day	Inches/week
Bahiagrass	0.25	1.75
Bermudagrass	0.12	0.84
Centipedegrass	0.15	1.05
Ky. bluegrass	0.15	1.05
Perennial ryegrass	0.15	1.05
Seashore paspalum	0.25	1.75
St. Augustinegrass	0.13	0.91
Tall fescue	0.15	1.05
Zoysiagrass	0.14	0.98

*The combined loss of water by evaporation from the soil and transpiration from the leaves.

Typically, you should plan to water two to three times per week in the summer and once every 10-14 days in the winter. If there is rainfall, adjust the irrigation rate accordingly.

Deciding How to Water

Water should never be applied faster than it can be absorbed by the soil. If a sprinkler applies too much water, it runs off and is wasted. This seldom happens with small sprinklers unless the lawn is thick or the soil is compacted. If your soil's infiltration rate is low, you may have to water less at a time but more frequently to allow the water to soak in.

Avoid extremes in irrigation frequency and amount. Light, frequent watering is inefficient and encourages shallow root systems. Excessive irrigation, which keeps the root system saturated with water, is harmful to the lawn and encourages pests such as weeds and disease. Roots need a balance of water and air to function and grow properly.

The time of watering is important. Water late in the evening after dewfall or early in the morning; these are the most efficient and beneficial times because they minimize water evaporation, allowing the plants to maximize their intake. Also, early morning irrigation may curtail the development and spread of diseases, because grass blades dry off quickly, reducing the probability of fungus spores from germinating and infecting the leaf tissues. Watering in late afternoon or late morning may be detrimental if it extends the time the lawn is wet. However, you may have little or no control over watering times if you use municipal water and have to schedule your watering to avoid peak residential water use.

After irrigating, do not water again until you observe symptoms of water deficiency. Avoid watering grass every day except during the establishment of newly seeded, sodded, or sprigged lawns. Otherwise, watering just a little every day encourages shallow rooting, making the grass less drought tolerant. Try to stretch the interval between waterings to as many days as possible to encourage the development of a deep, extensive root system.

Once you choose to water your lawn during the summer months, continue watering. Encouraging the lawn to break dormancy and then not watering again will exhaust the plant, resulting in injury or death.

Calibrating Your Sprinkler System

To water efficiently, you need to know how much water your irrigation system applies over a set time. Most people irrigate their lawn for a specific amount of time without knowing how much water they are applying during that period. This watering method can provide too much or too little water. Excess water can run down sidewalks and streets or through the root zone and deep belowground—out-of-reach of shallow turfgrass roots.

Calibrating your sprinkler system, or rather, determining the rate of water your sprinkler system applies over time, is easy (Figure 4.18). Follow these steps to calibrate your sprinkler if you have an in-ground irrigation system or a sprinkler at the end of a hose.

Step 1. Gather 5-10 coffee cans, tuna fish cans, or other straight-sided containers to catch the irrigation water. The containers should be identical and about 3-6 in. in diameter.

Step 2. If you have an in-ground system, place the containers in one zone at a time. Randomly place the cans within the zone. Repeat the following procedure in every zone individually, as the irrigation rates may differ.

If you use a hose-end sprinkler to water your lawn, place the containers equal distances apart in a straight line from the sprinkler to the edge of the watering pattern.

Step 3. Turn on the water for 15 minutes.

Step 4. After the 15 minutes, collect the cans and pour all the water into a single can.

Step 5. Measure the depth of the combined water collected during the 15-minute period.

Step 6. Calculate the average depth of water by dividing the amount of collected water (in inches) by the number of cans you used.

Step 7. Multiply the average depth by 4 to determine the application rate in inches per hour.

Now that you know the irrigation rate of your sprinkler system, you can irrigate your turf more efficiently. Use Table 4.13 as a guide for how long to water using your sprinkler. For example, if the sprinkler system applies water at the rate of 2 in. per hour and you want to apply ½ in., then run the sprinklers for 15 minutes. To determine how long to run a sprinkler system for irrigation rates not listed in the table, use the following equation:

Figure 4.18 Step 4 of calibrating your sprinkler systems begins with collecting the containers used to catch the water.
Image Credit: Terasa Lott and Kayla Murphy, Clemson University

Minutes required to run each zone=(Amount of water to be applied × 60)/(Your calibrated irrigation rate)

Aerifying

Core aeration, or aerification, is the practice of physically removing cores of soil and leaving holes or cavities in the lawn. Aerification can benefit lawns because it:

- Loosens compacted soil and increases the availability of water and nutrients;
- Enhances oxygen levels in the soil, stimulating root growth and enhancing the activity of thatch-decomposing organisms;
- Severs roots, rhizomes, and stolons, which stimulates the grass plants to produce new roots and shoots that fill up the holes in the lawn and increase the density of the turf;
- Reduces water runoff; and
- Increases the lawn's drought tolerance and improves its overall health.

TABLE 4.13 Time required to apply water for a given irrigation rate.

Amount of water to be applied	Irrigation Rate (Amount of water per hour)			
	½ inch	1 inch	1½ inch	2 inches
	Minutes to run each zone			
¼ inch	30	15	10	8
½ inch	60	30	20	15
¾ inch	90	45	30	23
1 inch	120	60	40	30

Aerification of home lawns is used primarily to correct soil problems and relieve compaction. Although aerification is not considered a routine practice for most turf, it may become a routine management practice in situations of poor-quality soil or excessive traffic.

It is best to aerify cool-season lawns in the fall, when there is less danger of invasion by weedy annuals; try to schedule aerification to allow at least four weeks of good growing weather afterwords to help the plants recover. It is best to aerify warm-season lawns in late spring and summer when they are actively growing. Regardless of grass type, the soil should be moderately moist, allowing for easier tine penetration and removal of soil core with minimal crumbling.

To aerify large lawns, professionals use a power-driven machine called a core aerator or aerifier. The working parts of these machines are spoon-shaped tines or hollow tubes; as the tube or tine is driven into the lawn, they remove cores of soil from the ground and strew them across the lawn (Figure 4.19). Both types of tines work well, but the hollow tine makes a somewhat cleaner hole than the spoon type and brings up less soil. Tine size varies up to 0.75 in. in diameter and penetrates up to 3 in. in depth, depending on the aerifier manufacturer. The closer the tines are spaced together, the more soil will be removed; the more soil is removed, the more soil surface area is exposed for water and fertilizer movement and the more quickly the compaction is alleviated.

Penetration depth depends on soil type, soil moisture, tine diameter, and the weight and power of the aerifier. Soil cores may be left on the lawn and they will break down with rainfall and traffic, or you can speed up their disappearance by mowing over cores with a rotary mower and then brushing them into the grass or raking and removing the cores from the turf. Regardless of the type of machine you use, you'll need to go over the lawn at least twice: first in one direction and then perpendicular to the first, as you would when fertilizing.

You can combine the aerification and seeding processes, particularly on sparse or bare areas. If you are going to seed the lawn, make 6-10 passes over the area with an aerifying machine. You need to produce many holes, at least 4 in. apart, to improve the appearance and density of the stand. Allow the holes to heal for about a month before seeding. If you overseed immediately after coring, seeds that land in or near the aerifier holes will germinate and grow much better than those between the holes, giving the lawn an uneven appearance. The benefit to aerifying before seeding is that you won't need to till the soil; with a fraction of the effort and expense, you can combine aerification and seeding to give the lawn a brand- new look.

Dethatching

Thatch is a dense, spongy collection of living and dead grass stems and roots lying between the soil surface and green grass leaves and stolons in established lawns (Figure 4.20). There is a gradual decrease in size of organic matter pore spaces from the top of the thatch layer to the bottom of the mat. A mat is a very fine, dense, and peat-like layer that cannot be easily compressed and does not provide an ideal situation for the growth of the turf roots.

Thatch originates from old stems, stolons, roots, and rhizomes shed by grasses during the development of new plant parts. The sloughed-off plant matter collects at the soil surface and gradually decomposes. Grass leaves or clippings decay rapidly, because they have the lowest amount of lignin in their tissues whereas stems, stolons, rhizomes, and roots decompose slowly, in part because of the high levels of lignin present in their tissues. When the accumulation rate of plant litter exceeds the decomposition rate, a thatch layer develops.

Thatch is not omnipresent; lawn grasses differ in their propensity to produce thatch. Highly vigorous cultivars or turfgrass species that experience quick growth rates, such as Kentucky bluegrass and hybrid bermudagrass cultivars, are heavy thatch-builders. Slower-growing grasses, such as red fescue and zoysiagrass, also produce thatch, because their fibrous tissues are highly

Figure 4.19 Core aerification removes sections of soil up to 3 inches deep and improves the movement of air and water into the soil profile.

Image Credit: Adam Gore, Clemson University

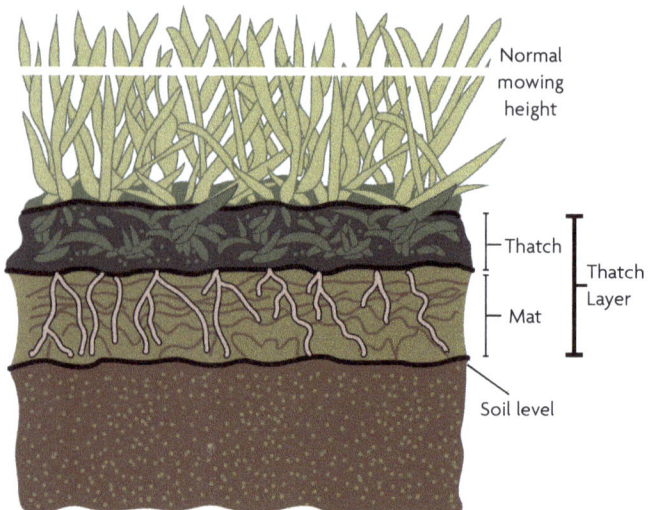

Figure 4.20 A thatch layer separates the growing point of a plant from the soil.

resistant to decomposition and quickly collect on the soil surface. Tall fescue, perennial ryegrass, bahiagrass, centipedegrass, and St. Augustinegrass also form thatch, but at a slower rate. Thatch problems generally arise from poor management practices such as over-fertilizing, over-watering, and infrequent mowing. Promoting turfgrass growth rates above natural decomposition rates will lead to a thatch layer.

Advantages of Thatch

Not all turfgrass thatch is bad. A shallow thatch layer—up to 0.5 in. thick—will benefit the lawn. Thatch acts like a natural cushion, enabling the lawn to endure wear and tear; helps the soil retain moisture; and insulates the soil from extreme temperatures. Unfortunately, shallow thatch layers usually evolve into thick, destructive ones that affect the health, vigor, and appearance of a lawn.

Disadvantages of Thatch

If the thatch layer is more than 0.5 in. thick, the disadvantages outweigh the advantages. Heavy thatch forces turfgrass plants to grow within the thatch layer. Their roots rely on the thatch for nutrients and moisture, but thatch usually either does not retain nutrients well or holds them too tightly, making them unavailable to plant roots; thatch also retains moisture poorly.

Irrigation is difficult on heavily thatched lawns. Thatch dries out easily and is difficult to re-wet. Eventually, localized dry spots develop. The lawn becomes less tolerant of drought and more susceptible to heat injury, wilting, and drying out. A "Catch-22" situation arises: the lawn needs to be irrigated frequently to keep it alive, but watering repeatedly causes the few available nutrients to leach out of the thatch and into the soil, which contains few grass roots. Sometimes, the thatch is so thick and the turf so established in the thatch that you can simply scrape the turf off the soil; the grass roots no longer anchor the plant to the soil.

While a thick thatch layer hinders grass growth, it provides a safe haven for insects and diseases. Thatch acts like an organic barrier, blocking the movement of pesticides and reducing their effectiveness. Because of this, lawns with thick thatch layers are plagued with pest problems.

Reducing Thatch Buildup

A thatch layer signals an imbalance between decomposition and accumulation of plant litter. To speed up decomposition, maintain an environment that encourages the proliferation of thatch-decomposing organisms; this is a natural way to keep the thatch layer at the recommended level. Maintaining your soil pH at the recommended level will also aid in natural thatch decomposition, as extremely acidic or alkaline soils hamper the activity of earthworms, insects, and microbes involved in natural thatch decomposition.

Highly compacted or finely textured soils, particularly heavy clay soils, impair the activity of soil-borne organisms due to restricted oxygen levels. Periodic core aerification, also called coring, will alleviate compaction and facilitate the movement of air and water into the soil. Coring is a cultural practice that does not remove substantial amounts of thatch but does improve the soil environment and benefits lawn grasses and the earthworms and microbes engaged in breaking down thatch. If you use pesticides, use them sparingly and locally to control specific pest problems; judicious pesticide use can minimize the destruction of thatch-decomposers in the lawn.

Thatch accumulation can be controlled by applying appropriate levels of nitrogen and water to meet the needs of the lawn. Lavish amounts of nitrogen and water produce an excessive amount of succulent growth, which increases thatch and often makes the lawn more susceptible to pests.

Mow at the proper height and mow frequently. Remove no more than one-third of the grass height each time you mow. Excessive thatch layers may accumulate if you mow infrequently or leave the grass too tall, particularly on warm-season grasses like bermudagrass and zoysiagrass. The use of a mulching mower alone will not prevent a thatch problem.

Thatch Removal

Examine the depth of a thatch layer by cutting out a wedge of sod (like a slice of pie or pizza) from the lawn using a knife or spade. If the layer is thicker than 0.5 in., you need to dethatch—or physically remove the thatch—from the lawn. Remember that thatch buildup is gradual and occurs over a period of years, so a thatch removal program should also be gradual.

For small areas or lawns, consider using a dethatching rake. As you pull the rake across the lawn, the sharp, curved blades slide through the thatch and lift it from the lawn. Larger areas will require power-driven dethatching equipment and know-how. Improper dethatching can devastate a lawn. If you'd prefer to dethatch the lawn rather than hire a reputable commercial lawn maintenance company, choose the most effective dethatcher available: a vertical mower (Figure 4.21). Select a vertical mower with revolving, straight fixed blades; the spacing between the knives and depth should be adjustable. Vary the spacing of the blades according to the kind of grass in the lawn.

For cool-season grasses like Kentucky bluegrass and tall fescue, the blades should be spaced 1-2 in. apart. Warm-season grasses are more varied; space blades 1-2 in. apart for bermudagrass, 2-3 in. for centipedegrass and zoysiagrass, and 3 in. for St. Augustinegrass. The blades should cut into the thatch layer and approximately 0.25 – 0.5 in. into the soil. Expect the vertical mower to lift the thatch to the surface and cultivate the top 0.25 – 0.5 in. of soil without causing serious injury to the turf, although the turf will look thin. The blades will cut into the thatch layer and lift it to the surface so you can rake away the debris; you can add broken-up thatch to a compost pile, but be careful if you want to use it as a mulch—some herbicides will bind to organic material of thatch layer can cause problems for ornamentals.

You can mow lawns containing grasses with rhizomes—such as Kentucky bluegrass and bermudagrass—with a vertical mower in several directions without killing the lawn. However, using a vertical mower several times on grasses with only stolons, such as centipedegrass and St. Augustinegrass, may kill them. Only vertically mow these grasses in one direction to avoid removing too much plant material and reducing the turf's recovery rate.

If the thatch layer is thicker than 2-3 in., widen the spacing of the blades to reduce injury to the grass plants

Figure 4.21 A vertical mower uses blades to cut and lift the thatch from the turf area.
Image Credit: Adam Gore, Clemson University

and remove only a portion of the thatch layer at a time. Allow the lawn to fully recover before you attempt to reduce the depth of the layer any further.

The best time to remove thatch from cool-season lawns is late summer or early fall. Dethatch warm-season grasses in spring after greenup or in early summer when the grass is growing rapidly but before the weather gets so hot that the lawn is under drought stress. Since vertical mowing is a traumatic experience for the lawn, plan to dethatch with a cushion of at least a month of favorable growing conditions, avoiding excessively hot or dry periods.

After dethatching, thoroughly water the lawn to prevent the exposed roots from drying out. About a week after dethatching, apply 1 lb. of actual nitrogen (<50% quick-release, water-soluble nitrogen) per 1,000 sq. ft. of lawn and irrigate afterwards to minimize burn. A good lawn management program includes both preventive practices to reduce thatch accumulation and curative practices to remove any excess.

Power raking follows the same mechanical principles as vertical mowing. These specialized machines use evenly spaced, flexible spring steel tines that revolve at high speed to strip through turf and loosen debris for its subsequent removal. The machine and procedures are often confused with vertical mowing. Power raking does not involve a cutting action; vertical mowing does. Therefore, power raking is not a substitute for vertical mowing and thatch removal.

Close mowing is a procedure in which turf is mowed to a much shorter height than normal. It is a poor substitute for vertical mowing, but its use, especially in early spring—when or just before new growth begins to appear—may delay the need for vertical mowing where a shallow thatch layer exists. Of course, how close of a mow is required depends on the species of turfgrass. Turfgrasses with rhizomes, like bermudagrass and zoysiagrass, may be mowed close to the soil surface. Centipedegrass and St. Augustinegrass spread by stolons, and their removal would kill the turf; they cannot handle as close of a mow as bermudagrass or zoysia. Zoysiagrass is not as sensitive to close mowing as centipede and St. Augustine, but it is more sensitive than bermuda. Mowing below the crown or green growing points of zoysiagrass will cause extensive damage. After mowing, collect and compost or remove the dead plant material.

Topdressing

Topdressing is the application of a thin layer of sand, compost, or another media to an area of turfgrass. Topdressing a lawn or sports field serves to:

- smooth out and level uneven areas of the turf;
- assist in thatch reduction;
- modify underlying soil texture, especially in clay soils after an aerification; and
- cover turf stolons or sprigs, allowing them to root better.

Topdressing soil, especially clay soils, with sand after aerification can beneficially modify the soil. When the sand penetrates the aerification holes, it creates columns of sand that improve water infiltration and percolation rates. However, this modification process is slow and may take several years to see satisfactory results.

Topdressing is often a routine management practice on sports fields such as golf course putting greens. However, topdressing is generally used sparingly for home lawns—serving primarily to smooth out rough or bumpy areas.

Usually, a topdressing material is distributed to a depth of approximately 0.125 - 0.25 in. and worked it into the turf with a drag mat. This mat can be made of old carpet or a piece of chain-link fencing. Use a topdressing material with a texture similar to that of the underlying soil to avoid soil layering. Soil layering occurs when soils of two different textures are placed on top of each other. These layers can inhibit the movement of water through the soil.

You can apply topdressing material by hand, but using a topdressing machine will be more precise; these machines dispense the desired amount of material onto the turf. Walking topdressers are available for use on smaller lawns or commercial turf, while larger turf areas may require topdressing by a tractor-pulled machine.

Practicing Integrated Pest Management

Integrated pest management (IPM) is essentially common-sense pest management practiced by most lawn owners, even if they don't realize it. IPM utilizes biological, cultural, mechanical, and chemical control options to achieve the best long-term results with minimal environmental disruption.

Cultural and mechanical pest-control methods reflect the basic agronomic principles covered previously, such as proper turfgrass selection, good establishment and soil management practices, proper mowing, fertilization, and irrigation; these practices all lead to promoting a healthy, dense stand of grass. These control actions create an environment that favors the competitive advantages of desired turfgrass plants.

Biological control relies on naturally occurring enemies of pests to reduce pest presence. One commonly used biological control for turfgrasses is the use of milky-spore disease-causing bacteria (*Bacillus papillae*) to control white grubs. Biological control can provide effective long-term control of pests; however, many biological control methods take time to have an effect, which may not be ideal or sufficient during a rapid outbreak.

Chemical control is the final control option in the IPM toolkit; while these methods are effective, use them judiciously. Before using a pesticide, make a few decisions:

Does the Problem Warrant Chemical Control?

Identify the pest plaguing your turf. How much damage is it doing? How many are there? Decide if the population and level of damage is sufficient to warrant pesticide use.

When Should I Apply Pesticides?

Treat the pest when it is most susceptible and the turfgrass is most tolerant. Pests—whether weedy plants, insects, or diseases—tend to be most vulnerable in their early stages of development; during this time, they are often referred to as "young and immature." For example, mole crickets are most susceptible to chemical control when they are small, usually during the months of May and June; chemical applications at other times are less effective.

What Pesticide Should I Apply?

Select the most effective but least toxic and persistent pesticide for your lawn's pests. Read the label completely and thoroughly. Determine the size of the affected are and treat only those locations. If you are uncertain about the best pesticide for your situation, contact your local county Extension agent.

Weed Management

A weed is any plant whose presence is unwanted or not valued in an area. Weeds are considered pests in most home lawns because they differ in color, leaf size, leaf shape, and growth habits from the turfgrasses that were placed there intentionally. Weeds also compete with the desired grasses for sunlight, soil moisture, and nutrients. A healthy, dense lawn crowds out most weeds. To avoid grassy and broadleaf weeds in an above-average quality lawn, some form of weed control may be necessary.

Development of Weed Problems

Most turfgrass weeds develop from seeds that were present but inactive in the soil, popularly called the "seed bank." Some weeds develop from seeds introduced in contaminated topsoil, manure, compost, mulch, turfgrass seed, or sod. Other weeds are introduced by wind, equipment, or animals. Regardless of their origin, millions of seeds are present in the soil and can compete for its resources.

Weed Establishment and Competition

In a healthy, dense stand of turf, little light reaches the soil surface. Most weed seedlings that do emerge from the soil surface are short-lived, because their leaves do not receive enough light for photosynthesis. However, if a lawn is thin or bare, weedy plants capitalize on the favorable conditions and establish themselves. Once established, weeds compete with surrounding plants for available light, water, and nutrients.

Cultural Practices for Weed Control

The first step in reducing weed pressure is selecting a grass species adapted for a particular site and maintaining it at the proper height (Figure 4.22). Turfgrasses that thrive in their site's growing conditions and are maintained at proper height will have more expansive and competitive root systems and be more capable of shading out

Figure 4.22 St. Augustinegrass is able to outcompete weedy plants in areas receiving 4 to 5 hours of sunlight.
Image Credit: Adam Gore, Clemson University

germinating weed seedlings. For example, if you plant bermudagrass in a shaded area, it will be thin and weak from a lack of sunlight; its lack of vigor would allow weedy plants to establish.

Proper fertility and irrigation practices promote overall health and aid in reducing the presence of lawn-damaging insects and diseases. Certain insects and diseases will attack lawn grass and leave it thinned, weakened, or dead; this allows weeds to germinate and establish.

Mechanical Practices for Weed Control

Frequent mowing can control many weed species due to their inability to tolerate a low growing height or the traffic associated with mowing. Hand weeding is an effective but time-consuming practice. Take care to remove as much of a weed's root system as possible. Perennial weeds such as Virginia buttonweed (*Diodia virginiana*) can propagate and regrow from a single remaining stem.

If complete removal isn't possible, the simple action of removing the flower of the plant or mowing prior to seed production aids in reducing the number of future offspring.

Chemical Practices for Weed Control

Only use herbicides when necessary and in conjunction with good agronomic practices. Herbicides are applied at specific times of the year and vary in what weed species they control based on individual chemistry. Also, many herbicides are not appropriate or safe for every turfgrass species. An herbicide's label is the best reference for its safe and effective use; always read the label prior to applying any herbicide to your turf.

Before purchasing or applying any herbicide, identify the target weed and the turfgrass species it is in and identify the surrounding landscape. Grassy weeds often require different herbicides than broadleaf weeds, and turfgrass species have varying sensitivities to the different ingredients. Additionally, plants in nearby vegetable gardens or nearby trees and shrubs may be sensitive to components. Protect your own health by ensuring you have the appropriate equipment to apply the selected herbicide.

The timing of the herbicide application is also an important consideration. Herbicides are formulated to work on certain growth stages of weeds. Apply preemergence herbicides to an existing turf before weed seeds germinate to control the emerging seedlings. Apply postemergence herbicides to actively growing weeds that have emerged from the soil surface.

Preemergence Herbicide. Preemergence herbicides form a chemical barrier in the soil. As weed seeds germinate, the developing shoots and roots contact and absorb the herbicide, resulting in death of the seedling. Apply preemergence herbicides according to the following schedule:

Fall. When nighttime temperatures drop to 55-60°F, apply preemergence herbicides to control winter annual weeds such as annual bluegrass, henbit, chickweed, and lawn burweed. From the Coastal Plains to the Sandhills, this period often lasts from September 15th-October 1st; in the Piedmont and Mountain areas, this period usually lasts from September 1st-September 15th.

Spring. When daytime temperatures reach 65 - 70°F for 4-5 consecutive days, apply preemergence herbicides to control summer annual weeds such as crabgrass and goosegrass. These temperatures often coincide with the blooming of other early spring plants such as redbuds, pears, and forsythia. Coastal Plains to the Sandhills typically experience this weather between February 15th-March 1st; Piedmont and Mountain areas normally see this weather from March 1st-March 15th.

With preemergence herbicides, it is important to remember that timing is strongly related to weather; recommended dates are not set in stone. Apply the herbicide uniformly across the lawn; most applications will require approximately 0.5 in. of water after the application to ensure the chemical moves into the thatch and soil layers. Some preemergence herbicides will break down during the summer months, potentially resulting in the need for a repeat application 2-3 months after the initial application.

Several preemergence herbicides are formulated with granular fertilizers to create fertilizer-herbicide mixtures called "weed 'n feed" products. While these mixtures are convenient, you should consider your species of turfgrass and the time of year you are applying, as a mixture like this may not be appropriate. For example, centipedegrass should not be fertilized until it fully greens up, which typically occurs in April. However, waiting until April to apply a preemergent herbicide may be too late.

Read the pesticide label for specific restrictions, but follow these general guidelines:

- Read the label for the time that must elapse between herbicide application and future seeding.
- Do not apply a preemergence herbicide at the time of turfgrass seeding unless it is specifically labeled for that scenario. If a preemergent is applied after seeding or sprigging, it can result in severe injury to the turfgrass.
- Mow new turfgrass seedlings at least three times before applying a preemergence herbicide.
- Do not apply a preemergence herbicide to the soil prior to laying sod.
- Return grass clippings to the lawn for 2-3 weeks after application to help ensure that any herbicide adsorbed to the leaf blades is returned to the soil.

Postemergence Herbicides. Postemergence herbicides control only weeds that have emerged from the soil and are actively growing at the time of application. Application rates of herbicides have been tested and evaluated for efficacy so there is no need to apply excess prodiuct or "drown" the weed; often any sprays that run off the weed is rendered useless resulting in wasted product with no increase in control.

Some herbicides, such as atrazine, display both preemergence and postemergence activity on a variety of annual broadleaf weeds. When these atrazine-fertilizer products are applied to centipedegrass and St. Augustinegrass after complete green-up, it controls many annual broadleaf weeds both before and after emergence.

Before applying any postemergence herbicide, read and understand the label. To improve the efficacy of postemergence herbicides:

- Apply postemergence herbicides in the fall and late spring. The cooler temperatures will improve turfgrass tolerance to herbicides, and perennial weeds and many annual weeds actively grow at this time of year, making them easier to control.
- Do not apply postemergence herbicides to turfgrasses that are under stress from high temperatures or drought. Turfgrasses become less tolerant to postemergence products when air temperatures exceed 85-90°F or when they are drought-stressed. These environmental conditions also reduce the active growth of weedy plants rendering herbicides less effective.
- Do not apply postemergence herbicides when the warm-season lawn is greening up in the spring. Turfgrass that is coming out of winter dormancy is at greater risk of being injured by herbicides than when fully dormant or actively growing.

Application Equipment. Applying herbicides successfully requires that you use the right equipment and application technique.

The amount of herbicide that needs to be applied to the lawn will be listed on the product's label. For home lawns, the recommended rate will often be given in an amount (pounds, fluid or dry ounces) of product per 1,000 sq. ft. of lawn area. Only apply the recommended rate. The adage that says "if some is good, more is better" does not apply here and can result in severe injury to your lawn and other desirable plants. Use the right equipment to apply the herbicide evenly to the lawn. Improper selection or use of herbicide equipment can be ineffective and cause damage to your lawn.

Dilute liquid formulations of herbicides with water before applying them to the lawn. Handheld pump-up sprayers and hose-end applicators are often used to apply liquid products. Know the square footage of your lawn to apply the herbicide at the correct rate. The addition of a spray indicator marker, normally a green or blue dye, can aid in even coverage.

Granular herbicides can be applied with a drop-type or rotary spreader. To ensure uniform distribution and help prevent skips or excessive overlap, divide the required amount in half. Apply one-half the required amount in one direction and the remaining amount in a perpendicular direction, as you would with a fertilizer.

Herbicide Safety Precautions. Always read and follow labeled directions regarding the handling, storage, and application of herbicides. Mix and use only the amount you need for your lawn. Store the herbicide in its original container in a dry place that's protected from freezing temperatures. All pesticides should be kept out of reach from children, pets, and livestock.

Insect Management

Many insects and similar live pests are common in lawns (Table 4.14). Southern chinch bugs, spittlebugs, grass scales, and bermudagrass mites suck juices from the plant; mole crickets, white grubs, and billbugs live in the soil and damage grass roots. Other pests, including sod webworms, grass loopers, cutworms, and armyworms, eat the grass leaves. Additional insects and related pests such as ants, fleas, ticks, millipedes, and snails do not damage lawns but may become nuisances by biting people or crawling into houses, garages, and swimming pools.

Cultural and Mechanical Practices for Insect Control

A properly managed lawn can tolerate more damage from insect pests before symptoms are evident. Excessive nitrogen fertilization of grasses encourages the presence of some insects and—along with inappropriate irrigation strategies—can encourage the development of a thick thatch layer which serves as an excellent habitat for insects. This thatch layer also reduces the efficacy of applied insecticides, as it binds up the active chemicals.

Consistently monitor your lawn for signs of insect damage. If you suspect a damaging insect is present, make a proper diagnosis and, if needed, apply a recommended treatment. Early detection lessens the chance of extensive turfgrass loss.

Biological Practices for Insect Control

Several predatory and parasitic insects are often associated with chinch bugs and webworms. The most prominent predator of chinch bugs is the big-eyed bug. One of the earwigs (*Labidura*) is a very good predator of both chinch bugs and webworm larvae as well as several other turfgrass insects. Spiders and ground beetles are also efficient predators that can be beneficial in warding off more harmful insects.

The fungus *Beauveria* causes a disease in which fungal threads fill the body cavities of chinch bugs, causing death in about three days. You can also use beneficial nematodes to control chinch bugs, sod webworms, billbugs, cutworms, and armyworms. The presence of these beneficial organisms will often prevent insect pests from reaching damaging levels.

TABLE 4.14 Periods of insect activity and treatment timing chart for South Carolina[1].

	Jan	Feb	Mar	Apr	May	June	July	Aug	Sep	Oct	Nov	Dec
Fire ants				■	■	■	■	■	■	■	■	
Fall armyworm						■	■	■	■	■		
Chinch bugs					■	■	■	■	■			
Cutworms					■	■	■	■	■	■		
White Grubs			■	■	■		■		■	■		
Mole Crickets			■	■	■	■	■	■	■	■	■	
Sod webworm					■	■	■	■	■	■		
Spittlebugs & Leafhoppers					■	■	■	■	■	■		

■ = Insect Present
▒ = Periods when control most likely needed

[1]Periods of activity will vary up to 3 weeks from the Mountains to the Coast

Chemical Practices for Insect Control

Insecticides labelled for home lawns are available in several formulations: baits, emulsifiable concentrates, wettable powders, soluble powders, and granules. The active ingredient and its formulation both play a major role in level of efficacy.

To help prevent unnecessary environmental contamination and reduction of beneficial insects, make spot treatments when you first notice infestations and the damaged area is still small. Treat the off-color area and a ten-foot buffer area surrounding it. Only if damage is widespread or you detect many infested areas should you treat the entire lawn. Inspect the area 2-3 times bi-weekly to determine if the infestation is under control.

Read the manufacturer's label carefully before opening the pesticide container and follow all instructions and precautions. Take care to avoid application of broad-spectrum insecticides during peak times of pollinator activity.

Detecting and Identifying Turfgrass Insects

Look for pests before serious infestations ravage your lawn. Look for damaged, injured areas, sod torn up by animals feeding on insects, the presence of moths flying over the lawn at night, and birds frequenting a particular area of the lawn, as these are conditions that indicate the potential presence of a lawn pests. By detecting and identifying insect pests early, you should have sufficient time to correctly identify the pest and follow through with a selected control strategy before severe damage occurs.

Insects are one of many causes of discolored areas in grass. Be sure of the cause before treating so the proper treatment can be applied to correct the trouble and avoid the use of unnecessary pesticides and extensive damage to the grass.

If you suspect an insect pest, use a sampling technique that will capture the insect causing the damage. The sampling technique must match the type of insect that may be present. Here, we describe a few common turfgrass insect pests and the sampling techniques used to confirm their presence.

Insects Pests Found on Leaves and Stems.

Bermudagrass Mite.

Time of damage: Typically active during hot, dry spells.

Identification: Normally found on bermudagrass—and occasionally zoysiagrass—in the Coastal region. Extremely small (1/130th in.), yellowish-white, and somewhat wormlike in shape. Microscopic; only visible under a microscope.

Detection: Unless you have access to a microscope, identify by turf symptoms: blades turning light green with an abnormal curl, creating a "witch's broom" appearance.

Bermudagrass Scale.

Time of damage: Prolonged periods of high temperature and drought

Identification: Found on multiple turf species, most often bermudagrass. Rhodesgrass mealybug is the most frequently encountered scale insect and is roughly the size of a BB, dark colored, and covered in a white, cottony secretion (Figure 4.23). Bermudagrass scale is oval to circular and 1/25-1/15 (0.04 – 0.067) in. in diameter.

Detection: Scale insects consume plant fluids, and infested grasses turn yellow and thin out. Rhodesgrass mealybug is often found at the nodes of grass stems. Bermudagrass scale is found on the crown, stolons, and underneath leaf sheaths of infested plants.

Chinch Bugs.

Time of damage: Late May through October

Identification: Major pest of St. Augustinegrass. Adults are about 1/5 in. long with small, black triangular patch on wings. Nymphs are 1/20 - 1/5 (0.05 – 0.2) in. and vary in color as they age, from reddish with a white band to black.

Detection: Damage typically appears in high sunlight areas during periods of high temperature and little to no

Figure 4.23 Rhodesgrass mealybug on bermudagrass.
Image Credit: Adam Gore, Clemson University

Figure 4.24 Damage from chinch bugs results in yellowed and thinned turf, particularly in sunny areas on St. Augustinegrass
Image Credit: Adam Gore, Clemson University

Figure 4.26 Ground pearls on centipedegrass.
Image Credit: Meg Williamson, Clemson University

Figure 4.25 Float test tecchnique used to determine presence of chinch bugs.
Image Credit: Turf-Tec International

rainfall. Symptoms first appear as slight yellowing on leaf blades and grass may also appear wilted (Figure 4.24). Perform float test on border between damaged area and healthy grass (Figure 4.25). To perform a float test:

- Cut out both ends of a metal can, such as a 2-3 lbs. coffee can. Push one end about 2-3 in. into the soil. If it is difficult to pass the can through the St. Augustinegrass runners, use a knife to cut a circle in the grass the size of the can.
- Fill the can with water. If bugs are present, the adults and nymphs will float to the top within 5 min. It may be necessary to add more water to keep the level above the grass surface. Perform

this in multiple sites.

Insects Found in Thatch and Soil.

Ground Pearls.

Time of damage: Typically seen during hot, dry spells

Identification: Most commonly seen in centipedegrass but also found in bahiagrass, St. Augustinegrass, and carpetgrass; most commonly found in sandier soils. These are scale insects that feed on roots. Round in shape, ranging in size from a grain of sand to 0.17 in. in diameter, very much like small pearls (Figure 4.26). Egg-laying females are 0.17 in. long, appear pink in color, and have well developed forelegs and claws.

Detection: Symptoms appear as general yellow color turning to brown; more noticeable in drought-stressed or nutrient-deficient grass areas. To detect, dig up and inspect roots and rootzone.

Mole Crickets.

Time of damage: March to November

Identification: The most damaging species, Southern and Tawny, are most serious in sandy soils of the Coastal Plain but also found farther inland. Most damage is caused by the insects' tunnelling, causing plants to be uprooted and dry out. The tawny mole cricket will feed on roots, whereas the southern is carnivorous. Tawny mole crickets are dark brown and can reach 1.5 in. in length; southern mole crickets are smaller and grayer. Identifiable by the distinct pattern on pronotal (area behind head) (Figure 4.27).

Figure 4.27 Southern and tawny mole crickets can be distinguished by pronotal pattern.
Image Credit: Casey Reynolds, Texas A&M University

Figure 4.28 Soap flush technique used to determine the presence of insect pests such as mole crickets and some caterpillars.
Image Credit: Clyde Sorenson, NC State University

Detection: Look for burrowing and tunneling activity of adult mole crickets in late winter and early spring. Map these areas for potential treatment, as these locations are where most of offspring will be found. In early morning or late afternoon in late June and early July, use a soap flush to sample any damaged areas (Figure 4.28):

- Mix 1-2 fl. Oz. of liquid dish detergent per gallon of water.
- Apply slowly to 2 sq. ft. of damaged area.
- Observe affected area for the presence of the pests.

The soap solution irritates the mole crickets, forcing them to the surface within 3-5 minutes.

Sod Webworms and Fall Armyworms.

Time of damage: Late April to October (most damage is noticeable in August)

Identification: Adult forms are moths, but damage is caused by caterpillar forms.

Sod webworm moths are small and dingy brown in color, with snout-like projections from front of heads; they fly over grass in the evening. The larvae are small, cream to green in color, with several black spots and range from 1/25 - 3/4 (0.04 – 0.75) in. in length depending on age.

Fall armyworm adults are light brown moths with a wingspan of 1.5 in. The oldest larvae stages can reach 1.5 in. in length. Armyworm larvae change in color as they age, starting out greyish green with a stripe on their side and maturing to a pale brown to black with large stripes on sides (Figure 4.29). Easiest identifier for armyworms is an inverted "Y" marking on the front of their head.

Detection: Inspect lawns weekly during spring and summer months, particularly in areas where you have noticed moth activity above the grass surface. Examine areas that appear off-color to determine if grass blades appear chewed. Sod webworm larvae rest in a curled position on the soil surface during the day and feed at night or during cloudy and rainy periods. Small green

Figure 4.29 Young, immature armyworm
Image Credit: Adam Gore, Clemson University

pellets of excrement will be numerous on soil surface. Armyworms do not rest in a curled position but feed during the day and may be seen crawling over the grass.

If no larvae are noticed, their presence or absence can be confirmed by a soap flush as described above.

Spittlebugs.

Time of damage: May to October

Identification: Adult two-lined spittlebugs are black with red eyes and legs and have two orange transverse stripes across their wings (Figure 4.30). Adults are approximately 0.25 in. long. Nymphs are yellow or white in color with a brown head; often, they are enveloped in a mass of white frothy spittle—which they excrete—and therefore not visible (Figure 4.31).

Detection: The majority of the spittle masses are not readily visible, as they are usually located near the soil surface or in the thatch layer. Infested turf wilts and the tips turn yellow, then brown. Traffic through the area—such as a mower—can cause the adults to fly up and land elsewhere, providing a visual of their presence.

White Grubs and Billbugs.

Time of damage: Late spring and early fall

Identification: White grubs are the larval form of scarab beetles such as Japanese beetles, green June beetles, Asiatic garden beetles, and northern and southern masked chafers. The grub forms are normally plump with distinctive brown heads, and usually lie in a curled or C-shaped position. A majority of their body is a dirty white color with dark areas visible on the rear abdomen (Figure 4.32).

Adult billbugs are black snout beetles approximately 0.375 in. long (Figure 4.33). Larvae are white, legless,

Figure 4.30 Spittlebug adult.
Image Credit: Adam Gore, Clemson University

Figure 4.32a Typically white grub larva of one of the scarab beetles.

Figure 4.31 Spittle mass that envelopes spittlebug nymph.
Image Credit: Adam Gore, Clemson University

4.32b Adult Japanese Beetle.
Image Credit: Paul Thompson, Clemson University

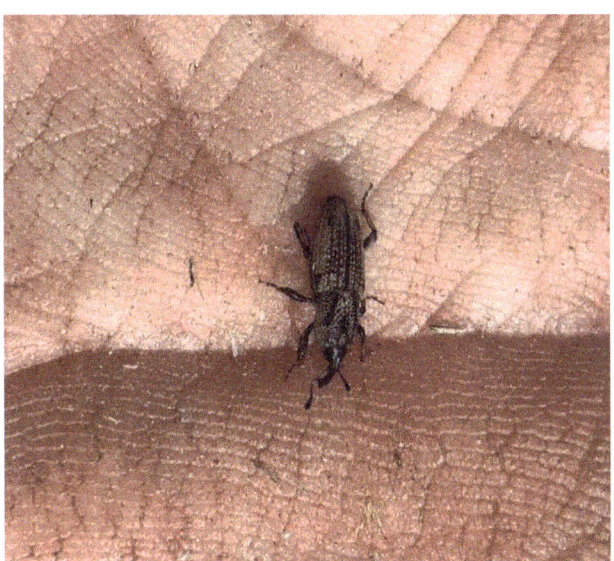

Figure 4.33 Adult hunting billbug.
Image Credit: Terri Billeisen, NC State University

and have hard, yellowish- or reddish-brown heads.

Detection: Most damage from white grubs and billbugs results from their feeding on roots about an inch below the soil surface; this causes grass to appear wilted, yellow, and thin. Inspect for these pests by using a knife or spade shovel to cut three sides of a 12-in. square at the edge of the damaged patch. Pry back this flap and examine the roots and upper 3 in. of soil for white grubs. Heavily infested patches can be lifted and rolled back like a throw rug.

Managing Disease

Diseases damage and thin-out lawns and are often the first factor that homeowners blame when they observe weakened areas of grass stands. Fortunately, diseases are less severe on properly managed lawns than on grasses that do not receive appropriate care. Because of the cost of pesticide applications, it is important to follow good cultural practices that enhance the vigor of the grasses and increase their tolerance to diseases.

Fungi cause the most common and severe diseases for turfgrasses. Fungi are unique, threadlike organisms that cannot produce their own food; they survive on dead or living plant and animal matter. Many fungi reproduce by forming spores, which are microscopic, seedlike bodies. These spores can be spread by wind, water, mowers, and other equipment. Fungi can also be introduced to a lawn through planting material such as infected sprigs, plugs, or sod.

Environmental Conditions That Increase Disease Risk

Light, temperature, and moisture not only influence the health of turfgrass plants and their ability to resist diseases, but also the growth of pathogens—disease-causing organisms. Moisture is necessary for the germination, infection, reproduction, and spread of disease-causing fungi. With a few exceptions, fungi are most damaging to turfgrass plants during wet or humid weather or when dew or irrigation remains on leaves for a long time.

Fungi also have specific temperature ranges within which they are most active. The fungi that cause snow mold are active only during cold weather, whereas the fungi that cause dollar spot and Pythium blight are most active during warm, humid weather. Some species of specific fungi are active at different temperature levels. Different species of *Pythium* and *Rhizoctonia* fungi cause Pythium blight and brown patch at distinct temperatures.

Cultural and Mechanical Disease Control

Just as humans weakened from fatigue or malnutrition are more vulnerable to illnesses, turfgrasses stressed by environmental factors are more susceptible to infection by diseases. Drought-stressed turf is more susceptible to damage from diseases such as red thread or dollar spot. Mowing too short weakens turf and makes it more susceptible to leaf spot diseases. Excessive fertilization encourages the development of diseases such as Pythium blight or brown patch, but inadequate fertilization promotes red thread and dollar spot.

Turfgrasses more easily resist diseases when a properly selected turf species is grown under adequate environmental conditions. If the site is shady, establish a lawn grass that will tolerate the amount of shade. Provide appropriate air circulation by selectively thinning out limbs or removing dense vegetation around the site. If drainage is a problem, the soil may need to be internally drained using tile drainpipe or a French drain system.

Reducing thatch, increasing sunlight, regulating fertilizer applications, and mowing properly promotes vigorous turfgrass growth and reduces the environmental factors that favor fungal development.

Detecting and Identifying Turfgrass Diseases
There are two types of disease symptoms to look for in turfgrass when you suspect a disease problem: symptoms that affect the lawn as a whole, creating patterns in the grass itself, and symptoms that affect each grass plant individually.

TABLE 4.15 Disease calendar for cool-season grasses

Disease	Jan	Feb	Mar	Apr	May	June	July	Aug	Sep	Oct	Nov	Dec
Brown Patch						█	█	█				
Dollar Spot					█	█	█	█	█	█	█	
Helminthosporium Leaf Spot			█	█	█			█	█	█		
Helminthosporium Root Rot					█	█	█	█	█	█		
Pythium Blight					█	█	█	█	█			
Fusarium Patch	█	█	█							█	█	█
Fairy Ring	█	█	█	█	█	█	█	█	█	█	█	█
Rust			█	█	█	█			█	█	█	
Stripe Smut	█	█	█	█	█	█	█	█	█	█	█	█
Slime Mold					█	█	█	█	█			
Red Thread	█	█	█	█	█	█						
Nematodes					█	█	█	█	█	█	█	

TABLE 4.16 Disease calendar for warm-season grasses

Disease	Jan	Feb	Mar	Apr	May	June	July	Aug	Sep	Oct	Nov	Dec
Large Patch				■	■	■			■	■	■	
Dollar Spot				■	■	■			■	■	■	
Spring Dead Spot			■	■	■							
Leaf Spots				■	■	■	■	■				
Gray Leaf Spot						■	■	■				
Fairy Ring	■	■	■	■	■	■	■	■	■	■	■	■
Zoysia Rust						■	■	■	■	■		
Pythium Blight					■	■	■	■				
St. Augustine Decline				■	■	■	■	■	■			
Slime Molds				■	■	■	■	■				
Centipede Decline			■	■	■	■	■					
Nematodes				■	■	■	■	■	■	■	■	

Figure 4.34 Many diseases have noticeable symptoms to circlular or ring-shaped damage.
Image Credit: Adam Gore, Clemson University

Figure 4.35 Large patch disease in zoysiagrass.
Image Credit: Adam Gore, Clemson University

First, look at the entire turf area to identify any visible patterns, such as a circular patch, spots, rings, or circles (Figure 4.34). Sometimes, disease symptoms do not show any type of pattern.

After examining the entire lawn, inspect individual plants in the affected area. On individual plants, look for leaf spots, leaf blighting, wilt, yellow, stunting, and root rot. Leaf spots can be an important diagnostic clue, as spots of different diseases are usually unique in shape, size, and color. Also take note of the infected grass type and determine if any surrounding weeds are also affected. Consider recent weather conditions.

For specific chemical control recommendations for individual pests, consult with your local county Extension agent. Below are some of the diseases often found in South Carolina lawns.

Brown Patch or Large Patch.

Time of damage: Cool-season grasses are attacked during warm, humid weather and the disease develops rapidly when nighttime temperatures reach or exceed 78°F. Warm-season grasses typically show damage during the spring, when grasses emerge from dormancy, or in fall, as grasses transition to dormancy. Infections on warm-season grasses normally occur during fall transition.

Symptoms: Individual diseased patches of turf may be several feet in diameter (Figure 4.35). Under drier conditions, affected areas may be smaller and appear sunken due to collapse of diseased leaves. Grass in the center of patches may appear unaffected or recover more rapidly than grass at the margins; this results in ring- or doughnut-shaped areas. Sometimes an area may be thinned and eventually killed by the pathogen. This is often seen in St. Augustinegrass growing in moist, shady locations.

Examination of individual infected leaves reveals gray or tan lesions with tan or brown borders. If conditions are only marginally favorable for disease development, only leaf lesions may develop. However, if conditions remain favorable for disease development, entire leaves may be consumed.

Control: Avoid high-nitrogen fertilization, especially to cool-season grasses during warm temperatures—when they're under stress—and to warm-season grasses in the fall or spring—when the disease is likely to appear. Monitor irrigation cycles, as the disease thrives on excessive moisture. Preventative fungicide treatments provide the best control.

Pythium Blight.

Time of damage: Though warm-season grasses are susceptible to some *Pythium* species—particularly as seedlings—cool-season grasses are more commonly damaged by Pythium blight. Pythium blight can be devastating to swards of ryegrass during hot (80-95°F), wet, or very humid weather, especially when air movement is limited. Young ryegrass or bluegrass plants used for overseeding are most susceptible in late summer or early fall. Large areas of turf can show damage overnight.

Symptoms: Round or irregular spots, from an inch in diameter on closely mowed turf up to several inches in diameter on higher cut turfgrass, can appear suddenly. The leaves in affected spots appear water-soaked, slimy to the touch, and copper colored, dark brown, or black when the disease is active. As humidity and/or temperature decreases, spots appear straw-colored and lesions on leaves are tan and lack a distinct border between diseased and green tissue. Generally, leaves in the centers of diseased patches or spots are completely blighted and do not show distinct lesions.

Control: Good surface and subsurface drainage are paramount. Increase air movement and light availability; decrease nitrogen fertilization. When practical, delay seeding cool-season grasses to avoid high temperatures in late summer. When conditions favor disease development, apply fungicide.

Dollar Spot.

Time of damage: Occurs during warm, humid weather (on most South Carolina turfgrass species).

Symptoms: On closely mowed turf, small patches of 1-2-in. diameter spots develop. On higher cut turf, patches may exceed 5 in. in diameter (Figure 4.36). Individual diseased grass leaves exhibit characteristic lesions which are tan or bleached with distinct reddish-brown or purplish margins. Leaves may be girdled and collapse at the lesions even though the leaf tips remain

Figure 4.36 Dollar spot on zoysiagrass is often associated with insufficient nitrogen fertilizer and thatch buildup.
Image Credit: Adam Gore, Clemson University

green. When active, tufts of fungal growth that look like shredded cotton are visible, frequently in early morning. Often confused with Pythium blight.

Control: Balance fertility to avoid nitrogen deficiencies and reduce the severity of the disease. Irrigate during early morning hours to limit periods of high humidity and leaf wetness. Mow regularly and at correct height and manage thatch regularly to reduce disease pressure. Several fungicides provide excellent control, but their use is generally unnecessary for home lawns.

Helminthosporum Diseases (Melting Out, Leaf Spot, Net-Blotch, Crown and Root Rot).

Time of damage: These diseases are caused by various species of *Bipolaris, Curvularia*, and *Drechslera*; because there are multiple species and genus represented, temperature ranges vary substantially—allowing for the possibility of damage throughout the year. However, all of these related diseases require films of moisture to be present on leaf tissues for spore germination and infection. Thus, these diseases are more common during prolonged periods of wet or humid weather.

Symptoms: Gradual browning and thinning occur over a period of weeks or months. As the disease progresses, larger irregular areas turn tallow, then brown, and thin out. On bermudagrass or zoysiagrass, small linear brown lesions appear on leaf blades and sheaths in spring or fall and may expand to larger irregular lesions with tan, white, or straw-colored centers.

Drechslera species, which primarily cause disease on cool-season grasses, cause leaf spots during cool, humid conditions, with crown and root phases occurring in warm, dry weather or during wet periods following dry periods. Leaf lesions are generally distinct and begin as tiny water-soaked areas that become dark brown to purplish black. These lesions are usually surrounded by a yellow area of carrying width that fades to the normal green of the leaf tissue. Older lesions may have a white or bleached area in the center.

Control: Avoid high-nitrogen fertilization and watering practices that leave plants wet for prolonged periods. Frequent mowing at proper heights will help grass dry more quickly in the turf canopy. Fungicides are necessary for high-maintenance turf areas.

Spring Dead Spot.

Time of damage: Symptoms appear during spring transition on bermudagrass, particularly on sterile hybrid cultivars. Infection occurs during the fall and generally begins to appear in bermudagrass that is 3-6 years old. More common in the Piedmont and Mountains than in the Coastal Plains.

Symptoms: Dead, sometimes sunken, circular areas of turf present as bermudagrass breaks dormancy in spring. Patches may be 2-3 ft. in diameter with some healthy grass in center.

Control: Maintain a balanced fertilization program, avoiding high rates of nitrogen in late summer. Avoid practices that increase thatch development and follow appropriate thatch mitigation strategies. Many fungicide applications vary in efficacy from year to year but applications should be made in the fall when soil temperatures are between 60-80°F.

Gray Leaf Spot.

Time of damage: This disease is most commonly seen on St. Augustinegrass and tall fescue during very hot and humid weather.

Symptoms: Infected leaves and stems have small, tan, oblong lesions with purple borders (Figure 4.37). The gray spores are sometimes visible during warm, wet weather. When the disease is severe, the entire lawn may look scorched.

Control: Collect and dispose of infected clippings while mowing. During growing season, use moderate amounts of nitrogen fertilizer, preferably that contains 25-50% of the nitrogen in a slow-release form. Improve air movement and light penetration. Schedule irrigation for early morning hours to promote maximum drying during the day. Equipment moved between properties should be washed before entering new property.

Figure 4.37 Leaf lesions of gray leaf spot on St. Augustinegrass
Image Credit: Adam Gore, Clemson University

Fairy Rings.

Symptoms: Fairy rings appears as rings or arcs of green, stimulated turf which may or may not be accompanied by adjacent areas of dead or declining grass. There may also be large mushrooms visible along these edges.

Some fungi associated with fairy rings produce toxic substances which can accumulate in the soil and kill turfgrass. More often, problems develop when mushroom mycelia accumulate in the soil and cause the soil to become hydrophobic (hard to wet). The turfgrass becomes stressed and declines due to the lack of water. Fairy rings may persist from year to year and usually increase in diameter each year. The fungi that cause fairy rings feed on old roots, stumps, thatch, and other organic accumulations.

Control: Fairy rings are difficult to control; you may have limited success by tilling the area thoroughly and deeply. Sometimes, prolonged irrigation that saturates the soil for several hours or days can mask toxins or leach them from the soil. If fairy rings are occurring consistently around trees over several growing seasons, it may be futile to try eradicating the fungi. In this case, consider mulching underneath the trees or planting ground covers.

Managing Nematodes

In many sandy soils in the southeastern United States, nematodes are among the most noteworthy and least understood turfgrass pests. Nematode damage is more common in the South than in most other places. Sandy soils, drought conditions, and a long growing season foster high nematode populations and make turfgrasses more sensitive.

Nematode Life Cycles

Nematodes are tiny, unsegmented roundworms, generally transparent and colorless. Most have slender bodies that are 1/100-1/8 in. in length. This makes them nearly invisible to the unaided eye.

Plant-parasitic nematodes have a simple life cycle consisting of six stages: the egg, four juvenile stages, and adulthood. Inside the egg, the embryo develops into a first-stage juvenile. The first-stage juvenile then molts within the egg to become a second-stage juvenile, which then hatches from the egg. In most species, this second-stage juvenile must feed before continuing its development. The nematode will then molt three more times before reaching its adult stage.

Male and female nematodes occur in most species, and both are often required for reproduction. Reproduction without males is common, however; some species are hermaphroditic, so "females" produce both sperm and egg.

The length of a nematode's life cycle varies considerably depending on the species, its host plant, and the temperature of its habitat. Rates of activity, growth, and reproduction increase as soil temperature rises from about 50-90°F. Under optimum conditions—usually 81°F—it takes at least four weeks for nematodes to generate.

Nematode Habitats and Their Effects on Plants

Plant nematodes are aquatic animals that live in soil water or plant fluids and feed on living plant tissues to survive. All have some form of a hollow oral stylet or spear, like a hypodermic needle, used to puncture the host cell wall (Figure 4.38). Many nematodes inject enzymes into the host cell before feeding. These enzymes partially digest the cell contents before they are sucked into the nematode gut. Most of the injury that nematodes cause to plants is related in some way to this feeding process.

Growth-regulating chemicals in the saliva of some nematodes causes root galling while the feeding of others can stop the growth of roots, causing stubby, swollen root tips and lateral root proliferation. As they move within the roots, endoparasitic nematodes can cause open wounds that allow organisms that cause rot and wilt diseases to invade. The wounds and other effects of feeding often cause physiological changes in plants, making them more susceptible to many diseases—sometimes even breaking the disease-resistance of cultivars. Some plant nematodes can serve as a vector for plant viruses. Nematodes feed on plant tissue from outside the plant (ectoparasitic) and within the plant tissue (endoparasitic). Migratory species refer to those in which the adult females move freely through the soil of plant tissue; sedentary species are those in which the females become permanently immobile.

Nematode Species

Below, we list the nematode species that affect turf and indicate the lowest numbers of each kind of nematode that will likely cause significant damage. Properly maintained turf can often withstand much higher populations than the minimal actional levels cited (AL = number of nematode per 100 cc soil).

Sting Nematode (*Belonolaimus longicaudatus*). Sting nematodes damage all common grasses in South Carolina, although bahiagrass is somewhat tolerant. Generally, they are only found in very sandy soils; given favorable conditions, the sting nematode is the most damaging nematode pest of lawn grasses (AL = 10).

Lance Nematode (*Hoplolaimus spp.*). Lance nematodes are common due to their willingness to attack all commonly grown grasses. They are easily distributed with sod, sprigs, and plugs and adapt readily to many soil conditions. They are the most noteworthy nematode pest found in St. Augustinegrasses (AL = 40).

Ring Nematode (*Criconemella spp.*). Ring nematodes are widely distributed. They are found on all turfgrasses but are only considered a major pest on centipedegrass. If populations are high enough, they can also damage bermudagrass and zoysiagrass (AL = 150 for centipedegrass; 500 for most others).

Root-Knot Nematode (*Meloidogyne spp.*). Root-knot nematodes are widely distributed but are most frequently found on St. Augustinegrass, zoysiagrass, and bermudagrass. The effects of these nematodes on turf are not well known, but they are believed to be injurious at high population densities (AL = 80).

Stubby-Root Nematode (*Paratrichodorus spp.* and related genera). Stubby-root nematodes live in most soils in the Coastal Plain. Damage appears similar to that caused by sting nematodes. (AL = 40).

Diagnosing Nematodes

Plant-parasitic nematodes—alone and in combination with other stressors, such as drought, insufficient nutrition, and fungal diseases—can cause serious damage to lawns. The largest problem in identifying nematodes as the cause of damage is that symptoms of nematode damage look exactly like symptoms of several

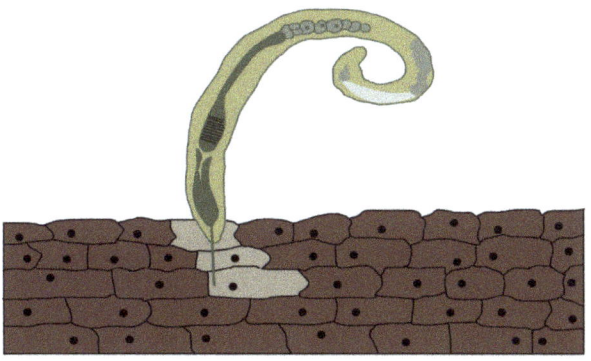

Figure 4.38 Stylets are used by nematodes to pierce cell walls in order to feed.

Figure 4.39 Zoysiagrass that has thinned out due to nematode infestation.
Image Credit: Barry McGrath, Cold Creek Nursery

Figure 4.40 Side by side bentgrass cores showing sting nematode damage compared to normal roots.
Image Credit: Joseph Roberts, Clemson University

other environmental problems, such as nutritional deficiency, drought, and heat stress.

Above-Ground Symptoms. Nematodes can cause wilting, thinning, gradual decline, and yellowing of leaves, but do not cause lesions or deformities. Since most plant-parasitic nematodes affect roots, most above-ground symptoms are the result of inadequate water supply or mineral nutrition, such as wilting under moderate moisture stress, recovering slowly after rainfall or irrigation cycles, and thinning in the canopy (Figure 4.39). Turfgrass weakened by nematode damage is unable to compete with invading weeds such as sedges, spurges, and Florida pusley.

Root Symptoms. Root systems injured by nematodes are usually dark, short, and lacking normal lateral or "feeder" roots (Figure 4.40). Some nematodes feed on root tips and induce a short, excessively-hairy root system. These symptoms are typical of damage by sting, awl, or high populations of stubby-root nematodes. Some nematodes induce swellings, root lesions, and stubby, swollen root tips; the result is accelerated rotting or blackening of roots and a propensity for wilting. Heavily affected root systems have much less soil clinging to them than do unaffected turfgrass stands; you can see this in plugs.

Damage Patterns. Nematode populations are unevenly distributed in soil, so there is great potential for encountering large variations in numbers even within the same few feet of soil. Nematode movement within soil is slow. In undisturbed turf, visible symptoms may appear as round, oval, or irregularly lobed areas that gradually increase in size. Nematode damage is often seen first and most pronouncedly in areas under stress from traffic, excessive drainage, or insufficient irrigation.

Sampling for Nematodes

Performing a soil assay for nematode identification is the surest way to determine whether a problem in the turf is caused by plant-parasitic nematodes. To collect a sample for assay:

- Take samples when soil is moist but not wet. A single sample should include 10-20 smaller samples from the root zone of symptomatic and non-symptomatic areas. The composite sample should be one quart of soil. Ideally, gather samples using a 1-in. core sampler; if that is not available, use a shovel to cut through the soil profile and take a 1-2-in. slice from the edge of the opening to simulate a soil core.
- Sample turf sites in a zig-zag pattern. If there are dead or dying areas, take the sample from along the border between the good and poor areas.
- Place the mixed sample in a sealed plastic bag, labeled with your name and sample number.

Label the outside of the bag with location information using a permanent marker. Fill out the submission form as completely as possible. Accurate information helps the diagnosticians do a better job for you.
- Keep samples cool—below 80°F—and out of direct sunlight. Do not put samples in the back of trucks, in car trunks, or on non-insulated floorboards of vehicles. Take the samples to your county Extension office for processing.

Managing Nematodes

A nematode assay identifies the species of nematode infesting a lawn, but it also identifies the approximate size of the nematode infestation. When considering what or how much action to take to control a nematode population in your turfgrass, consider professional advice alongside personal preference, aesthetic standards, and budget. Due to heavy restriction, no nematicide is available for use by homeowners; only certified pesticide applicators can apply nematicides. This excess cost places a greater emphasis on managing nematodes through cultural practices.

Cultural Practices. The goal of cultural practices in nematode management is to minimize stress on the turfgrass. To facilitate the deeper penetration of roots into the soil, irrigate deeply and less frequently rather than providing a shallow, daily watering. However, sandy soils with significant nematode infestations may require more frequent irrigation to compensate for the soil conditions and damaged root system. To achieve adequate filtration oxygen levels in the soil, core with narrow, hollow tines or spikes in late spring and early summer. Cultivate during times of the year when turf can best recover: late spring and early summer for warm-season grasses and mid-spring or early fall for cool-season grasses.

Avoid excessive fertilization with water-soluble nitrogen, since succulent growth causes a flush in nematode population. Turfgrass also benefits from the addition of organic matter to improve soil structure and moisture- and nutrient-holding capacity.

Diagnosing Turfgrass Damage

Often, the sudden appearance of thin, yellowing, or damaged turf causes alarm. A gardener's mind may jump immediately to disease or insects; in truth, a majority of damage or problems in turf management is related to human error and poor management.

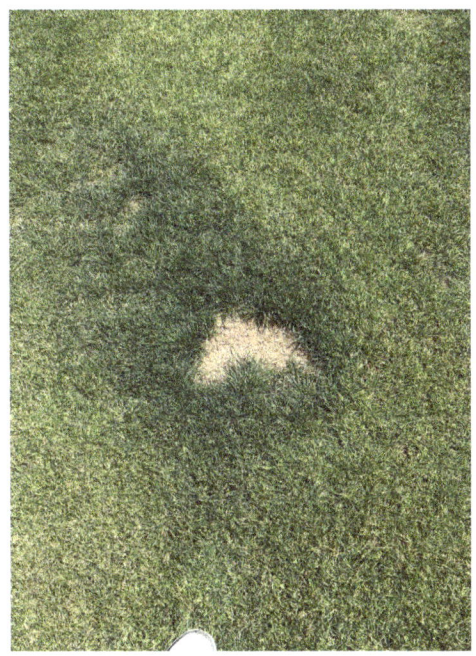

Figure 4.41 Ryegrass damaged by the dumping of leftover fertilizer into a single pile.
Image Credit: Adam Gore, Clemson University

Figure 4.42 Damage to bermudagrass as a result of wet tires carrying carrying excess soluble nitrogen fertilizer onto wet grass resulting in burning of foliage.
Image Credit: Adam Gore, Clemson University

When diagnosing problems, look for patterns. Damage resulting from humans is normally uniform, with a distinct pattern of straight lines. Living organisms damaging turf—whether they are diseases, insects, or something else—have more scattered symptoms. The following figures show how poor management, accidents, and carelessness can cause as much damage as a living pest.

Figure 4.43 Zoysiagrass failing to break dormancy due to the presence of excessive chaff from excessive mowing heights.
Image Credit: Adam Gore, Clemson University

Figure 4.44 St. Augustinegrass damaged by metal siding laying on grass during high temperatures.
Image Credit: Adam Gore, Clemson University

ORGANIC LAWN CARE

"Organic" is defined as containing carbon or carbon-composed compounds. Most products used in lawn care contain carbon; technically, they are organic. However, in a broader sense, "organic" refers to "natural" or "naturally-derived" products or those products not grown with "synthetic" inputs.

Organic lawn care relies on the same basic principles and techniques of turfgrass culture discussed previously in this chapter. As with conventional lawn care, each maintenance practice influences another. When and how much you fertilize affects how often you mow; your mowing height affects how often you need to water and how many weeds you have. However, unlike conventional lawn care—which involves synthetic fertilizers and pesticides—organic lawn care relies on organic or naturally-derived products to fertilize the lawn and cultural or biological techniques to manage pests. This natural approach promotes the long-term benefits of a healthy soil—which creates favorable growing conditions for the turfgrass and the soil-dwelling inhabitants.

The main goal of organic lawn care is to work with nature to create a healthy, well-managed lawn that can resist invasion from weeds and attacks from insects and diseases. Organic lawn care works like preventive healthcare: prevent problems from occurring to avoid having to treat them. The suggestions below will help you establish and maintain a healthy, attractive organic lawn.

Develop Healthy Soil

Good soil is the foundation of a healthy lawn. Have your soil analyzed for organic matter content, soil pH, and nutrient content. If you are establishing a new lawn, add organic matter such as compost. Organic matter improves drainage in clay soils and water retention in sandy soils. It also improves soil structure, which benefits the lawn and the earthworms and microbes that break down thatch and organic matter and make the nutrients available to the grass plants.

Add organic matter to established lawns by topdressing regularly with no more than 0.25 in. of compost at a time, worked into the turf. Topdress cool-season lawns in the fall and warm-season lawns in late spring to early summer, after they emerge from dormancy. Aerify on a regular basis, especially if the lawn is subject to traffic.

Choose Appropriate Grasses for Your Region and Management Style

Select a turfgrass that is adapted to the soil and climate of your specific site. Choose a turfgrass variety that can tolerate or resist pest pressures. As described previously in this chapter, grasses differ in their appearance, adaptation, ability to tolerate pests, and ideal growing conditions.

Use Organic Fertilizers Derived from Natural Sources

Organic fertilizers are derived from naturally occurring sources, usually waste or the byproducts of processing organic goods; they could include composted animal manure, cottonseed meal, blood meal, and other substances (Table 4.17). Although organic fertilizers contain relatively low concentrations of nutrients—usually 2-10% nitrogen—compared to synthetic fertilizers, they increase the organic matter content of the soil and improve soil structure. Be careful with organic fertilizers to ensure they do not contain weed seeds. Excessive nitrate or uric acid present in the fertilizer, as is often found in poultry manure, can burn the lawn if not applied correctly.

Organic fertilizers rely on soil microorganisms to slowly break down the materials and release the nutrients. This can take several weeks or longer for the nutrients to become available to the grass plants. Extended dry periods or cold temperatures may hamper the activity of microorganisms, further delaying the release of nitrogen

TABLE 4.17 Potential organic fertilizer sources.

Nutrient	Product	Source(s)	Comments
Nitrogen	Natural organic fertilizers	Municipal sludge, composted poultry litter, animal proteins, bone meal, wheat germ, manure, feather meal	Most contain a complete N-P-K ratio, but N rates are low (2 to 10%); some also supply micronutrients.
		Seaweed, kelp extracts	Source of N, Fe, and some micro- nutrients; often mixed with organic matter sources to encourage rooting and stress resistance.
Phosphorous	Bone meal	Pulverized poultry bones	More readily available P; dust; often hard to apply.
	Colloidal phosphate	Mine industry by-product	Contains 0-20-0. Slow-acting, long-lasting.
	Rock phosphate	Mining	Contains 0-33-0. Slow-acting, long-lasting.
Potassium	Wood ash	Fireplaces	Contains up to 4% elemental K; also a source of lime to raise soil pH.
	Sul-Po-Mag	Mining	Available as 0-0-21. Fast-acting, high burn potential.
	Granite dust	Mining by-product	Contain 0-0-5. Slow acting, long-lasting.
	Greensand	Mining	Contains 0-1-6. Slow-acting, long-lasting.
	Compost	Home and lawn trimmings	Contains up to 1% elemental K.
Iron	Humates	Mined extractions	Sources of various nutrients including iron.

from organic fertilizers. Before fertilizing your lawn, have your soil tested every two or three years through your local Extension service. Maintain the appropriate soil pH for your lawn grasses and select fertilizers that will apply minerals that are deficient in the soil. A soil pH between 6-6.5 (or 5.5-6.0 for centipede and carpetgrass), adequate moisture and oxygen, and temperatures of at least 50-55°F enhance microbial activity and the release of nutrients.

Mow Appropriately

Follow these basic rules of proper mowing to maintain a healthy, dense lawn.

Use a Sharp Mower Blade

Sharp blades cut grass cleanly, ensuring rapid healing and regrowth. When dull blades tear and rip the leaves, the wounded grass plants are weakened, appear ragged, and become more vulnerable to weeds, disease, and insects.

Mow Your Lawn Regularly, but Only When Dry

A good rule of thumb is to remove no more than 1/3 of the grass height at any single mowing. For example, if you are maintaining your centipedegrass lawn at 1.5 in., mow the lawn when it is about 2 in. tall. Following the 1/3 rule produces smaller clippings that disappear more quickly by filtering down to the soil surface. Mowing when grass is wet encourages clumping of clippings leading to potential ripping and uneven mowing. Additionally, most fungal spores prefer higher levels of moisture thus mowing in wet areas can serve as a mean for fungal dispersion.

Mow Your Lawn to the Proper Height

By maintaining a lawn to the appropriate height, you will create a dense lawn that can outcompete weeds for sunlight, water, and nutrients. In the summer, gradually raise the mowing heigh by ¼-½ in. A higher mowing height encourages deeper root growth and greater access to water and nutrients. Refer to the previous section on "Mowing" for suggested mowing practices.

Recycle Grass Clippings While Mowing

Returning your grass clippings to the lawn saves time, energy, and money. Additionally, using clippings as a fertilization source can provide up to 25% of a lawn's annual nutrient requirement.

Water Wisely

Irrigate your lawn only when it truly needs water. Irrigate when the lawn shows the signs of moisture stress listed in the "Irrigating" section above: bluish-gray color; footprints that remain imprinted on the lawn; and wilted, folded, or curled leaves. Water deeply, 0.75-1 in. of water at a time, or until runoff begins to occur. Deep watering encourages deeper roots and stronger plants.

Aerify Compacted Soils

Soil compaction occurs when particles in the top 4 in. of soil are compressed, reducing the size of the pore spaces between them and impeding the movement of air, water, and nutrients to grass roots. In turn, this impeded movement stresses the grass plants, making them less able to compete with weeds and slowing recovery from injury. In time, a compacted lawn needs renovation.

Compaction is likely in areas with high traffic; when heavy equipment rolls repeatedly over an existent or soon-to-be lawn—especially when it's wet—it compresses and compacts the soil. Sandy soils are less likely to become compacted than those comprised of clay and silt. See the previous section, "Aerifying," for more information on alleviating compaction.

Correct Thatch Buildups

For most turfgrasses, thatch causes problems when it exceeds ½ in. in thickness. The grass develops roots within the thatch layer, where it's unable to obtain adequate moisture or minerals. The thatch also provides a habitat for destructive insects and disease-causing organisms. Prevent a thatch problem by properly maintaining your turf using cultural practices.

Work with nature to manage pests. A healthy, organic lawn is likely to have some type of pest problem. However, it will also have beneficial insects and other organisms that help keep pests under control. Maintain a strong, healthy lawn to help it ward off weed invasions or cope with insects or diseases. When pest problems need attention, use cultural and biological controls to manage them.

Figure 4.45 Cuticle burning of bermudagrass and weedy plant species resulting from a single application of an organic herbicide product such as vinegar.
Image Credit: Adam Gore, Clemson University

Manage Weeds

The best form of weed control is prevention. Follow good cultural practices that favor the growth and development of the lawn grasses; simply mowing with a sharp blade at the recommended height and frequency helps lawns fight weeds naturally.

When weeds occur, figure out what sparked the invasion. If you don't address the cause, weeds will continue to grow despite attempts to remove them. Weeds often appear because of poor management techniques, such as improper mowing, watering, or fertilizing. Other factors that can indirectly lead to a weak or thin stand of grass include insects, disease, compacted soil, and thatch. Weeds will eventually invade weak areas. Several weed species serve as indicators of the surrounding environment and may serves as clues to the lawn's weakness.

Although it can be time consuming, hand pull weeds when the soil is moist. For perennial weeds that come back year after year from underground plants parts, remove as much of the root system as possible; any remaining pieces of rhizomes or roots will develop into new plants. If you choose to use a nonselective herbicide to control weeds, spot-treat with a postemergent herbicide containing ingredients such as potassium salts of fatty acids or acetic and citric acids. Organic pesticides primarily use salts or various pH levels to burn plant tissue (Figure 4.45). This provides a burndown effect but has little impact on plants with an extensive root system.

A preemergence herbicide containing corn gluten meal inhibits root development in certain germinating weed seeds. This yellow powder, which is a by-product of corn processing, has long been used as an additive to animal feed. It's labeled as a preemergent herbicide for use on turfgrass, field crops, and home gardens. Corn gluten meal can control crabgrass, dandelions, smartweed, redroot pigweed, purslane, lamb's-quarters, foxtail, and barnyard grass. Both powdered and pelleted forms of corn gluten meal are available.

Timing is important to best control weeds. Corn gluten meal must be applied just prior to weed seed germination. If applied too early, the corn gluten meal has a limited effect due to soil microbes; if applied too late, it will do little to reduce root growth.

Corn gluten meal is most effective at controlling weed emergence during periods of drought; when soil particularly moist, many weeds survive despite their stunted root systems. Nevertheless, research indicates that corn gluten meal grants up to 80% control of weeds over a three-year period. Corn gluten meal herbicide, which contains 10% nitrogen by weight, must be applied at a higher rate than conventional herbicides. This translates to as much as a threefold increase in cost per square foot. Nevertheless, you can experiment with this organic herbicide by trying it on small areas to see if you're pleased with the results.

Manage Insects

A variety of insects attack lawn grasses. By maintaining your lawn, you can reduce your lawn's susceptibility to insects, allowing it to tolerate and bounce back from the damage caused by the insects' feeding. All other basic maintenance techniques—including proper fertilization, watering, mowing, and thatch control—can contribute to insect tolerance. Organic, slow-release fertilizers are a good choice, because they do not increase the succulence of the turf like fast-release synthetic fertilizers—which make the grass more attractive to some insects.

Follow an IPM approach to manage insect pests. First, grow an adapted, competitive grass. Then, monitor your lawn frequently for signs of insect damage. If you suspect the presence of a damaging insect, confirm your suspicion before taking appropriate action. Early detection and control lessen the chance of losing a large amount of lawn to an infestation.

Botanical pesticides are naturally occurring pesticides derived from plants. Two common botanicals include pyrethrins—insecticidal chemicals extracted from the pyrethrum flower (*Tanacetum cinerariifolium*)—and neem—a botanical insecticide and fungicide extracted from the tropical neem tree (*Azadirachta indica*) which contains the active ingredient azadirachtin.

Microbial insecticides combat damaging insects using microscopic living organisms like viruses, bacteria, fungi, protozoa, or nematodes. Although they may look like out-of-the-ordinary insecticides, they can be applied in ordinary ways—as sprays, dusts, or granules. The naturally occurring bacteria (*Bacillus popilliae*), which primarily infects Japanese beetle grubs, is a popular pathogen sold as milky spore powder that serves as a long-term biological approach to manage Japanese beetle grubs. However, milky spore has been only marginally effective in the South.

Parasitic nematodes (*Steinernema carpocapsae*) have proven to be quite effective against adult and very large mole cricket nymphs. However, as biological control agents and living organisms, they need to be handled carefully and according to manufacturer's instructions to ensure their survival.

In recent years, plant breeders have been working on creating varieties of lawn grasses that resist insects. This is done by introducing a fungus (endophyte) into the grass plant; the fungus produces a chemical toxic to insects. Because the toxin does not move to underground plant parts, this insect resistance is limited to surface feeders such as sod webworms and chinch bugs.

Disease Management

Proper lawn management practices will reduce the prevalence of disease in your lawn. Reducing thatch, increasing sunlight, fertilizing appropriately and at the right times of year, watering the soil deeply and infrequently—and late at night or early in the morning when dew has formed—and mowing properly all help reduce disease and ensure a vigorous lawn that can recover well from injury caused by disease.

Grow disease-resistant grasses to reduce the chances for disease outbreaks. When possible, use a blend of three or more varieties of cool-season grasses to take advantage of their varying levels of disease resistance.

An organically managed lawn requires a rich, healthy soil that harbors high populations of microorganisms that are antagonistic toward plant pathogens that cause lawn diseases. Research shows that well-aged compost contains organisms that suppress disease; these microorganisms starve the plant pathogens by feeding on nutrients that would otherwise support the growth and spread of fungal diseases.

Recently, several commercial fungicides have become available that differ from traditional fungicides in that their active ingredients are derived from wood-decaying fungi. They include active ingredients such as azoxystrobin and trifloxystrobin. These fungicides help control brown patch, pythium blight, snow mold, leaf spot, rust, take-all patch and some fairy rings. Although these new fungicides are not organic in their composition, there is an organic fungicide called a Bordeaux mixture that is made from copper sulfate and lime and is effective against some diseases in crops.

Set Realistic Goals

Be realistic about the quality of lawn that you want and the amount of time or money you have available to maintain that look. An organic lawn is unlikely to look like a perfect golf course putting green. A healthy lawn is likely to have some weeds or insect pests, but it will also have beneficial insects and other organisms that help keep pests under control.

Chapter 5
Trees and Shrubs

Revised and updated by: Paul Thompson, James F. Hodges, Laura Lee Rose, Barbara Smith, and Jordan Franklin

Previous version by: James F. Hodges, Ellen A. Vincent, and Bob Polomski

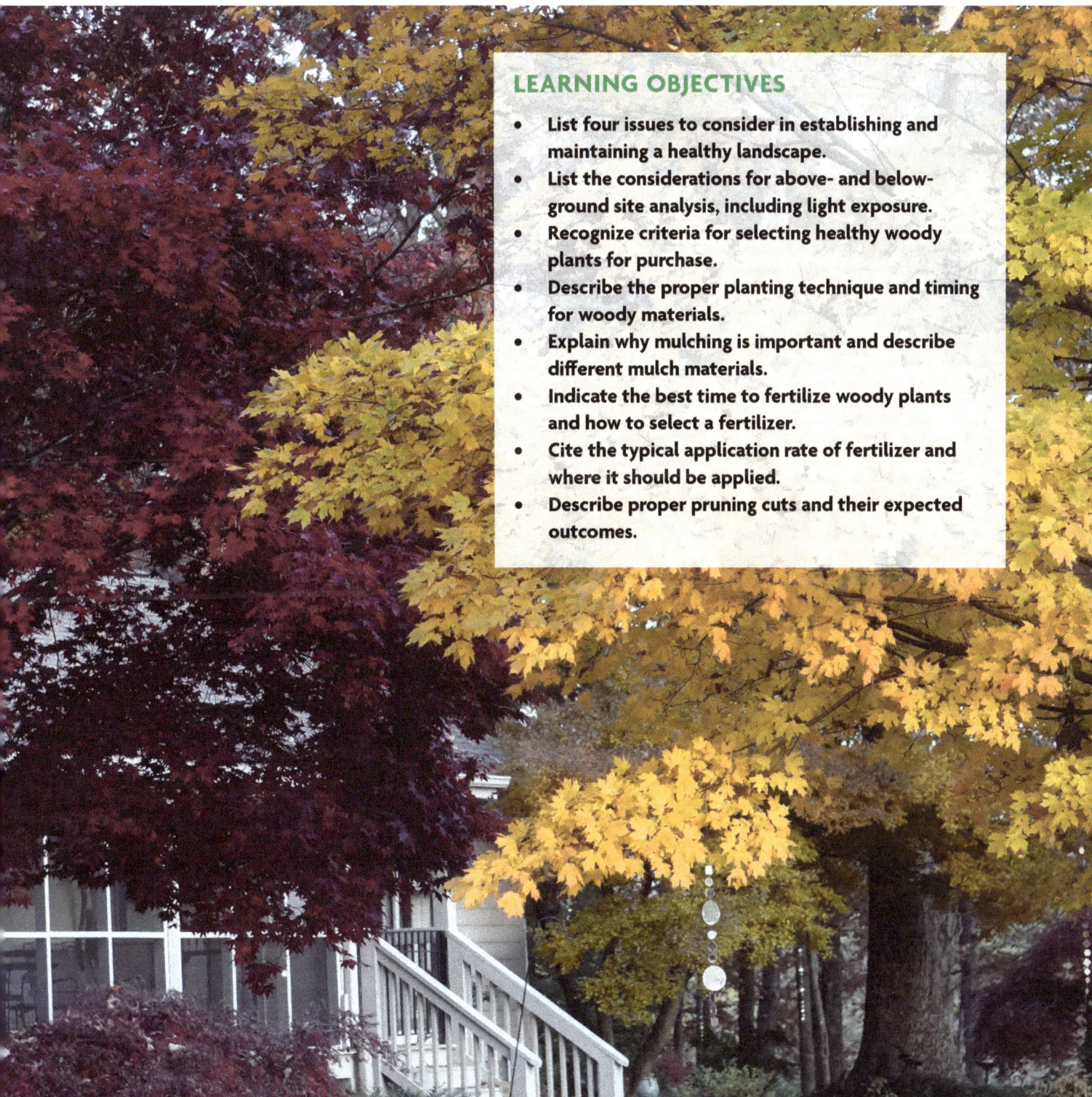

LEARNING OBJECTIVES

- List four issues to consider in establishing and maintaining a healthy landscape.
- List the considerations for above- and below-ground site analysis, including light exposure.
- Recognize criteria for selecting healthy woody plants for purchase.
- Describe the proper planting technique and timing for woody materials.
- Explain why mulching is important and describe different mulch materials.
- Indicate the best time to fertilize woody plants and how to select a fertilizer.
- Cite the typical application rate of fertilizer and where it should be applied.
- Describe proper pruning cuts and their expected outcomes.

INTRODUCTION

Public lands and gardens represent between 15-20% of the land area of South Carolina. We can no longer think of home landscapes and gardens as private islands (Figure 5.1). Our collective actions on the landscape are multiplied by the increasing number of managed home landscapes appearing as the state's population grows. Our actions in our own landscapes and home gardens affect our stewardship of the natural resources on which we depend. Sustainable landscaping has environmental, economic, and social dimensions.

Environmental

Plants provide many ecological benefits; from the oxygen we breathe to the food we eat. The fallen leaves and branches produced by plants enrich the soil, and beneficial soil microorganisms feed on decaying plant matter and add humus to the soil, which benefits plant growth. Plant roots hold soil particles and reduce soil erosion, and trees provide shade to counteract the heat that accumulates on and around hard urban surfaces. If you regularly compost, practice integrated pest management, or plant trees, you are enhancing the ecological services provided by plants.

Plants are the keystone of all life; they transform inorganic and organic nutrients and minerals into living tissues, wood, fibers, and leaves capable of synthesizing sugars, oils, and proteins. Plants produce fruits, nuts, flowers, and nectar, which are not only attractive landscaping features but also food for wildlife. If you grow food for yourself; cultivate plants that attract hummingbirds, butterflies, bees, and other pollinators; incorporate water features; or harvest rainwater from your roof with rain barrels or rain gardens, you are incorporating environmental sustainability into your landscape.

Figure 5.2 It only takes 1/10th of an inch of rainfall on a 1000ft^2 roof to fill a standard rain barrel
Image Credit: iStock

Figure 5.1 Although landscapes can be private islands, our actions impact the natural resources on which we depend.
Image Credit: Paul Thompson, Clemson University

Economic

Sustainability is an important consideration in selecting plants, maintaining existing features of a landscape, and planning future landscapes. Sustainable practices include conducting a proper site analysis, using locally sourced and sustainably produced materials, and choosing the right plants for the right places. The most sustainable plants can survive with little or no additional fertilization, pesticides, or irrigation. There are low-maintenance native plants and specific communities of plants to fill any niche in a landscape.

Plan your landscape depending on the level of maintenance you are willing and able to provide—or willing and able to pay someone else to provide. Consider a reasonable expectation of the effort and cost for weekly, monthly, quarterly, or yearly maintenance. Choosing woody plants of the appropriate mature size and growth habits for your site will reduce the need for pruning.

In the future, governments or communities may pass stricter regulations regarding water use; Municipalities

Figure 5.3 What a great place to read a book!
Image Credit: Paul Thompson, Clemson University

Climate

The plants you select should be suited to the climate of your region.

As referenced in Chapter 2: Botany and Plant Physiology, the United States is divided into a series of cold hardiness zones based on average minimum winter temperatures. A plant that is adapted to your hardiness zone can tolerate the lowest average winter temperatures, as indicated on the map.

In the Southeast, heat tolerance is also an important trait, since some plants native to colder climates suffer in the hot, humid summers of South Carolina. Information for specific climate zones for plant species and cultivars is usually indicated with a zone range; this range provides an indication of heat and cold tolerance. For example, sugar maple has a hardiness zone range of zone 3 to zone 8A, meaning that all or parts of 16 counties near the South Carolina coast do not have a summer climate suitable for growing a healthy and vigorous sugar maple tree.

In addition to the larger climate that governs the planting site, plants will be affected by factors within the site that modify the overall conditions, which are called microclimates (Figure 5.5). Taller plants will have a totally different microclimate than those at or near ground level. These microclimates may vary by several degrees, a difference that can mean life or death in extreme weather for marginal species.

Microclimates are influenced by sun exposure, existing vegetation, and nearby buildings. Take note of the differences on your site; keep in mind that generally,

and public service authorities already encourage the use of plants that establish quickly and need little or no supplemental irrigation.

Social

Gardens can provide cultural, intellectual, and spiritual inspiration, and they host a variety of recreational opportunities. If your home landscape inspires you to interact with the natural world, host outdoor gatherings, or spend quiet mornings in your garden, then it likely improves mental and physical well-being.

SITE ANALYSIS

Several factors should contribute to the creation of an attractive and successful landscape. Chief among them is a thorough assessment and understanding of the particular conditions of a site. These conditions include amounts of direct and indirect sunlight received throughout the day, exposure to wind—or salt spray in coastal areas —, and various above- and below-ground features, both natural and manmade, within the landscape.

The lack of a proper site analysis is often the cause of landscape problems and failures. Take time to evaluate your landscape site and envision what it will need and how it may change during different stages and seasons. Consider the following factors included in site analysis.

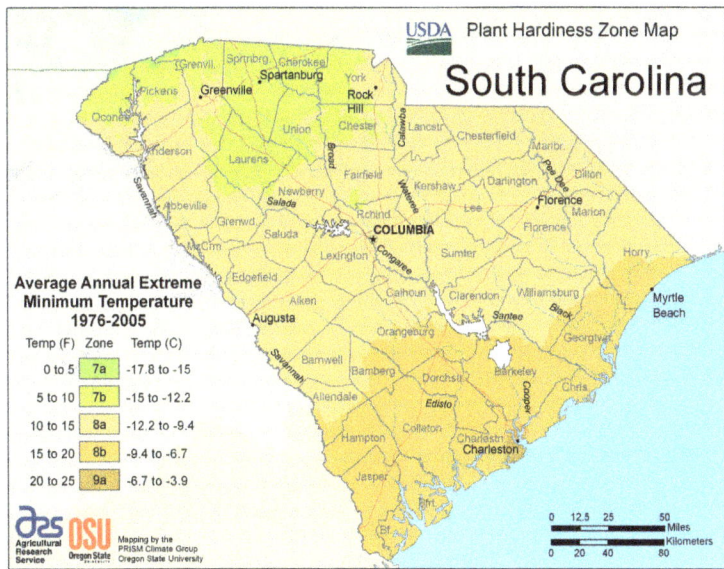

Figure 5.4 USDA Hardiness Zone Map for South Carolina
Image Credit: USDA Plant Hardiness Zone Map, 2012. Agricultural Research Service, U.S. Department of Agriculture. Accessed from https://planthardiness.ars.usda.gov/

Figure 5.5 Landforms, existing vegetation and structures create microclimates within a landscape.
Image Credit: Paul Thompson, Clemson University

minimum summer and winter temperatures occur on the north side of a house and maximum summer and winter temperatures occur in unshaded southwestern exposures. On the south side of a home, temperature fluctuations on a given winter day can be dramatic and may predispose plants to winter damage.

Tree canopies protect neighboring plants by reducing their radiant heat loss. In winter, the microclimate beneath a tree may be several degrees warmer than the surrounding air, and this small increase in temperature may be just enough to prevent winter injury. Furthermore, the tree's shade during the early morning slows the rate of thaw and can reduce the amount of cold damage to some species. Building overhangs, arbors, walls, and fences may provide similar kinds of protection.

Above-Ground Site Analysis

Exposure to Sunlight

All plants require sunlight, but some species need many hours of full sun while others do best largely in shade. Before choosing plants for your landscape, observe how many hours of sun and shade occur in different parts of your site. Remember to take into account that the angle of the sun changes with the time of year; you will probably have more hours of direct sun in summer than in other seasons, although plants growing in the shade of deciduous trees will receive more, less-intense sun in the winter months.

Plants requiring full sun, such as junipers, need at least 6 hours of direct sun daily. Often, they will produce the best form and growth if they receive sun the entire day. Most large trees grow best in full sun, while some small trees—such as dogwoods or Japanese maples—will often do best in sites that are shaded in the afternoon.

Plants that can tolerate full sun to partial sun/partial shade will need 3-4 hours of direct sun. Shade-loving plants will adapt to sites with less than 2 hours of direct sun or with filtered sun/filtered shade. Some shade-loving plants can tolerate direct exposure to early morning sun, but they may suffer if directly exposed to 2 or more hours of midday or afternoon sun.

Wind

Wind increases the amount of water lost from a plant to the atmosphere. If roots can grow into the surrounding area, uninhibited by compacted soil or by structures such as curbs, sidewalks, patios, buildings, and streets, water loss to wind may be inconsequential. However, the root systems of plants growing in confined situations, such as cutouts in city sidewalks, dry out the little available soil quickly and are highly vulnerable to wind desiccation. Likewise, plants in very sandy, well-drained soils are in a perilous situation if they do not receive adequate irrigation.

Well-managed irrigation systems can partially make up for these water deficits, but this may be difficult to accomplish in highly urbanized sites. The best way to manage water loss on a windy site is by selecting drought-tolerant species. If the site is poorly drained, select a species that can tolerate both dry and wet conditions.

Salt Spray

Airborne salt affects leaves and shoots; once it's deposited on the ground, it may also damage roots. Plants within 1/4 mi of saltwater coastlines should be somewhat tolerance to salt spray. Those exposed to direct spray along dunes need to be highly salt tolerant. Salt-tolerant plants can survive and grow in—but are often deformed by—direct exposure to salty air. Salt-sensitive plants grow poorly or die when exposed to salty air.

Overhead Power Lines

Plant trees that mature to a small height directly under or within 6 ft of overhead power lines. When planting within 6-50 ft of a utility line, size at maturity is still a critical consideration. Remember that a tree with a wide-spreading canopy must be planted further from

Figure 5.6 Pay attention to overhead utilities when selecting trees to avoid drastic pruning needs to protect electrical service.
Image Credit: Paul Thompson, Clemson University

the wire than a tree with a narrow, more upright canopy. For example, if a planting site is 20 ft from a power line, select a tree that—at maturity—will have a canopy that is less than 40 ft in diameter.

Existing Trees

When young trees or shrubs that require full sun are planted under or near the canopy of established trees, they will grow in the direction of the sunlight. Without adequate light reaching a plant from all sides, the plant tends to become one-sided. Although the plant is not necessarily damaged by this, it can be unsightly. Shade-tolerant plants are a better choice for planting in the shade of established trees.

Below-Ground Site Analysis

Soil and below-ground characteristics that significantly affect the growth and well-being of plants include soil pH level, drainage capacity, depth of topsoil, salinity, distance to the water table, and rooting-space limitations. Recent surveys show that most people do not take these factors into consideration when selecting plants, which may explain why so many plantings fail.

High-quality soil is precious and should not be wasted. When deciding to build on a site, planning before construction starts enables you to identify and preserve good soil. Make provisions to save and store high quality soil for use when construction is completed. Do not permit this soil to be hauled away or buried. Work with contractors to prevent excessive soil compaction in areas where trees currently exist or will be planted. These areas can be isolated with fencing with the understanding that fines will be levied for violations.

Often, plants must be selected for a site where construction has already been completed and the soil and terrain have been modified. Equipment operations may have caused problems, such as turning a moderately well-drained clay soil that would have been capable of supporting tree growth into compacted, poorly drained soil. Simply layering topsoil over the compacted soil will not promote healthy plant growth. Compacted soil must be broken up and mixed with loose soil or compost.

Landscapes in highly urbanized areas require more soil tests and site evaluation than older or undisturbed sites. Poor-quality subsoil is sometimes substituted for topsoil, and rubble or other debris is often mixed with soil. Examine soil throughout the planting site and test each type you find.

Soil pH

Soil pH governs the availability of nutrients to plants and affects the activity of microorganisms in the soil. It is the most important component of a soil test; don't assume you know or can guess the pH of a site's soil.

Conduct soil tests in several different areas of the planting site—wherever the soil color or texture appears distinctly different from elsewhere on the site. Soil pH may be lower or higher next to a building because of the sand or other materials used near the footings, or it may vary too much across the site to permit planting of the same species or cultivar throughout the entire landscape.

Soil Texture

While soil texture alone is not a growth-limiting factor, it does indicate other soil attributes that influence plant growth. For example, the dense texture of clay often drains poorly if the terrain is flat or if the soil has been compacted by heavy equipment. When planting in clay soil, determine whether drainage is poor or appropriate, and select plants that are adapted to the prevailing moisture level. On the other hand, many sandy soils drain quickly. If irrigation will not be provided on a regular basis after plants are established, choose drought-resistant species for a sandy-soiled site.

Nitrogen, potassium, and other essential elements leach more quickly from sandy soils. These elements can migrate below the root zone, which affects fertilization recommendations. A controlled, slow-release fertilizer is best for sandy soil, because soluble, fast-release nitrogen fertilizers leach quickly.

You can also consider choosing a native or adapted species that may be more tolerant of these infertile soils.

Compacted Low-Oxygen Soils

Compacted and poorly drained soils contain little oxygen, which plant roots need to survive and grow. Though some plants tolerate soils with low oxygen, most grow poorly or eventually succumb to disease or insect problems when planted in soil that is too compacted or too wet during certain times of the year. Although any type of soil can become compacted, clay is the most problematic.

To check for compaction and drainage, conduct the percolation test. Video 4 on the Clemson Extension Virtual Rain Garden web page will walk you through the process (https://www.clemson.edu/extension/raingarden/virtual_rain_garden.html). Another method for determining if a soil is poorly drained is to smell it. A sour smell and a gray color indicate low oxygen content. Occasionally, the sour smell may be strong enough to detect while standing near a dug hole. More often, you must break a soil clump close to your nose to detect the smell.

A site with a high water table or poor soil drainage can be altered to accommodate plants that are intolerant of wet, waterlogged soils. Create raised beds to elevate the plants' root systems. Crown beds with gently sloping sides to facilitate surface drainage. Often, you will also need to install subsurface drainage.

Compacted and poorly drained soils may be improved by the incorporation of organic matter via tilling. A ripping tool, which is dragged behind a bulldozer, can be used to loosen soil on a large site. Do not use the tiller or ripping tool under the drip line of trees and shrubs or you will cause serious damage to the root systems. Air spades are professional tools that can be used under the canopy of the tree. You can use these tools to expose the root collar and inspect for root problems, but you can also use them to loosen compacted soils and add organic amendments within the tree's root zone. Air spade services are available from specialty arboriculture firms. Remember that an ideal soil only contains 5% organic matter by weight; incorporating too much organic matter leads to soil subsidence as it breaks down and becomes consumed by microorganisms.

Subsurface Compacted Layers. Loose topsoil spread over compacted soil creates special challenges. Often, roots grow only in the loose soil and fail to penetrate the compacted subsoil; the resulting root system is shallow and can create unstable and potentially hazardous large trees. Consequently, it is best to plant only small- and medium-sized trees where there are less than 2 ft of loose soil spread over compacted subsoil.

In landscapes with subsurface compacted layers, the lowest areas are likely to be wet during certain times of the year. Within a day or two after a significant rainfall, evaluate the site and decide if it is necessary to choose plants more tolerant of wet conditions. If you conduct your evaluation during a drier time of the year, you may mistakenly conclude that your drainage is fine; consider how the site will change over time.

Artificial Soil Horizons

Most soils in urban areas—and many in suburban landscapes—are disturbed by heavy equipment before planting. This disturbance often brings poor quality subsoil with a fine texture, high clay content, or high pH to the surface. Construction debris and soils from other sites may be layered on top of one another to create an artificial soil profile or horizon. This structure disrupts the flow of water through the soil and can create areas that drain poorly. If there are abrupt changes in soil color as you dig a hole, this may indicate a drainage problem. If soil is mixed with bricks, concrete, or other construction debris, consider replacing the soil or sifting out the debris.

Soil Salinity

Some soils in coastal areas have a high salt content. If you are unfamiliar with the area or suspect that salts could be a problem, have the soil tested. Be mindful that irrigation water may also be salty. When using well water along the coast, have it tested. If fresh water is not available, choose salt-tolerant plants or those that have been growing well in your area with the available irrigation water.

Soil Depth

In the ideal planting site, the layer of soil above bedrock is at least 5-6 ft deep. Dig a hole to learn the depth of your soil layer. If bedrock is close to the surface or there is little soil for other reasons, it is best to plant only small- to medium-sized trees that will not grow into large trees. Trees that are large at maturity will likely form large surface roots when planted in shallow soil; these can disrupt foundations, driveways, sidewalks, curbing, and gardens. Furthermore, large trees with shallow root systems can topple over in storms.

Distance to the Water Table

Below-ground variations within a planting site and the surrounding terrain affect the distance between the soil surface and the top of the water table. The distance to the water table often varies throughout the year; you may find that the water table was within inches of the surface in one season but has dropped several feet below it during another. For the purposes of plant selection, consider sites with water within 1-2 ft of the soil surface (during at least part of the year) poorly drained.

To determine the distance to the water table, use a shovel or a 4-in. auger to dig several holes 2-3-ft deep around your planting site. Wait for 2 hr. If water appears in the hole, the water table is high, suggesting a need to select plants that tolerate wet sites. If the distance from the soil surface to the surface of the water is less than 18 in., only plant small- or medium-sized wet-site trees. Large, mature trees will adapt to wet sites by developing shallow root systems, which become unstable in storms.

The possible exceptions to these guidelines are trees that grow with submerged root systems, such as bald cypress (*Taxodium distichum*), and black gum (*Nyssa sylvatica*). If water does not appear in the hole, you will not have to consider the water table in choosing plants for that site.

Underground Utilities

Before digging or planting, determine the location of underground electric, telephone, and television cables, and water, sewer, and gas lines. Call 811—a single toll-free telephone number that will notify all companies at once—before you dig. Call several days before you plan to start digging. Digging holes without regard for underground utilities can cause serious personal injury as well as damage to the lines; the person(s) causing the damage pays for repairs.

Plant large, mature trees at least 12 ft from major underground utility lines; it is best to plant them as far away as possible. No tree should be planted directly over a utility line because the tree might be damaged or need to be removed if the line needs to be serviced.

Do not plant trees that are medium to large at maturity near septic tanks and drain fields, as they can cause damage with their roots. Although the roots of small maturing trees and shrubs can also invade septic tanks, they seldom cause extensive problems. To be safe, plant a tree at least as far from a potential underground trouble spot as the diameter of its canopy at maturity. For example, a tree expected to produce a 40-ft diameter canopy should be planted at least 40 ft from a septic tank or drain field.

SITE PREPARATION AND SOIL AMENDMENTS

Many planting sites require preparation before planting can begin. Preparations may include grading, tilling compacted soil, installing irrigation or other utilities, adding gutters to a roof to control runoff during heavy rains, terracing to retain runoff, amending soil, or other projects that will affect the conditions of the planting site.

Grading the soil to achieve the desired aesthetic is the first step in preparing the site. You must also create or install adequate surface drainage that directs water flow away from structures and planting beds and into an appropriate water path.

Compacted soil may be loosened by plowing or tilling, which can dramatically increase the rate of root growth and root penetration into the soil. Establishment takes less time, which reduces the period of the tree's vulnerability to pests, disease, and drought. Loosen the soil in at least a 15-20 ft diameter space around the area where you plan to plant the tree.

Most landscape soils are not modified with soil amendments prior to planting, and the plants grow well. However, adding organic matter such as compost to large planting beds will improve soil structure and increase fertility. Research shows that amending individual planting holes for trees and shrubs provides no increase in growth or survival of plants compared to un-amended backfill; in clay soils, amendments can increase plant mortality by retaining too much moisture. Adding compost to the planting hole increases drainage of surface water into the planting hole but does not improve drainage out of the planting hole.

PLANT SELECTION

You can plant only native plants, or you can combine them with adapted, nonnative, ornamental plants. Regardless of the plants' origins, it's most important that you select plants that are adapted to the environmental conditions in your area and that are non-invasive. From an aesthetic viewpoint, select plants that appear to fit comfortably and naturally into the surrounding landscape.

In selecting appropriate plants for a landscape, consider:

- how much maintenance the plant will require and its susceptibility to insects and diseases;
- if the wood is strong enough to withstand damage by wind and ice;
- if the fruits or seeds are large, messy, smelly, or otherwise undesirable; and
- if the tree is prone to abundant shedding of twigs and small branches.

For example, Indian hawthorn is prone to defoliation and dieback caused by *Entomosporium* leaf spot (See Figure 5.7). The limbs and trunks of Bradford pears are easily damaged by wind and ice. Female gingko trees, Gingko biloba, produce a particularly bad-smelling fruit. Even mulberry trees (*Morus spp.*) can be undesirable, because they produce a fruit that attracts birds and—when soft and ripe or decomposing—attracts flies and other insects.

Select plants according to their size at maturity, growth rate, and lifespan. Choosing a plant based on its mature size, not its size at the time of purchase, assures that you will have sufficient room for the plant to spread roots and that its ultimate height and spread will be compatible with buildings and surrounding areas. One common mistake is to choose plants that quickly outgrow their location. Drastic pruning becomes necessary, adding to maintenance costs and potentially altering the overall aesthetic. Overgrown plants left unpruned alter the balance and accent of the design and may partially hide the house or features they are meant to complement.

Consider the size of mature trees and shrubs and where they will be. Trees that mature to a size greater than 50 ft might be suitable beside two-story houses and larger buildings, but they tend to dominate and look out of scale beside one-story houses. For an attractive balance in the landscaping around single-story buildings, plant trees that do not grow to be over 35 ft tall. Shrubs that outgrow their spaces can hide windows, block walkways, or crowd out other plants (see Figure 5.8). You can sometimes prune shrubs to keep them small, but in this case, the shrub will require regular maintenance. Careful consideration of mature sizes will reduce the need for constant pruning.

Overplanting is another common mistake. It is difficult to visualize a young, one-gallon shrub reaching 5-6 ft in diameter at maturity. Learn the mature spread of plants and be sure to space each plant at least one-half the total spread of each plant. For example, if a plant spreads 4 ft at maturity, plant it at least 4 ft away from the next plant of the same species; this leaves 2 ft on either side of the plant for it to spread, and another 2 ft for the next plant to do the same.

Also consider a plant's lifespan. Many plants grow fast but have short lives. If you choose a fast- growing tree because you are desperate for shade, you may solve the shade problem quickly but have to replace the tree in 15 years. Rapid-growing trees such as Siberian elm (*Ulmus pumila*), poplar (*Populus spp.*), and willow (*Salix spp.*) are brittle. High winds, ice storms, and other natural events can damage them severely.

Figure 5.7 Avoid plants that are disease prone requiring preventative fungicide applications every year
Image Credit: Paul Thompson, Clemson University

Figure 5.8 The two large evergreens where probably not the best selections for these locations.
Image Credit: Paul Thompson, Clemson University

Choosing the Right Size Tree or Shrub

What is a Tree, What is a Shrub?

Trees and shrubs are generally categorized by their height or size at maturity, but there are large shrubs and small trees that may overlap within a given height and width range. Generally, plants that mature to be 10-12 ft tall are classified as shrubs, but under the right growing conditions, many large shrubs can grow larger and more tree-like.

Certain woody plants—such as dwarf cultivars of Japanese maple trees—may grow very slowly and rarely reach 10 ft, but they are still referred to as trees and pruned to maintain their tree form.

Choosing Trees by Size

Table 12.1 outlines the differences in culture, cost, and use between small- and large-sized trees. Newly planted trees require regular watering; smaller trees require regular irrigation for several months following planting, while larger trees will require this for far longer. If you cannot meet the watering requirements of a given tree, choose it in a smaller size. You can estimate the approximate time it will take a tree to establish by its trunk diameter: as a general rule, the tree will require 8 months per inch of trunk diameter. See Table 5.1 for an example

Drainage also affects what size tree is best for your site. On sites with poor drainage, smaller trees with shallower root balls often do better than larger nursery trees. A nursery tree is considered large if its trunk is more than 2 in. in diameter. The larger root balls of big trees can become submerged in water if a site has poor drainage; this will kill the roots at the base of the root ball and stress the tree, slowing the rate of establishment and making it more vulnerable to injury from insects, disease, and drought. If you must plant large trees in a poorly drained site, select trees specifically grown to have shallow root balls or plant them in shallow holes to keep their roots above the water level.

Choosing Shrubs by Size

Choose the appropriate size shrub for your site; don't think that just because a shrub looks small in the nursery, it will not rapidly outgrow its allotted area after a few years. Decide what size plant to purchase by considering its final height and spread as well as how long it will take to reach that size. Often, dwarf cultivars of shrubs are good choices. You don't need to prune dwarf cultivars frequently; because they stay small, you will not have to replace them or cut them back with time.

Base the number of plants you purchase on the mature spread of the plant, the space you will plant it, and the planting density of the final layout. In areas where you want to create a mass effect, plant shrubs closer together. In other instances, space plants far enough apart to allow each plant to develop its own natural form or shape.

Methods of Tree and Shrub Production

When a tree or shrub will be planted in a well-drained site and receive regular irrigation, the production method is of little consequence; however, when watering will be infrequent, the method by which a tree was grown or harvested will affect its chances of surviving transplanting.

Field-Grown Trees and Shrubs

Trees grown directly in the ground are referred to as **field-grown** (Figure 5.9); field-grown trees are properly harvested, hardened off, and strong and sturdy. They are good choices for any site type—and usually the best choice for sites that you will water only infrequently or irregularly. Compared to trees grown by other methods, the root ball of a harvested field-grown tree is larger and capable of storing more water, and thus slower to dry out. The root balls are also much heavier than those of container-grown trees, so they are significantly harder to handle.

TABLE 5.1 Landscape Establishment Period and Tree Size

Criteria	½"dia.	2"dia.
Establishment period	4 months	16 months
Regular Irrigation after planting	2 months	8 months
Cost of nursery stock	<$50	>$200
Number of trees planted per dollars spent	4+	1

Figure 5.9 Balled-in-burlap and container grown trees available at a garden center.
Image Credit: Paul Thompson, Clemson Universtiy

Field-grown trees that receive drip irrigation and fertilization near the base of the trunk during the first several years in the nursery's field will develop fine root growth near the trunk. This denser root system contributes to a healthy root ball.

Field-grown trees should be hardened-off before going to market. By dealing with an established, reliable nursery, you minimize the risk of buying a field-grown tree that has not been hardened off. Hardened-off trees have had their roots pruned several weeks or months prior to being dug up. In the hardening-off period, the newly harvested tree slows down the growth of its leaf shoots and can even drop leaves. Meanwhile, the root ball is regenerating new roots to replace those severed in pruning so the tree survival rate will be more successful when transplanted. During this time, the tree needs frequent and carefully managed irrigation, something a good nursery is equipped to handle. Remember, do not plant a freshly dug but not hardened-off tree unless you can meet its special irrigation needs. Certain palms, such as the cabbage palm, are exceptions to this rule and do not require hardening-off.

Once field-grown trees have been hardened-off, they are more tolerant than container-grown trees of transplantation into dry landscape soil.

When field-grown trees are harvested, their root balls are balled and burlapped (B&B). That is, burlap is wrapped around the root balls and secured with nails, string, or wire. Take care to avoid breaking or crushing the root ball during transport and handling.

Container-Grown Trees and Shrubs

Container-grown trees and shrubs are most commonly grown in plastic containers that are placed either above ground or below ground; if they are below ground, they are placed inside permanent, installed containers with specially designed underground drainage systems. This latter method, known as **pot-in-pot**, insulates the root system and should produce roots that are more uniformly distributed than those found in above-ground containers; pot-in-pot growing also prevents blow-over of trees or large shrubs in the nursery. Whether a containerized tree or shrub is grown above or below ground should not affect how it transplants, but there are few published comparative tests or experiments on the subject to confirm this.

Growing containers are usually filled with an artificial or soilless growing medium composed of one or more materials like bark, peat moss, compost, and sand. These media tend to be coarser than soil, which permits them to drain quickly and, in turn, prevents root rot. Because of this rapid drainage, containerized trees require daily or even more frequent irrigation in the summer.

When a container-grown tree or shrub is transplanted, moisture is drawn out of the container's growing medium into the more finely textured landscape soil; this causes the root ball to dry out even faster than it did in the container. To maintain optimum growth after planting, water container-grown plants at least as often as they were watered in the nursery. In the summer, these plants may require frequent irrigation on well-drained, sandy soils for weeks or months after planting—especially trees with trunks over 2 in. in diameter. You can reduce the frequency of irrigation as roots grow out into the soil of the landscape.

Standard plastic containers have smooth sides and are about as deep as they are wide. Roots of plants in these containers frequently grow along the outside of the root ball and eventually encircle it. At the time of transplanting, Circling roots should be disturbed and either straightened or pruned. This will prevent the roots from girdling the trunk of the plant as it grows. Another root defect that is especially important to watch for in container-grown trees are plunging roots. (Figure 5.11). As with encircling roots, once surface roots reach the wall of the container, they may bend and grow straight down, or plunge. This can cause instability in the root flare, which acts as a pedestal to support the tremendous weight and spread of the trunk and branches.

Figures 5.10 a&b The root flare on the left is not visible and would require further investigation. The root flare on the right is obvious, which makes this a better choice.

Image Credit: Paul Thompson, Clemson Universtiy

Bare-Root Trees and Shrubs

As the name suggests, bare-root plants are sold with roots that are not encased in soil. They are field-grown, hardened off, and commonly sold via mail order. If their roots are kept shaded, moist, and cool until planting, bare-root trees should perform as well as container-grown or balled-and-burlapped trees—and sometimes better.

Checking a Root Ball for Defects

Some root ball defects are obvious; you'll only discover others with careful observation and inspection. Because the health of a plant's root ball is critical to its ultimate survival, insist that you be able to look at the root ball of a container-grown plant before you purchase it. Always ask permission before removing plants from their containers, as sellers may want that to occur elsewhere in the garden center. You should buy from a nursery that knows what cultivation methods were used to grow their stock. Tree roots deformed within the first several months of propagation in the nursery can doom a tree, but the consequences of such root deformations may not become evident until the trees are older. A thorough inspection before planting helps prevent future disappointment.

Check for the location of the root flare (Figure 5.10 a&b) and the top-most root, which should be visible at or slightly below the surface of the soil. If the root flare is not visible in the pot, slip your fingers along the trunk and down into the soil until you feel the first root growing from the trunk. If the root flare and topmost root are below the soil surface, the plant has been planted too deeply; this can happen to both field-grown and container-grown plants.

Once the tree is out of the container, the root ball should stay together but be somewhat pliable. You should be able to pick the root ball up and gently place it back in the container without losing much of the planting medium. If the root ball falls apart when you remove it, particularly with shrubs, it may have just been "stepped up" to a larger container. You could be buying a large container of potting media with very few roots.

If many large-diameter woody roots circle around the outside of the root ball or the root ball is very dense and hard, it is said to be **pot-bound** or root-bound. A

Figure 5.11 Avoid plants with plunging roots (red arrow) and potential girdling roots (blue arrow). Prune out the defects if unavoidable.

Image Credit: Paul Thompson, Clemson University

Figure 5.12 Significant numbers of roots growing out drainage holes often indicate the plant is rootbound.
Image Credit: Paul Thompson, Clemson University

mass of circling roots on the outside of a root ball can act as a physical barrier to root penetration into the landscape soil after planting. The circling roots can also choke and kill the tree as it grows older. Do not purchase pot-bound plants.

Examine the roots on the surface of the root ball. Do not buy a plant with black roots. These roots were probably killed by heat stress, freezing temperatures, or overwatering. Bare-root trees should have living, small-diameter roots growing from the larger roots. The insides of living roots are whitish and moist.

Trunk Form and Structure

Strong trunks are thickest near the ground and taper towards the top. They do not require stakes for support (Figure 5.13). Trees that are staked at the nursery may not develop proper trunk taper and may bend over when stakes are removed; the trunks of these trees are often the same diameter at the ground as they are several feet up the tree. This is a sign that the trunk may be weak. One of the major causes of this weakness is the removal of lower lateral branches too early in the life of a young tree. Lower branches on a young tree should be left to help the trunk develop a taper that will not require staking.

Single-Trunk Trees

Trees with one trunk are usually considered more structurally sound than multi-trunk trees and are more durable in the landscape. Certain small trees—such as crape myrtle (*Lagerstroemia indica*), southern wax

Figure 5.13 The tree on the left will not stand erect without the bamboo stake. Removing all lower branches on a young tree is a poor production practice.
Image Credit: Paul Thompson, Clemson University

myrtle (*Morella cerifera*), and other landscape trees—usually grow with several trunks but can be trained in the nursery as a single trunk specimen.

A large tree that will grow to be more than 40 ft tall should have a single trunk at least 2/3 the height of the mature size, but the trunk does not have to be straight—a slight bend is acceptable. A tree with a forked trunk is said to have co-dominant stems (Figure 5.14 a&b); if co-dominant stems are so large in diameter that you cannot easily remove one with a pair of hand pruners, choose another tree.

Trees with a single trunk are usually more appropriate for planting along streets and near walks; they are easier to train so that the branches grow well above vehicles and pedestrians. Lower branches and entire trunks on multi-trunked trees often obstruct pedestrians and traffic; eventually, these branches or trunks must be removed. This removal often disfigures the tree and compromises its health.

Multi-Trunk Trees

Small multi-trunk trees under 40 ft tall at maturity have a definite place in the landscape. They make nice

Figures 5.14 a&b The tree on the left has good structure with a dominant central leader and lateral branches that are less than half the diameter of the trunk where attached. The tree on the right has three codominent stems which will lead to the formation of included bark.
Image Credit: Paul Thompson, Clemson University

specimens—especially those that have attractive, showy bark or trunk structure.

Trees with several trunks often develop **included bark** (Figure 5.15) in the branch crotches. Included bark appears as a crease running several inches to many feet down from the crotch. Bark is pinched into the crease. This condition can cause one of the trunks to split from the rest of the tree during a storm or strong winds. When a major branch or trunk splits, the break can significantly alter the character and health of a tree.

A multi-trunked tree is well-formed if it has wide branch angles, branches less than half the diameter of the main trunks, and no included bark.

Branch Size and Arrangement

Branches should be distributed along a tree or shrub's trunk, not clumped toward the top. Branches in the lower half of ta tree help distribute the stress placed on the trunk when the wind blows. At least half of the foliage should originate from branches on the lower two-thirds of the tree.

Branches that are less than half the diameter of the trunk and those with a U-shaped crotch are stronger than those that grow larger than half the trunk diameter and those with a V-shaped crotch (Figure 5.16).

Branch arrangement and spacing is especially important on trees that will grow to over 40 ft at maturity. On saplings with trunk diameters of less than 2 in., the main or largest-diameter branches should be about 6 in. apart; smaller branches can be closer than this. Inferior branch arrangements can split apart when they get older if they are not properly pruned.

Figure 5.15 The two branches on the flowering pear tree failed because of included bark (brown-colored areas) between the stems.
Image Credit: Paul Thompson, Clemson University

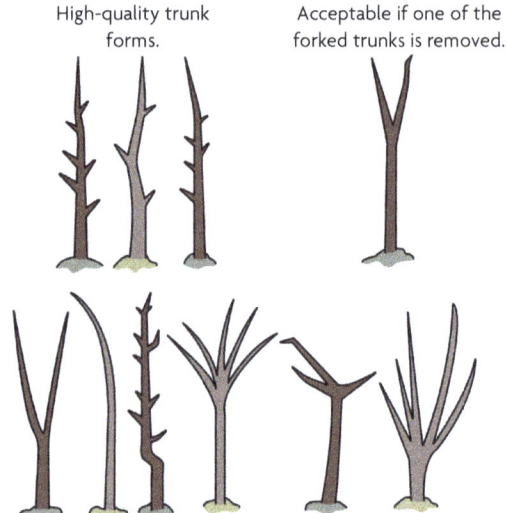

Figure 5.16 Some trees species are genetically prone to produce upright branch angles. Select well-spaced branches with U-shaped crotches as permanent branches.

Trees with trunk diameters between 2-4 in. might have only one or two permanent branches near the top. Permanent branches should be at least 18 in. apart and should not have included bark in the branch crotches. Trees with trunks larger than 4 in. in diameter are likely to have several permanent branches; these should also be at least 18 in. apart.

Branch arrangement and spacing is less crucial for trees that will remain small at maturity. You can choose any small tree with a pleasing branch arrangement that will fit the needs of the planting site.

Evidence of Pests and Damage

Examine a tree's leaves, trunk, and branches for evidence of disease, insects, or other injury. You want to select a tree that is healthy so that it grows well, but you also want to avoid exposing the other plants in a landscape to a contaminated specimen.

Many mites and insect pests are tiny and/or well camouflaged. Look carefully at both sides of a tree's leaves, especially if the foliage is speckled or spotted. Speckling may be the result of a generally harmless leaf spot disease. Spotted foliage may be an indication of sunburn or chemical injury—or an infestation of scales, spider mites, lace bugs, or some other pest that sucks sap from foliage. Such pests may be visible upon close inspection; if you see signs of pests, do not purchase the affected trees.

Because their color is often similar to twigs and branches, the presence of scale insects is one of the more difficult infestations to detect. Look for raised ridges or bumps on the tree's twigs. To determine if these are scales or a normal part of the tree, pick several off with your fingernail. If the bump is a normal part of the tree's bark, you will expose the green or white tissue that grows beneath the bark; if the bump is a scale insect, the twig's bark will remain more or less intact, and there will be no exposed tissue.

Scale insects are easier to see when they are on foliage because their color is usually quite different from that of the leaves. Do not plant trees with scale infestations—the stress of defending against the infestation may prove excessive in the vulnerable period following transplanting.

Except in their dormant season, nursery trees should have leaves to the ends of all their branches. Dead tips indicate problems that you should investigate further. If the tree is dormant and has no leaves, scrape several of its twigs with your thumbnail. If the tissue revealed is greenish or white, the twig is alive; dry, brown tissue indicates that the twig or branch is dead from that point to the tip. As a rule, do not purchase trees with dieback.

Avoid trees with scars, open wounds, or cankers along the trunk. If there is material covering the trunk, ask nursery personnel for permission to remove the trunk wrap and inspect the trunk; you can replace the wrap to help prevent damage during shipment to the planting site, if necessary. Open pruning wounds are fine if they are small, but the presence of large open pruning wounds (Figure 5.17) could indicate a poor or unplanned pruning program at the nursery. Small broken branches should be pruned back to healthy tissue; leave trees with large broken branches at the nursery. Do not

Figure 5.17 This tree has a canker developing on the trunk from improper pruning.

Image Credit: Paul Thompson, Clemson University

purchase trees with bark stripped down the trunk from an improper pruning cut.

Evaluate old pruning cuts as well. Proper pruning cuts display round cross sections; improper cuts are often oval. Properly made pruning cuts indicate that the nursery has high pruning standards and is capable of growing high-quality trees.

Check for injuries to the trunk from stakes rubbing against it; also, be sure the tree was not harmed in the nursery by stake ties that were left on for too long. By the time of purchase, a tree should usually be able to stand without stakes.

Leaves should have the same coloration as those of other trees of the same type. If leaves are smaller, lighter colored, or yellower than others, the tree may lack vigor and grow poorly.

Major branches should not have included bark in the crotch; this indicates that the branch is not attached well to the trunk and could separate from the tree as it grows.

CARE BEFORE PLANTING

How a tree or shrub is handled between the time it leaves the nursery and the time it is planted will affect its health and chances of survival after planting. Before purchasing plants, decide how to provide the appropriate transportation to the planting site and the correct storage for the tree if it will not be planted immediately upon arrival.

Transport

Never pick up a tree by the trunk; always lift and carry it by the root ball or container. Never drop a tree, as this will disrupt contact between fine roots and soil; these must be in intimate contact with each other for the roots to absorb water.

Root balls in plastic containers or boxes are more resistant to rough handling than those in fabric containers or balled and burlapped. With the latter, be sure that burlap is secured tightly or soil within the root ball could shift, causing cracks in the root ball and root breakage. A cracked root ball dries out quickly; to reduce water loss during shipping, some nurseries shrink-wrap the root balls of trees that are balled and burlapped.

When taking a tree or shrub home in a car, don't lash it to the roof or let foliage hang out of windows or an open trunk; exposure to wind causes rapid moisture loss and may result in

Trees hauled in open trucks lose more water through their foliage and twigs and can arrive at in poor condition with scorched leaves or dieback of young twigs. Many nursery operators cover trees with a fabric or cloth designed to reduce wind damage to the foliage.

Some nursery operators routinely spray trees that are in leaf with antitranspirants before shipping. **Antitranspirants**, or antidesiccant sprays, leave a transparent film of wax, plastic, or resin on the leaves that slows the loss of water through a plant's pores. These sprays are useful when transplanting trees in leaf during the summer, often benefitting the trees for several weeks.

Storage and Irrigation at the Planting Site

If trees or shrubs are not planted the day they arrive at a planting site, they need a holding area that is shaded and screened from the wind. Container-grown trees and shrubs dry out very quickly. A single day without water can cause significant root death, depriving the tree of vigor and magnifying the stress of the establishment period. Several days without water could mean death. Any plastic coverings used to protect the tree's foliage or roots during transport should be removed as soon as the tree reaches the holding area—plastic coverings can raise temperatures to lethal levels.

Balled-and-burlapped trees and shrubs should have their root balls surrounded by soil, compost, mulch, or sawdust as soon as they arrive to the holding area, especially if they have roots growing through the burlap. This will help prevent the roots from drying out and will facilitate the absorption of water by the root ball. If the root balls have been enclosed in a layer of plastic, either remove the plastic or provide complete protection from direct sun to avoid overheating.

Keep bare-root trees, especially their roots, covered with moistened burlap and in the shade prior to planting. Fine roots can dry out and die if exposed to direct sun for even a few minutes. Spray roots with water often enough to keep them moist; determine how often based on the weather and the characteristics of your holding area. Use a sharp hand pruner to remove damaged or broken portions of the roots.

Planting Time

In the professional landscape industry, planting occurs all throughout the year. You can plant container-grown plants with well-developed root systems at any point. Balled-and-burlapped plants, on the other hand, are best planted during the fall and winter months. Balled-and-burlapped trees in full leaf have been successfully transplanted during spring and summer months, but establishment requires special care. The degree of "transplant shock" a tree will experience varies based on the plant's species and the care and handling of the tree in the nursery, during transport, and in the landscape.

The very best time of year to plant, in terms of root growth and plant establishment, is during the fall. Unlike the tops of ornamental plants—that go dormant and cease growth for the winter—roots of landscape plants in the Southeast continue to grow throughout the winter months. Fall planting allows the carbohydrates produced during the previous growing season to be directed to root growth, since there is little demand from the top. When spring arrives, a well-established root system will be ready to provide the necessary water and nutrients to help the plant thrive.

Organic Amendments

Whether a specific soil or plant will benefit from the addition of organic matter must be considered on a case-by-case basis. There is no recipe for amending all soils. The type and amount of amendment used depends on the structure and texture of the existing soil, soil drainage, and the type of plant to be grown.

Many gardeners apply organic amendments such as peat moss, rotted animal manure, or compost to soils to improve the nutrient and water-holding capacity—in other words, to improve soil tilth. When adding organic matter to a soil, research shows that it is best to incorporate it throughout the rooting zone instead of placing it directly in the planting hole; by incorporating it uniformly in the soil, the entire rooting area becomes a homogenous growing environment.

On the other hand, amending only the planting hole causes the structure and texture of the soil to differ from that of the surrounding native soil. This difference encourages the roots to stay within the confines of the hole and discourages them from exploring the surrounding soil. It also upsets the water equilibrium between the surrounding native soil and the soil in the hole. For instance, fine-textured organic matter in the planting hole can act like a sponge in a bathtub, holding excess moisture after rainfall or irrigation.

Extensive research on planting indicates that organic amendments placed in the planting hole do not result in a larger root system, do not encourage root penetration into the native soil, and are not cost-effective. If you choose to add organic matter to the soil, incorporate it uniformly throughout the planting area or projected rooting zone.

Organic matter should comprise no more than 20% of the total soil volume. For example, preparing a bed 8 inches deep requires incorporating about 2 in. of organic matter such as compost or shredded leaves. You can improve drainage in clay soils by subsoiling or deep tilling before adding organic matter.

Do not use uncomposted products as amendments. Fresh organic materials that have not been composted rob plants of nitrogen when added to the soil. As microorganisms in the soil feed on bark and decompose it, they use nitrogen in the soil. Well-composted organic products have a rich, earthy smell and a crumbly appearance; the original organic materials are no longer recognizable.

PLANTING TREES AND SHRUBS

Always plant trees and shrubs at the appropriate depth and water them adequately during the establishment period if you want them to flourish. Under- or overwatering are often equally damaging to newly planted trees and can delay normal establishment or cause plant death. Planting too deeply, failure to recognize and cut deformed circling roots within the root ball at planting, improper mulching, uncontrolled grass, and weed competition are common and serious planting errors that contribute to poor establishment. Use of quality planting stock will increase the likelihood of quick establishment and healthy plants in the future.

Planting Depth

Do not plant trees or shrubs below their original soil level. Because root balls can settle after planting, it is better to place them slightly above grade. Measure the root ball height and dig the planting hole 1-2 in. shallower than the height of the root ball. In well-drained soil, the goal is to plant them at the original soil line. Do not plant them deeper than the soil line (Figure 5.18).

Locate the topmost root in the root ball and ensure it is level with the soil surface when setting the root ball. It is better to have it slightly above grade than below the soil surface. The soil in the bottom of the hole should not be loose or disturbed.

When finding the topmost root, remove any excess soil or planting media that has been added to the pot; even a little extra soil can inhibit water infiltration into the root ball, especially those that have developed in containers. In well-drained soil, the planting hole should be two-five times the width of the root ball. New roots will have an easier time penetrating this loosened soil, which will speed up establishment.

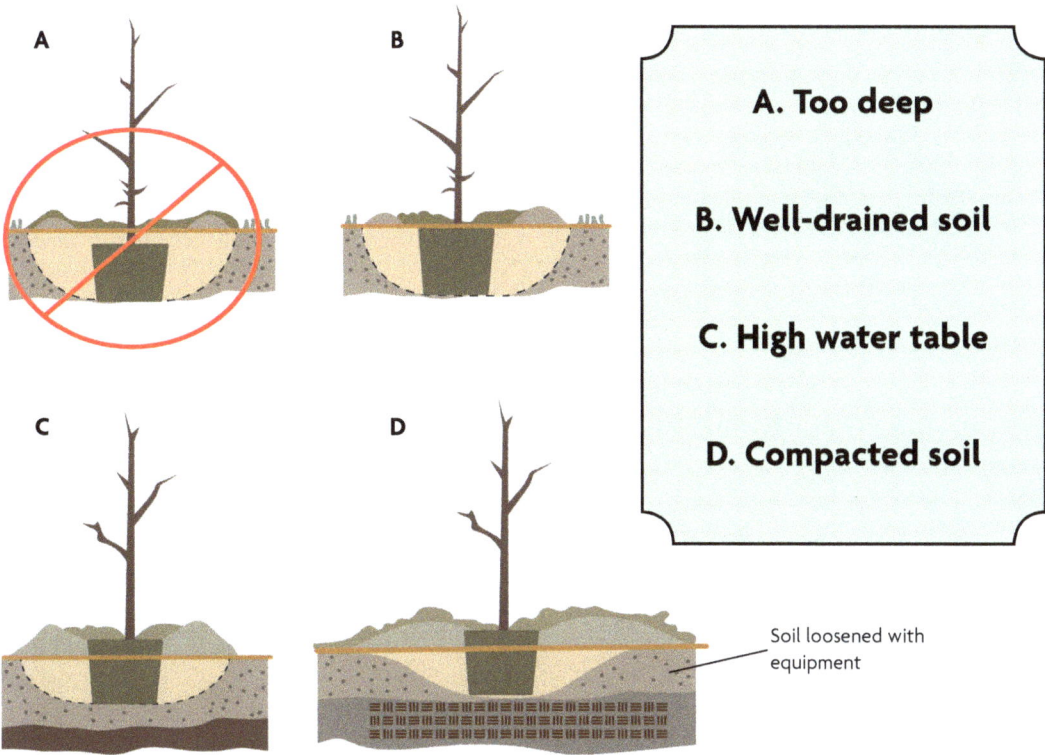

Figure 5.18 Plant trees and shrubs at the appropriate depth.

Where there is flooding during heavy rains, add gutters and downspouts to buildings to direct surface water away from planting areas. In poorly drained soils or compacted soils, it is better to plant on a berm or raised bed. Place the root ball 2-4 in. higher than the original grade. This allows oxygen to reach the roots in the upper surface and excess water to drain away from the root ball.

Do not disturb soil in the bottom of the planting hole; this could allow the root ball to settle. Planted higher, the root ball may dry out more quickly in the summer when there's more direct sunlight; be prepared to check and irrigate more often.

Soil Conditions and Contributing Factors

Soil type and planting stock size have a major effect on how much water young transplants require. Plants require more water at each watering, and sandy soil that drains more quickly requires more frequent watering. Clay soils typically have slow water percolation rates and become saturated when overwatered; plant roots must have air as well as water, so be aware of natural rainfall and check the root ball for moisture before irrigating shrubs or trees on clay sites. Roots submerged in water for too long can be damaged or die.

Woody plants establish more quickly and develop a better root structure if their roots can spread quickly into the surrounding soil and absorb necessary water and nutrients for the stressed plant. This is one important reason to till or loosen the soil for three-five times the width of the plant root ball size. Often, gardeners build raised beds with added organic matter for groups of shrubs, such as several azalea plants.

Step by Step Tree and Shrub Planting

Step 1: Dig a Wide, Shallow Hole (Figure 5.19.1)

Dig a wide, shallow hole. The hole should be 1-2 in. shallower than the height of the root ball to ensure it will remain at ground level or slightly above if the root ball settles. Ideally, the hole should be three to five times as

Figure 5.19.1 Dig a wide, shallow hole

wide as the width of the root ball. We do not recommend adding compost or other organic matter directly to the planting hole.

Step 2: Check and Remove Circling or Damaged Roots from the Root Ball (Figure 5.19.2)

Circling roots are common in container-grown plants and can be worse on large potted plants that are transplanted several times as they grow. Past recommendations specified cutting circling roots with a knife or pruning clippers in multiple places around the root ball; more recent studies show better results from shearing or shaving all outside circling roots on the root ball with a tool such as a machete, serrated knife, or small pruning saw. Shearing all the roots at the same point causes new roots to regenerate and grow away from the stem to spread into surrounding soil. Also shave any large roots from the bottom of the container.

Figure 5.19.2 Check and remove circling or damaged roots from the root ball

Step 3: Ensure the Topmost Root on the Stem is 1-2 In. Above Soil Level (Figure 5.19.3)

Trees and large shrubs develop a natural **root flare** (or buttress) around the plant to support the weight of the top (or crown) as it grows. Plant trees at the same height as they develop naturally. The processes of growing, potting, transporting, and planting often cover the root flare with soil. Remove soil from the top of the root ball until you expose the top root. Then, gently place the tree into the middle of the planting hole. Move it by lifting the root ball, not the stem. Position it with the top root exposed 1-2 in. above grade to account for settling of the root ball. If it is too deep, move it slightly to the side while you pack more soil underneath, then recenter it.

Figure 5.19.3 Ensure the topmost root on the stem is 1–2 in. above soil level

Step 4: Remove Synthetic Materials from the Root Ball

Some trees and large shrubs are dug and sold with a synthetic burlap material or straps or ties holding the root ball together. This material does not deteriorate quickly; remove it from the root ball after the plant is in the hole so that the roots can expand freely. Very large plants may sit in a wire basket; if this is the case, remove the upper two-thirds of the burlap and basket after placing the tree in the hole.

Step 5: Fill the Hole and Firm the Soil Around the Root Ball (Figure 5.19.4)

It is important to replace the soil from the hole around the planted root ball only to the level of the root ball or slightly below it; do not pile soil on the root ball or the stem. Soil removed from the hole is used to backfill around the root ball. Tamp down the soil around the root

Figure 5.19.4 Fill the hole and firm the soil around the root ball

ball to remove air pockets and make it firm. Do not add organic matter directly to the root ball or planting hole.

Step 6: Add Organic Mulch, Berm the Soil, and Irrigate (Figure 5.19.5)

A 2-3 in. berm is optional, but you can add one around the edge of the planting hole to improve moisture retention. Regardless, apply 2-4 in. of loose mulch to hold moisture and inhibit grass and weed invasion. Your mulched area should form a donut shape; the tree stem is in the middle, and the mulch ring begins several inches away from the trunk.

Water the root ball slowly and thoroughly until saturated after planting. Since roots are restricted to the root ball at this stage, water it directly. The most critical part of the planting process is irrigating sufficiently and as needed after planting. Many plants die or are severely damaged when watered too little or too much; at first, plan to check the plant daily or every other day and soaking the root ball as needed. Plants in poorly drained soils will require less frequent watering than those in well-drained sites.

Figure 5.19.5 Add organic mulch, berm the soil, and irrigate

The size of the mulched area is critical when trees are added to turfed or grassy areas; turf can be a strong competitor for water and nutrients necessary for newly planted trees with limited root systems. Trees planted without mulch or surrounded by very little mulch are also more easily damaged by string trimmers and lawn mowers.

ESTABLISHMENT PERIOD

The time between planting a tree or shrub until they can flourish on their own is called the establishment period. Larger plants take longer to establish. Establishment rate is affected by soil conditions, local climate, and plant care. Following beneficial, recommended practices can make the difference between long-lasting, healthy trees and struggling, vulnerable plants. A tree's establishment period can be as short as one year or last for several growing seasons.

Watering During Establishment

Soil type and planting stock size determine how much water is necessary for young transplants. Larger plants require more water each time, while sandy soil—which drains more quickly—requires more frequent watering. Frequency of watering is usually more important than the amount of water provided at each watering. Start by checking soil moisture and watering the root ball daily if it is drying out. Under warm, dry conditions, continue daily watering for several weeks; eventually, you can begin to gradually increase the number of days between irrigation, but continue monitor the plant regularly.

Clay soils typically drain slowly and become saturated when overwatered. One benefit of tilling or loosening the soil in a large area before planting is that it allows rainfall or irrigation water to disperse around the root ball instead of pooling below it.

You can check for moisture near the root ball before you water using a long screwdriver or similar object; just push down near the root ball before you add water. Soil should be moist but not saturated. Plant roots must have air as well as water, so irrigate regularly but in moderation. Establishment rate can vary between different trees and shrubs on the same planting site, so check each plant regularly and create your watering schedule depending upon their individual needs.

Staking or Supporting Trees

Where you can, avoid staking and guying as much as possible. Smaller trees and well-balanced, stocky trees—that are not skinny or top heavy—usually don't need much or any support. There are several staking methods that allow trees to sway in the wind but do not use wire; flexible straps are better but attach them loosely so the tree has enough room to sway in the wind. Check and adjust straps often and don't leave them on for more than a year or girdling may occur (Figure 5.21).

LANDSCAPE MANAGEMENT PRACTICES

Once you've planted and established your landscape, the job isn't done. Provide regular management as necessary based on the following guidelines.

Irrigating

Irrigating Established Shrubs and Trees

Established, drought-tolerant shrubs and trees may not require water during dry, rainless periods; others,

Figure 5.21 Anchoring straps should be checked several times during the year and removed after one growing season to avoid girdling the trunk.
Image Credit: Paul Thompson, Clemson University

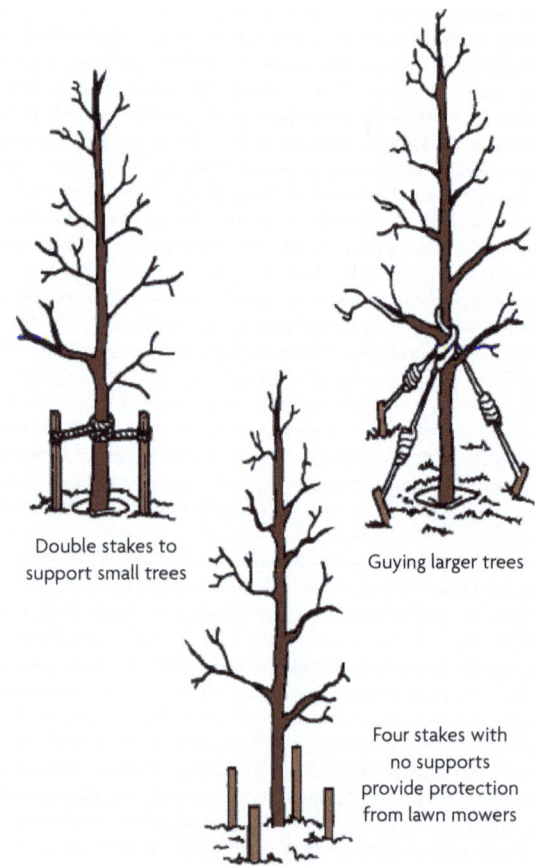

Figure 5.20 Although usually not needed, different methods of staking can be used which depends on the size of the tree and wind exposure.

however, may need to be watered. The best guide for determining when to water a plant is the plant itself. Wilting or leaf rolling are the most common symptoms of a plant's need for water. Certain plants in a landscape will need more water than others. By watering only those plants that need water, you save water, time, and money—and avoid overwatering plants that do not need a lot of moisture.

The amount of water an ornamental plant requires depends on the type of plant, the soil type, the amount of existing moisture in the soil, and the time of year. Generally, 6 gal of water per 10 sq ft of bed area or canopy area will saturate most soils to a depth of about 12 in.; for most ornamental plants, this area contains 80% of all roots.

The best time to water is at night or in the very early morning. As much as 30% of all water provided at midday is lost to accelerated evaporation due to the sun. Keep the root collar dry between times you irrigate, as wet soil or mulch in contact with the lower trunk or root collar may lead to infection by soil-borne pathogens.

To avoid runoff and water loss, apply water slowly to the base of the plant using a hand-held hose, drip or trickle irrigation, micro-sprinklers, or a soaker hose (a fibrous tube that "sweats" or allows water to seep out along its length and is suitable for dense plantings). Do-it-yourself drip irrigation systems, available from most garden centers, use 30-50% less water than overhead sprinklers.

Avoid watering with a sprinkler or in-ground irrigation system designed for turf. In addition to wasting water and watering weeds, wetting leaves encourages diseases. When tree trunks are watered rather than roots, it may cause root or collar rot. Also avoid shallow watering; it encourages surface rooting and may cause the entire root system to dry out during extended dry periods. Infrequent deep soaking develops deeper, more extensive root systems and more drought-tolerant shrubs and trees.

Xeriscaping

A xeriscape, which means "dry landscape," combines sound horticultural principles with water conservation while maintaining a beautiful landscape. Xeriscaping incorporates the following seven basic principles:

Careful Planning and Design. Planning and designing a xeriscape takes into account which plants have similar irrigation needs. Creating xeriscapes incorporates seven basic principles. The landscape is divided into these groups, called "hydrozones"—specific areas that receive either low, moderate, or high amounts of water. Hydrozones are usually divided into three categories: those that require regular irrigation (high-moisture zones), those that need irrigation only during long dry spells (moderate-moisture zones), and those that rarely or never require irrigation outside of establishment or severe drought (low-moisture zones).

Use of Lawns as Functional Spaces. Xeriscapes reduce lawn areas to functional spaces and make use of drought-tolerant lawn grasses that require much less irrigation.

Soil Preparation with Organic Matter. Using organic matter such as compost improves soil structure and maximizes moisture retention where it's most needed.

Efficient Watering Methods. Drip and micro irrigation help conserve water by reducing runoff or oversaturation.

Mulch. Mulching soil around trees, shrubs, and flower beds conserves moisture, suppresses weeds, and enhances plant growth.

Proper and Timely Maintenance. Fertilizing, pruning, mowing, and watering the plants in a landscape keeps them healthy, reducing the need for excess or urgent care.

Research indicates that incorporating these principles into landscaping reduces water consumption by at least 30-60%.

Evaluate your plants during dry spells. While many well-established trees and shrubs can survive drought without irrigation, others are harmed by extended periods of drought that injures root systems and causes premature leaf drop, twig dieback, and eventual death. Look for leaves that wilt or droop during hot summer afternoons. If leaves are not turgid or fully hydrated by the next morning, the plant may be experiencing drought stress. Leaves may turn brown and fall. Without supplemental irrigation, small roots will die, and the tree's health will decline. Irrigate these drought-sensitive trees and shrubs to avoid additional damage.

Be careful determining if a plant is showing drought symptoms or symptoms of another condition that only mimics drought. When trees lose water at a faster rate than the roots can replace it—often under hot, dry, windy conditions— leaf scorch symptoms develop even if there is adequate moisture available. Also, if any conditions affect water transport within the shrub or tree—such as girdling roots, trunk injury, or damaged roots—they affect the uptake and movement of water within the vascular system and cause some symptoms of dehydration even though the water is available in the soil.

Fertilizing

Plants growing in high-quality soil may require little or no fertilizer; plants growing in poor, infertile soil with little or no organic matter may require periodic fertilization to maintain growth. Keep two key points in mind when considering fertilization:

1. Fertilizer is only beneficial when it is needed.
2. Use the right amount of fertilizer at the right time and in the right place.

Fertilizer is not a cure for ailing plants when the plants themselves are poorly adapted to the environment, unhealthy, planted carelessly, or watered improperly. Adding too much fertilizer produces excessive growth in plants. This may sound good, but this growth is weak, easily broken, and more susceptible to injury from cold, drought, and pests. Sometimes, fertilization attracts or sustains pests or decreases a plant's resistance. Excessive rates of fertilizer that are not absorbed by the plant—and instead remain in the soil—can contaminate ground and surface water.

Establish a Need for Fertilizer

Consider the following conditions to decide if you should fertilize your trees and shrubs.

Soil Test. Test your soil. Depending on the results, you may need to add specific nutrients to make up for any deficiencies in the soil. If a soil analysis doesn't indicate nutrient deficiencies, it's possible the soil is adequate on its own.

Growth. Look at shrubs and trees for signs of poor growth progress such as: poorly colored leaves (pale green to yellow), smaller leaf size than usual, earlier onset of fall coloring and leaf drop, little annual twig growth, or twig or branch dieback. These symptoms are not always related to low levels of nutrients in the soil, nor is it certain that fertilizers would cure these problems. Heavily compacted soil, insect-induced stressors, diseases and weeds, and even adverse weather conditions can all cause these same symptoms. Before fertilizing, determine the cause of the problem; decide how to correct it based on this cause.

Planting Age. Applying fertilizer in the early years of established, transplanted trees and shrubs can speed up top growth and help young trees fill their space in the landscape. Slow-release fertilizers are best for recently planted trees and shrubs.

Location. If shrubs or trees grow in a regularly fertilized lawn, there is usually no need to fertilize them separately; the roots of trees and shrubs will absorb some of the fertilizer applied to the lawn. However, trees and shrubs growing in planting beds may require fertilizer, especially if the soil is sandy and has little or no organic matter.

Timing of Fertilizer Applications

If you're fertilizing shrubs and trees growing in lawns, apply the fertilizer as you would for the turfgrass species. If you're fertilizing woody landscape plants not growing in lawn areas, time the application so that their roots can readily absorb the nutrients.

Although nutrient uptake occurs between bud break in the spring and when the leaves change color in autumn, efficient absorption coincides with intense root growth: when soil temperatures are between 68-84°F and there is adequate moisture available. The best times of year to apply fertilizer are late spring-early summer, after new shoot growth has ceased, and from late summer to fall, when shoot growth has ceased but roots are actively growing. This fall application is particularly important, because research indicates that early spring growth depends almost exclusively on nutrients that were absorbed and stored the previous year. Try to split your application of fertilizer so that half of the total annual amount is applied during one season and the other half in the other season, especially if your soil is sandy. Always be sure that adequate moisture—supplied by rainfall or irrigation—is available so the fertilizer dissolves in the soil solution and can be taken up by the roots. Avoid fertilizing trees and shrubs that are stressed by drought. If water is unavailable, do not fertilize at all; plants will not be able to absorb the nutrients.

Fertilizer Type

A complete fertilizer with a ratio around 3:1:2 or 3:1:3 (such as 16-4-8, 12-6-6, or 12-4-8) tends to be best unless a soil test reveals adequate levels of phosphorus and potassium.

Two kinds of fertilizers are available: fast-release and slow-release. Fast-release or water-soluble fertilizers are less expensive than slow-release products, which release nitrogen over an extended period; however, the nutrients in a fast-release fertilizer leach more quickly through the soil. In sandy, well-drained soils, the soluble fertilizer may move past the root system after only a few inches of rainfall or irrigation. In fine-textured clay soils, leaching is slower, but runoff may be greater.

Slow-release or controlled-release fertilizers have longer release periods. The nitrogen in slow-release fertilizers may be sulfur coated or included in a form like IBDU or urea-formaldehyde. One-half or more of the total amount of nitrogen in controlled-release fertilizers should be water insoluble (slow release). Slow-release fertilizers are a particularly good choice for newly planted shrubs and trees or in areas where the potential for runoff is very high, such as slopes or compacted soil. Since the nutrients are released more slowly, there is a lower potential for fertilizer damage (fertilizer burn) or water contamination.

Natural fertilizers—such as composted sewage sludge, cow manure, or complete fertilizer blends—also provide nitrogen and other nutrients slowly. One advantage of these natural "nutrient suppliers" is that they provide minor nutrients such as iron or zinc that are usually not found in synthetic fertilizers. Natural fertilizers also improve soil structure.

One disadvantage of natural fertilizers is that usually, the concentration of nitrogen, phosphorus, and potassium are low. Therefore, a greater amount of a natural fertilizer must be applied to provide the same amount of nutrients that would be obtained from a synthetic nutrient source.

Many fertilizers are formulated for use on lawn grasses. Some, known as "weed-and-feed" fertilizers, may contain an herbicide that can damage ground covers, vines, shrubs, and trees. Read all labels carefully and follow the directions.

Fertilizer Amount

As with lawn fertilization, the recommended rates for fertilizing woody plants are based on actual pounds of nitrogen. Shrubs and trees can receive 2-4 lbs of actual nitrogen per 1,000 sq ft of root zone per year. Generally, younger shrubs and trees should receive more nitrogen than mature plants. Established trees in lawn areas typically do not need additional fertilizer if the lawn is fertilized.

Fertilizer Placement

Use a drop-type or cyclone spreader to apply fertilizer to the root zone of the shrub or tree over the mulched areas. The **root zone** is a roughly circular area that extends beyond the **drip line** (outermost branches), about 1.5 times the area of the branch spread (Figure 5.22). For example, if the distance from the trunk of a tree to the drip line is 8 ft, the "feeder" roots that absorb minerals can extend an additional 4 ft (one-half of 8 ft) beyond the drip line. So, the root zone can occupy an area up to 12 ft away from the trunk; this is the area you need to fertilize.

When fertilizing individual shrubs, follow the directions given above for trees to determine their root zone area. When several shrubs or ground covers are grouped together in a bed or natural area, simply measure the area of the entire bed to determine the amount of fertilizer to apply. When fertilizing over the top of shrubs and groundcovers, make certain the leaves are dry and use a leaf rake or broom to brush fertilizer off the leaves and onto the ground after application.

Refer to the fertilizer label to determine the appropriate setting for the amount of nitrogen you want to apply. If your fertilizer spreader is not listed on the label, you will have to calibrate your lawn spreader to ensure that you apply the right amount. Adding too much fertilizer can harm the plants and the environment.; excessive fertilizer produces weak growth that breaks easily and is susceptible to injury from cold, drought and pests and may contaminate ground and surface water.

You can also have a commercial arborist inject fertilizer below the surface of the soil under high pressure. **Subsurface injection** can be successful when fertilizer is injected 4-8 in. below the soil surface, where most of the fibrous feeding roots are. Fertilizer injection aerates the soil as it fertilizes it.

Another kind of subsurface fertilizer application involves drilling 2-in.-diameter holes in the ground to a depth of 3-12 in. (though preferably 4-8 in.) and pouring fertilizer in each hole, leaving 2 in. of space between the top of the fertilizer and the soil surface. For best results, drill the holes in a grid pattern, spaced 1-3 ft apart. One drawback to this method is the potential for overstimulating or burning turfgrass near the hole with the high concentration of fertilizer.

The two methods of belowground fertilization are typically unnecessary unless trees have excessive nutrient deficiencies and surface plants may intercept other fertilizer treatments.

Fertilizer spikes are favored by some homeowners. These spikes are composed of fertilizer that is compressed and molded into stakes or spikes that can be hammered into the ground. These stakes are convenient, but the manufacturing process causes them to be expensive, too. When using fertilizer spikes, create a basic grid pattern to ensure adequate fertilizer coverage and contact with the roots.

When fertilizing the soil is impractical or ineffective for your plants, consider foliar applications. Foliar application is the application of a liquid fertilizer to the leaves of shrubs and trees; it is commonly used to correct micronutrient deficiencies such as iron chlorosis in azaleas, with displays as yellow (chlorotic) new leaves with green veins. Applying fertilizer to the leaves will not cure the reason behind the micronutrient deficiency; the cause of the deficiency may be anything from the soil pH to an impaired root system. To find the underlying problem, have the soil tested and examine the results.

Pruning & Training

What is Pruning?

Pruning is a regular part of urban plant maintenance. It involves the selective removal of specific plant parts.

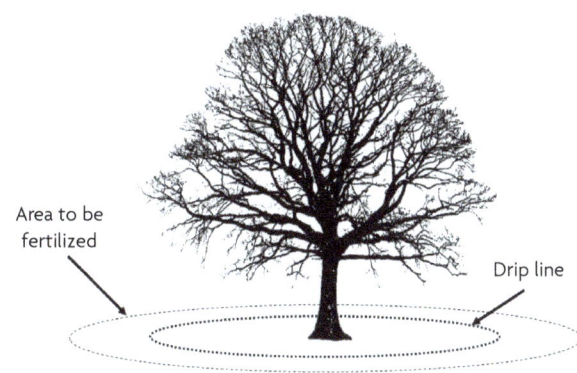

Figure 5.22 Recommended area to fertilize a tree or shrub is 1.5 times the spread of the branches.
Image Credit: Paul Thompson, Clemson University

Although shoots and branches are the main targets for pruning, you can also prune roots, flower buds, fruits, and seed pods.

Pruning creates wounds that can make plants more vulnerable to disease. Unlike animals, whose wounds heal, plants must grow new tissue around and over the wound; this callus tissue is called a seal because it forms around the damaged area and eventually covers and seals the damaged area against infection by diseases and rot fungi.

Another response to pruning occurs inside plants. Chemical boundaries form around wounded areas, walling off or compartmentalizing the wounds. Compartmentalization limits the decay that results from wounding or through the natural death of branches. Always use pruning techniques that limit wounding.

Pruning is much more than controlling plant size, even though many plants are pruned routinely to maintain a desired size or shape. This is why it's important to consider a plant's mature size and form when planting; if a shrub or tree is placed in the landscape with plenty of space and with its final form in mind, there will be little need to prune it.

In today's market, production nurseries are breeding, selecting, and producing many more small-maturing shrubs and trees that can be substituted for large-maturing plants and reduce the amount of pruning needed for size control.

Reasons for Pruning

Landscape plants are pruned for many reasons. Pruning, when done properly, is an important cultural practice in landscape management. Proper pruning can keep plants attractive and within bounds. It can add years to a plant's usefulness. Proper pruning allows you to control and direct a plant's growth, but improper pruning can cause a loss of control.

The most common reasons to prune are:

- To maintain plant health—the first cuts should aim to remove dead, damaged, and diseased branches and tissue;
- To remove crossing branches and branches with narrow crotch angles, as this will help to improve plant structure and shape;
- To increase flower and fruit production;
- To train plants such as hedges, espalier forms, and topiary plants to a particular size or shape;
- To rejuvenate shrubs that have overgrown their space, as large, vigorous plants often regrow quickly where a smaller plant may be more appropriate; and
- To remove lower tree limbs that interfere with lawn management or pedestrian or vehicle traffic.

Plants vary in their need for pruning. Each plant type in the landscape has its own growth habit that requires a different pruning regimen. Slow-growing or dwarf-type plants require little or no pruning, while fast-growing, vigorous plants often require frequent pruning to not outgrow their allotted space.

Pruning a plant is a deliberate act to satisfy various types of landscape management objectives. Before you prune, be certain that your pruning methods and timing will meet your objectives and avoid serious permanent damage to shrubs or trees.

The Three Ts of Pruning

The three Ts of pruning are the three important considerations to keep in mind before making a cut: tools, timing, and techniques.

Tools. Pruning tools are available in a wide range of brand names, styles, and prices. When possible, shop for durable, high-quality tools rather than those that are most affordable. Look for tool companies that offer replacement parts and provide good warranties on their products. You can accomplish most pruning tasks with hand pruners, lopping shears, pruning saws, pole pruners, or hedge shears (Figure 5.23).

There are two basic types of hand pruners: scissor-action (or bypass) pruners and anvil-action (or snap-cut) pruners. Scissor-action pruners have a sharp blade that cuts by sliding past a hooked blade; anvil-action pruners have a sharp blade that cuts against a flat anvil of softer metal. Scissor-action pruners usually cost more than anvil-action pruners, but they make closer, smoother cuts.

Smooth pruning cuts at the right locations are important to the plant's ability to close the wound with the growth of response tissue (called **woundwood**). Using the appropriate size tool facilitates better pruning cuts. Using a small tool for large cuts can lead to ragged cuts or—if you apply too much pressure—damage to tools. Hand pruners cut small twigs and branches up to ½ in. in diameter and are the best tool for routine pruning, because smaller cuts mean smaller wounds. For branches ½-1½ in. in diameter, lopping shears may be best. Cut large branches that measure more than 1½ in. in diameter with a pruning saw.

Handle shapes vary among pruning saws and are a matter of personal preference. The bow saw is another type of pruning saw; it makes large cuts but cannot be maneuvered in tight spaces.

Pole pruners aid in removing tree branches that you cannot reach from the ground. Most pole saws have both a lopping blade and a pruning saw. The lopping blade is operated from the ground by a long rope or lanyard that is pulled downwards to cut. The pole can be aluminum, fiberglass, or plastic. Some poles fit together in sections, while newer models have telescoping extensions. Because of the risk of electrocution, avoid using aluminum-handled pole pruners near power lines.

Pruning Timing. Flowering ornamentals form their flower buds at different times of the year, so pruning times must be adjusted accordingly so as not to lose flowers for a season. Many spring-flowering plants, such as azaleas, dogwood, forsythia, and redbud, produce flower buds in the late summer and fall, so pruning during fall or winter months eliminates or reduces their spring flower displays. Some plants—such as crape myrtle, Abelia, and Indian hawthorn—form flower buds on new growth, so they can be pruned in late winter to early spring and will still produce summer flowers.

Figure 5.23 Common pruning tools

Lopping shears operate like hand pruners, but they have larger blades and long handles to increase leverage. As previously mentioned, bypass lopping shears will make smoother cuts and cause less tissue damage than anvil types.

One caution: there is a wide range of density between various woody shrubs and trees; this can affect which tool size is best for the task. Trees such as oaks have harder, higher-density wood and may require larger tools even when they are smaller than a yellow poplar that is not as dense or difficult to cut.

Use a pruning saw for branches larger than 1½ in. in diameter. There are many variations of pruning saws, but essentially, a pruning saw has a narrow blade for easy maneuvering and coarser teeth than a common carpentry saw; most pruning saws also have curved blades that cut on the draw stroke as you pull the blade toward you.

Generally, plants that flower before June 1st should be pruned after they bloom; those that flower after June 1st are considered summer-flowering and can be pruned just prior to spring growth. There are exceptions, including oakleaf hydrangea or gardenias; they are summer-flowering shrubs that form flower buds the previous season.

You can prune landscape plants not grown for their flowers during late winter, spring, or summer. Avoid pruning during fall or early winter, because it may encourage tender new growth that may not harden sufficiently to resist cold injury.

Some trees—such as maple, birch, dogwood, beech, elm, willow, flowering plum, and cherry—bleed or excrete large amounts of sap from pruning wounds. Sap excreted from the tree is not harmful, but it is unsightly. To minimize bleeding, prune these trees after the leaves have matured, in early summer. Leaves use plant sap when they expand, so the tree excretes less sap from its wounds.

Pruning Techniques. There are several ways to prune plants. To understand why one pruning technique is preferred over another for a specific plant and why cuts are made the way they are, it helps to understand a few physiological principles of pruning.

Figure 5.24 shows the effect of apical dominance on lateral buds. The terminal bud is the bud at the top of a woody plant or the end of a branch or twig. It produces a hormone called auxin that directs the growth of lateral buds below it. This auxin inhibits growth in the lower branches if the terminal bud is intact. However, when the terminal bud is removed and auxin no longer flows downward to inhibit the lateral buds and shoots, they grow more vigorously. Shoots or buds within 6-8 in. of the pruning cut are the most vigorous.

Making the Cut. A second physiological principle explains what happens when you make a pruning cut and why certain cuts are better than others. When you cut a branch back to the main stem, a lateral branch, or a lateral bud, the wound seals rapidly due to a higher concentration of hormones in these areas. When you leave a stub, the distance from the hormonal source increases and the process of sealing the wound slows—if it seals at all. Insects or diseases may enter the cut portion of the stub and cause it to die back. Therefore, regardless of whether you are pruning a small twig or large branch, avoid leaving a stub by always cutting back to a bud, a lateral branch, or the main trunk outside the branch collar.

When you prune back to a bud, make the cut at a slight angle ¼ in. above a bud (Figure 5.25). A hormonal stimulus from the nearby bud accelerates the sealing process. However, avoid making the cut at a sharp angle, as it will produce a larger wound.

Heading and Thinning Cuts. When shrubs are headed back or sheared routinely—which is the indiscriminate cutting of the ends of twigs or young branches to a bud or node—it produces a lot of dense, thick, new growth near the outer portions of the canopy. As a result, less light reaches the interior portions of the plant, foliage within the canopy becomes sparse, and the plant appears twiggy and top-heavy. To avoid this problem, head back the shrub's shoots to several different heights.

Heading back or stubbing trees is rarely warranted in landscape sites and often results in undesirable multiple leaders and trunks. If it is necessary, for instance, to prune beneath power lines or to clear a tree from interfering with a structure, always prune back to a fork where there is a live branch at least one-third the diameter of the limb or stem being removed. This technique is called a reduction cut, or "drop-crotching." (Figure 5.26) Within several months, prune out all sprouts from the cut. Never "hat-rack" or "top" (Figure 5.27) a landscape tree by cutting its branches back to an arbitrary length.

Minimize Wounding and Speed Wound Closure. It is important to make pruning cuts that minimize injury to woody stems, buds, and bark. Current pruning recommendations advise against pruning branches

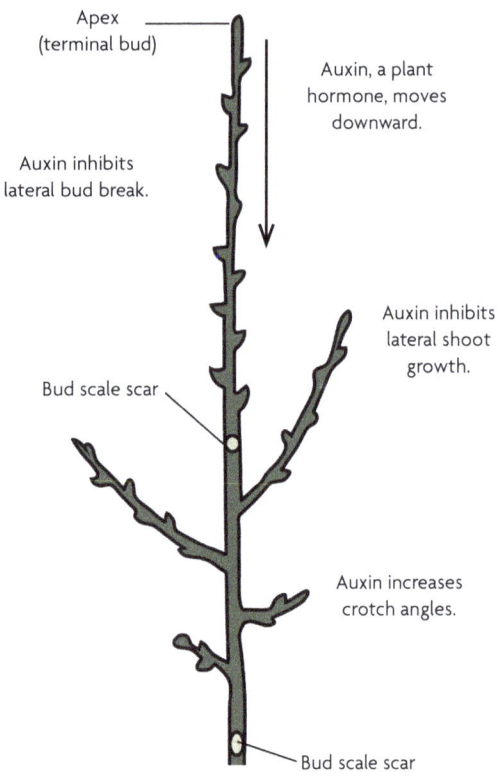

Figure 5.24 **Effect of pruning on apical dominance of stems.**

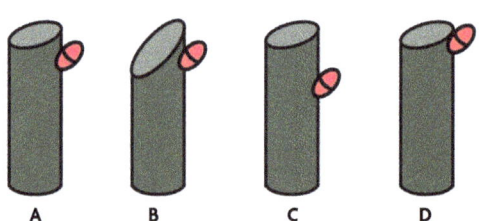

(A) Proper location and angle of pruning cut. (B) Too slanted. (C) Too far from the bud. (D) Too close to the bud.

Figure 5.25 **Heading back to a bud**

CHAPTER 5 - TREES AND SHRUBS • 165

Figure 5.26 Reduction cuts
Image Credit: Paul Thompson, Clemson University

Figure 5.28 The branch collar is the swollen area at the base of the branch which is highlighted in yellow. The branch bark ridge (highlighted in red) is an area of pushed up bark at the top of the collar angling down the trunk on each side of the branch.
Image Credit: Paul Thompson, Clemson University

Pruning Trees

Become familiar with the characteristics of the forms of different trees before removing any branches. In many landscapes, it's best not to alter a tree's basic form, as that stems from its genetic growth habit. Instead, prune trees in a way that enhances and encourages their natural shapes.

Also consider the genetics of a particular species or cultivar and how they influence tree form, size potential, and tree position within a landscape. Many plant species can be considered large shrubs or small trees depending on their genetics, the quality of the planting site, and whether the plant is left as a small tree or pruned into a shrub form.

When pruning, first remove dead, diseased, or broken twigs or branches. Then, study the tree's form and identify the permanent branches that are best spaced and positioned; only remove or shorten the others. To shorten, use reduction cuts. Permanent branches should be 6-24 in. apart on the trunk, depending on the ultimate mature size of the tree. On small trees like dogwood, 6 in. between branches is adequate, whereas large, maturing trees like oaks may require that branches be 18-24 in. apart. Remove fast-growing watersprouts that appear at the base of and along tree trunks or on large interior branches.

Figure 5.27 Topping or "hatracking" a tree introduces decay and leads to a better chance of limb failure from regrowth and increasing decay.
Image Credit: Paul Thompson, Clemson University

flush to the trunk. Flush cutting is harmful because it damages bark when pruning tools rub against the trunk, it removes the branch collar, and it goes behind the branch bark ridge.

The branch collar is the swollen area of trunk tissue that forms around the base of a branch. If you prune away the branch collar, you remove not only branch wood but trunk wood, which opens the plant to more extensive decay. The branch collar is what produces woundwood (Figure 5.28), which covers and seals the wound.

The branch bark ridge on trees is a line of rough bark running from the branch-trunk crotch into the trunk bark. It is less prominent on some trees than on others. The best pruning cuts start just outside the branch bark ridge and leave the collar intact.

Check young trees for multiple leaders; prune all but one to develop a single strong, permanent trunk. Keep the straightest and healthiest leader. When shaping a tree crown, remove lateral branches that grow upright; these can compete with the leader and form weak trees with multiple leaders. Most trees can be grown to have a single leader when they are young, but some spread to include multiple leaders at maturity. No branches should grow from the trunk at an acute angle or into narrow forks between branches or between a branch and the trunk. Branches that are less than one-half the diameter of the trunk are less likely to split off than larger branches.

When training young trees after establishment, prune back each branch in the bottom one-third of the tree's height to remove at least half the leaf area; this is referred to as making subordination cuts (Figure 5.29 a & b). The pruned branches are temporary and will be removed later as the tree grows. Young trees need lower branches to develop strong trunks, but subordinating the branches slows their growth so they don't get too big. Monitor and remove any temporary branches that become one-half as thick as the trunk where they attach.

By keeping the thinner branches on the trunk, the tree stands erect and develops a thicker trunk and more extensive root system. The lower trunk is also better protected from sunburn, vandalism, and accidental damage. Removing the lower branches too soon will result in a poor-quality plant that will not stand erect without a stake. When the tree trunk approaches 2 in. in diameter as measured 6 in. from the ground, remove all temporary branches.

Once the framework—the trunk and main branches—of a tree is established, the tree will still require some annual maintenance pruning. Each tree is different in its growth habit, vigor, and pruning requirements. Below are some general considerations to guide your pruning:

- Major limbs growing at a narrow angle to the main trunk (less than 45°) are more likely to develop weak crotches, and they may split during heavy winds and ice loads. Remove branches that have narrow crotches.
- Remove branches that grow inward or threaten to rub against nearby branches.
- Remove branches that grow downward from the main limbs, as they may interfere with mowing and other maintenance.
- Prune any branches damaged by insects, diseases, winter cold, or storms below the damaged area. Prune branches of pear, pyracantha, or loquat damaged by fire blight disease at least 8 in. below the symptomatic area. To prevent spreading disease, sterilize pruning tools between cuts by dipping the blades in Lysol® or a solution of 1 part household bleach to 9 parts water.
- Trees such as Bradford pear, ornamental cherry, crabapple, and ornamental plum form vigorous shoots or suckers at the base of the trunk and upright succulent shoots (water sprouts) along the main branches; these shoots starve the tree of valuable nutrients and detract from the tree's overall appearance. Remove them while they are young.
- Some trees develop upright shoots that compete with the main trunk for dominance. Remove these shoots to maintain conical, pyramidal growth.
- Large, maturing trees planted within turf areas with dense foliage often need more branches

Figures 5.29a&b This newly planted 8 foot tall tree will one day mature to over 50 feet. All the current branches are temporary but important for trunk development. The image on the right shows a subordination of lower branchs to slow their growth but still feed the trunk. Competely remove the branches one at a time as they approach 1/2 the diameter of the trunk where they are attached such as the branch with the red arrow. the branch with the blue arrow was a codominent stem which has been subordinated for now until a branch collar forms.
Image Credit: Paul Thompson, Clemson University

removed as they grow to allow adequate sunlight to reach nearby turf. Failure to remove these branches often results in gradual decline the turfgrass.

Removing Large Tree Branches. Large branches that are too heavy to support by hand require pruning via the 3-cut method (Figure 5.30) to prevent trunk bark stripping. Make the first cut on the underside of the branch six to eight inches out from the branch collar. Cut through the branch until the weight of the branch begins to bind the saw. Make the second cut downward from the top of the branch, several inches beyond the first cut so the limb splits cleanly between the cuts and falls to the ground without damaging the trunk. You can then hold the remaining stub with one hand as you cut it from the tree. Your final cut begins just outside of the branch bark ridge and ends just outside the branch collar that swells on the lower side of the branch.

It is no longer best practice to paint wounds with a tree wound dressing. Previously, it was standard to paint wounds with a high-quality wound dressing to protect the cut surface from rotting due to pests and cracking when dry. However, research shows that wound dressings do not prevent decay. When exposed to the sun, the protective coating often cracks and allows moisture to enter and accumulate in pockets between the wood and the wound covering. These moist pockets are often more attractive to wood-rotting organisms than undressed wounds.

Pruning Broadleaf Evergreen Trees. Broadleaf evergreens, like magnolias and hollies, usually require little or no pruning. In fact, most evergreens develop a naturally symmetric growth habit when left alone. Low-sweeping branches at ground level lend a natural southern charm to South Carolina landscapes.

However, you may want to prune some during the early life of the tree to balance the growth or to eliminate multiple trunks and/or leader branches. Otherwise, routine annual pruning is unnecessary. Allowing the crown of southern magnolia to remain at ground level is the longtime norm and reduces the necessary cleanup of their long-lasting, leathery leaves.

Pruning Conifers. The branches of most upright conifers—such as spruce, pine, cedar, and fir—grow evenly-distributed around the main trunk. They develop a symmetrical growth habit and become very large at maturity. If planted in open areas and given plenty of room, they require minimal pruning. However, to encourage compact, bushy growth, you can trim the new growth (called "candles") (Figure 5.31). Do this in spring, when the candles are soft and succulent. As a rule of thumb, do this when the new needles are about one-half the length of the old needles. Pruning at this time allows buds to develop on the new shoots below the cut, around needle fascicles that will sprout the next season.

You can prune spruces back to a lateral bud. Avoid cutting into hardened, older wood, though, because new shoots will not grow; this will ruin the plant's form.

Upright and broad-spreading juniper cultivars, such as Torulosa, Pfitzeriana and Hetzii sometimes outgrow their sites and must be pruned. You can make thinning cuts within a plant's canopy to reduce the size of a plant without destroying its natural shape. You can shear these plants, but it's best to shear only when creating formal shapes or topiaries.

Figure 5.30 The 3-cut method is used to remove a large limb while keeping the branch collar undamaged.
Image Credit: Paul Thompson, Clemson University

Figure 5.31 The new "candles" of a pine tree can be cut back to induce branching. Cut when candle needles are about halg the size of mature needles.
Image Credit: Paul Thompson, Clemson University

Like pines and spruces, junipers do not generate new growth from old wood. You can reduce the length of individual branches by cutting them back to a smaller lateral branch; this technique maintains a plant's natural appearance while decreasing its size.

One way to hide the cut stems on larger branches is to select smaller branches that are farther back on the stems and above the main branch. Once the larger branches are cut, the smaller branches above will grow outward and cover the pruning cuts.

Pines, spruces, firs, and most junipers should not be pruned back to older, bare branches; they will not produce new growth, and the needleless branch usually dies. Only prune these trees back to a green side branch or some foliage on the stem. Latent or dormant buds along the length of their needle-bearing branches will grow. Young arborvitae, false cypress, and yew are exceptions to this rule: when dormant, they can be cut back to one- or two-year-old wood that lacks foliage, and latent buds will sprout and fill in the gaps.

Pruning Shrubs

A properly pruned shrub is a work of art and beauty; it does not look like it has been pruned. Pruning cuts should not be visible, but rather, located inside the plant and covered by remaining foliage. The first step in pruning a shrub is to remove all dead, diseased, or injured branches. Remove branches that cross or touch each other and those that look out of place. If the shrub is still too dense or large, remove some of the oldest branches. Head back excessively long branches to a bud or lateral branch 6-12 in. below the desired plant height. You may also want to thin the shrub. Do not use hedge shears; cut each branch separately to different lengths with hand pruners. This will maintain a neat, informal shrub with a natural shape. Plants sheared to hard geometric shapes look out of place in a landscape designed to look natural. If you must prune dwarf shrubs, thin their growth instead of shearing whenever possible.

Pruning and Training Hedges

Because hedges are primarily used as privacy screens, begin pruning early to encourage compact growth. Head back newly planted hedge plants to within 12 in. of ground level, and prune shoot tips during the growing season to encourage branching. To develop a dense, compact hedge that provides privacy, prune regularly as the plants mature. Figure 5.32 illustrates a 3-year pruning sequence to produce a hedge.

Once a hedge reaches the desired height, decide whether to maintain an informal or formal pruning style. An informal style is best for a low-maintenance landscape; informally pruned hedges assume a natural growth habit. Prune only as needed to remove dead or diseased wood, and head back just enough to maintain a desired height and width.

Formal or clipped hedges require specialized pruning which may require constant work during the growing season. Usually, the desired appearance of a formal hedge is a sharply defined geometric shape. There are two important factors to remember when pruning formal hedges:

- Clip hedges while new growth is green and succulent.
- Trim plants so the base of the hedge is wider than the top.

Hedges pruned with a narrow base will lose their lower leaves and branches, because top growth will shade the growth below it and not permit sufficient light to penetrate (Figure 5.33). This condition will worsen with age, resulting in sparse growth at ground level and an unattractive hedge that does not provide privacy. Flowering hedges grown formally should be sheared after they bloom, as more frequent shearing reduces the number of blooms.

Shearing vs. Thinning

When shrubs are sheared routinely, it produces a lot of dense, thick new growth near the outer portions of the canopy. As a result, less light reaches the interior of the plant and foliage within the canopy becomes sparse; the plant appears hollow.

Do not attempt to cut large branches with hedge

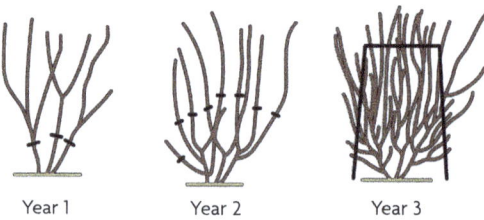

Figure 5.32 Developing a dense hedge over a three year period.

Figure 5.33 This image shows the effect of outward sloping sides (fullness to the ground) vs vertical or undercut sides (thin/leggy on the bottom) on one sheared hedge.
Image Credit: Paul Thompson, Clemson University

Figure 5.35 Hedge shears should only be used on succulent tissue but not on thick woody stems which cause a lot of ragged cuts.
Image Credit: Paul Thompson, Clemson University

clippers. Over the last few years, the electric and gas power shears available for sale have gotten longer and begun to have increasingly larger cutting edges. They are now routinely used to shear larger woody stems in addition to succulent new growth on shrubs. Unfortunately, their use often results in damage to larger woody stems due to poor technique.

Use thinning cuts if you want to maintain the natural form and shape of shrubs and trees. Thinning—cutting back selected branches to a lateral branch or the main trunk—is usually better than shearing. Thinning encourages new growth within interior portions of a shrub, reduces size, and creates a fuller, more attractive plant.

Renewal Pruning

Homeowners and inexperienced landscapers sometimes make the mistake of planting large-growing shrubs along the foundation of a building or home. As the plants mature, they overgrow the site, crowd other plants, hide windows, and appear out of scale with the building and landscape. When this occurs, it may be necessary to prune severely—called renewal pruning (Figure 5.37 a, b &c)—to bring the plants within bounds.

Renewal pruning refers to cutting plants back to within 6-12 in. of ground level. For renewal pruning, timing is more important than technique. The best time to prune severely is before spring growth begins. Pruning in the late fall or midwinter may encourage new growth that can be injured by cold. Renewal pruning results in abundant new growth by midsummer. Once the new shoots are 6-12 inches long, prune the tips to encourage lateral branching and a more compact plant.

Most broadleaf shrubs—such as azaleas, camellias, privets, glossy abelias, nandina, and cleyera—respond well to renewal pruning. Boxwoods, junipers, pines, cypress, cedar, arborvitae, yews, and other narrow-leaf evergreens do not respond well to severe pruning and may decline. Transplanting may be a better option than pruning if these plants overgrow a site.

Figure 5.34 Shearing creates a shell of full sun leaves with no foliage inside the plant. This makes the plant less photosynthetically efficient when the sun leaves shut down due to water loss on a hot day. It also causes plants to continuously use resources to regrow due to the continuous removal of terminal buds.
Image Credit: Paul Thompson, Clemson University

Figures 5.36a&b Using thining cuts opens up plant for interior leaf growth and leaves plants with a natural form.
Image Credit: Paul Thompson, Clemson University

Figure 5.37ab&c The shrubs in image (A) have become overgrown outside of bed areas and growing into the house. Image (B) shows a severe renewal pruning done in late winter before spring growth. Image (C) shows the regrowth of the pruned shrubs by early spring. A late frost nipped the newest growth, but the plant recovered nicely.
Image Credit: Adam Gore, Clemson University

One alternative to the drastic removal of top growth on multiple-stem shrubs is to cut back all stems at ground level over a period of 3 years (Figure 5.38). At the first pruning, remove one-third of the old, mature stems. The following year, remove one-half of the remaining old stems and head back long shoots growing from the previous pruning cuts. At the third pruning year, remove the remaining old wood and head back the long new shoots.

Skirting—lifting a plant's canopy by removing low-growing branches and shaping it into a tree form—is

CHAPTER 5 - TREES AND SHRUBS • 171

Figure 5.38 This boxwood is in its second year of a three-year renewal pruning. Half the taller branches will be removed this year, and the remainder next year.
Image Credit: Paul Thompson, Clemson University

another alternative to renewal pruning. A tree form may adapt well to a landscape scheme and appear less harsh than a severely pruned shrub.

Shaping Tree-Form Shrubs. Common larger-maturing landscape shrubs—like crape myrtle, camellias, yaupon holly, wax myrtle, and wax-leaf privet—are often pruned into tree forms: shrubs shaped like trees with one or more main trunks. The best time to begin a tree form is in late winter, before spring growth begins.

It is best to start a tree-form shrub from a young, one-year-old old plant, because it has not been pruned previously to a shrub form. These are then pruned to develop one to three stems that become the trunks. As the plant increases in height, more side branches are removed to raise the crown and develop the desired tree form.

However, more often than not, the decision to convert a plant to tree form comes after years of heavy pruning to restrict large shrub growth. If they are healthy, you can convert older, mature plants into small trees (Figure 5.39); you should replace any trees with significant insect, disease, or adaptability problems. When pruning a shrub into a tree form, select one to three of the most vigorously growing branches, depending on how many trunks you want. Prune all others to ground level. Remove any lateral branches on these retained stems that are less than 4 ft off the ground, and thin the canopy by removing inward-growing or crossing branches. Prune the plant each season as the stems grow to maintain tree form and remove any stump sprouts.

You can also develop a multi-trunk tree form by pruning back to ground level and selecting three to five of the most vigorous new shoots during the growing season; these serve as the main trunks, and you can remove the rest. In the spring, it's easy to remove undesirable shoots by hand while they are young and succulent. It may take 3-5 years to shape a tree-form plant, but the interest and accent it lends to the landscape may be worth the extra effort.

Pruning Vines and Ground Covers

Certain vines in a landscape—such as honeysuckle, English ivy, clematis, winter creeper, euonymus, and trumpet creeper—climb trees and other supports; they can grow rampant if they are not controlled (Figure 5.40 a & b). If you are unable to maintain them, it is wise to avoid planting them or remove established plants.

The amount of pruning these plants need every year depends on their vigor, growth habit, and spread. Vines trained to an arbor to shade a patio or deck may require only minor thinning or tip pruning to encourage branching, while those growing in trees or competing with other plants may need more severe pruning to control their size.

Figure 5.39 This overgrown sasanqua has been limbed up into a tree form to allow the canopy to grow above the sidewalk and driveway traffic.
Image Credit: Paul Thompson, Clemson University

Figure 5.40 Be careful where you plant vines; this house is just a big tree trunk to this native cross vine. The crossvine on the right is pruned about six times each year to keep it in check.
Image Credit: Paul Thompson, Clemson University

The timing of pruning is important for flowering vines. Prune summer-blooming vines (such as some hybrid clematis and trumpet creeper) before new growth begins. Prune spring-blooming vines (like crossvine, native honeysuckle, evergreen clematis, and yellow jessamine) after they flower.

There are three main reasons to prune ground covers:

- to thin their canopy when they grow thick and dense,
- to keep them within bounds, and
- to rejuvenate their growth after a harsh winter damages their foliage.

Horizontal junipers varieties such as Blue Rug, Bar Harbor, and Prince of Wales tend to form new needles on top of older ones and become thick and dense when their canopies meet. Thinning cuts improve air circulation within the canopy and suppress insect and disease problems.

In early spring, before growth begins, prune ground covers whose foliage has been damaged by harsh winter temperatures, as is common with plants such as pachysandra, Algerian ivy, and St. John's wort. Remove the old leaves of liriope in early spring, before new growth emerges. You can mow the foliage of these ground covers with a lawnmower set at the highest possible cutting height, but be careful not to injure their crowns.

Pruning and Training Crape Myrtles

Crape myrtles are a prime example of what can occur when a plant group has numerous cultivars that range in mature size from 3-ft shrubs to 30-40-ft medium-sized trees.

All too often, flower color is the only characteristic used to select plants; gardeners often select cultivars that quickly outgrow their expected or desired size. Thus "Crape Murder" (Figure 5.41) becomes the method for yearly size control of plants that are not suited to their planting space and intended function.

"Crape Murder" is a term used to describe the annual severe cutting back of thick stems. In these cases, the pruner gives little or no regard to forming, shaping, or training the plant. Severe topping creates basal sprouts and multiple vigorous sprouts below the cuts; these grow as a reaction to replace the photosynthetic tissues removed by topping. Unfortunately, it is very difficult and time-consuming to reshape a topped tree and recover a graceful form.

The popularity and widespread use of Crape myrtle began with the release of new cultivars from the National Arboretum. These new cold-hardy and disease-resistant hybrids quickly gained popularity; many wonderful cultivars have beautiful bark and showy flowers, but mistakes made in placement in the landscape can require drastic pruning that often ruins these desired characteristics.

Figure 5.41 This crapemyrtle has been "crape murdered."
Image Credit: Paul Thompson, Clemson University

Figure 5.42 The palmetto palm, South Carolina's state tree in its classis form.
Image Credit: Paul Thompson, Clemson University

Pruning Palms

Palms are like grasses and are monocots, while most ornamental shrubs and trees are dicots. There are physiological differences between these two classes in the plant kingdom. Palms have a physiology more like a lily, yucca, or grass; they grow all year and produce about one whorl of fronds each year. The South Carolina state flag shows how a mature palmetto is supposed to look (Figure 5.42). The form of the state tree is naturalistic and loose. The new growth at the top comes from the growth bud, or apical meristem. As they mature, the secondary fronds provide most of the nutrition for the palm. The older green fronds provide sugars and other metabolites (fats, oils, proteins) that are available to the rest of the plant's roots and stems. When the fronds turn brown and no longer produce sugars for the plant, they begin to hang down. They don't need to be pruned to benefit to the palm, but some remove them for purely aesthetic reasons.

Removing a green frond is a disservice to the palm (Figure 5.43). Older leaves provide a supplemental source of potassium, magnesium, and other elements for the growing palm. There is also evidence that over-trimming makes palms more susceptible to cold damage. Removal of leaves too soon results in previously healthy leaves in the canopy becoming nutrient deficient. Regular removal of declining leaves can cause premature death due to potassium deficiency. Removal of living leaves can create wounds through which serious disease pathogens can enter.

When removing fronds that are diseased or damaged by insects, use a sharp, clean pruning saw. Undercut the

Figure 5.43 Even though the older frond of this palm are spotted and looking a little ragged, they should not be removed because it will result in nutrient deficiencies. Never remove a frond until it is brown.
Image Credit: Paul Thompson, Clemson University

frond's petiole about 12 in. from the "boot," or attachment to the trunk. Then, make a top cut 1-2 in. distal to the undercut. Make the third cut at a slight angle toward the trunk. Remove only diseased fronds and clean up debris.

To keep unwanted palm sprouts out of flower beds and lawns, use a telescoping pole saw or pruner to remove the flower stalks before the seeds are released.

Sustainable Pruning and Training

If you only prune your plants to control their size or combat disease, it may be time to evaluate the long-term utility of your plants. It is always an option to remove or replace plants that require excessive pruning.

Mulching

Mulch is any material applied to the soil surface for protection or improvement of the covered area. Mulches are usually applied around plants to beautify plant beds, modify the soil environment, and enhance plant growth. The mulch material is often organic, such as bark, wood chips, leaves, pine needles, and grass clippings. Inorganic mulches do not decay and include gravel, pebbles, plastic film, and woven landscape fabric.

Benefits of Mulching

There are many benefits to soil and plants when much is used correctly. These include:

- Mulches can prevent water loss from the soil by evaporation. Moisture moves to the soil surface by capillary action and evaporates in the sun if the soil is not covered by a mulch.
- Mulches suppress weeds, though only when the mulch material itself is weed-free and applied deeply enough to prevent weed germination and smother existing weeds.
- Mulches aid in maintaining a more uniform soil temperature. The mulch acts as an insulator that keeps the soil cool under intense sunlight and warm during cold weather. As a result, mulched plants have more roots than un-mulched plants.
- Mulching prevents crusting of the soil surface, thus improving the absorption and movement of water into the soil while reducing erosion.
- Mulching can prevent soil splashing, which not only limits erosion but also keeps soilborne diseases from splashing up onto plants.
- Mulches composed of organic materials can improve soil structure as decomposing mulch adds nutrients to the soil.
- Mulches beautify the landscape by providing a cover of uniform color to the landscape.

Organic Mulching Materials

You can recycle pine needles, leaves, and other yard trimmings back into your landscape as mulch either alone or in combination with other materials. Fine-textured mulches do a better job of holding moisture in the soil than large particle mulches. Table 5.2 lists some advantages and disadvantages of common mulches.

Inorganic Mulching Materials

Gravel, pebbles, and crushed stone are permanent, fireproof, and available in many colors to complement the features of a home, patio, or landscape. When used near a lawn, there is some danger that lawn mowers will pick up and throw the stones. These materials reflect solar radiation and can create a very hot landscape during the summer (Figure 5.44), so limit their use to small, shaded areas. They do not benefit the soil like organic mulches do.

The best features of black plastic, and the reasons for its continued popularity, are its abilities to suppress weed growth and retain soil moisture. It is commonly used in vegetable and small fruit plantings and applied as a layer under wood, bark, or mineral chips.

Unfortunately, although black plastic prevents water from exiting the soil, it also prevents water from entering

Figure 5.44 Rock mulches such this southwest facing foundation planting, create a very hot and dry environment in the summer which is extremely stressful on the plants.
Image Credit: Paul Thompson, Clemson University

TABLE 5.2 Comparison of Mulch Materials

Mulch	Advantages	Disadvantage
Pine straw (needles)	Attractive. Not easily removed from beds by wind or rain. Doesn't mat down excessively.	Flammable. Fades with age. Decomposes rather quickly and requires annual top-dressing to maintain fresh appearance.
Leaves and grass clippings	Readily available. Shredded leaves stay seated and conserve moisture better than unshredded leaves.	Not as neat and attractive as commercial mulches. Could serve as a base layer with a thin layer of more attractive material on top. Grass clippings can mat if applied in a thick layer, excluding air and water.
Pine bark	Mini-nuggets conserve moisture and stay seated better than large nuggets. Longer lasting than pine straw.	May be dislodged by rain.
Wood chips	Attractive. Tends to stay in place even in windy conditions.	Decomposes more rapidly than bark.
Gravel, marble chips, volcanic rock	Attractive and long lasting.	Absorbs and re-radiates heat. May appear unnatural.

the soil. This is acceptable in crop plantings, where rows covered with black plastic are normally alternated with rows of bare ground or drip irrigation, but it is a problem in wide landscape beds.

Geotextiles or landscape fabrics are alternatives to black plastic. These woven and nonwoven fabrics of polypropylene or polyester are an improvement over traditional black plastic. They not only block most weed growth and reduce surface evaporation, but they also allow water, fertilizer, and oxygen to penetrate through to the soil, at least for a few years. In areas that will be devoid of plant material or under inorganic mulches, this cloth can be very effective for a long time.

However, when geotextiles are used under organic mulches, weed seeds will eventually germinate in the mulch as it breaks down into smaller particles (Figure 5.45). These fine particles can plug up the porous fabric and reduce the air exchange with the soil. The roots of the weeds will penetrate the fabric, making them difficult to remove. Fabric also creates a barrier that does not allow the normal processes that continuously add organic matter to the top of the soil as mulch. Usually, this process mimics the natural recycling and soil building that happen on the forest floor.

Although geotextiles are a great advance in mulching technology, they do not prevent all weed growth. Troublesome weed species such as nutsedge and bermudagrass will not disappear. Nutsedges will pierce and emerge through most fabrics. The extensive

Figure 5.45 after a period of time, mulch breaks down on top of landscape fabrics and weeds now germinate in the much with their roots growing through the fabric.
Image Credit: Paul Thompson, Clemson University

rhizome growth of bermudagrass allows it to grow laterally until it finds an opening to emerge; the most common openings are where the fabric has been cut to plant shrubs and trees.

One last consideration: landscapes change over time. If plants die, become overgrown, and need to be replaced, the fabric riddled with plant roots is extremely difficult to remove.

Where to Use Mulch

Mulching is extremely important when establishing plantings, as it helps to conserve moisture in the root ball of the new plant until its roots have grown out into the adjacent soil of the landscape. Without the competition for water and nutrients by turf and weeds, the growth rate and health of trees and shrubs increases. Mulch also helps to prevent injury to tree trunks caused by mowers and line trimmers (Figure 5.46). Mulch entire beds of shrubs, trees, annuals, herbaceous perennials, and ground covers.

In addition to benefiting plants, mulch can create a ground cover for walks, trails, driveways, play areas, and natural areas. Using mulch has less of an impact on tree roots than laying concrete surfaces. By allowing for more even water percolation, it is also less disruptive to drainage patterns. Lightweight mulch such as pine straw or grass clippings can temporarily cover low-growing tender plants to protect them from frost injury, and organic mulch be composted and serve as a soil amendment.

When and How Often to Mulch

You can apply mulch around established plants at any time. Mulch new plantings immediately after they are planted and thoroughly watered. Fall is an excellent time to collect fallen leaves and pine needles to use as mulch.

Organic mulches will gradually decompose and need replenishing to function effectively. Shallow plant roots grow up and into moist mulch and will die if the mulch is allowed to decay or wash away. How often mulch needs to be replenished depends on the mulching material. Grass clippings and leaves decompose very rapidly and need to be replenished frequently; other organic mulches, such as pine bark, break down very slowly and only need to be replenished to maintain a 2-3-in. depth. Once plants in a ground cover or shrub bed have formed a solid mass by touching one another, it reduces the amount of mulch necessary; the plants create their own mulch by dropping leaves, flowers, and fruit. Leaves from surrounding trees may also fall in the beds and provide additional free mulch.

Most organic mulches will change from their original colors to a weathered gray color with age. There are several ways of restoring color to mulches. One approach is to apply a thin (1 in. or less) layer of fresh mulch to the surface of the existing mulch; never exceed 2-3 in. of total depth. This approach is labor intensive and expensive.

Another approach is to shallow rake the existing mulch to restore the appearance of fresh mulch.

A third choice is to use a mulch colorant. Mulch colorants are dyes that are sprayed on the mulch to restore its color. Manufacturers claim they are harmless to both plants and animals but be cautious if you choose to apply them as they can cause skin and eye irritation. Dyes may also stain sidewalks and other surfaces.

Inorganic mulches such as gravel, pebbles, and stones are considered permanent mulches; they rarely need replenishing. Still, unless you use landscape fabric, small particles will eventually move down into the soil, and you may need to add a thin layer of new material. To maintain a neat appearance and prevent future weed growth, regularly remove leaves and other debris from the surface of inorganic mulch.

How to Apply Mulch

Spread a layer of mulch over the entire plant bed. When mulching newly planted individual trees in lawns, create a circle of mulch at least 2 ft in diameter for each inch of trunk diameter as measured 6 in. above the soil

Figure 5.46 Mulch not only helps conserve moisture and moderate soil temperature, but also help protect the trunks from lawn mowers and string trimmer damage.
Image Credit: Paul Thompson, Clemson University

surface. Increase the size of the mulched area as the tree grows, extending up to or beyond the dripline on established plants. This mulched area promotes faster tree establishment by eliminating competition for water and nutrients from grass roots.

Pull mulch 3-6 in. away from the stems and trunks of plants. If mulch is placed too close, the moist environment it creates increases the chance of stem or trunk rot; trunk rot can result in plant death. Keep organic mulches at least 12 in. away from the foundations of houses.

How Deep to Apply Mulch

The amount of mulch you should apply will depend on the texture and density of the mulch you plan to use. Many wood and bark mulches are composed of fine particles and should not be more than 2-3 in. deep after settling. Excessive amounts of these fine-textured mulches around shallow-rooted plants can suffocate the roots and cause yellowing of foliage (chlorosis) and poor growth. Coarse-textured mulches such as pine needles and pine bark nuggets allow for adequate air movement and can be maintained as deep as 4 in.

Mulches composed solely of shredded leaves, small leaves, or grass clippings should never be deeper than 2 in. These materials have flat surfaces and tend to mat together, restricting the water and air supply to plant roots. Rather than raking, which can damage the root systems that have grown into the mulch, you can punch the mulched area with a pitchfork to counteract the suffocating effects of matted mulches or gently rake the surface of the mulch to ventilate.

How Much Mulch to Acquire

Use this formula to determine how much mulch you'll need for your site:

(Length (ft) x Width (ft) x Height (in)) / 12 = cubic feet of mulch

Cubic feet may be useful when purchasing bagged mulch. If you plan to buy in bulk, you'll want to convert cubic feet into cubic yards. To do this, simply divide by 27.

For example: if a garden bed is 15 ft long by 3 ft wide and your desired depth of mulch is 3 in., you would calculate:

(15 ft x 3 ft x 3 in.) / 12 = 11.25 cubic feet

To convert this measurement to cubic yards, divide by 27:

11.25 cubic feet / 27 = .42 cubic yards

South Carolina is covered with forests and has a thriving forestry industry. Bark mulches and pine straw are biproducts of the timber industry. Many areas have local mills nearby, and bark mulches are readily available in bulk. Because of availability, over-application of mulch is a common practice at planting and on reapplications. Bark is often used around tree trunks in such large amounts that it inspired a new term: mulch volcanoes. Mulch volcanoes increase the likelihood of circling roots and stem girdling.

The first photo below (Figure 5.47) shows a very neat planting and mulching that, to a novice, would appear excellent. The tree appears snug, with plenty of mulch to protect it. However, this "deep mulching" creates a very wet environment around the crown of the tree, which can increase problems with circling roots, root rot, and crown diseases. When a lawn is irrigated with sprinklers, wet mulch is constantly in contact with the stems of trees. Heavy mulching along with deep planting predispose trees to future problems, particularly when trees are planted in clay or otherwise poorly drained soils that hold water near the base of the crown. Over-watering only increases the likelihood of future problems. Circling roots can also re-develop under these conditions (Figure 5.48).

LONG-TERM BENEFITS OF GOOD PRACTICE

Correct tree and shrub planting and aftercare practices are extremely important to a sustainable landscape.

Figure 5.47 Mulch volcanoes can lead to problems.
Image Credit: Paul Thompson, Clemson University

Pruning any circling roots at planting, planting at the right height—leaving the top root at or above ground line—, light mulching away from the stem, and irrigating properly can reduce or eliminate the potential for many future problems. Mulch provides other benefits, such as some protection from string trimmers and lawn mower damage, reduced competition from weeds and grass for water and nutrients, and improved rooting conditions.

Figure 5.48 Deep mulching can cause girdling roots which can pinch water nutrient and carbohydrate conduction tissues in the stem leading to decline.
Image Credit: Paul Thompson, Clemson University

Chapter 6
Herbaceous Plants

*Updated and revised by Amy L. Dabbs, M. S.,
and Anthony P. Keinath, Ph. D.*

Originally prepared by Bob Polomski and Anthony P. Keinath, Ph.D.

LEARNING OBJECTIVES
- Select appropriate herbaceous plants for various landscaping sites.
- Understand the basic requirements for soil preparation.
- Identify the basic maintenance requirements of herbaceous plants.
- Understand the basics of designing landscapes with herbaceous plants.

INTRODUCTION

Herbaceous ornamental plants—including seasonal annual bedding plants, flowering perennials, tropical foliage plants (Figure 6.1), vines, ornamental grasses, ferns, and succulents—are the horticultural equivalent of the icing on a cake. Gardeners use these plants to create colorful seasonal displays, functional landscapes such as rain gardens and pollinator gardens, and attractive container gardens.

While botanists have specific criteria for what defines annual, perennial, and biennial plants, horticulturists have blurred these definitions in the way they utilize plants in the landscape. Tropical plants are typically grown as **summer** or **warm season annuals** in South Carolina, where even the coastal region receives killing frosts. Plants that thrive in other parts of the world, where there are relatively cool summers and low humidity, are grown as short-lived, cool-season annuals in South Carolina, planted in fall and removed as summer temperatures rise. Taking advantage of commercially available transplants and fluctuations in temperatures, gardeners in South Carolina can induce flowering in fall-planted biennials within one year instead of two. In this chapter, we provide both the botanical and horticultural definitions of each herbaceous plant category.

FLOWER BED PREPARATION AND ESTABLISHMENT FOR ANNUALS AND HERBACEOUS PERENNIALS

Since annual plants spend a relatively brief time growing in the landscape, a gardener must prepare the soil in advance to facilitate rapid growth. Good soil preparation is even more important for perennials and bulbs. The goal is to create a garden that will grow and thrive over a long period of time; it is easier and less disruptive to improve soil and correct drainage problems before planting.

Begin any planting project with a soil test. Soil testing is the only way to determine a soil's pH and nutrient levels. Without a soil test, any application of fertilizer or other amendments could be detrimental to the landscape. Over-applying or adding unnecessary nutrients can injure plants, cause nutrient imbalances, harm the environment, and waste money. Follow recommendations provided by soil test results rather than guessing at how best to prepare your soil.

A soil pH of 5.8-6.5 is satisfactory for most annuals. Most South Carolina soils are acidic and require the addition of lime to correct pH. Some loamy or sandy soils may have a pH above 7.0. Adding sulfur or a small amount of aluminum sulfate will lower the pH of the soil. If the soil test indicates a need for phosphorus and calcium, incorporate these nutrients into the top 6-10 in. of the soil, as they move very slowly through the soil profile. If these elements are only applied to the surface of the soil, the nutrients will not be as readily available to the plants.

Most annuals grow well in a variety of soil types as long as the soil is capable of holding a sufficient amount of water, oxygen, and nutrients. Fine-textured clay soils typically have poor drainage and inadequate aeration; the opposite is true for coarse-textured sandy soils, which have good drainage and plenty of oxygen but retain little water. These problems can be combatted by amending the soil. Properly amended clay soils will have adequate drainage to supply both water and oxygen. The best amendments for clay soils are pine bark humus, composted organic matter, or small pea gravel; deeply spade the beds to a depth of 6-10 in. when possible.

When selecting compost, make certain that the material is fully composted and not merely "aged."

Figure 6.1 Tropical foliage plants such as copperhead (*Acalypha wilkesiana*) add bold color and texture to the landscape and in container gardens.
Image Credit: Amy Dabbs, Clemson University

Decomposing plant materials utilize nutrients such as nitrogen and sulfur to complete the decomposition process, which means nearby plants may suffer from nutrient deficiencies and the resulting poor growth.

When adding compost to amend clay soils, the resulting soil should comprise 20-30% compost by volume. For example, to amend 8 in. of soil, add a minimum of 2 in. of compost into the top 6 in. of soil. Incorporating up to 50% may have a negative effect on plant growth, while incorporating less than 20% by volume is a waste of time and material.

Peat moss, sand, hardwood bark, sawdust, wood chips, and pine straw are not recommended amendments for clay soils. These materials will not adequately improve the physical properties of a clay soil.

Improve water retention in sandy soils with amendments such as pine bark hummus or compost. Like clay soils, these amendments should comprise 20-30% of the soil by volume.

In some situations, it may be necessary to construct raised beds or install underground drainage lines to insure sufficient drainage. Commercial landscapes often utilize berms or raised beds to ensure adequate drainage; soil conditioner and compost are mounded 3-6 in. higher than the soil line to create well drained planting beds. You can also install drainage tiles; this is an expensive option, but it may be necessary if other alternatives are not available or sufficient.

Figure 6.2 *Nemesia* is a recently introduced cool-season annual that flowers prolifically in mild winters.
Image Credit: Anthony Keinath, Clemson University

best in cool weather (Figure 6.2). For example, annual phlox and calendula usually decline in the heat of summer but may bloom again in the late summer or fall.

Tender or summer annuals cannot tolerate freezing temperatures (Figure 6.3).

Annuals

Annuals can provide more color in a landscape more quickly and for longer periods of time than any other garden plants. They are versatile, sturdy, and inexpensive (HGIC #1152).

Botanically, annuals are plants that complete their entire life cycle from seed to flower to seed again within a single growing season. All roots, stems, and leaves of the plant die at the end of the growing year. Only the dormant seed bridges the gap between one generation and the next. Horticulturally, annuals are as seasonal plants that occupy a particular niche in the landscape prior to death by high or low temperature extremes.

Annuals are further categorized by their ability to tolerate cold temperatures, labeled as hardy, half-hardy, or tender.

Hardy annuals are those that can withstand temperatures below 26°F. Most hardy annuals are not very heat tolerant and usually decline or die with the onset of summer.

Half-hardy or **cool-season annuals** are those that can tolerate freezing temperatures above 26°F and grow

Figure 6.3 The star-shaped flowers of pentas, a tender annual, attract hummingbirds, butterflies, and bees.
Image Credit: Amy Dabbs, Clemson University

Growing Annuals from Seed

You can grow many annuals from seed. They may be seeded directly in their final locations in the garden or grown indoors and eventually transplanted outside (Figure 6.4).

Seed packets provide a wealth of information about planting, including when plants should be planted, how deeply to plant them, and how far apart to space them. Before sowing seeds, carefully prepare the bed and pay close attention to it during germination and the initial growth of the seedlings. Often, the gardener must thin or remove seedlings that are too close together. When most outdoor-sown annuals develop the first pair of true leaves, thin them to the recommended spacing found on the seed packet. This spacing offers the plants adequate light, water, nutrients, and space to fully develop both above and below ground. If you sow your seeds in furrows filled with vermiculite, you can transplant excess seedlings to another area without injury.

Many home gardeners prefer to sow seeds indoors and transplant them into the garden. There are two distinct advantages to sowing seeds indoors:

- You can more closely control the environmental conditions for germination and growth; and
- You can sow seeds earlier than outdoor conditions may permit.

It is critical to provide sufficient levels of light when growing seedlings indoors. Insufficient light will result in weak, spindly seedlings that will not recover. You can use adjustable fluorescent lights, but keep seedlings within 6 in. of the light at all times. Be sure to provide at least 16 hr of light daily to newly emerging seedlings. Sunny windows typically do not provide sufficient light to grow strong, vigorous seedlings.

Timing is also critical when growing seedlings indoors. Seeds sown too early may produce seedlings that need to be transplanted before weather conditions permit. As a rule, you can seed most annuals indoors 6-8 weeks before the last frost. Sow seeds according to the directions on the label in clean, sterile media such as bagged, soilless seed-starting media. Always use fresh, high-quality seeds; for highest germination rates, check the date on the packet to ensure the seed is fresh.

There are a variety of seeding flats to choose from. Many commercial products are available, or you can improvise and create homemade flats. In all cases, provide good drainage. You may want to seed directly into individual containers or small pots and eliminate the need to transplant. There are a variety of small plastic pots, peat pots, and formed pots—and combinations of planting media—available or easily made at home.

Harden off new transplants prior to planting by placing flats outdoors in a shaded location for a few days; then, move them to a sunnier location for a few more days. Avoid shocking plants by moving them from the greenhouse or indoor location to the garden without a transition period. Maintain consistent moisture during the hardening-off phase and after planting.

Transplanting Annuals

Many home gardeners purchase annuals as transplants or bedding plants. Countless varieties are available through retail outlets like greenhouses, garden centers, mass merchandisers, and grocery stores. Transplants have the advantages of being less susceptible to damping-off than young direct-seeded annuals and easier to space uniformly in more formal beds.

Do not plant tender annuals outdoors until the danger of frost has passed. The last frost date varies by several weeks between coastal South Carolina and the mountains (and everywhere in between). There is always the urge to plant too soon, but many annuals will not grow well until the soil warms sufficiently; when young plants are growing slowly or not at all, they are more susceptible to diseases such as root rot.

Figure 6.4 Zinnias are among the easiest annuals to grow from seed sown directly in the garden or started indoors and transplanted after the chance of frost has passed.
Image Credit: Amy Dabbs, Clemson University

If plants are pot-bound at planting time, simply loosen the roots around the bottom and sides of the root ball and spread them out in the bottom of the planting hole. Cover and firm the soil lightly around the plant. Be sure the crown of the plant is at or slightly above ground level in sandy soil and ½-1 in. above ground level in heavy soil. In raised beds, ensure that the crowns are slightly above the level of the bed.

If annuals are in fiber pots, remove the paper from the outside of the root mass and set the plant in a prepared planting hole. When setting out plants in peat pots, set the entire pot in the planting hole but remove the upper edges of the pot so that all of the peat pot is covered when you firm the soil around the transplant. If the lip of the peat pot is exposed above the soil level, it may act like a wick and draw water away from the plant, resulting in rapid drying of the soil and roots.

Once transplanting is complete, mulch the bed and water the plants thoroughly. If using pine straw mulch, it may be easier to mulch the bed before transplanting annuals rather than trying to fit mulch between closely spaced plants. Plants need to be watered thoroughly after planting to settle the soil around the roots. Check your plants every few days after planting to prevent them from drying out. Supplying adequate water during the establishment period is essential, but avoid overwatering.

Spacing Annuals

The most effective spacing plan for a bed of annuals is off-center or triangular rather than straight rows or square spacing (Figure 6.5). Triangular spacing requires more plants per square foot, but the resulting effect will be more attractive than plants placed in rows. In a triangular spacing, the rows are staggered, leaving no gaps or holes in the beds. The close spacing reduces opportunities for weed growth between plants.

To determine how many plants you need for a given area using triangular spacing, use the following formula:

Area of bed (in square feet) x spacing multiplier = the number of plants needed (Table 6.1).

Using the calculation above, 6-in. spacing in a 40-ft^2 bed requires 184 plants: 40 x 4.6= 184.

Growing Annuals in Containers

Many annuals grow well in a variety of containers, including large pots, urns, window boxes, and hanging baskets. You can also add perennials to containers for added height and variety. Containers are a convenient alternative when garden soil has poor texture or is infested with root-rotting fungi or root-knot nematodes.

Don't choose containers based only on aesthetics; containers should be proportional to the type and number of plants you plan to grow. The prerequisite for any container is that it has one or more drainage holes to allow excess water to leave the soil.

When designing container gardens, use a variety of plant sizes. Place plants in smaller pots in front of larger ones to eliminate some of the visual blank space created by the surface of the pot and relegate plants in large pots to the floor or base of your space. To tie containers into in-ground landscapes, use some of the same plants or the same colors in the containers as in the beds nearby. Place trailing plants at the edge of pots so they can

Figure 6.5 An alternating arrangement of annuals provides the maximum amount of space for each plant in the group.
Image Credit: Anthony Keinath, Clemson University

TABLE 6.1 Triangular Spacing Chart for Annuals

In Row Spacing (inches between plants)	Spacing Multiplier (# of plants needed/1 sq. ft.)
4	10.4
6	4.6
8	2.6
10	1.7
12	1.2
14	0.8
16	0.7
18	0.5
24	0.5

Figure 6.6 A container illustrate the "thriller", "filler", "spiller" concept.
Image Credit: Barbara Smith, Clemson University

gracefully flow over the rim. Use hanging baskets and vines for vertical accents.

One simple formula for creating interesting containers is to use one tall "thriller" plant, several low "filler" plants, and several trailing or "spiller" plants. Depending on the size of the container, use one, two, or three complementary colors and always choose plants that have the same light requirements or tolerances.

Soilless media is easy to use and gives superior results. A variety of ready-to-use products are commercially available. Avoid heavy muck soils or insufficiently aged compost, both of which are sometimes sold as potting soils. Watering and fertility requirements differ among containers, but generally, annuals in containers require more water and fertilizer than similar annuals grown in garden beds.

Fertilizing Annuals

Slow and controlled-release fertilizers are more expensive than conventional fertilizers, but they reduce the need for supplemental applications of fertilizer throughout the growing season and prevent fertilizer from leaching into the soil or entering drainage easements or ponds during heavy rains.

When using complete fertilizers, such as 10-10-10, reapply approximately every 4-8 weeks during the growing season at a rate of 1 lb. fertilizer per 100 ft². This will deliver 0.1 lb. of actual nitrogen per 100 ft² of bed area. Apply no more than 0.4-0.6 lb. of nitrogen per 100 ft² during the growing season. You can apply liquid, water-soluble fertilizers every 2-4 weeks, following label directions and labeled rates. Before making any supplemental fertilizer applications, observe the plants and let their appearance guide your decision to fertilize. If their growth and overall appearance look normal, fertilization is unnecessary. If you do deem fertilizing necessary, use soil test recommendations in deciding application rates.

Deadheading Annuals

Many modern cultivars are **self-cleaning**—meaning dead flowers drop quickly on their own—and others are sterile and produce no seeds; some species and cultivars, however, require the removal of spent flowers. This removal of spent flowers is called deadheading and improves the health and appearance of plants by channeling the plants resources away from seed production and into vegetative growth. This task is particularly popular for calendula, cosmos, geranium, marigold, pansy, and zinnia. Deadheading not only prevents the formation of seeds but stimulates additional flowering. For some plants, removing the flowers stimulates the growth of side shoots on which new, additional flowers will form.

Herbaceous Perennials

Herbaceous perennials are available in an incredibly wide variety of flowers, colors, textures, forms, and heights. Herbaceous perennials include bulbs, culinary herbs, ferns, grasses, ground covers, succulents, wildflowers, and the more traditional flowering perennials. Individually, they may bloom for a few days or several months, but together, these plants offer a continuity of bloom in a bed or border.

Perennials are herbaceous—non-woody—plants that live for more than two years. Depending on how well they are adapted to the region, perennials typically flower each year.

Herbaceous perennials have soft, fleshy stems that differentiate them from woody trees and shrubs. The top growth of many perennials is killed by freezing temperatures, while belowground structures such as crowns and roots survive the winter months and produce new growth in the spring. Although bulbs behave similarly, they are classified separately because they have a unique system of storing food, retaining it in thick, bulb-like structures.

Perennials return each year, unlike annual plants. However, many have shorter flowering periods and last only 2-6 weeks, while many annuals bloom for 3-5 months. Fortunately, perennials deliver more than just flowers; they are constantly changing, providing variety each season before, during, and after flowering. Even in the winter months, some perennials—such as sweetgrass and coneflowers—provide architectural interest with their leaves, stems, and seed heads (Figure 6.7). Perennials provide gardeners a wide range of design options for container, meadow, rock, shade, pollinator, rain, wildflower, and traditional perennial border gardens.

Today, there are more choices available for low-maintenance, sustainable, herbaceous perennials than ever before. There is an increasing demand for plants that are native, pollinator friendly, or more adapted to the landscape—and therefore require less water, fertilizer, and pesticide usage to thrive (Figure 6.8).

Characteristics of Perennials

The characteristics of herbaceous perennials are as varied as the number of species available. The term "herbaceous" originates from "herb": any seed-producing annual, biennial, or perennial that does not produce woody stems. Historically, herbs are used for culinary, medical, religious, romantic, and aesthetic reasons. These plants take one or more seasons to go from seed to seed and then can often live for three or more seasons, hence the term "perennial." Some perennials, such as columbine, are short-lived; others, such as peonies, will outlast several generations of the same family, in the same site, without needing to be divided or moved.

Figure 6.8 Eastern bluestar (*Amsonia* sp.), a native perennial that prefers partial shade and moist soils, is especially attractive to native pollinators.
Image Credit: Amy Dabbs, Clemson University

Herbaceous perennials, like annuals, are grouped by their winter hardiness. Those that survive the winter with little or no protection are considered hardy (Figure 6.9); those that need some protection to survive the winter outdoors are said to be half-hardy (Figure 6.10), while tender herbaceous perennials cannot survive in the garden overwinter. To maintain tender perennials from year to year, you must lift or dig them from the ground

Figure 6.7 Upland river oats (*Chasmanthium latifolium*) a native perennial grass performs well in full sun to part shade. Cut back previous year's growth in spring to allow the graceful drooping seed heads to provide winter interest in the garden. Be aware some seed may germinate.
Image Credit: Terasa Lott, Clemson University

Figure 6.9 Daylilies are among the hardiest perennials available to gardeners throughout the state. Their wide range of sizes, colors and shapes make them excellent choices for many gardens.
Image Credit: Amy Dabbs, Clemson University

Figure 6.10 *Lantana* cultivars such as 'Chapel Gold' are considered tender perennials, surviving all but the lowest winter temperatures.
Image Credit: Amy Dabbs, Clemson University

and store them indoors or propagate them before cold weather arrives. Many of these tender perennials grow from bulbs or bulb-like storage organs such as tubers, corms, or rhizomes. Some herbaceous perennials are so cold hardy and heat tolerant that they remain semi to completely evergreen throughout the year; examples of these particularly hardy plants include holly fern and Lenten roses.

Biennials are like perennials, as they complete their life cycle in two years. The first year, they develop leaves (often a rosette); in the second year, biennials produce flowers, develop seeds, and die. Because of South Carolina's mild winter climate, a biennial's life cycle can be viewed in a couple of seasons rather than calendar years. For example, if you sow biennial seeds in midsummer, plants develop during the fall months; exposure to a cold period during the winter months forces these biennials to bloom the next season.

Plant breeders have successfully developed biennials that now more appropriately fall into the annual or perennial category. For example, there are now annual strains of sweet William and hollyhock, both traditionally considered biennial plants. Common foxglove, often cited as the "classic" example of a biennial, is now also available as a short-lived perennial, *D. x mertonensis*; this plant is actually a cross between common foxglove (a biennial) and yellow foxglove (an annual).

Staking Herbaceous Perennials

Although plant breeders have developed cultivars of most species that are compact and sturdy and require no support, certain plants do still need extra support for protection. Tall-growing annuals like larkspur and tall cultivars of marigold or cosmos, as well as some particularly top-heavy species, need support to protect them from bending or falling in strong winds and rain.

You can support tall plants using wooden, bamboo, or plastic stakes or wire large enough to hold the plants upright yet remain inconspicuous (Figure 6.11). Stakes should be about 6 in. shorter than the mature plant so their presence does not interfere with the plant's aesthetic; when staked correctly, the plants grow to cover the stakes. Begin staking when plants are about one-third their mature size. Place the stakes close to the plant, but take care to avoid damaging the main roots. Secure the stems of the plants to stakes in several places with paper-covered wire or other materials that will not cut into the stem. Be careful not to twist the ties too tightly or you risk injuring the stem. You can use wire hoops to support plants with multiple stems, like peonies and salvias.

Pruning Herbaceous Perennials

Pruning herbaceous perennials can include deadheading spent flowers, pinching stems or buds, and cutting back leggy plants. Pruning improves the appearance of many perennial plants by extending their bloom period,

Figure 6.11 Support hoops can be used to easily protect tall flowers on single stalks from damage by strong wind.
Image Credit: Anthony Keinath, Clemson University

increasing the size and number of flowers, encouraging repeat flowering, and improving air circulation to aid in the control of insects and diseases.

Some perennials, especially those that are low-growing, edging, or mat-forming plants, benefit from shearing shortly after flowering. This drastic form of deadheading involves removing spent flowers, stems, and leaves with a pair of hedge shears. It improves their appearance, encourages the production of attractive new growth, and prevents them from thinning in the center. Sheared plants should be watered well to help them recover and produce new growth.

In the fall, remove dead foliage and stems of herbaceous perennials. Remember that it is natural for the tops of many perennials to be killed to the ground by frost, although other herbaceous perennials have evergreen foliage. Some perennials should not be pruned back completely in the fall, because they survive cold temperatures better with their stems left on; these include salvias, lantanas, chrysanthemums, verbenas, and Russian sage. To improve their appearance, these perennials may be cut back partially, but leave a 12-in.-long section of stem to heal before heavy frost.

Dividing Perennials

Over time, most perennials outgrow their allotted space or become overcrowded. Cramped quarters can cause perennials to decline and produce few, if any, flowers. When overcrowded, some perennials begin to look like donuts with empty centers surrounded by a ring of stems and leaves.

Separating or splitting apart herbaceous perennials helps to control their size and invigorate them and allows gardeners to propagate more plants for the garden. Dividing short-lived perennials or older perennials that have become crowded, with sparse flowers, can keep them vigorous and blooming. Divisions typically contain three to five shoots, or growing points, that—when planted—show more vigorous growth and better flowering than the parent plant.

Divide hardy ferns (Figure 6.12) like most other perennials. Ideally, dig and divide in early spring before new growth emerges. Cut ferns with branching rhizomes or underground stems on or near the soil surface into sections with a growing tip and one or two intact fronds to divide or propagate.

For ferns that develop a tangle of rhizomes and roots, dig them as a clump and cut them into sections. Occasionally, ferns develop multiple crowns—these can be cut apart and planted individually. Do not cover the

Figure 6.12   Native cinnamon ferns prefer shade and moist to wet soil. The lush foliage adds drama and depth to shade gardens.
Image Credit: Amy Dabbs, Clemson University

crowns of new transplants with more than ½ in. of soil and keep them well watered until they are established.

As a general rule, divide spring- and summer-blooming perennials in the fall and early winter. Divide fall-flowering perennials in early spring, when the new shoots are a few inches high, to avoid interrupting flowering. Most importantly, divide plants when they are not flowering.

We recommend taking these steps to divide and replant perennials:

1. Water the plant 1-2 days before dividing it.
2. Using a trowel, shovel, or spading fork, dig around the plant about 3-4 in. away from the shoots. If the clump is too big, slice the clump into manageable sections and pry them out one at a time. Lift the plant from the ground and shake the loose soil from the roots. If the soil hides the roots, hose away the soil so you can get a better look at the roots.
3. Plants with numerous shoots and loose spreading crowns can be teased apart by hand or cut into sections with a sharp knife.
4. Make sure each division has one or more shoots of healthy leaves and an adequate cluster of roots.
5. Replant the divisions at the same depth they were growing, water them in, and keep them moist until they settle in. Apply a light layer of mulch around the base to help retain moisture.

6. During the first month after replanting, check the divisions frequently to ensure that the soil remains moist but not soggy.

Propagating Perennials from Seed

You can propagate many perennials from seeds. In many cases, however, vegetative propagation is better. Vegetative propagation ensures that new plants retain the desirable characteristics of the parent plants, while seedlings can be inferior to parent plants.

Seed propagation techniques for perennials and annuals are essentially the same. However, perennial seeds often require a chilling period or **cold stratification** treatment to germinate. Perennials that rely on seeds to self-propagate often produce many seeds as insurance against the cold, animal predation, and other forces of nature. They often produce these seeds in late summer or early fall. The seeds scatter onto the soil and are covered with leaves until the spring, when conditions are right for germination. Gardeners can mimic this process and propagate more plants by simply collecting seeds in fall and sowing them in flats or screen-covered containers over the winter. The seeds will break dormancy in spring and sprout in the container, and when they are large enough, you can lift and transplant them into the garden.

Many perennials are produced in containers that aid in transplanting and establishment, but some are still grown in fields and shipped bare root and dormant. Most perennials can be planted in the fall or early spring. Fall planting is often best, because it gives plants more time to establish before the start of active growth in the spring. Perennials established in fall continue to develop after planting. They produce an extensive root system during fall and spring, enabling them to establish before hot weather arrives. In general, you should plant perennials at least six weeks before a hard freeze.

Insects and Diseases Affecting Annuals and Perennials

Herbaceous ornamentals vary in their susceptibility to insects and diseases. Some are virtually trouble-free in the landscape, whereas others require regular maintenance to look their best. The most common insect pests are aphids, spider mites, white flies, and caterpillars. Common leaf diseases include powdery mildews and rusts, while gray mold attacks flowers. Various fungi that live in the soil cause damping-off of seedlings and root or crown rot. It is easiest to remedy pest problems early, before the pest population grows or the plant is severely affected.

There are several conventional and alternative pesticides available for controlling insects and diseases that affect herbaceous ornamentals. The first step, though, is accurately identifying the insect or disease. If cultural or mechanical controls are ineffective or inappropriate, select an appropriate pesticide that is labeled for control of the pest and approved for use on the given plant. Misuse of pesticides can not only fail to control the problem but may cause injury to desirable plants. Always read the label carefully. Consult the Clemson Extension Home and Garden Information Center for current pesticide recommendations.

To manage insect, weed, and disease pests in herbaceous garden plants, practice Integrated Pest Management (IPM). This commonsense approach focuses on establishing and maintaining healthy plants and understanding pests. Reduce or avoid pest damage by selecting well-adapted species and cultivars—especially those with documented disease resistance—and planting them appropriately. Maintain plants properly, meeting their needs for light, water, and nutrients. Inspect for pests regularly, since it is easier to control small outbreaks than to wait and be surprised by full-scale attacks. Instead of immediately treating plants with insecticides, begin by pruning out affected plant parts or completely removing the first affected plants from the bed. Rake and remove fallen leaves and remove spent flowers, as both can harbor pests.

When deciding about pest control, start with the least-toxic solutions—such as handpicking large insects, removing old or diseased leaves, or hand weeding. Use insecticidal soap in a hose-end sprayer to control soft-bodied insects such as aphids and whiteflies; completely cover the undersides of leaves where the insects live.

Only use synthetic chemical insecticides as a last resort or when pest populations exceed acceptable levels of damage. Gardeners must decide if the plant should be saved with a pesticide application or removed. If annuals are near the end of their blooming season, it is often better to remove them rather than to try and cure a severe insect or disease infestation.

Good soil drainage can prevent many plant diseases. Well-drained soil is key to preventing and reducing root, stem, and crown rot. Good drainage is also critical for bulbs and perennials during the dormant seasons. Keep plant foliage dry when watering by using proper irrigation practices (as described later in this chapter). Maintain proper spacing between plants to allow for adequate air circulation that reduces foliar diseases.

Bed or crop rotation is important in the control of

certain diseases. It is generally unadvisable to plant the same annual species in the same bed each year. Remove all roots when removing old annuals at the end of the season (or whenever dead or dying plants are replaced). Disease and nematode problems may spread via roots left in the ground.

Root-knot nematodes are a persistent soil pest. Simply not planting in infested areas does not eliminate them. To manage root-knot nematodes, inspect roots of all plants when digging or removing them. Look for round or oval swellings (called galls) on fibrous or secondary roots. If you find galls, remove all traces of the root system from the bed.

Choose herbaceous ornamentals that are resistant to root-knot nematodes such as marigolds, coreopsis and calliopsis, black-eyed Susans, ageratum, blanket flowers, four o'clocks, cosmos, sweet alyssum, mealy-cup sage, and all bulbs. You can safely plant these plants in infested areas.

Remove cool-season annuals—like calendula, larkspur, lobelia, pansy, and snapdragons—that are susceptible to root-knot nematodes before soils warm and nematodes become active. Plant French (*Tagetes patula*) or African (*T. erecta*) marigolds in infested areas to starve root-knot nematodes. Nematode eggs hatch when marigold roots grow near them, but the hatchlings cannot infect marigold roots, so they starve. Planting marigolds following susceptible annuals can help to prevent a buildup of root-knot nematodes.

Irrigation

Herbaceous ornamentals vary in their drought tolerance, but most require an ample moisture supply, at least during periods of active growth. Natural rainfall is sometimes sufficient, but it is unwise to rely upon rainfall as the plants' sole source of water. As a rule, most herbaceous ornamentals require 1-1½ in. of water per week during dry weather. More water may be necessary during periods of extreme heat. Frequent light watering is not appropriate for herbaceous ornamentals; this wets only the upper soil layers and results in shallow root growth.

Soaker hoses or drip irrigation systems are ideal approaches to watering garden beds. Water from a soaker hose or drip emitter seeps directly into the soil without wetting leaves and flowers. The slow-moving water does not disturb the soil or reduce its capacity to absorb water.

Oscillating or overhead sprinklers are less effective. Water from sprinklers wets the flowers and foliage, making them susceptible to diseases. They may also destroy soil structure with the impact of water drops falling on the surface; the soil can puddle or crust, preventing free entry of water and air. The least-effective method for watering is with a handheld nozzle. Watering with a nozzle has all the disadvantages of watering with a sprinkler. In addition, gardeners are seldom patient enough to water thoroughly with a nozzle and often do not apply enough water. In addition, the water that is applied is usually distributed poorly throughout the bed. When watering, moisten the entire bed thoroughly and deeply. Allow the soil surface to dry before watering again.

Mulch

Mulch helps conserve moisture, moderate soil temperatures, control weeds, and improve the overall appearance of a garden. Mulches help prevent soil crusting, which slows water penetration, and prevents soil from splashing on lower leaves and flowers. For perennials, mulch also provides an added degree of winter protection. Heavy mulches that hold too much moisture can be detrimental, however, as heavy mulching may encourage crown rot if mulch is pressed too close to the crown. There are many satisfactory mulch materials, including compost, pine or hardwood bark, and pine straw. A 1-in. layer of compost, 2 in. of bark, or 3 in. of pine straw is sufficient.

A clean, weed-free, properly mulched bed should eliminate the need for cultivation. If cultivation is necessary, it should be shallow to avoid disturbing plant roots. Deep cultivation is likely to injure roots and often uncovers weed seeds, which can then germinate.

Occasional hand weeding should keep weeds in check. Some herbicides are approved for use in herbaceous ornamentals, but use them with extreme caution. Read and follow all label directions before using any herbicide.

BULBS

A wide variety of flowering herbaceous bulbs grow well in South Carolina, primarily chosen for their flowers but sometimes for their foliage. You can grow bulbs in pots, borders, naturalistic plantings, and mass displays. Bulbs come in varying forms, fragrances, colors, and seasonal interest.

In this manual, the term "bulb" is used in a horticultural sense, encompassing both true bulbs and other bulblike structures such as corms, tubers, tuberous roots and stems, and rhizomes. The primary function of these modified plant parts is food storage that ensures the plant's survival during adverse conditions. It is important, nevertheless, to distinguish between these structures, since each requires different culture, propagation, and care.

Botanically, **true bulbs** are comprised of a compressed stem—or **basal plate**—and modified leaves—or **scales**—which store carbohydrates, providing energy for the bulb for the next season of growth. Examples of true bulbs include daffodils, tulips, lilies, onions, Dutch irises, and hyacinths.

There are two types of true bulbs: **tunicate** and non-tunicate. The outermost scales of tunicate bulbs are covered in a papery skin, or tunic, that protects the fleshy scales. Onions and daffodils are both tunicate bulbs. Non-tunicate bulbs such as lilies (*Lilium spp.*) have thick, loosely arranged scales that lack a protective covering and are often have a scaly appearance.

Many species of bulbs produce thickened **contractile roots** that shorten and pull the bulb to a given level in the ground. Tulips produce stolon-like structures called droppers from the bulb instead of contractile roots; they produce bulbs at the tips of droppers.

During the growing season, lateral buds on the basal plate produce small, new bulbs called **bulblets** (Figure 6.13). Some plants, such as lilies, can produce stem bulblets along the underground stem and small aerial bulbs (called bulbils) in the axils of their leaves.

Like a true bulb, a corm is a modified stem with a basal plate. However, the primary storage tissue in a corm is the swollen stem tissue rather than the leaves. Gladiolus, freesia, and crocus are all corms. Corms may also be tunicate or non-tunicate. On top of a corm are one or more meristems, or growing points referred to as "eyes," from which the top growth emerges. During the growing season, the corm is depleted of food reserves and replaced by a new corm formed from buds on top of or beside the old one. In addition, stolon-like structures bearing miniature corms—called cormels—on their tip develop from the base of the new corm.

A tuber is a thickened underground stem swollen with carbohydrate reserves. Unlike a corm, a tuber has no basal plate or tunicate covering. Meristems or growth buds are scattered over the surface and, on potato, are commonly called "eyes." Both roots and shoots emerge from these eyes. A caladium is a tuber.

A **tuberous root** consists of enlarged, fleshy root tissue that is modified to store food. Tuberous roots only produce buds on their crown or stem end; usually they produce fibrous roots on the opposite end. Tuberous roots are biennial; they are produced in one growing season and then go dormant when the herbaceous shoots die. The tuberous roots store food materials that allow the plant to survive the dormant period. The following spring, buds from the crown produce new shoots that rely on the reserves from the old root during their initial growth. The old root then breaks down, and new tuberous roots are produced to begin the cycle again. Dahlia, anemone, and ranunculus are all tuberous roots.

A rhizome is a modified stem that grows horizontally, usually below the soil surface. Roots grow from the lower surface while shoots develop from buds on the upper surface or sides, usually at the tip. Cannas, certain species of iris, oxalis, and calla lily are all rhizomatous (Figure 6.14).

In some plants, the hypocotyl—the portion of the stem below the cotyledon and above the roots in a seedling—enlarges to become a fleshy storage site as the plant develops. This enlarged hypocotyl is perennial and continues to enlarge laterally every year. Cyclamen, gloxinia, and "tuberous" begonia have enlarged hypocotyls.

In this chapter, we use the term "bulb" in a broad sense to include all six of the storage organs described above.

Bulbs are often categorized according to their hardiness, time of bloom, and size. Under normal conditions, hardy bulbs are those that survive cold

Figure 6.13 Daffodil bulbs that are in the process of dividing have two or three "noses," which are the tips of the new bulbs.

Image Credit: Anthony Keinath, Clemson University

Figure 6.14 Louisiana iris are rhizomatous.
Image Credit: Amy Dabbs, Clemson University

Selecting a Site for Bulbs

The key to successful gardening with bulbs lies in site selection. The four major factors to consider are drainage, soil conditions, weeds, and sunlight.

Drainage

Well-drained soil is critical to bulb growth. The majority of bulbous plants are actually less particular about soil than many other cultivated plants, but good drainage is essential to all bulbs. Test how the site drains before planting by digging a hole about 1 ft deep and filling it with water. The next day, fill the hole with water again and see how long it remains. If the water drains away in 8-10 hr, the soil drains sufficiently to grow most bulbs. For waterlogged soils, cultivate adapted bulbs such as canna, summer snowflake (*Leucojum aestivum*), Dutch iris (*I. x hollandica*), rain lily (*Zephyranthes spp.*), crinum (*Crinum spp.*), and spider lily (*Hymenocallis spp.*)

Soil Conditions

Perform a soil test before planting. Bulbs perform best when soil pH is between 6-7. Based on the results of the soil test, add recommended lime, fertilizer or other material.

Weeds

Weeds can compete with bulbs. Remove perennial noxious weeds and eliminate weeds such as nutsedge (*Cyperus spp.*), quackgrass (*Elytrigia repens*), bermudagrass (*Cynodon dactylon*), and Johnsongrass (*Sorghum halepense*) prior to planting flowering bulbs.

Sunlight

Bulbs need sun to flower. Most spring-flowering bulbs prefer light shade to full sun. Select a site that provides at least 6-10 hr of direct sunlight per day. This requirement does not restrict their planting to areas that are in full sun throughout the year; because many spring-flowering bulbs bloom and produce foliage well before most deciduous trees leaf out, they get plenty of sun under the canopy of such trees that offer dense shade later in the season.

Light requirements for other bulbs, especially summer bulbs, are more variable. Select a spot where they will receive the recommended amount of light. Insufficient light usually results in poor flowering, but

climates, semi-hardy bulbs are those that are hardy in milder climates but not reliable in colder climates without protection, and tender bulbs do not tolerate freezing and can only be left in the ground in warm climates.

Spring-flowering bulbs consist largely of the so-called Dutch bulbs. Planted in the fall, they bloom the following spring. Most spring flowering bulbs are completely hardy in South Carolina, but some do not survive the hot, wet summers along the coast.

Summer-flowering bulbs include hardy, semi-hardy, and tender bulbs that flower in the summer; some summer flowering bulbs continue to flower until there is frost.

Fall-flowering bulbs consist largely of a few hardy bulbs and flower in late summer or early fall. The term "winter flowering" generally refers to tender bulbs simply forced out of season indoors, but a few bulbs—such as *Cyclamen coum*—bloom outdoors between early winter and very early spring and are sometimes called winter flowering.

Minor or underused bulbs are small in stature compared to the larger, showier bulbs. They can be used to great advantage in the landscape. Many, such as crocus and spring star flower, are especially valued for their early flowering habit.

too much light will bleach the flowers and foliage of some species. Keep in mind that you'll want to establish flower beds and plantings where they will be aesthetically pleasing, but not at the expense of plant quality.

Fertilizing Bulbs

If necessary, adjust the soil pH to be between 6-7 and add the nutrients recommended by the soil test results. In the absence of a soil test, there are two fertilizer systems suggested for spring-flowering bulbs.

The first system requires a single fall application of a complete, slow-release fertilizer at planting time. The second system incorporates bone meal into the rooting area at planting time, accompanied by a quick-release, complete fertilizer such as 1-2 lb. of 8-8-8 or 10-10-10 per 100 ft^2 of bed space; the fertilizer is applied again as soon as the shoots break the ground in the spring.

Organic fertilizers such as bonemeal are often recommended for bulbs; however, bonemeal releases phosphorus at a slower rate than inorganic sources. With either source, apply according to the recommended rates listed on the product labels. Under conditions where spring-flowering bulbs become perennial, they should receive an annual fall application of a complete slow-release or quick-release fertilizer.

Incorporate lime, fertilizer, and any soil amendments thoroughly and deeply to at least 12 in. Do not attempt to work the soil when it is too wet. If you can crumble the soil between your fingers, it is dry enough for digging and planting; otherwise, wait it out.

Fertilize most summer-flowering bulbs monthly from shoot emergence until the plants reach full flower. Usually, 1-2 lb. of 10-10- 10 per 100 ft^2 per application is sufficient. Additionally, some available slow-release fertilizers require a single application. This is a general fertilization recommendation; fertilizers are not necessary when plants show no symptoms of nutrient deficiencies and are growing in fertile soil.

Selecting Bulbs

Select and purchase firm bulbs. Avoid bulbs that are soft, moldy, or discolored. Bulbs are generally graded and sold according to size (usually circumference). Large bulbs produce larger and/or multiple flowers. The largest bulbs are not necessary for good landscape effect; in most cases, medium grades are entirely satisfactory.

Planting Bulbs

Plant spring- and early-summer-flowering bulbs in the fall. This allows the bulbs to develop a good root system and satisfy the cold requirement of their specific species. During this cool period, the plants roots form and the stem elongates. The cold requirement for most bulbs ranges from 6-20 weeks, depending on the species or cultivar. The exact time to plant these bulbs depends on the prevailing soil temperature. In general, it is best to wait until the soil temperature is below 60°F at the ideal planting depth. In most of South Carolina, this is between October and December.

Coastal gardeners can refrigerate tulips and other spring-flowering bulbs for at least 6-8 weeks prior to planting in December. When bulbs do not receive sufficient weeks of cold treatment, they produce flowers on shortened stalks, close to the ground, that are often hidden by leaves.

If you cannot plant bulbs right away, store them at around 60-65°F in a dry area. Temperatures above 70°F may damage the flower buds. Plant summer- and fall-flowering bulbs—except for colchicum and crocus—in spring, after the danger of frost has passed. Lilies are especially delicate; set them into the ground immediately.

Plant small bulbs, less than 1 in. tall, 2 in. deep; plant bulbs 2 in. or taller 6 in. deep. When in doubt, follow this simple rule of thumb: plant bulbs at a depth three times the bulb's height, measured from the base to the "nose" (or top) of the bulb. In heavy soil, set bulbs at two-thirds the recommended depth to ensure their survival during wet periods.

Plant bulbs upright and press the soil firmly around them. Water the planting area thoroughly to settle the soil around the bulbs. When planting in crowded areas among other plants, cultivate as large an area as possible and dig each hole with a trowel or a special bulb planter.

Caring for and Maintaining Bulbs

Mulching bulbs is important to conserve moisture (especially during periods of drought), protect them against extreme cold and heat, and control weeds. Apply a 2-3 in. layer of organic mulch after planting.

You may need to use mechanical methods of protection against wind damage. Tall plants such as lilies may require windbreaks or staking. Once the plant is in bloom, there is no effective means of providing cold protection; but while late or severe cold waves occasionally spoil spring-flowering bulbs, the bulbs are amazingly resilient—many do withstand severe cold.

A well-prepared bed should require little cultivation apart from periodic weeding. Many spring-flowering bulbs are inter-planted with other plants, frequently annuals. When planting annuals, be careful not to damage the bulbs.

Normal rainfall usually provides enough moisture for spring-flowering bulbs, but that's not the case for summer-flowering bulbs. During dry weather, provide supplemental irrigation weekly. Soak the ground thoroughly; bulbs have a much higher water requirement when in active growth than when dormant.

When the flowers fade, cut them off to prevent seed formation. Don't cut or remove the foliage until it dies naturally. Most spring-flowering bulbs produce foliage in fall or early spring that dies by late spring or early summer. Summer- and fall-flowering bulbs produce their foliage in spring; it usually remains until cold weather kills it in the fall.

To camouflage or reduce the negative impact of old bulb foliage, consider the following:

1. Interplant early-flowering species such as crocus with perennials that will overgrow the bulb foliage.
2. Interplant the bulbs with clumping forms of grasses, sedges, liriopes, and daylilies.
3. Plant bulbs behind the leading edge of a border so that as the foreground develops, attention is drawn away from the declining foliage.
4. Plant taller flowering bulbs behind lower foreground shrubs.
5. Underplant low-growing groundcover shrubs; when the bulb foliage becomes distracting, tuck the leaves beneath the sprawling branches of adjacent shrubs.

Dividing and Propagating Bulbs

Nearly all bulbs eventually become overcrowded and must be divided and replanted for best results; how long this take depends largely on the propensity of the bulbs to produce bulblets. Some may remain undisturbed for many years, while others may require division every 2-3 years. Do not dig bulbs until the foliage has turned yellow and withers, but dig them before the foliage disappears completely. Be cautious when digging so as not to damage the bulbs.

You can gently pull apart bulbs and corms. Cut tubers and rhizomes into pieces, with each division containing at least one eye. Split apart tuberous roots; some, like dahlia, require that a small piece of crown tissue remain attached.

It is generally best to wash off any soil that clings to the bulb you're dividing. You can replant bulbs immediately or store them to plant later. Store in a dry place away from sunlight, preferably at 60-65°F. Be sure to provide good air circulation and discard any bulbs that appear diseased. Remember that you need to dig tender bulbs in early fall and store them over the winter to replant them the following spring.

Controlling Infection and Infestation of Bulbs

Good cultural conditions eliminate many disease problems with bulbs; discard any diseased bulbs at planting. Aphids, thrips, Japanese beetles, slugs, stem and bulb nematodes, narcissus bulb fly larvae, wireworms, bulb mites, mosaic virus, botrytis, and various bacterial and fungal rots can sometimes be problematic. Because the recommendations for controlling these pests change over time, consult the Clemson University Home Garden Information Center for current recommendations.

Protecting Bulbs from Animal Predation

Many flowering bulbs and their flowers are eaten by animals such as voles, rabbits, and deer. Consider their susceptibility when planning your garden. Several rodent-resistant bulbs grow well in South Carolina, and although no system can totally exclude animals, covering bulbs with heavy wire mesh screening that allows the shoots to grow through can often afford some protection. A simpler but less effective method is to spread a handful of sharp, crushed, fingernail-sized gravel around the bulbs at planting.

Chapter 7
Home Vegetable and Herb Gardening

By Zachary B. Snipes and J. Powell Smith, Ph. D.

LEARNING OBJECTIVES

- Describe basic vegetable gardening techniques such as seeding, transplanting, cultivation, fertilization, and harvesting.
- Plan and plant a traditional, raised-bed, or container vegetable garden.
- Recommend the different vegetables and herbs typically grown in South Carolina and their appropriate growing season.
- Choose appropriate vegetables for warm- and cool-season gardens.
- Identify common vegetable pests and discuss management recommendations using IPM.
- Describe the benefits of crop rotation, intercropping, relay planting, and succession planting.

INTRODUCTION

If you care for them properly, you can grow plenty of home garden vegetables throughout the year in South Carolina. Beginning and experienced gardeners alike can benefit from this chapter's discussion of growing and harvesting vegetables and herbs.

PLANNING A VEGETABLE GARDEN

When planning a garden, start by asking yourself a few basic questions:

- Who will do the work? Will the garden be an individual project, or a group effort alongside family or friends willing to work through the season? A small garden free of weeds produces a greater harvest than a large garden suffering from weed competition.
- What do you and your family like to eat? Make a list of your family's favorite vegetables, ranked in order of preference. This will be a useful guide when deciding how much of each vegetable to plant.
- Which vegetables are worth growing? Grow the expensive, unique, and flavorful vegetables that you can't always find or afford in the grocery store. Consider growing high-value vegetables such as colored sweet peppers, gourmet lettuces, tomatoes, certain melons, cucumbers, and some squash.
- How much nutrition do you hope to provide with your garden? Some vegetables pack more vitamins and minerals than others. Nutrient-dense vegetables include sweet potatoes, carrots, spinach, collards, red pepper, and kale.
- What do you want your garden to look like? The flowers, leaves, and fruits of some vegetables add beauty to a landscape or are more aesthetically pleasing.
- How will you use the produce from the garden? If you plan to share, can, freeze, dry, or store all or part of your produce, this will affect the size of the garden and the vegetable varieties you select. Some varieties keep better than others.
- What are the characteristics of your planting site? Be sure to choose seeds of varieties that are adapted to the planting space and the eventual vegetable use.
- How much space is available? How many plants can you reasonably care for?

Once you've established what size and type of garden are most practical for you, begin to plan the garden's layout and care schedule.

Plan the garden on paper first. Graph paper, where ¼ in. represents 1 ft, works well. A 12x16-ft space is usually sufficient to grow a selection of greens, some herbs, and a supply of tomatoes, peppers, beans, and cucumbers. If you're planting in rows, orient them north-to-south so that both sides of the rows receive sunlight, this orientation also speeds up drying of the leaves to thwart diseases. If a garden is planted on a slope, the rows should extend across the slope at right angles to reduce erosion. Remember to allow room to walk between rows while providing maintenance.

Draw maps showing how you will arrange and space the crops. You can use a separate sheet of paper for each season to show how the layout will change over time. Place tall and trellised crops on the north side so they won't shade the shorter vegetables, and group plants by growing period; if you plant spring crops together, you can plant later crops in this area after the early crops mature. Place perennial crops to one side, so you don't disrupt them with annual tillage. Consider maturation and harvest times for various crops to place similar ones together (Figure 7.1).

Vegetables are categorized as light, medium, and heavy feeders (Table 7.5) depending upon their fertilization needs. Consider grouping similar feeder types together so you can fertilize whole sections of the garden together.

Practice crop rotation to avoid planting the same or related vegetables in the same location every year (Table 7.1).

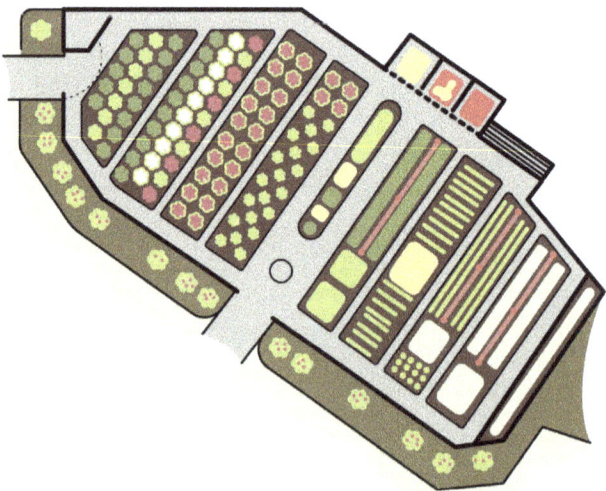

Figure 7.1 An example of a well-mapped garden plan.

TABLE 7.1 Vegetables and their Families

Monocots (Monocotyledonae)

Family	Crop(s)
Grass (Poaceae)	Sweetcorn
Onion (Alliaceae)	Chives, Garlic, Leek, Onion, Shallot

Dicots (Dicotyledonaea)

Family	Crop(s)
Mustard or Cole Crops (Brassicaceae)	Arugula, Brussels Sprouts, Broccoli, Cabbage, Cauliflower, Collard Greens, Horseradish, Kale, Kohlrabi, Mustard Greens, Radish, Rutabaga, Turnip
Cucurbit or Gourd (Cucubitaceae)	Cantaloupe, Cucumber, Gourd, Honeydew Melon, Pumpkin, Squash, Watermelon
Goosefoot (Chenopodiaceae)	Beet, Spinach, Swiss Chard
Mallow (Malvaceae)	Okra
Nightshade (Solanaceae)	Eggplant, Pepper, Potato, Tomato
Pea/Bean (Fabaceae)	English Pea, Lima Bean, Peanut, Snap Bean, Southern Pea
Sunflower (Asteraceae)	Endive, Escarole, Jerusalem Artichoke, Lettuce

TABLE 7.2 Vegetable Planting Chart Per Person

Vegetable	Number of Plantings	Total Feet (includes all plantings)	Yield (lbs)/ Processed Yield (pt)
Asparagus	1	25	15
Beans (snap)	3	75	30/30
Beans (pole)	1	20	12/15
Beans (lima)	2	50	16/8
Beets	2	12	17/17
Broccoli	2	16	9/9
Cabbage	2	13	21/15
Cantaloupe	2	6 hills	12 melons
Carrots	2	20	17/13
Collard Greens	2	24	30/15
Cucumber	2	10 hills	10
Eggplant	1	8	9/8
Kale	2	18	13/10
Lettuce	3	12	17
Mustard/Turnip Greens	2	12	11/10
Okra	1	25	17/20
Onions (dry)	1	20	20
Onions (green)	2	20	100 onions
Peas (English)	1	50	15/7
Peas (Southern)	1	50	20/10
Pepper	2	16	10
Potato (Irish)	1	75	50
Radish	3	15	150 radishes
Spinach	2	20	6/5
Squash (Summer)	2	6 hills	30/25
Squash (Winter)	1	6 hills	30
Sweet Corn	1	60	40/20
Soybean (Edamame)	1	30	15/10
Sweetpotato	1	30	20
Tomato	2	6 plants	40
Turnip	1	12	8/8
Watermelon	1	3 hills	6 melons

Plan the garden early and order seeds by January or February. You can start some plants indoors as early as January. You can plant some crops, such as beans, repeatedly or successively and harvest them over a longer period of time, increasing overall yields. Consider planting dates and days to maturity of your desired or recommended varieties while planning.

SELECTING YOUR SITE

Your garden should be as small as possible to eliminate unnecessary work. Decide on the quantity of vegetables you hope to grow and allocate the necessary garden space for each crop. Table 7.2 lists the space requirements of various vegetables on a per-person basis—that is, how much space you need to grow enough vegetables for each person you hope to feed. You'll need less space if you don't plan to preserve food.

In South Carolina, gardens should receive at least six hours of direct sun each day. Leafy vegetables can tolerate partial shade; vegetables which produce fruit, such as peppers and tomatoes, must be grown in full sun (Table 7.3).

TABLE 7.3 Light Requirements of Selected Vegetables

Full Sun Required	Partial Shade Tolerated
Beans, Broccoli, Cantaloupe, Cauliflower, Cucumber, Eggplant, Okra, Onion, Peanut, Pepper, Potato, Pumpkin, Squash, Sweet Potato, Sweetcorn, Tomato, Watermelon	Beets, Brussels Sprouts, Cabbage, Carrots, Celery, Collard Greens, Kale, Lettuce, Mustard Greens, Radish, Spinach, Swiss Chard, Turnips

Avoid planting your garden close to or beneath trees and shrubs, as shade and competition for nutrients and water may reduce vegetable growth. If a garden must be planted near trees, reserve the sunniest spot for vegetables grown for their fruit. Plants grown for their leaves can be grown in partial shade.

Gardeners with poorly drained sites or sites on steep slopes can improve them by using raised beds (Figure 7.2). You can create a permanent raised bed using treated lumber, cypress, watering troughs, concrete blocks, or similar rot-resistant material. Beds should be at least three feet deep so that they will not dry out during the day. Fill beds with raised bed mixes found at local supply retailers; alternatively, fill beds with alternating layers of carbon sources with nitrogen rich materials. This is known as the lasagna bed method. If you plan to use top soil as a fill material, ensure it does not contain weeds, herbicides, or other unwanted material.

Permanent raised beds are easy to maintain, require less effort to control weeds, and overcome poor soil or site problems. Raised beds can be any size, but narrow beds (about 3-4 ft wide) allow the gardener to reach the center of the bed without stepping into it.

Because vegetables require irrigation, especially during drought, consider a planting site close to the house; usually, this ensures access to an abundant water supply. People are also more likely to work in the garden and check for pests when the garden is conveniently located.

When soil or landscape space is unavailable, you can grow vegetables in containers. See "Container Gardening" for more information and instructions.

CREATING YOUR PLANTING SCHEDULE

When to plant vegetables outdoors depends on the cold hardiness of a particular species or cultivar. Vegetables are divided into two categories based on temperature requirements: cool-season and warm-season crops (Table 7.4).

TABLE 7.4 Classification of Vegetables According to Temperature Requirements at Time of Planting

Cool-Season Crops		Warm-Season Crops	
Hardy	Half-Hardy	Tender	Very Tender
4-6 weeks before last expected freeze	2-4 weeks before expected freeze	Not sooner than after the last freeze	1-2 weeks after the last freeze in Spring
Broccoli	Beet	Southern Pea	Cucumber
Brussels Sprouts	Carrot	Snap Bean	Eggplant
Cabbage	Cauliflower	Edamame (Soybean)	Lima Bean
Collards	Celery	Sweet Corn	Okra
Garlic	Chinese Cabbage		Pepper
Kale	Mustard		Pumpkin
Kohlrabi	Parsnip		Squash
Leek	Potato		Sweet Potato
Lettuce	Rutabaga		Tomato
Onion	Salsify		Watermelon
Pea	Swiss Chard		
Radish			
Spinach			
Turnip			

Cool-season vegetables originate in temperate climates and show the most favorable growth during the cool parts of the year. Cool-season crops grow poorly in summer heat. Though cool-season crops continue to grow well past the earliest freeze in the fall, be sure to

Figure 7.2 Creating raised beds on a sloped site.

start them early enough that they mature before hard freezes are expected—especially in the Piedmont and Central regions of the state.

Warm-season crops primarily came from subtropical and tropical regions and require warm weather for seed germination and plant growth. They are injured or killed by freezing temperatures and should not be planted outdoors in the spring without protection or until the danger of freezing temperatures is past. If you plant warm-season crops in the summer to mature in the fall, be sure to plant early enough that you can harvest them before they are killed by freezing temperatures in the fall.

If you know the number of days required by a plant to reach maturity, determine the appropriate planting time for seeds and transplants by using the average dates of the first and last freezes in the area. HGIC 1256, Planning A Garden, will help you determine when to plant cool- and warm-season vegetables.

PREPARING A VEGETABLE GARDEN

Improving the Soil

Healthy soil includes organic matter. South Carolina soils range from a fine clay to a coarse sand. To improve their fertility and productivity, add organic matter; this also improves the soil's tilth, its physical condition or structure.

When added to clay soil, organic matter holds the clay particles apart, improving air and water movement in the soil; this contributes to deeper and more extensive root development. On the other hand, coarse-textured sandy soils have excellent drainage—so excellent that they hold little water. Adding organic matter increases the soil's water retention and fertility.

Good sources of organic matter include animal manures and compost. Soil organisms break down these materials in the soil. Other relatively inexpensive sources of organic matter include cover crops, or "green manure." These plants protect the soil from erosion and, when tilled under, improve the soil (Figure 7.3).

When you incorporate a cover crop into the soil at the end of the season, it is converted into soil organic matter. The use of a cover crop for only one year will not have much impact on the soil's organic matter content; regular use over several years, however, slowly raises the overall levels of organic matter in the soil and increases the activity of soil organisms, such as earthworms and fungi. As these organisms decompose organic materials, they help improve soil structure and tilth, making the soil a more favorable place for root development. It is important to understand, however, that organic matter is continually decomposing and cannot be built up permanently in the soil. Soil building is a continual process in the garden.

Figure 7.3 A winter legume cover crop of Austrian Winter Peas being turned into the soil.
Image Credit: Zachary Snipes, Clemson University

Before sowing the cover crop, turn over the garden with a rotary tiller or spading fork. Dig under weeds and any remaining refuse from the vegetables or flowers that were not thrown into the compost pile. Level the soil with a garden rake. Sow the seed by hand, broadcasting as evenly as possible. Broadcast back and forth over the area several times to distribute the seed evenly.

About three weeks to one month before planting the garden for the next season, till the cover crop under if the soil is not too wet. Refer to Chapter 1, "Soils and Plant Nutrition," for more information about cover crops.

Testing the Soil

Get your soil tested by the county Extension office, as described in Chapter 1. Results from a soil test will indicate the amount of limestone or sulfur required to bring the soil pH to an ideal range, which is between 5.8-6.5 for vegetable gardens. Maintaining the right soil pH is very important, as it affects plant health and the availability of nutrients, eliminates problems with aluminum toxicity, and creates an environment that supports helpful soil-dwelling organisms, such as earthworms.

Cultivating the Soil

To prepare the soil for planting seeds or transplants, dig the soil to a depth of at least 8-10 in. The deeper the soil is prepared, the greater its ability to hold air and moisture, which provides a healthy environment for root growth and microorganisms.

To avoid damaging the soil structure, never dig or cultivate when the soil is too wet or too dry. Follow this simple test: if the soil sticks to the shovel, the soil is too wet. Postpone digging until the soil dries out.

When preparing a garden, add organic matter—such as rotted straw, compost, or manure—as mentioned previously; compost bulky material, such as leaves and hay, before adding them to garden soil.

The trenching, or double-dig, method may be useful for gardeners dealing with heavy soil. This method involves breaking up the soil to a depth of 18-24 in. First, remove the top 12 in. of soil. Insert a spade or fork into the next 10-12 inches and break up the soil. Mix in organic matter, lime, or fertilizer as needed. Mix the soil you removed with a generous amount of organic matter and return the mixture to the bed. This type of garden soil preparation requires a lot of effort, but preparing heavy soils in this manner improves drainage, aeration, moisture retention, and root penetration for many years. You can double-dig soil over a period of several years by focusing on one sector of the garden at a time.

Some gardeners may prefer to use a rototiller rather than a spade or shovel. Though a rototiller reduces the amount of physical effort expended in preparing the soil, the gardener should be aware of a few potential problems:

- Rototillers only till the soil to a depth of 4-6 in.
- Routine rototilling at a shallow depth may cause a hardpan layer to form.
- Excessive rototilling may pulverize the upper few inches of soil, destroying the natural granular or crumb structure of the soil; this can also lead to crusting.

Fertilizing Before Planting

Fertilizers are nutrients added to the soil. The three nutrients needed in the highest levels—nitrogen (N), phosphorus (P), and potassium (K)—are represented on a fertilizer bag by three numbers. Besides the primary elements, the fertilizer may contain secondary plant nutrients like calcium, magnesium, sulfur, or minor nutrients such as manganese, zinc, copper, iron, and molybdenum.

If you plan to maintain an organic vegetable garden, check with Clemson's Agricultural Service Laboratory for recommendations for organic fertilizers. Organic fertilizers derived from naturally occurring sources are a good alternative to inorganic fertilizers. They include composted animal manure, cottonseed meal, and blood meal, among other ingredients. Although they contain relatively low concentrations of actual nutrients compared to inorganic fertilizers, they do increase the organic matter content in the soil and improve soil structure.

In addition, organic fertilizers release nutrients over a long period of time. Organic fertilizers depend on soil organisms to break them down to release nutrients, so most of them are effective only when the soil is moist and warm enough for the soil organisms to be active.

The amount of fertilizer to apply to a garden depends on the natural fertility of the soil, the amount of organic matter, the type of fertilizer, and the kinds of vegetables (Table 7.5).

TABLE 7.5 Relative Fertility Needs of Commonly Grown Vegetables

Heavy Feeders	Medium Feeders	Light Feeders
Asparagus	Beans	English Peas
Broccoli	Beets	Okra
Brussels Sprouts	Carrots	Peanuts
Cabbage	Cucumber	Pepper
Cauliflower	Eggplant	Radish
Irish Potatoes	Greens	Southern Peas
Lettuce	Melons	Spinach
Onions	Swiss Chard	Sunflower
Pumpkins		Sweet Potatoes
Squash		Turnips
Sweetcorn		
Tomatoes		

There are two methods of applying fertilizer before planting: broadcasting and banding.

Broadcasting refers to spreading the necessary fertilizer over the garden and incorporating it into the soil with a shovel or rototiller.

Banding is an alternative approach in which the gardener applies the fertilizer in narrow bands in furrows several inches to the side and below the seeds or plants; placing the fertilizer closer to the seed may injure or kill emerging plants. The best technique is to stretch a string along the row where the seeds will be planted. With the corner of a hoe, dig a furrow 3 in. deep and 3 in. to one side of but parallel with the string. Spread the fertilizer in the furrow and cover it with soil. Repeat the banding operation on the other side of the string, then sow your seeds directly underneath the string. For plants that require a lot of space, such as tomatoes, place the fertilizer in 6-in. bands alongside each plant, about 4 in. from the base of the plant.

Banding is one way to satisfy the phosphorus needs of many plants, especially tomatoes, as the first roots develop. When fertilizers are broadcast and worked into the soil, much of the phosphorus is absorbed by the soil and not immediately available to the plant. By concentrating the phosphorus near the roots, the plant receives what it needs even despite the phosphorous being tied up. Banding is a particularly effective method of supplying phosphorus to early-planted vegetables when the soil is still cold.

If you tested your soil the previous year but not the year you're preparing for, apply fertilizer at the same rate as you did the previous year. Do not apply lime until conducting another test, as over-liming can result in poor growth and nutrient deficiencies.

Applying limestone as needed according to soil test results benefits gardens in two ways: it eliminates some acid in the soil, and it makes plant nutrients more available to the plants. Limestone is a form of fertilizer because it contains calcium, a necessary nutrient for plant growth; dolomitic limestone contains calcium and magnesium, other essential nutrients for plant growth. Grinding lime makes it more effective; the smaller the particles, the faster the lime begins to actively reduce acid.

Pulverized limestone is the most effective form of agricultural limestone. Other types of lime are sold, but the application rates differ for each. Our recommendations are based on the use of agricultural limestone.

If a recent soil test is not available, make a pre-plant application of 5-10-10 at the rate suggested in Table 7.6. Refer to Table 7.7 for information on converting weights to volumes.

PLANTING A GARDEN
Seeds

Choosing and purchasing fresh, high-quality vegetable seeds is important to successful gardening. Purchase seed from a dependable seed company to increase your chances of a bountiful harvest. Keep notes about the seeds you purchase: their germination, the vigor of the plants, and any tendencies toward insects and disease. Even under the best storage conditions, seed vigor will start to decline after 2-3 years.

Using this information, it is easy determine which seed company best meets your needs and which vegetable varieties are most suited to your area or gardening style. Always choose a seed variety adapted to South Carolina, as environmental conditions can cause unsuitable seeds to perform poorly.

Indoor Seeds as Outdoor Transplants

If a gardener has plenty of time and space available, they can start vegetable seeds indoors and later transplant them to the garden. Growing transplants from seed gives greater access to many cultivars and produces many transplants inexpensively. To ensure the successful production of transplants, the gardener needs to meet the following requirements: insect-, weed-, and disease-free growing medium; adequate heat and moisture; enough light to grow a stocky plant; and the time or materials to harden off the transplants prior to planting them outdoors. Some vegetables transplant to the field more easily than others. Refer to Table 7.8 to determine which vegetables should be transplanted or directly seeded into the garden.

There are two basic methods of growing transplants from seed. In the one-step method, seed directly into a container and then plant the container or transplant the full plant into the garden. The container could be a peat pot, peat pellet, or a container with a hole punched in the bottom for drainage. Some common household containers include cut-off milk cartons, plastic jugs, yogurt cups, and margarine tubs. Place the container in a plastic bag that is closed at the top with a twist-tie to keep the soil moist. When planting peat pots directly into the garden soil, cut or remove one side and do not allow the edges of the pot to stick out above the soil.

In the two-step method, sow the seeds in a flat. Because seeds are extremely sensitive to drying out, cover the flats with plastic wrap to retain moisture until all the seeds have germinated. When one or two sets of true leaves appear, transplant the seedlings into larger

TABLE 7.6

Plant Family (examples)	Soil Considerations	Pre-plant Fertilizer per 100 ft^2	Additional Fertilizer	Watering
Cole Crop (cabbage, kale)	Well-drained 5.8-6.5 pH	3 lbs 5-10-10	2 lbs calcium nitrate per 100 feet of row 3-4 weeks after planting More fertilizer will be needed on sandier soils	Consistent soil moisture levels down to 6 inches
Squash (cucumber, squash)	Well-drained Use raised beds to promote drainage 5.8-6.5 pH	3 lbs 5-10-10	2 lbs calcium nitrate per 100 row feet For vining cucurbits, side-dress when plants begin to "run" and again after bloom Too much nitrogen will result in vegetative growth and reduce yield	Consistent soil moisture Use organic or man-made mulches Increase water during fruiting periods Keep foliage dry
Goosefoot (beet, spinach)	Fertile sandy loam High organic matter Well-drained 5.8-6.5 pH	3 lbs 5-10-10	Side-dress once with 2 lbs of calcium nitrate halfway through the growing season	Consistent soil moisture levels down to 6 inches Increase water as plants get larger
Grass (sweetcorn)	Seed germinates at 60-95 degrees Fahrenheit	3 lbs 5-10-10	Side-dress three times with calcium nitrate at 2 lbs per 100 row feet	Moisture levels are critical during pollination and ear fill
Morning Glory (sweet potato)	Well-drained	3 lbs 5-10-10	Side-dress with 4 lbs of 5-10-10 per 100 row feet before vines cover row.	At least 1 inch of water per week Moisture levels are critical during root development and for sizing of sweet potato.

containers. Hold each seedling by the cotyledons (or "seed leaves"), not by the stem. The stem is fragile, and the slightest injury could cause permanent damage. Finish growing the plants in these larger containers until they are ready to plant outdoors.

Whether planting directly into the garden or in a container inside, it is important to start seeds in a sterile media. The media should be well-drained and well-aerated. There are a wide variety of commercially available and homemade soilless mixtures suitable for planting vegetables (Table 7.9); soilless mixtures reduce the chances of damping-off. See "Damping-off and Root Diseases" for more information.

Transplants grown indoors need adequate light. In low light, vegetable seedlings become leggy and weak and tend to topple over when they are a few inches tall. Seeds

TABLE 7.6 Continued

Plant Family (examples)	Soil Considerations	Pre-plant Fertilizer per 100 ft^2	Additional Fertilizer	Watering
Nightshade (pepper, tomato)	Well-drained Sandy loam or loam Fairly high organic matter 5.8-6.5 pH Avoid areas where members of the nightshade family have grown in the past two years	3 lbs 5-10-10 or liquid starter fertilizer when setting transplants	Side-dress with 1.5-2 lbs of calcium nitrate per 100 row feet when first fruits are quarter sized Side-dress again 2-3 weeks later with 5-10-10 Too much nitrogen will cause vegetative growth	It is extremely important to have adequate moisture from flowering to harvest
Onion (onion, garlic)	Well-drained 6-7 pH	3-5 lbs 10-10-10	Side-dress 1-2 weeks after bulb enlargement with 2 lbs 10-10-10 per 100 sq ft.	Needs consistent soil moisture Best to let soil dry before harvest
Pea (beans)	Well-drained 5.8-6.5 pH Avoid soils infested with nematodes Add Rhizobium bacterium as an inoculant for enhanced nodule and nitrogen fixation	3-5 lbs 10-10-10	Side-dress before first bloom.	Critical moisture periods are during pollination and pod development

require a total of 16-18 hr. of natural or artificial light to produce stocky seedlings. You can place containers near a south-facing window and provide supplemental light with fluorescent bulbs, or you can grow your seedlings under fluorescent light alone. Place 40-watt, 48-in. fluorescent tubes with a timer just above the seedlings; you can also attach aluminum foil to the light fixture to reflect more light onto the plants.

Fertilize seedlings growing in soilless mixes when the first true leaves appear. Feed them a water-soluble starter fertilizer every other time you water to promote faster plant growth; do this until the plants are ready to plant outdoors. Wash the seedlings with plain water to remove any fertilizer from the leaves. Water between feedings with plain water to prevent any salt from accumulating in the media. Seedlings growing in mixes containing compost, rotted manure, or commercially prepared soil may not need fertilizer.

Water the transplants before they begin to wilt and stop watering when water runs out of the bottom of the container. You can water transplants overhead or from the bottom. To water transplants from the bottom, fill a container or lid with 1-2 in. of water and set the transplant tray into the water reservoir. Allow the transplant tray to absorb water for 3-10 min before placing the tray back under the grow lights. Larger-celled trays and pots may appear dry at times, but due to the large volume of soil, they can be moist while the top of the cell appears dry. Avoid excess watering when plants are small or if algae appear on the soil surface.

Before moving the transplants to the garden, they need to be hardened off. When the plants have two true

TABLE 7.7

Fertilizer	Cups per Pound	Tablespoons per Pound
Ground limestone	1.5	24
Nitrate of soda	1.5	24
Potassium sulfate	1.5	24
Calcium nitrate	2	32
Superphosphate	2.25	36
10-10-10	2.25	36
5-10-10	2.25	36
Borax	2.75	44
Ammonium nitrate	2.5	40
Epsom salts	2.5	40
Aluminum sulfate	2.75	44

TABLE 7.8 Degree of Difficulty in Transplanting Common Vegetables

Easily Survive Transplanting	Require Care in Transplanting	Not Successfully Transplanted by Usual Methods*
Broccoli	Celery	Beans
Brussels Sprouts	Cucumbers	Beets
Cabbage	Melons	Carrots
Cauliflower	Pumpkin	Corn
Eggplant	Spinach	Peas
Kale	Squash	
Lettuce	Swiss Chard	
Onion (dry)		
Okra		
Pepper		
Sweet Potato		
Tomato		

* = These crops are best sown directly in the garden or planted in individual containers because any root disturbance hinders growth.

TABLE 7.9 Recipe for Soilless Seed-Starting Medium

Material	Amount
Shredded sphagnum peat moss*	19 qt.
Horticultural vermiculite (#4 particle size)	19 qt.
5-10-10 fertilizer**	8 tbsp.
20% powdered superphosphate (0-20-0)	3 tbsp.
Ground dolomitic limestone	5 tbsp.
Chelated iron	½ tbsp.

*If peat moss is very dry, dampen by sprinkling with a gallon of warm water before mixing. Blend the peat and vermiculite thoroughly before adding the dry fertilizer materials.
**At least half of the nitrogen should be in the nitrate form.

leaves, place a fan near the seedlings to produce a gentle sway; leave the fan there and on until you transplant the plants. The fan will cause higher transpiration rates and dry the seedlings out, so pay close attention to moisture management during this time. Once plants are about 3 in. tall, begin conditioning them to grow outdoors. Outside, the seedlings are exposed to varying temperatures, increased sunlight, drying winds, and moisture stress. Start by placing the seedlings outdoors during the day and bringing them inside before sundown. Gradually expose the plants to more and more direct sun to avoid injuring the plants. Continue this routine for 2-3 weeks to condition the seedlings. This adjustment may result in a temporary decrease in growth rate, but it helps the plant successfully adapt to outdoor conditions. The adjustment must be gradual, or the plant will be damaged by the sudden onset of outdoor conditions; this could result in delayed growth, reduced fruiting, and reduced yields when the plants are set out. It is best to transplant on cool, cloudy days to avoid transplant shock.

Starting Seeds Outdoors

Many seeds can be sown directly in the garden. Generally, the rule of thumb is to cover seeds to a depth four times their diameter. The seed package likely also provides the appropriate planting depth. In heavy soil or wet weather, plant seeds closer to the surface; in dry weather or sandy soil, plant the seeds deeper. It may be helpful to apply a band of sand, fine compost, or vermiculite about a hand's width and ¼-in. thick along the row after the seeds are planted. This thin mulch layer helps retain soil moisture and reduce crusting, making it easier for the seedlings to push through the soil surface.

When planting a fall garden in midsummer, you may need to plant seeds deeper below the warm, dry soil. Keep the soil moist by watering, sprinkle the row with a shallow layer of mulch, or cover the row with a board until the seeds germinate and break through the soil surface. Seeds need good seed-to-soil contact for proper germination, so lightly pack the soil before and after planting.

Transplanting

Transplants of annual vegetables should be stocky, healthy, and disease-free, with good color and white roots. Transplant vegetables on cloudy days, in late afternoon, or in early evening to prevent wilting. It helps to water the plants several hours before planting. Dig a hole large enough to hold the roots of the plants or to completely bury a biodegradable pot. Slide the transplant out of plastic, paper, or clay containers and crack peat pots so the roots can grow easily into the soil. Do not pull the plants by their stems. The roots of cucumbers, watermelons, cantaloupes and squash are easily damaged, so never break the peat cup or destroy the roots. Set transplants of these crops while the plants are small, as once they become large or stunted, they do not grow as well.

Set the plants slightly deeper than they were planted previously. Press soil firmly around the roots of the transplants, then water to eliminate large air pockets and improve root-to-soil contact. For a few days after transplanting, keep the transplants well-watered and, if possible, protected from excess heat or cold; you can protect plants from extreme temperatures by covering them with newspaper or cardboard tents, jugs, baskets, or flowerpots.

Mole crickets, ants, and cutworms can be problems after transplants are set into a garden. These pests girdle, smother, or cut off transplants, leaving empty spaces when the plants die. Gardeners should rotate garden areas away from sites where mole crickets, ants, and cutworms have been problematic in previous seasons. Several granular insecticides are approved for use in vegetable gardens for these pests, but always read the label before applying insecticides.

Planting Patterns

There are several planting patterns or layouts that home gardeners use. This section describes some of the most popular methods, all of which are illustrated in Figure 7.4. The spacing of vegetables varies and depends on the cultivation method; for example, tractors require particularly wide rows, while rows in small gardens may be placed close together if weeding is done by hand. Spacing recommendations can be found in HGIC 1256. For individuals with restricted space, more intensive gardening may be in order. This could range from planting several tomato plants in containers to planting a dozen or more different types of vegetables in a small, raised bed.

Row Planting

When row planting, seeds or transplants are placed in straight, single rows. Tie a string between two stakes to serve as a guide and keep the row straight. Below the string, use the end of a rake or hoe to create a furrow or trench at the appropriate depth.

Broadcast Planting

Broadcast planting is also called wide-row planting; to broadcast seeds, the gardener sows them in rows at least 10 in. wide. Sow the seeds evenly over the area and then rake them in. Firm the soil to improve seed-to-soil contact and water the bed. When the plants are ½-1-in. tall, thin them out by hand or with a garden rake dragged across the row. This planting pattern can produce more growth than does a single row. Also, the closely growing plants in a broadcast planting shade the soil, which reduces weed growth and conserves moisture. Crops that grow well in the broadcast pattern include beans, spinach, collards, beets, lettuce, carrots, chard, dill, onions, turnips, and peas.

Hill Planting

When hill planting, plants grow in hills about 6-9 in. high and slightly wider in diameter. If using seeds, plant 7-10 seeds per hill in a 12-18-in. circle. Once the seeds have become seedlings, thin the hill to three or four of the best seedlings. Sprawling vegetables such as melons, squash, corn, and cucumbers grow well in hill plantings.

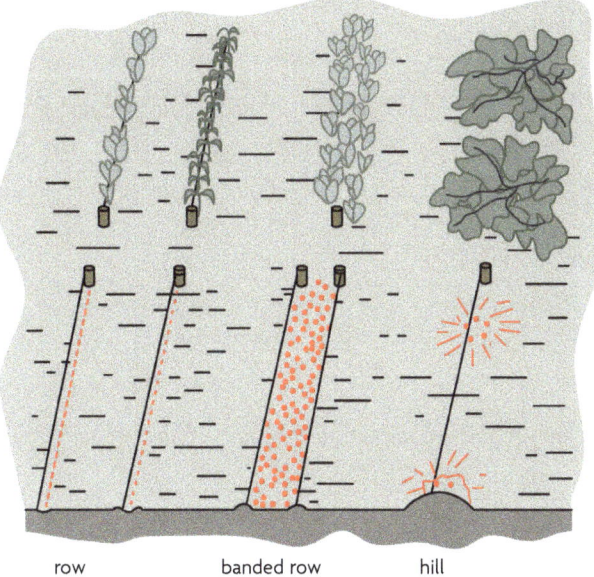

Figure 7.4 Three common vegetable planting methods.

TABLE 7.10 Commonly Available Side-Dressing Fertilizers and Rates of Application

Fertilizer	%N	Lbs/100 ft. row
Calcium Nitrate	15.5	2
Ammonium Nitrate	33.0	1
10-10-10	10.0	3
15-0-14	15.0	2

Fertilizing During the Season

Vegetables need to be side-dressed, a practice in which nutrients are applied to established plants. Calcium nitrate is one of the more popular side-dressing materials, but there are many others. Table 7.10 lists some side-dressing fertilizers and the suggested application rates. Compare the nitrogen content of other materials to see alternatives.

Side dress by applying the fertilizer in a band along one side of the row, about 4-6 in. from the crop depending on plant size (Figure 7.5). Incorporate the fertilizer using a hoe. If it is unlikely to rain, lightly water the fertilizer to make it quickly available to the roots. Side dress vegetables after 3-5 weeks of growth. Table 7.6 provides a general idea of required side-dressing applications based on the kind of vegetables grown.

Irrigation Methods

A home gardener has several options by which they can irrigate their garden; watering cans, garden hoses with fan nozzles or spray attachments, portable lawn sprinklers, soaker hoses, and drip or trickle irrigation systems are all appropriate for irrigating vegetables.

Figure 7.5 Corn sidedressed with ammonium sulfate.
Image Credit: Zachary Snipes, Clemson University

Most of these options are simple to use. Drip or trickle irrigation requires special equipment, but it is the best method for conserving water.

Watering cans and hoses are fine for small gardens. When watering with a hose, direct a low-pressure stream of water to the base of the plant, not the foliage.

Overhead sprinklers offer a wide range of watering patterns and area coverages. They are convenient, though they are not very efficient. During hot, windy days, especially when the sprinklers produce small droplets, a considerable amount of water is lost to evaporation. Also, many sprinklers deposit less water the farther they are from the water source. Place sprinklers at staggered locations to provide adequate overlap; this usually results in an over-application of water. Oscillating sprinklers apply water more evenly than overhead sprinklers and can be easily adjusted to cover square or rectangular areas. Watering foliage with a sprinkler may increase disease problems; however, watering in early morning should reduce the chances for disease outbreaks, as the foliage dries more quickly in the sun.

A soaker hose is a hose made of plastic or canvas tubing that allows water to seep out all along its length at a slow rate. They are not pressure- or volume-compensated, and they result in overwatering at the inlet of a row and underwatering at the end of a row.

Finally, the drip or trickle system has pressure/volume compensated emitters ideally suited for raised bed or container gardens. Emitters are either embedded in hose (called tape) or consist of small buttons with short tubes punched into hoses that come off a main water supply hose. The emitter places the water directly at the roots of the desired plants and leaves foliage and

TABLE 7.11 Critical Watering Periods for Vegetable Crops

Critical Period	Crops
Germination	All, particularly summer or fall crops
Pollination	Lima beans
Pod enlargement	Lima and snap beans, edible podded peas
Head development	Broccoli, cabbage, cauliflower
Root, bulb and tuber enlargement	Carrot, onion, parsnip, potato, radish, turnip
Fruit set and early development	Muskmelon
Uniform supply from flower to harvest	Eggplant, pepper, tomato

fruits dry. The drip system allows the gardener to replace the water lost by the plants on a daily basis. By including a filter or self-flushing hose in the system to prevent clogging, the drip system is a cost-effective irrigation tool that uses the minimum amount of water necessary.

A gardener should be aware of the periods in the development and growth of vegetables that require more water (See Tables 7.6 & 7.11). Generally, the first few weeks after planting and transplanting and during the development of fruit or storage organs, plants may be adversely affected by water shortages.

Reducing Water Demands

Adding organic matter to soil prior to planting conserves water and reduces the amount of water that must be added. The moisture-holding capacity of sandy soils is improved by adding organic matter; though most water in sandy soil is available, it drains so quickly that the water moves below the root zone within a few days of rainfall. Crop residue and other rough organic matter in sandy soil improve the water-holding capacity of such a soil.

Mulching also decreases the amount of supplemental irrigation needed. A 2-3-in. layer of organic mulch suppresses weed growth and reduces water evaporation from the soil.

Intensive Gardening Methods

The purpose of intensive gardening is to harvest as many vegetables as possible from a given space. Traditional gardens consist of long, narrow rows of vegetables spaced widely apart. Much of the garden area is just space between the rows. An intensive garden minimizes wasted space. The practice of intensive gardening is not just for those with limited garden space; rather, an intensive garden concentrates work efforts to create an ideal plant environment, growing better yields with less labor.

Though intensive gardening can be highly beneficial, it isn't for everyone. Some people enjoy the sight of long, straight rows in their gardens; others prefer machine cultivation to hand weeding. The few pathways and closely spaced plants in intensive gardens minimize weed growth, but weeding is usually done by hand or with hand tools. Still other gardeners like to get their gardens planted quickly and harvest everything at once. The ideal intensive garden has something growing in every part of the garden at all times during the growing season.

A good intensive garden requires early, thorough planning to make the best use of time and space in the garden. The gardener must consider interrelationships between plants, such as their nutrient needs, shade tolerance, above- and below-ground growth patterns, and preferred growing season. The following systems or techniques are particularly suited to maximize yields in limited spaces. These approaches allow gardeners to concentrate their efforts on producing more vegetables than they would in a traditional row-planted garden.

Interplanting

Also known as intercropping, interplanting involves growing different kinds of vegetables together at the same time. Plants grow in separate rows or alternate within the same row.

The basic idea of interplanting is to combine a slow-growing or late-maturing crop with a fast- growing or early maturing crop. The quick-growing vegetable matures and is harvested before the slow-growing crop needs the space; thus, two crops can grow in the same area without crowding each other.

For example, you can plant fast-growing and slow-growing vegetables in alternate rows, such as a row of radishes beside a row of tomatoes; you can harvest the radishes in time to make room for the later-maturing tomatoes. You can also alternate vegetables within the

Figure 7.6 Bell pepper double cropped with arugula.
Image Credit: Zachary Snipes, Clemson University

TABLE 7.12 Combinations of Vegetables that Perform Well in an Intercropping System

Cabbage & Lettuce	Carrot & Radish	Tomato & Spinach
Corn & Lettuce	Onion & Radish	
Tomato & Lettuce	Parsnip & Radish	Swiss Chard & Pepper
	Cabbage & Radish	
	Tomato & Radish	Cabbage & Onion

same row; for example, one row could alternate radishes or lettuce with caged tomatoes, okra, or cucumbers (Figure 7.6).

The vegetable pairs in Table 7.12 complement one another in growth habit and maturity. Besides maturity, consider shade tolerance (refer to Table 7.3). Plant shade-tolerant crops such as lettuce and spinach in the shadow of taller crops like pole beans and tomatoes.

Combining different kinds of vegetables together can help reduce insect and disease problems. Often, a pest affecting one type of crop takes more time to spread to another row or plant of the same crop when there is a different vegetable in between. This delay provides the gardener with more time to address the infestation.

When gardens are interplanted, vegetables grow closely beside each other; the leaves come close to touching at maturity. Thus, the leaves act as a living mulch that shades the soil to reduce water evaporation and weed growth. Be careful that plants do not crowd each other so much that it causes disease or competition.

Consider an equidistant spacing pattern in which plants are the same distance from each other within the bed; that is, plant so that the center of one plant is the same distance from the centers of plants on all sides of it. In beds of more than two rows, stagger the rows so that the plants in every other row are between the plants in the adjacent rows. Table 7.13 provides spacing for interplanting.

Succession and Relay Planting

In succession planting, the gardener plants, grows, and removes one crop before immediately placing another in its space. In South Carolina, successively planted garden space can produce a continuous supply of fresh vegetables throughout the year. For the succession planting scheme to work, the gardener needs to know the length of time required for the vegetables to mature and the most favorable times for growth.

Planting successively reduces insect or disease problems. Do not replace a vegetable with another from the same family. For example, after harvesting peas (*Fabaceae*), you can plant okra (*Malvaceae*) and cucumbers (*Cucurbitaceae*) but not peanuts or beans (both *Fabaceae*).

Planting a spring, summer, and fall garden is another form of succession planting. Cool-season crops like broccoli, lettuce, and peas are replaced by warm-season crops such as beans, tomatoes, and peppers; these may be followed by more cool-season plants or a winter cover crop.

TABLE 7.13 Intensive Interplanting Spacing Guide

Crop	Spacing (in.)
Asparagus	15-18
Beans (lima)	4-6
Beans (pole)	6-12
Beets	2-4
Broccoli	12-18
Brussels Sprouts	15-18
Cabbage (Chinese)	10-12
Carrots	2-3
Cauliflower	15-18
Cucumber	12-18
Collards	12-15
Endive	15-18
Eggplant	18-24
Kale	15-18
Kohlrabi	6-9
Leeks	3-6
Lettuce (head)	8-12
Lettuce (leaf)	4-6
Melons	18-24
Mustard	6-9
Okra	12-18
Peas (garden)	2-4
Peas (southern)	3-4
Peppers	12-15
Potatoes	10-12
Pumpkins	24-26
Radishes	2-3
Spinach	4-6
Squash (summer)	18-24
Squash (winter)	24-36
Swiss Chard	6-9

Note: To determine spacing for interplanting, add the inch(es) for the two crops to be planted together and divide the sum by 2. For example, if radishes are planted next to beans, add 2 inches + 4 inches = 6 inches, then divide 6 inches by 2 inches = 3 inches. The radishes should be planted 3 inches from the beans.

Relay planting consists of staggering the planting times of one type of crop to extend the harvest season over a longer period rather than harvest all at once.

One approach to relay planting is to plant one variety several times, at about two-week intervals. Bush beans, cucumbers, and other crops that yield for two weeks or less are all good candidates for relay planting.

Square-Foot Gardening

Square-foot gardening is an intensive form of gardening that blocks off squares of space for crops rather than planting them in rows. The name comes from partitioning a garden into 1 ft² spaces (or sometimes, larger spaces at the same 1:1 ratio). One common arrangement is to mark off squares that measure 4x4 ft (16 ft²) (Figure 7.7). Then, this area is divided into four parts, each 2x2 ft, with walkways around each main 16-ft² section. The gardener plants a different crop in each 4-ft² block. Although plant or seed count depends on crop size, square-foot gardening usually allows for more individual plants than row gardening, which increases yield per unit area. Each plant or seed is planted an equal distance from all other plants or seeds of the same variety.

Vertical Gardening

The use of trellises, nets, strings, cages, or poles to support growing plants is called vertical gardening (Figure 7.8). This technique is especially suited to, but not limited to, gardeners with a small space. Vining and sprawling plants such as cucumbers, tomatoes, melons, and pole beans are obvious candidates for this type of gardening. Some plants climb the support themselves, while others need to be tied.

Vertical planting does cast a shadow, so beware of shading sun-loving crops; take advantage of the shade by planting shade-tolerant crops near the vertical ones.

Plants grown vertically take up much less space

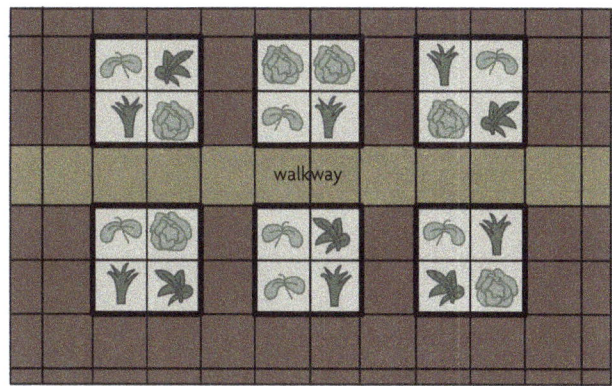

Figure 7.7 A common square-foot gardening arrangement.

on the ground and increase the yield per square foot of garden space. Because vertically growing plants are more exposed, they dry out faster and require more water than they would if spread over the ground; however, this fast drying is an advantage to plants susceptible to fungal diseases.

Container Gardening

Growing vegetables in containers is a viable option and helps overcome problems with poor soil, soil-borne diseases, and nematodes. A windowsill, patio, balcony, or even a doorstep can provide space for a productive container garden. Vegetables that don't require a lot of space—such as carrots, radishes, and lettuce—are well-suited for container gardens, as are crops that bear fruit over a longer period, such as tomatoes and peppers. Container gardening is also appropriate for varieties of carrots that produce short roots ideal for heavy soils.

Dwarf or miniature varieties often mature and bear fruit quickly, but most produce less fruit than standard varieties. Dwarf (determinate) character is also found in tomato, eggplant, and pepper. Look for cultivars labeled "bush," "baby," or "patio." There are cultivars of cherry tomatoes, Roma (paste) tomatoes, and round (slicing)

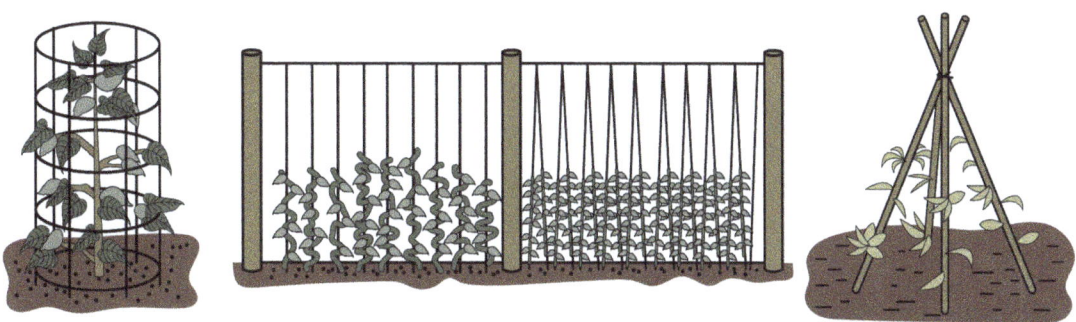

Figure 7.8 Structures used in vertical gardening.

tomatoes suitable for containers. Many ornamental peppers are compact; all are edible, and most are quite hot.

The various vine crops show the greatest advantage of dwarf varieties; there are dwarf varieties of high-quality cucumber, and compact yellow squash produce bountiful harvests of yellow straight-neck squash. As with many other compact plants, over-fertilization can overcome compactness.

We do not recommend planting short-season corn or midget corn. When planting in vertical space, the dwarf character is of little value. As interest in container gardening increases, plant breeders and seed companies are working to develop vegetables specifically designed for container gardens. These varieties are not necessarily miniature or dwarf plants, so they may produce as much or as well as standard types if cared for properly.

The amount of sunlight that a container garden spot receives determines which crops you can grow. Generally, leaf crops—and to a lesser degree, root crops—can tolerate partial shade, but vegetables grown for their fruits generally need at least 6 hr of full, direct sunlight each day and perform better with 8-10 hr. You can increase available light by placing reflective materials such as aluminum foil, white-painted surfaces, or marble chips around the plant or container.

Container gardening lends itself to attractive plantscaping. You can brighten a dull patio with baskets of cascading tomatoes or a colorful herb mix. Planter boxes with trellises can create a cool, shady place on an apartment balcony. Containers present opportunities for innovation and creativity.

Containers for Planting. There are many containers appropriate for gardening. Clay, wood, plastic, and metal are all suitable materials. Containers for vegetable plants must:

- be big enough to support plants when they are fully grown,
- hold soil without spilling,
- have adequate drainage, and
- never have held products that are toxic to plants or people.

Consider using barrels, flowerpots, cut-off milk cartons, recycled Styrofoam coolers, window boxes, baskets lined with plastic (with drainage holes), pieces of drainage pipe, or cinder block. When building a planting box out of wood, use rot-resistant redwood, cedar, or cypress. No matter the type of container, be sure that there are holes in the bottom for drainage; plant roots must not stand in water. Most plants need containers at least 6-8 in. deep for adequate rooting; the deeper, the better.

The imaginative use of discarded items or construction of attractive patio planters can be an enjoyable aspect of container gardening. To facilitate plant care and maintenance, use dollies or platforms with wheels or casters to move the containers from place to place. This is especially useful when your containers are in apartment or on a balcony, as it makes it easier to move plants to maximize available space and sunlight and avoid damage from inclement weather.

Media for Container Planting. Use a fairly lightweight potting mix for container vegetable gardening. Do not use soil straight from the garden in a container unless the soil is sandy or has sandy loam, as it may be too heavy. Clay soil consists of microscopic particles. In a container, the undesirable qualities of clay are magnified; it holds too much moisture when wet, which results in too little air for the roots, and it pulls away from the sides of the pot when dry. Using garden soil can also spread soilborne pathogens that will exploit the "biological vacuum" present in mostly sterile potting soil.

Container planting media needs to be porous, because roots require both air and water. Packaged potting soil available at local garden centers is relatively lightweight and may make a good container medium; however, if the container is also lightweight, strong winds can blow plants over and cause major damage. Some soilless mixes contain few nutrients, so even though major nutrients are added, there are no trace elements available to the plant.

For a large container garden, the expense of prepackaged or soilless mixes may be high. Try mixing equal parts peat moss, potting soil, and clean, coarse builders sand or perlite with a slow-release 14-14-14 fertilizer. You may also need to add lime to raise soil pH to around 6.5. In any case, a soil test is just as helpful in determining nutrient and pH needs for a container garden as in a larger or in-ground garden.

Planting Container Gardens. Plant container crops at the same time you would plant them in a regular garden. Fill a clean container to within ½ in. of the rim with the slightly damp soil mixture. If you add peat moss to the planting media and soak the mix in water, it absorbs water much more readily. Sow the seeds or set transplants according to the instructions on the seed package and place a label with the name, variety, and date of planting on or in each container. After planting, gently soak the soil with water—being careful not to wash out or displace seeds! Thin the seedlings to obtain proper spacing when the plants have two or three leaves. If you plan to use cages, stakes, or other supports, provide them when the plants are very small to avoid damaging the roots once they're more extensive.

Watering. Pay particular attention to watering container plants. Because the volume of soil is relatively small, containers can dry out very quickly, especially on a concrete patio in full sun. It may be necessary to water daily or twice a day. Apply water until it runs out the drainage holes. On an upstairs balcony, this runoff could create problems with downstairs neighbors; plan your drainage system in advance. Large trays filled with coarse marble chips work nicely for attractive but effective drainage solutions.

The soil in container gardens should never be soggy or have water standing on top of it. When the weather is cool, container plants may be subject to root rots if they stay too wet. Clay pots and other porous containers allow additional evaporation from the sides of the pots and require more frequent watering. Small pots also tend to dry out more quickly than larger ones. If the soil appears to be getting excessively dry—for example, if plants are wilting every day—, group the containers together so that the foliage creates a canopy that shades the soil and keeps it cool. On a hot patio, consider putting containers on pallets or other structures that allow air movement beneath the pots and prevent direct contact with the cement. Check containers at least once a day—twice if the day is particularly hot, dry, or windy. Feel the soil to determine if it is damp. Mulching and windbreaks can help reduce water requirements for containers; if you plan on being away for more than a few days at a time, use an automatic drip emitter irrigation system.

Fertilizing Container Gardens. If you plant your gardens with a soil mix that includes fertilizer, plants have enough nutrients for 8-10 weeks. If the plants grow for longer than this, add a water-soluble fertilizer at the recommended rate. Repeat the application every 2-3 weeks. An occasional dose of fish emulsion or compost can add other trace elements to the soil. Do not overfertilize, as this may cause fertilizer burn and kill the plants. Container plants do not have the buffer of large volumes of soil and humus to protect them from overfertilization or excessive lime.

Caring for Container Gardens. The same insects and diseases common to in-ground gardens can attack vegetables grown in containers. Periodically inspect plants for signs of foliage- and fruit-feeding insects and disease. Protect plants from very high temperatures caused by light reflection from pavement; move them to a cool spot or shade them during the hottest part of the day. Move plants to a sheltered location during severe rain, hail, windstorms, and fall frosts.

PLANT FAMILIES

Plants that are members of the same families (as classified by scientists) often require similar care and planting conditions.

COLE CROP FAMILY (BRASSICACEAE)

Collards and Kale

Planting. Collards (*Brassica oleracea* Acephala Group) and kale are cool-season plants that grow best in early spring or fall, ideally in temperatures from 60-65°F.

There are both traditional, open-pollinated collard and newer hybrid varieties of collard on the market. There are four distinct horticultural types of kale that are most popular:

Figure 7.9. Dinosaur or lacinato kale is a beautiful and tasty addition to the garden.

Image Credit: Zachary Snipes, Clemson University

- Green to blue-green "curly" kale (Scots kale, *Brassica oleracea*) with ruffled leaves;
- "Dinosaur" kale (*Brassica oleracea*), also called Tuscan kale or lacinato kale, with wavy, narrow, exceptionally dark green leaves;
- "Red" kale (*Brassica napus*) with flat green leaves and red-violet leaf veins and petioles; and
- Siberian kale (*Brassica napus*).

Leaves of red, Tuscan, and Siberian kale tend to be more tender than those of curly kale.

You can grow and set out kale and collard transplants in early spring. It takes about 6-8 weeks to produce plants ready for transplanting. Plant collards and kale in rows that are 3 ft apart; spacing within the row depends on when you plan to harvest the crop. If you want to harvest half-grown plants, space them 10-15 in. apart; If harvesting full-grown plants, space them 15-18 in. apart.

It is possible to directly seed kale and collards, especially for a fall harvest.

Loamy to sandy soil is best for direct seeding. It is critical to keep the soil moist during seedling establishment. It is also desirable to have an area that is protected from the wind when seeding these crops. Plant seeds about ½-¾ in. deep in moist soil, but never deeper than 1 in.

When direct-seeded plants are in the three-leaf stage, thin them to the desired stand. If you plan to harvest young, direct-seeded plants like mustard greens, space the plants 2-4 in. apart. Maintain 3-ft spacing between rows.

Harvesting and Storing. Collards should be ready for harvest 70 days after direct seeding. You can cut entire plants when they are very young, half-grown or full-grown. You can also harvest tender leaves from full-grown plants. Store all harvested collards in the refrigerator.

Problems. Most pest-related damage to collards and kale stems from worms (imported cabbageworm, cabbage looper, and diamondback moth caterpillar) and harlequin bugs. Aphids can also become a serious problem, especially during cool weather.

Common disease problems include black rot, downy mildew, and Alternaria leaf spot. Summer-grown collards may suffer from fusarium yellows.

SQUASH FAMILY (*CUCURBITACEAE*)

"Cucurbit" is the term vegetable scientists use to refer to all crops in the squash or gourd family. Another common term is "vine crops."

Cucumber

Planting. Cucumber (*Cucumis sativus*) is a warm-season vegetable that grows best at temperatures between 75-85°F. They are very tender; even light frosts can kill them. Start cucumbers in the garden either from seed or transplants.

Plant seed after the danger of frost has passed and the soil has warmed. Seeds will not germinate at soil temperatures below 50°F; the ideal soil temperature is 70°F. Grow transplants indoors in peat pots 2-3 weeks prior to outdoor planting time. You can grow cucumbers as both spring and fall crops.

If the cucumber plants are un-trellised, space them 8-10 in. apart along rows that are 5 ft apart. If the plants are trellised, plant four to five seeds per foot of row in rows spaced 30 in. apart. When plants are 4-5 in. high, thin them to be 9-12 in. apart. It is often better to plant a second crop around August 1 rather than try to continue harvesting an early planting until frost.

Types. Burpless cucumbers are long and slender with tender skin. Bush varieties produce well and take up less space, so they are a good alternative when trellising is not possible. There are new varieties of cucumber advertised as all-female or gynoecious. These plants tend to bear fruit earlier, with a more concentrated fruit set and better yield, since they have more or only female flowers.

Maintenance. Most varieties of cucumber vines spread from row to row. Training vines on a trellis or fence along the edge of the garden corrects this problem and lifts the fruit off the soil. A satisfactory trellis is about 6 ft high, with a top and bottom wire and plastic twine tied between the two wires at each plant. Posts should be no more than 15 ft apart, and the top wire must be very tight.

Harvesting and Storing. Depending on the variety, cucumbers are ready for harvest in about 50-70 days. Pick them as frequently as necessary to avoid oversized fruit. The more cucumbers you pick, the more the vines will produce. Harvest when cucumbers are at least 2 in. long or up until they begin to turn yellow, generally within about 15 days. Remove fruit by turning cucumbers parallel to the vine and giving a quick snap. This removal method prevents vine damage and results in a clean break. Store cucumbers in the refrigerator, ideally between 45-50°F with 95% relative humidity.

Problems. Low fertility and poor pollination often cause misshapen fruit. Too few bees for adequate pollination, no pollinating plants for gynoecious hybrids, and changes in temperature often cause a failure to set. Fruit is only produced when insects carry pollen to a female cucumber flower, and honeybees are essential for this purpose. The first 10-20 flowers on a plant are male and will not produce fruit. Temperature variations of more than 20°F or storing cucumbers near other ripening vegetables can cause bitterness.

The major pests that feed on cucumber are cucumber beetles, pickleworms, aphids, mites, whiteflies, and the squash vine borer (Table 7.14).

Diseases that may occur in home gardens include powdery and downy mildew, anthracnose, gummy stem blight, bacterial wilt, mosaic viruses, target spot, belly rot, and nematodes. Most of these diseases—bacterial wilt being the exception—are not a problem in the spring. Look for downy and powdery mildew in late spring; the others are mainly problems during the fall. Root-knot nematodes can also cause problems.

Summer Squash

Planting. Summer squash (*Cucurbita pepo*) includes yellow squash (straight and crookneck), zucchini, and scallop squash. Some varieties of summer squashes grow in a bush form instead of on vines, which is useful in small gardens. Summer squash is a warm-season crop that grows best at average temperatures between 65-75°F; squash seeds do not germinate well in cold soil. In the spring, do not plant this crop until after the last chance of frost has passed and the soil temperature is 60°F about 4 in. below the surface.

Maintenance. A common problem with summer squash is the rotting of the blossom end of the fruit, called blossom-end rot. Read more in "Abiotic Vegetable Disorders" at the end of this chapter.

Figure 7.10. Harvest squash when they are small and have a glossy appearance.
Image Credit: Robert Polomski, Clemson University

Squash have separate male and female flowers on the same plant, and pollen must be transferred from the male flowers to the female flowers by bees. Poor pollination can result in misshapen fruit. Observe plants closely when they begin to bloom to determine if there are bees present. When using insecticides, apply them late in the evening to prevent killing bees.

Harvesting and Storing. You can harvest summer squash about 55 days after planting. For optimum quality, harvest while fruits are tender and still have a shiny or glossy appearance. When growing conditions are favorable, harvest the crop daily or every other day. Harvest crookneck and straight-neck squash when fruit is 1½-2 in. in diameter.

Harvest zucchini when fruit is 7-8 in. long and scallop types when they are 3-4 in. in diameter. Do not leave large summer squash fruit on the plant, as this will inhibit the development of additional fruit. Store summer squash in the refrigerator.

Problems. Insect problems include spotted cucumber beetles, striped cucumber beetles, pickleworms, squash vine borers, aphids, and squash bugs. Aphids are especially dangerous, because they can transmit viruses to plants. Squash vine borers can cause total collapse of the plant; plant summer squash early, as squash vine borers and pickleworms are bigger problems later in the season. Common disease problems for summer squash include powdery mildew and various viruses.

NIGHTSHADE FAMILY (SOLANACEAE)

Pepper

Planting. Peppers (*Capsicum annuum*) are warm-season plants that grow best at temperatures between 70-85°F during the day and 60-70°F during the night. Peppers generally require a long growing season and grow very slowly during cool periods. To make up for this and get a head start towards your harvest, set out 8-10-week-old transplants after the soil has thoroughly warmed in the spring. Do not plant peppers in the garden until after the last chance of frost.

Space most peppers 12 in. apart along rows that are 3 ft apart. Pimento peppers require 18-24-in. spacing along rows that are 42 in. apart.

Types. Although there are six categories of pepper, most are classified according to their degree of hot or mild flavor. Mild peppers include bell, banana, pimento, and sweet cherry; hot peppers include the cayenne, celestial, large cherry, and tabasco.

Bell peppers measuring 3 in. wide by 4 in. long usually have three or four lobes and a blocky appearance; they are commonly harvested when green, yet they will turn red or yellow when fully ripe if left on the plant. Other sweet peppers are conical and 2-3 in. wide by 4 in. long; they have thick walls and are harvested and used when red and fully ripe. Banana peppers are long and taper at the end; they are harvested when yellow, orange, or red. Hungarian wax peppers are a mild hot pepper variety. Cherry peppers vary in size and flavor, but they are usually harvested when orange to deep red.

The hot cayenne pepper group is characterized by slim, pointed, slightly twisted fruits. You can harvest cayenne peppers when green or red; the cayenne pepper group includes varieties such as Anaheim, cayenne, serrano, and jalapeño. Celestial peppers are cone-shaped, ½-2 in. long, and very hot. They vary in color from yellow to red to purple, making them an especially attractive plant. Slender, pointed, 1-3-in. tabasco peppers are extremely hot; chili pequin and small red chili are both varieties of tabasco peppers.

Harvesting and Storing. Harvest peppers about 70-85 days after transplanting or 100-120 days after planting from seed. Harvest sweet peppers when they reach full size, the fruit walls are firm, and the peppers are still in the green or yellow state. The stems of pepper plants are brittle; when harvesting the fruit, cut the stems instead of pulling to avoid breaking the branches.

Varieties turn from green to red, yellow, or chocolate when allowed to mature on the plant. Bell peppers can be left on the plant to turn color; however, they should be picked as soon as they change to the desired color.

Hot peppers, except for jalapeños, are allowed to ripen and change colors on the plant. Harvest jalapeño peppers when the fruit turn blackish green. You can pull and hang entire plants just before full frosts. Yields are smaller for hot peppers.

Store peppers in the refrigerator, ideally from 45-50°F and between 80-90% relative humidity, for up to 2-3 weeks.

Problems. Blossom-end rot is a common problem that causes a brown-to-black sunken rot at the blossom end of the fruit. It is caused by calcium deficiency. Blossom drop occurs when night temperatures are above 75°F or when a crop of fruit set is excessive.

Insects that may be problematic for peppers include European corn borers, corn earworms, and armyworms. See Table 7.15.

You can avoid many disease problems by using certified disease-free seed and transplants. Do not use tobacco products near peppers, since tobacco mosaic virus can spread to plants from tobacco. The two most troublesome diseases of peppers in home gardens are bacterial wilt and bacterial spot. Other disease problems include Pythium root rot, Cercospora leaf spot, Southern blight, and anthracnose (on fruit). Root-knot nematodes can also be a problem (Table 8.15).

Tomato

Tomatoes (*Lycopersicon esculentum*) are valuable garden plants in that they require relatively little space to provide a large yield. Each plant, properly cared for, yields 10-15 lb of fruit or more.

Planting. Tomatoes are warm-season plants that grow best at temperatures between 70-80°F during the day and 60-70°F at night.

If you plan to stake or trellis plants, space them 24 in. apart in rows 3 ft apart. Although it requires more initial work, staking makes it easier to take care of tomatoes than letting them sprawl; since they are off the ground, there is reduced fruit rot, spraying is easier and possibly required less frequently, and harvesting is much less work. Use wooden stakes 6 ft tall and 1½-2 in. wide. Drive them one foot into the soil, about 4-6 in. away from the plant, soon after transplanting. Attach heavy twine or strips of cloth to the stakes every 10 in.

Prune staked tomatoes to one or two main stems. A new shoot will develop at the junction of each leaf and the first main stem. If plants are trained to two stems, remove all other shoots (called suckers) weekly to maintain the two main stems. You can pinch shoots off with your fingers (Figure 7.11).

Figure 7.11 The small shoot coming off at a 45° angle should be pinched or pruned off.
Image Credit: Zachary Snipes, Clemson University

Growing tomatoes in wire cages is a popular method among gardeners because of its simplicity. Cage-growing allows the tomato plant to grow in its natural manner while maintaining the fruit and leaves off the ground. Using wire cages requires initial expenditure, but they last many years. Be sure to get fencing with at least 6-in. spacing between the wires so you can harvest more easily.

If you choose to prune tomato plants in wire cages, once is enough; prune to three or four main stems. Wire-cage tomatoes develop a heavy foliage cover, reducing sunscald on fruits. Caged plants are less prone to the spread of disease from plant handling, since they do not have open wounds and are handled less frequently than staked plants. However, it helps to space the plants somewhat further apart—about 3 ft—to allow adequate air circulation between plants. Humidity is higher around caged tomatoes because of the foliage density; diseases, such as late blight, spread rapidly in humid situations.

Types. There are an almost overwhelming number of varieties of tomato plants, but there are seven overarching type categories:

- Midget, patio, or dwarf varieties have compact vines and grow well in hanging baskets or containers. They can produce cherry tomatoes (1 in. in diameter or less) or larger tomatoes.
- Cherry tomatoes produce small fruits often used in salads. Cherry tomato plants range from dwarf varieties like the Tiny Tim to 7-ft plants called Sweet 100.
- Compact or determinate tomato plants grow to a certain size, set fruit, and then decline. Most of the early-ripening tomato varieties are determinate and will not produce tomatoes throughout a South Carolina summer.
- Beefsteak tomato plants produce particularly large fruit that are usually late to ripen.
- Paste tomatoes have small, pear-shaped fruits with meaty interiors and few seeds, making them ideal for canning.
- Some tomatoes are orange or yellow.
- Winter storage tomatoes are set out later in the season than others, and their fruits are harvested when partially ripe. If stored properly, they stay fresh for 12 weeks or more. While the flavor is not equal to that of summer vine-ripened tomatoes, many people prefer them to grocery store tomatoes in winter.

Varieties. Always choose disease-resistant tomato varieties, as indicated by the letters after the cultivar name. For example, VFN means the plants are resistant to Verticillium, Fusarium, and nematodes; VFNT adds tobacco mosaic virus to the list. Pay particular attention to disease issues in your garden and aim to purchase plants that have resistance to those diseases.

Maintenance. Blossom-end rot can cause serious problems for tomatoes. The main symptom of blossom-end rot is a dark-colored dry rot on the blossom end of the fruits. It occurs when there are extremes in soil moisture that cause calcium deficiency in the fruit. When rain or irrigation follows a dry spell, the roots cannot take up calcium fast enough to keep up with the rapid fruit growth. If the delicate feeder roots are damaged during transplanting or deep cultivation near the plants, this can also cause blossom-end rot.

The following measures can help prevent blossom-end rot:

- Test your soil. Maintain a pH between 6-6.5 and an adequate calcium level by liming or applying gypsum.
- Add organic matter to the soil. This helps loosen clay soils and improves water retention in sandy soils. Regardless of the soil type, organic matter increases plants' uptake of water and calcium.
- Apply 2-3 in. of mulch material such as grass clippings, pine straw, or leaves. Mulching prevents soil from drying too rapidly and allows roots to take up available calcium more efficiently.
- Do not overfertilize tomato plants with nitrogen or potash. Excessive amounts of these nutrients depress calcium uptake.
- Maintain uniform moisture levels by watering regularly and maintaining a mulch layer around the base of each plant. Water plants during extended dry periods—tomatoes need 1-1.5 in. of water per week.

Harvesting and Storing. Depending on the variety of tomato, it takes between 55-105 days for plants to mature. Pick fruit when it is fully vine-ripened but still firm; most varieties ripen to a dark red. Place picked tomatoes in the shade; light isn't necessary for immature tomatoes to ripen.

You can pick some green tomatoes before the first killing frost and store them in a cool (55°F), moist (90% relative humidity) place. Do not store green tomatoes in the refrigerator, since the red coloration does not develop at less than 50°F. When necessary, you can ripen fruits at 70°F. Store green tomatoes between

50-70°F for 1-3 weeks; store ripe tomatoes at 45-50°F for 4-7 days.

Common Problems. Some of the most common problems with tomato plants are blossom-end rot, catfacing, growth cracks, and leaf roll (a physiological condition caused by excess water).

Tomato blossoms are also very sensitive to temperature. Temperatures of 55-60°F can severely impair pollination and limit fruit formation. Temperatures between 90-95°F are also unfavorable for pollination.

See the section "Abiotic Vegetable Disorders" later in this chapter for more information.

SUNFLOWER FAMILY (ASTERACEAE)

Lettuce

Lettuce (*Lactuca sativa*) is one of the easiest cool-season vegetables to grow. Although lettuce can withstand light frost, sunlight and high summer temperatures usually cause seed stalk formation (bolting) and a bitter flavor. There are slow-bolting or heat-resistant varieties available that can extend the lettuce-growing season.

Most gardeners who grow lettuce raise loose-leaf-type lettuce with either green or reddish leaves. This type is a fast-growing, long-lasting lettuce used for salads and sandwiches that can be harvested over an extended period of time.

Figure 7.12 Lettuce comes in a variety of shapes, sizes, colors, and textures.
Image Credit: Zachary Snipes, Clemson University

Butterhead or Bibb lettuce is a loose-heading type with dark green leaves that are somewhat thicker than those of iceberg lettuce. Butterheads develop a light yellow, buttery appearance and are very attractive in salads. Bibb lettuce quickly develops a bitter taste if temperatures rise above 95°F.

Romaine or cos lettuce is less common despite being relatively easy to grow. It forms upright heads with wavy, attractive leaves.

Crisphead lettuce, also known as iceberg, has a tight, compact head with crisp, light green leaves. Many South Carolina gardeners find it difficult to grow iceberg lettuce in the state's high temperatures.

Planting. Lettuce is a cool-season crop that grows best at temperatures between 55-65°F. This crop prefers a loamy soil with a high content of organic matter. Protect lettuce seedlings from wind, as young plants dry out rapidly in windy conditions.

The optimum soil temperature for lettuce seed germination is between 60-80°F. Lettuce seed will not germinate at a soil temperature above 95°F. Lettuce seeds are small, so they are difficult to space precisely; usually, one must plant many seeds and thin the area later. Thin leaf lettuce when the plants are 1-2 in. tall. You can also plant leaf lettuce by broadcasting it over 12-in.-wide beds.

Plant head lettuce 12 in. apart in parallel rows 3 ft apart. It is best to grow head lettuce from transplants purchased from a reputable garden center.

Prepare soil well before planting lettuce to ensure good seed-to-soil contact and rapid stand establishment. Soil crusting over the tiny seeds or developing seedlings may make it difficult to obtain a good stand, especially if the soil is a heavy clay. Covering the seed with potting soil instead of garden soil will eliminate crusting problems.

Maintenance. To have a continuous supply of leaf lettuce during the spring and fall, it is best to grow several plantings during each season. Head lettuce is generally more difficult to grow than leaf lettuce. Lettuce does not tolerate hot weather; if this crop experiences temperature or moisture stress, it usually develops a bitter flavor.

Lettuce seedlings are poor competitors with weeds, so weed control is very important. Any cultivation to control weeds should be shallow to prevent root injury.

Problems. Aphids, cabbage looper, corn earworm, and leafhoppers are common insects that cause problems for lettuce plants; gray mold, Rhizoctonia bottom rot, and Sclerotinia drop are common diseases that do the same. Tipburn is a physiological disorder related to calcium nutrition that occasionally occurs on lettuce;

you can combat tipburn by maintaining a proper soil pH and watering well.

Harvesting and Storing. Leaf lettuce should be ready to harvest about 45 days after planting; you can harvest and use it as soon as plants are 5-6 in. tall. Bibb lettuce is mature when leaves begin to cup inward to form a loose head. Romaine is ready to use when the leaves have elongated and overlap to form a fairly tight head about 6-8 in. tall.

Head lettuce matures in as few as 55 days, depending on the variety. It is mature when leaves overlap to form a head like those available in stores.

Store lettuce in the refrigerator in the coolest area. Leaf and Bibb will store as long as 3 weeks if the leaves are dried before bagging.

INTEGRATED PEST MANAGEMENT

Integrated Pest Management (IPM) is a viable way to successfully manage garden pests without harming the environment. IPM incorporates a variety of mechanical, biological, cultural, and chemical controls into a pest management regimen. A successful IPM program involves identifying the insect, disease, or weed and becoming familiar with its life cycle.

IPM Cultural Practices

Soil Management

Maintain the appropriate soil pH for plants by testing garden soil every year. The appropriate pH gives vegetable plants access to all the necessary nutrients in the soil and provides a suitable environment for earthworms and microorganisms. Add generous amounts of organic matter, such as compost, to build up soil fertility and improve tilth.

Plant Selection

Choose plants that are suited to the soil and climate of your garden. Also select species and cultivars that are resistant to pests; these plants are resistant—not immune—to damage, so they have stronger defenses against and are less-severely injured by insects or diseases than susceptible varieties in the same environment. Select sturdy plants with well-developed root systems. Diseases and insects in young seedlings may start in greenhouses or plant beds and cause heavy losses in the garden. Buy plants from a reputable grower with assurance that plants are free of disease. Avoid accepting plants from friends if there is a chance you could unknowingly receive insects or diseases along with them.

Crop Rotation

Do not grow vegetables from the same family in the same place year after year. Rotate species within the garden or, where space permits, rotate the entire garden. Divide small gardens into quarters and plant vegetables from one plant family in each quarter each season or year. Refer to Table 7.1 for a list of vegetable families to rotate between garden plots.

Plant Timing

Select planting dates that are both favorable for the crop and unfavorable for pests. For example, plant squash as early as possible to avoid squash vine borers, which lay eggs in early summer. Keep a record of the dates around which you tend to notice insect problems and use this list when planning for the following year.

Interplanting

Plant different kinds of vegetables together in the same part of your garden, since many insect pests attack all plants belonging to a certain family and reject others. A plant that the pests don't like can act as a buffer and slow the spread of harmful insects to other vulnerable plants.

Thinning

Thin young plants to a proper stand, which differs depending on the crop. Overcrowding causes weak growth and makes plants more susceptible to problems caused by insects and disease.

Watering

Water plants late at night or early in the morning (when dew has formed). Avoid watering plants in early evening, as leaves could remain wet for an extended period of time. Wet leaves are highly susceptible to fungal infections. Water after dewfall or early in the morning so plants have time to dry out before warm, humid evenings when fungal infection is most likely. Use a soaker hose or drip irrigation to prevent leaves from getting wet when watering. For plants such as tomatoes that are particularly susceptible to diseases caused by bacteria, fungi, and water molds, leave extra space between plants to allow for adequate air flow and orient rows so that

CULINARY HERBS

Planning and growing a kitchen herb garden can reward both the eye and the palate. Fresh herbs can be used fresh from the garden in salads and sauces. Dried herbs may be used for teas, vinegars, or flavored oils. Many edible herbs are ornamental as well as functional.

Plant herb gardens as close to the kitchen as possible. Sunny porches, patios, or balconies are all suitable for growing herbs. Growing herbs close to the kitchen makes them more convenient to use. Use clean kitchen shears to cut fresh herbs for cooking.

Most herbs prefer full sun, good drainage, and moderately fertile soil with a pH between 6.5-7.5. Dill, parsley, and mint are the exceptions, growing well in partial sun and moist—but not soggy—soil. Use fertilizers sparingly or not at all, as most herbs thrive on low soil fertility.

The flowers of many edible herbs, such as bee balm, basil, thyme, and rosemary, attract and sustain pollinators such as bees, butterflies, and hummingbirds.

Easy-to-grow culinary herbs include basil, thyme, oregano, marjoram, chives, and parsley.

Basil (*Ocimum spp.*) is an annual warm-season herb grown from seed or transplants. Plant basil after all danger of frost has passed and allow it to grow in full sun with plenty of moisture and good drainage. Look for cultivars that have resistance to basil downy mildew. Harvest basil early in the day when aromatic oils are present in the leaves and remove flowers to prolong the life of the plant. Lemon basil (*Ocimum x citriodorum*) has a delightful citrus flavor perfect for summer salads and cold beverages.

Thyme is an aromatic evergreen perennial herb; plant thyme in full sun in well-drained soil. Thyme grows in a mound form, making it very pretty in containers and raised beds. The small white or purple flowers attract bees. There are several non-culinary varieties of thyme used in landscaping, but when planting for flavor, try:

- Common thyme (*Thymus vulgaris*), the classic thyme used in traditional dishes such as eggs, soups, and stews.
- Lemon thyme (*Thymus × citriodorus*), widely used when cooking fish and mixing herbal teas.
- Variegated lemon thyme (*Thymus × citriodorus 'Aureus'*), a yellow-edged lemon thyme that is as pretty as it is delicious.

Figure 7.13 A container of herbs located in close proximity to the house for convenience.
Image Credit: Amy Dabbs, Clemson University

Oregano and **marjoram** are thought of as two different herbs, but taxonomically, they share the same genus: Origanum. Plant either one in the fall in full to partial sun; they thrive in well-drained soils with a neutral pH. There are several varieties of oregano and marjoram, too. The most common include:

- Sweet marjoram (*Origanum majorana*), a sweet, mild herb that is wonderful with vegetables and in desserts.
- Oregano (*Origanum vulgare*), the spicy herb used in Italian, Greek, and Mexican foods.
- Greek Oregano (*O. vulgare subsp. hirtum*) which has a sharper flavor than most other oreganos.
- Italian oregano, also called hardy sweet marjoram (*Origanum x majoricum*), which combines the best of both the spicy and sweet and creates the perfect oregano for cooking. Italian oregano, also called "Hilltop," is considered the most reliable in the South.

> **Common (or onion) chives** (*Allium schoenoprasum*) impart a sweet green-onion flavor when snipped and used fresh. Chives grow from seed easily, but they take so long to establish that impatient gardeners may choose to purchase potted plants. Chives bloom from mid-May through June, with cheery pink flowers pretty enough to cut for arrangements.
>
> **Curled-leaf parsley** (*Petroselinum crispum var. crispum*) is a biennial herb that is wonderful when used fresh in a variety of dishes. Flat-leafed or Italian Parsley (Petroselinum crispum var. neapolitanum) has a stronger flavor, upright growth habit, and less finely dissected leaves. Parsley is best harvested and eaten the first year of its biennial life cycle and tends to get bitter the second year as it prepares to flower and produce seed. Start new parsley from seed each fall in the coastal region, or in the spring for a fresh supply.
>
> Source:
> The American Herb Society provides a wealth of information, learn more at http://www.herbsociety.org/.

prevailing winds help foliage dry quickly after a rain or watering. While this may reduce the number of plants per square foot, yields may still be higher due to reduced crop loss via disease. To prevent spreading diseases, stay out of the garden when plants are wet with rain or dew.

Staking Plants

Staking or planting crops in wire cages prevents the fruit from touching the soil. It also helps prevent fruit rots. Caging helps reduce the sun scald often seen in staked tomatoes, since caged plants do not require as much pruning and maintain a heavier foliage cover.

Injury Prevention

Cuts, bruises, cracks, and insect damage—just like open wounds on humans or animals—often host disease-causing organisms. When fruit like pumpkins and watermelons are difficult to remove, cut them instead of pulling them from the plant. When cultivating a garden, avoid cutting into the plant roots or damaging nearby stems.

Mulching

Mulch with compost, pine needles, or other materials to suppress weeds, conserve moisture, and prevent soil splashing (which brings soilborne diseases into contact with lower leaves and fruits).

Weed Control

Control weeds and grasses. They often harbor insects or disease and compete for necessary nutrients and water; they also provide an alternate source of food that can contribute to pest buildups and can provide cover for cutworms and slugs.

Sanitation

Remove infected leaves from diseased plants as soon as you see them. Dispose of severely diseased plants before they contaminate others.

Clean up crop refuse as soon as the harvest is over. Many insects and diseases will mature or overwinter in the stems, leaves, and roots of the plants they feed on; removing debris will reduce pest populations. Organisms that cause disease will survive at least as long as crop debris remains intact, so remove diseased plants from the garden area and discard them. Do not put diseased plants in a home compost pile, as it will not reach a high enough temperature to kill pathogens.

IPM Mechanical Controls

Handpicking

Inspect plants for egg clusters, bean beetles, caterpillars, and other insects as often as possible. Handpick to remove as many as possible. If you do not want to squash the pests, knock the insects and egg clusters into a quart jar of soapy water or knock insects off with a strong spray of water from the hose.

Traps

Use appropriate insect traps to reduce specific insect populations. Upturned flowerpots, boards, or newspaper will trap earwigs, sowbugs, and slugs; collect the trapped pests every morning.

Barriers

Aluminum foil and other reflective mulch can repel aphids. However, consider the environmental impact and energy consumption involved in making aluminum foil. Spread crushed eggshells or diatomaceous earth around plants to discourage slugs—while heavy mulch is good for weed control, it gives slugs a place to hide.

Exclusion

Physically block insects from attacking plants. Place cardboard tubes, orange juice cans, or aluminum foil collars around seedlings to keep cutworms away from plant stems. Use paper bags over ears of corn to keep birds and insects out (but do not cover them until pollination is complete). Netting or floating row covers can protect plants from insects during critical times for plant development.

Biological Controls

Predators and Parasites

Beneficial insects or natural enemies of damaging insects fall into two main categories: predators and parasites. Predators hunt and feed on other insects; they include spiders, praying mantids, lady beetles, and green lacewings. Parasites, such as Braconid and Trichogramma wasps, hatch from eggs inside or on another insect and eat the host as they grow (Figure 7.14). Releasing beneficial insects into landscapes or gardens may offer some benefit, but it is better to conserve the beneficial insects already present. To augment the beneficial insects in a garden or landscape, be sure to have flowering plants year-round—as they provide food and shelter for adults. Plants with small flowers, including but not limited to dill, cilantro, buckwheat, and sweet alyssum, attract many beneficial insects and maintain populations throughout the year. It is important to learn how to distinguish between pests and beneficial insects in gardens and landscapes. Conserve beneficial insect populations by avoiding the application of broad-spectrum insecticides that could harm beneficial insects.

Chemical Controls

Botanical Pesticides and Insecticidal Soaps

Botanical pesticides, or botanicals, are naturally occurring pesticides derived from plants. One common botanical is pyrethrin, an insecticide extracted from the pyrethrum flower (*Tanacetum cinerariifolium*). Insecticidal soaps are formulated specifically for their ability to control insects. Soaps are only effective against soft-bodied insects that come into direct contact with the spray droplets before they dry. These natural pesticides break down rapidly when exposed to sunlight, air, and moisture and are less likely to kill beneficial insects than insecticides that have longer residual activity.

Microbial Insecticides

Microbial insecticides combat insect infestations with microscopic living organisms such as viruses, bacteria, fungi, protozoa, or nematodes. The bacterium *Bacillus thuringiensis* (Bt) is the most popular pathogen. Formulations from *Bacillus thuringiensis var. kurstaki* (Btk) are the most widely used in controlling caterpillars, the larvae of butterflies and moths.

Synthetic Pesticides

Synthetic pesticides should be a last resort against damaging pests. Use these pesticides sparingly and target specific pests. Avoid broad-spectrum pesticides—such as insecticides in the pyrethroid, organophosphate, and neonicotinoid families—so as not to wipe out beneficial insect populations. We do not include the specific names of synthetic pesticides in this book, because products and their labels change rapidly, along with the pesticide registration and their use process. Always implement appropriate cultural practices before resorting to chemicals to control pests.

Apply chemicals according to label directions and with a sprayer. When used properly, output from sprayers can adequately cover plant surfaces and deliver an effective dose of the pesticide to the target site. Pesticides that are mixed with water tend to stick to the leaves better and resist wash-off by rain better than dust/powdered formulations. Before using any chemicals, read the labels

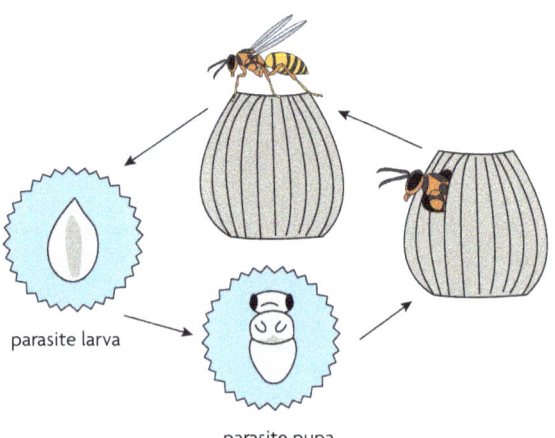

Figure 7.14 Life cycle of Trichogramma wasp.

thoroughly; always follow the directions precisely. When buying any pesticide, read the label beforehand; follow all directions and heed all precautions while mixing, applying, storing, or disposing of the pesticide.

ORGANIC GARDENING

The simple definition of organic gardening is gardening without the use of synthetic fertilizers or crop protection materials. Organic gardening, however, is much more than a simple replacement of synthetic inputs with natural ones; a philosophy of co-existence with natural systems prevails across the spectrum of organic gardening systems. Several organizations establish regulations and approve materials for certified organic agriculture, although there are no requirements for an organic gardener to be certified in any way. Organic gardening is an information-based system that uses knowledge of natural cycles, processes, and materials (or IPM) to improve and maintain soil health, provide necessary plant nutrients, and promote a habitat that naturally reduces pests and diseases.

Although some pesticides had been used for centuries, increased use of synthetic insecticides, fungicides, and herbicides began in earnest in the 1940s; during this time, Robert Rodale began to strongly promote 'non-chemical' farming methods. The early workers taught the use of rotation, crop residues, green manures, animal manure, and deep-rooted cover crops to provide plant nutrition and create a diverse habitat to reduce pest and disease pressure.

The movement gained momentum in the 1970's, and now there are established standards for organic production practices and materials. The National Organic Program (NOP) (www.ams.usda.gov/nop) publishes the National Organic Standards (NOS), and the Organic Materials Research Institute (OMRI) (www.omri.org) publishes a list of certified products. The NOS outlines both approved materials (such as natural pesticides and crop inputs) and sanctioned production practices. These organizations are excellent sources of information about organic agriculture for gardeners. Another good source of information is the National Center for Appropriate Technology (http://attra.ncat.org/organic.html).

One fundamental aspect of an organic gardening system is a concept known as soil health. Nutrients needed by plants are available in a variety of natural materials; in some cases, they are in the actual garden soil or subsoil, and the use of natural processes or certain cover crops can make them available to the garden crops. Most organic fertilizers must be mineralized—that is, converted from an organic form to an inorganic form—for the nutrients to become available to the crop. A soil enriched by the addition of necessary amendments that maintain the proper pH, levels of organic matter, and drainage supports an active and diverse microbial community—an essential part of nutrient mineralization and release. Such a soil also supports a diverse community of larger soil organisms such as fungi, worms, insects, and mites. This enriched soil ecosystem is the basis of soil health and therefore the goal of organic gardening. Maintaining a diverse plant community of both edible plants and non-edible plants (such as cover crop, green manure, and nectar) in a garden creates a habitat that encourages natural enemies, which helps limit insect and mite pests on the garden crops.

Pest and disease management in the garden is a complex process that requires knowledge about the impact of plant selection, crop spacing, crop timing, and the biology of pests and disease organisms. More information about organic gardening is available at the sources shown above, as well as at many university and Extension websites, including Extension Organic Agriculture (http://extension.org/organic_production). Local information is often more pertinent than that from distant locales.

COMMON VEGETABLE GARDEN PESTS

Insects

The table below groups the insect and mite pests common to home vegetable gardens in South Carolina by type. Some insects prefer one crop or one group of crops, whereas others are less picky and can damage almost any plant. Table 7.14 lists the insects commonly found on members of different vegetable families. For more information on these pests, please visit the Home and Garden Information Center.

Diseases

A lack of adequate disease control may be the limiting factor to gardening efforts. The key to controlling vegetable garden diseases is preventing them from the beginning. There are many different diseases that affect the wide variety of plants found in home gardens. Certain diseases occur each year, while other diseases only appear occasionally. Under certain weather conditions and to particularly susceptible plants, some uncommon diseases may cause serious problems. All it takes for a

TABLE 7.14 Common Insect Pest of Vegetable Plant Families

Plant Family	Lepidopteran Pests	Coleopteran Pests	Hemipteran Pests	Other Pests
Cole Crop	Cabbage Looper, Diamondback Moth, Cabbage Webworm, Cross-Striped Cabbageworm, Imported Cabbageworm	Yellow-Margined Leaf Beetle, Flea Beetles	Harlequin Bug, Cabbage Aphid, Turnip Aphid	
Squash	Melon Worm, Pickleworm, Squash Vine Borer	Cucumber Beetle (spotted, striped, and banded), Squash Beetles	Melon Aphid, Squash Bug, Leaf-footed Bug, Stink Bugs (many species)	Nematodes, Two-spotted Spider Mite
Goosefoot	Cutworms, Armyworms (many species), Cabbage Looper, Diamondback Moth		Aphids	Nematodes
Grass	Armyworms (many species), Corn Earworm, Cutworms	Southern Corn Billbug, Rootworm, Wireworm Complex	Stink Bugs (many species)	
Morning Glory	Armyworms (many species)	Wireworm Complex (potato, tobacco), Cucumber Beetle, Flea Beetles, Grubs, May and June beetles, Sweet Potato Weevil	Potato Leafhopper	
Nightshade	Hornworm, Tomato Fruitworm	Colorado Potato Beetle	Potato Aphid, Stink Bugs (many species), Leaf-footed Bug	Nematodes, Two-spotted Spider Mite
Pea	Lesser Cornstalk Borer, Cabbage Borer, Corn Earworm	Mexican Bean Beetle, Cowpea Curculio	Aphids (many species), Stink Bugs (many species), Tarnished Plant Bug	Thrips, Two-spotted Spider Mite

disease to spread in a plant is the right environment, a susceptible host, and a disease organism. By altering this disease triangle, you can prevent disease. See Chapter 5, Basic Plant Pathology, to review the different types of pathogens and disease symptoms.

The best way to control disease is by growing resistant plant varieties. Certain highly desirable horticultural types may not carry needed disease resistance. When a plant is not particularly resistant, depend on cultural practices and chemicals for disease control. Review the list of cultural pest-control practices in the section "Integrated Pest Management."

Three general types of vegetable diseases are discussed in more detail in the following pages: damping-off and root diseases, leaf and fruit diseases, and nematodes. Refer to Table 7.15 for a summary.

Damping-Off and Root Diseases

Seedling damping-off, root rot, and stem rot cause serious damage to garden plants. These diseases occur when crops are not rotated—that is, when the same vegetables are planted the same areas from one year to the next (Figure 7.15).

The most common cause of root disease is the water mold Pythium. Pythium minimizes the emergence of seedlings or causes young seedlings to die or "damp off" with a water-soaked lesion at the soil line. On older plants, infected feeder roots turn brown and rot. On some plants, long, water-soaked lesions move up the stem and cause young plants to collapse. Pythium diseases can occur any time during the growing season.

Root-rotting fungi include Rhizoctonia and Fusarium. These common soil-inhabiting fungi are

TABLE 7.15 Common Diseases and Disorders of Vegetable Plant Families

Plant Family	Disease Caused by Fungi	Diseases Caused by Water Molds	Diseases Caused by Bacteria	Diseases Caused by Viruses	Abiotic Diseases
Cole Crops	Alternaria Leaf Spot, Wirestem*, Sclerotinia Stem Rot*	Pythium Damping Off*, Downy Mildew	Black Rot	Cucumber Mosaic Virus (CMV)	Calcium and Magnesium Deficiency, Hollow Stem
Squash	Powdery Mildew, Gummy Stem Blight, Alternaria Leaf Spot, Anthracnose, Fusarium Wilt*	Downy Mildew	Bacterial Wilt	Cucumber Mosaic Virus (CMV), Watermelon Mosaic Virus (WMV)	Blossom End Rot, Poor Pollination, Ozone Injury
Goosefoot	Cercospora Leaf Spot, Damping Off*	Downy Mildew			Boron Deficiency
Grass	Corn Smut, Rust, Southern Corn Leaf Blight	Pythium (seedling, root, and stalk rots)*			
Morning Glory	Scurf, Black Rot, Fusarium Wilt*				
Nightshade	Early Blight, Southern Blight*, Fusarium Wilt, Verticillium Wilt	Late Blight	Bacterial Wilt*, Bacterial Spot, Bacterial Soft Rot	Tomato Spotted Wilt Virus (TSWV), Tobacco Mosaic Virus (TMV)	Blossom End Rot, Growth Cracks, Sunscald, Poor Fruit Set, Catfacing, Herbicide Injury
Pea	Anthracnose, Root Rots (Rhizoctonia, Fusarium)*, Rust, Powdery Mildew, Cercospora Leaf Spot, White Mold*	Pythium (root rot)*	Bacterial Blights	Mosaic Viruses	

*indicates the disease is caused by a soil borne pathogen

present in most areas and can cause serious problems when weather conditions are right. Rhizoctonia causes damping-off, normally after emergence. Sunken, dark brown lesions form on the lower stems of young seedlings and on roots. Fusarium may cause damping-off, but more often, it causes root rot or clogging of water-conducting tissues, thus reducing the growth rate of the plant.

Prevention and Treatment. You can prevent damping-off by sowing fungicide-treated seed. Seed treatment usually allows young seedlings to establish before root-rotting pathogens can cause serious problems. Because organic seed is not treated with fungicide, seedlings may be more susceptible to damping-off.

You can also avoid damping-off and root rot by planting in raised beds. If root rot and stem rot are a serious problem, fill raised beds with a soilless potting mix. Add compost to soil before planting each season to improve soil drainage. Fresh compost that contains beneficial microorganisms promotes healthy root growth and allows plants to compensate for some roots lost to root rot. Some of the beneficial microorganisms in compost are also antagonistic towards root-rot pathogens.

Leaf and Fruit Diseases

Once vegetable crops have outgrown their juvenile susceptibility to pre- and post-emergence damping-off, most crops remain healthy for several weeks during vegetative growth. Once fruiting vegetable crops set fruit, they tend to become more susceptible to leaf and

Figure 7.15 Damping-off on brassica transplant seen after cool soil temperatures and excessive rain.
Image Credit: Zachary Snipes, Clemson University

Figure 7.16 Anthracnose fruit rot seen on eggplant.
Image Credit: Zachary Snipes, Clemson University

fruit diseases caused by fungi, water molds, and bacteria (Figure 7.16).

Pathogens that cause leaf spots, leaf blights, fruit spots, and fruit rots often spread to the garden via wind or wind-blown rain. If crops are not properly rotated, some pathogens may stay in the soil. Infrequently, diseased seeds or transplants are the source of problems. Viruses can arrive via insect vectors.

Foliar diseases caused by fungi, water molds, and bacteria are more prevalent when leaves remain wet from dew, rain, or poorly timed irrigation. One exception to this is powdery mildew, which occurs during dry weather. Some pathogens that cause fruit rots originate on leaves, reproduce, and then spread to fruit.

Prevention and Treatment. Increase spacing around plants. Open space allows air to circulate more freely than if plants are spaced too closely together; more air movement means leaves dry faster, which reduces the chances of disease.

Avoid handling plants when they are wet. Infection spreads more when leaves are wet. Staying out of the garden until leaves are dry will reduce the spread of disease-causing organisms, particularly bacteria.

Rotating crops allows time for foliar pathogens to die out in soil before their host vegetables are replanted. Most foliar pathogens cannot survive in soil after the infested crop debris decays.

Use fungicides if foliar diseases appear early in the season when plants start to flower or if diseases have become severe in previous years.

Disease Control and Irrigation

Irrigation is necessary to supplement natural rainfall in growing a garden, but free moisture on foliage increases the chances of disease. Without free moisture, disease-causing organisms cannot germinate or penetrate the host. The best time to irrigate a garden is either late at night after the dew has formed or in the morning after the garden has dried. Make sure leaves have dried before dew wets the plants in the evening. Direct the stream of irrigation water to the base of the plant; use a soaker hose or drip irrigation to avoid wetting the leaves. It takes 1-9 hr of constant wetness for a fungal spore or a bacterium to germinate and penetrate a leaf. Breaking the cycle of wetness can help to prevent or limit disease.

Nematodes

Nematodes attack a wide variety of plants and can cause considerable damage in home gardens. Nematodes are microscopic roundworms that live in the soil and on plant roots. They injure plants by feeding on root cells with their needlelike mouthparts (stylets). They can damage the root system until it cannot properly absorb water and nutrients for the plants. Although they are widespread in South Carolina and elsewhere, nematodes are more common in the sandy soils of the Coastal Plain and river deltas. The most common nematode in home gardens is the Southern root-knot nematode (*Meloidogyne incognita*), which can severely gall roots and stunt plants (Figure 7.17).

Symptoms

You can confirm the presence of root-knot nematodes by physically examining the roots for knots or by submitting a sample for laboratory testing. Often, you can see symptoms of nematode infestations on plants both above and below ground.

Above the ground, plants may appear stunted and discolored and may die. In hot, dry weather, plants will wilt and have noticeable nutrient deficiencies. But do not depend only on above-ground plant symptoms when trying to determine if nematodes are damaging the plants.

Beneath the ground, the roots may have knots or galls (swollen areas). Both large and small roots will have round swellings on them, and the entire root system may be shallow with areas that are dead or branched excessively. County Extension offices provide guidelines for nematode sampling. Samples are analyzed to determine the types and quantities of nematodes present in the soil and make appropriate recommendations for control.

Prevention

Where root-knot nematodes are not present, take measures to ensure that they do not appear. Rotate susceptible plants to different areas of the garden each year so that one area isn't vulnerable longer than others. Carefully examine the roots of transplants for signs of very tiny knots and avoid planting those that look suspicious. Check for bumps on the surface of Irish potatoes. Whenever possible, purchase certified disease-free transplants and seed potatoes. Destroy roots by pulling up or tilling immediately after harvest is complete.

Treatment

Once you confirm a nematode problem, you can implement some or all of several different management options; the more controls you implement, the more likely you truly wipe out the nematode population.

Remove all plants immediately after harvest, including all root fragments. Do not let stalks stand through the winter. Work the soil two to four times during winter and allow the sun and weather to exert their killing effect.

Use root-knot-nematode-resistant plant varieties. A few varieties of tomato, pepper, and Southern pea are resistant to root-knot nematodes. In seed catalogues or on plant tags, look for the "N" code on tomato, but know that resistant tomato may not be as effective at high soil temperatures.

Establish a rotation system. Rotate the garden to a new location to prevent nematodes and diseases from establishing in one area. If new space is not available, rotate plants so that resistant plants are moved to an area where susceptible ones had grown previously. Usually, it takes three years of growing non-susceptible plants in a

Figure 7.17 This plant was stunted and upon examining the roots, found to have gall-like symptoms associate with root-knot nematode.
Image Credit: Zachary Snipes, Clemson University

particular garden space to reduce nematode populations.

You can reduce root-knot nematode populations in infected soils using French marigolds (*Tagetes patula*) or their hybrids. For the first year, plant a solid stand of marigolds in areas of greatest damage or plant marigolds in strips several feet wide across the garden to establish a rotation scheme. Keep marigolds free of grass and weeds to prevent nematodes from feeding on roots other than marigolds. Plant vegetables particularly susceptible to root-knot nematodes in the marigold area the following spring. Plant marigolds in the same area at least every other year as long as the nematode problem continues.

Weeds

Weeds compete with vegetables for water, nutrients, and light. Weeds also harbor insects and diseases that can spread to vegetables. Efforts made early in the growing season reduce the time required for hand weeding later in the season and in following years.

Common Weeds in Vegetable Gardens

The most common weeds found in the garden can be divided into summer annuals, winter annuals, and perennials.

Summer Annual Weeds. Summer annuals are weeds that germinate in spring or early summer and flower in the summer or fall. These are the most common type of weed found in gardens, particularly at the end of the spring gardening season or in abandoned plots. You can further divide this group into summer annual grasses and summer annual broadleaf weeds. Common summer annual grasses include large crabgrass, goosegrass, and giant foxtail.

Annual grasses are easy to control if you take appropriate measures early in the growing season but can quickly become a more severe problem if left to grow. Large crabgrass, for example, roots into the soil where the nodes of the stem contact the soil, allowing the grass to quickly cover open ground. The fibrous root systems of grasses make them more difficult to remove from the ground. Weedy grasses have multiple shoots and can become large clumps.

Common summer annual broadleaf weeds include smooth pigweed, common lambsquarters, purslane, galinsoga, common ragweed, and tall morning glory. When controlling purslane by hoeing, remove all stems from the garden; purslane can re-root if left on the soil surface because the thick, succulent stem can survive a period of drought. Galinsoga is often called quickweed, perhaps because it develops quickly and grows flowers while still a small plant. Small-seeded broadleaf weeds like pigweed are easier to control than large-seeded broadleaf weeds like morning glory. Larger-seeded weeds can germinate from a greater soil depth and can push through a shallow layer of mulch.

Winter Annual Weeds. Winter annuals are weeds that germinate in fall and flower in the spring. These weeds grow in fall gardens and are often present when the garden is prepared for spring planting. Annual ryegrass is a common winter annual grass; henbit, common chickweed, and wild mustard are common winter annual broadleaf weeds. Tilling soil kills existing stands of common chickweed and other winter annuals. Weeds in this category are generally not as troublesome in the garden as summer annuals, since they do not produce as much biomass. However, they compete with slow-growing cool-season vegetables like carrot, beet, and onion.

Perennial Weeds. Herbaceous perennial weeds can be especially difficult to manage in gardens. These plants are killed back to the ground by hard frosts and over-winter using underground plant parts such as tubers or rhizomes. Tilling the garden may spread these weeds by fragmenting and moving root pieces. Each of the root pieces can develop into a complete plant. The most common perennial weeds are common bermudagrass and yellow nutsedge. Bermudagrass, often called wiregrass, spreads by creeping stolons and rhizomes. Thoroughly remove all plant parts from the garden when hand-weeding, because bermudagrass can re-root into the soil. Yellow nutsedge is often called nutgrass; however, this plant is a member of the sedge family, not the grass family. Yellow nutsedge reproduces via underground tubers.

Weed Control in Vegetable Gardens

Mulches. Mulches fit into two basic categories: organic and inorganic. Mulches are one of the easiest and most effective way to control annual weeds in the garden and can also suppress some species of perennial weed. Mulches control weeds by preventing sunlight from reaching the soil surface. Certain weeds require light to germinate, and all green plants require light to grow.

Organic Mulches. Organic mulches include grass clippings, pine bark, straw, compost, or similar materials. Organic mulches cool the soil surface, which is beneficial during hot summer days, but may reduce crop growth in the spring by shading the soil and preventing warming.

Avoid over-mulching, which can reduce oxygen

levels in the soil. Crop roots require oxygen for growth, so limit the mulch layer to a maximum of 3 inches. Organic mulches provide good control of annual weeds, but perennial weeds may be able to push through the mulch layer. Occasionally, annual weeds will germinate and grow in the mulch layer. When using an organic mulch, make sure that the source is not contaminated with weed seed, rhizomes or tubers. Weeds are often spread by contaminated mulch, making weed control harder than if no mulch was used.

Grass clippings from lawns make great organic mulches, but be sure that the lawn has not been treated with a broadleaf herbicide such as 2,4-D. Tomatoes, peppers and most other vegetables are very sensitive to 2,4-D and could absorb residues of the compound from the treated grass clippings.

Inorganic Mulches. Inorganic mulches are synthetic; this group includes black plastic and geotextiles.

Black plastic, a solid sheet of polyethylene, effectively controls annual weeds. The disadvantage of black plastic is that water and oxygen cannot pass through this material. The soil must be moist prior to laying this synthetic material, and the gardener must check the soil under the black plastic during the growing season to ensure that the soil remains moist. Black plastic warms the soil, which is an advantage in the spring but can be harmful in the summer. Clear plastic—which increases soil temperature more than black plastic—will not control weeds, since sunlight can reach the soil surface. Black plastic can suppress perennial weeds, but plants like yellow nut sedge can push through the material.

Geotextiles, also called weed barriers, are woven or spun-bonded fabrics containing polypropylene or polyester; they are available in both black and white. These fabrics are more expensive than black plastic, but they allow water and gases to pass through to the soil surface. Research indicates that black plastic is mostly effective against annual weeds; however, some weeds are able to germinate above the fabric and grow roots through to the soil. Other weeds, such as large crabgrass, are able to germinate below the fabric and push their shoots through holes in the material. As with black plastic, perennial weeds can often penetrate these fabrics.

Physical Weed Controls. Since mature weeds extract large quantities of moisture and nutrients from the soil, it is important to remove weeds when they are young. Hand-pulling weeds suffices for small gardens and raised beds, but a hoe is critical for larger gardens. Cut off weeds just below the soil surface with a sharp hoe. Hoeing must be shallow, as most vegetable roots are near the soil surface and easily damaged (Figure 7.18).

Figure 7.18 Rows of arugula were spaced appropriately for easy cultivation with a long-handled stirrup hoe.
Image Credit: Zachary Snipes, Clemson University

You can save time in larger garden areas by using wheel hoes. Wheel hoes come in a variety of different models, and each model has an assortment of removable attachments for specific garden tasks. Manual rotary cultivators do a good job on long rows and pathways, provided that the soil is not too wet or dry and the weeds are small. In large gardens with widely spaced rows, an appropriately sized rotary tiller makes the work easy and fast. Manual and powered rotary cultivators are usually unable to turn under weeds close to vegetable plants without damaging the vegetables, so hand-pulling and hoeing are best for removing weeds near vegetable plants. Deep cultivation with any instrument is likely to damage roots or stems of crop plants.

While cultivating, try to move as little soil as possible to limit the amount of weed seed brought to the soil surface where it can germinate. It's best to cultivate when the soil is moist but not wet. After removing weeds from the garden, apply mulch to control future germinating weeds.

Crop Competition. Once vegetable plants establish, their foliage begins to shade the ground. This shading effect reduces the amount of light available for weed germination and development. Close spacing of vegetables decreases the amount of time required for the crop canopy to significantly shade the soil. Once vegetable plants establish, they can reduce the growth of weeds that have previously been controlled by other means. In small gardens, planting vegetables in square blocks leaves less open space for weeds to grow than traditional row culture.

Chemical Control. Most gardens don't require herbicides; a combination of mulch and hand weeding is sufficient to control annual weeds. The difficulty with herbicides in a vegetable garden is that not many are safe for the wide range of plant species grown in a garden. Herbicides are not universally labeled for use on all vegetable crops, because (among other reasons) different crops differ in tolerance just as weeds do.

You can use glyphosate in conjunction with appropriate cultivation techniques to control hard-to-kill perennial weeds—such as bermudagrass or nutsedge—when the garden plot is fallow (not planted in a crop).

ABIOTIC VEGETABLE DISORDERS

Blossom-End Rot

Blossom-end rot is a physiological disorder of many fruiting vegetables, including tomato, pepper, melons, and squash. This disorder causes water-soaked spots on the blossom end of the fruit that enlarge and turn black. Usually, secondary infection by decay-causing organisms follows soon after.

Blossom-end rot stems from calcium deficiency in developing fruit. When a plant is growing rapidly, it may not supply enough calcium to the blossom end of the developing fruit. Extreme fluctuations in moisture, root pruning, and excessive nitrogen fertilization can also enhance blossom-end rot.

Prevention and Treatment

Lime soil according to the recommendations provided by a soil analysis report. Using gypsum (1-2 lb per 100 ft^2) as a supplement to lime on calcium-deficient soils is also beneficial. Apply the lime or gypsum before planting crops.

Maintain uniform moisture by irrigation and mulching. After plants set fruit, increase the amount of water. Applying calcium sprays to foliage will not prevent or cure blossom-end rot.

Growth Cracks

Cracking is a physiological disorder that describes the splitting of the outer skin or epidermis of tomato fruit. Two kinds of cracks occur in tomatoes:

- Radial cracks are deep, v-shaped splits that begin at the calyx (or stem end) and radiate out towards the blossom end.

- Circular cracks are a series of concentric rings that appear between the stem end and the shoulders of the fruit.

Tomato fruits crack in response to environmental conditions that encourage rapid fruit growth or expansion, such as wide fluctuations in moisture or temperature. For example, when the epidermis cells have "hardened" during a slow growth period, excess water encourages rapid growth that can cause the skin to split. Hot daytime and cool nighttime temperatures can also result in expansion and contraction of the fruits and the development of cracks. High nitrogen and low potassium levels are also linked to fruit cracking.

Some tomato varieties resist cracking better than others. Highly susceptible tomatoes develop cracks while the fruit is still green; crack-resistant varieties show no signs of stress until they start turning red. Ripe tomatoes tend to develop circular cracks after remaining on the vine too long. Cracking is particularly severe on heirloom tomato varieties.

Sunscald

Sunscald occurs when tomatoes, peppers, melons, and other fruiting vegetables are exposed to the direct rays of the sun during hot weather; it is most common on green fruit. Decay-causing fungi frequently invade the damaged tissue.

Prevention

Cover exposed fruits with a kaolin clay compound. Control leaf diseases that destroy the foliage canopy to retain this additional shade cover.

Poor Fruit Set

Poor fruit set occurs in tomato, pepper, beans, cucumber, melon, and squash for several reasons.

Extreme temperatures can cause poor fruit set. Generally, blossoms drop off without setting fruit when temperatures are below 55°F or above 90°F for extended periods. To avoid this, plant hot-set varieties of tomato and replant beans, cucumber, and squash crops later in the season for a fall garden.

Dry soil can also cause poor fruit set when blossoms dry and fall due to dehydration. However, too much shade can also cause poor fruit set; few blossoms are produced when the plants receive less than six hours of sun a day.

Excessive nitrogen can cause poor fruit set, because high nitrogen levels in the soil promote leaf growth at the expense of blossom and fruit formation.

Catfacing

Catfacing is caused by cold temperatures during fruit set of tomato. It causes the fruit to be extremely malformed and scarred, usually at the blossom end. Fruits that develop later in the season will not be affected; regardless, catfaced fruit are safe to eat.

Hollow Stem

Hollow stem is exactly what it sounds like: the formation of a hollow, discolored stem in broccoli and cauliflower, sometimes with discoloration of the florets. A deficiency of boron or an excess of nitrogen can cause hollow stem.

Bolting

Bolting, or premature flowering, occurs when there are major fluctuations in temperature or changes in daylength. Plants sense these environmental cues and try to produce seeds before the crop is fully developed. This phenomenon is commonly seen in lettuce, spinach, and plants from the cole crop family. Seeding these crops at the recommended times will reduce the chances of bolting, though unseasonably cold or hot weather may still trigger bolting (in cole crops or lettuce and spinach, respectively).

Cole crops will bolt if exposed to a prolonged cold period following a favorable growing period, followed by warm conditions. This is a problem of spring-planted and overwintered crops. Lack of nitrogen or other nutrient stressors, as well as competition from weeds, insects, or diseases that slow vegetative growth, can also promote flowering. Some varieties are more susceptible to bolting than others.

Chapter 8
Fruit Gardening

By Dave Ouellette

LEARNING OBJECTIVES

- Give examples of common fruits and nuts that can be grown successfully in South Carolina.
- Understand and be able to explain best practices for growing fruit and nut crops, including site selection, care, maintenance, and pest management.

INTRODUCTION

A gardener can cultivate a wide variety of fruits in South Carolina gardens and landscapes. Fruit crops require proper care to produce a yearly, high-quality harvest. Regular maintenance keeps them healthy and productive and includes pruning and training, pest management, and thinning fruit.

Maximize your success by selecting fruit crops that match your level of commitment. Some types of fruit require a higher level of commitment than others. For example, fruits such as figs and persimmons require less training, pruning, fertilizing, and pest management than apples, peaches, or bunch grapes, all of which require intensive management. The chances of having a successful harvest are greatly improved if your site's climate and soil are suitable for growing that particular fruit crop.

This chapter explains some of the challenges and opportunities that gardeners encounter when selecting, planting, and maintaining fruit crops.

GENERAL FRUIT CROP CONSIDERATIONS

Location

Planting fruit crops close to home is convenient, especially at harvest time. You can grow fruiting plants next to or in place of ornamentals in a home landscape, use strawberries as a ground cover or as a border for a flower bed, plant grapes and blackberries alongside the garden on a trellis or fence, and place blueberries to form a hedge or as part of a foundation planting around a home.

Always plant fruit crops in areas that receive full sun (6-8 hr per day). Just a few extra hours of shade can negatively impact growth and fruiting potential. Assess the amount of sunlight that falls on different parts of your site and select the sunniest areas for fruit crops.

Always consider the mature size of the fruit tree or shrub when evaluating a potential planting location. Consider planting dwarf fruit trees or small fruit crops in smaller spaces. Dwarf apples and pears occupy less space than standard-sized trees and produce fruit sooner after planting. Plants growing in insufficient space require either severe pruning or eventual relocation. If planted too close together, plants can weaken and be less fruitful due to inadequate sunlight and increased competition for nutrients and water. Very dense plantings see more disease outbreaks because insufficient air movement allows leaves to remain wet for longer. To avoid these problems, plant fruit crops at the recommended distances (Table 8.1).

TABLE 8.1 Spacing Recommendations for Fruit Crops in South Carolina

	Planting Distance	
	In-row (ft)	Between row (ft)
Tree Fruit		
Apple		
Semi-dwarf	15-20	20-25
Dwarf	6-10	12-15
Pear	15-20	20-25
Peach/Nectarine	15-20	20-25
Plum	12-20	20-25
Persimmon		
American	20-30	20-30
Asian	15-20	20-25
Pawpaw	10-15	18-20
Pomegranate	10-12	14-16
Fig	10-20	18-20
Mulberry	15-30	20-30
Pecan	40-60	40-60
Small Fruit		
Blackberry		
Erect or Semi-erect	3-5	8-12
Raspberry		
Erect or Semi-erect	2-3	8-12
Trailing	8-10	8-12
Blueberry		
Rabbiteye	6-8	10-12
Highbush	4-5	8-10
Grape		
Muscadine	15-20	8-10
Bunch	6-8	8-10
Strawberry		
Matted row	2	4
Annual hill	1	1
Elderberry	6-8	10-12

Avoid planting fruits in low areas or "frost pockets," where early spring frosts may kill flowers and reduce or eliminate the year's crop. In sloping landscapes, plant fruits at the highest elevation or on the sides of slopes, away from cold air (which drains downhill to low spots). On south-facing slopes, fruits tend to bloom earlier and are therefore more likely to be injured by freezing temperatures. Late-flowering cultivars may be most appropriate for these locations.

Low areas in a landscape tend to drain poorly and should be avoided. Planting in areas of poor drainage often results in stunted growth and eventual death of fruit crops. On heavy or compacted soils, consider planting in raised beds or on soil berms to improve drainage.

Some fruit crops grown in other areas of the country are not recommended or suited for gardens in South Carolina. For example, it is challenging to grow cherries in South Carolina; they do not reliably produce fruit. Cherry trees, especially sour types, have a higher chilling requirement than can be consistently fulfilled year after year in South Carolina except in the highest elevations. An early spring blooming period makes them very vulnerable to frost damage. Cherry trees are also very susceptible to a wide array of diseases that affect fruit and branches, including brown rot and bacterial canker. Birds are another common problem and can consume an entire crop if trees are not protected with netting. Fruit splitting or cracking caused by untimely rainfall can also result in complete crop losses.

Apricots are also likely to be damaged by frost in South Carolina because of their very early bloom period. Apricots are very susceptible to many diseases when grown in the heat and high humidity of South Carolina.

Citrus fruit crops—even the more cold-hardy types—require relatively mild winters. Satsuma mandarins, especially those cultivars that ripen in the fall, can be grown successfully in the state's coastal regions. Outside of the coastal zones, South Carolina gardeners should grow citrus in containers to allow the option of moving plants inside during the coldest parts of winter. In-ground citrus plantings are much more challenging to protect from the cold.

Fertilization

Applying fertilizer without knowing if it is needed can result in excessive growth and poor-quality fruit. Avoid the temptation to make routine fertilizer applications, as they may encourage leafy, vegetative growth at the expense of fruit production and fruit quality. Never apply large amounts of fertilizer to a small area, as this can injure roots. If your fruit crops are near a fertilized lawn, additional fertilizer applications may be unnecessary.

Determine the pH and fertility of the soil at your site by having the soil tested. A soil pH between 6.0-6.5 is optimum for most tree fruits and many small fruits. Blueberries prefer more acidic conditions, with a soil pH between 4.5-5.5. Plant nutrient availability directly relates to soil pH—if soil pH is not in the optimum range, required nutrients may be unavailable to plants.

Fertilize according to the recommendations of your soil test report.

Generalized fertility recommendations are made for the various fruits and nuts discussed in this chapter. A soil test combined with periodic plant tissue testing is the best way of knowing the fertility needs of your soil and plants. For information regarding soil testing and plant tissue sampling guidelines, contact the HGIC.

Irrigation

A shortage of soil moisture can reduce growth, fruit size, and yield. Watering is especially important for newly planted fruit trees, shrubs, and vines. Generally, fruit crops require about 1- 1.5 in. of water per week during the growing season. A rain gauge is helpful for keeping track of daily rainfall accumulations and determining how much additional water to apply.

Drip or micro-sprinkler irrigation is convenient and easy to install. Such systems apply water only to the base of plants, improving irrigation efficiency and reducing disease outbreaks. An organic mulch applied 2-4 in. deep in a doughnut shape—with the trunk at its center and stretching to the dripline—is another excellent strategy for improving water penetration, conserving moisture, and reducing watering requirements. Maintain a 4-6-in. gap of bare ground between the mulch and plant stems.

Fruit Thinning

Under favorable conditions, most fruit trees produce more fruit than can mature to a desirable size. Fruit thinning—removing some of the developing, immature fruit from the tree—increases the size and quality of the remaining fruit at harvest. Fruit thinning also reduces limb breakage and stimulates flower bud production for next year's crop. Thinning allows apple trees to maintain a regular bearing cycle, which is particularly important in apple cultivars that only produce a crop every other year if fruits are not thinned adequately.

Sanitation

A good sanitation program can reduce the need for chemical controls and improve the effectiveness of other practices for managing disease and insect pests. Your sanitation regimen should include:

- Collecting and removing fallen leaves, fruit, and other plant debris;

- Pruning out all dead, diseased, and insect-infested limbs and branches;
- Burning or removing all infected plant material from the area (do not compost!);
- Disinfecting and sterilizing pruning tools to prevent the spread of disease-causing pathogens—this is especially important when pruning out bacterial diseases, such as fire blight, or canker-affected branches. Wipe or dip your pruning tools using a 20% chlorine bleach-water mixture (1 part household bleach to 4 parts water) or less corrosive household disinfectants such as Lysol or 70–100% ethanol or isopropyl alcohol; and
- Removing weeds to prevent the establishment of a "green bridge" between plants, which provides a host for pathogens and can trigger future disease outbreaks.

Pruning and Training

Pruning and training are essential practices for growing fruit successfully. Pruning is the process of selectively cutting or removing individual branches, whereas training is a practice that directs plant growth into a desired shape. Procedures for pruning and training vary according to the type, variety, and age of the fruit crop.

The primary objective of pruning and training is to develop a framework in young trees and shrubs that is strong enough to support future fruit production. When done properly during the early years, pruning and training minimize the amount of effort required to care for plants in the future. Untrained and unpruned fruit crops can become entangled masses of shoots and branches that produce little or no fruit and harbor insects and disease. Trees and shrubs that have been neglected or improperly pruned for several years will need more aggressive corrective pruning.

Proper training and pruning expose the interior canopy of fruit trees and shrubs to more sunlight. For many fruit crops, flower buds for the current season's crop form during the previous summer. Light penetration is essential for flower bud development and optimal fruit set, flavor, and quality. Opening the canopy also increases air movement through the plant. This minimizes disease infection and allows thorough spray penetration. Another goal of annual pruning is to remove dead, diseased, and broken limbs. Removal helps to minimize the potential spread of opportunistic pathogens and insect pests.

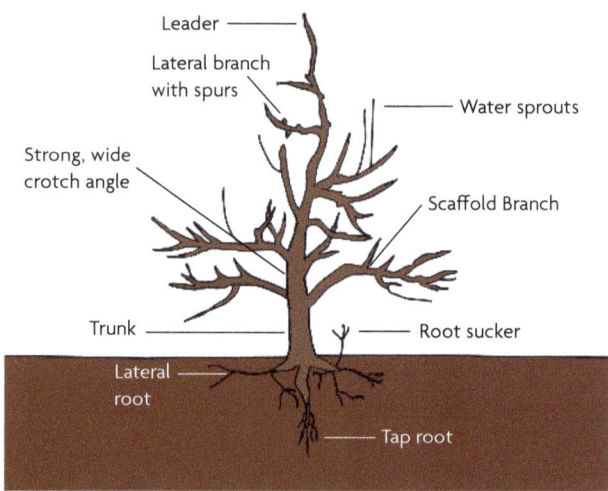

Figure 8.1 Major parts of a fruit tree.

Figure 8.1 illustrates the major parts of a tree discussed in the following sections.

Pruning is an annual management practice. Here, we discuss three basic pruning cuts—heading, reduction, and thinning (Figure 8.2).

Heading (or heading back) removes only the terminal portion of shoots or limbs. This increases side bud growth and results in denser growth where the pruning cut was made.

Reduction cuts remove a larger branch or trunk

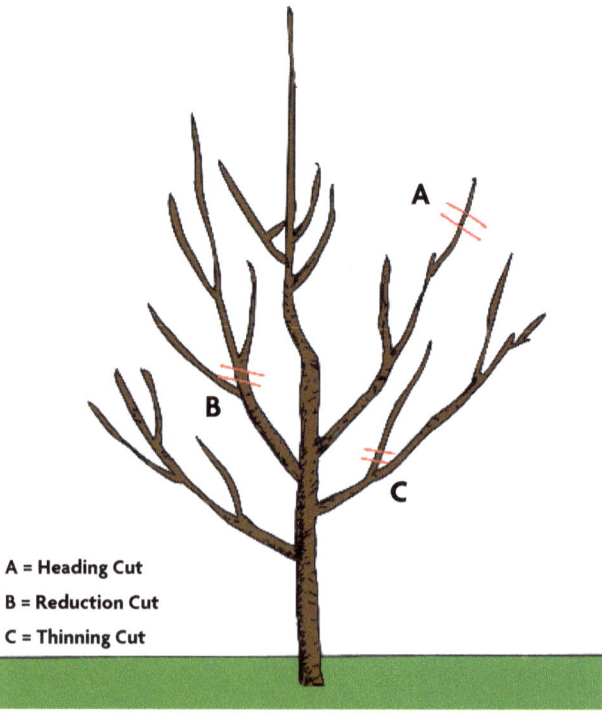

Figure 8.2 Types of pruning cuts.

back to a side branch that is typically one-third to one-half the diameter of the removed branch. Reduction cuts are commonly used in training young fruit trees. These types of cuts are useful for lowering tree height and improving the tree's overall shape.

Thinning removes an entire shoot or limb to its point of origin on the main branch or trunk. Thinning cuts reduce canopy density but have little impact on height. This type of cut improves light penetration and airflow into the plant canopy.

Most fruit crop pruning is best done the winter before active growth begins, called dormant pruning. Pruning during the growing season—summer pruning—focuses on removing undesired upright and overly vigorous current-season growth in tree fruits. You can perform light pruning throughout the growing season to remove broken, injured, or diseased branches and improve air circulation and light penetration.

Cultivar Selection

Select fruit cultivars—commonly referred to as varieties—that are adapted to the soil conditions and climate of your area. Consider varieties with the fewest insect and disease problems. If you want to extend your harvest season, plant several cultivars of the same kind of fruit but that mature at different times.

Be aware of the pollination requirements of each cultivar. Fruit cultivars may be either self-fruitful or self-unfruitful. A self-fruitful (or self-fertile) cultivar can reproduce sexually by itself; a self-unfruitful cultivar requires pollen from another cultivar to produce fruit.

TABLE 8.2 Pollination Requirements for Tree Fruit Crops in South Carolina

Crop	Remarks
Apple	Apples are self-unfruitful, and therefore need to be cross-pollinated by another apple variety. Two or more varieties with overlapping bloom periods should be spaced less than 50 feet apart to ensure the transfer of pollen between trees in backyard settings. Some varieties may be listed as partially self-fruitful, but will set more fruit if cross-pollinated. Additionally, some varieties, such as 'Winesap', 'Stayman', 'Mutsu' and 'Jonagold', produce sterile pollen and therefore cannot be used to pollinate other varieties. Many nursery catalogues include pollination compatibility charts to help determine appropriate pollinizer varieties.
Pear	Most varieties of pear are self-unfruitful, and therefore need to be cross-pollinated with another pear variety with a similar bloom period. Pear blossoms are not as attractive to bees as other blooming fruit trees. Although 'Anjou' and 'Bartlett' are partially self-fruitful, they should be cross-pollinated to produce regular and more productive crops. 'Bartlett' and 'Comice' may set crops of parthenocarpic fruit without pollination. European and Asian pears will cross-pollinate only if blooming at the same time.
Peach/Nectarine	Self-fruitful. Bee activity may increase fruit set.
Plum	Most plum varieties are considerd to be partially or completely self-unfruitful. Planting two or more cultivars for cross-pollination is highly recommended to ensure fruit set, good yield and proper fruit sizing. Japanese plums and European plums do not cross-pollinate. Many nursery catalogues include pollination compatibility charts to help determine appropriate pollinizer varieties.
Persimmon	American persimmons are generally self-unfruitful, having male and female flowers on separate trees. Both a male and female tree are usually required for cross-pollination and fruit production. There are a few self-fruitful varieties of American persimmons, including 'Meader' and 'Prok' that will produce seedless fruit without pollination. However, pollinated persimmons will often also grow larger and have better flavor.
	Asian persimmons are likely to have perfect flowers and have the potential to be self-fruitful. Certain cultivars of Asian persimmons, such as 'Fuyu', 'Ichi-Ki-Kei-Jiro', and 'Hachiya' produce seedless fruit without pollination. However, pollinated fruit are less likely to abort and more likely to size properly. Fruit of some Asian persimmons such as 'Chocolate' change appearance and flavor depending on whether or not pollination has occurred. These pollination-variant persimmons have light-colored seedless flesh when unpollinated, and darker brown flesh with seeds when pollinated. American and Asian persimmon trees do not cross-pollinate.

continued

TABLE 8.2 Continued

Crop	Remarks
Pawpaw	Self-unfruitful. Two or more varieties should be planted to ensure cross-pollination. Pollination is performed by flies and beetles. Hand pollination is a viable option to obtain better fruit set.
Pomegranate	Self-fruitful. There are two types of flowers: perfect and functionally male. The perfect, fruit-bearing flowers have a full, rounded base. Male flowers will be more narrow and vase-shaped. Bees and hummingbirds serve as pollinators.
Fig	All common fig varieties, including 'Brown Turkey', 'Celeste', 'Brunswick' and 'Mission' set fruit parthenocarpically, not needing pollination for fruit development.
Mulberry	Most modern mulberry varieties are self-fruitful, but a pollination partner may increase the size and quality of the harvest. Wind pollinated.
Pecan	Self-unfruitful and require cross-pollination. Wind-pollinated. Pecan varieties are classified into two broad categories based on flowering habit. In Type I varieties, pollen is matured and released first, and female flowers become receptive several days later. In Type II varieties, female flowers are receptive first, and then pollen is released after the female flowers are no longer receptive. Planting two or more varieties of each type ensures pollen is available throughout the flowering season. Choosing which varieties to grow is helped by using pollination charts listing the pollen shedding and pistil receptivity times of cultivars.

Both self-fruitful and self-unfruitful cultivars can pollinate self-unfruitful cultivars. Fruit varieties that can pollinate one another have compatible pollen and overlapping flowering dates. Refer to Table 8.2 and Table 8.3 for a list of fruit crops and their pollination requirements.

Choose fruit cultivars that have the appropriate chill-hour requirement for your region. Chill hours are the number of hours below 45°F experienced by fruiting plants during winter. To overcome dormancy in spring and then bloom and set fruit, fruit and nut trees require a certain number of chill hours. This requirement varies by fruit type and is specific to each cultivar; different cultivars of the same fruit require different numbers of chilling hours. For example, peach trees may require anywhere from 200-1,200 chill hours depending on the cultivar.

The lower the chill-hour requirement, the earlier growth may begin once temperatures are warm enough. Low-chilling cultivars may have their chill requirement met too early in the winter. A warm period during the remainder of the winter may result in open flowers that are then threatened by freezing temperatures. Likewise, fruit crops will suffer if their chilling requirement is not met. They may bloom erratically, produce deformed leaves, and have little to no fruit set.

A cultivar developed in the northern United States or Florida may have too high or too low of a chilling requirement for it to grow successfully in your region. The Piedmont region typically accumulates about 800-1200 chill hours per year, the Midlands region typically receives 600-900 chill hours per year, and the Coastal Plain may receive as few as 300-500 chill hours per year. These chilling hour ranges are estimates and vary from year to year.

Rootstocks

Grafting is commonly used to propagate most fruit and nut tree cultivars. Grafting involves joining together parts of two closely related plants to function as a single unit. One of the plants —the rootstock—provides the lower trunk and root system. The other plant—the scion—provides the upper trunk, stems, leaves, flowers and fruit. As in other methods of vegetative or asexual plant propagation, grafting creates genetic duplicates of superior plants.

Select scion varieties based on what fruit traits you find desirable, such as large size, high yields, or extended shelf life. Select a rootstock based on its resistance to pest problems, performance in certain soil conditions, or effect on the mature size of the tree.

TREE FRUITS AND NUTS

Apples

Growing apples in a home garden requires a high level of commitment. It is necessary to follow a regular spray program to control the many destructive insects

TABLE 8.3 Pollination Requirements for Small Fruit Crops in South Carolina

Crop	Remarks
Blackberry/Raspberry	Most blackberry and raspberry varieties are self-fruitful, however planting two or more varieties for the purpose of cross-pollination will improve fruit set, size, and yield. Bees are the primary pollinators.
Blueberry	Most varieties of rabbiteye blueberry (*Vaccinium virgatum*) are partially or completely self-unfruitful and must be cross-pollinated by another cultivar with a similar timing of bloom.
	Highbush blueberries (*Vaccinium corymbosum*) are considered self-fruitful but benefit from cross-pollination. Planting two or more cultivars with similar bloom periods will allow for cross-pollination, improving fruit set, size, and yield. Bees are the primary pollinators.
Grape	Muscadine grapes (*Vitis rotundifolia*) can be self-fruitful or self-unfruitful. Modern varieties either have all female flowers or perfect flowers (containing both functional male and female parts). Female flowering vines can set fruit but must be in close proximity to a perfect-flowered vine. Perfect-flowered vines are self-fruitful. Pollination is primarily performed by wind but can benefit from bee activity.
Strawberry	Self-fruitful. Pollinated by wind, rain, and insects. Lack of complete pollination can result in smaller or misshapen fruit.
Elderberry	European elderberry (*Sambucus nigra*) and American elderberry (*Sambucus canadensis*) are only partially self-fruitful and therefore require cross-pollination for best results. Pollination is primarily due to wind, but insects also can play a role.

and diseases in apple plantings in South Carolina. The gardener must be attentive to tree needs such as pruning, training, and fruit thinning.

Site and Soil Requirements

Apple trees grow well in a wide range of soil types, though they suffer in poorly drained soils. Most fruit crops, including apples, grow best when soil pH is between 5.5-6.5. Since the natural pH of most South Carolina soils is below that level, it may be necessary to incorporate lime into the soil before planting to raise pH to the appropriate level. A soil test report will indicate if lime is necessary and, if so, how much to apply to your site. Retest soil pH levels every 2-3 years.

Soil Preparation and Planting

Test soil several months prior to planting apple trees. If test results recommend adding lime or phosphorus to the soil, incorporate these into the soil prior to planting.

If planting dormant, bare-root trees and the roots are not already moist, soak the roots in water for 6-12 hours. Then plant the trees, though only if the soil is not wet. If the soil is not yet prepared at the planting site or the ground is too wet, heel the trees in by placing them in an open trench deep enough to cover all roots. The best place for heeling-in is the north side of a building, as the trees will remain dormant longer.

Before planting, cut off any damaged roots at the point of injury. Shorten roots that are especially long and do not fit in the hole. Roots that are not shortened can wrap around the tree hole and girdle the root system, eventually killing the tree. Dig a hole large enough to receive the roots freely without bending from their natural position. Set the plants with the graft union at least 2 in. above the soil line. Work soil in and around the roots.

When the hole is half-filled, firm the soil with your feet before completely filling the hole. When the hole is filled, pack the soil firmly again. Do not leave a depression around the tree. Do not place fertilizer in the planting hole or fertilize immediately after planting.

Purchasing Trees

The best apple trees for transplanting are 1-2 years old and 4-6 ft tall, with vigorous root systems. Older trees do not usually grow as well as younger trees; frequently, older trees do not have sufficient buds on the lower portion of the trunk to develop sufficient fruit-bearing limbs. A small tree with a robust root system is better than a large tree with a poor root system. Purchase trees from a reliable source and check labels carefully to ensure trees are of the desired cultivar and rootstock.

Apple Varieties. There are apple varieties adapted to all parts of South Carolina. Variety selection should be based on your geographic region. The Coastal Plain is not ideally suited for apples, but there are some varieties—such as the low-chill 'Anna' cultivar—that can be grown successfully in this region. Table 8.4 lists the apple varieties that grow best in the various regions of South Carolina.

Some apple varieties—such as 'Red Delicious,' 'Gala,' and 'Fuji'—are available in various strains. A strain (or sport) is a mutation of a certain cultivar selected for an improved characteristic and vegetatively propagated by grafting. A strain may differ in fruit or tree characteristics. Fruiting characteristics that may differ between strains include fruit coloring and ripening time. The main vegetative difference is spur-type versus non-spur (or standard) type. Spurs are short, stubby, slow-growing branches that support multiple flower and fruit clusters and can remain productive for 7-10 years. A spur-type apple has more fruit spurs and leaf buds more closely spaced than those on non-spur types. Spur-type apple varieties have a stiff, upright growth habit that minimizes limb breakage. They offer an advantage to home gardeners with limited space due to their compact growth form. Generally, spur-type strains of a cultivar result in trees that are only 60-70% as large as non-spur types.

Dwarf and Semi-Dwarf Rootstocks. There are three general categories of apple tree size: standard, semi-dwarf, and dwarf (Figure 8.3). Standard trees are grafted on to seedling rootstock and produce trees that may grow 20 ft tall or more. Semi-dwarf trees are grafted on to one of several rootstocks that produce trees about 60-80% the size of standard trees. The most common semi-dwarf rootstocks used for apples in South Carolina are MM.106, MM.111, and M.7; trees on M.7 will produce the smallest trees in the semi-dwarf category. Dwarf trees are about 30-50% as large as standard trees. The most common dwarf rootstocks are M.9 and M.26; trees grown on M.9 are smaller.

Several newer rootstocks have become available in recent years. The Budagovsky series, designated as

TABLE 8.4 Recommended Apple Varieties for Home Gardens in South Carolina

Variety[1]	Area[2]	Bloom Season[3]	Harvest Season	Characteristics
Anna	CP	Early	Very early	Medium-sized, green-yellow skin with red blush. Crisp, sweet-tart flesh. Partially self-fruitful. Very low chilling requirement.
Dorsett Golden	CP	Early	Very early	Medium-sized, green-yellow skin with red blush. Slightly smaller and firmer than 'Anna'. Very low chilling requirement.
TropicSweet	CP	Early	Very early	Medium-sized, green-yellow skin with red blush. Sweet, low acid. Very low chilling requirement.
Sansa	P, M	Early-Mid	Early	Medium-sized, yellow-green covered in dark red-orange striping and blush. Crisp, sweet, aromatic flesh, similar to 'Gala'. Resistant to cedar-apple and fire blight.
Mollie's Delicious	P, M	Early-Mid	Early	Medium-large, conical shaped with aromatic, sweet-tart flavor. Yellow-green, covered in pink-red striping and blush. Resistant to cedar-apple rust, but susceptible to fire blight.
Ginger Gold	P, M	Early-Mid	Early	Large, green-yellow with slight red blush. Crisp, sweet-tart. Flesh browns very slowly, excellent choice for fresh-cut use. Susceptible to fire blight.
Gala	P, M	Mid	Early-Mid	Medium-sized with thin skin and crisp, sweet, aromatic flesh. Yellow-orange with red blush, streaks, or striping. There are numerous sports (strains) with varied appearance. Susceptible to fire blight.
Ozark Gold	P, M	Mid	Early-Mid	Golden Delicious type with earlier, firmer and less russeting. Large fruit with a firm, crisp texture. Bright-yellow, waxy skin with slight red blush.

TABLE 8.4 Continued

Variety[1]	Area[2]	Bloom Season[3]	Harvest Season	Characteristics
Red Delicious	P, M	Mid	Mid	Medium-large, conical shaped with sweet but very mild flavor and tough skin. Numerous sports (strains) with varied appearance including spur-types. Very important commercial apple variety. High resistance to fire blight.
Golden Delicious	P, M	Mid	Mid	Medium-large with crisp, light yellow flesh. Mild flavor but very sweet if allowed to mature fully on tree. Susceptible to russeting. Partially self-fruitful. Medium resistance to fire blight.
Jonagold	P	Mid*	Mid-Late	Large, yellow apple with red striped blush and firm, sweet-tart flesh. Produces sterile pollen and therefore not a suitable pollinizer for other varieties. Resistant to cedar-apple rust but susceptible to fire blight.
Fuji	P, M	Mid-Late	Mid-Late	Medium-large with light red blush, often with stripes. Numerous sports (strains) with varied appearance. Dense, crisp, very sweet flesh. Susceptible to fire blight.
Mutsu (Crispin)	P, M	Mid-Late*	Mid-Late	Similar in appearance to Golden Delicious but larger and rounder. Stores extremely well. Produces sterile pollen and therefore not a suitable pollinizer for other varieties.
Rome Beauty	P	Mid-Late	Late	Solid red, with thick skin and firm flesh. Primarily used for baking and cooking, holding its shape well. Numerous sports (strains) with varied appearance including spur-types. Susceptible to fire blight.
Stayman Winesap	P	Mid-Late*	Late	Solid red, with a thick skin and sweet-tart, crisp flesh. Stores extremely well. Produces sterile pollen and therefore not a suitable pollinizer for other varieties.
Arkansas Black	P	Late*	Late	Dark red and very firm. Reaches full ripeness after about three months in storage, when flesh is a creamy yellow color and flavor sweetens. Produces sterile pollen and therefore not a suitable pollinizer for other varieties. Spur-type strains available. Highly resistant to cedar-apple rust and fire blight.
Granny Smith	P, M	Mid-Late	Very Late	Large, green, and thick-skinned. Flesh is firm, crunchy, and tart. Does acquire some sweetness and pink blush when allowed to fully ripen on tree. Stores extremely well. Resistant to cedar-apple rust but susceptible to fire blight.
Goldrush	P	Late	Very Late	Medium-large, yellow-green with an orange-red blush, becoming all bronze in storage. Flesh is very firm, crisp, and tart at harvest, turning sweeter in storage. Stores extremely well. Resistant to apple scab and fire blight.
Cripps Pink (Pink Lady)	P, M	Mid-Late	Very Late	Medium-large, golden-yellow skin with pink blush. Crisp, aromatic, sweet-tart flesh. Susceptible to fire blight.

[1] Listed in approximate order of ripening.
[2] P – Piedmont; M – Midlands; CP – Coastal Plains
[3] Overlapping bloom periods are necessary for successful cross-pollination. Cultivars with sterile pollen are noted with an asterisk.

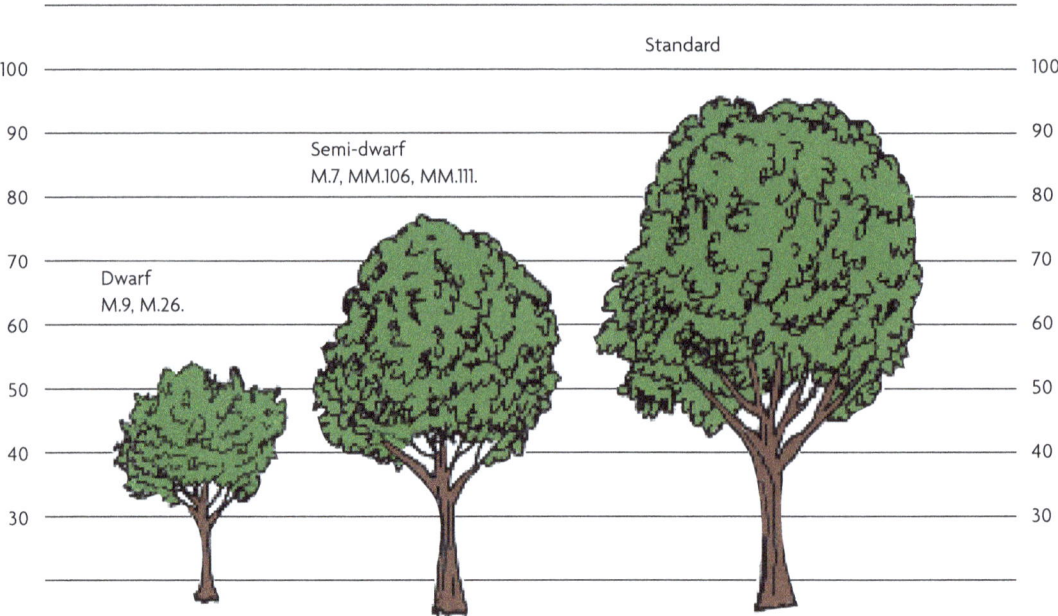

Figure 8.3 Size classes of different apple rootstocks.

either Bud or B, was developed for dwarfing ability and cold hardiness; B.9 and B.118 are both in this series. An ongoing breeding program at Cornell University, in cooperation with the USDA, develops size-controlling rootstocks with resistance to fire blight, crown and root rots, and woolly apple aphids. This rootstock series is designated as either Geneva or G and includes the dwarfing G.214 and G.935 and the semi-dwarfing G.210 and G.890.

Dwarf Apple Trees

Gardeners in the United States, Europe, and elsewhere have grown dwarf apple trees for many years. These trees are advantageous because:

- They are easier to prune and spray,
- Most fruit can be harvested from the ground,
- They grow bigger and higher-quality fruit, and
- They begin to bear fruit from an earlier age.

Dwarf trees are produced by grafting a scion (or fruiting cultivar) onto a dwarfing rootstock or by grafting an interstem—a small section of stem—between the rootstock and the scion; either method restricts top growth (Figure 8.4). Depending on the combination of rootstock and scion or interstem, the resulting apple tree will be dwarf or semi-dwarf.

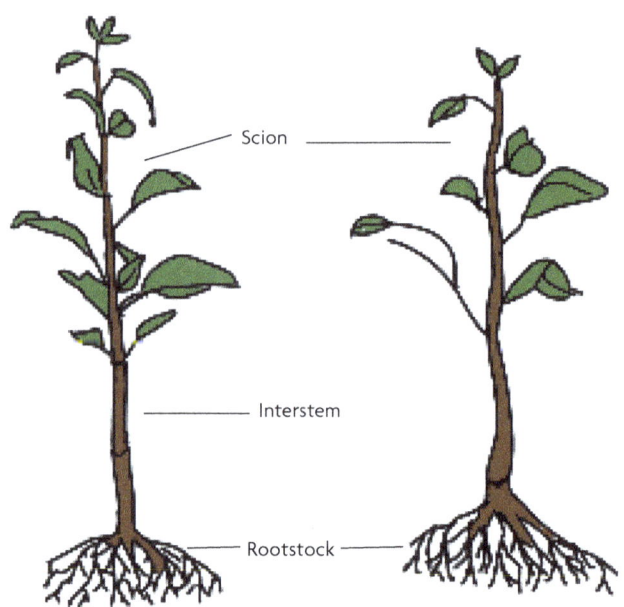

Figure 8.4 Tree at left illustrates the interstem method of dwarfing. The rootstock is a vigorous seedling or a semi-dwarfing rootstock. The tree on the right shows a scion variety grafted directly onto a dwarfing rootstock.

To produce a dwarf tree using an interstem, use a semi-dwarfing rootstock such as MM.111 or MM.106 and graft on a stem piece of a dwarfing M.9 or M.27. Then graft the desired variety onto the M.9 or M.27 interstem piece; size control is directly related to the length of this piece. Interstem apple trees offer a strong root system while reducing the size of the overall tree.

Using an interstem piece to induce dwarfing may be less desirable because of the added propagation expense of making two grafts instead of one. Trees propagated directly onto dwarfing rootstocks are typically more desirable, but they require support from a stake or trellis.

Post-Planting Care

After planting, apply sufficient water to thoroughly soak the soil. Watering helps bring the soil into closer contact with the roots and eliminate air pockets. Maintain a weed-free area around the tree to minimize competition for moisture and nutrients during the growing season. This weed-free area also keeps mowers away from the tree and reduces trunk damage.

Apples on dwarfing rootstocks should have a permanent anchoring system to stand up to high winds. Without permanent staking, dwarf trees can struggle under the heavy weight of fruit and the graft union is vulnerable to breakage in high winds.

Use 8-ft or 10-ft wooden or metal stakes and drive them 2 ft into the ground about 6-8 in. from the trunk. Common stakes are ¾- or 1-in. aluminum electrical conduit or ½-in. angle iron. Secure the trees to the stakes using flexible ties to avoid rubbing and girdling damage.

Training and Pruning

Proper training and pruning develop a strong framework in young apple trees that supports future fruit production. The purpose of training and pruning is to maintain a desired tree shape that is capable of early production of high-quality crops by balancing vegetative and reproductive growth.

Apples are often trained to a central leader system. The tree should develop with one dominant central leader in the center with several wide-angled limbs spaced around it. A mature apple tree should be cone-shaped with a narrow top and a wide base, somewhat resembling a Christmas tree (Figure 8.5).

Training and pruning are easier in home landscapes when using spur-type strains or growing apples on dwarfing rootstocks. Spur-type and dwarf trees produce fruit at an earlier age than full-sized trees; moreover, these trees are easier to manage and harvest than full-sized types.

Figure 8.5 Properly trained central leader apple tree exhibiting a pyramidal shape.
Image Credit: Dave Ouellette, Clemson University

If you plant 1-year-old, unbranched trees, make a heading cut 30-36 in. above the ground. When new growth is 4-6 in. long, select a central leader and side branches. These branches should be spaced at least 6 in. apart vertically and at even distances around the trunk. You can select four to six branches as scaffolds during the first summer or leave them all to grow throughout the season and prune them out selectively during the next dormant season.

If young trees are already branched when planted, remove any broken branches and those which form narrow angles with the main trunk (Figure 8.6). Eliminate forked terminals by removing one of the least desirable branches. Heading back the central leader is optional during the first year, but you can make this cut about 12 in. above the highest branch to stimulate additional branching. It is important to minimize any competition between side branches and the central leader. The central leader should be dominant and form a single trunk for the tree.

Figure 8.6 Prune young apple trees by removing narrow-angled branches and eliminating forks.

Figure 8.7 Using limb spreaders to widen branch angles.
Image Credit: Dave Ouellette, Clemson University

Keep pruning to a minimum during the first few years to encourage the trees to produce fruiting wood. Apples generally bear fruit on short spurs that form on 2-year-old wood. Some cultivars also flower and set fruit on terminal shoots from the previous season's growth.

You can encourage the formation of early fruit buds by training limbs to form angles 45-60° from vertical. Training growth outward forms the strong, wide crotch angles needed to support future fruit. Spreading out branches reduces overall tree vigor, balancing vegetative and reproductive growth. Limb spreading is especially useful in training varieties such as 'Red Delicious' and 'Fuji,' both of which have a very upright growth habit and a tendency to form branches with narrow crotch angles. Begin training the limbs with the first dormant pruning. You can insert wooden strips with finishing nails in each end between the selected scaffold limb and the central leader of the tree to form a wider crotch angle (Figure 8.7). Plastic limb spreaders of various sizes are also available and work well with young trees. Do this while branches are still pliable enough to be trained into a new position. You can train new shoots during the growing season using wooden spring-type clothespins or toothpicks; place the clothespin or toothpick between the central leader and the new succulent growth.

To develop a well-shaped central leader tree, be sure to:

- Control any branch that is competing with the central leader by removing it completely, heading it back, or bending it. The central leader should always be dominant and the highest point on the tree.
- Keep top growth under control. Do not allow over-vigorous growth to shade out the bottom portion of the tree. Focus on creating a cone-shaped tree made up of a framework of well-shaped horizontal branches radiating from the central leader. Upper branches should be shorter than those lower in the canopy.
- Remove watersprouts and broken, diseased, or injured branches.

Pruning Neglected Trees. Overgrown, neglected apple trees require extensive corrective pruning during the dormant season. The main objective in pruning such trees is to open the canopy to allow better light penetration.

The first step is to remove all upright, vigorously growing shoots at their bases. As with young apple trees, it is necessary to select four to six lower scaffold branches with wide crotch angles that are well-spaced around the tree. Remove extra scaffold limbs and branches with narrow angles. Spread major corrective pruning over two or three seasons to minimize stress to the tree.

Fertilizing

Always consider tree vigor and soil fertility before applying fertilizer. A soil test combined with periodic plant tissue testing is the best way of knowing the fertility needs of your soil and trees.

To fertilize newly planted apples, broadcast 1 cup (½ lb) of 10-10-10 fertilizer about one month after planting. Apply 1 cup (½ lb) of 10-10-10 fertilizer again in early summer. Apply all fertilizers evenly beneath the dripline of the branches, at least 12 in. from the trunk.

In early spring of the second season, broadcast 2 cups (1 lb) of 10-10-10 fertilizer. Repeat this application again in June. In succeeding years, apply fertilizer in early spring and increase the amount applied by 1 cup (1/2 lb) of 10-10-10 per year, up to a maximum of 5 cups (2½ lbs) 10-10-10 per dwarf tree, 10 cups (5 lbs) 10-10-10 per semi-dwarf tree, and 15 cups (7½ lbs) 10-10-10 per standard-sized apple tree. It may be best to split the total amount of fertilizer into two or more applications per year in sandy soils.

Use shoot growth to determine if you need to reduce or supplement these suggested fertilization rates. Reduce nitrogen fertilizer rates if trees become overly vegetative and produce more than 12-18 in. of new shoot growth per year. Do not apply any fertilizer to a tree that, in the same year, receives a severe corrective pruning.

Fruit Thinning

Apple trees typically set more fruit than they are capable of successfully carrying to maturity. Thinning an apple tree involves selectively removing some of the developing fruits to improve the quality of the remaining fruit and prevent overbearing. Fruit thinning helps ensure that the apple tree allocates its resources more efficiently, resulting in larger, higher-quality fruits. It also helps prevent branches from breaking due to excessive fruit weight and promotes better airflow, reducing the risk of fungal diseases. Failure to remove excess fruit may decrease flower and fruit formation the following year.

The earlier in the growing season that you thin the fruit, the more effective it will be. Fruit thinning should be done within 4-6 weeks after full bloom. Hand-thin young apples when they are about the size of a dime, leaving one fruit per cluster and 6 in. between fruits. The center apple in each cluster is derived from the "king flower" and is the best apple to leave; it usually develops into the largest fruit. Aim to keep the largest, healthiest-looking apples with proper spacing between them. Remove the smaller, weaker, or damaged fruits. Thin evenly across the entire tree canopy.

Harvesting

Proper technique is important when harvesting apples (Figure 8.8). Simply pulling apples from the tree is likely to bruise fruit and remove fruit stems. Pulling also tends to remove spurs from the tree. These fruit spurs represent next year's crop and removing them results in fewer apples the following year. Always pick apples with their fruit stems attached; otherwise, they do not store as long.

Figure 8.8 **Proper harvesting technique in the apple orchard is essential.**
Image Credit: Dave Ouellette, Clemson University

Grasp the apple with the palm of your hand. Remove the apple from the spur by pulling upward and outward while rotating the fruit slightly. Some cultivars, such as 'Golden Delicious,' sometimes require a firmly placed finger at the point of attachment between the stem and spur to prevent breaking off the spur. Do not squeeze, throw, or drop apples while harvesting, as this will cause bruising and reduce storage life.

Pest Management

A gardener must manage several diseases and insects to produce high-quality apples. It is helpful to follow a regular preventative spray program; these sprays are usually a combination of fungicide and insecticide that is applied simultaneously. However, never apply insecticides during bloom.

In home gardens, plant apple varieties that are resistant to certain diseases. For example, some cultivars are resistant to diseases such as apple scab, cedar apple rust, powdery mildew, or fire blight. However, all varieties are susceptible to summer diseases such as black rot, bitter rot, white rot, sooty blotch, flyspeck, Brooks fruit spot, and black pox. Summer diseases are particularly devastating in South Carolina and can result in complete crop loss.

Take action to prevent the diseases most common to apples—scab, black rot, bitter rot, and fire blight—and the insects that most often damage them—apple tree borers, spider mites, scales, aphids, and fruit worms. Controlling these diseases and insect pests with chemical applications may be difficult on large trees.

Below, we discuss some of the most common disease and insect pests. For more detailed information about the biology, prevention, and treatment of these pests, refer to the HGIC website.

Diseases. Various types of apples are susceptible to any of several diseases that can harm a tree's aesthetic, crop, or lifespan.

Apple Scab (*Venturia inaequalis*). Apple scab is especially problematic in areas that experience cool, wet weather in spring and early summer. The main source of infection is fruiting bodies that overwinter on fallen leaves and fruit. When leaf litter is moistened by rain or heavy dew in late winter, the fungus begins to grow and eventually discharges wind-borne spores that land on emerging leaves and flowers.

The spores discharge over a 5-9-week period, and the peak infection occurs between the pink stage to petal fall stage of apple flowering. Infected leaves and fruits become sources of secondary infections that occur throughout the summer and early fall.

Velvety brown to olive spots develop on the undersides of leaves as they emerge in the spring and turn greenish-black to black. Severely infected leaves fall. Infected fruits have lesions that eventually turn brown and corky.

Apple scab will not kill trees, but it can affect the next year's crop due to a lack of flower bud formation on defoliated trees. Reduce future infections by collecting and disposing of fallen leaves. Prune trees to improve air movement and sunlight penetration to help to dry off leaves quickly. Plant apple varieties that are resistant to minimize infection and damage. If disease is severe enough to warrant chemical control, apply a recommended fungicide. The most important time for application begins in the tight cluster stage of flowering and ends three weeks after petal fall.

Cedar-Apple Rust (*Gymnosporangium* spp.). Cedar-apple rust is a fungal disease that requires another host plant—eastern red cedar (*Juniperus virginiana*) or other ornamental junipers—to complete its life cycle. The disease spreads from the cedar to the apple and then back to the cedar. It can be a severe problem on sites where these two are grown together, and most apple varieties are susceptible to the disease.

The symptoms of cedar-apple rust are raised, bright orange-yellow spots on leaves. Leaves and fruit can drop from the tree, and severe defoliation can lead to reduced bloom and harvest the next season. Spots develop primarily on leaves in mid to late spring. Infected fruit is often small and distorted. On Eastern red cedar, hard brown galls up to 2 in. in diameter form near the ends of branches in the summer. Following a rain in the spring, the galls produce large, orange, gelatin-like tendrils full of spores that can blow up to ½ mi and infect other apple trees.

Plant apple varieties that are resistant to this disease. If possible, remove red cedars from the area or prune out galls on nearby cedars. If disease symptoms are severe enough to warrant chemical control, apply a recommended fungicide.

Fire Blight. Fire blight is a destructive disease caused by a bacterium (*Erwinia amylovora*). This disease develops rapidly in early spring during rainy weather when temperatures are above 60°F and the tree is in bloom. Blossoms and young shoots show the first symptoms, appearing wilted or shriveled and then turning brown or black. The tips of infected young shoots wilt and die, forming a shepherd's crook, as the disease progresses down the branch. Dead leaves often remain attached to the branch.

Branches and fruit are more susceptible to fire blight

infection if injured by insects, hail, or wind. Avoid high nitrogen fertilization, which increases succulent growth that is most susceptible to infection. Unfortunately, pollinators can carry the fire blight bacterium from flower to flower.

Remove all infection sources, such as blighted branches and cankers, before growth starts in the spring. Make pruning cuts 12-18 in. below any blighted tissue, as the bacterium usually penetrates beyond any physical sign of infection. Disinfect all pruning tools by dipping them in 70% isopropyl alcohol (rubbing alcohol) or a 10% bleach solution (1 part bleach to 9 parts water) between each cut.

Chemical control is not always effective against fire blight; apply chemicals preventively. In years when warm, humid, wet weather coincides with flowering and leaf emergence, spray plants with a fungicide containing basic copper sulfate or an antibiotic (streptomycin) to reduce infection. Applications of streptomycin should begin at the start of blooming and continue every 3-4 days during the bloom period. Application of copper sulfate should begin at bloom and continue every 7 days during bloom.

Powdery Mildew (Sphaerotheca spp. or Podosphaera spp.). Powdery mildew is most prevalent during dry, hot periods. The fungus causes gray-white powdery patches on leaves and new shoots. New growth is often stunted, curled, and distorted. Fruit may turn russet-colored and develop poorly.

Prune out branches or infected twigs early in the season. If disease is severe enough to warrant chemical control, use a recommended fungicide.

Black Rot (Physalospora obtusa). Black rot (or Frogeye leaf spot) is a fungal disease that begins on the leaf as a purple speck that enlarges to have a brown or tan center that looks like a frog's eye. Heavily infected leaves drop from the tree. Limbs may have slightly sunken, reddish-brown cankers.

Infected fruits begin by showing tiny red or purple spots on the non-stem end. After a few weeks, the spots enlarge and have alternating zones of black and brown. The rot eventually affects the entire fruit, which wrinkles, mummifies, and often remains attached to the tree.

Remove and discard dead branches and diseased fruit (called mummies) where the fungus overwinters. Recommended fungicides are effective if applied early and at regular intervals throughout the season.

Flyspeck (Schizothyrium pomi) and Sooty Blotch (Gloeodes pomigena). Flyspeck and Sooty Blotch infect the surface of the fruit and are mainly cosmetic problems. They often occur together, although they are distinctive fungal diseases. Although unsightly, the fruit is still edible. Sooty blotch can be wiped from the fruit, but flyspeck cannot be removed.

True to its name, flyspeck disease looks like groups of very small, superficial black dots on the surface of the fruit; the dots are slightly elevated. Sooty blotch appears as a ¼-in.-diameter brown or black blotch on the fruit; spots may coalesce to cover the entire fruit.

These summer diseases develop during cool, rainy weather, particularly in dense, unpruned trees with poor air circulation. Maintain good air circulation throughout the canopy by pruning and thinning branches and fruit. If disease is severe enough to warrant chemical control, use an appropriate fungicide.

Insects. Insects are the culprits of other significant injury to apple trees.

Green Apple Aphid (Aphis pomi) and Spirea Aphid (A. spiraecola). Green apple aphid and spirea aphid are two kinds of aphids that affect apple trees, especially during the summer. Both species are green and commonly found on watersprouts and the tender young leaves on branch tips. While feeding, the aphids produce honeydew, which is often colonized by black sooty mold. Aphids produce several generations in a season.

Rosy Apple Aphid (Dysaphis plantaginea). Rosy apple aphid is potentially the most damaging aphid to apples. Newly hatched rosy apple aphids are dark green and found on new growth in early spring. Mature rosy apple aphids are purplish and covered with a waxy, powdery bloom. Winged forms develop on apple trees in late spring and migrate to plantain, where they are found in summer. In fall, winged forms develop and migrate back to the apple trees. They lay overwintering eggs on fruit spurs and shoots.

Rosy apple aphids cluster on leaves of fruit spurs and growing shoots, where they cause severe leaf curling. Fruits on heavily infested fruit spurs fail to properly develop and become misshapen.

Woolly Apple Aphids (Eriosoma lanigerum). Woolly apple aphids are covered with a mass of long, waxy filaments. They feed on the bark of small twigs, around pruning cuts, and on the roots of apple trees. The feeding causes the tree to form knobby galls on twigs and roots. Heavy feeding damage reduces the vigor of the tree. You can control above-ground woolly apple aphids with an insecticide, but root-feeding colonies are much more difficult to control.

Among the most important predators of aphids are lady beetles, lacewings, syrphid fly larvae, and soldier beetles. Applying pesticides in summer can kill these predators and allow apple aphid populations to increase. In many cases, these beneficial insects keep aphid populations under control as long as they don't fall victim to insecticide treatments.

Two-Spotted Spider Mites (Tetranychus urticae) and European Red Mites (Panonychus ulmi). Two-spotted spider mites and European red mites can be serious pests of apples. If mite populations are high, feeding activity can reduce the quality of the current crop and the number of flower buds the following year.

Japanese Beetle (Popillia japonica). Adult Japanese beetles feed on leaves during June and July. The beetles "skeletonize" the leaves, eating the soft leaf tissue and leaving the leaf veins behind; this gives the damaged leaves a lacy appearance. They may also feed on damaged fruit.

Japanese beetle traps may suppress populations, but always place traps at least 30 ft away from the plants to protect them; if the trap is too close to the tree, the beetles may still stop and feed on the tree before entering the trap.

Leafrollers (Archips spp., Choristoneura rosaceana, and Sparganothis sulfureana). Leafrollers tie leaves to the fruit with a silky web and feed on both the surface of the fruit and the leaves. There are several predators and parasites that feed on leafroller caterpillars; if applying an insecticide, any of the Bacillus thuringiensis materials (Dipel®, among others) do not harm the natural enemies of the leafrollers but will kill the young caterpillars.

Codling Moth (Cydia pomonella). Codling moths are responsible for producing the proverbial "wormy apple;" this worm is actually the moth's caterpillar stage. The mature larvae emerge from apple fruit in the fall and spin a silk shelter under loose bark to overwinter. Adult moths emerge shortly after bloom and lay eggs on leaves near fruit clusters, where larvae enter the young fruit. A second generation of moths hatch in mid-summer and lays eggs directly on the surface of the fruit; again, the larvae burrow to the core of the fruit and feed. A third generation hatches in late summer.

Direct insecticide treatments toward the adult moths or the newly hatched larvae. Once the larvae enter the apples, they are protected. Parasites and predatory insects feed on eggs and larvae.

Tarnished Plant Bugs (Lygus lineolaris) and Stink Bugs (Acrosternum species and Euschistus spp.). Tarnished plant bugs and stink bugs feed on young fruit. As the bugs fsuck juices from the fruit with their needlelike mouthparts, they inject a saliva that kills the plant cells around the puncture. As the fruit continues to grow, discolored depressions appear around the feeding sites.

Eliminating broadleaf weeds, especially legumes, can reduce stink bug populations; many insecticides are ineffective. Stink bugs are very mobile insects and may reinfest treated areas quickly.

Plum Curculio (Conotrachelus nenuphar). Plum curculio is a native weevil that attacks apple fruit. The adult weevils spend the winter in protected areas near the apple trees; soon after bloom, female weevils make a crescent-shaped cut through the fruit skin and insert eggs under a flap of skin. Infected fruits are misshapen and often drop to the ground.

Insecticide sprays applied at petal fall may reduce plum curculio damage. Removal of wild plums in the area and practicing sanitation around the apple trees reduces pest populations.

San Jose Scale (Quadraspidiotus perniciosus). San Jose scale is one of the most notable pests affecting apple trunks and branches. The adult scale insect is about 1/10 in. in diameter. Scale insects have threadlike mouthparts that they insert into the bark to feed on sap. There are four generations of San Jose scale insects per year in South Carolina. A single female scale can produce about 400 young, called crawlers, over a 6-week period. These crawlers move to a new area to feed and secrete a protective covering over their body. If scale populations are high, they may feed on fruit and produce red measles-like spots.

Heavy scale infestations can kill individual branches. The best control is a thorough application of dormant oil in the late winter before buds begin to open. Insecticide sprays during the growing season are effective against crawlers but does not kill scale insects once they secrete the protective cover.

Flatheaded Appletree Borers (Chrysobothris femorata). Flatheaded appletree borers are attracted to weakened or stressed apple trees. Adult beetles are about ½-in. long, somewhat flattened, and vary from dark metallic brown to dull gray. Adults appear throughout the summer and lay orange to reddish brown eggs under bark scales or in crevices of the main trunk and larger branches. Yellow to yellowish-white larvae bore into the trunk and main branches. Their tunnels, or galleries, are often 3 in. long or more, especially in young trees. Eventually the galleries can cause girdling and the tree's death.

You can protect trunks and larger branches with insecticides during the plant's first year or two in the landscape. Alternatively, you can wrap trunks to prevent adult flatheaded borers from laying eggs on stressed trees. Keeping newly planted trees vigorous by watering and mulching sufficiently reduces the chances of an infestation of adult borers.

Pears

Pears were once grown commercially throughout the United States. However, the prevalence of fire blight disease in the humid eastern and southern states pushed most commercial production to the drier areas of California, Oregon, and Washington.

Pears can be an excellent crop for backyard growers if the gardener is committed to the attention to detail and pest management that the crop requires. Pears share many cultural similarities and pest problems with apples. Selecting pear varieties that are disease-resistant greatly increases the chance of success.

Site and Soil Requirements

Pear trees bloom relatively early—from one to several weeks before apples—and are more subject to the hazards of early spring frosts. For optimal flowering and fruit production, choose an area where pear trees will be in full sun. Most pear rootstocks have some tolerance to poorly drained soils, but well-drained areas are best.

Types of Pears

There are two main types of pears: European and Asian.

European pears (*Pyrus communis*) are the most common type in US markets. They produce traditional pear-shaped fruits that have a soft, buttery texture and sweet, aromatic flavor when properly ripened off the tree. Fruits are harvested, placed in cold storage, and then ripened at room temperature. Most varieties require 600–1000 chill hours.

Asian pears (*Pyrus pyrifolia*) typically produce round fruits with crisp, juicy, very sweet flesh (Figure 8.9). Fruits ripen on the tree and are ready to eat when harvested. They do not change texture after harvest or short-term storage. Asian pears typically require 300-800 chill hours, depending on the cultivar.

Variety Selection and Pollination Requirements

Many pear varieties, including 'Bartlett,' are extremely susceptible to fire blight, a disease that kills limbs or entire trees. There are varieties of pear that are less susceptible to this disease or are considered fire blight resistant. See Table 8.5 for a list of recommended pear varieties and their characteristics.

Some pear varieties are partially self-fruitful but set better crops when two or more varieties are planted

Figure 8.9 'Hosui' Asian pear near harvest time.
Image Credit: Dave Ouellette, Clemson University

together. Pear flowers are not as attractive to bees as many other flowers. Some varieties, such as 'Magness,' do not produce viable pollen and therefore cannot serve as a pollinizer for other varieties. Plant trees of several different pear varieties together to ensure overlapping bloom periods; most combinations of pear varieties are satisfactory for cross-pollination.

Rootstocks

Asian pear varieties are typically grafted onto *Pyrus calleryana* or *P. betulifolia* rootstock to produce standard-sized trees that often grow 18-20 ft tall and 10-12 ft wide. *P. calleryana* imparts some fire blight resistance to the tree and *P. betulifolia* increases tree vigor and fruit size. However, because of concerns about its invasiveness, *P. calleryana* is no longer available for sale in South Carolina—even as rootstock.

European pears are available on dwarfing Quince rootstocks that reduce tree size by about 50%. Semi-dwarfing rootstocks such as OHxF 87 (*P. communis* Old

TABLE 8.5 Pear Varieties for Home Gardens in South Carolina

Variety[1]	Bloom Season[2]	Harvest Season	Characteristics
European Type			
Harrow Delight	Mid	Early	Medium fruit, greenish-yellow with red blush, fire blight resistant.
Maxine (Starking Delicious)	Mid	Early	Medium fruit, greenish-yellow, fire blight resistant.
Harvest Queen	Mid	Early	Medium fruit, yellow with no russet, fire blight resistant.
Sunrise	Mid	Early	Large fruit, green-yellow with red blush, stores 2-3 months, fire blight resistant.
Ayers	Early-Mid	Mid	Large fruit, green-yellow with red blush, fire blight resistant.
Moonglow	Mid	Mid	Large fruit, green-yellow with red blush, store 1-2 months for best flavor, fire blight resistant.
Honeysweet	Mid-Late	Mid	Med-large fruit, reddish-brown russet, fire blight resistant.
Bell	Mid	Mid	Medium-large fruit, green-yellow with red blush, fire blight resistant.
Harrow Crisp	Mid	Mid	Medium-large fruit, yellow skin blushed with red, self-fruitful, fire blight resistant.
Blake's Pride	Mid	Mid	Medium-large fruit, yellow with tan russet, fire blight resistant.
Potomac	Mid	Mid	Large fruit, green with slight red blush, fire blight resistant.
Seckel	Mid	Mid	Small-medium fruit, reddish-brown russet, naturally semi-dwarf tree, fire blight resistant.
Magness	Mid*	Late	Large fruit, yellow with red blush, sterile pollen, fire blight resistant.
Harrow Sweet	Mid	Late	Medium fruit, yellow with red blush, stores, fire blight resistant.
Shenandoah	Mid-Late	Late	Large fruit, greenish-yellow with red blush, stores 4-5 months, fire blight resistant.
Orient	Early-Mid	Late	Very large fruit, greenish-yellow, semi-hard flesh with thick skin, fire blight resistant.
Kieffer	Early-Mid	Late	Very large fruit, greenish-yellow with red blush, fire blight resistant.
Asian Type			
Shinseiki	Early-Mid	Early	Medium-large fruit size, smooth yellow skin, stores 2-3 months, susceptible to fire blight.
Hosui	Early-Mid	Early	Medium-large size fruit, brown-orange skin, does not store well, susceptible to fire blight.
Yoinashi	Mid	Mid	Large size fruit, orange-brown skin, stores 3-4 months, fire blight resistant.
Atago	Mid	Mid	Very large size fruit, golden-brown skin, fire blight resistant.
Shinko	Mid	Late	Large size fruit, golden-brown skin, fire blight resistant.
Olympic	Mid-Late	Late	Very large size fruit, golden-brown skin, fire blight resistant.
Shin Li	Mid	Late	Very large fruit size, greenish-yellow skin, fire blight resistant.

[1]Listed in approximate order of ripening for each type.
[2]Overlapping bloom periods are necessary for successful cross-pollination. Cultivars with sterile pollen are noted with an asterisk.

Home x Farmingdale) produce trees about 70% standard size and offer fire blight resistance. Trees grafted onto OHxF 97 have only a slightly reduced vigor compared to those on seedling or standard rootstocks. As with apples, dwarf and semi-dwarf pear trees produce fruit at an earlier age than standard trees.

Planting and Training

If planting unbranched trees, head them back to 30-36 in. from the ground to encourage several buds to grow from below the cut; these new branches will form the framework of the tree. If planting a branched tree, retain three to five well-positioned primary scaffolds and head back to 24-30 in. above the uppermost retained branch. Plant trees so graft unions are 2-3 in. above the soil surface.

In the second year, head back the leader to 24-30 in. above where the tree was cut back the previous year. Select three to five scaffold branches and head these back if necessary to encourage the formation of secondary branches. Remove all other unwanted growth, including broken or diseased branches, watersprouts (vigorous upright shoots), and rootsuckers (Figure 8.10).

Pear trees generally grow more vigorously and upright than apple trees. If left alone, this growth pattern results in narrow branch angles and poor light penetration, reducing fruit quality. Train limbs to 45-60° from vertical to develop wider, stronger scaffold branches. This serves to open up the tree to sunlight, reduce vigor, and increase fruit production. Remove branches that are very upright. Pear trees are typically trained according to the same central-leader system used to train apple trees (Figure 8.11).

Figure 8.10 One-year-old pear tree before (A) and after (B) dormant pruning.

Figure 8.11 Flowering mature Asian pear trained to central leader system.
Image Credit: Dave Ouellette, Clemson University

Pruning Bearing Trees

Allow the tree to bear its first crop in its third or fourth year. Prune bearing trees to maintain a balance between vegetative growth and fruit production. Older trees require moderate pruning to maintain the established shape. Most pruning in older trees should be thinning cuts, not heading cuts. Control tree height by cutting back the top portion of the tree to a short, non-vigorous lateral branch.

Only prune pear trees in summer to remove watersprouts, rootsuckers, and fire-blight-infected wood. Make pruning cuts to remove diseased wood 12-18 in. below any blighted tissue; the bacterium tends to penetrate beyond any physical signs of infection. Disinfect all pruning tools by dipping them in 70% isopropyl alcohol (rubbing alcohol) or a 10% bleach solution (1 part bleach to 9 parts water) between each cut.

Fertilizing

Consider tree vigor and soil fertility before applying fertilizer. A soil test combined with periodic plant tissue testing is the best way to know the fertility needs of your soil and trees.

Pear trees growing too vigorously are more susceptible to fire blight than those growing more moderately. Reduce nitrogen fertilizer rates if trees become overly vegetative and produce more than 12-18 in. of new shoot growth per year.

Fruit Thinning

Pear trees often set more fruit than they are capable of successfully carrying to maturity. Remove excess fruit to ensure satisfactory development of the remaining fruit. The earlier in the growing season that you thin the fruit, the more effective it will be.

Remove fruit by hand, leaving one pear per cluster when fruit reach ¾-1 in. in diameter. Space the remaining fruit 6-8 in. apart along the branch. To remove fruit without damaging the spur, hold the fruit stem between your thumb and forefinger and push the fruit from the stem with the other hand.

Harvesting

Harvest European pears when they are mature but not ripe. If picked too early, fruit may develop undesirable flavors and lack sweetness; when picked too late, the fruit may be gritty and is susceptible to a disorder called "internal breakdown"—when the flesh around the core becomes soft and brown. When mature, the skin color changes from dark green to a lighter green and lenticels on the skin often darken in color. For the highest-quality pears, harvest slightly before they are ripe, store in the refrigerator, and ripen at room temperature for up to a week before eating or canning. You can store many varieties of European pears in the refrigerator for several months.

Asian pears should ripen on the tree. The skin color of most Asian pears changes from green to yellow or golden-brown when ripe. Fruits are very delicate; handle them carefully during harvest and storage to prevent bruising. You can store Asian pears in the refrigerator for 1-2 months.

To harvest a pear, gently take the fruit in the palm of your hand and lift and twist in a single motion. Alternatively, use one hand to hold the spur and the other hand to lift and twist the fruit from the tree.

Pest Management

Pears suffer from some of the same pest and disease issues as apples, but generally, they are not as susceptible. However, many varieties of pears are particularly susceptible to fire blight.

Fire blight is a destructive disease caused by a bacterium (*Erwinia amylovora*). This disease develops rapidly in early spring during rainy weather when temperatures are above 60°F and the tree is in bloom. Blossoms and young shoots show the first symptoms, appearing wilted or shriveled and then turning brown or black. The tips of infected young shoots wilt and die, forming a shepherd's crook as the disease progresses down the branch. Dead leaves often remain attached to the branch.

Branches and fruit are more susceptible to fire blight infection if they have been injured by insects, hail, or wind. Avoid high-nitrogen fertilization, which increases succulent growth susceptible to infection. Unfortunately, pollinators can carry the fire blight bacterium from flower to flower.

Once a tree is infected, cut out and discard the diseased portions. Remove blighted branches and cankers before growth starts in the spring. Make pruning cuts 12-18 in. below any blighted tissue, as the bacterium can penetrate beyond the physical signs of infection. Disinfect all pruning tools by dipping them in 70% isopropyl alcohol (rubbing alcohol) or a 10% bleach solution (1 part bleach to 9 parts water) between each cut.

Chemical control is not always effective; apply it preventively. In years when warm, humid, wet weather coincides with flowering and leaf emergence, spray plants with a fungicide of basic copper sulfate or an antibiotic (streptomycin) to reduce infection. Begin applications of streptomycin at the start of blooming and continue every 3-4 days during the bloom period. Application of copper sulfate should begin at bloom and continue every 7 days during bloom.

Pear leaf spot begins as small purplish-black spots on the leaves or fruit. The spots gradually enlarge to form brown lesions about 1/8-1/4 in. in diameter. A small, black blister may appear in the center of these spots. You can only control leaf spot with a spray program that begins as the first leaves appear and continues through summer.

Much like apples, pear trees are subject to infestations by mites and scales. Dormant oil applications during the dormant season suppress these pests. Mite infestations during the growing season sometimes require miticide treatments.

Plum curculio and caterpillars sometimes scar pear fruits as they do apples. These pests typically cause little internal injury to pears, but their feeding and egg laying frequently cause cosmetic scarring. Late-maturing pear varieties often suffer more serious damage, as the caterpillars reach and damage the core of the fruit.

Damage from feeding stink bugs is the most common insect injury to pears in South Carolina. The bugs produce shallow depressions in fruit that are often corky or woody in texture.

Peaches and Nectarines

Growing peaches and nectarines can be both fun and rewarding. However, your success depends largely on the care and attention you give your trees. Nectarines are essentially peaches without their characteristic fuzz, and their maintenance and care are the same as peaches. For simplicity, the term "peach" is used in this section to refer to both peaches and nectarines.

Site and Soil Requirements

For optimal flowering and fruit production, choose a site where trees receive full sun. Early-morning sun is particularly important, because it dries the dew from trees, reducing the incidence of disease. Peach trees grow well in a range of soil types but are very sensitive to poor drainage.

Peach trees perform best when soil pH is between 6.0-6.5. Since the natural pH of most South Carolina soil is below this level, you may need to incorporate lime before planting to raise the pH. Follow the recommendations of a soil test to adjust pH and fertility levels.

Peach trees bloom relatively early in the season, from one to several weeks before apples, and are often subject to the hazards of early spring frosts. Select a planting site on a slope or high elevation to allow cold air to flow downhill away from the trees on a cold night during bloom.

Soil Preparation and Planting

Test the soil at your site several months prior to planting. If the results recommend adding lime or phosphorus, incorporate these into the soil in advance.

If planting dormant, bare-root trees, check the roots to see if they are moist; if not, soak roots in water for 6-12 hours. Then, plant trees only if the soil is not wet. If you still have to prepare the soil or the ground is too wet, heel the trees in by placing them in an open trench deep enough to cover all roots. The north side of a building is the best place to heel-in the trees, as they remain dormant longer. Leave the trees there until you are ready to plant.

Before planting, cut off any damaged roots at the point of injury. Shorten roots that are especially long and do not fit in the hole. Roots that are not shortened can wrap around the tree hole and girdle the root system, eventually resulting in tree death. Dig a hole large enough to receive the roots freely without bending from their natural position. Set the plants at about the same depth they were planted at the nursery so that the uppermost root is not more than 1-2 in. underground.

Peach and Nectarine Varieties

There are peach varieties adapted to all areas of South Carolina. Table 8.6 lists recommended peach and nectarine cultivars. Varieties with low chilling requirements grow best in coastal areas.

Pollination. Peach flowers are self-fruitful, so it is not necessary to plant more than one peach variety for fruit set.

Chilling Requirements

Fruit crops such as peaches develop their vegetative and fruiting buds in the summer; as winter approaches, buds go dormant in response to the shorter days and cooler temperatures. This dormancy stage protects buds from cold weather. Once buds enter dormancy, they can tolerate temperatures far below freezing and do not grow in response to midwinter warm spells. These buds remain dormant until they have accumulated sufficient chilling hours—temperatures at or below 45°F. Once enough chilling hours have passed, buds are ready to grow in response to warm temperatures. As long as there have been enough chilling hours, the flower and leaf buds develop normally. If the buds do not receive sufficient chilling temperatures during winter to completely release dormancy, trees develop one or more of the physiological symptoms associated with insufficient chilling: delayed leafing-out and flowering; reduced fruit set and increased "buttoning" that produces small, misshapen fruit; and reduced fruit quality.

Rootstocks

In the past, 'Lovell' was the preferred rootstock in most regions of South Carolina; gardeners in the Coastal Plain used 'Nemaguard' because of widespread problems with root-knot nematodes. Researchers at Clemson University and the USDA-ARS developed a rootstock called Guardian®, which is now the recommended rootstock for all of South Carolina and the southeastern United States. Guardian® rootstock shows superior resistance to certain types of nematodes and bacterial canker disease.

TABLE 8.6 Peach and Nectarine Varieties for Home Gardens in South Carolina

Variety[1]	Harvest Season	Flesh Color	Chill Requirement[2]
Peaches			
Gulfking	Early	Yellow	Low
Flordaking	Early	Yellow	Low
Flavorich	Early	Yellow	Medium
Flordacrest	Early	Yellow	Low
Springprince	Early	Yellow	Medium
Carored	Early	Yellow	Medium
Crimson Lady	Early-Mid	Yellow	Medium
Gulfcrimson	Early-Mid	Yellow	Low
Junegold	Early-Mid	Yellow	Medium
Rubyprince	Early-Mid	Yellow	High
Gulfprince	Early-Mid	Yellow	Low
Gulfsnow	Early-Mid	Yellow	Low
Juneprince	Early-Mid	Yellow	Medium
Coronet	Early-Mid	Yellow	Medium
Redhaven	Early-Mid	Yellow	High
Harvester	Mid	Yellow	Medium
White Lady	Mid	White	Medium
Blazeprince	Mid	Yellow	High
Winblo	Mid	Yellow	High
Redglobe	Mid	Yellow	High
Southern Pearl	Mid	White	Medium
Scarletprince	Mid	Yellow	High
Bounty	Mid	Yellow	Medium
Loring	Mid	Yellow	Medium
Julyprince	Mid-Late	Yellow	High
Contender	Mid-Late	Yellow	High
Cresthaven	Mid-Late	Yellow	High
Augustprince	Late	Yellow	High
Flameprince	Late	Yellow	High
Snow Giant	Late	White	Medium
Big Red	Late	Yellow	Medium
Autumnprince	Late	Yellow	Medium
Nectarines			
Sunbest	Early-Mid	Yellow	Low
Snow Queen	Mid	White	Medium
Juneprincess	Mid	Yellow	Medium
Fantasia	Mid-Late	Yellow	Medium
Redgold	Mid-Late	Yellow	High

[1] Listed in approximate order of ripening.
[2] Low chill = <500 hrs; Medium chill = 500-800 hrs; High chill = >800 hrs.

Figure 8.12 Blooming mature peach tree pruned to the open-center system.
Image Credit: Dave Ouellette, Clemson University

Training and Pruning

Peaches are typically trained to an open-center system (Figure 8.12). This system produces a vase-shaped tree. Open-center trees allow better air circulation and light penetration within the tree's canopy.

The best time to prune peach trees is in late winter, just before spring budbreak. This timing minimizes winter injury and infection due to bacterial canker disease.

Cut back newly planted trees to 30-36 in. above the ground. If the tree is branched when it arrives from the nursery, select three to five branches with wide-angle crotches spaced evenly around the trunk to serve as permanent scaffold limbs. The lowest limb should be about 15 in. from the ground and the highest about 30 in. from the ground. Remove all other branches. If there are no desirable branches available, head the tree to the desired height and prune all branches back to very short stubs. Several new shoots will develop at the stubs, from which you can select future scaffold limbs.

At the beginning of the second year, it is necessary to remove the upright, vigorous middle section of the tree with a large pruning cut to create an open-center vase shaped tree (Figure 8.13). Prune out any extra scaffold branches, rootsuckers, and growth from the lower trunk.

At the beginning of the third year, remove any vigorous upright shoots developing on the inside of the tree to maintain the open-center shape; leave the smaller shoots for fruit production. Continue to remove any extra scaffold branches, rootsuckers, and growth from

Figure 8.13 Training a two-year-old peach by pruning out the central part of the tree.
Image Credit: Dave Ouellette, Clemson University

the lower trunk. Prune out poor-quality fruiting wood, such as branches that hang downward and are shaded. The desirable wood left for production should be about the diameter of a pencil and 12-18 in. long. If the length exceeds 18 in., cut off about one-third of this fruiting branch. Peaches are only produced on wood that grew during the previous season. At the beginning of the third year, the tree should resemble Figure 8.14. Finally, prune the vigorous upright growth on the ends of scaffold branches by cutting them back to an outside growing shoot.

You may crop peach trees during their second growing season if they are vigorous and have well-developed scaffold branches. However, it's often best that the first crop occurs in the third season.

The same principles used to develop trees are used to annually maintain the size and shape of mature peach trees. Lower tree height by pruning each scaffold back to an outward-growing lateral branch to maintain an open-center vase shape.

Figure 8.14 Three-year-old peach tree pruned to the open-center system.
Image Credit: Dave Ouellette, Clemson University

Fertilizing

To fertilize newly planted peaches, broadcast 2 cups (1 lb) of 10-10-10 fertilizer over an area about 3 ft in diameter when growth begins in spring. Apply 2 cups (1 lb) of 10-10-10 fertilizer again in early summer. Apply all fertilizers evenly beneath the dripline of the branches, at least 12 in. from the trunk. Never apply large amounts off fertilizer in a small area, as it may cause root injury.

In early spring of the second season, broadcast 3 cups (1 1/2 lbs) of 10-10-10 fertilizer. Repeat this application again in early summer for a total of 6 cups (3 lbs) during this second year.

In succeeding years, apply a maximum of 10 cups (5 lbs) 10-10-10 per tree per year. Split the total amount of fertilizer between two or more applications per year, especially if your soil is sandy. Splitting applications allows the gardener to reduce or eliminate applications if the crop is lost to a freeze event.

Always consider tree vigor and soil fertility before applying fertilizer. A soil test combined with periodic plant tissue testing is the best way to know the fertility needs of your soil and trees.

Fruit Thinning

Peach trees often set more fruit than they are capable of successfully carrying to maturity. To prevent limb breakage and ensure good fruit quality, remove (thin) excess fruits. Hand-thin peach trees about 4-6 weeks after full bloom, leaving the remaining fruit about 6 in. apart along the branches. You can space early-maturing peach varieties to about 8 in. apart to ensure proper sizing.

Harvesting

There is a fine line to the timing of harvesting peaches. It's best for fruit to remain on the tree long enough for flavor and sugar content to peak, but not so long that it becomes overripe. Overripe fruit develop undesirable flavors, have reduced storage life, and are more susceptible to disease, insect, and bird damage. Peaches lose firmness as they ripen, and it can be best to harvest when the fruit yields slightly to pressure.

The degree of red skin coloration, or blush, is generally not a reliable indicator of peach maturity. Many peach varieties produce fruit that turns solid red several weeks before they are ready to harvest (Figure 8.15). Fruit position in the canopy and sunlight interception can both affect changes in blush. A more reliable indicator of ripeness is background color. Peaches are ripe when the background skin color changes from green to yellow for yellow-fleshed peaches or to a cream color for white-fleshed peaches. Changes in background color are not affected by exposure to sunlight.

The best indicator of the correct harvest time in a home orchard is a taste test. You can harvest mature but slightly underripe fruit and allow it to ripen fully once

Figure 8.15 Ripening peaches.
Image Credit: Dave Ouellette, Clemson University

indoors. If the fruits lack flavor and are too firm and crunchy, wait a few days before harvesting. A peach tree typically ripens its fruit over 10-14 days, so it's best to harvest every 3-4 days. Fruits from the exterior of the trees's canopy receive more sunlight, and usually ripen earlier, than fruits from the interior.

To harvest, grasp a ripe peach gently in the palm of your hand to avoid bruising. Twist the peach gently while pulling it away from the branch.

Pest Management

It is difficult to grow top-quality peaches in home orchards without maintaining a rigid pest control program throughout the growing season.

Diseases. One of the most damaging peach diseases is a fruit rot commonly called brown rot; other diseases that affect peaches include scab, bacterial spot, Rhizopus rot, leaf curl, and Phony Peach disease.

Brown Rot. Brown rot infects flowers, shoots, and fruit. Diseased flowers wilt and turn brown very quickly. Shoot infections result in gummy, 1-3-in.-long cankers. These cankers provide the disease spores for fruit rot. Infected fruits rot completely to become "mummies," which carry the disease over the winter. Sanitation is a valuable component of brown rot control. Collect diseased fruit as soon as it appears and remove infected twigs and mummies from trees to reduce the carry-over of brown rot disease into the next season.

Peach Scab. Peach scab appears as small, dark, velvety spots on fruit. Numerous closely spaced scab lesions may form large black areas. It is easy to control peach scab using chemical sprays applied at the "shuck split" stage and every 14 days for the next 4-6 weeks. Shuck split is the stage after bloom when the dry flower parts split and fall free of the small, immature fruit. Disease symptoms occur only on the outer skin; peel fruit to remove all traces of the disease, as the quality or flavor of the flesh is unaffected.

Bacterial Spot. Bacterial spot infects peach fruit and leaves. Infected leaves develop small reddish-purple spots, often with white centers. These spots often drop out to give the leaf a tattered or "shot hole" appearance. Infected leaves eventually turn yellow and drop. Infections on fruit appear as small dark spots; very close examination reveals that these spots resemble open sores rather than the velvety spots characteristic of peach scab. In years of severe infection, diseased areas of the fruit may develop severe cracks. The best way to control bacterial spot is to select resistant peach varieties. Fortunately, spots seldom penetrate beneath the skin; peeling fruit removes most traces of the disease.

Plum Pox (Sharka). Plum pox is a viral disease transmitted and spread by aphids and the movement of infected plants. Peach fruit may develop lightly pigmented yellow rings or line patterns. Report any sighting of this very serious disease to your Clemson Extension agent or HGIC specialists.

Peach Leaf Curl. Peach leaf curl is a disease of peach leaves and occasionally green, immature fruit. Leaf infections occur at budbreak, and disease symptoms become evident around bloom time. Infected leaves appear thickened, puckered, or twisted and are often tinged with red. Infected leaves usually drop in early summer. The disease seldom kills trees, but the early defoliation weakens them. Infected fruit has raised, wrinkled areas that are often reddish in color. Chemical sprays before budbreak provide good leaf curl control.

Phony Peach. Phony peach is a bacterial disease transmitted to healthy trees by sharpshooter leafhoppers. Sharpshooter vectors transmit the bacteria to peaches from wild hosts and among peach trees in orchards. Infected trees initially appear healthy, with abundant, dark green foliage; however, they are dwarfed and produce limited fruit of poor size and quality. Chemical sprays do not control this disease.

Oak Root Rot. Oak root rot is caused by a soilborne fungus that attacks and kills peach roots. The fungus survives for many years in the soil on roots of hardwood trees that have long since been removed. There is currently no effective control. It is recommended that peaches not be planted on land recently cleared of hardwood trees, or planted in spots where peach trees have been removed.

Insects and Nematodes. There are also several insects and nematodes that damage peach flowers, fruit, branches, and trunks. Among the most destructive insects include plum curculio, borers, scale insects, catfacing insects, and oriental fruit moths.

Root-Knot Nematodes. Root-knot nematodes are microscopic soilborne roundworms that attack the roots of numerous plants—including peach—and shorten their lifespans. The roots of infested trees show numerous small swellings or knots. Diseased trees may grow poorly and appear nutrient-deficient. Obtain information on nematode sampling from the HGIC.

Peach Tree Short Life. Peach tree short life (PTSL) is responsible for changing the face of the peach industry in the Southeast. This replant disease is associated with sites infested with ring nematodes (*Mesocriconema xenoplax*). Trees planted in soil infected with ring nematodes are more likely to acquire the disorder if they are pruned in October-December or if they develop bacterial canker. This disease can be avoided by planting trees on Guardian® rootstock.

Plum Curculio. Plum curculio is the key fruit insect pest affecting peaches in South Carolina. These small, native weevils (snout-beetles) are present on numerous wild hosts. Plum curculio can cause injury all season long.

Peaches often produce gum at the sites of curculio wounds. The larvae mature in the dropped fruit, so promptly remove any infested fruit from the ground or tree. Preventative insecticide sprays are the only means of effectively preventing plum curculio damage.

Peachtree Borer and Lesser Peachtree Borer. Peachtree borers are caterpillar pests that feed on the inner bark of trees, causing major damage to the tree's vascular system. Peachtree borers attack the lower trunk and major roots; whereas, lesser peachtree borers attack the structural wood throughout the tree. Adults lay eggs in the wound areas, and larvae bore into the vascular tissue and impair the flow of water and nutrients, ultimately killing the limb or even the entire tree. Late summer application of insecticides can help. Avoid making large pruning cuts that leave excessive wounds.

Scale Insects. Scale insects are very small insects that attach to limbs and trunks. Heavy scale infestations can kill individual branches and sometimes entire trees. The best control is a thorough application of dormant oil in the late winter, before buds begin to open. Insecticide sprays during the growing season are effective against the crawler stage but will not kill scale insects once they secrete their protective covers.

Catfacing Insects. Catfacing insects such as stink bugs (*Acrosternum species and Euschistus spp.*) feed on young fruit. As the bugs feed with their needlelike mouthparts, they inject a saliva that kills the plant cells around the puncture as they suck juices from the fruit. As the fruit continues to grow, discolored depressions appear around the feeding sites.

Eliminating broadleaf weeds, especially legumes, contributes to stink bug management. Many insecticides are ineffective at controlling stink bug populations; the bugs are very mobile insects and can quickly reinfest treated areas.

Oriental Fruit Moth. The caterpillars of oriental fruit moths attack and tunnel within the stems of succulent new vegetative growth and also damage the fruit. Though typically regarded as the most impactful fruit-feeding pest of peaches worldwide, this moth is only a minor fruit pest in South Carolina. The caterpillar does modest injury to the terminals of new shoots in the spring and again during the annual vegetative growth flush.

Plums

Growing plums in a home landscape comes with a number of challenges. Many varieties flower very early in the season, and this often results in crop losses from freezes in early spring. Plums are highly susceptible to bacterial diseases and can have short lifespans.

Site and Soil Requirements

Plant plums in full sun. Plum trees grow well in a range of soil types but are very sensitive to poor drainage.

Plum trees perform best when soil pH is between 6.0-6.5. Since the natural pH of most South Carolina soil is below this level, you may need to incorporate lime before planting to raise the pH. Follow the recommendations of a soil test to adjust pH and fertility levels.

Plum trees bloom very early in the season, often one or two weeks before peaches, and are often subject to the hazards of early spring frosts (Figure 8.16). Select a planting site on a slope or high elevation to allow cold air to flow downhill away from the trees on a cold night during bloom.

Figure 8.16 Japanese plum tree flowering in early spring.
Image Credit: Dave Ouellette, Clemson University

Soil Preparation and Planting

Test your soil several months prior to planting. If the results recommend adding lime or phosphorus, incorporate them into the soil prior to planting. The recommended soil pH for plums is 6.0-6.5.

Before planting, cut off any damaged roots at the point of injury. Shorten roots that are especially long and do not fit in the hole; roots that are not shortened can wrap around the tree hole and girdle the root system, eventually resulting in tree death. Dig a hole large enough to receive the roots freely without bending from their natural position. Set the plants at about the same depth they were planted at the nursery so that the uppermost root is not more than 1-2 in. underground.

Types of Plums

There are many species of plums with different origins and diverse fruit types. Most commercially grown varieties are derived from either Japanese plums (*Prunus salicina* and hybrids) or European plums (*P. domestica*). Japanese plums are used primarily for fresh consumption, and European plums are used for both processing and fresh consumption. One product obtained from processing plums includes prunes, which are dried fruit of certain varieties of European plums. European plums generally bloom 10-14 days later than Japanese plums.

Home gardeners have limited access to varieties of plum-apricot hybrids. These interspecific hybrids range from predominantly plum to predominantly apricot and are known as plumcots, pluots, and apriums.

Plum Varieties and Pollination Requirements. Many plum varieties are not self-fruitful and require appropriate pollinizers for reliable cropping. Fruit set of partially self-fruitful varieties such as 'Methley' improves when multiple varieties are planted in a single location. It is more common for European varieties to be self-fruitful; however, planting two or more cultivars still improves production. European and Japanese varieties will not cross-pollinate. Most recommended plum varieties will have sufficient bloom overlap to ensure cross-pollination. See Table 8.7 for a list of the plum varieties best suited to South Carolina.

Rootstocks

Plums are commonly propagated onto the same rootstocks used for peaches and nectarines. The most commonly used peach rootstocks are Guardian®, 'Lovell,' and 'Halford.'

Training and Pruning

Plum trees are typically trained and pruned to the same open-center (open-vase) system as peaches. Plum varieties can differ significantly in growth habit, and the gardener will have to adjust pruning and training based on how upright or spreading the tree is. Most plum varieties naturally have a more upright growth habit than peaches, so you can leave scaffold branches to grow at a more upright angle. The best time to prune plum trees is in late winter, just before spring budbreak. This timing minimizes winter injury and infection by the organism responsible for bacterial canker disease.

Cut back newly planted trees to 30-36 in. above the ground. If the tree is branched when it arrives from the nursery, select three to five branches with wide-angle crotches spaced evenly around the trunk to serve as permanent scaffold limbs. The lowest limb should be about 15 in. from the ground and the highest about 30 in. from the ground. Remove all other branches. If there are no desirable branches available, head the tree to the desired height and prune all branches back to very short stubs. Several new shoots will develop at the stubs, from which you can select future scaffold limbs.

At the beginning of the second year, it is necessary to remove the upright, vigorous middle section of the tree with a large pruning cut to create an open-center vase shaped tree. Prune out any extra scaffold branches, rootsuckers, and growth from the lower trunk.

At the beginning of the third year, remove any vigorous upright shoots developing on the inside of the tree to maintain the open-center shape; leave the smaller shoots for fruit production. Continue to remove any extra scaffold branches, rootsuckers, and growth from the lower trunk. Prune out poor-quality fruiting wood, such as branches that hang downward and are shaded. The fruiting habit of plums differs from that of peaches; plums bear fruit on last year's growth—as do peaches—and on spurs growing on older wood—as do apples.

You can crop plum trees during their second growing season if tree vigor is sufficient and trees have well-developed scaffold branches. However, it's usually best that the first crop occurs during the third season in the orchard.

Maintain the size and shape of mature plum trees following the same annual principles used to develop the tree (Figure 8.17). Shorten the tree and maintain an open-center vase shape by pruning each scaffold back to an outward-growing lateral branch.

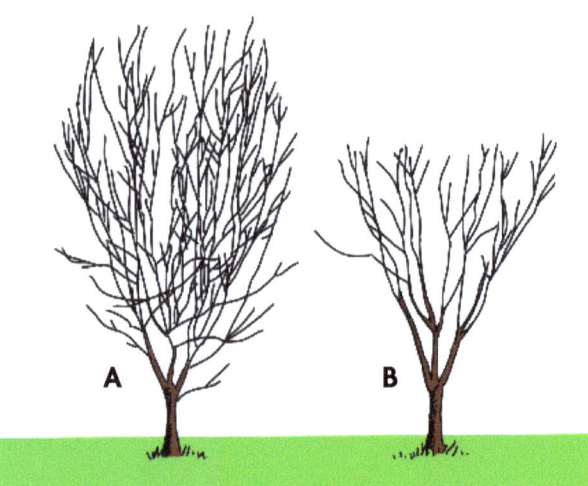

Figure 8.17 Mature plum tree before (A) and after (B) dormant pruning.

Fertilizing

To fertilize newly planted plums, broadcast 2 cups (1 lb) of 10-10-10 fertilizer over an area about 3 ft in diameter when growth begins in spring. Apply 2 cups (1 lb) of 10-10-10 fertilizer again in early summer. Apply all fertilizers evenly beneath the dripline of the branches, at least 12 in. away from the trunk.

In early spring of the second season, broadcast 3 cups (1 1/2 lbs) of 10-10-10 fertilizer. Repeat this application again in early summer for a total of 6 cups (3 lbs) applied in the second year.

In succeeding years, apply a maximum of 10 cups (5 lbs) 10-10-10 per tree per year. It's best to split the total amount of fertilizer between two or more applications per year, especially if your soil is sandy. Splitting applications also allows you to reduce or eliminate an application if the crop was lost to a freeze event.

Consider tree vigor and soil fertility before making fertilizer applications. A soil test combined with periodic plant tissue testing is the best way to know the fertility needs of your soil and trees.

Fruit Thinning

Plum trees often set more fruit than they are capable of successfully carrying to maturity. To prevent limb breakage and ensure good fruit quality, remove or "thin" excess fruits. Hand-thin trees about 4-6 weeks after full bloom, leaving the remaining fruit about 3-4 in. apart on the limb.

Harvesting

Plums are ready for harvest when the fruit begins to soften slightly and separates easily from the tree with a slight twist. Fruit mature to be blue, purple, or red, depending on cultivar. Green plum varieties often develop yellow highlights when ripe. Fruits from the exterior of the tree receive more sunlight and ripen earlier than fruits from the interior. A plum tree typically ripens its fruit over 14-21 days. It's best to harvest every 3-4 days. Alternatively, you can use a "shake and catch" method to make harvesting easier (especially from very tall trees); place a tarp underneath the tree and gently shake limbs to dislodge the ripe fruit. This is a useful method, especially if you plan to process the fruit into preserves.

Pest Management

Plum trees are susceptible to several diseases and insect pests. Many of these also affect peach trees.

Brown rot attacks flowers, shoots, and fruit; bacterial spot infects fruit and leaves. See "Brown Rot" and "Bacterial Spot" in the Peach section for more information about these stone fruit diseases.

Bacterial canker is a very invasive disease and can kill a tree if left untreated. The first sign of a problem occurs when orange-reddish gum starts oozing from the infected area.

Black knot (*Dibotryon morbosum*) forms elongated swellings or knots on twigs and branches. In the spring, the fungus ejects spores that splash or blow onto the current season's growth. Although infections can occur any time when shoots are actively growing, most infections occur from just before bloom until after petal fall.

After the spore germinates, it penetrates the tree's tissues and stimulates the cambium to grow abnormally, producing a tumorlike knot that expands rapidly in length and girth. Eventually, the swollen bark tissue splits open to reveal a soft, corky, olive-green fungal mass. This darkens over the course of the season, and by autumn, it turns into a black, hard, woody growth. Two years from the time of initial infection, the knot becomes mature and capable of producing spores. The active margins of the knot continue to grow and enlarge.

Before budbreak in late winter, prune out knot-infested twigs and limbs. Burn or bury the infected

TABLE 8.7 Plum Cultivars for Home Gardens in South Carolina

Cultivar[1]	Harvest Season	Chill Requirement[2]	Comments
Spring Satin	Early	Medium	Dark reddish-black skin and firm yellowish-red flesh. Resistant to bacterial fruit spot, bacterial leaf spot, bacterial canker, and Plum leaf scald. Plumcot (plum x apricot hybrid).
AU Amber	Early	Medium	Self-fruitful. Dark red skin, yellow flesh. Medium-large fruit. Clingstone. Resistant to bacterial fruit spot, bacterial leaf spot, bacterial canker, and Plum leaf scald.
Methley	Early	Medium	Self-fruitful. Dark red-purple skin, dark red flesh. Small-medium size fruit. Clingstone.
Robusto	Early	Low	Red skin and flesh. Medium size fruit. One of the cultivars grown for green plums.
Rubysweet	Mid	Low	Red-bronze skin, red flesh. Medium sized fruit.
Segundo	Mid	Medium	Yellow-red skin and flesh. Large fruit. Grown for green plums.
AU Rubrum	Mid	Medium	Self-fruitful. Dark red skin, red flesh. Large fruit. Resistant to bacterial fruit spot, bacterial leaf spot, bacterial canker, Black knot. Clingstone.
Shiro	Mid	Medium	Self-fruitful. Yellow skin and flesh. Medium size fruit. Clingstone. Spreading growth habit.
Morris	Mid	Medium	Light red skin and flesh. Large fruit. Clingstone. Tolerant to bacterial fruit spot.
AU Homeside	Mid	Medium	Self-fruitful. Light red skin, amber flesh. Large fruit. Resistant to bacterial fruit spot, bacterial leaf spot. Good tolerance to bacterial canker, Black knot, Plum leaf scald. Clingstone.
AU Roadside	Mid	Medium	Self-fruitful. Dark red skin, red flesh. Large fruit. Resistant to bacterial fruit spot, bacterial leaf spot, bacterial canker, Black knot. Semi-clingstone.
AU Producer	Mid	Medium	Self-fruitful. Dark red skin and flesh. Medium size fruit. Resistant to bacterial fruit spot, bacterial leaf spot, bacterial canker. Clingstone.
AU Rosa	Mid	Medium	Self-fruitful. Red skin, light yellow flesh. Large fruit. Resistant to bacterial fruit spot, bacterial leaf spot, bacterial canker, Black knot, Plum leaf scald, Brown rot. Clingstone.
AU Cherry	Mid	Medium	Self-fruitful. Dark red skin and flesh. Small fruit. Resistant to bacterial fruit spot, bacterial leaf spot, bacterial canker, Black knot, Plum leaf scald, Brown rot. Clingstone. Good selection for canning and processing.
Ozark Premier	Mid	Medium	Dark red skin, yellow flesh. Large fruit. Resistant to bacterial fruit spot. Semi-clingstone.
Byrongold	Late	Low	Yellow skin with red blush, yellow flesh. Medium-large fruit.
Black Ruby	Late	Low	Purple-black skin, yellow flesh. Large fruit. Very upright growth habit. Skin can be a bit sour tasting.
Ruby Queen	Late	Medium	Dark red skin, red flesh. Large fruit. Excellent storage life.
Flavorheart	Late	High	Dark reddish-black skin and yellow flesh. Heart-shaped fruit with short shelf life. Pluot (plum x apricot hybrid).
Flavorich	Late	High	Dark reddish-black skin and firm yellow-orange flesh. Pluot (plum x apricot hybrid).

[1]Listed in approximate order of ripening.
[2]Low chill = <500 hrs; Medium chill = 500-800 hrs; High chill = >800 hrs.

knotty wood, as the knots are capable of sporulating for some time after being pruned out. When knots are present on major scaffold limbs or on the trunk, remove them by cutting out the diseased tissue down to bare wood and at least 4 in. beyond the edge of the knot; fungicides cannot completely control black knot in the absence of this pruning.

Black knot-resistant plums include the Japanese plums 'AU-Rubrum,' 'AU-Rosa,' and 'AU-Cherry'.

Plum pocket (*Taprina communis*) causes fruit to become distorted—enlarging up to 10 times their normal size—about 6-8 weeks after budbreak. Plum-pocketed fruit have spongy or hollow centers and may have pits. Early symptoms of fungal infections are small, light-colored spots that may become blisters. They enlarge rapidly and become reddish with a velvety-gray appearance. Affected fruit then dry out, leaving only the outer fruit wall; this eventually turns brown to black and falls off the tree.

Remove wild plums in and around the orchard to reduce potential inoculum. Applying fungicide in the fall or before budbreak in the spring reduces the incidence of plum pocket in affected orchards.

Plum leaf scald (*Xylella fastidiosa*) is caused by a xylem-limited bacterium that spreads from tree to tree via the glassy winged sharpshooter and other sharpshooter leafhoppers. The first symptom is fading or bronzing along the margins or tips of leaves. Leaves may die inward from the margin in several steps. The trees shed diseased leaves in late summer. This disease cannot be controlled by chemical sprays or other means, and it affects some varieties of plum more severely than others.

There are other conditions that mimic plum leaf scald. Some of these include nutrient deficiency or toxicity, drought stress, herbicide toxicity, root death, or a delayed reaction to winter cold damage. Before concluding that plum leaf scald is the problem, eliminate all other possibilities.

Plum pox (Sharka) is a viral disease. It is transmitted and spread by aphids and the movement of infected plants. Peach fruit may develop lightly pigmented yellow rings, or line patterns resulting from several rings running together, on the surface of the fruit. Report any sighting of this very serious disease to your Clemson Extension agent or HGIC specialists.

There are a number of insects that damage plum flowers, fruit, limbs, twigs, and trunks. Among the most destructive include plum curculio, borers, scale insects, catfacing insects, and oriental fruit moths, all of which you can read more about in the previous section, "Peaches and Nectarines."

Pecans

The pecan tree is native to the southern United States. Growing pecans is a long-term endeavor that requires patience, as pecans typically take longer to start bearing than most fruit crops. It's helpful to think of pecans as shade trees in the landscape with the eventual added benefit of harvestable nuts (Figure 8.18).

Site and Soil Requirements

Pecans grow well in home landscapes from the Coastal Plain to the Piedmont; they do not grow well in the Mountain region because of inconsistent cropping due to late freeze events.

When selecting a planting site, consider the eventual size of the tree. Pecan trees may eventually reach a height of around 100 ft, so they require a large space to grow. Spacing pecan trees at least 40 ft apart provides sufficient room for future growth. It is important to plant pecan trees well away from structures, buildings, and overhead power lines.

Soil Preparation and Planting

Test the soil several months prior to planting; if the results recommend adding lime or phosphorus, incorporate them into the soil prior to planting. The recommended pH range for pecans is 6.0-6.5. Soil analysis reports include liming and nutrient recommendations based on site soil and crop.

Pecan trees are typically planted bare-root, but some suppliers also sell container-grown transplants. Bare-root pecan trees have long taproots and require a deep planting

Figure 8.18 Cluster of ripening pecan nuts in their husks.
Image Credit: Dave Ouellette, Clemson University

hole. The planting hole should be at least 3 ft deep and 12-24 in. wide so that you can properly position all roots as the hole is refilled. Trim twisted, broken, or excessively long roots to fit in the hole. Make every effort to keep the taproot intact, but you may shorten it if it is excessively long.

Plant the tree at the same depth that it grew in the nursery, usually indicated by a color change on the bark. Fill the hole about one-third full of soil and saturate with water to settle, repeating this process until the hole is filled. Mulch with a 2-3-in. layer of pine straw, leaves, or other organic material to conserve moisture and reduce competition from grass and weeds.

Container-grown pecan trees are planted similarly. After removing trees from containers, check for pot-bound roots. Pull circling roots away from the root ball and prune them. If the taproot has become twisted at the base of the container, straighten or cut it to encourage new taproot growth.

Pecan Varieties and Pollination Requirements

Pecan trees are monoecious, meaning male flowers (catkins) and female flowers are borne separately at different locations on the same tree (Figure 8.19). The tree bears female flowers in clusters near the ends of the current season's shoots in the spring and catkins at the base of the shoot and along the length of the supporting 1-year-old wood.

Pecans are pollinated by wind. When catkins mature, they shed huge quantities of pollen; the sheer amount of pollen increases the chance that, when blown by the wind, some lands on the stigmas of female flowers. Should the catkins mature before or after the female flower is receptive, pollination does not occur. Usually, within a pecan cultivar, pollen shedding does not closely overlap the period when the stigma is receptive. This condition, called dichogamy, helps ensure cross-fertilization.

Pecan cultivars differ in the order that the male and female flowers mature. When pollen is shed early, before the female flowers are receptive, the cultivar is considered protandrous. When pollen is shed late, after the female flowers are receptive, the cultivar is protogynous. Protandrous cultivars are commonly referred to as Type I and protogynous cultivars as Type II. For adequate cross pollination between pecan trees, it is best to grow at least one of each type.

Table 8.8 lists recommendations for pecan varieties to grow in South Carolina.

Alternate Bearing

Alternate bearing refers to the tendency of certain fruit and nut trees to follow a cycle of high production one year followed by one or more years of relatively low production. Growth regulators produced by developing pecan nuts can suppress the formation of flower buds for the next season. Additionally, excessive crop loads can leave trees depleted of stored carbohydrates so that flower buds are aborted the following spring. All pecan trees tend to bear alternately, but some varieties are much more consistent than others at producing regular crops.

Watering

Young pecan trees lose a large percentage of their roots during transplanting. It is important to water them thoroughly and at regular intervals the first year. On bearing trees, drought during the nut sizing and kernel fill periods (July to September) often results in premature nut drop. Supplemental irrigation during this time can improve healthy nut development.

Training and Pruning

Remove one-third to one-half of the top of a newly planted pecan tree to encourage vigorous growth and rapid establishment. Young pecan trees typically do not require pruning, because they naturally develop a full canopy. You can remove lower branches to raise the height of the canopy as the tree grows.

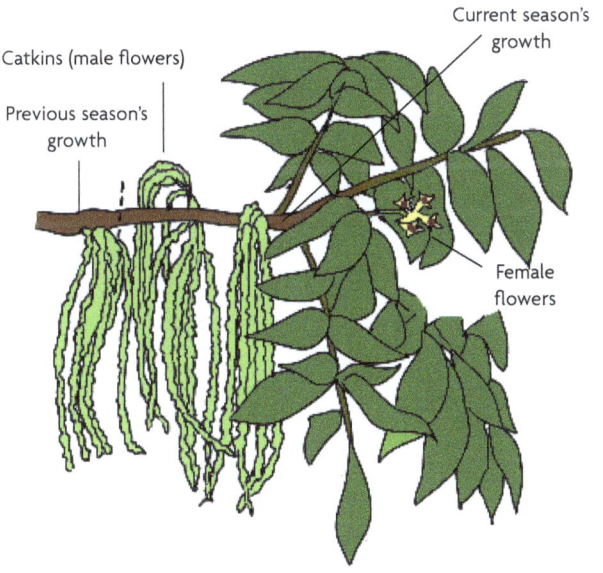

Figure 8.19 Pecan flowering habit. The non-showy female (pistillate) flowers are borne separately from the male (catkin or staminate) flowers.

TABLE 8.8 Pecan Cultivars for Home Landscapes in South Carolina

Cultivar	Nut Size	Scab Resistance	Comments
Type I – Protandrous Cultivars			
Amling	Small	High	One of the best cultivars for home production. Little to no pest issues. Moderately low yields. Pollinated well by Excel, Stuart and Sumner. Good pollinizer for McMillan and Elliott.
Caddo	Medium	Moderate	Precocious and productive. Mid-season harvest. Low tendency to alternate bear. Pollinated well by Elliott, Kanza and Stuart.
Cape Fear	Medium	Variable	Very precocious and productive. Becomes strongly alternate bearing with age.
Eclipse	Medium	High	Similar to Pawnee but higher yields and less alternate bearing. Very early harvest time.
Lipan	Large	High	High nut quality and yields. Not prone to alternate bear. Good companions are Kanza and Lakota.
Mandan	Large	High	High yield potential. Very early harvest.
Oconee	Large	Moderate	Precocious and productive. Low tendency to alternate bear.
Pawnee	Large	Moderate	Precocious, medium yields. Tendency to alternate bear. Very early harvest date.
Syrup Mill	Medium	High	One of the best cultivars for home production. Little to no pest issues. Moderate yields. Pollinated well by Excel, Lakota and McMillan.
Type II – Protogynous Cultivars			
Avalon	Large	High	Late to leaf out and flower in the spring. Excellent quality.
Elliott	Small	High	Early to leaf out in the spring, can be damaged by late spring freeze. Slow to bear. Excellent quality, but not heavy bearer. Alternate bearing.
Ellis	Large	High	Large, oblong nuts with very good nut quality.
Excel	Large	High	Late to leaf out and flower in the spring. Thin branches give tree "weeping" appearance. Pollinated by Elliott, Kanza and Mandan. Pollinizer for Caddo and Mandan.
Forkert	Medium	Moderate	Nut shell is very rough, with prominent dark stripes. Very good quality kernel. Pollinated by Elliott and Cape Fear.
Gloria Grande	Large	High	Thick shell, smooth with dark stripes. Not prone to alternate bear.
Kanza	Small	High	Tendency to alternate bear.
Kiowa	Very Large	Moderate	Tendency to alternate bear. Pollinated by Caddo and Pawnee. Pollinizer for Pawnee and Forkert.
Lakota	Medium	High	High nut quality, high yield potential. Early nut maturity.
McMillan	Medium	High	Precocious and productive. Alternate bearing. Similar in appearance to Stuart, but slightly smaller nut and darker kernel. Pollinated by Caddo, Cape Fear, Creek, Amling, Pawnee and Mandan.
Nacono	Large	High	Precocious, good early yields. Likely to alternate bear. Pollinated by Amling, Mandan and Pawnee.
Stuart	Medium	Moderate	Standard cultivar, most widely planted across the Southeast. Late to leaf out in the spring.
Sumner	Medium	High	Productive, but prone to alternate bear. Late harvest season.

Fertilizing

Fertilization is one of the most important practices for growing pecans. Young trees should make 2-4 ft of terminal growth each year. In the absence of a leaf tissue analysis or soil test, broadcast 4 lbs of 10-10-10 or an equivalent complete fertilizer for each inch of trunk diameter (measured 4½ ft above soil level) before budbreak in early spring, up to a maximum of 25 lbs per tree. Do not place fertilizer within 12 in. of the trunk.

Zinc nutrition is particularly important for pecans. Rosetting in pecan is caused by zinc deficiency and produces several symptoms: bronzing and mottling of leaves; small, yellowish-green leaves at tips of short, thin shoots; and abnormally small nuts. Leaf sample analyses taken in summer best determine the zinc needs of a specific plant. For more information regarding plant tissue sampling guidelines, contact the HGIC. In the absence of a plant tissue analysis, apply 1 lb of zinc sulfate each year to young trees and 3-5 lbs to older trees.

Harvesting and Storing

Harvesting pecans is easy: just wait until the nuts begin to drop from the tree. Because pecan trees become very large over time, shaking the tree and branches is not feasible in home landscapes.

After pecans have begun to fall, harvest daily to avoid predation by wildlife. Inspect all fallen nuts for signs of insect damage. Newly dropped pecans will look brighter and cleaner than older, duller nuts from previous seasons. Once harvested, allow nuts to "cure" in a dry location for 7-10 days prior to storing. This process eliminates excess moisture that can lead to spoiling.

Pest Management

The most notable pecan disease is pecan scab, a fungus prevalent throughout the southeastern United States that can devastate unsprayed, susceptible cultivars. The best solution is to plant scab-resistant varieties. Spraying is the only way to control pecan scab on susceptible cultivars, but sanitation can almost always help reduce losses from scab and other minor diseases. Nearly all fruit and foliage diseases that affect pecans, including scab, overwinter on plant parts infected the year before. Rake and remove leaves and shucks in the winter to reduce disease carry-over.

Pecan scab occurs on leaves, twigs, and nut shucks. Scab lesions are typically small, brown or black spots, often with a velvety or rough appearance. If conditions favor further scab development, the lesions can coalesce to cover much of the leaf or nut surface. The severity of pecan scab each year is determined by the frequency of rainfall.

Spraying lower limbs with fungicide helps with disease control on those limbs. Make the first application at bud swell and continue every 14-21 days.

The main insect pests that affect pecans are the pecan nut casebearer, shuckworms, stinkbugs, leaf-footed bugs, and pecan weevils. Usually, spraying is the only way to control these insects.

Common Problems with Pecan Nut Development

Failure to Fill. Insect and disease damage to leaves or insufficient foliage can cause nuts not to fill. Early defoliation caused by diseases or insects and nutrient deficiency directly influence filling. Drought may also cause a failure to fill, especially when it occurs late in the growing season.

Premature Nut Loss. Pecan trees naturally drop nuts several times each growing season. Lack of pollination causes the greatest loss of nuts. Since pecans are pollinated by wind, excessive rain during bloom prevents pollination, and the unfertilized nuts fall. Weather conditions can also cause the male and female flowers to mature at different times and fail to pollinate.

Premature defoliation, drought stress, and disease also cause nut drop or reduce nut quality, as do insect pests such as the pecan nut casebearer, black aphids, pecan weevils, stink bugs, and shuckworm.

Figs

Figs are a great addition to the home landscape. They require minimal care and maintenance, yet they provide a reliable, bountiful harvest. Figs produce delicious fruit with flavors best experienced ripe from the tree. They blend easily into shrub borders and grow well in containers.

Site and Soil Requirements

Plant figs in a well-drained location in full sun. They grow well in many soil types, but need a site free of root-knot nematodes. Figs can grow into trees or shrubs 15-20 ft. tall, but pruning can maintain them at a manageable height.

Figs thrive in areas with long, hot summers. They can also grow in colder areas if they are properly insulated against freezing temperatures or grown in containers and brought indoors as needed.

Soil Preparation and Planting

Always start preparing your soil based on a soil analysis test; adjust the pH and other qualities based on the results of the test. In warmer areas, you can set out bare-rooted trees in winter; in the Mountains and Piedmont regions, it is best to set them out in early spring after the danger of severe winter freezes has passed. You can plant out container-grown plants later in the growing season if desired.

Types of Figs

There are four main types of figs grown around the world: the Caprifig, the Smyrna fig, the San Pedro fig, and the common fig. Common figs (*Ficus carica*) are the only type of fig that can be successfully grown in South Carolina. Its flowers do not require pollination to produce figs. Other species of figs either do not produce edible fruit or have very specific pollination requirements, such as requiring pollination by a certain type of wasp not native to South Carolina.

Purchasing or Propagating. Nurseries sell fig trees bare-root or in containers. See Table 8.9 for a list of suitable fig varieties that can be grown in South Carolina.

Fig trees are easy to propagate, and a home planting can be started at very little expense. You can use dormant cuttings of 1-year-old wood for propagation.

TABLE 8.9 Fig Cultivars for Home Gardens in South Carolina

Cultivar	Skin Color	Harvest Season	Fruit Size	Comments
Alma	Yellow/Tan	Late	Medium-Large	No breba crop, only main crop.
Brown Turkey	Tan/Violet	Mid	Medium	Small eye. Most popular fig in the Southeast. Light breba crop and heavy main crop. Very cold hardy.
Celeste	Tan/Violet	Mid	Small-Medium	Small eye. Very popular fig in the Southeast. Very cold hardy. Tends to drop fruit during extremely hot and dry weather.
Chicago Hardy	Purple/Black	Mid	Medium	Small eye. Very cold hardy.
Conadria	Yellow/Green	Late	Medium-Large	Light breba crop, medium to heavy main crop. Small eye. Very cold hardy.
Excel	Yellow	Mid	Medium	Light breba crop, medium to heavy main crop. Very cold hardy.
Florea	Tan/Violet	Mid	Medium	Very cold hardy.
Green Ischia	Green/Yellow	Late	Large	Also known as Strawberry Verte. Late harvest season.
Hunt	Tan/Violet	Late	Medium	Small eye. Not a heavy bearer. Well suited to rainy environments.
Kadota	Yellow/Green	Late	Medium-Large	Prone to split and sour in heavy rains.
LSU Gold	Yellow/Green	Mid	Large	Cold hardy.
LSU Purple	Purple/Black	Mid	Medium	Small eye. Cold hardy.
Malta Black	Purple/Black	Mid	Medium-Large	Small eye. Cold hardy.
Marseilles	Yellow/Green	Late	Medium	Small eye. Cold hardy.
O'Rourke	Tan/Violet	Early	Medium-Large	Also know as Improved Celeste. Partial closed ostiole. Cold hardy. Very early harvest season.
Sals	Purple/Black	Mid	Medium	Small eye. Cold hardy.

Cuttings should be ½-¾ in. diameter and 8-12 in. long. For best results, prepare cuttings in late winter or early spring, well before bud break. Grow cuttings for one season before transplanting to a permanent location. You can also propagate figs by mound layering or by transplanting rootsuckers.

Winter Protection

Fig trees are susceptible to cold damage during unseasonably cold winters. Even the most cold-hardy varieties are likely to suffer damage when temperatures fall below 15°F, but you can protect fig trees from excessive cold damage.

If you have smaller plants, cover them completely with a heavy cloth or floating row cover. Secure the cloth along the ground to prevent movement in the wind. If using a non-breathable cloth, remove it as soon as temperatures are above freezing.

Alternatively, mound the base of the fig plant with an organic mulch such as straw or chopped leaves. This provides cold protection to the crown and roots, which can still send out vigorous new growth in the spring if the top portion of the plant does not survive.

Training and Pruning

Figs require some pruning to keep growth within bounds and maintain an open canopy. Prune in the winter months, preferably after the coldest weather has passed but before growth starts in the spring.

Figs are typically grown as multi-trunked trees or shrubs. Begin training at the time of planting by cutting off one-third of the young plant, forcing shoots to grow from the base. Let these shoots grow through the first season. During late winter before the second growing season, select three to eight vigorous, widely spaced shoots to serve as the main branches and remove all other shoots.

Ensure the main branches are far enough apart to grow to 3-4 in. diameter without crowding each other. If you desire more branching, head back the plant each spring. Do this by removing about one-third to one-half the length of the annual growth. Prune out all dead wood, low-growing branches, and rootsuckers.

Fertilizing

Figs grow well in moderately fertile soils without any fertilizer applications. A fig tree that receives too much nitrogen produces fewer fruit and is more susceptible to cold weather damage. No additional nitrogen is necessary if terminal shoots grow at least 12 in. annually.

Fruit Drop or Absence of Fruiting

A number of conditions may cause fig fruit not to ripen or to drop prematurely. Young, vigorous plants often produce figs that do not fully ripen. It may be 3 or 4 years before a plant matures a quality crop. Dry, very hot periods can result in poor fruit quality, but mulching and supplemental watering during dry spells reduce this problem. The 'Celeste' variety often drops fruit prematurely in very hot weather regardless of how well the plants are maintained. An infestation of root-knot nematodes can intensify fruit drop.

Harvesting

Many fig cultivars bear two crops a year: a light crop (called a breba crop) in early summer borne on the previous season's wood and a main crop in mid or late summer borne on wood from the current season. Figs must ripen fully on the tree before harvest (Figure 8.20). They do not ripen if picked before they are mature. A ripe fruit is slightly soft and starts to bend at the neck. Harvest the fruit gently to avoid bruising. Fresh figs do not keep well; you can store them in a refrigerator for no more than two or three days.

Pest Management

Root-Knot Nematodes. Root-knot nematodes are especially problematic for fig plants. These microscopic,

Figure 8.20 Ripe fruit on 'Chicago' fig.
Image Credit: Dave Ouellette, Clemson University

wormlike creatures can cause significant damage to the plant's root system. Their feeding causes significant decline within the plant and results in poor growth, leaf discoloration, low yield, poor fruit quality, and potentially, death. Chemical treatment does not cure fig trees infested with root-knot nematodes. However, it is possible to prolong the life of an infested tree. Prune back the top of the tree to balance it with the weakened root system and be attentive to irrigation needs.

Fig Rust. Fig rust can be a serious fungal disease in figs. Severely infected leaves turn yellow-brown and drop. The undersides of fallen leaves have numerous small, raised, reddish-brown spots that are often covered with a yellow mass of rust spores. Fig rust is usually not fatal, but repeated epidemics defoliate and weaken plants. Unless fig rust is an annual problem, you do not need to spray. Sanitation is the best way to reduce the incidence of this disease.

Fig Fruit Souring. Fig fruit souring is caused by yeasts spread by insects. Souring becomes noticeable as the figs begin to ripen; souring figs often show gas bubbles or scummy masses oozing from the eye. These figs give off an offensive fermented odor. You cannot control souring with chemical sprays; the only control for souring is to grow fig cultivars that have tight or closed eyes that prevent insects from entering the fruit.

Pink Blight. Pink blight appears as a white to pink velvety growth on dying and dead twigs. It usually occurs in the interior of the tree. To control pink blight, remove infected branches and prune the tree to allow adequate air movement.

Leaf Blight (Thread Blight). Leaf blight is a fungal disease that attacks leaves and fruit. Infection may start as a semicircular brown spot at the base of the leaf. Some leaves shrivel and die, while others are covered with brown spots that leave irregular holes. During hot, wet weather, leaves quickly die and drop. Dead leaves are often matted together and held to the tree by threadlike strands like spider webs. Sanitation is the best way to reduce pathogen levels.

Borers. Borers occasionally harm figs. Signs of their activity include the presence of sawdust at the base of the trunk.

Scale Insects. Scale insects are sometimes present on fig trees. Heavy infestations can cause plants to decline. Control scale by applying dormant oil in late winter.

Spotted Wing Drosophila (SWD). SWD have become a major nuisance in fruit crops across the United States. Thin-skinned, soft fruit such as figs are especially attractive to this pest.

Wasps. Wasps can be a pest when they are attracted to overripe or soured fruit on the tree. Remove overripe and soured fruit during harvest.

June Bugs and Japanese Beetles. June bugs and Japanese beetles feed on foliage and fruit, which can reduce yield and quality. They can be especially problematic during harvest.

Persimmons

Persimmon trees can be an excellent addition to a home landscape (Figure 8.21). Growing persimmons requires less attention to training and pruning, fertilizing, and pest management than growing most other types of fruit trees.

Site and Soil Requirements

Persimmon trees grow best in loamy soils rich in organic matter. Trees are tolerant of heavy clay soils if they are well-drained, but light, sandy soils are not ideal. Persimmon trees grow best in a slightly acidic to neutral soil with a pH between 6.0-6.5.

American persimmon trees are especially cold hardy and able to tolerate temperatures as low as -25°F. In contrast, Asian persimmons can be sensitive to cold winter temperatures and are injured by temperatures below 10°F.

Types of Persimmons

Persimmons belong to one of two distinct groups: American persimmon (*Diospyros virginiana*) and Asian persimmon (*D. kaki*).

Figure 8.21 Ripening fruit of 'Hana Gosho' Asian persimmon.
Image Credit: Dave Ouellette, Clemson University

The American persimmon is native to the eastern half of the United States. The fruit is small, seedy, and astringent until fully ripe. American persimmon trees can grow to be more than 50 ft tall and have a spread of up to 30 ft. Asian persimmon trees are shorter, usually 15 ft or less. Asian persimmon fruit are larger, and some cultivars are seedless under certain pollination conditions.

Asian persimmon cultivars are classified as either astringent or non-astringent. Tannins in the fruit produce an astringent taste and cause the mouth to pucker and feel dry. Fruit of astringent varieties remain astringent until they ripen completely and become soft. This can occur whether fruit are on or off the tree, since persimmons continue to ripen after harvest. Fruit of non-astringent varieties are firm; you can eat these fruits prior to softening, but allow the fruit to fully color and soften for best flavor.

Pollination. Persimmon trees are considered dioecious, although that is not entirely accurate. Male trees can have the occasional female flower or perfect flower (having both male and female parts); female trees are similar and develop primarily female flowers with the occasional male flower or perfect flower.

American persimmon trees are typically not self-fruitful and do require cross-pollination. The Asian persimmon is usually self-fruitful. Many Asian cultivars produce fruit without pollination, which results in seedless fruit. However, pollinated fruit is usually larger and less likely to drop prematurely. American and Asian persimmons will not cross-pollinate.

Refer to Table 8.10 for persimmon varieties recommended for South Carolina.

Post-Planting Care

Persimmons are not very demanding and require relatively little care. Fertilization, pruning, and pest management are usually minimal.

Persimmon trees do not require high levels of nutrients. First-year fertilization should consist of a single application of 1 cup (1/2 lb) of 10-10-10 fertilizer per tree applied in the spring. Second-year fertilization should increase to 2 cups (1 lb) 10-10-10 fertilizer per tree. Every year after, increase the amount by 1 lb 10-10-10, up to a maximum of 10 pounds per tree. Split applications for trees planted in in lighter, sandy soils. Watch for excessive fruit drop throughout the season, which may be caused by excessive nitrogen.

Minimal pruning, consisting of limb removal to prevent crossing and to remove dead or broken limbs, may be necessary. You may also need to prune to control the size of the tree as it ages.

Persimmon trees may develop a biennial bearing habit, bearing heavily one year and not much the next. To reduce this, thin fruit, leaving one every 6 in. along the branch. Remove fruitlets by clipping, not pulling them from the limb.

Harvesting

A common misconception is that persimmons require frost to become edible; the truth is that persimmons naturally lose astringency as they ripen—often well in advance of frosts.

Persimmons continue to ripen after they are harvested. Fruit of astringent cultivars must be allowed to soften to lose enough astringency to be edible. Harvest persimmon fruit by clipping them from the tree, leaving the stem intact on the fruit. Take care to prevent bruising.

Pest Management

Insect pests of persimmons include scale, persimmon psyllid, caterpillars, and persimmon borer.

Scale Insects. Natural parasites and predators often keep scale insect populations under control. Apply dormant oil shortly before bud swell to continue to limit infestations.

Persimmon Psyllid. Persimmon psyllids are tiny, leaf-feeding, aphid-like pests that cause leaf deformation. Infested leaves roll and curl up on themselves. Natural parasites often limit psyllid infestations.

Caterpillars. Caterpillars such as fall webworm, red-humped caterpillar, and variable oak leaf caterpillar will occasionally infest persimmons. There tend to be many natural caterpillar parasites that limit caterpillar populations and damage.

Persimmon Borer. One serious pest of persimmons is the persimmon borer. The larvae of persimmon borers attack the lower trunk and tap roots. Preventative insecticide treatments may be required to avoid infestations.

Pawpaws

Pawpaws (*Asimina triloba*) are well-suited to edible landscaping due to their tropical appearance, unusual fruit, and lack of insect and disease problems. They are the exclusive larval host plant of zebra swallowtails and a great addition to butterfly gardens.

Pawpaw fruit are typically 3-6 in. long, 2-4 in. wide, and between 8 oz-2 lb. They often grow in clusters that

TABLE 8.10 Persimmon Cultivars for Home Gardens in South Carolina

Cultivar	Astringency	Comments
American		
Dollywood	Astringent	Heavy producer of very large fruit. Spreading growth habit with drooping branches.
Early Golden	Astringent	First named cultivar. Productive with medium sized fruit. Early harvest season.
Early Jewel	Astringent	Productive with large fruit. Ripens early in the season and is seedless without a pollinator.
Elmo	Astringent	Productive with very large fruit. Ripens mid-season and is seedless without a pollinator.
John Rick	Astringent	Productive. Excellent flavor and firmness.
Meader	Astringent	Reliably self-fruitful.
Mohler	Astringent	Medium size fruit. Early harvest season.
Morris Burton	Astringent	Small to medium sized fruit.
Prok	Astringent	Heavy producer with large fruit. Late harvest season.
Yates	Astringent	Heavy producer with large fruit. Low seed number.
Asian		
Eureka	Astringent	Flattened round-shaped, red fruit. Small tree size.
Fuyu	Non-Astringent	Medium-sized, red, blocky fruit. Fruit is edible even when green and firm.
Giombo	Astringent	Large, oval-shaped orange fruit.
Great Wall	Astringent	Small, flattened round orange-red fruit. Greater tolerance of cold weather than many other cultivars.
Hachiya	Astringent	Large, oval-shaped, seedless orange fruit.
Hana-Fuyu	Non-Astringent	Also known as Giant Fuyu. Large, round, yellow-orange fruit.
Hanagosho	Non-Astringent	Medium-large, orange-red fruit. Mid to late- season ripening.
Izu	Non-Astringent	Large, round, yellow-orange fruit. Ripens early season.
Jiro	Non-Astringent	Possibly same cultivar as Fuyu. Medium-sized, flat round fruit.
Matsumoto	Non-Astringent	Large, round, yellow-orange fruit.
Saruga	Non-Astringent	Large, flattened round-shaped, red fruit.
Sheng	Astringent	Large, flat orange fruit with lobed sections.
Tamopan	Astringent	Large, flat orange fruit with constriction around the middle of the fruit.
Tanenashi	Astringent	Large, oval-shaped, orange-yellow seedless fruit. Early harvest season.

resemble "hands" of bananas (Figure 8.22). The fruits have thin green skin and yellow, orange, or white flesh depending on variety. The highly aromatic fruit has flavor notes similar to a banana, mango, or pineapple.

Site and Soil Requirements

Pawpaws naturally grow in deep, fertile river-bottom lands of hardwood forests in the eastern United States, where they grow as shrubby thickets due to prolific root suckering. Although an understory tree in the native habitat, pawpaw trees require full sun for best fruit production. In sunny locations, trees form a dense pyramidal shape with a short, single trunk and typically grow to be 15-20 ft tall. The ideal soil for pawpaw growth is well drained and slightly acidic (pH between 5.5-6.5).

Figure 8.22 **Pawpaw fruit near harvest time.**
Image Credit: Dave Ouellette, Clemson University

Planting

Transplanting pawpaw trees from the wild is often unsuccessful, because their large taproot and brittle roots are easily damaged. Container-grown, grafted cultivars are strongly recommended, as they will transplant more successfully and produce higher quality fruit compared to bare-root seedlings.

Trees are sensitive to full sunlight their first year or two, so its often best to keep them in partial shade during this time and then transplant to a location receiving full sun. Once established, pawpaws produce numerous root suckers around the trunk. Remove these root suckers to maintain a single trunk for faster growth and earlier fruiting. Pawpaw trees require 3-4 years of growth to develop the physical structure to produce and support large fruiting clusters.

Mulch to help maintain soil moisture, reduce weed growth, and cushion ripe fruit that drop from the tree.

Pawpaw Varieties

Pawpaws grow well in all of South Carolina except the Coastal region, as most varieties require more chill hours than that region can provide. However, there are some varieties that require only 400-600 chill hours and may grow adequately in coastal climates.

Trees must cross-pollinate for fruit production, so always plant more than one variety. Table 8.11 lists some of the best pawpaw varieties to grow in South Carolina.

Flowering and Pollination

Flowers emerge before leaves in mid-spring, and the flowering period often extends over several weeks. The downturned flowers have dark, maroon-colored petals and a weak, unpleasant aroma. Flowers grow on the previous year's branches and may be up to 2 in. wide.

Trees must cross-pollinate with genetically different pawpaws for fruit set to occur. In general, scientists believe that small sap beetles or bottle flies pollinate pawpaws. In the wild, fruit set is usually low due to a scarcity of these pollinators. If pollinators are scarce in a home garden, it may be worthwhile to pollinate by hand.

Harvesting and Storing

Do not harvest fruit until they are slightly soft or drop from the tree. Fruit do not ripen properly if picked when very firm. The skin of ripening fruit of most varieties turns yellowish when fully ripe. The flesh has a custard-like consistency and is best eaten with a spoon; seeds are large, but easily discarded when eating. Do not eat the seeds and skin, as they contain alkaloids.

Their tropical flavor and aroma make pawpaws ideal for eating fresh or processing into blended fruit drinks, ice creams, and desserts. You can substitute pawpaw for banana (in equal parts) in most recipes. The shelf-life of tree-ripened pawpaw fruit stored at room temperature is 3-5 days; if refrigerated, fruit lasts up to 3 weeks.

Pest Management

Pawpaws are naturally resistant to disease and other pests. They produce natural compounds in leaf, bark, and twig tissues that possess anti-tumor and pesticidal properties that protect them from most infestations.

One fungal disease, bordered leaf spot (*Phyllosticta asiminae*), causes hard black spots to form on the fruit skin. These spots often merge, which leads to premature cracking. Another fungal disease, known as flyspeck (*Zygophiala jamaicensis*), can also infect pawpaws. Both diseases typically result in only minor damage to leaves and fruit. Pawpaw is a larval host plant for the zebra swallowtail and pawpaw sphinx moth, but their feeding causes only minor damage to leaves.

Foxes, feral pigs, opossums, and raccoons will eat the fruit. Deer do not feed on leaves or branches but will eat the ripe fruit.

TABLE 8.11 Pawpaw Cultivars for Home Gardens in South Carolina

Cultivar	Fruit Size	Comments
Alleghany	Medium	Fruit skin retains its green color when ripe. Flesh is yellow and sweet with a hint if citrus flavor. Seedier than most cultivars.
KSU-Atwood	Large	Greenish-blue skin. Yellow-orange flesh with few seeds. Flavor reminiscent of mango.
KSU-Benson	Medium	Very productive. Orange flesh with few seeds and rich, tropical flavors.
KSU-Chappell	Large	Very vigorous tree with sweet, mild banana-pineapple flavored fruit.
Mango	Medium-Large	A selection from the wild. Vigorous, large tree with flavorful fruit that has a mango-like taste. Does not store well and better for processing or freezing.
NC-1	Large	Yellow skin and flesh with few seeds. Very ornamental, with large, dark blue-green leaves. Stores well with refrigeration.
Overleese	Large	A selection from the wild. Fruit with exceptional flavor and fruit quality. Parent to many other improved selections.
PA Golden	Medium-Large	Very productive. Doesn't store well. Flavor is good, but can sometimes be a little bitter. Thought to be a very good pollinizer for other cultivars.
Potomac	Very Large	Strongly upright growth habit. Sweet, rich flavor with firm, smooth texture. Yellow flesh with few seeds.
Prolific	Medium-Large	Productive and fast growing. Light yellow flesh with firm, chewy texture and sometimes bitter.
Rappahannock	Medium-Large	Very productive. Unusual horizontally held leaves. Yellow, firm, sweet flesh with very few seeds. Fruit stores well.
Shenandoah	Large	Similar to Overleese, but more productive.
Sunflower	Large	Wide spreading growth habit. Yellow skin and yellow flesh with few seeds. Partially self-fruitful.
Susquehanna	Large	Yellow, firm flesh with few seeds. Very sweet, rich flavor.
Tallahatchie	Large	Sweet and aromatic with melon-like flavor and few seeds. Often bears large fruit clusters.
Taylor	Medium	A selection from the wild. Fruit skin remains green when ripe. Yellow flesh.
Taytwo	Medium	A selection from the wild. Fruit skin remains green when ripe. Yellow flesh.
Wabash	Very Large	Very productive. Yellow-orange flesh with sweet, rich flavor and a firm, smooth texture.

Mulberries

Mulberries come in many shapes and forms, including dwarf, weeping, and high-quality fruiting varieties. They are extremely adaptable trees and require minimal care.

Site and Soil Requirements

Plant mulberry trees in full sun for best fruit production. They grow well in a wide range of soil types but perform best in well-drained soils with a pH between 6.0-7.5.

Mulberries have extensive root systems that can cause damage to structures such as driveways, foundations, utilities, and septic systems. Plant trees far away from these structures to avoid potential damages. Consider the tree's mature height and spread and choose a planting location where the tree can grow freely to encourage it to produce an abundance of fruit. Fallen mulberry fruits can stain surfaces—another reason it's best to avoid planting them close to driveways, sidewalks, and patios.

Types of Mulberries

Most mulberries sold for fruit production in the United States are cultivars of the native red mulberry (*Morus rubra*), the white mulberry (*M. alba*), the black mulberry (*M. nigra),* and the Himalayan or Tibetan mulberry (*M. macroura*). Many cultivars are hybrids and do not represent any one species.

Red mulberry is native to a wide swath of the eastern United States. White and black mulberry have naturalized in some areas of the United States, but both were originally imported from Asia for silk production. There is widespread hybridization between red and white mulberries in the wild.

White mulberry trees get their name from the color of their flower buds. Fruit from white mulberry trees can be black, purple, lavender, or white. Red and white mulberries can grow to be 70-80 ft tall; the smaller, slower-growing black mulberry and Himalayan mulberry may reach 25-30 ft.

Mulberry Varieties. There are many different cultivars of Himalayan mulberry—often referred to as white, red, or black 'Pakistan' or 'Shahtoot'—that bear fruit up to 4 in. long. The fruit is generally firmer than others and stains less. Some cultivars or hybrids of white mulberry are also called 'Pakistan' if they grow elongated fruit.

There are also many "everbearing" varieties of mulberry, such as 'Illinois Everbearing,' 'David Smith,' and 'Silk Hope;' which produce fruit over a period of several months. 'Dwarf Giraldi,' 'Shangri-La,' and the many weeping mulberry varieties take up much less space than other varieties, though it's important to note that many weeping or contorted mulberry varieties are fruitless.

Pruning

The best time to prune a mulberry tree is in late winter or early spring, when the tree is still dormant. Mulberry trees require minimal pruning, but perform light pruning when trees are young to create a strong framework of branches.

Mulberries naturally produce a dense canopy of crossing branches. Use thinning cuts to remove crossing branches and open the canopy; heading cuts will make the canopy even more congested than it was before pruning. Remove dead, damaged, or diseased branches as well as any rootsuckers that emerge from the tree's base. Avoid excessive pruning, as this reduces fruit production.

Mulberry trees have milky sap that can cause skin rashes for some people. Wear gloves and long sleeves while pruning to protect your skin.

Harvesting

Mulberry trees produce a heavy crop of white, red, purple, or black fruit that resemble long, thin blackberries. The berries ripen in stages and drop from the tree as they mature. Fully ripe fruits easily separate from the tree.

To speed up the mulberry harvest, place sheets under the trees and shake the limbs to harvest large quantities of berries. The sweet, flavorful fruits are eaten fresh, juiced, and used in preserves.

Pest Management

Mulberries are an important source of food for many species of birds. Unfortunately, fruit-laden bird droppings can discolor or stain pavement and patios. Birds are a particular problem for smaller trees; it may be best to cover them with netting during the harvest season. Large trees shouldn't require netting, as they generally produce more than enough fruit for humans and birds alike.

Mulberries do not experience as many disease or insect problems as other fruit trees, but they are susceptible to leaf spot, bacterial blight, scale insects, mealybugs, and fall webworms. These are typically minor issues and have minimal impact on fruit production.

Pomegranates

Pomegranates (*Punica granatum*) have been popular throughout history and are experiencing a surge in popularity due to the health benefits associated with their juice. Pomegranates also have a long history in South Carolina; they are often found around old home sites and plantations, especially in the Midlands and Coastal Plain. Pomegranates require minimal maintenance and are long-lasting, drought tolerant plants once established.

Widely grown for their edible fruits, pomegranates are equally valuable as ornamental plants. Their scarlet, tube-shaped flowers are attractive to hummingbirds and other pollinators. There are dwarf forms suitable for containers.

Site and Soil Requirements

Pomegranates perform best when planted in full sun. They are adaptable to most soils but require good drainage. Pomegranates are tolerant of moderately brackish water, making them good candidates for coastal landscapes. They grow best in a soil with a pH between 5.5-7.0.

Pomegranates often fruit poorly in humid climates; they are best suited to warm, arid regions. They do grow successfully in South Carolina, but they often experience greater issues with fungal pathogens and fruit splitting.

In cooler areas of South Carolina, grow pomegranates near a south-facing wall or in a large container that can be moved to a protected location during cold weather. Some cold-hardy varieties can tolerate temperatures as low as 10°F.

Pomegranate Varieties

There are numerous pomegranate cultivars, but South Carolina gardeners—particularly those in the western half of the state—should seek out those that are most cold-tolerant. The "Russian series" of cultivars were selected for greater cold hardiness, high yields, and excellent flavor; 'Afganski,' 'Salavatski,' 'Parfianka,' and 'Surh-Anor' are some of the varieties that tolerate humid summers and cold winters.

Pomegranate fruits come in a wide range of colors: red, purple, pink, or yellow. Seeds can be clear, red, pink, or yellow and soft, semi-soft, or hard. Dwarf varieties such as 'Nana,' 'State Fair,' and 'Purple Sunset' bear small, edible fruit and are planted mainly for their ornamental value. Ornamental varieties with double flowers, resembling carnation blossoms, typically do not produce fruit.

Planting and Post-Plant Care

Plant pomegranates in the spring after any danger of frost has passed. Fertilize plants in spring and again in mid-summer, using 1 lb of 10-10-10 per 3 ft of plant height. Fertilize established plants as needed to maintain 12-18 in. of terminal shoot growth. Irrigating and mulching to maintain soil moisture reduces fruit drop and fruit splitting.

Pruning and Training

Pomegranates flower on new growth, so always prune in early spring before growth begins. However, if winter temperatures reach 15°F, at least part of the plant may experience cold damage. Pomegranates usually re-sprout vigorously from the crown after such events, so wait to see where new spring growth is located before pruning.

Pomegranate trees produce fruit on short spurs found on 2- to 3-year-old branches. Light annual pruning encourages the development of new fruiting spurs. Avoid heavy pruning, which reduces fruiting.

Train pomegranates to multi-trunk plants with five or six strong branches that grow directly from the ground. Make efforts to maintain an open, vase-shaped canopy. Prune annually to maintain major branches, thin out interior growth, and remove dead or damaged shoots. Pomegranates naturally sucker profusely from the base; routinely remove these suckers or plants quickly become overly dense.

Flowering

Pomegranate flowers are 1-2 in. wide and typically orange-red with crepe paper-like petals. Pomegranates produce two types of flowers. Fruit-bearing flowers have a fuller, more rounded base that appears somewhat bell-shaped; male flowers are narrower and vase-shaped.

Pomegranates do not have a single spring bloom but often have shoot flushes that bear flowers throughout the summer. Although pomegranates are self-fruitful, the chance of pollination and fruit set increases if there is more than one cultivar present.

Harvesting

Pomegranates typically begin producing fruit 3-4 years after planting. It is not uncommon for some fruit to develop in the first 2 years, but most is low quality and drops prematurely.

Arils are edible, seed-containing capsules inside the pomegranate fruit; each aril is a small, translucent sac filled with sweet, tart juice. The juice typically varies from light pink to dark red but can also appear yellow or clear in some varieties.

Harvest begins in late summer for cultivars that mature more quickly and continues through mid-autumn for late-maturing cultivars. Plan to harvest two to four times per plant. To harvest, cut off the fruit as close to the branch as possible.

Because pomegranate fruit do not ripen after being picked, harvest only after fruit reach full maturity. Color changes of the rind and arils indicate that fruit are ready for harvest. The glossy sheen of the skin changes to a matte or rough finish. As a pomegranate fruit ripens and the seeds swell, it changes from round to more hexagonal in shape. Fruit that is ready to pick may make a metallic sound when lightly tapped. Fruit left on the tree too long can begin to split, but they are still edible.

Many people say that pomegranates are difficult to peel. Try this technique to successfully remove arils from fruit with minimal mess:

- Slice off the calyx end of the fruit with a knife and carefully score the exposed surface into quarters.
- Fill a container with water and submerge the fruit.
- Pry open the fruit along the score lines and remove the arils with a rolling motion under your thumb.
- The arils sink to the bottom of the container and all the pulp, peel, and damaged seeds float to the top. Remove the floating debris and pour the water through a strainer to retrieve the arils.

Store whole fruit in the refrigerator for up to 2 months. Juice and seeds removed from the fruit have about a 5-day storage life.

Pest Management

Pomegranates are relatively trouble-free when proper conditions are provided. Leaf and fruit spots are common in South Carolina, but do not require treatment. Pomegranates may be attacked by insects such as mealybugs, scale, aphids, and whiteflies, but these are typically minor problems.

SMALL FRUIT

Blueberries

Blueberry plants can be a great addition to edible landscaping in home gardens. Growing blueberries can be challenging, because blueberry plants require soils that are acidic, well-drained, and high in organic matter; these types of soils are not common in most areas of South Carolina. Taking the time to properly amend the soil for blueberries is well worth the effort. Once established, blueberries are not difficult to maintain and produce reliable, bountiful harvests.

Types of Blueberry

There are two main types of cultivated blueberries that grow successfully in South Carolina: rabbiteye and southern highbush.

Rabbiteye blueberries (*Vaccinium ashei*) are the most adaptable, productive, and pest-tolerant of the two blueberry types. This type is native to the Southeastern United States and can grow successfully in all regions of the state. They are adaptable to various soils and tolerant of disease. Rabbiteye blueberries are somewhat self-incompatible; at least two varieties are required for cross-pollination and an abundant harvest.

Flowers of rabbiteye blueberries can be damaged by spring frosts; their fruit begin to ripen in late May or early June in the Coastal Region and last through July; in the Piedmont region, they begin to ripen in mid-June and continue into August.

Refer to Table 8.12 for rabbiteye blueberry cultivars that grow in South Carolina.

Southern highbush blueberries are hybrids derived from crosses between northern highbush blueberries (*Vaccinium corymbosum*) and native southern species—mainly Darrow's evergreen blueberry (*V. darrowii*). The resulting hybrids are plants that produce very high-quality fruit, have a very low chilling requirement, and produce fruit very early in the season. Southern highbush blueberries are self-fruitful, but their berries ripen earlier and grow to be larger if several cultivars are interplanted for cross-pollination.

Southern highbush are not as tolerant of disease as rabbiteyes, nor are they as tolerant of soils that are low in organic matter. Flowering and fruiting occur very early in spring, and freezing temperatures often damage the crop. Southern highbush can grow across South Carolina, but selection of appropriate cultivars is very important. Choosing a cultivar that blooms too early may result in crop loss. Southern highbush blueberries often have difficulty adapting to suboptimal sites, so it can be difficult to establish a planting.

Refer to Table 8.13 for a list of southern highbush cultivars recommended for South Carolina.

Recently, there has been an effort to increase the ornamental value of the blueberry plant through breeding. Compact growth habit, vibrant autumn color, evergreen foliage, and unusually colored flowers and fruit are some of the desired ornamental traits.

Site and Soil Requirements

Soil requirements for blueberries differ from those of most fruiting plants. Blueberry plants require low pH soils that contain a relatively high level of organic matter. Blueberries are very sensitive to saturated soils and must be grown on well-drained sites.

There are slight differences in soil requirements for different types of blueberry plants. Highbush types require low pH soils with high organic matter, whereas rabbiteyes have some tolerance to more average soil conditions.

When growing highbush varieties, maintain soil pH between 4.0-5.0 and organic matter content higher than 3%. Highbush blueberry plants begin to show nutrient

TABLE 8.12 Rabbiteye Blueberry Cultivars Recommended for South Carolina

Season	Cultivar	Chill Requirement (hrs)	Comments
Early	Climax	400-450	Standard cultivar. Fruit is medium in size with good color, flavor and firmness. Can bloom very early and is susceptible to late frost/freeze. Cane development from the ground is poor, must manage cane renewal differently. Upright, open habit.
	Alapaha	450-550	Blooms 7-10 days later than Climax, but produces fruit at the same time. Fruit is medium in size with good color, firmness and flavor. Upright habit with narrow base.
	Premier	550	Standard cultivar. Fruit is medium-large to large in size with good flavor and color. Vigorous, upright growth habit. Ripe fruit must be picked frequently or becomes slightly soft.
	Vernon	500-550	Blooms 7-10 days after Climax, but fruit matures at the same time. Fruit is large in size with excellent color, firmness and flavor.
	Titan	500-550	Very large fruit size. Fruit is very firm with good color and flavor. Plants are vigorous and upright, with narrow crowns. Fruit can split if heavy rain occurs during harvest time.
	Krewer	400-450	Very large fruit size. Fruit is very firm with good color and flavor. Fruit is less prone to splitting than Titan.
	Montgomery	550	Fruit is medium-large with good color and flavor. Firmness is average. Plants are vigorous and semi-upright.
	Austin	500	Blooms 5-7 days after Climax but fruit matures about same time. Fruit is medium-large with good color and flavor. Firmness is fair to good. Moderately vigorous and upright.
Mid	Brightwell	350-400	Standard cultivar. Dependable crop even after late freeze events. Begins ripening approximately 14 days after Climax. Fruit is medium-large and has good color, flavor, and firmness. Plants are vigorous and upright. Ripe fruit can split in heavy rain events. Leaf spot can be a problem.
	Ira	700-800	Blooms late, so it escapes most late freezes. Berries are medium in size, with good firmness.
	Chaucer	350-400	Berries are medium in size with wet stem scar. Plants are vigorous and spreading.
	Columbus	600-700	Fruit is very large with good flavor, excellent color, but can be somewhat soft. Less susceptible to fruit splitting during heavy rain events.
	Tifblue	600-700	Standard cultivar. Blooms late, so it escapes most late freezes. Fruit is small to medium in size, with good flavor and firmness. Fruit is tart unless allowed to fully ripen. Plants are vigorous and upright, and produce an excessive number of new canes. Ripe fruit is prone to splitting in heavy rain events.
	Yadkin	650-750	Blooms late, so it escapes most late freezes. Berries are medium in size and somewhat darker than average.

TABLE 8.12 Continued

Season	Cultivar	Chill Requirement (hrs)	Comments
Late	Powderblue	550-650	Standard cultivar. Very tolerant to splitting due to heavy rain events. Fruit is light blue and medium in size. Plants are vigorous, upright, and spreading.
	DeSoto	600-650	Newer cultivar. Plants are vigorous, but semi-dwarf, having a mature height of about 6 feet tall. Highly productive. Fruit are medium-large in size. Fruit have excellent color, flavor and firmness.
	Baldwin	550-650	Fruit are medium-large and dark blue in color. Good firmness and flavor. Plant is vigorous and upright.
	Centurion	550-650	Fruit are medium in size and can split in heavy rain events. Plants are vigorous and narrowly upright.
	Ochlockonee	650-700	Fruit are large with good color, flavor, and firmness. Fruit splitting is low. Plant is vigorous and upright.
	Onslow	500-600	Fruit are large in size, and medium blue in color. Fruit have good firmness and flavor. Plants are vigorous and upright.

deficiencies such as iron chlorosis when grown in soils with a pH above 5.0. In soils with less than 3% organic matter, highbush plants can be difficult to establish. Amending the soil only within the planting hole is not sufficient; you must incorporate amendments into a larger area for highbush blueberries to thrive.

When growing rabbiteye blueberry varieties, soil pH should be between 4.5-5.5. Plants can develop nutrient deficiencies if soil pH is higher than 5.5. Rabbiteye blueberries can tolerate soils with low organic matter, but they do benefit from its presence.

Site Preparation and Planting

Perform a soil test on any potential blueberry planting site before planting. When submitting the sample for analysis, request an organic matter test in addition to the standard soil test. On sites where organic matter is lower than ideal, add pine bark, peat moss, or well decomposed softwood sawdust. These materials further decompose and mimic the soil conditions found in the blueberry's native environment. You can also apply and incorporate elemental sulfur into soil prior to planting to lower soil pH, though this may require multiple applications.

Amended soil and raised beds are important to the success of a blueberry planting. Planting on raised beds provides extra drainage. Apply one or more of the recommended soil amendments in a layer 3-4 in. deep and 2-4 ft wide in the planting area and incorporate it into the soil. If you are planting individual blueberry plants into your landscape, incorporate 1½-2 ft^3 of material per plant. Create a raised mound at least 6 in. high and plant in the center.

The best plants to transplant are 2-3 years old and 1-3 ft tall. Always keep roots moist during the planting process.

Plant bare-root plants between late winter and early spring. You can plant potted plants throughout the year, but they do best when planted between fall and early spring. Ensure that the uppermost roots are just below the surface of the soil when planted. The root system of blueberry plants is naturally shallow, and planting too deeply increases the potential for root rot and lowers the plant's survival rate. Apply a 3-in. layer of organic mulch such as bark, wood chips, or pine straw to the surface of the soil after planting.

Pruning

Blueberries require annual pruning to prevent overbearing and maintain vigor. Do not let blueberry plants flower or fruit for the first two years. Remove flowers and immature fruit to allow the plant to focus its energy on root and shoot development. After planting, remove two-thirds of the top growth from bare-root plants and one-third of top growth from potted plants.

Blueberries require minimal pruning the second year. Remove all flower buds and any weak, damaged, or diseased growth. After two growing seasons, retain some flower buds on vigorous shoots to produce a small crop in the third year.

TABLE 8.13 Southern Highbush Blueberry Cultivars Recommended for South Carolina

Season	Cultivar	Chill Requirement (hrs)	Comments
Early	Rebel	400-450	Very early blooming and ripening. Fruit is large and light to medium blue in color. Fruit has good firmness but flavor is somewhat bland. Plants are very vigorous, with a spreading, bushy habit.
	Star	400-500	Standard cultivar. Early bloom. Fruit is large to very large with good flavor, color, and firmness. Plants are vigorous and upright.
	O'Neal	400-500	Early bloom. Blooms over a longer period than many other early cultivars. Fruit is medium-large with good flavor and firmness. Plant is moderately vigorous and upright. Can be a bit slow to leaf out in the spring.
	Farthing	300	Early bloom. Fruit is medium-large and darker blue than average. Fruit is very firm to crisp, with a mild tart flavor. Plant is shorter and has more disease resistance than most cultivars.
	Suziblue	400	Early bloom. Fruit is large with good firmness and flavor. Plants are vigorous, with a semi-spreading bushy habit.
	Palmetto	400-450	Early bloom. Fruit is medium in size with good firmness and flavor. Plants are vigorous, with a narrow crown, and an open and spreading habit.
	Abundance	300	Early bloom. Fruit is very large with good flavor and firmness. Plant is very vigorous and upright.
	Southern Splendour	450-500	Blooms after most early-season cultivars. Fruit is medium-large and very firm and crisp. Plant is vigorous, with a narrow crown and semi-upright, bushy habit.
Early-Mid	Pinnacle	600-700	Fruit is large in size and light blue. Fruit is firm and has excellent flavor. Plant is semi-upright.
	Camellia	450-500	Fruit is large and very light blue in color. Fruit has good firmness and flavor. Plant is very vigorous, is upright and bushy, and has a narrow crown.
	New Hannover	500-600	Fruit is large and has good flavor and firmness. Plant is vigorous and semi-upright.
	Southern Belle	400-500	Fruit is large to extra-large with good firmness and flavor. Plant is vigorous but can have problems with root rot. Plant is semi-spreading in habit and can get quite bushy from excessive cane development and heavy lateral branching.
	Gupton	500-550	Fruit is medium-large and light blue in color. Fruit has good firmness and flavor. Resistant to rain splitting. Plant is vigorous and upright, with a narrow crown.

TABLE 8.13 Continued

Season	Cultivar	Chill Requirement (hrs)	Comments
Mid	Norman	500	Fruit is medium-large to large in size and light blue in color. Fruit has excellent flavor and firmness. Plant is moderately vigorous and upright, with good cane development.
	Legacy	700-800	Blooms late enough to escape many freezes. Fruit is large at first harvest, but size is reduced on later harvests. Fruit is light blue in color with excellent flavor and good firmness. Plant is highly vigorous and upright. Plants are more adaptable to different soil types than other cultivars.
	Summit	800	Blooms and ripens later than most other southern highbush cultivars. Late freezes do not pose a significant threat. Fruit is large in size, with good flavor, color, and firmness. Plant is moderately vigorous and semi-upright.
	Ozarkblue	800-1000	Blooms and ripens later than most other southern highbush cultivars. Due to high chill requirements, would be best suited in the western portion of the state. Fruit is large in size with good color, flavor and firmness. Plants are fairly vigorous and semi-upright.

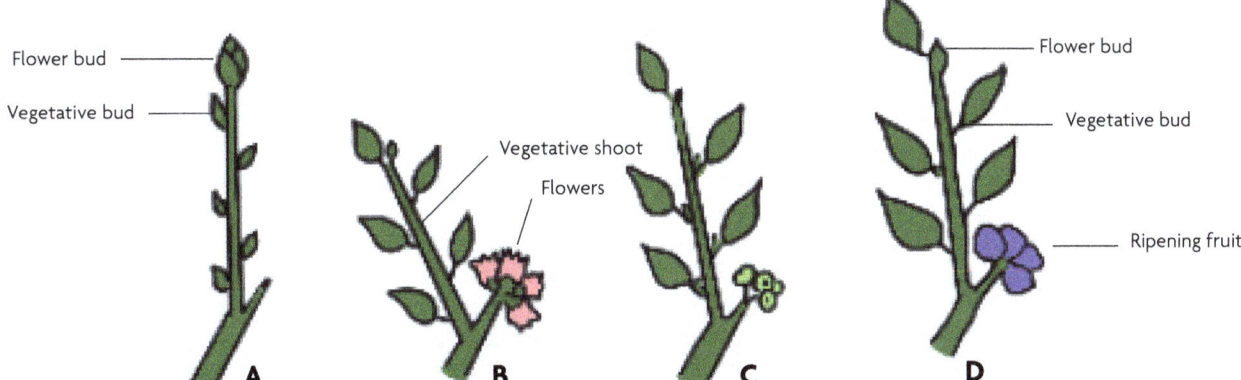

Figure 8.23 Stages in fruit development and vegetative growth in blueberries: (A) dormant stage after leaf drop showing one flower bud; (B) blooming stage that shows the cluster of flowers and vegetative shoot that developed from the top two buds in the dormant stage; (C) fruit set stage where pollinated flowers begin developing into small fruits; (D) fruit development stage that extends from fruit set to mature fruit.

To prune plants of bearing age, remove low spreading branches and branches growing through the center of the plant. Remove very slender or twiggy growth, dead or damaged shoots, and crossing branches. Head back excessively long shoots to stimulate lateral branching. Remove any rootsuckers that appear more than 18 in. away from the crown of the plant. After pruning, all remaining canes should be vigorous and upright.

Blueberry flower buds grow near the ends of shoots that grew the previous year (Figures 8.23 and 8.25). Most pruning cuts should be thinning cuts that remove an entire shoot back to a branch or to ground level. Too many heading cuts remove an excessive amount of flower buds and reduce the harvest (Figure 8.24).

Practice renewal pruning to maintain vigor and the production of high-quality fruit. Begin the renewal process when plants are in their fifth or sixth year. Aging canes produce a large percentage of twiggy growth with undersized fruit. Remove canes that have fruited for more than three or four years to allow for vigorous new canes to replace them. Completely remove one or two of the oldest canes to the ground every year.

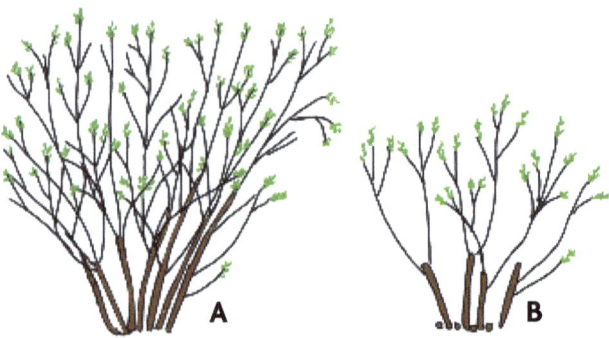

Figure 8.24 Blueberry plant before (A) and after (B) dormant pruning.

Fertilizing

Even though blueberries have evolved in low-nutrient environments, they respond well to fertilization. The sensitivity of blueberries to elevated levels of salt in the soil warrants multiple light fertilizer applications throughout the growing season. Overfertilization can injure roots, resulting in shoot dieback and leaf scorch.

Do not fertilize plants immediately after planting; wait until the first leaves have reached full size. Apply 2 tbsp (1 oz) of 10-10-10 or 12-4-8 evenly in a 1-ft circle around the plants. Fertilize at this same rate in late spring and again in mid-summer during the first year.

In the second year, apply 4 tbsp (2 oz) of 10-10-10 or 12-4-8 evenly over a 2-ft circle in early spring and mid-summer. For older plants, apply 1 oz of 10-10-10 or 12-4-8 per foot of plant height in early spring and then again in summer after harvest. Do not apply more than 6 oz of fertilizer per plant per application.

If soil levels of phosphorus and potassium are excessive, use ammonium sulfate at one-half the rate of 10-10-10 with plants of bearing age. Avoid using nitrate-based fertilizers such as calcium nitrate.

Harvesting

Wait to harvest until berries turn completely blue and readily detach from the plant (Figure 8.26). Using your thumb, roll the berry off the stem and into your palm. Harvest twice weekly if possible, picking all ripe fruit. Blueberry plants typically reach their peak production between 8-10 years of age.

Birds also eat blueberries—often the complete crop from smaller plantings. Control birds' access to the berries by draping netting over the plants.

Figure 8.25 Blueberry flower buds before bloom.
Image Credit: Dave Ouellette, Clemson University

Figure 8.26 Ripening fruit on rabbiteye blueberry plant.
Image Credit: Dave Ouellette, Clemson University

Pest Management

Blueberries are affected by relatively few pests in home garden settings. The primary insect pests are larvae that feed on the fruit, foliage, and stem interiors. Blueberry diseases include those typical to fruiting plants: cankers, root rot, fruit rot, and leaf spots.

Blueberry Maggot. Blueberry maggot is the larva of the adult Blueberry maggot fly (*Rhagoletis mendax*). The female flies lay eggs into the fruit that then hatch and feed upon the pulp. Often, larvae are present in the fruit at harvest.

Blueberry Stem Borer. Blueberry stem borers can build up to become significant, localized pests. These insects bore into the canes of blueberry plants and tunnel upwards, killing the terminal tip of the cane before tunneling down towards the crown of the plant. Borers leave an accumulation of sawdust and frass below the entry point on the infested cane. To control them, remove and destroy the infested cane.

Spotted wing drosophila. Spotted wing drosophila (SWD) is an invasive pest throughout the United States. Female flies use a specialized sawtooth-like ovipositor to cut through the skin of ripening fruit and place eggs inside. Upon hatching, larvae tunnel their way through the fruit and remain there until harvest. Control SWD with regular cover sprays of labeled insecticides throughout the ripening season and proper cooling and storage of fruit after harvest.

Stem Cankers. Stem cankers first appear as red splotches or rough, raised grey bumps and ridges along canes. Advanced cankers encircle the stem, restricting the flow of water and nutrients to the upper parts of the plant and causing severe decline. Cane removal is the best control method.

Phytophthora Root Rot. Phytophthora rot root often occurs in areas where blueberries are planted in poorly drained soils. Early above-ground symptoms include yellowing of leaves and lack of new growth. The terminal leaves become small as the disease progresses and excessive defoliation occurs. Older, chronically affected plants appear stunted and are prone to wilting. Chemical control measures are not realistic long-term solutions.

Mummy Berry. Mummy berry is a fungal disease that affects shoots and berries. The causal fungus (*Monilinia vaccinii-corymbosi*) overwinters on the ground, and in spring produces a cup-shaped mushroom that releases spores. These spores infect and kill emerging shoots, causing the shoot blight phase of the disease. Blighted shoots then produce a second type of spore that is carried by insects to the flowers, where fruit infection takes place. This results in "mummies," berries that turn pink or salmon-colored (instead of blue) and fall to the ground. Sanitation is key in controlling infections. Rake and destroy mummied fruit each season.

Septoria Leaf Spot. Septoria leaf spot causes defoliation and poor growth. The small spots on leaves have white to tan centers and reddish-brown margins. The fungus overwinters in infected leaves on the ground, so sanitation is important in controlling future infections.

Blackberries and Raspberries

Blackberries and raspberries are among the easiest fruit crops for home production (Figure 8.27). Most varieties of blackberries perform well in South Carolina, whereas raspberries are best suited for the Mountain region due to their intolerance to summer heat.

Caneberries are members of the genus *Rubus*, which includes blackberry and raspberry. Raspberries are distinguished from blackberries by fruit type: raspberry fruit separate from a central core, or receptacle, when harvested and look like a thimble; the receptacle of a blackberry remains with the harvested fruit.

Figure 8.27 **Flowers and maturing fruits on 'Osage' blackberry.**
Image Credit: Dave Ouellette, Clemson University

Site Selection

Blackberries and raspberries grow well in a wide range of soil types, but they do best in sandy loam or clay loam soils with a pH between 6.0-6.5. Avoid planting these fruits in low areas where water may stand after heavy rains. Test the soil before planting to allow for adequate time to amend the soil if necessary.

Life Cycle of Canes

Blackberry and raspberry shoots have biennial life cycles. Those that emerge and grow the first year are called primocanes. In the second year, these same shoots are called floricanes. Flowers and fruit grow on the tips of short lateral branches that grow on floricanes. After fruiting, floricanes begin to age and eventually die; they are removed by pruning. New primocanes are produced each spring, and the cycle continues.

TABLE 8.14 Blackberry and Raspberry Cultivars for Home Gardens in South Carolina

Cultivar	Harvest season	Habit	Comments
Blackberry - Floricane Fruiting			
Arapaho	Early	Thornless, erect	Medium-size, firm fruit. Good flavor, sweet and mildly subacid. Low yielding, benefits from planting at a closer spacing. Moderate resistance to anthracnose. High resistance to orange rust.
Natchez	Early	Thornless, semi-erect	Large fruit, medium firmness. Very high yielding. Vigorous, arching canes. Winter hardiness can be an issue, best suited for warmer regions of the state.
Ponca	Early	Thornless, erect	Newer cultivar. Medium-sized, very sweet fruit with excellent postharvest quality. High yielding.
Caddo	Mid	Thornless, erect	Newer cultivar. Medium-large fruit. Sweet with very good flavor.
Osage	Mid	Thornless, erect	Medium-sized fruit with excellent flavor and good firmness. Vigorous, very productive. Excellent postharvest quality.
Ouachita	Mid	Thornless, erect	Medium-large fruit. Very sweet berries with low acid. Flavor can be a little variable after a heavy summer rain. Vigorous, very productive.
Kiowa	Mid	Thorny, erect	Very large fruit, good flavor, fairly firm fruit. Vigorous. Susceptible to rosette/double blossom disease. Semi-evergreen on warmer, coastal sites. Early trellising is necessary due to early (first year) trailing habit. Becomes erect with age.
Navaho	Mid	Thornless, erect	Medium-sized fruit, good firmness. Can be weak in primocane development, sometimes only 1-2 new canes. May need to be planted at a closer spacing. High chill cultivar so better suited to western portion of the state. Susceptible to orange rust.
Von	Mid	Thornless, erect	Medium-sized fruit with small drupelets and small seeds. Very high yielding. Vigorous. Long harvest window. Sweet, low acid. Very good postharvest quality. High chill cultivar so best suited to western portion of the state.
Apache	Mid	Thornless, erect	Large fruit. Vigorous, high yielding. Can develop white drupelets on fruit in hot weather. Moderately resistant to anthracnose.

TABLE 8.14 Continued

Cultivar	Harvest season	Habit	Comments
Hull	Late	Thornless, semi-erect	Medium-large fruit. Good flavor but should be allowed to ripen until dull black. Can be rather acidic if harvested early. Fair to good firmness. Fruit subject to sunburn. Vigorous, good yield. Best suited for the western portion of the state.
Triple Crown	Late	Thornless, semi-erect	Medium to large fruit with good flavor and fair firmness. Fruit can ripen unevenly and can be subject to sunburn. Seed can be a bit large. Vigorous, high yielding.
Chester	Late	Thornless, trailing	Large fruit, with good firmness and good flavor. Skin can be tough. Fruit can sunburn. Very high yielding. Best suited to the western portion of the state. Resistant to Botryosphaeria cane blight and crown gall.
Blackberry- Primocane/Floricane Fruiting			
Prime-Ark Freedom	Very early/Late	Thornless, erect	Very large fruit with medium firmness. Floricane crop bloom time is very early and can be damaged by late freezes in the spring. Primocane crop produces well into the fall. Floricane production - all regions of the state. Primocane production - best potential in the Upstate.
Prime-Ark Traveler	Very early/Late	Thornless, erect	Medium-large fruit with very good firmness and good flavor. Fruit is sweet and subacid. Floricane crop bloom time is very early and can be damaged by late freezes in the spring. Very good postharvest quality. Floricane production - all regions of the state. Primocane production - best potential in the Upstate.
Prime-Ark 45	Early/Late	Thorny, erect	Floricane fruit is medium in size. Primocane fruit size can be variable. Fruit is firm and has good flavor. Good floricane crop yield. Floricane production - all regions of the state. Primocane production - best potential in the Upstate.
Raspberry - Floricane Fruiting			
Dormanred	Mid	Thorny, trailing	Medium-sized fruit with fair flavor. Flavor improves with cooking. Attractive fruit.
Raspberry - Primocane Fruiting			
Heritage	Late	Thorny, erect	Small fruit size. Average quality. Medium to dark red in color. Very productive. Root rot can be an issue. Best suited for Mountain region of South Carolina.
Caroline	Late	Semi-thornless, trailing	Medium-sized berries with average quality. Fruit is medium red in color. Very vigorous, good yields. Good tolerance to Phytophthora root rot. Not very tolerant of heat and drought. Best suited for Mountain region of South Carolina.
Nantahala	Late	Thorny, erect	Medium-large berries with excellent flavor. Light red fruit. Very good quality. Excellent postharvest quality. Best suited for Mountain region of South Carolina.

Types of Blackberries and Raspberries

Some varieties of blackberries and raspberries produce flowers at the tips of primocanes, usually in regions with long growing seasons. These primocane-fruiting or "fall-bearing" cultivars bear fruit that ripens in late summer to fall, after the main crop ripens on the floricanes.

Canes have one of three different growth habits: erect, semi-erect, or trailing. Some varieties of each of these types can grow in South Carolina (Table 8.14). Trellising is not required for erect and semi-erect varieties, but many gardeners prefer to trellis to facilitate management and harvesting.

Planting

Trellising blackberries and raspberries allows for easier harvesting and better disease control. To construct a simple trellis, set 6½- or 7-ft posts 1½-2 ft in the ground, 10-20 ft apart. The recommended number of trellis wires varies depending on the plant's growth habit (Figure 8.28). A single top wire may be sufficient for erect types, whereas two or three wires may be more suitable for semi-erect and trailing types respectively. Set multiple wires 18-24 in. apart.

Plant erect or semi-erect blackberries 3-5 ft apart. Plant erect or semi-erect raspberries 2-3 ft apart and trailing types 8-10 ft apart. The crown of the plant should be ½ in. below the soil line. Mulch the planting to conserve moisture and reduce weed pressure.

Training and Pruning

In the first year of planting, tie all developing primocanes to the trellis as they grow. You can fan out canes of trailing-type raspberries (Figure 8.29).

In the second year, before growth begins, select five to eight of the most vigorous desirable shoots from each crown to serve as floricanes and remove all others. Shorten any long, lateral branches on these floricanes by one-third to one-half. Tip new primocanes periodically during the growing season to encourage lateral branching. Allow rootsuckers to develop in an 18-in.-wide row and remove any that grow beyond this width. After harvest is complete, cut out all the floricanes and discard them.

Figure 8.30 illustrates an erect-type blackberry plant before and after dormant pruning.

To produce a single late summer or early fall crop on primocane-fruiting varieties, mow or cut all canes to within 2 in. of the ground before new growth emerges in

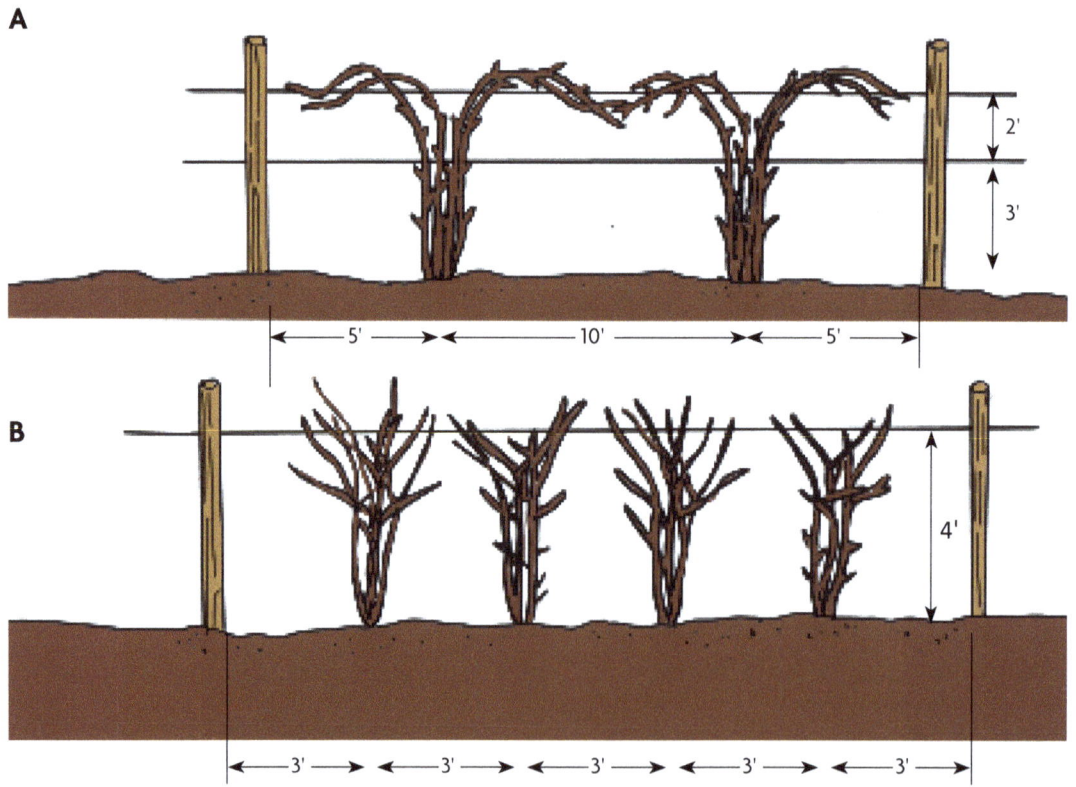

Figure 8.28 Train trailing types of blackberry and raspberry to a multiple wire trellis (A). Erect or semi-erect types can be trained to a single wire trellis (B).

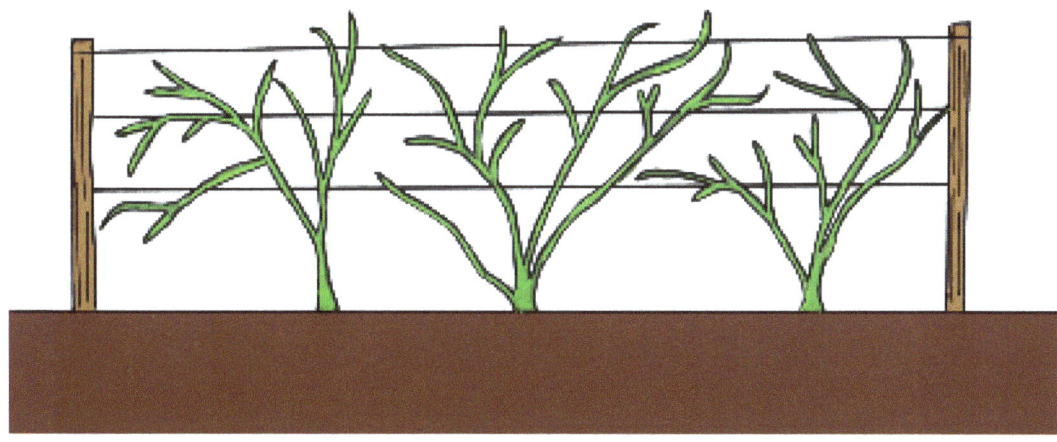

Figure 8.29 3-wire trellis for trailing vines such as 'Dormanred' raspberry.

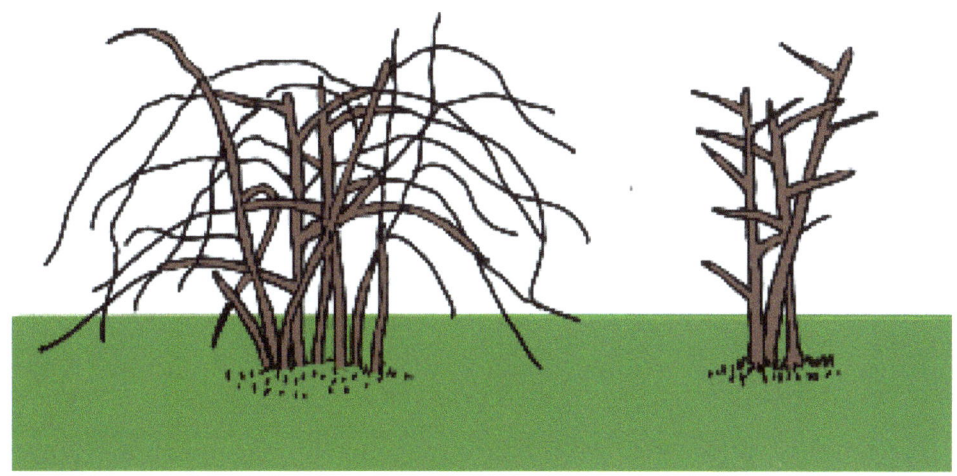

Figure 8.30 Erect type blackberry before (A) and after (B) dormant pruning.

early spring. This approach sacrifices the spring or early summer main crop but simplifies management.

Fertilizing

Blackberries and raspberries should receive about 4 oz of 10-10-10 fertilizer per plant in early spring and again in mid-summer the year of planting. Scatter the fertilizer evenly over a 2-ft circle centered on each plant. In future years, apply 1 lb of 10-10-10 per 10 feet of row in early spring and 1 lb of 10-10-10 per 20 ft of row in mid-summer. Spread the fertilizer evenly over the row in a 2-ft-wide band.

Harvesting

Harvest blackberries and raspberries in the morning after dew dries. This minimizes field heat buildup in the fruit and results in longer shelf life. Roll or gently pull berries off the plant and place in shallow containers. Blackberries are ripe when they turn fully black and detach easily. Raspberries are ripe when slightly soft, fully colored, and separate easily from the stem with the core remaining on the plant. It is best to harvest every 2 or 3 days to avoid overripe fruit. Berries should be as dry as possible before storing in the refrigerator. Freshly harvested raspberries can be refrigerated for up to a week and blackberries several days longer.

Pest Management

Anthracnose. Anthracnose first appears as small, purplish spots on new canes. As the disease progresses, the spots enlarge and become grayish in the center with raised purple edges. It is common for the bark on diseased canes to crack; infected canes may wilt and die. Infections in the berry clusters result in dry, withered berries.

Rosette (Double Blossom). Rosette infects buds on vegetative canes during the spring and summer. The following season, numerous short, leafy shoots grow from the infected leaf buds and become broomlike in appearance. Blossoms from infected buds are abnormal, often with numerous extra petals. These flowers do not produce fruit. Cut any infected canes back to 12 in. above the ground immediately after harvest.

Orange Rust. Orange rust is a fungal infection that results in orange pustules covering the undersides of leaves in the spring. Diseased shoots may recover by midsummer, but developing canes are smaller than normal and bear no fruit the following year. The fungus that causes orange rust is systemic and remains in the host plant. Remove and destroy infected plants, including the roots. Fungicides are not helpful in controlling orange rust. Orange rust does not affect red raspberries.

Crown Gall. Crown gall results in tumorous growths in plant crowns and root systems. Once infected, plants cannot be cured. Crown gall reduces plant vigor, which in turn increases mortality and decreases productivity. Do not transplant any plants with galls on them or transplant any plants—even those that appear healthy—out of fields where crown gall is present.

Strawberry Clipper Weevils. Strawberry clipper weevils injure caneberries by laying eggs in flower buds and chewing through pedicels, causing buds to drop from the plant. Larvae develop in the dropped flower buds over the course of 3-4 weeks. Adults emerge in midsummer, briefly feed on pollen, and then overwinter in wooded areas.

Red-Necked Cane Borers. Red-necked cane borers are small black beetles with red "necks" (structurally, they are thoraxes). Adults are generally present in late spring and early summer. Larval feeding causes swellings and splits in canes. Infested canes are unproductive and, if not destroyed, may reinfest other canes for years. Always remove and discard infested canes.

Blackberry Psyllids. Blackberry psyllids are small, aphid-like insects with three reddish stripes running lengthwise on the wings. Adults jump when disturbed. Psyllids overwinter in conifers. Feeding stunts plants and causes tightly curled leaves.

Raspberry Crown Borer. Raspberry crown borer is a black, clear-winged moth. Females have yellow legs and rings around their abdomens. Larvae are yellowish white with brown heads; larval feeding results in weak, spindly canes that break easily. Pull up and discard infested canes and roots.

Grapes

Grapes can be a great addition to home gardens and landscapes. You can eat harvested fruit fresh or process it into products such as jellies, juice, or wine. For best results, choose the type and variety of grape recommended for your region of the state.

Types of Grapes and Selecting Grape Varieties

There are three species of grapes grown in the United States: the European bunch grape (*Vitis vinifera*), the American bunch grape (*V. labrusca*), and the muscadine grape (*V. rotundifolia*). There are also many varieties of grape that are interspecific hybrids. French-American hybrids are crosses between the wild American grape and the European bunch grape. These combine the excellent wine quality of the European bunch grape with the cold-hardiness and pest resistance of native American species.

South Carolina is not well-suited to production of European bunch grapes, but it is possible to successfully grow some American bunch grapes and hybrids between the two species. Pierce's disease, a widespread systemic bacterial disease, severely limits the areas where bunch grapes can grow. Planting resistant varieties is the only control; there are no cultural practices, sprays, or rootstocks that reduce the probability of the disease. Varieties that show tolerance to Pierce's disease are still susceptible to the many other diseases that afflict bunch grapes, such as anthracnose and fruit rots. Some cultivars of bunch grapes that are considered resistant to Pierce's disease are: 'Victoria Red,' 'Suwanee,' and 'Daytona' (for fresh use) and 'MidSouth,' 'Black Spanish,' 'Lomanto,' and 'Blanc duBois' (for wine, juice, and jellies).

Muscadine grapes are native to the southeastern United States and are well adapted to all areas of the state except for those at high elevations. Considerable injury typically occurs where winter temperatures drop below 0°F. Muscadine grapes are much more resistant to diseases—including Pierce's disease—than bunch grape species and hybrids. Muscadine cultivars are traditionally sorted into four categories: two based on fruit color (purple/black or bronze) and two based on flower type (perfect-flowered and female-flowered). Muscadine skin color varies widely and can be bronze, pink, purple, or black. It is very important to know the flower type of a particular muscadine variety; if you plan to grow only one vine, it must be perfect-flowered to produce fruit. Female-flowered cultivars produce no pollen and need to

TABLE 8.15 Muscadine Grape Cultivars for Home Gardens in South Carolina

Cultivar	Color	Harvest season	Berry size	Use	Comments
Female Flowering Types					
Big Red	Red	Mid	Large	Fresh	High fruit quality. Dark red-black color. Dry stem scar.
Black Beauty	Purple/Black	Early-mid	Very large	Fresh & wine/juice	Very vigorous, moderate yields. Very good disease resistance. Dry stem scar.
Black Fry	Purple/Black	Mid	Large	Fresh	Vigorous, productive. Good cold tolerance. Good disease resistance.
Darlene	Bronze	Mid	Large	Fresh	Vigorous growth, but inconsistent yields. Fruit can be varable in size but can produce some very large berries.
Early Fry	Bronze	Early	Very large	Fresh	Medium vigor, very productive.
Fry	Bronze	Mid	Large	Fresh	Known as the standard for bronze fresh fruit muscadines. Medium vigor. Susceptible to fruit rot, especially ripe rot.
Scarlett	Red	Mid	Large	Fresh	Low productivity, but excellent quality.
Scuppernong	Bronze	Late	Small	Fresh & wine/juice	Very old cultivar, selected from the wild. Many associate all bronze muscadines with the name 'Scuppernong', instead of a particular cultivar. Vigorous, but low yielding. Small fruit. Not very sweet, rather acidic.
Summit	Bronze	Mid	Large	Fresh	Very vigorous, productive. Slightly smaller than Fry but better productivity, fruit rot resistance and drier stem scar. Slightly pinker than Fry.
Supreme	Purple/Black	Mid	Very large	Fresh	Medium-low vigor. Good productivity. Excellent quality with crisp, edible skin.
Sweet Jenny	Bronze	Mid	Large	Fresh	Very vigorous, but subject to variable yield.

continued

TABLE 8.15 Continued

Cultivar	Color	Harvest season	Berry size	Use	Comments
Perfect-flowered Types					
Carlos	Bronze	Mid	Medium	Wine/juice	The standard for bronze juice muscadines. Very vigorous and productive. Juice has good flavor, but skin can be very bitter. Has dry stem scar, but not well suited for fresh use.
Dixie Red	Red	Mid	Large	Fresh & wine/juice	Very vigorous, very productive. Good cold hardiness.
Doreen	Bronze	Late	Medium	Fresh & wine/juice	Good vigor, productive. Better fruit rot resistance than Carlos. Excellent selection for wine and juice.
Granny Val	Bronze	Very late	Large	Fresh	Medium high vigor, very productive. Average flavor. Produces crop at a time when few other cultivars of quality are producing. Dry stem scar.
Hall	Bronze	Early	Large	Fresh	Newer cultivar. Moderate vigor, productive. Excellent quality.
Ison	Purple/Black	Late	Large	Fresh & wine/juice	Very productive. Can be subject to cold damage.
Lane	Purple/Black	Early	Large	Fresh	Newer cultivar. Moderate vigor, productive. Fruit has a tendency to split and tear during harvest.
Late Fry	Bronze	Late	Very large	Fresh	Good vine vigor, productive. Ripens within a late window. Dry stem scar.
Nesbitt	Purple/Black	Mid-late	Large	Fresh	Moderate vigor, very productive. Skin can be a bit tough. Good resistance/tolerance to fruit rots. Long harvest season.
Noble	Purple/Black	Mid	Small	Wine/juice	The primary red cultivar for juice and wine, very stable red color. Vigorous, very productive. Very good disease resistance/tolerance.
Oh My!	Bronze	Mid	Medium	Fresh	Vigorous, and productive. Tender skin, seedless.
Paulk	Purple/Black	Mid-late	Large	Fresh	Newer cultivar. Good vigor and productivity.
Razzmatazz	Red	Continuous	Small	Fresh	Moderate vigor, very productive. Crisp texture, thin skin, seedless. Produces fruit from mid-summer until first frost.

TABLE 8.15 Continued

Cultivar	Color	Harvest season	Berry size	Use	Comments
RubyCrisp	Red	Mid	Very large	Fresh	Newer cultivar. Good vigor, excellent productivity. Crisp flesh with distinctive taste without traditional muscadine flavor. Dry stem scar.
Southern Home	Purple/Black	Mid-late	Medium	Fresh	Overall good fruit quality. Leaves have ornamental cut-leaf pattern.
Tara	Bronze	Early	Large	Fresh & wine/juice	Moderate vigor, productive. Only slight color difference exist between underripe and ripe fruit. Flavor can be quite variable.
Triumph	Bronze	Early	Medium	Fresh	Vigorous, very productive. Noticeable pink-bronze color.

be interplanted with perfect-flowered cultivars for proper pollination and fruit set. Table 8.15 lists several muscadine grape cultivars recommended for home gardens in South Carolina.

Site and Soil Requirements

A planting location with full sun and well-drained soil is best. The optimal soil pH for grapes is between 5.5-6.5.

Grapevine Terminology

To understand how to train, grow, or care for a grape vine, it's important to know the names of its various parts. The following terms are used in training bunch and muscadine grapes:

- Cane: a mature woody shoot after leaf fall.
- Cordon: a horizontal extension of the trunk trained along a trellis wire.
- Lateral: the side branch of a shoot or cane.
- Node: the thickened part of a shoot or cane where leaves, buds, or branches attach.
- Shoot: current-season growth arising from a bud, including stem, leaves, and fruit.
- Spur: a cane severely shortened by pruning back to a few nodes.
- Sucker: a shoot that arises from the base of the trunk or root system.
- Tendril: a long, slender, stringlike organ of shoots, located opposite leaves at nodes, that can coil around objects and provide support.
- Trunk: the permanent vertical structure of the vine that connects the root system with the cordons and fruit-bearing wood.
- Watersprout: a vigorous, non-fruitful shoot from the upper part of the vine.

Trellis Systems

Grapevines do not have rigid trunks; you must provide the plant with a trellis or some other support. Trellis design should maximize light penetration inside the canopy to expose the buds, leaves, and fruit clusters to as much sunlight as possible. A trellis must be strong enough to support large crops, withstand high winds, and last 20 years or more. Many types of trellising are successful, but an equal number are impractical for long-term vine management. For example, growing muscadine vines over a garden arch or pergola can be aesthetically pleasing and provide shade, but managing vines on these structures is impractical.

Although several trellis systems are available, there is no single system that is appropriate for all grapes in all situations. American bunch grapes and muscadine grapes perform well on the High Cordon (HC) or Geneva Double Curtain (GDC) systems, since these grapes naturally tend to grow downward. European bunch grapes are predisposed to upward growth and typically are not as vigorous; the Vertical Shoot Positioning (VSP) system is a good fit for this type. There are numerous interspecific grape hybrids available, and their growth habits vary with cultivar.

High Cordon (HC). HC is a system that establishes cordons 5-6 ft above the ground (Figure 8.31a). Cultivars suited to the HC system are very vigorous and have a

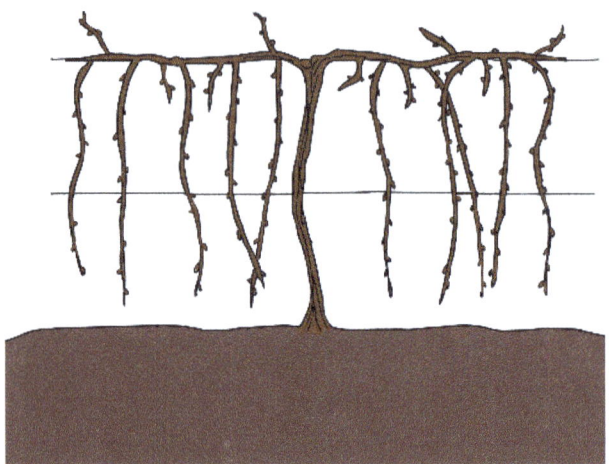

Figure 8.31a High Cordon trellis system

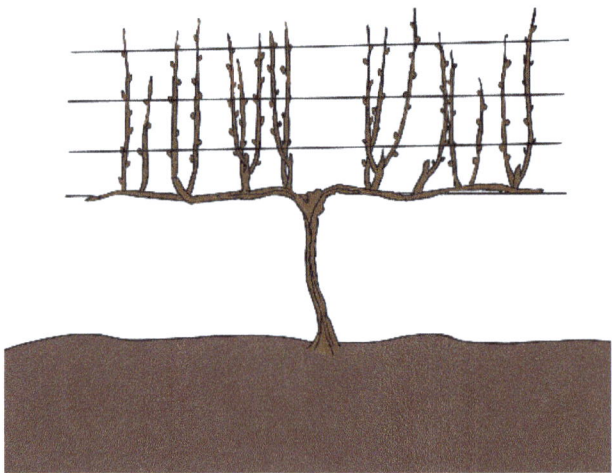

Figure 8.31b Vertical Shoot Position (VSP)

trailing growth habit. The vigorous downward growth of American bunch grapes and muscadine grapes is well suited to this system. The HC training system consists of one to three wires; the top wire is 4-6 ft above the ground. Muscadines are typically trained to a single wire stretched 5-6 ft above the ground. Lower wires provide support for young vines in the process of reaching the top wire and for older vines that become heavy with fruit. This high positioning allows for good sun exposure to fruit. This system is also ideal for its simplicity of pruning practices and shoot positioning.

Vertical Shoot Position (VSP). Gardeners often use VSP as a trellis system for European bunch grapes. In the VSP system, shoots are trained upward in a vertical, narrow curtain above the fruiting zone (Figure 8.31b). A VSP trellis system can consist of four to six levels of wire. The cordon, or fruiting wire, is typically about 3 ft above the ground. Above the cordon wire are two movable catch wires at different heights that train the growth of the shoots in an upward direction. The top wire is often about 60-70 in. high. This system promotes vertical growth and results in a narrow, upright vertical canopy. This form encourages the drying of leaves and fruit and helps to reduce disease outbreaks. The VSP system may be more difficult to manage with high vigor cultivars or on fertile sites that produce large vines.

Geneva Double Curtain (GDC). GDC trellis systems use two wires spaced 4 ft apart horizontally, 5 ft above the ground (Figure 8.32). The goal of the GDC system is to manage a dense canopy by dividing it horizontally in two, allowing more sunlight to reach the fruiting zone. This system trains vines from the trunk to bilateral cordons and positions shoots downward to create a canopy that has the appearance of two "curtains." The GDC trellis system can result in higher yields than other systems, but it is more costly to establish than other trellis systems and requires appropriate maintenance for the divided canopy.

Trellis Construction and Planting

To simplify installation and to avoid damaging young vines, build and erect your trellis before planting your vines. For a top trellis wire positioned 5 ft above the ground, establish 8-ft-long, 5-6-in. diameter, pressure-treated wooden posts. Set them 3 ft deep and angle them slightly away from each other.

Line posts should be 4 in. in diameter and 7 ft long, set 2 ft deep in a vertical position. Set line posts at 20-30-ft intervals down the row and brace end posts as shown in Figure 8.33. Use high tensile galvanized steel wire and wire strainers to maintain tension. The number of wires installed, and their tension, depend on the selected trellis system.

Plant grape vines in late winter or early spring. Vigorous one-year-old plants are best. Keep the roots moist until planting to prevent them from drying out. Plant grafted vines with the graft union 2-3 in. above soil level. For non-grafted vines, set vines so that the crown is 1-2 in. above soil level. Tamp the soil firmly around the roots and water immediately afterwards. After planting, remove all stems except one; prune this back to two or three buds.

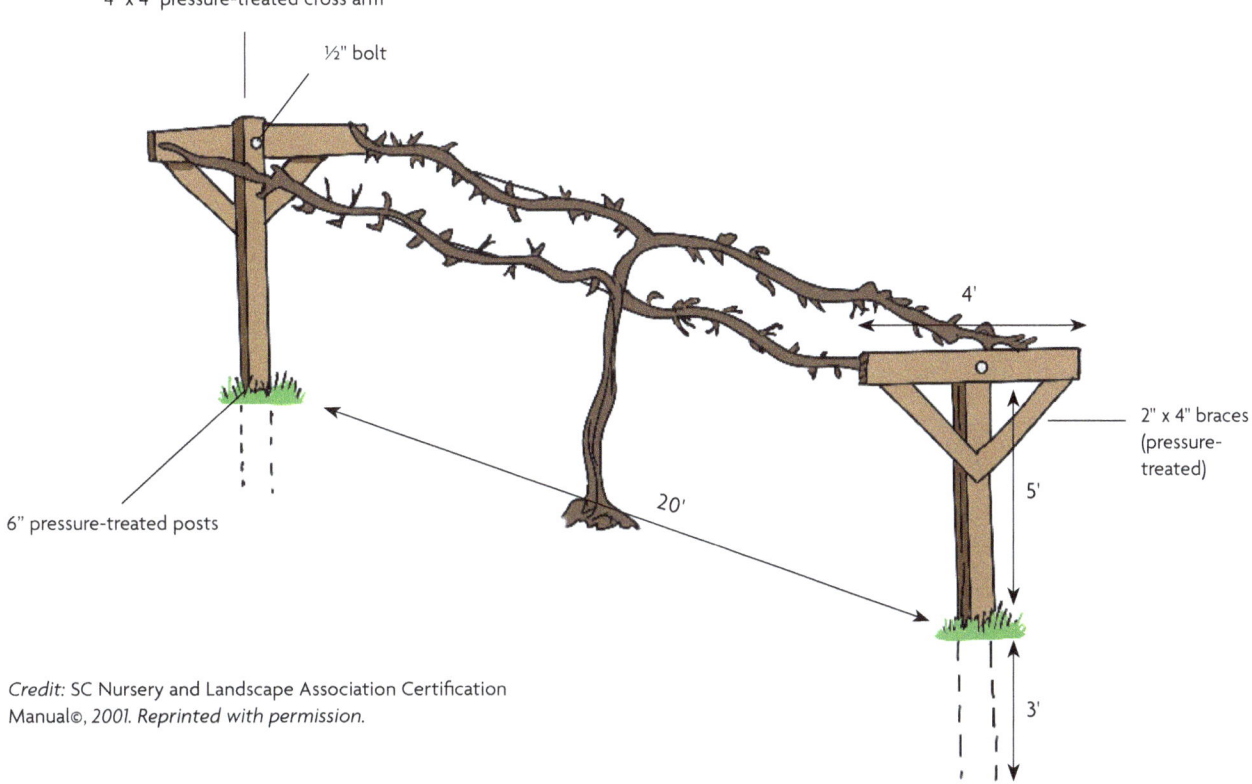

Credit: SC Nursery and Landscape Association Certification Manual©, 2001. Reprinted with permission.

Figure 8.32 Geneva Double Curtain trellis.

Training and Pruning

The basic framework of a vine consists of the trunk, permanent arms or cordons, and the fruiting spurs and canes. Flower and fruit clusters form on current-season shoots. These shoots develop from buds formed on last year's growth.

During the first season, the primary objective of training and pruning grapes is the development of a large root system and a strong vertical trunk. When new growth begins, train two or three new shoots to a training stake that is long enough to be tied to the trellis (Figure 8.34). A bamboo stake driven 3 in. away from the plant is convenient for attaching the growing vine. Tie the shoots loosely to the stake several times during this first growing season to maintain vertical growth. Pinch back any side branches to a leaf to encourage rapid extension growth of the vertical shoots.

In the second year, in late winter, evaluate the amount of growth produced during the first year. If no shoot reached the cordon wire, remove all but one. Prune this shoot back to two buds and treat it as a first-year vine. If a shoot is long enough to reach the cordon wire, retain it as the permanent trunk and remove the others. Prune this trunk back to the first node above the cordon wire (Figure 8.35).

When new growth emerges from below this pruning cut, select two shoots that are about 5-10 in. below the cordon wire and on opposite sides of the trunk. When these shoots are about 18-24 in. long, gently bend and tie them to the cordon wire (Figure 8.36). As these cordon shoots continue to grow, continue to loosely tie them to the wire. To avoid damaging the tender shoots, tie them at least 12 in. from the tip. Allow the cordon shoots to grow to the halfway point to the adjacent vine. Once the framework of trunk and cordons is established, let side shoots along the cordons develop. Rub off all flower clusters as they develop during this second year.

In late winter of the third year, head back canes that developed on the cordon to spurs of two or three buds for bunch grapes or three to four buds for muscadines (Figure 8.37). Space the spurs at regular intervals of 4-6 in. along the cordon by removing all extra shoots. Also remove any extra growth that has developed on the trunk. To maintain this framework, prune the vines each dormant season.

If using the VSP training system, train the growth of the shoots in an upward direction between the two catch wires at each level and tie if necessary (Figure 8.38 and Figure 8.39). You can trim these shoots above the uppermost wires to give the vineyard row a hedge-like appearance.

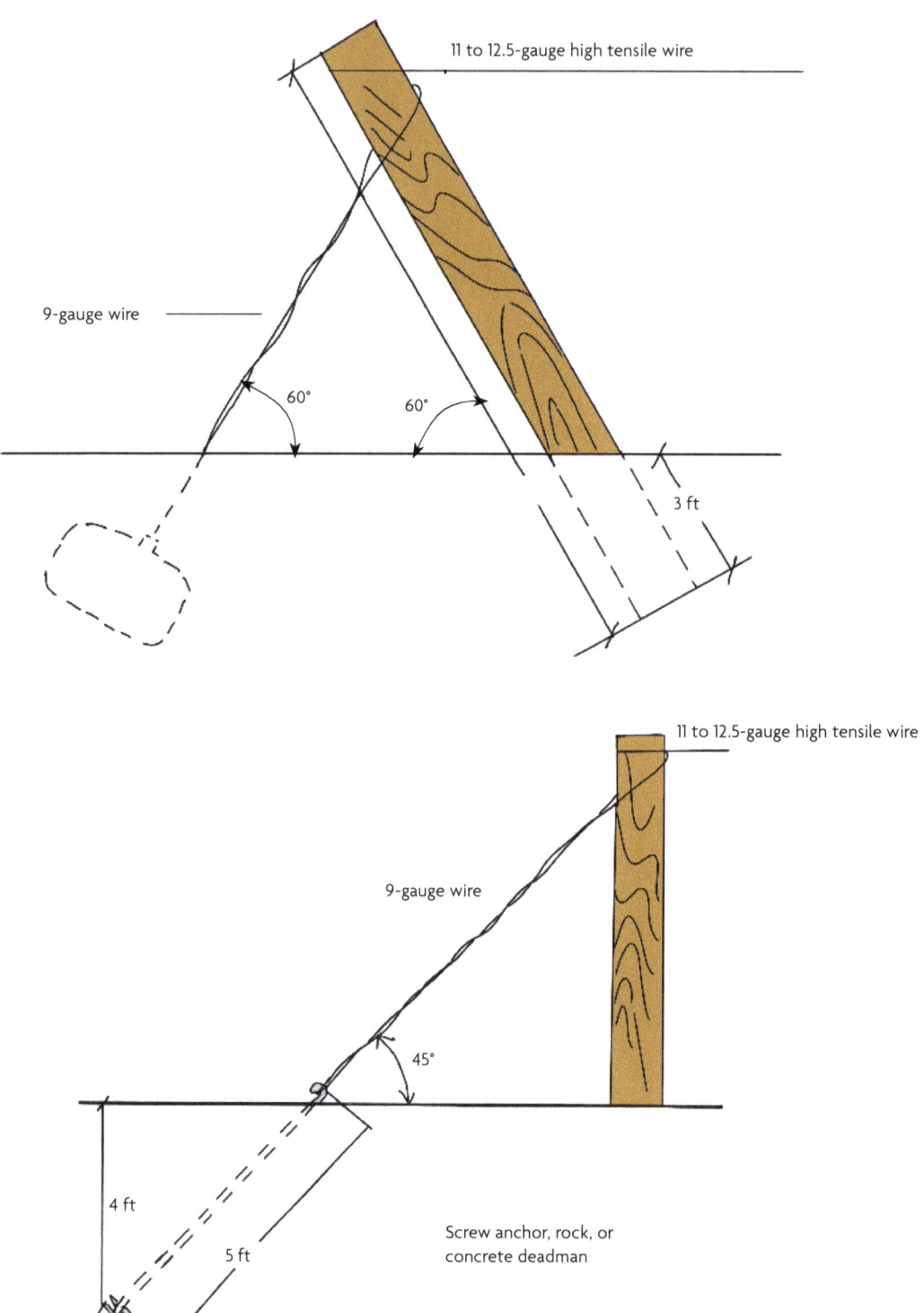

Figure 8.33 (a & b) Inverted "V" bracing system and vertical end post system.

CHAPTER 8 - FRUIT GARDENING • 291

Figure 8.34 Train two or three shoots that grow the first season to a training stake.

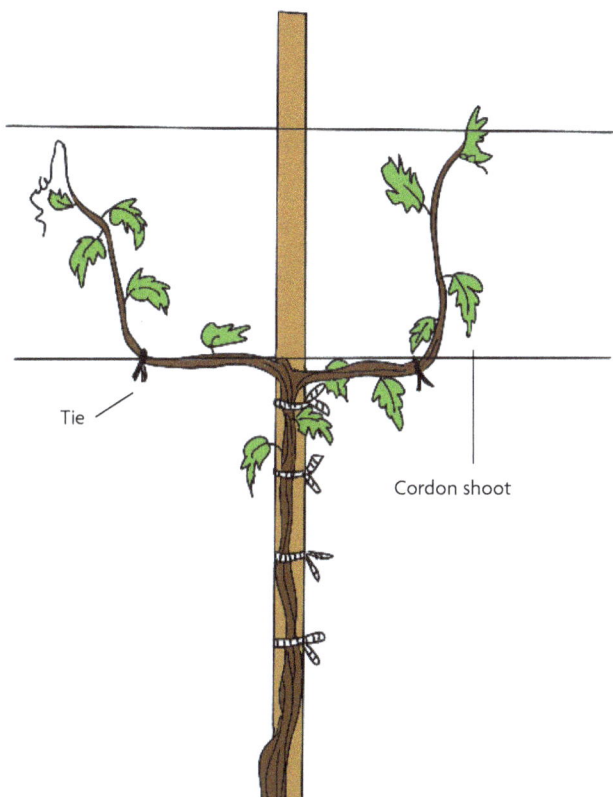

Figure 8.36 Tie new cordon shoots and train horizontally along lower wire.

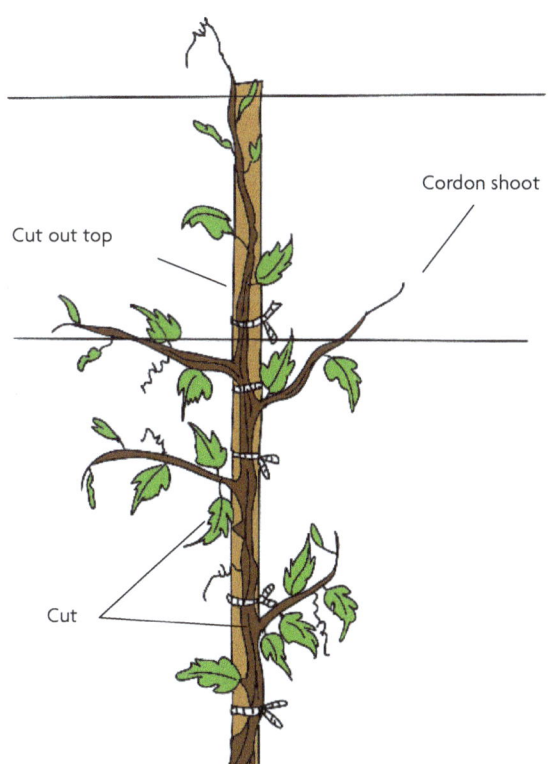

Figure 8.35 Remove trunk growth above first wire and select one lateral branch on left and right sides as cordons.

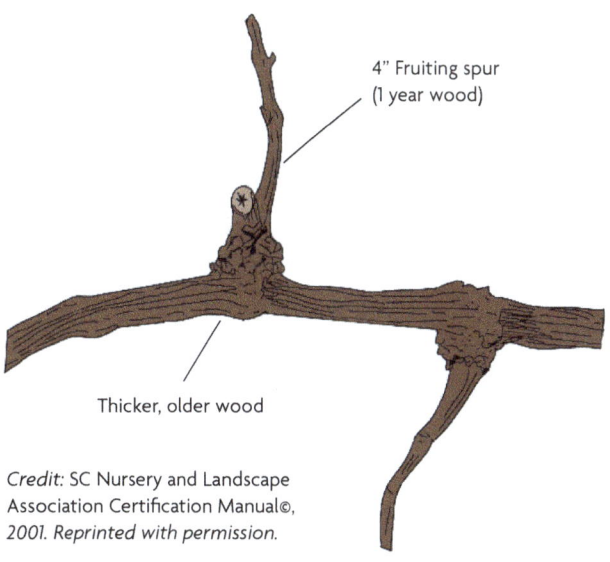

Credit: SC Nursery and Landscape Association Certification Manual©, 2001. Reprinted with permission.

Figure 8.37 Muscadine grape fruiting spur.

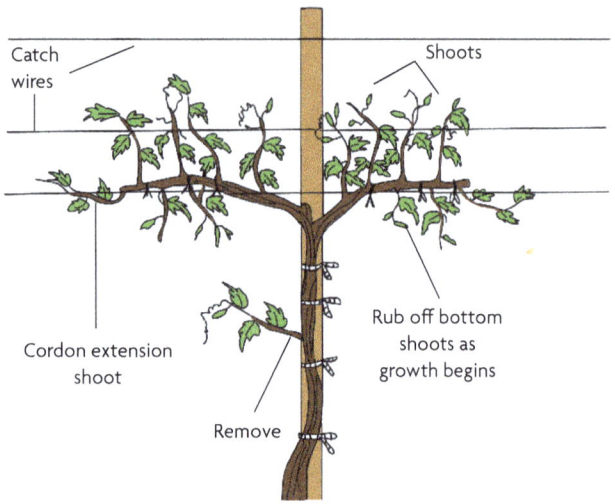

Figure 8.38 Select upward-growing shoots in a Vertical Shoot Position (VSP) trellis system.

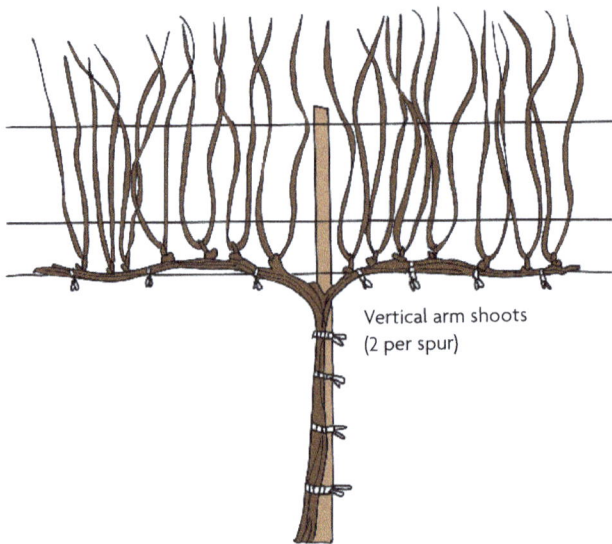

Figure 8.40 Dormant vine trained to Vertical Shoot Position (VSP) system at end of growing season before pruning.

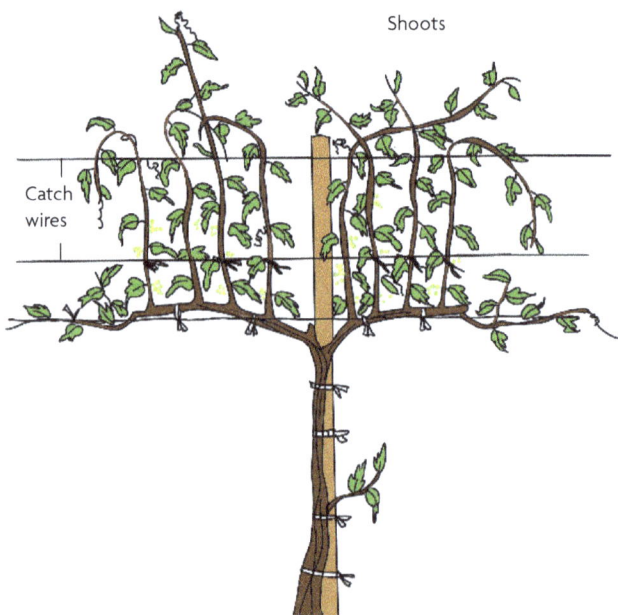

Figure 8.39 Tie selected vertical shoots to the catch wires.

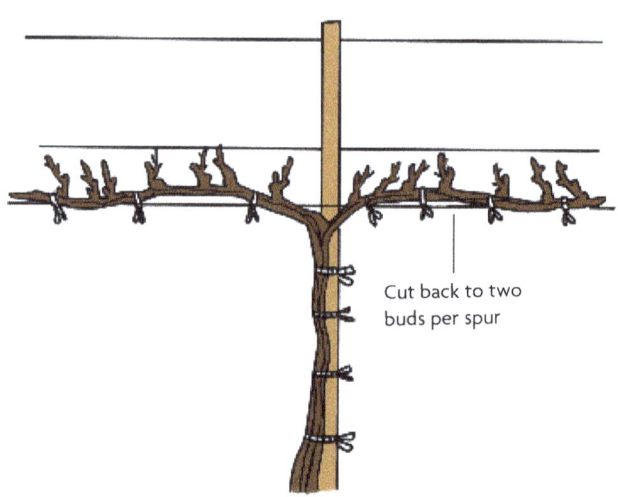

Figure 8.41 Dormant vine trained to Vertical Shoot Position (VSP) system after pruning

Figures 8.40, 8.41, and 8.42 illustrate a mature vine trained to the VSP system before and after dormant pruning, and its growth and fruiting the following summer.

Figure 8.43 illustrates a mature muscadine grape vine before and after dormant pruning.

As you prune new shoots back to spurs in successive years, a single spur can become a many-branched spur cluster. Unless some of these spurs or clusters are removed, the vine may become an entangled, unmanageable mass. Remove every other spur cluster on the cordon, or portions of each cluster, each year. You can develop new shoots growing from the cordon into new spurs to replace the older ones.

Remove tendrils that have wrapped around the cordons. These tendrils become extremely tough and wiry and can girdle shoots or cordons. Removing old fruit stems minimizes sites for overwintering diseases.

Neglected Vines. The first step in managing neglected vines is to return each vine to the basic framework of a main trunk that branches into two permanent arms or cordons. If this framework is not present within the mass of vines, create it by selecting a pair of young canes that arise from the top of the trunk.

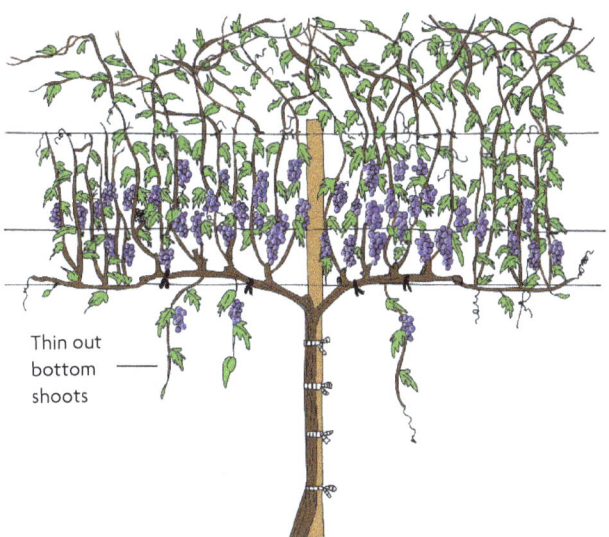

Figure 8.42 Growth and fruiting the following summer.

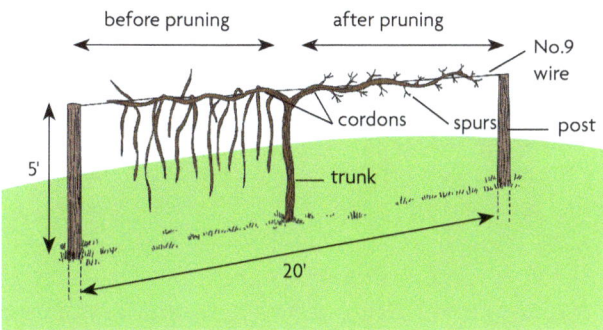

Figure 8.43 Unpruned (left) and pruned (right) cordons of a mature muscadine grape vine trained to a one-wire trellis.

Tie these shoots to the trellis wire when they are 3-5 ft long. Prune out all other shoots that arise from the base or side of the trunk to concentrate growth along the cordons.

Fertilizing

Grape vines require minimal fertilization after they begin fruiting. Too much fertilizer can stimulate excessive vegetative growth at the expense of fruit production, but moderate amounts of fertilizer during the first and second years after planting can result in earlier fruit production.

After planting, but before growth starts, apply 1/2 cup (4 oz) of 10-10-10 fertilizer around each vine. Repeat this application in early summer. Keep the fertilizer at least 6 in. away from the plant.

In the second year, apply 1 cup (8 oz) of 10-10-10 fertilizer around each plant in early spring and again in early summer. For bearing vines, you can apply 2 cups (1 lb) of 10-10-10 per plant in early spring.

Harvesting

It can be challenging to know when to harvest grapes. Many grape varieties dramatically change color to indicate that fruit is beginning to ripen; this color change is called veraison. The best way to find out when grapes are ready to pick is to continually taste a small sample until you find that they are sweet and flavorful. Determining the harvest time of wine grapes requires experience and a means of measuring sugar and acid content.

Harvest bunch grapes by removing entire clusters from the vine with sharp shears. Muscadine grapes typically have an extended ripening period; harvest them every 3-5 days. Harvest individual muscadine berries when ripe (Figure 8.44). Alternatively, harvest ripe berries more quickly by placing a drop cloth underneath the plant and gently shaking the vine. Muscadine fruit with dry stem scars will store well for 7 days or more if refrigerated.

Pest Management

Bunch grapes are susceptible to many diseases, but fungicide sprays can help control disease when used properly. Contact the HGIC for specific fungicide recommendations.

Diseases affect European bunch grapes more severely than American bunch grapes. Downy mildew, Phomopsis cane and leaf spot, and Botrytis blight are serious problems for European bunch grapes, but only

Figure 8.44 Muscadine grapes at harvest time.
Image Credit: Dave Ouellette, Clemson University

minor problems for American bunch grapes. Black rot, anthracnose, powdery mildew, and Pierce's disease can cause devastating damage to all bunch grapes. Muscadine grapes are much less susceptible to disease compared to bunch grapes.

Black Rot. Black rot is a particularly notable disease for bunch grapes and can also be problematic on muscadine grapes. The fungus overwinters in infected canes and fruit and spreads to new growth early in the spring. The fungus reproduces in great quantity and spreads rapidly in recurring waves during each rain, infecting all parts of the vine. Leaf infection appears as tiny, reddish-brown spots on the upper surface of the leaf in early summer; the lesions enlarge and become brown with black borders. A ring of black fungal bodies develops near the outer edge of the brown area. Stem lesions are narrow, sunken, and often split lengthwise on the vine. Small white spots are the first symptom of fruit infection. Affected fruit turn black, shrivel, and dry up. Sanitation is vital in controlling black rot.

Grape Anthracnose. Grape anthracnose overwinters on infected canes and spreads to all new growth during wet periods in early spring. The appearance of anthracnose on fruit, stems, and leaves is easy to distinguish from black rot and other diseases. Fruit infection spots look like bird's eyes with light gray centers and reddish-brown borders. Stem lesions are similar in color and sunken with slightly raised borders. Severely infected leaves become distorted and curl down from the margins. Individual leaf spots are gray with dark borders. Dead areas of leaves may drop out and leave a "shot hole" appearance. Sanitation is vital in controlling anthracnose.

Downy Mildew. Downy mildew attacks all green tissues of grapevines. Initially, lesions are yellowish and oily; eventually, they become angular, yellow to reddish-brown spots. Infected shoots thicken and curl before turning brown and dying. Young fruit become gray when infected. All infected parts, except older fruit, are covered with white fungal growth during moist weather. The fungus overwinters primarily in infected leaves on the ground. Control downy mildew with pre-bloom fungicide sprays.

Powdery Mildew. Powdery mildew also infects all green parts of vines. Symptoms are a white powdery growth on infected parts. When infected before maturity, fruit split and dry up or rot. Infection of mature fruit results in a blotchy appearance or a netlike pattern of scar tissue. The fungus overwinters as black fruiting bodies on the vines and in dormant buds. Control powdery mildew infection using sprays starting at petal fall.

Pierce's Disease. Pierce's disease is caused by a bacterium (*Xylella fastidiosa*) that lives in the xylem of host plants and spreads to grapes via sap-feeding insects such as the glassy-winged sharpshooter. Symptoms appear when bacteria grow and cause significant blockage within the xylem vessels. Symptoms can vary depending on when a vine is infected. During the summer, any of the following symptoms may indicate the presence of Pierce's disease:

- leaves becoming slightly yellow or red along leaf margins, which eventually dry or die in concentric zones.
- fruit clusters shriveling.
- dried leaves falling but leaving the petiole attached to the cane ("matchsticks").
- wood on new canes maturing irregularly, producing patches of green surrounded by mature brown bark.

Shoot growth of infected plants becomes progressively weaker as symptoms become more pronounced. One year after vines are infected, some canes or spurs may fail to bud, and shoot growth may be stunted. New leaves become chlorotic between leaf veins, and scorching appears on older leaves. From late spring through summer, infected vines may grow at a normal rate, but the total new growth is less than that of healthy vines. In late summer, leaf burning symptoms reappear. In chronically diseased vines, portions of the vine may be dead. The last part of the vine to die is often the crown near the soil line; rootstock or scion suckers at the base of the vine may be present for a year or two prior to vine death.

The only control for Pierce's disease is to plant resistant grape varieties. There are no cultural practices, sprays, or rootstocks that reduce the probability of the disease.

Phomopsis Cane and Leaf Spot. Phomopsis cane and leaf spot is especially destructive. Leaves develop small, chlorotic spots with dark centers. Spots may also occur on veins and petioles, and leaf margins may turn under. Dead areas of leaves may drop out, leaving "shot holes." Infected stems have dark brown or black streaks or blotches. Infected fruit become dark brown and brittle. Early-season fungicide sprays are particularly important for control.

Botrytis Blight. Botrytis blight primarily infects at bloom, killing flowers. Fruit may also be infected as the disease progresses through the entire cluster. White berries turn brown, and dark berries become reddish. The fungus overwinters on canes or soil surface. Bloom sprays are essential for control.

Angular Leafspot. Angular leafspot is the primary disease that infects muscadines. Leaf spotting can lead to rapid defoliation that reduces fruit quality and yield.

Bitter Rot. Bitter rot can be problematic for susceptible muscadine cultivars. Bitter rot causes significant fruit losses beginning at bloom and continuing through harvest. Fungicide sprays are particularly important for control. Infection begins during or shortly after bloom.

Ripe Rot. Ripe rot overwinters in stems that carried rotten fruit and can be a problem in muscadines. The fungus can infect fruit at any stage of development, but symptoms are not apparent until the fruit ripens.

Macrophoma Rot. Macrophoma rot can also be a problem for muscadines, particularly for susceptible cultivars. Some years, the infection may be severe enough to warrant spraying.

Grape Root Borer. Grape root borers are very difficult to control and can destroy entire vineyards. The adult grape root borer is a moth that resembles a wasp. Larvae drop from eggs down to the soil, where they begin to feed on the small feeder roots and eventually move into the crown of the vine. Infested vines lose vigor and usually die.

Cultural control measures include mounding soil directly beneath the vines in summer to prevent adult emergence. Landscape fabric may be an alternative to mounding soil; these materials are porous and will allow water penetration, but the weave is too tight for adults to pass through. While these cultural controls can eliminate the adults, they offer no control of moths flying into the vineyard and laying eggs on leaves. The larvae may be small enough to reach the roots through landscape fabric.

Other Insects. Green June beetles, Japanese beetles, and wasps may swarm plants shortly before and during harvest. They are attracted to and feed on ripening fruit. Moderate defoliation is seldom damaging.

Strawberries

Strawberries can be a great addition to South Carolina gardens. They are the first fruit to ripen in the spring, and no other fruit produces berries as soon after planting. They can grow in small spaces and thrive in pots, hanging baskets, and window boxes.

Soil and Site Requirements

Choose a planting location that receives full sun. Strawberries grow best in well-drained soils with a pH between 5.5-6.5. Do not grow strawberries in areas that have previously grown potatoes, tomatoes, peppers, or eggplants; both these vegetables and strawberries are susceptible to verticillium wilt disease.

Types of Strawberries and Selecting Strawberry Varieties

The Alpine strawberry (*Fragaria vesca sempervirens*) originated in the mountains of Italy and is cultivated for its intensely flavored, miniature fruits. Alpine, or "wild," strawberries ripen only a few berries at a time. These make attractive ornamental plants often used as groundcovers, edging plants, and container plants. A wide variety of alpine strawberries can be grown successfully from seed. Unlike other strawberries, alpine varieties grow and produce well in partial shade, especially in warm climates.

The modern hybrid garden strawberry (*Fragaria x ananassa*) is derived from two native strawberries: the Virginia strawberry (*F. virginiana*), found on the east coast, and the Chilean strawberry (*F. chiloensis*), found on the Pacific coast. These hybrids combine the size and firmness of the Chilean strawberry with the high productivity, flavor, and disease resistance of the Virginia strawberry.

The main type of strawberry suited for South Carolina gardens is called a June-bearer. The name June-bearer can be misleading, because these varieties bear most of their crop well before June in South Carolina. June-bearing varieties produce a single, large crop in the spring.

Everbearing or day-neutral types are not affected by daylength and produce smaller harvests throughout the growing season. Most varieties of everbearing strawberries are poor choices for South Carolina, but a few of the newest 'day-neutral' types of strawberries—such as 'Albion' or 'Monterrey'—can grow spring and fall berry crops.

Both climate and soil type affect the performance of strawberry. It is important to plant varieties best suited to your area (Table 8.16). Some cultivars can adapt to many environments, but most have been bred to produce in relatively specific climates.

Purchase certified virus-free strawberry plants from a reputable nursery. Bareroot transplants are most common, but "plug" transplants in plastic trays or pots are also available.

TABLE 8.16 Recommended Strawberry Cultivars for South Carolina

Variety	Region[1]	Comments
June-bearing		
Camarosa	All	Standard cultivar. Large fruit with long spring harvest window. Excellent shelf life.
Camino Real	All	Medium-large, firm fruit with average flavor. Resistant to Verticillium wilt and Phytophthora crown rot (red stele).
Chandler	All	Standard cultivar. Medium-large fruit with medium firmness.
Earliglow	P, M	Medium-large, firm fruit. Resistant to Phytophthora crown rot (red stele).
Ruby June	All	Large fruit. Disease resistant. Considered an alternative to Chandler.
Surecrop	P, M	Resistant to Verticillium wilt, Phytophthora crown rot (red stele), leaf spot and leaf scorch.
Sweet Charlie	M, CP	Medium-large fruit with medium firmness. Resisistant to Phytophthora crown rot (red stele) and powdery mildew. Fruit ripen 7-10 days before Chandler.
Everbearing		
Albion	All	Medium-large, firm fruit. Resistant to Verticillium wilt and Phytophthora crown rot (red stele). Produces large number of runners for an everbearing variety. Best results if planted in fall. Very susceptible to mites.
Eversweet	All	Large fruit. Bred especially for hot southern climates.
Monterey	All	Similar to Albion with slightly larger, but less firm, fruit. Best results if planted in fall.

[1]P – Piedmont; M – Midlands; CP – Coastal Plain

Figure 8.45 Strawberry crowns give rise to leaves, runners, flowers, and fruit.

Growth Cycle

The strawberry crown grows leaves, runners, flowers, and fruit (Figure 8.45). Temperature and daylength greatly affect the growth of strawberry plants. In new plantings, runner production occurs during the longer days and warmer temperatures of summer. In the shorter, cooler days of fall, runner production stops and flower buds form. The flower clusters that develop inside the crown in the fall emerge in early spring. Harvest begins 4-5 weeks after the first flowers open.

Growing Systems

Two different growing methods are used in South Carolina: the matted row system and the annual hill system.

Matted Row System. In the matted row system, plants are grown as perennials. Plants are set out in the spring and fruited the following spring; production may continue for several years. It is a common system in regions with colder climates.

To use this production method, set out strawberry plants at regular intervals within regularly spaced rows, creating a grid pattern. Allow this initial planting to grow, produce runners, and establish daughter plants that produce their own harvest the following spring (Figure 8.46). This crisscrossed network of runners creates a matted tangle of strawberry plants, hence the name. Each matted row produces until the plants become unproductive, usually in 3-4 years. This system is likely the best option for home gardens, as it minimizes annual costs and maximizes garden space.

Planting. The objective during the first growing season is to develop matted 2-ft-wide rows 2 ft apart. In the spring, mark off two rows that are 4 ft apart and 2 ft from the edge of the bed. Set the plants 2 ft apart in the rows so the base of the crown is at soil level (Figure 8.47).

Remove any flowers that grow in spring of the first

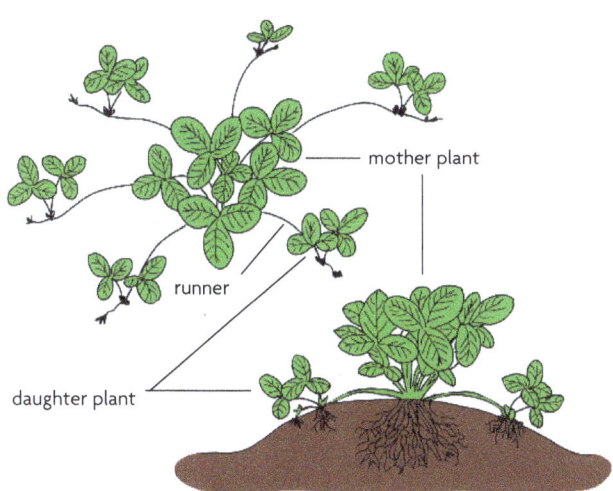

Figure 8.46 Matted row system with mother and daughter plants.

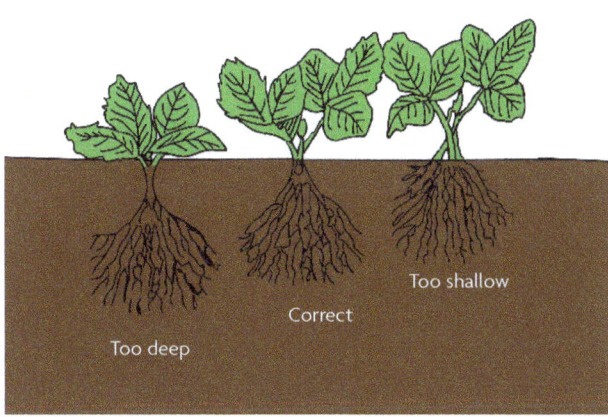

Figure 8.47 Strawberry crowns should be planted at soil level.

year. This improves establishment and channels food reserves into the production of vigorous runners. Allow the runners to develop and form the matted row.

Mulching. Freezing temperatures damage the flowers and fruits of strawberry plants, but the crowns and leaves survive temperatures as low as 15-20°F. In winter, before temperatures fall below 20°F, apply a 2-4-in. layer of wheat straw or pine needles to both the row middles and tops of planted rows. This mulch layer offers adequate cold protection for the strawberry crowns during the winter months. Rake away all but a thin layer of mulch from plants in the spring when there are signs of new growth. This mulch will prevent berries from contacting the soil, helping to reduce fruit rots. If you do not spread mulch in the winter months, apply a 1-2-in. layer to the soil as growth resumes in the spring.

Renovating. Matted row strawberry plantings bear fruit for more than one season and may be productive for up to 3-4 fruiting seasons if properly renovated. The main purpose of renovation is to keep plants from becoming overcrowded.

Renovate strawberry beds after the final harvest following these four steps:

1. Mow the leaves from the strawberry plants. Set the mower blade high enough to avoid damaging crowns.
2. Narrow the 2-ft matted rows into 12-in. strips with a rototiller or hoe. Remove about two-thirds of the plants.
3. Rake out the discarded plants and smooth the soil surface.
4. Broadcast 2 lbs. of 10-10-10 fertilizer per 100 ft^2.

Annual Hill System. In the annual hill system, plants are set out in the fall and fruited the following spring. This system is most efficient when using plastic-mulched beds, as this encourages significant root growth and crown development during the winter. Use drip irrigation under the plastic mulch. Discard strawberry plants after harvest and establish a new planting in the fall.

Planting. When following the annual hill system, set strawberry plants in the fall. Beds should be about 6 in. high at the shoulder, 8 in. high in the center, and 24-26 in. wide (Figure 8.48). For easiest access to the plants, leave an aisle about 24 in. wide between beds.

Obtain best results by mulching the bed with plastic before planting. Place drip irrigation tubing under the plastic. Be sure the bed is well-formed, firm, and moist before installing the plastic. Set plants through slits in the mulch, 12 in. apart, in double rows. Cut off all runners as they form during the season.

Fertilizing and Watering

If using the matted row system, broadcast 2 lb of 10-10-10 fertilizer per 100 ft^2 about two weeks before planting. Fertilize again in early summer and late summer this first year according to the same rate. In late winter of the following years, broadcast 4 lb of 10-10-10 fertilizer per 100 ft^2. Apply fertilizer when leaves are dry and sweep the plants with a broom immediately after the application to prevent fertilizer burn.

Consider watering every day for the first week after planting to help newly set plants establish. Strawberries require 1-1.5 in. of water per week during the growing season.

If using drip irrigation according to the annual hill

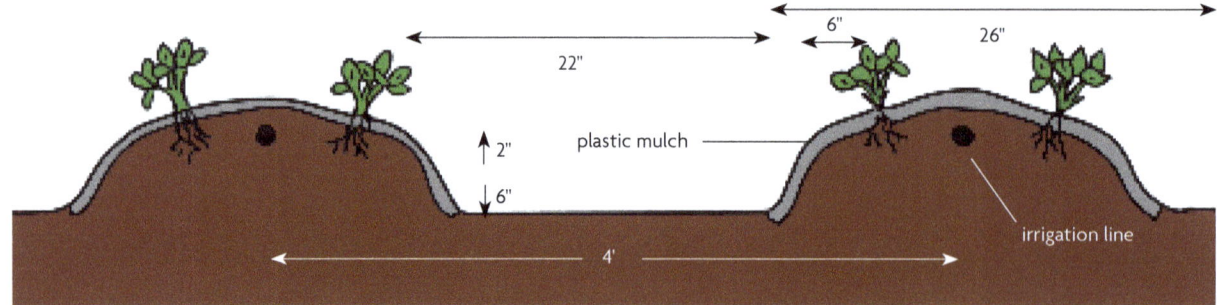

Figure 8.48 Cross-section of bed construction for annual hill system. Note the plastic mulch and drip irrigation tubing which allow beds to be watered without wetting fruit or leaves.

system, it is important to check regularly to determine if the selected time intervals are satisfactory. Irrigation time intervals depend on the temperature, the stage of plant development, and the flow rate of the drip tube. The interval starts out short and increases as the plant develops and daily temperatures rise.

Use an injector, available at many garden centers, for fertigation—the application of fertilizer through a drip irrigation system. Inject calcium nitrate or other water-soluble fertilizer during fall planting and then again weekly between bloom and final harvest.

Harvesting

For best results, harvest strawberries every other day. Leave about one-quarter of the stem attached to the fruit when you pick it. The best time to harvest is in early morning when berries are still cool. Pick only the berries that are fully red. Harvest and discard any diseased or damaged fruit to reduce the incidence of disease and insect pests.

Pest Management

Birds. Birds can cause serious problems during strawberry harvest. The most effective control measure against birds is covering the entire planting with bird netting between harvests.

Mites and Insects. Two-spotted spider mite can cause significant damage to strawberries. Inspect plants and monitor the planting for early signs of mite infestations. Soil insects that affect strawberry plants include ants, white grubs, root weevils, crown borers, and mole crickets. Other pests, such as plant bugs, sometimes feed on flowers and young fruit; this causes a condition known as "catfacing" in which areas of the fruit surface appear deformed or unripe.

Diseases

Botrytis Fruit Rot. Botrytis fruit rot, or gray mold, is the most common fruit disease that affects strawberries. Spores favor cool temperatures and high humidity and are carried by wind and rainfall onto flower parts. The fungus eventually infects the developing fruits, producing soft, light brown areas. With time, the rot spreads over the entire fruit, causing it to shrivel and mummify. It becomes coated with a gray dusting of spores. Handling diseased fruit while picking spreads the disease to healthy berries. The fungus eventually infects emerging leaves in the fall, overwinters, and continues the cycle in the spring.

Sanitation is an important part of managing this disease. Collect and discard any diseased fruits, dead leaves, and other plant debris. Apply protective fungicide sprays starting before bloom and continuing through harvest.

Anthracnose (Colletotrichum acutatum). Anthracnose infects runners, leaf petioles, crowns, fruit, and leaves. Small, dark lesions girdle petioles and runners in the summer, killing the leaves and unrooted daughter plants. The fungus spreads from the infected petioles and runners into the crown of the plant, causing the plants to wilt and die. Round, brown sunken spots appear on infected fruit. Normally, plants die the year after they are infected. Buying disease-free plants is the best control measure.

Verticillium Wilt. The symptoms of verticillium wilt include marginal and interveinal browning and eventual death of outer leaves; inner leaves are stunted and may wilt but tend to remain green. Plants that are fruiting are most severely affected. The first symptoms become noticeable as temperatures increase in late spring. A wide range of annual and perennial crops and weeds, particularly in the tomato family, host the fungi.

The fungus overwinters in soil or plant debris and can penetrate root hairs either directly or through breaks or wounds in roots. Once inside the root, the fungus invades the vascular system, causing plants to wilt and collapse.

Rhizoctonia Root and Crown Rot. Rhizoctonia root rot favors cool weather, while Rhizoctonia crown rot is more prevalent during hot weather. Plants typically collapse as fruiting starts. The undersides of leaves turn purple, and the leaves curl. The disease kills the original crown, and numerous side crowns may develop. It is important to purchase and plant disease-free plants to avoid the introduction and spread of both diseases.

Red Stele Root Rot or Phytophthora Crown Rot. Red stele root rot is caused by *Phytophthora fragariae* and *P. cactorum* and affects plants in poorly drained soils or during long periods of rain. Advanced symptoms include a collapse of plants and a dark red discoloration of the crown. Stunting of plants or wilting of young leaves are the first symptoms, and may appear at any point during the season. Infected plants may remain stunted, or foliage may turn bluish as the entire plant wilts rapidly until total collapse. Wilting is often accompanied by drought symptoms on the leaves, such as browning of leaf margins that progress between the veins.

Phomopsis Leaf Spot. Phomopsis leaf spot has become increasingly prevalent in recent years. The disease starts to develop in the fall, or spring shortly after planting. It spreads rapidly and can kill significant foliage. It remains active as long as there is green foliage on the plants. The earliest symptom is the development of circular, red-to-purple spots on leaflets. The spots enlarge and develop gray centers. Older spots along veins develop into large V-shaped lesions. Flower and fruit infection also occurs. The fungus survives in dead leaves attached to the plants. Apply fungicides when new growth starts and continue in the spring when the disease is a problem. Prevent fruit infection by controlling foliar infection.

Angular Leaf Spot. Angular leaf spot is a bacterial disease that survives in dead plant tissue. It starts as small, angular, water-soaked spots on the undersides of leaves. Spots enlarge but are limited by the veins. Spots coalesce to cover large portions of the leaf and appear as irregular reddish-brown spots on the top of leaves. Heavily infected leaves usually die. The disease favors wet weather with day temperatures of 70°F and night temperatures near or below freezing.

Leaf Spot and Leaf Scorch. Leaf spot and leaf scorch are fungal diseases that cause similar damage and spread in a similar manner. Insects, birds, new plants, and farm equipment carry the fungal spores into new areas. They both cause a loss of foliage that can stunt the entire plant. Severely infected plants may die. During early spring rains, spores from just a few diseased plants can multiply and spread through an entire planting.

Leaf spot shows up first on the upper leaf surface as tiny, round purple spots. The center of the spot becomes gray and then almost white; the border remains purple.

Leaf scorch forms small, dark purple spots on upper leaf surfaces. These spots remain dark purple and have an irregular outline. When numerous spots form and coalesce, the leaves appear to be scorched.

Plant-Parasitic Nematodes. Many nematodes—such as root-knot, lesion, and sting nematodes—are problematic in strawberries. Injured plants appear stunted and may develop symptoms of nutrient deficiency. No chemical control for nematodes is currently available to homeowners. Proper crop rotation is the best way to prevent the build-up of plant-parasitic nematode populations.

Elderberries

Elderberries have a long history of use as both medicine and food and can be a great addition to landscapes and gardens. Elderberries are attractive landscape plants with large compound leaves, large showy flower clusters, and an abundance of dark-colored berries. Bees and butterflies frequently visit the edible flowers, and the fruit is highly attractive to many birds and other wildlife.

Site and Soil Requirements

Elderberries grow best in moist, well-drained soils with a pH between 5.5-6.5. They can tolerate occasional drought and temporarily wet soils, but they are not a good choice for very sandy or marshy sites. Elderberries are tolerant of partial shade conditions but require full sun for optimal flowering and fruit production.

Elderberries grow and spread quickly via suckering, often resulting in an unruly appearance. Whether they enhance your landscape or become a bothersome feature depends largely on their location. With mature heights of 6-10 ft and widths reaching 8 ft, they are not recommended for foundation plantings or inclusion in formal gardens.

Types of Elderberries and Selecting Varieties

Two species of elderberry are commonly grown in gardens and landscapes: American elderberry (*Sambucus canadensis*) and European elderberry (*S.*

nigra). American elderberry is native to the eastern United States.

The elderberry varieties commonly found in garden centers and nurseries are predominantly American elderberry. Varieties such as 'Johns,' 'Adams,' 'Nova,' 'York,' 'Bob Gordon,' 'Ranch,' and 'Wyldewood' all produce well. Some varieties of the European species are grown for their fruit-bearing capabilities, but most are prized for their ornamental features such as purple or lacey foliage.

Elderberries are pollinated by wind and insects. Although they are partially self-fruitful, having more than one cultivar will result in better pollination and higher yields.

Planting and Post-Planting Care

You can purchase elderberries as either bare-root or potted plants. You can also easily propagate plants from softwood or hardwood cuttings.

Plant elderberries at the same depth as their roots. Elderberries have shallow roots, and it's beneficial to irrigate the first year and during dry periods. Mulching helps conserve soil moisture and build up organic matter. Elderberries typically require very little fertilizer.

Pruning

Elderberries require pruning to keep plants attractive and productive. Elderberry plants flower on new growth, so prune during the dormant season. Remove damaged or weak stems and older canes to produce vigorous new growth that produces flowers and fruits.

Elderberries sprout new canes each spring. Second-year canes with lateral branches are usually the most fruitful. Canes become less productive after three or four years; you can prune these back to ground level in the dormant season. It is possible to renovate an overgrown planting by cutting all stems to the ground. Remove rootsuckers at any time to contain the plant's lateral spread.

Harvesting

Harvest elderberry fruit once they are dark purple or black. Individual plants typically ripen over a three-week period. Harvest the fruit by removing the entire berry cluster. Removing the individual berries from clusters can be time consuming; try freezing the entire fruit cluster and then removing the berries while frozen, a method that is quick and leaves little mess.

Avoid green berries, as these are toxic. Harvest with caution, examine fruit clusters carefully, and remove any unripe berries. It is not uncommon for a fruit cluster to contain both immature, green berries and ripe, black berries. Even ripe fruit can be mildly toxic and cause illness if eaten raw in large quantities. The fruit becomes edible through the process of cooking or drying.

Elderberries are excellent for making juice, wine, extracts, syrup, and jam. Mature elderberries can produce about 12-15 lb of fruit per plant.

Pest Management

Elderberries experience relatively few pest and disease problems. However, plants can be susceptible to insects such as the spotted-wing drosophila fly, Japanese beetles, and borers. Cankers, leaf spots, and powdery mildew are the most common diseases, but they are not significant issues in home landscapes.

Chapter 9
Watering Plants and Landscapes

By W. Bryan Smith

LEARNING OBJECTIVES
- Understand the principles of residential irrigation, including basic design.
- Identify types of irrigation, their applications, and basic components.
- Recognize factors that affect irrigation scheduling.
- Be able to explain the process of calibration.

INTRODUCTION

Water is widely considered the most limiting factor in plant growth. Proper irrigation of landscape plants, lawns, and vegetable gardens is one of the most poorly understood aspects of home landscape maintenance. This chapter is divided into several sections that introduce the basic concepts of landscape irrigation. There is a great deal more to proper irrigation design and management than is covered in this chapter, but the concepts introduced here provide a foundation that allows homeowners to keep their home landscape beautiful and vigorous.

IRRIGATION MANAGEMENT

Many in the Southeast view irrigation as a quick fix for problems encountered during a hot, dry summer. Others see it as a method to provide all the water a plant may need on a daily basis. Neither of these views is accurate.

Irrigation is a balancing act. It is an attempt to maintain a given soil moisture range for optimum plant growth.

When the gardener applies too much water, the excess water saturates the root zone and replaces oxygen in the rooting area. Plant roots require oxygen, so the anaerobic (without oxygen) conditions in a saturated or flooded landscape do not provide the ideal growing medium for a plant. Plants in a flooded or saturated area are often referred to as "drowned," which is an apt expression.

When the gardener applies too little water, plants begin to dry and wither. Every plant transpires an amount of water through the stomata in the leaves as a part of the plant's water use and transport/production processes. When a plant finds itself in drought conditions, it usually begins to hoard its water supply by partially closing the stomata. This restricts water flow through the plant and results in slower internal transport processes and wilting. If we allow the plant to be drought-stressed for too long, the plant is weakened and may die. Review Chapter 2 for more information about transpiration.

Irrigation is one method of replacing the water in the soil used by the plants. As previously mentioned, this is a balancing act (Figure 9.1). The gardener must apply enough water to maintain a plant's growth but not so much that the soil is saturated, and the plant drowns. It's important to consider other additions to and subtractions from the landscape's water supply.

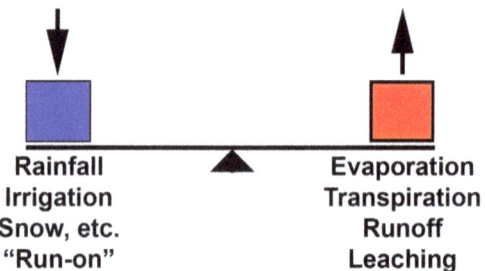

Figure 9.1 The residential landscape water "balancing act."
Image Credit: W. Bryan Smith, Clemson University

Water Additions to the Landscape

Rainfall

Rainfall is an obvious contributor of water to a landscape. Nice, gentle showers provide a great deal of water over a longer period of time, most of which stays in the landscape. Intense thunderstorms, however, often provide water more quickly than it can be absorbed. In this case, the landscape may not receive the full benefit of all the water that fell in the rain gauge. Excess water "runs off" (explained later in the text) and leaves the landscape.

Snow, Sleet, and Hail

Frozen precipitation also contributes water to the landscape, albeit during times of the year when plants may not require very much. "Wet" snow that falls when the temperature is near freezing may contribute up to 1 in. of water for every 6 in. of snowfall, while "dry" snow that falls during much colder weather may contribute just 1 in. of water for every 12 in. of snowfall. Sleet and hail also contribute water, although hail doesn't usually fall in a large enough quantity to provide an appreciable amount of water.

Irrigation

Irrigation is the man-made method of applying water to the landscape. Some concerns that apply to rainfall also apply to irrigation. For example, if water is applied too quickly, some of it may "run off" and provide no benefit to the landscape.

Run-On

To understand run-on, think of the following example:
Assume that one yard is a few feet higher in elevation than the neighboring yard. If there is hard rainfall, some

of the water may "run off" that yard and subsequently "run on" to the lower yard. If the water stays in the lower yard, it contributes to the soil moisture in that landscape. This "run-on" may be beneficial in a dry year, but it may be a continual problem in a wet year if it regularly saturates landscape soil or creates a wet spot. If run-on becomes problematic, some form of drainage (drain tile, etc.) or runoff water diversion (terrace, etc.) may be necessary.

Water Subtractions from the Landscape

Evaporation

Evaporation of water—from puddles, beverage glasses, ponds, and swimming pools—is likely a familiar process. Soil moisture can also be lost from a bare soil surface due to evaporation. Only the top inch or so of soil is subject to evaporation, but in a drought situation, every drop counts. Mulches help reduce soil moisture loss due to evaporation.

Transpiration

Transpiration refers to plant water use. In transpiration, water is taken up by plant roots, moves through plant tissues, and leaves as water vapor through stomata. The term "evapotranspiration," also called "ET" in irrigation publications, refers to plant transpiration plus soil evaporation.

Runoff

Soil accepts water at a certain speed or rate, called the **infiltration rate**. This rate of water movement into the soil varies with soil type, ground cover, previous moisture content, and other factors. When water is applied to the landscape more quickly than the soil can accept it, the excess water "runs off" across the landscape, hence the term "**runoff**."

Water that "runs off" leaves the landscape and is not there when plants need it. If runoff occurs during a thunderstorm, some portion of the rainfall received will benefit the landscape, but not the full amount found in a rain gauge. Quickly moving runoff can also cause soil erosion, creating rills and small gullies in the landscape.

The same principle applies to irrigation. Irrigation generating runoff is not providing moisture for plants. If water is running off during irrigation, stop the irrigation system, allow the water to soak in for an hour or so, and then resume irrigating. If the runoff is due to a steep slope or heavy soils (clays, etc.), consider adjusting the irrigation schedule to water for a shorter amount of time twice a day rather than once for a longer time. This conserves water and ensures the landscape receives all the purchased or pumped water.

Driveways and sidewalks also contribute to runoff losses if sprinklers are not adjusted correctly. Any water applied to a concrete or asphalt surface immediately runs off to the nearest ditch or culvert. Water applied to these areas also create liability problems for the homeowner, especially if an irrigation system turns on unexpectedly while pedestrians are using the sidewalk. Make sure all sprinklers and spray heads are adjusted correctly so they apply water to the landscape, not the pavement.

As runoff moves across a landscape, it can transport substances such as fertilizers and pesticides. The Environmental Protection Agency (EPA) considers runoff to be the leading threat to water quality. Reducing runoff conserves water and protects water quality.

Leaching

Assume that a yard is completely level, the soil is somewhat coarse or sandy, and no runoff occurs during irrigation. If more water is applied than the soil can hold (more on this later in the chapter), the excess water must go somewhere. In this case, the water moves downward through the soil profile. When the excess water moves past the root zone, it has "leached" out of the root zone. The water is still in the soil, but it is too deep for the plants to retrieve. This water has left the landscape just as effectively as if it had run off over the top of the ground. In this case, the threat is to groundwater rather than surface water, as the leached water transports water-soluble compounds.

Determining When to Irrigate

A great deal of irrigation mismanagement occurs simply because few homeowners know when to begin irrigating. Some gardeners wait until plants begin to wilt before adding water, while others are convinced that watering very frequently is beneficial to the plants. There are several ways to determine if a section of the landscape needs water.

Screwdriver Test

Walk around your landscape once or twice a week with a standard screwdriver. Push the screwdriver 4-6 in. into the soil in several places in the lawn and flower beds, digging up a small amount of soil. Feel the soil for moisture. If it feels too dry, it may be time to turn on the irrigation system; if it feels relatively moist, it doesn't require additional irrigation. If the soil feels quite wet, there may be a drainage problem that requires attention.

The screwdriver method has the added advantage of requiring the homeowner to "tour" the landscape regularly, seeing problems or potential problems that may otherwise go unnoticed.

Footprint Test

Walk across the lawn, then turn around and look for footprints (Figure 9.2). If the lawn has adequate moisture, the footprints spring back readily and are not noticeable. If the lawn is stressed due to lack of water or some other condition, the footprints remain obvious for some time. When grass blades are compressed by shoes or feet, low water levels prevent the grass blades from springing back up. If the footprints remain, water the lawn.

Obviously, there are some portions of a yard that do not lend themselves to this method, such as flower beds. Use the screwdriver method in those areas to check soil moisture. Footprinting the lawn provides a good preliminary indication of the moisture condition of flower beds and foundation plantings, but nothing replaces feeling the soil to be sure.

Figure 9.2 Footprints are readily visible in a stressed lawn.
Image Credit: Lambert McCarty, Clemson University

Leaf Check

During dry periods, grass leaves wilt, roll, or fold; use these symptoms as a signal to irrigate to prevent the turfgrass from becoming further stressed or dormant.

Actual Plant Water Use

There are methods available to determine the actual daily water use of various plants. These methods (Penman-Monteith, etc.) are quite involved and require a large amount of information, including solar radiation, wind speed, relative humidity, temperature, and other measurements. This information aids in calculating daily plant water use, and then the land is irrigated according to calculations that show how much water has been removed from the soil.

This method usually requires more daily work than the average homeowner cares to invest. An entire book found on the United Nation's Food and Agriculture website is dedicated to the proper use of the Penman-Monteith method (available free of charge at http://www.fao.org/3/x0490e/x0490e00.htm). Be aware that these methods are available but not practical for residential landscapes.

Measuring Soil Moisture

Since the objective is to maintain soil moisture levels within a certain range to keep plants healthy, one obvious way to determine when to irrigate is to measure the soil moisture. There are many different types and models of soil moisture monitoring devices on the market, ranging from inexpensive plastic devices of questionable accuracy to fully automated, computer-controlled systems that use radio links to turn on the irrigation system and cost thousands of dollars. A happy medium between these two options that might be useful to the homeowner is called a tensiometer.

It is very easy for a plant to withdraw water from saturated soil. As the soil dries, the soil moisture is held more tightly to the soil particles and is increasingly difficult for a plant to withdraw. The tensiometer device measures this soil moisture tension and helps determine how difficult it may be for a plant to retrieve water from the soil.

A **tensiometer** is a hollow, plastic tube with a porous, ceramic tip on one end and a small water reservoir on the other (Figure 9.3). There is a vacuum gauge attached to the side of the tube. The tube is pushed into the soil, ceramic tip first, until the tip is approximately in the center of the plant's root zone (more involved methods use two tensiometers, but that is not necessary for landscapes). The tube and reservoir are filled with water, and a stopper is screwed into the reservoir to seal the tensiometer.

Water is drawn, or wicked, from the inside of the hollow tube through the porous, ceramic tip as the soil around the tip dries. Since the water reservoir connected to the tube is sealed with a stopper, this removal of water creates a vacuum inside the tube, which registers on the vacuum gauge. As the soil dries more, the reading on the vacuum gauge increases. When the vacuum gauge

CHAPTER 9 - WATERING PLANTS AND LANDSCAPES

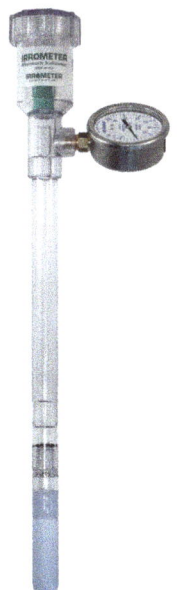

Figure 9.3 A tensiometer used to measure soil moisture. Notice the porous ceramic tip and the vacuum gauge.
Image Credit: IRROMETER Company, Inc.

reading reaches a certain level—indicating a certain minimum level of moisture in the soil—the irrigation system is turned on to replenish the soil moisture.

This is a fairly effective method of monitoring soil moisture and is not too expensive. Tensiometers usually cost between $100-150. The gardener must check the tensiometer at least once each day, though twice a day is better during hot summer months.

The tensiometer may be a tool some homeowners would like to use, but the majority prefer the screwdriver method; it works well and is inexpensive.

Plant Water Needs Vary

Some plants require a great deal of water; others require a very little. A mature pecan tree may use 140-320 gal of water per day depending on tree spacing. A drought-tolerant yaupon holly requires very little water. Homeowners may not have access to the research that provides estimated water needs for all landscape plants, but many can tell from their own experience which plants seem to use more water and which plants use less.

Consider the relative water needs of potential plants for a landscape before designing the landscape. If a pecan tree and a yaupon holly are planted in the same bed, neither receives appropriate irrigation. If the bed is irrigated for the needs of the pecan tree, the holly drowns; if the bed is irrigated for the needs of the holly, the pecan tree withers and dies. Plan bed plantings with an idea of the plants' water requirements as well as the color and foliage to make the best use of the irrigation system and ensure a healthy landscape.

How Much Water?

Quite a bit of water use information is available for agronomic crops such as tomatoes, cotton, and peaches. Most of this information comes from research that compares crop yields (and other factors) to the amount of water applied. However, there are many landscape plants for which it is hard to find water use information. Homeowners simply don't know if plant A requires 2 gal or 10 gal of water each week. Finding all available figures and trying to apply them to a landscape irrigation schedule can be overwhelming.

Fortunately, there is a rule of thumb for residential irrigation. If the water requirements of a plant are unknown, start by applying 1 in. of water per week (Figure 9.4). Monitor the landscape at least weekly and adjust the amount as needed for each section. Note that this is a starting point; some plants may take more, and others may require less.

The amount of water required by any plant varies with type of plant, stage of plant growth, climate, and time of year. An irrigation system programmed to apply the correct amount of water to a landscape each week in

Figure 9.4 One inch of water per week is a good starting point for any Southern landscape.
Image Credit: W. Bryan Smith, Clemson University

April will fall far short of the landscape's water need in July. The climate in July is warmer, less humid, and more stressful to the plant, all of which increase the plant's water needs. Likewise, an irrigation system programmed to apply the correct amount of water in July greatly overwaters the landscape in October. Again, the 1 in. per week is simply a starting point. Adjust the irrigation schedule throughout the year to match the varying water needs of the landscape.

How does 1 in. of water translate into time on an irrigation timer? Quite simply, it doesn't.

Each section, or "zone," of irrigation may have different nozzles, closer or wider sprinkler spacing, and a host of other factors that change the application rate of that zone. The only way to determine how much water is applied in a given time period is to calibrate the sprinkler system.

Begin by randomly placing six to eight straight-sided cans in a particular irrigation zone (Figure 9.5). Irrigate that zone for the time currently set on the timer and measure the depth of water in each can with a tape measure. The average depth found in the cans is the actual amount of water applied to that zone of the landscape. This method is a quick and easy way to determine the amount of water applied to a zone with no math required. If the average amount measured in the cans is not enough, increase the time the zone operates and measure again. If the amount in the cans is too much, decrease the time the zone operates and measure again. This method can help homeowners find the proper starting point for their irrigation system.

Do not use a single can in this method; it is too likely that the homeowner will unintentionally choose the driest or wettest spot in the sprinkler zone. Use several cans to get a good idea of the average water depth applied to the entire zone. Repeat this process in each zone to account for differences in nozzle sizes and spacings (Figure 9.6).

The key word for an irrigation system is management.

Figure 9.5 Place several cans in random spots when calibrating your sprinkler system.
Image Credit: Kayla Rutherford, Clemson University

Figure 9.6 Measure the amount in each can. The average is how much water was applied.
Image Credit: Kayla Rutherford, Clemson University

An unmanaged irrigation system can be more of a hindrance than a help. Walk through your landscape every week or two and note the condition of the plants. If the soil appears drier than it should be and the plants seem stressed, increase the amount of water applied. If the plants seem to be suffering and the soil seems too wet, decrease the amount of water.

Automatic irrigation timers relieve homeowners of the burden of turning valves on and off. They do not consider a landscape's changing needs and therefore cannot replace a homeowner's management. The key to irrigation and a healthy landscape is management, management, management.

One Inch of Water

Most homeowners have no idea how many gallons of water are required to properly irrigate their landscape. A simple comparison may help by providing a frame of reference and prevent a nasty shock from an unexpected water bill.

An average household in South Carolina uses 120-150 gal of water per person per day. Using the 150 gal per person per day figure, a four-person household uses 4,200 gal of water each week.

When a homeowner applies 1 in. of water each week to 1 acre of land, the homeowner uses 27,154 gal of water. This is approximately six times the normal water use for a four-person household.

The moral to this example is simple: if a landscape is irrigated properly, the homeowner will receive a higher water bill.

Winter Irrigation

Winter landscape irrigation has long been considered something of an oxymoron in the Southeast. A good portion of South Carolina's 48-52 in. of annual rainfall finds its way to earth during this time. Plant growth slows considerably during this time—or stops if a plant is dormant—and temperatures are cool. Plant water needs during the winter should be met by rainfall.

There is a time in the winter when it may be beneficial to irrigate lawns in the South. First, note that water holds heat energy. One simple example of this: heat a wet dish towel and a dry dish towel to the same temperature. Place both towels on the counter and check them for warmth 30 min later. The wet dish towel will be warmer simply because the cotton and water in the wet dish towel retains more heat than the cotton alone in the dry dish towel.

Similarly, moist soil retains heat more readily than dry soil. During a winter day, the sun can warm the soil surface. If the soil is moist, it absorbs more heat and loses heat more slowly during the evening and night. Lawn grasses subject to cold damage may suffer less cold injury after irrigation due to the longer heat retention of the moist soil.

It is not necessary to irrigate weekly or even bi-weekly during the winter. However, if there has been an extended dry period (about 3 weeks or more), adding 1 in. of water to the landscape during a warm winter day may help prevent cold injury to cold-sensitive lawns.

Irrigation Frequency

Homeowners often ask how frequently they should irrigate a particular plant or lawn. There are a few rules of thumb to use as starting points. Adjust these general rules based on planting practices, climate, and plant size—or root ball size, if planting new material.

New Sod

Irrigate new sod daily with 0.2 in. of water each day for 10-14 days or until established.

Newly Planted Ornamentals

Irrigate newly planted ornamentals as needed. Smaller plants may need water added once or twice per week; large plants installed with small root balls may need water daily. Test the root ball with your finger before watering, but do not allow the root ball to dry out.

Landscapes With High Water Use Plants

Irrigate landscapes planted with high water use plants once or twice a week depending on soil type (more on that in the next section).

Landscapes With Moderate Water Use Plants

Irrigate landscapes with medium water use plants as needed based on signs of drought and soil moisture.

Landscapes With Low Water Use Plants

Do not irrigate landscapes planted with low water use plants. Generally, rainfall alone is sufficient.

Time of Day and Irrigation

The best time of day to irrigate is the subject of some debate. One group suggests that early morning is the best time, while another group claims that afternoon is best. Very few people consider night irrigation to be a viable alternative due to concerns of increased disease pressure.

From a conservation standpoint, daytime is a poor time to irrigate. Daytime temperatures and wind speeds are higher, resulting in increased evaporative water loss. Daytime humidity is lower, which accelerates evaporation. Solar radiation from the sun also contributes to a higher evaporative loss. Estimates of water loss during daytime irrigation range from 20-30%, depending on humidity, wind speed, and temperature. In effect, the homeowner paid for 1 in. of water and received the benefit of just 0.7 in.

Instead, irrigate at night. Nighttime temperatures and wind speeds are much lower, which means lower evaporative losses during irrigation. Nighttime humidity is higher, which also reduces evaporation. There is no sun, so solar radiation does not contribute to water evaporation. Estimates of water loss during nighttime irrigation range from 10-15%—once again depending on humidity, wind speed, and temperature. The homeowner paid for 1 in. of water and received the benefit from 0.85 in. or more by irrigating at night.

So a homeowner conserving water will have more disease problems, correct? Consider a commonplace, unremarkable event that happens each evening in South Carolina—dewfall. If a person walks across a lawn in the evening, their shoes quickly become wet. The leaves of the plants in the landscape are moist from dewfall and remain that way until the dew naturally dries in the morning. For simplicity, call this time frame the "leaf wetness period." This is not a true "wetting" event, but moisture does remain on the leaves for this entire period.

If you add water to the landscape during this time by irrigating, you are not introducing a new factor to the disease equation—moisture already exists on the leaves. However, if irrigation begins in the evening before dewfall, it can extend the leaf wetness period and provide more time for fungi and bacteria to sporulate, germinate, and get a foothold on the plant to start a disease. Likewise, if irrigation begins later in the morning before the dew has dried, the leaf wetness period is extended due to the extra volume of water that must dry from the leaves.

With these concepts in mind, it is apparent that irrigating during the night should not cause an increase in disease pressure. There are microclimates in certain landscapes that may react adversely to nighttime irrigation, but the majority of landscapes in South Carolina respond well with no disease increase. However, if you extend the leaf wetness period by irrigating before dewfall or before the dew completely dries, there is a risk of increasing disease problems.

From a conservation standpoint, the best time of day to begin irrigating is any time after dewfall. The irrigation cycle should end several hours before sunrise to allow excess water to soak into the landscape so the leaves dry within the normal time period the next morning. Many irrigation system installers program systems to begin irrigation between 11:00 p.m. and 2:00 a.m.

As with any new practice, try this irrigation timing for your landscape and monitor plants for several weeks. If you notice an increase in disease pressure, irrigate in the morning after the dew dries from the plant leaves.

Turf diseases seem to flourish when temperatures are moderately warm and the turf is moist, which describes spring and fall nighttime climates in South Carolina. Monitor the landscape carefully during these times. If disease pressures increase, change the irrigation schedule to late morning, watering for a month or two in the early spring and again in the late fall. Move back to nighttime watering during the summer months, after the temperatures raise and the climate becomes less humid.

One final caution: do not program your system to begin watering between 4:00 a.m. and 7:00 a.m.

Local municipalities try to keep reservoirs filled for the "morning rush" of showers and baths in the community. If several residents have irrigation systems running during this time, the reservoirs quickly deplete and the water pressure for the community is much lower than it would be otherwise. Be a good neighbor.

IRRIGATION AND SOIL TYPE

The soil type found in a landscape is the most frequently overlooked aspect of irrigation design and operation. The most important property of a soil for an irrigator is the water-holding capacity of the soil. Soils hold water!

Only by understanding that concept can homeowners create a well-managed irrigation system and healthy landscape.

Different soil types hold different amounts of water. As described in Chapter 1, sandy soil is made up of large particles that are visible to the naked eye. Large soil particles mean large pore spaces between the particles. These large pore spaces allow water to drain quickly and easily through the soil. Sandy soils also have very little charge (a low cation exchange capacity; see Chapter 1). Due to these factors, sandy soils drain quickly and do not hold much water.

Clay soils, on the other hand, are made up of very fine, microscopic particles. These tiny particles fit together tightly, resulting in tiny pore spaces. The tiny pore spaces do allow water to move through them but at a much slower pace than it would in sandy soils. Clay soils also have a much higher cation exchange capacity than sandy soils. Therefore, clay soils drain more slowly and hold more water than sandy soils.

There are established estimates of water-holding capacity based on soil texture—based on a given range of soil water tension, which is beyond the scope of this chapter. Coarse sands may hold 0.05 in. of water per 1 in. of soil depth; loams may hold up to 0.18 in. of water per 1 in. of soil depth, and clays may hold up to 0.17 in. of water per 1 in. of soil depth. Not all of this water is available to the plants in the landscape, but these figures help schedule irrigation frequency based on soil type.

How do these numbers help manage an irrigation system? First, assume that most landscape plants have a rooting depth of about 10 in. If the landscape has a coarse, sandy soil that holds 0.05 inches of water per 1 in. of soil depth, multiply the 10 in. of rooting depth times 0.05 in. of water per inch of depth of water holding capacity results in 0.50 in. of water held within that rooting depth. If more than 0.50 in. of water is applied at any one time, the excess water moves into the soil and down through the soil profile below the root zone. The extra water simply moves out of the root zone to an area that is not accessible by the plant. This is called **leaching**. The excess water can and will take some nutrients or fertilizer with it as it moves downward.

We previously presented the idea of applying 1 in. of water to the landscape each week; if homeowners can only apply ½ in. of water at any one time, they need to irrigate landscapes with sandy soils twice per week, ½ in. of water each time. This provides the 1 in. of water needed by the landscape and prevents leaching of water and nutrients out of the root zone.

A clay or clay loam soil holds 0.17 in. of water per 1

in. of soil depth. Using the same 10 in. of rooting depth times 0.17 in. of water per 1 in. of depth shows that the clay soil can hold 1.70 in. of water in the 10-in. root zone. The 1 in. of water required can be applied just once each week with little concern for leaching as long as runoff does not occur during irrigation.

From all this information, we can establish two rules of thumb. First, irrigate landscapes with sandy soils twice per week, about ½ in. of water each time. Second, irrigate landscapes with clay and clay loam soils once per week, about 1 in. at a time. Note that some very sandy coastal plain landscapes benefit from three irrigations per week due to microclimate and soil type. Monitor your landscape and discuss this with your irrigation contractor or Extension agent.

There is a popular misconception that you should water landscapes daily. Daily irrigation promotes shallow root growth and makes plants less drought tolerant, less stable, and much less hardy. The plants are forced to retrieve most of their nutrients from the tiny root zone, which gives them a limited window of opportunity to retrieve fertilizers. Daily irrigation can also encourage the growth of many weeds, such as nutsedge, crabgrass, and annual bluegrass. Wetting the foliage every day enhances the environment that diseases need to flourish and usually increases disease pressure in the landscape.

There are only a few times when daily irrigation is appropriate, as stated previously in this chapter:

- Newly Planted Sod. Irrigate new sod with 0.2 in. of water each day for 10-14 days or until established; this keeps the sod moist until the roots grow well into the native soil below the sod. After this time, gradually decrease irrigation to once or twice per week depending on soil type.
- Potted or Containerized Plants. The soil media used in many potted plants is very porous and well-drained, with very little water-holding capacity. There are cases where you should irrigate these plants daily or multiple times each week.
- Newly Planted Ornamentals. Irrigate these plants as needed. Some smaller plants may need water once or twice per week; other large plants installed with small root balls may need water daily. Test the root ball with your finger before watering, but do not allow the root ball to dry out.

Plants use more water in extremely hot weather. In a sandy soil, weather above 95°F may require irrigating three times per week. Since coarse sand will only hold about 0.5 in. of water in the rooting area, apply 0.4-0.5 in. three times per week. Clays hold more water, but during hot days, it may be helpful to water them twice a week. Do not water every day, but watch the landscape, dig into the soil with a screwdriver to check the soil moisture by hand, and adjust the irrigation schedule as needed.

Another often overlooked property of soil type is **infiltration capacity**, which is the rate at which a particular soil can absorb water. Most sandy soils have a high infiltration capacity. These soils can accept water quickly due to their large pore spaces, which means they seldom cause excessive runoff. Clay soils have a much lower infiltration rate; they can hold quite a bit of water, but due to their small pore spaces, they cannot absorb it quickly. If an irrigation system is designed to apply water too rapidly, it runs off. Runoff can be especially problematic in landscapes with clay soil and moderate to steep slopes.

If runoff does occur from a clay soil landscape, try splitting the irrigation cycle on the same day. For instance, apply ½ in. of water during the first irrigation cycle, then another ½ in. of water later that same day; this allows time for the previously applied water to soak into the ground before the second watering. Another option is to use smaller nozzles in the sprinklers to apply water more slowly and allow them to run longer. Be aware that smaller nozzles also decrease the wetted diameter of the sprinkler, so there is a limit to how much you can lower the application rate of the system while still uniformly applying water to the landscape.

Polyacrylamide

Polyacrylamide (PAM) is marketed in many areas as a water-saving soil additive. It is a synthetic compound typically sold as soft, translucent granules or beads. PAM is incorporated into the soil and soaks up moisture in wet soils, expanding somewhat as it does. As the soil dries out, the PAM releases moisture back into the soil. It could be considered an artificial organic matter in this regard, since it basically increases the water holding capacity of the soil in which it is incorporated.

In most instances, PAM does not reduce the water needs of landscape plants. Amending the soil with PAM simply helps the soil hold more water.

PAM breaks down over time and needs to be reapplied every 3-5 years. Due to this and the relatively high application expense, PAM is not considered a viable option for landscapes. Sufficient quantities of organic matter provide a similar—if not greater—benefit for a lower cost. PAM may be useful in containerized plantings, such as trees placed on city squares or hanging baskets in front of a home. The PAM increases the water holding capacity of the soil in the container, allowing more water to be added to the container at one time, reducing the irrigation frequency.

IRRIGATION EQUIPMENT

There are an incredible number of irrigation devices on the market today: sprinklers, spray heads, misters, spray stakes, and drip emitters are just a few. Many of these products are known by several different names. Some products are easy to confuse with another type of product that applies water in an entirely different manner. This section of the chapter does not cover every individual piece of landscape irrigation equipment, but it does cover the major types of equipment and help provide a good, basic understanding of proper application methods for each type.

Sprinklers

Impact Sprinklers

The typical yard sprinkler is the most common example of irrigation equipment. This device was originally developed by a citrus grower in Florida in 1932. Impact sprinklers are made of brass or plastic and come in many different sizes (Figures 9.7 and 9.8).

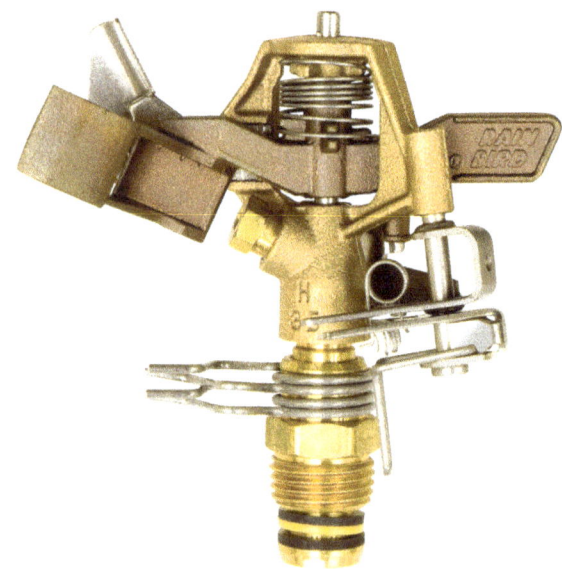

Figure 9.7 A typical brass impact sprinkler.
Image Credit: RainBird International, Inc.

Figure 9.8 A typical plastic impact sprinkler in operation.
Image Credit: W. Bryan Smith, Clemson University

As the name implies, the impact sprinkler operates using an impact motion. First, the curved arm of the sprinkler moves into the water stream exiting the sprinkler nozzle. The force of the water stream pushes against the curved sprinkler arm, forcing it away from the stream. The arm rapidly moves away from the stream but is slowed and eventually stopped by a large spring attached to the arm. The large spring then forces the arm back toward and into the stream of water. The "impact" of the arm hitting the sprinkler frame as it is forced back into the stream of water moves the sprinkler slightly to one side. The process then repeats itself, providing the sprinkler rotation and the familiar "chk-chk-chk" sound common to impact sprinklers.

The first impact sprinklers were of the "stand-up" variety, meaning they were permanently attached to standing pipes or risers in the area to be irrigated. Impact sprinklers are still used on risers today in many contexts, including vegetable gardens, frost protection systems for orchards and small fruits, and large landscape beds.

Mowing around permanent sprinklers in a landscape is difficult. Grass must be trimmed manually near the sprinklers and occasionally, one of the sprinklers falls victim to an inattentive worker on a mower. The "pop-up" sprinkler was developed to alleviate this problem (Figure 9.9).

Sprinkler manufacturers make cast iron or plastic recessed cases for sprinklers that can be placed directly into the lawn. Each case has a 4-6-in. diameter lid covering the opening and a spring-loaded extending sleeve inside. When water pressure is applied, the sprinkler extends approximately 4 in. above the landscape and irrigates the area. When the water pressure is removed, the spring pulls the sleeve down and lowers the sprinkler.

Figure 9.9 Typical plastic pop-up impact sprinkler.
Image Credit: RainBird International, Inc.

Figure 9.10 Typical rotor and gear drive pop-up sprinklers.
Image Credit: (A) RainBird International, Inc., (B) Hunter Industries

The pop-up impact sprinkler provides a convenient, inconspicuous way to irrigate lawns. Mowers can mow over the retracted sprinklers to eliminate a considerable amount of hand trimming. Pop-up impact sprinklers are still used in many areas today, especially to irrigate golf courses and sports fields.

There are two main drawbacks to pop-up impact sprinklers. First, a high-vacuum lawn mower can forcefully pull up on the sprinkler lid when passing over a retracted sprinkler. Occasionally, the intense suction of the mowers can draw up and chop off the sprinkler. This is not a regular occurrence but can happen often enough to irritate homeowners.

Second, in some landscapes, sand and dirt washes into the casing during irrigation, eventually lodging in the pop-up sleeve area and causing the sprinkler to remain extended when the water pressure is turned off. Some turf grasses can also grow into the casing and cause problems with sprinkler retraction.

Rotor and Gear Drive Sprinklers

Irrigation equipment manufacturers saw the drawbacks to pop-up impact sprinklers and the need for a different sprinkler design to overcome these problems. They sought to design a sprinkler without the large, open cavity of the pop-up impact. The answer was a sprinkler with an internal drive mechanism.

Rotor and gear drive sprinklers are similar in appearance and operation (Figure 9.10). The two designs have different internal drive mechanisms, but both operate based on a flow of water moving past some internal component.

When pressure is applied to the sprinkler, a single, 1-in.-diameter shaft extends 4 in. above the sprinkler body (Figure 9.11). A portion of this shaft rotates, driven by the internal drive mechanism below. There is a wiper seal around the shaft to prevent dirt and soil entry into the sprinkler, which eliminates many of the problems associated with pop-up impact sprinklers.

There is an additional benefit to this design. The 1-in. shaft has such a small top that it is almost impossible to see in the landscape when the sprinkler retracts.

Stream Rotors. Stream rotors are another type of gear drive or rotor sprinkler (Figure 9.12). The usually irrigate a smaller area than a standard pop-up impact, gear driven, or rotor sprinkler.

Figure 9.11 Gear drive sprinkler in operation.
Image Credit: W. Bryan Smith, Clemson University

Figure 9.12 Stream rotor sprinklers in operation.
Image Credit: Hunter Industries

Figure 9.13 A half-circle spray head in operation.
Image Credit: W. Bryan Smith, Clemson University

"Normal" sprinklers (impact, gear drive, and rotor) irrigate with a single stream of water that rotates back and forth. Stream rotors irrigate with multiple streams of water (usually six or more) that rotate over the area they irrigate. Many homeowners like stream rotors simply because they like to see the multiple streams of water.

Stream rotors will not replace the larger rotor or gear drive sprinklers because of the smaller diameter of throw. They are well-suited to smaller lawn areas where the normal diameter of throw of a standard gear drive or impact sprinkler is too large. Gardeners can use stream rotors throughout a lawn, but the smaller throw diameter means sprinklers must be closer together, there must be more of them, there are more trenches and pipes, and they are more expensive to install.

Spray Heads

Spray heads are aptly named: they quite literally spray a pattern of water over an area. There is no moving stream of water; the spray head simply pops up and sprays water, covering the entire area at once.

The pattern of irrigation for a spray head is determined by the nozzle. Sprinklers only offer a choice of nozzle sizes—pattern or arc adjustments are set in the sprinkler body. You can purchase spray head nozzles in a wide variety or patterns, including full circle, one-half circle, one-quarter circle, one-third circle, and a host of others (Figure 9.13). Larger and smaller nozzles are available in each pattern for different diameters of throw. Nozzles with 15-, 20-, 24-, and 30-ft diameters of throw are common. Adjustable-arc nozzles are also available, as are "rectangular-pattern" nozzles for areas between a sidewalk and a street.

You can place spray head nozzles on standing pipes or risers using an adapter if you don't need them to pop up. You can purchase spray head bodies in a number of different pop-up heights—typically from 2-12 in.—for different applications (Figure 9.14). Spray head bodies and nozzles are usually purchased separately due to the wide array of available body sizes and nozzle patterns.

Spray heads are usually placed in shrubbery and ornamental beds. They may also be used in lawn areas that are too small for sprinklers and stream rotors.

Do not place spray heads and sprinklers on the same irrigation section or zone. Spray heads apply water at a

Figure 9.14 Spray heads come in many different pop-up heights.
Image Credit: RainBird International, Inc.

much faster rate than stream rotors and sprinklers—in most cases, almost twice as quickly. Due to this, never attach spray heads to a sprinkler section or zone. A spray head added to the end of a sprinkler zone applies water twice as quickly as the sprinklers, flooding the area irrigated by the spray head. If the irrigation timing for that zone is decreased to prevent flooding the spray head area, the sprinkler areas suffer.

Sprinklers, spray heads, and drip irrigation components are three distinctly different types of irrigation equipment. Each should be the only type of irrigation equipment used in a specific zone or section.

Drip Irrigation

Drip irrigation is different from conventional irrigation methods. Sprinklers and spray heads apply water to an entire area, while drip irrigation components apply water only to the root zone of a plant. This provides needed water to the plant without irrigating large portions of unplanted ground that may harbor weeds and weed seed.

Drip irrigation systems apply water directly to the ground (with some exceptions). You can water an area or zone via a drip irrigation system at any time of day with little concern for disease pressure, since the irrigation does not wet the plant foliage. Applying water directly to the ground also makes drip systems highly efficient; generally, drip irrigation is considered 90-95% efficient.

Drip irrigation has gained wide acceptance in the residential irrigation market over the last few decades. Initially, many irrigation installers did not include drip irrigation in their designs simply because they were not familiar with the equipment or proper installation practices. However, the benefits of drip have slowly made it an indispensable part of an irrigation designer's toolbox.

There are a number of pieces of equipment that make up a successful drip irrigation system. Understanding what these pieces are and why they work better than simple "holes in a pipe" allows you to use a drip irrigation system to its fullest advantage.

Drip Emitters

The drip emitter is the heart of a drip irrigation system. A drip emitter "emits" water; more importantly, it regulates the water flow (Figure 9.15). Consider a long pipe placed in a flower bed with holes drilled every 1-2 ft. If you attach a garden hose to this pipe and turn on the water, a lot of water squirts out of the first hole in the pipe. The second hole also provides significant water, but not quite as much as the first; there is a slightly lower

Figure 9.15 A ½ gallon per hour drip emitter in operation.
Image Credit: W. Bryan Smith, Clemson University

water pressure. Each successive hole provides slightly less water than the one before it. The last hole in the pipe applies substantially less water than the first one.

A drip emitter overcomes this problem. Each emitter provides a given flow of water. The emitter is designed so that the flow rate changes very little with changes in pressure. If you installed emitters in each hole in the pipe in the previous example, the first emitter would regulate the water flow of the first hole, providing quite a bit less than the unregulated hole did. The second emitter would regulate the rate of flow from the second hole to approximately the same as the first. The last emitter would also regulate flow from the last hole to provide about the same flow rate as the first emitter. The irrigation system becomes one that applies the same amount of water to each plant simply by installing emitters.

Drip emitters come in a myriad of shapes, sizes and colors. Some are pressure-compensating, meaning their flow rate changes very little with variations in pressure. Others are of a turbulent-flow design, which is less expensive but allows a little more variation in flow with pressure change. Either type works well in a typical landscape.

There are three standard emitter flow rates: 1/2 gph (2 lph), 1 gph (4 lph), and 2 gph (8 lph) per hour. These flow rates are used internationally. Emitters made in the United States are sold with the "gallon per hour" flow listing, while emitters made overseas are sold with the "liter per hour" flow listing. A single manufacturer may make a number of different emitter styles, but each style is likely offered in these three flow rates (Figure 9.16).

A manufacturer normally uses the same emitter body of a given style for all three flow rates of emitters sold. Sometimes, the emitter body will be color-coded

Figure 9.16 Emitters come in all shapes and sizes. These emitter styles are made by different companies but provide the same flow.
Image Credit: W. Bryan Smith, Clemson University

based on flow rate; other times there is a tiny number stamped in the emitter body indicating the flow rate (such as "1" or "4," depending on where it was manufactured) (Figure 9.17). Multiple-outlet emitters are also available (Figure 9.18); these are simply five or six separate emitters placed inside a single body or housing. These are normally used with ¼-in. distribution tubing (called "spaghetti" tubing) to provide water to several plants or pots in a single location.

The incredible flexibility of a drip system is due in part to the three emitter flow rates. A shrub may require a 1-gph (gallon per hour) emitter, while a small tree may need a pair of 2-gph emitters and a flower may need just a ½-gph emitter—all on the same section of drip tubing. If the area is irrigated for one hour, the flower receives ½ gal of water, the shrub receives 1 gal, and the small tree receives 4 gal. The incredible flexibility of drip irrigation within a single zone makes it an attractive option.

Drip emitters typically have a plastic barb on the bottom that is inserted into a hole punched into the drip tubing (more on tubing later); they do not require glue, thread sealant, or Teflon tape. The hole in the tubing is made with a punch sized for that particular emitter (Figure 9.19). You can plug extra holes in the tubing with an inexpensive "goof plug."

Many emitters have a small shank or barb outlet on the top suitable for ¼-inch distribution or "spaghetti" tubing (Figure 9.20). This allows you to add a small amount of tubing to the emitter to distribute water farther away from it. Be careful when adding spaghetti tubing to an emitter outlet; the emitter provides only a tiny bit of pressure to the outlet, which is not enough to push the water very far. You can use 1-2 ft of spaghetti tubing on a level surface with few problems, but 6-10 ft of tubing does not allow the water to reach the end of the tubing. Also, the small amount of pressure on the emitter outlet is not enough to push the water very far vertically. The water

Figure 9.17 Three different flow sizes of the same style emitter, color-coded for identification.
Image Credit: RainBird International, Inc.

Figure 9.18 Multi-outlet emitters.
Image Credit: RainBird International, Inc.

Figure 9.19 Installation of a drip emitter using a drip hole punch.
Image Credit: W. Bryan Smith, Clemson University

CHAPTER 9 - WATERING PLANTS AND LANDSCAPES 315

Drip Tubing

Drip tubing comes in several sizes, ranging from ¼ in.-1.5 in. or more, and in various styles (Figure 9.22). It is almost always black in color, sometimes with a colored stripe or identifying mark that is a trademark of the company. It is normally sold in 100-, 500-, or 1,000-ft rolls. It is resistant to sunlight and lasts 30 years or more in direct sunlight.

Drip tubing is made for use with drip emitters and microsprayers. It is flexible and expands and contracts with heat. If you place the tubing in a bed on a hot summer day, run cold water through it before inserting emitters. A hot piece of drip tubing 100 ft long may shrink up to 1 ft when you add cold water, pulling the last emitter 1 ft away from where you intended it to be. The cold water—in this case, normal-temperature irrigation water—causes the sun-heated, expanded tubing to shrink or draw up to the length it will maintain during irrigation. Then you can place emitters in the tubing with confidence (after turning the water off).

The most common drip tubing sizes (sized by diameter) are:

- 3/8 in. (10 mm or "380" size)
- 1/2 in. (13 mm or "500" size)
- 5/8 in. (16 mm outside diameter or "600" size)
- 5/8 in. (16 mm inside diameter or "700" size)

The most popular sizes are 16 mm inside and outside diameters (600 and 700 sizes respectively). These sizes are large enough to provide adequate flow for an entire foundation planting of a normal house, yet small enough to be inconspicuous in a landscape. The 10 mm size is

Figure 9.20 Spaghetti tubing can be added to an emitter in small lengths to provide water some distance from the emitter.
Image Credit: W. Bryan Smith, Clemson University

may rise 6-12 in., but it will not reach a hanging basket 8 ft above the emitter. Barbed couplings, or "transfer barbs," allow the spaghetti tubing to attach directly to drip tubing for this application, with the emitter placed on the end of the spaghetti tubing. Even in this situation, minimize the length of the spaghetti tubing.

Always place drip emitters in the landscape above ground and under mulch (Figure 9.21). If the emitter is buried, dirt may plug the outlet or roots may grow into it. If the emitter is placed above a layer of mulch, the water has to completely saturate the mulch before any water reaches the soil. This degrades the mulch more quickly, and it requires much more water to properly irrigate a plant.

Figure 9.21 Mulch pulled back to reveal a drip emitter.
Image Credit: W. Bryan Smith, Clemson University

Figure 9.22 "630" size drip tubing in a 1000-foot roll.
Image Credit: W. Bryan Smith, Clemson University

also common but is small enough to restrict flow (due to **friction loss**) if used with too many emitters.

Each tubing size requires a specific size fitting. Fittings are available in tees, elbows, and adapters to male garden hose thread (MHT) and female garden hose thread (FHT) as well as a few others. The fittings attach to the drip tubing using a compression-type connection that does not require tools, thread sealants, or glue. A sharp knife can easily cut the tubing to the desired length (exercise care with all tools and sharp objects—safety first).

Plug the open end of the tubing with a figure 8 clamp (they actually look like the number 8!); insert 2-3 in. of the tubing through the bottom hole of the 8 and bend the tubing back to form a kink. Push the free, kinked end of the tubing through the upper hole of the 8 to hold it in place. There are no tools required and it is easy to do.

Drip tubing is generally "snaked" or curved through a landscape bed, leaving the tubing near the various plants that need irrigation. Tees and elbows are inserted where necessary to irrigate more than one row of plants in an area. A newly planted bed of closely planted groundcover, such as Allegheny spurge (*Pachysandra procumbens*), may require a 2x2-ft grid of tubing and ½ gph emitters until it becomes established. Place the drip tubing in 2-ft-apart rows throughout the bed and insert emitters 2 ft apart along each row of drip tubing. The 2x2-ft grid provides coverage to the entire area.

Figure 9.23 Dripline with emitters pre-installed inside the tubing.
Image Credit: RainBird International, Inc.

Dripline

Many companies provide 600 size drip tubing with pre-installed emitters spaced evenly inside the tubing, usually 12, 18, 24 in. apart (Figure 9.23). This dripline greatly reduces the amount of labor required to install a drip irrigation system. It is only sold in 1,000-ft or longer rolls.

Dripline may be a perfect fit for an orchard or an area with regularly spaced plants. In a landscape, dripline may provide too many or two few emitters to water randomly spaced plants in a bed. If a homeowner plans to irrigate the entire bed with a 2x2 grid of emitters, dripline is an excellent choice. If their preference is to water several different plants in various areas, drip tubing with separate emitters is better.

"Drip Tape" or Line Source Drip Tubing

There is another drip product used almost exclusively in commercial vegetable production called "drip tape," or line source drip tubing (Figures 9.24 and 9.25). This

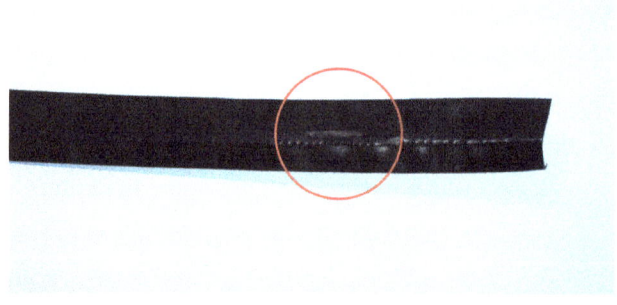

Figure 9.24 "Drip tape." The image shows the actual emitter made inside the "tape" and the slit that allows the water to exit.
Image Credit: W. Bryan Smith, Clemson University

is an extremely thin, extruded drip tubing; typical wall thicknesses are 8-10 thousandths of an inch, or 8-10 "mil"). Emitter outlets are typically installed on an 8-12-in. spacing, but longer spacings are available.

Drip tape was developed for use in a commercial vegetable bed for a single year on perhaps one or two crops. After the growing season is over, the drip tape is removed and recycled or discarded. The following year, new drip tape is installed in the new vegetable beds.

Commercial vegetable producers can replace this

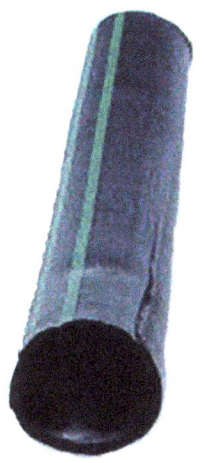

Figure 9.25 Drip tubing (left) and drip tape (right) side-by-side. Notice the very thin wall of the drip tape.
Image Credit: W. Bryan Smith, Clemson University

Figure 9.26 A microsprayer complete with spaghetti tubing and stake.
Image Credit: RainBird International, Inc.

product each year due to the high value of their crop and the low cost of the drip tape. An irrigation system failure for a commercial grower could mean a loss of millions of dollars in some cases. New drip tape each year helps prevent problems due to insect intrusion or physical damage over the winter. Drip tape is quite inexpensive due to the thin wall of the product—usually around $0.06 per foot in a full roll quantity of 7,500 ft.

Drip tape is suitable for use in home vegetable gardens, but since it should be replaced each year, there is no other practical application for it in home landscapes. There is some work being done that buries this product in the landscape to irrigate lawn areas (called subsurface drip irrigation or SDI), but this application is just now seeing wider acceptance in South Carolina due to our variable soil types and other factors. SDI is currently used successfully in row crop applications. Perhaps more work with SDI on lawn applications will be completed in the future.

Microsprinklers and Microsprayers

Microsprinklers and microsprayers are tiny, plastic sprinklers or sprayers, typically mounted on some type of plastic stake (Figure 9.26). The microsprinkler is connected to drip tubing with a barbed coupling and a length of spaghetti tubing. Microsprinklers are a compromise between drip irrigation and normal sprinkler irrigation—they are less efficient than drip emitters but considerably more efficient than sprinklers. Flow rates for microsprinklers range from 6-60 gph or more.

Microsprinklers are sold in a variety of styles, patterns, and throw diameters. They are used extensively in greenhouses and orchards.

Microsprinklers are especially useful in areas with coarse, sandy soils. Water applied to a sandy soil quickly moves downward through the soil. The application rate of a drip emitter is slow; so slow, in fact, that in a sandy soil, the water applied by the emitter moves downward into the soil with little lateral movement away from the emitter. In some coarse sands, the water may only move 6-12 in. horizontally in the ground away from the emitter. This minimal lateral movement may not provide water to enough plant roots for proper growth; the international design standard is to provide water to 50% of the plant's rooting area with drip irrigation.

The microsprinkler sprays water out over a large area, providing water to a much larger rooting area in sandy soils. Citrus groves in sandy areas rely almost exclusively on microsprinkler systems for this reason. This also regrettably provides some water to vacant areas and weeds.

In finer soils such as loams and clays, the water moves downward more slowly, which allows more lateral water movement from the emitter in the soil. Lateral movement 2-3 ft from the emitter are not uncommon in clays and clay loam soils. In this case, microsprinklers are not necessary.

Spray Stakes

The potting media used in many pots is porous and well-drained. In some instances, water provided by a drip emitter to these pots moves directly downward through the media with almost no lateral movement. Because of this, very few plant roots receive the water.

Spray stakes are a specialized type of microsprayer used for this application (Figure 9.27). The spray stake is

Figure 9.27 Spray stakes are used in pots to more evenly distribute water.
Image Credit: Sarah White, Clemson University

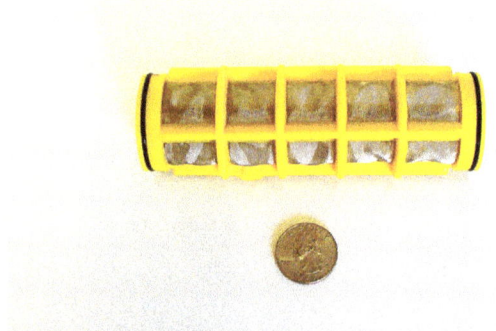

Figure 9.29 A 150-mesh filter element for a drip system.
Image Credit: W. Bryan Smith, Clemson University

placed in one edge of the pot and attached to drip tubing with a short piece of spaghetti tube. When the system is on, the spray stake sprays a very small pattern of water that covers the entire potting media surface and very little else. The spray stake irrigates the entire rooting area in the pot.

Filters

Irrigation water for sprinkler systems is not normally filtered. The large nozzle sizes (typically 7/64 in. and larger) usually pass any particles or sediment in the water with little problem. Drip emitters and microsprayers have much smaller outlets and pathways that can easily clog with small particles. The water provided to a drip system must be properly filtered (Figure 9.28).

A drip system requires a 150 mesh filter to prevent plugging problems, regardless of type (Figure 9.29);

Figure 9.28 Typical filters for a drip system.
Image Credit: W. Bryan Smith, Clemson University

the term "150 mesh" means that the filter screen has 150 openings per inch in a straight line. Some emitters and microsprayers require an even smaller screen—200 mesh. Do not depend on common sediment filters to provide adequate protection; purchase a filter with the proper mesh rating to protect your investment.

There are two special problems that may cause difficulty for drip systems. The first is pond or surface water. Surface water naturally contains a large amount of sediment and organic matter. The high sediment content can plug a normal-sized screen filter in a short time. Usually, users install some type of self-cleaning screen filter or sand media filter (like a pool filter) to prevent frequent plugging.

Surface water can also contain algae that may grow on the filter screen, causing frequent clogs. Usually, a small but continuous injection of chlorine into the irrigation water prevents algae problems. Chemical injection of any type requires the installation of certain safeguards in the irrigation system to prevent backflow into the water body. For a small drip system in a landscape, it may be less expensive and much more convenient to use well or municipal water for the drip system and use surface water for the sprinkler system. The two systems must be completely separate to prevent cross-contamination.

The second potential problem for a drip system is iron in well water. The iron remains in a liquid form and flows through the filter regardless of the mesh size. When the iron leaves the drip emitter or microsprayer and contacts the air, it will oxidize into iron oxide, which is a solid. In a normal sprinkler system with large nozzle openings, this is not a problem, but iron oxide deposits can plug the tiny opening in an emitter or microsprayer in a very short time.

If the homeowner suspects that iron is present in the well water used in a drip system, the first course of action is to have the water tested for iron. If the iron content is less than 0.1 ppm, there is no issue. If the iron content is 0.3 ppm or more, it will cause a plugging problem over time. Test the water before installing a drip system if there are reddish-brown stains in the sink or tub.

Pressure Regulators

Drip irrigation systems do not require as much pressure as normal sprinkler systems. Drip tubing and emitter systems work well with a pressure of 30 pounds per square inch (psi). A pressure higher than 45 psi can pop emitters out of the tubing and send them flying.

Drip tape has a much thinner wall and requires only 10 psi for proper operation. A pressure above 12-15 psi can quickly rupture the drip tape.

Pressure regulators are used to protect drip systems from excessive pressure (Figure 9.30). A 30-psi pressure regulator works well for most landscape drip irrigation systems, while a 10-psi regulator works nicely for a drip tape system in the garden. Expensive brass pressure regulators found at most hardware stores are not necessary for these systems. A simple, plastic, preset agricultural irrigation pressure regulator works well and costs about 50-75% less.

Some homeowners use a partially opened valve, instead of a pressure regulator, to restrict the pressure to their drip system. This may work well for a time, but it's all too easy to turn the valve just a bit too far and have to pay the price. The small amount of money required to purchase a pressure regulator is well worth the investment.

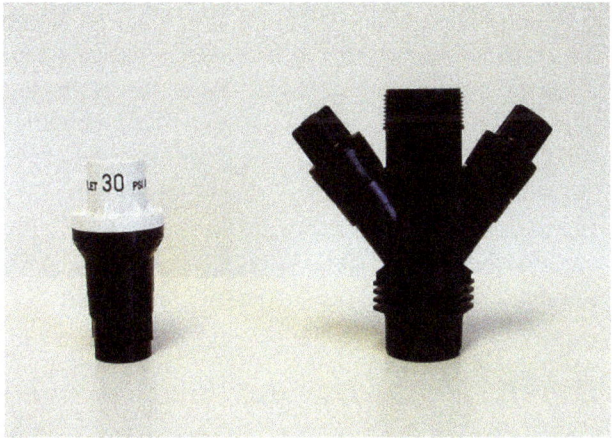

Figure 9.30 Drip irrigation pressure regulators from two different manufacturers.
Image Credit: W. Bryan Smith, Clemson University

Timers and Controllers

To properly irrigate a yard or crop, homeowners and growers need to know when to begin irrigation, how much water to apply, and how long to operate the system. Most irrigation systems are divided into zones that each require a different operating time to apply the correct amount of water. Manually turning a valve on and off works just fine, but it does require attention to the project at hand. It is easy to become involved in another project and then—oops—realize that time has slipped by and a zone has been irrigated for an extra 30 minutes.

Irrigation timers were developed to automate the irrigation process. Replace the manual valves with electric valves, add some wire, install the irrigation timer, and simply set the appropriate times for each zone. After setup, you're off the hook.

The first electric timers were electro-mechanical (Figure 9.31). A clock motor ran the entire timer, with a simple dial to set the current day and time, another dial to set the day and time the irrigation system should turn on, and one small dial for each zone to set the irrigation time. These timers are dependable, simple to set up, rugged and long-lasting, and still available from many irrigation manufacturers.

There are several limitations to an electro-mechanical timer. The timer is very inflexible. If the timer is programmed to begin irrigation on Tuesday at 9:00 p.m., it does so—and every zone is irrigated that evening. There is no way to program two zones to irrigate on Tuesday and three more to irrigate on Friday. Also, the timer does not allow different irrigation times for the same zone; it is not possible to irrigate zone 1 for 20 min on Tuesday and then again for 40 min on Friday with an electromechanical timer unless the time is manually

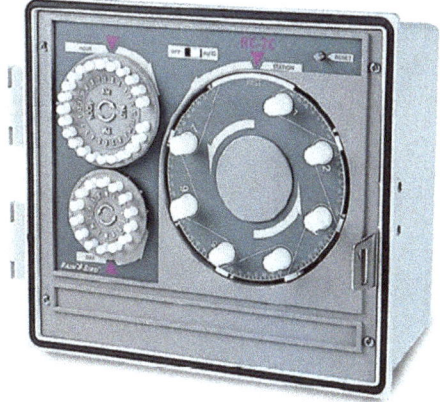

Figure 9.31 Typical electro-mechanical timer.
Image Credit: RainBird International, Inc.

reset. Finally, each zone has a maximum irrigation time of 60 min. This can be a problem, especially if some zones are drip zones.

The next advance in timers was the electronic timer. These timers, usually characterized by a L.E.D. readout, were very flexible and provided three available "programs". A homeowner might use "Program A" to set zones 1, 2, and 5 to irrigate on Tuesdays, "Program B" to set zones 3, 4, and 6 to irrigate on Fridays, and "Program C" to set zones 3 and 6 to irrigate again on Saturdays. These timers were very complex to program, but their primary fault was their susceptibility to voltage surges. If there was a thunderstorm in the area, there was a good chance that the electronic timer needed to be repaired.

The latest timer advancement is the hybrid timer (Figure 9.32). This timer combines the ruggedness and ease of programming of the electro-mechanical timer with the flexibility of the electronic timer. Most hybrid timers have a combination of dials, buttons, and an LCD readout that simplifies programming. There are usually three different programs to allow for irrigation flexibility. Hybrid timers have rapidly become the timer of choice for landscape irrigation.

Timers are both a blessing and a curse. The blessing is obvious: irrigation devices turn on and off automatically at the proper time. The curse of the irrigation timer is less obvious and is based on plant water use.

Homeowners typically begin irrigating during April or May, when humidity is relatively high, and the days are cool and pleasant. They check the system, set the times for the zones on the timer, and monitor the yard for a few weeks. Everything looks fine, so homeowners congratulate themselves on a job well done and forget about the timer for the rest of the year.

Enter the curse. Plants require more water when temperatures are higher and humidity is lower, as described previously. The plant transpires more water during these higher-stress times, so the roots take more up from the soil. It's easy to understand that the landscape requires more water during the higher temperatures and lower humidity of July and August—suddenly, the irrigation system doesn't provide enough water for the landscape.

Of course, the solution is to add time to the various irrigation zones to meet the higher water need. That works fine through July and August, but when late September arrives, the irrigation zone times should be reduced again.

Most homeowners want a completely automatic irrigation system for which the installation company installs the system and sets the timer; ideally, the system requires no further attention. Timers automatically turn valves on and off, but they cannot sense or measure the need of a landscape; software and sensors are available to do this, but they are usually cost-prohibitive for home landscapes. Timers are helpers, not schedulers. Homeowners must regularly monitor the landscape and change the irrigation zone times based on plant needs.

There is a bright spot in this picture. Most new hybrid timers have a "water budget" or "water efficiency" feature. The water budget in the timer comes from the factory set for 100%; that is, the timer irrigates each zone for 100% of the time programmed into the timer. As the season progresses, the homeowner may decide that the landscape needs more water. You can make these changes in one place on the timer: the water budget section. One setting could increase the water budget from 100% to 120%. This would increase the time each zone operates by 20%, regardless of how many zones are on the timer or when they are scheduled to operate. This is an extremely handy feature that saves a great deal of programming time.

Rain Sensors

There are many types of **rain sensors** on the market. Rain sensors actually do "sense" when rain is falling and prevent the irrigation system from operating during this time (Figure 9.33). This is usually as simple as interrupting or turning off the "common" wire that travels from the controller to all the electric valves in the

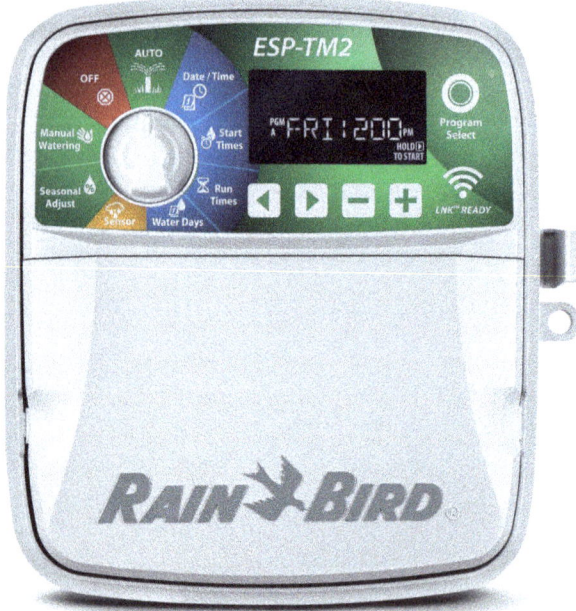

Figure 9.32 Typical hybrid timer.
Image Credit: RainBird International, Inc.

Figure 9.34 A gate valve. Notice the "gate" partially lowered inside the valve.
Image Credit: W. Bryan Smith, Clemson University

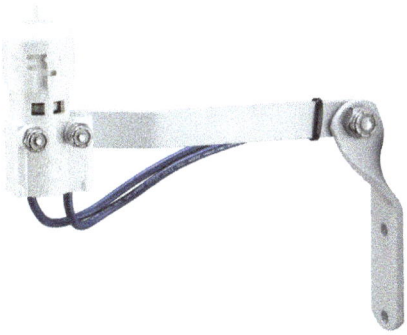

Figure 9.33 Typical wired and wireless rain sensors.
Image Credit: Hunter Industries

Figure 9.35 A ball valve with the "ball" partially closed.
Image Credit: W. Bryan Smith, Clemson University

yard. Rain sensors are an excellent tool for any system; some municipalities even require them. They are usually installed on the eaves of a roof or the side of a building. Some thought must go into placement—if the sensor is placed in the normal storm "lee" or protected area of a building, the sensor will seldom (if ever) prevent irrigation; it must be placed where it will be wetted by any rain that falls.

Valves

There are three basic types of valves used in irrigation systems: gate valves, ball valves, and electric valves. Gate and ball valves are both manual valves for use with manual (non-automated) irrigation system.

Gate valves have a simple "gate" inside the valve body that is raised or lowered into the water flow by turning the handle (Figure 9.34). When fully lowered, the gate stops the water flow.

Ball valves have a "ball" with a hole drilled through it (Figure 9.35). Turning the handle one-quarter turn lines this hole up with the piping and allows water to flow. Turn the handle back one-quarter turn to turn off the valve. This quick on-off action can cause water hammer problems in some systems, so to be on the safe side, always turn on and off ball valves slowly. Both gate and ball valves work well in manual systems.

Electric valves used with automatic timers are diaphragm valves with 24-volt solenoids (Figure 9.36). Apply 24 volts to the solenoid and the valve opens; remove the voltage and the valve closes. These valves also allow the owner to turn the valve on without electricity, if necessary, but if turned on manually, the valve must also be turned off manually.

Figure 9.36 Electric valves with and without manual flow control (center tower).
Image Credit: RainBird International, Inc.

Some homeowners are concerned about the electric wires in the yard used to connect electric valves to timers. The 24-volt system used to operate the valves is similar to those used for model trains, providing enough voltage to open the valves but not enough to pose a shock or electrocution threat should a wire be accidentally cut with a shovel.

Any valve installed in a landscape should be in a valve box for easy access (Figure 9.37). A valve box is simply a small bucket with an easy-to-remove top, no bottom, and openings in the sides to allow pipe to run through. Valve boxes are installed with the top at ground level and designed to allow lawn mowers to run over them without damaging them. The tops are usually green to make them less conspicuous in the landscape. Any valve requires maintenance at some point, so always install them in valve boxes so you can find and repair them easily.

Figure 9.38 Various sizes of PVC pipe.
Image Credit: W. Bryan Smith, Clemson University

Figure 9.37 A typical valve box. Some designs place one valve in each box across the landscape.
Image Credit: Cory Tanner, Clemson University

Piping

There are many types of piping available, including CPVC, PVC, galvanized iron, and polyethylene. The two most common piping types for irrigation systems are white PVC (polyvinyl chloride) and "black roll pipe" (polyethylene).

PVC is generally the most popular piping in the southern states (Figure 9.38). It is easy to work with, inexpensive, and common. PVC comes in a number of varieties, but the two used for landscape irrigation are Schedule 40 and 160 psi "pressure-rated" (or PR160) piping. Both of these types of PVC work well for landscape irrigation systems. Schedule 40 piping has a slightly thicker wall than PR160 in sizes less than 6 in. and can withstand higher pressures. However, the thicker wall also means that Schedule 40 is slightly more expensive and that more pressure is lost to friction. Schedule 40 is somewhat more forgiving if installed in rocky ground. Either type works well.

PVC comes in 10- or 20-ft lengths depending on the supplier and is glued together with PVC cement. Most PVC piping has one "belled end," or coupling made into the end of the pipe. Schedule 40 fittings are used on both PR160 and Schedule 40 PVC pipe. Be careful not to buy drain, waste, and vent (DWV) PVC fittings; they are less expensive but not designed to handle higher pressures, so they may fail over time.

"Black roll pipe" is commonly used for landscape irrigation systems in northern states (Figure 9.39). The pipe comes in 300-ft rolls and connects with insert fittings and clamps. Black roll pipe is somewhat more difficult to install but not appreciably so. Black roll pipe is used in Northern areas because it expands a small amount to allow the water in it to freeze without damaging the pipe, an important feature in the north. In the south, there are typically no issues with pipes freezing if the piping is installed at the recommended 12-in. depth. Both black roll piping and PVC piping work well in our climate, but PVC piping may be easier to install and repair.

Figure 9.39 "Black roll" polyethylene pipe.
Image Credit: W. Bryan Smith, Clemson University

"Swing" Pipe

Imagine that a residential sprinkler system is installed and working well. A friend stops by and accidentally backs into the yard, right over a sprinkler. The sprinkler is crushed, of course; but since the sprinkler was screwed directly into the PVC pipe, a good portion of the pipe is broken too.

There is no way to prevent a sprinkler from being broken in this manner, but you can protect the piping.

Most manufacturers offer a product called "swing pipe" or "funny pipe" (Figure 9.40). This piping looks much like drip tubing but has a much thicker wall and can handle greater pressure.

Swing pipe is installed between the PVC piping and the sprinkler to provide some flexibility if the sprinkler is crushed. Usually, 2 ft of swing pipe attach a sprinkler to the PVC, but you can install 3-4 ft if needed. Swing pipe also allows the installer to move the sprinkler around a little during installation if a planned sprinkler location turns out to be right behind or too near an obstacle.

Swing pipe is relatively inexpensive and pays for itself even if it only helps to avoid a single pipe break. There are special fittings for swing pipe to attach it to the sprinkler and the PVC piping.

Water Meters

Irrigation systems using municipal or county water are supplied through a water meter (Figure 9.41). Water meters range in size from 5/8-2 in. or more. In a typical landscape system, a 5/8-3/4-in. water meter allows adequate water flow.

In some areas with municipal water and sewer services, the homeowner may consider installing an additional irrigation-only meter for the irrigation system. The client pays for the water used through the second meter by the irrigation system but is not charged for sewer services (since that water does not return to the sewer system). This can be an attractive option if the installation cost of the second meter is relatively low. If the cost of installing the irrigation meter is high, it may

Figure 9.40 A flexible joint made with "swing" pipe.
Image Credit: Hunter Industries

Figure 9.41 A typical water meter.
Image Credit: W. Bryan Smith, Clemson University

be best to simply use the existing meter. Be sure to check your local regulations.

Backflow Preventers

All municipal water systems require some type of anti-siphon or backflow prevention device (Figures 9.42 and 9.43). This device prevents water from the irrigation system from re-entering and possibly contaminating the drinking water system.

The most common backflow-prevention device is the double check valve. This device contains two successive check valves. The theory is that should one check valve fail, the second one will still operate and prevent backflow and possible contamination.

All backflow-prevention or anti-siphon devices have a number of small test ports to allow testing. South Carolina law requires that these devices be tested annually to make sure they are operating properly.

Figure 9.42 A typical double check valve backflow preventer.
Image Credit: Zurn/Wilkes

Figure 9.43 A typical anti-siphon device.
Image Credit: Zurn/Wilkes

Pumps and Wells

Many homeowners want to irrigate their landscapes with existing wells. This is possible if the well has a flow rate of at least 15 gpm. Before making a decision, though, consider the following points to prevent confusion and problems:

- Pump size. Well drillers install 5-gpm pumps in most household wells regardless of the actual well flow rate. The well may be rated for 15-20 gpm or more, but you will probably have to replace the existing pump to obtain this flow rate for a new irrigation system.
- Pressure tanks. Pressure tanks are sized based on pump flow rate. The tank is simply there to prevent constant cycling—on and off, on and off—by a pump as water is used during the day. If you install a larger pump, you may also need to install a larger pressure tank (or more than one).
- Continuous use. Well pumps are made to run continuously. Allowing a pump to operate for 20 hr will not damage the pump in any way. However, the pump is not constructed to withstand constant starts. Each time the pump starts, the "start" windings in the motor heat up due to the large amount of electrical current used to start the motor. If the pump starts more than once every 5 min, the "start" windings become hot and burn out quickly. Installing the appropriate size pressure tank, a cycle-stop valve, or a system designed to pump continuously prevents this potential problem.

IRRIGATION DESIGN CONCEPTS

You must understand a few irrigation design concepts to properly evaluate an irrigation system. These concepts are only a few of the many issues considered when designing an irrigation system, but they are very important. If you ignore one of these concepts, the system will not work correctly.

Sprinkler Placement

Proper sprinkler placement is one of the most misunderstood irrigation concepts. Homeowners often set up a sprinkler, irrigate a circular area, and move the sprinkler to a new location. That circle of lawn was irrigated, but it was not irrigated uniformly. Understanding how a sprinkler applies water is critical to understanding proper sprinkler spacing.

Consider a race where sprinters compete on a circular track. Each sprinter is assigned a lane. The inside lane is 10 ft from the center of the track, while the outside lane is 100 ft from the center of the track. It is obvious that the sprinter in the outside lane is at a tremendous disadvantage. He or she has a much longer race to run because the outside lane is so far from the center of the track.

A sprinkler rotates in a circular pattern much like the racetrack mentioned above. The sprinkler irrigates with a single stream of water over this large area. The total amount of water applied per square foot near the outside of the irrigated circle is much less than that applied near the sprinkler simply because of the much larger area of lawn affected. This is true even if the sprinkler stream provides an even application of water under the water stream from one end to the other when held stationary (which is not generally the case anyway). This means that a single sprinkler is not capable of irrigating an area uniformly because of the circular irrigation pattern (Figure 9.44). The area near the sprinkler may receive 3/4 in. of water, while the outer edges of the irrigated circle receive 1/4 in. or less.

You can overcome this application uniformity problem by placing sprinklers so their streams overlap the watering

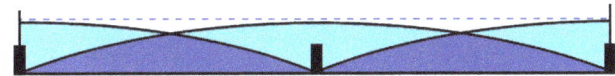

Figure 9.45 Sprinklers installed using the "head to head" spacing concept provide a uniform water application as indicated by the straight line, which is a total of all the water applied by the three sprinklers over the area.
Figure Credit: W. Bryan Smith, Clemson University

areas of adjacent sprinklers. Typically, one sprinkler is placed so that its stream of water just touches the next adjacent sprinkler body, called "head-to-head coverage" (Figure 9.45). Head-to-head coverage is when sprinklers are placed in a square pattern in which each sprinkler is placed one-half of its irrigating or wetted diameter from the next sprinkler in that row and from the parallel sprinkler in the next row (Figure 9.46). For example, if a sprinkler type provides a 70-ft wetted diameter, place it approximately 35 ft from the next sprinkler in the row and space the rows of sprinklers 35 ft apart.

For example, sprinkler 1 provides 3/4 in. of water near its body, gradually decreasing to 1/4 in. or less

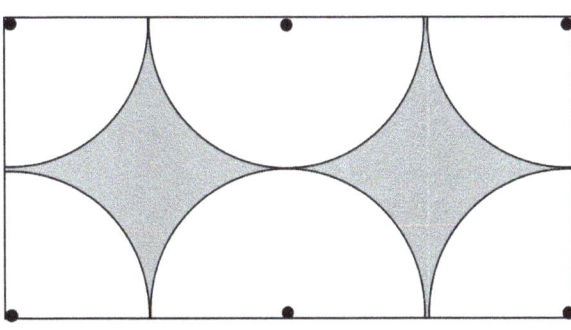

(A) Improper Spacing

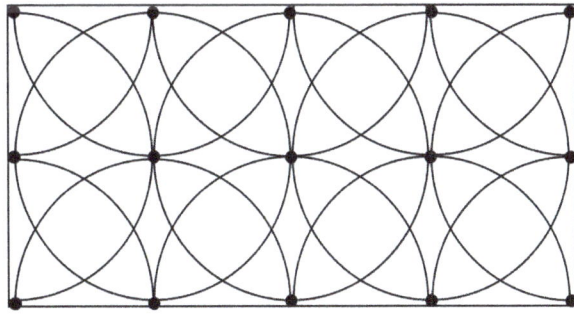

(B) Proper Spacing

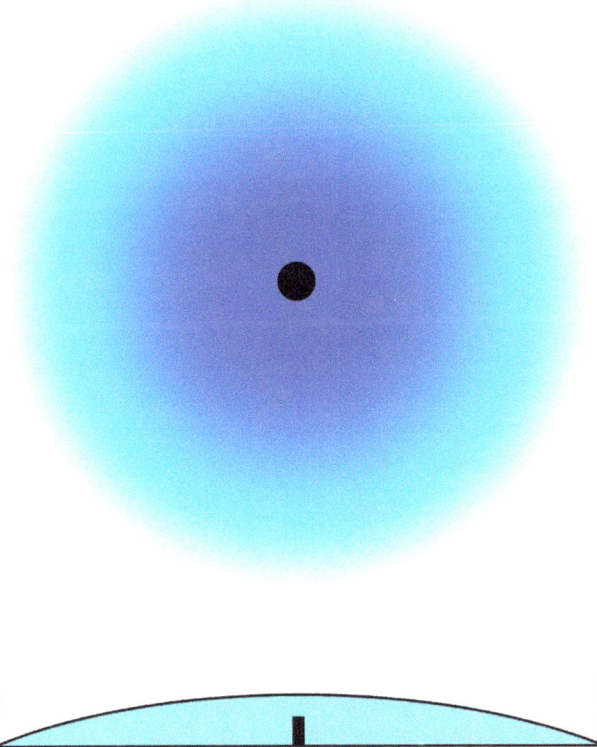

Figure 9.44 More water is applied near the sprinkler simply because of the circular irrigation pattern.
Figure Credit: W. Bryan Smith, Clemson University

Figure 9.46 Wetted lawn areas when sprinklers are (A) improperly spaced and (B) spaced using the "head to head" coverage concept. Notice the large dry areas in image (A) and the excellent coverage in image (B).
Figure Credit: W. Bryan Smith, Clemson University

near the edge of the circle irrigated. Sprinkler 2, by just touching sprinkler 1 with its stream of water, adds another 1/4 in. near sprinkler 1, for a total of 1 in. of water applied near sprinkler 1. Sprinkler 2's water application complements the water applied by sprinkler 1 along the path between the two sprinklers, resulting in an approximately uniform application of one inch of water over the area between the two sprinklers. The same spacing concept is used to place spray heads properly.

In some cases, this method seems use many sprinklers where fewer would suffice. However, dry weather quickly shows the inadequate coverage of sprinklers spaced farther apart, darker green circles in a light green or somewhat brown lawn are not very attractive!

Be aware that this is not a perfect world. The layout of a lawn may not allow exact head-to-head coverage placement of sprinklers. As long as the sprinklers are within 6-7% of the proper spacing distance (about 2 ft for a system spaced at 35 ft, as in the previous example), the system should work fine. If the system design spaces the sprinklers 10% or farther apart than the optimal head-to-head distance to fit the area, redesign to ensure uniform coverage.

A note of caution: some systems may be installed with wider, improper spacing to save money. These improperly spaced systems apply water, but there are always dry areas and areas of marginal water application (Figure 9.47). Applying excess irrigation water may help the marginal areas, but the areas closer to the sprinklers suffer from too much water and the leaching of nutrients through the soil profile. The excess water may cause excessive yellowing of the lawn near the sprinkler heads—more so than the slight amount that normally occurs in a well-designed system.

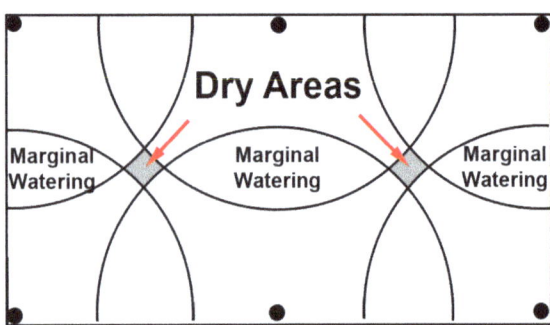

Figure 9.47 Spacing sprinklers farther apart to save money always results in poor irrigation uniformity and "dry" areas.
Figure Credit: W. Bryan Smith, Clemson University

Matching Precipitation Rates

Now that the sprinklers and spray heads are spaced properly, install properly sized nozzles—based on irrigation patterns—to provide uniform distribution.

A little common sense makes this a very simple job. For example, in one zone, a sprinkler placed near a road or sidewalk may be adjusted to irrigate a half-circle pattern; another sprinkler in the same zone, placed in the center of the lawn should irrigate a full circle pattern. The full circle sprinkler has twice as much ground to irrigate, so it must apply twice as much water as the half-circle sprinkler in the same amount of time (Figure 9.48).

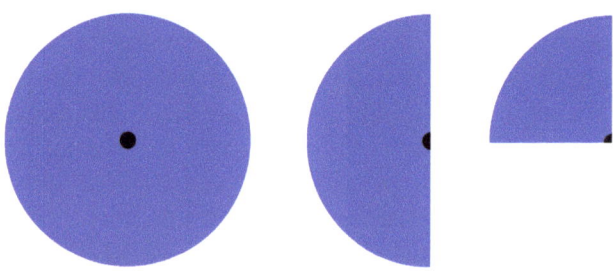

Figure 9.48 Full-circle sprinklers irrigate twice as much yard area as half-circle sprinklers and four times as much as quarter-circle sprinklers.
Figure Credit: W. Bryan Smith, Clemson University

The solution is quite simple: change the nozzle size. In a perfect world, the full circle sprinkler would use an 8-gpm nozzle, the half-circle sprinkler would use a 4-gpm nozzle, and a quarter-circle sprinkler would use a 2-gpm nozzle. Each sprinkler would apply the same total depth of water to the area covered if operated for the same amount of time. In the real world, an installer may use 6-, 3-, and 2-gpm nozzles to accommodate a small water meter or low well flow rate.

Remember these two points:

- Sprinklers with different irrigation areas will require different nozzle sizes.
- When replacing a broken sprinkler, always make sure the proper nozzle size is placed in the replacement.

Matching precipitation rates is quite simple for spray heads. Each spray head nozzle is purchased based on an irrigation pattern—half-circle, quarter-circle, etc. The flow rate of each nozzle is set by the pattern diameter. If the nozzles are purchased with the same wetted radius (10 ft, 12 ft, 15 ft, etc.), the precipitation rate automatically matches regardless of the spray pattern.

Piping Pressure Losses

There are two main reasons for pressure change in an irrigation system:

- Pressure loss or gain due to the elevation changes of a property.
- Pressure loss in the pipe due to friction.

There are other losses—valves, fittings, filters, backflow preventers, etc.—but these two main reasons usually comprise the bulk of the pressure change through a system.

Pressure Loss Due to Landscape Elevation

The total amount of rise or fall of a landscape impacts irrigation system pressure. The actual steepness of a slope does not. For instance, one property 50 ft wide has a slope that rises 20 ft from the lowest point on the property to the highest point. Another property that is 100 feet wide also rises a total of 20 feet from the lowest to the highest point, but over the entire 100-ft width. The steeper slope of the narrower property is more prone to runoff, but the actual 20-ft rise affects the irrigation system pressure, not the steepness or shallowness of the slope.

Pressure loss or gain due to elevation differences does not depend on pipe size or flow rate. The pressure change is simply due to the weight of water in the pipe. For example, think of a person swimming in a pool that is 10 ft deep. The water pressure on the swimmer's ears increases as the swimmer moves down through the water. If the swimmer stays 5 ft below the surface, the pressure on the swimmer's ears will be the same regardless of where he or she swims within the pool.

The same concept holds true for water in irrigation piping. A certain amount of elevation pressure is placed on the system simply due to the weight of the water in the system. This elevation pressure remains the same whether water flows through the system or not.

There are some basic numbers for elevation pressure. One vertical foot of water elevation equals 0.433 psi of water pressure. For example, if water is piped up a 1-ft-tall hill, the irrigation system loses 0.433 psi of water pressure due to the rise in elevation. If water is piped up a 10-ft hill, the system loses 4.33 psi of water pressure (Figure 9.49).

Elevation pressure works both ways: it reduces pressure as water is piped up hill, but it also adds pressure as water is piped downhill. If water is piped down a 1-ft hill, the system gains 0.433 psi of water pressure.

Any competent irrigation designer understands this concept and designs systems that consider the elevation changes in a landscape and provides uniform irrigation coverage. Just be aware that elevation changes in a yard affect system pressure and performance.

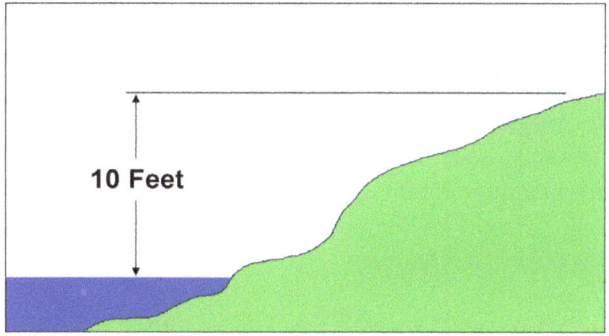

Figure 9.49 Simply pumping water up 10 feet of vertical elevation will require 4.3 psi in addition to the pressure losses due to pipe friction, valves, and other factors. The slope of the land surface does not change this elevation pressure loss.
Figure Credit: W. Bryan Smith, Clemson University

Piping Friction Pressure Losses

One of the more common misconceptions concerning water flow is that using a smaller pipe will increase pressure. This understanding is based on the fact that adding a nozzle to the end of a garden hose seems to increase pressure, creating a small stream of quickly moving water in the place of the large, slowly moving stream of water normally leaving the hose.

Adding a nozzle to a garden hose does not increase pressure. Instead, it increases water velocity. The nozzle simply converts water pressure inside the hose into water velocity. While the nozzle increases flow velocity, it actually decreases the flow rate of the water. The quickly moving water loses more pressure due to friction losses in the nozzle.

The same concept is true for irrigation pipe. The faster the water flows through a pipe, the more pressure is lost due to friction against the pipe wall. A smaller pipe size increases water velocity in the pipe but increases the pressure lost to friction. For instance, if water is pumped at a rate of 10 gpm through a ¾-in. pipe, about 8.7 psi of pressure is lost for every 100 ft of pipe. If the same flow is pumped through a 1-in. pipe, only about 2.6 psi of pressure is lost per 100 ft of pipe. For uniform irrigation, piping must be properly sized to provide adequate flow and pressure to each sprinkler in a zone.

Irrigation designers use equations such as Hazen-Williams or Scobey to determine the pressure loss due to friction in an irrigation system. A designer may also use pipe friction loss charts to determine pressure loss. Irrigation design concepts such as pipe friction loss equations and charts are beyond the scope of this chapter, but a simple pipe-sizing chart may be helpful for very small additions. This chart applies basic rules of thumb to make sure a pipe is not grossly undersized for a specific application.

The rules of thumb depicted in the chart are based on three assumptions:

- Water velocity in a pipe will be 5 ft per second or less (to minimize water hammer (pressure surge) problems);
- Water will be piped a short distance, usually 200 ft or less; and
- There are no friction losses or elevation losses to be considered.

These pipe-sizing rules of thumb are based solely on flow rate. Recommended maximum flow rates for common pipe sizes are illustrated in Table 9.1

TABLE 9.1 Pipe-Sizing Rules of Thumb

Minimum Pipe Size (in)	Flow Rate (gpm)
½	5
¾	10
1	15
1¼	25
1½	35
2	50

For example, a system with a flow rate of 40 gpm requires at least 2-in. mainline pipe. A system with a flow rate of 18 gpm requires at least 1¼-in. pipe. This is a very simplistic method of pipe sizing and is not intended to replace design methods considering friction loss and elevation. It is simply provided for understanding why it is so important to replace a broken irrigation pipe with one of the same size.

Irrigation System Design

As mentioned at the beginning of this chapter, this chapter is not intended to provide a full primer on irrigation design. Many entire books are available on the subject. However, we aim to provide a better understanding of proper irrigation system operation and maintenance with the basics covered in this chapter.

The first step to installing an irrigation system is to find a competent irrigation designer. The designer should consider available water flow, elevation differences in the landscape, available pressure from the water source, valve friction losses, and a number of other factors during the design of any system. The designer will usually use a scale drawing or map (a county tax plat of the property works well) to begin the design. The finished product should include zones based on homeowner preferences for irrigation of various sections or beds, a scale drawing of the design showing pipe sizes, sprinklers, spray heads, and valves, and a list of materials necessary to complete the project.

The second step is to choose a reputable irrigation installation company. There are usually a number of lower-price installers working in an area, but the adage "you get what you pay for" certainly applies to irrigation system installation. Choose a company that not only provides a professional installation job but that is available to repair problems and provide any necessary warranty work.

If a homeowner chooses to install an irrigation system on their own, they must be sure to understand basic piping and wiring concepts. South Carolina residents are required to call South Carolina 811 (dial 811 or 888-721-7877; online at https://sc811.com/) to locate any underground wires, pipes, or fiber-optic cables before digging trenches in the landscape. Repair of damaged buried utilities is the responsibility of the homeowner; in the event of a gas line break, this damage can be very dangerous. Call 811 to locate utilities before beginning to dig.

Homeowners may be required to hire a licensed plumber to connect the irrigation system to the water supply or have a licensed irrigation company inspect the system before the trenches are filled. Check with local city and county ordinances or municipal authorities before beginning the project to fully understand local requirements.

Finally, spend a little time caring for trees by planning the trenching plan for the yard. This should be done regardless of whether installation is done professionally or by the homeowner. Most tree roots grow in the top 12-16 in. of the soil. Twelve-in.-deep trenches that accommodate the irrigation pipes may sever most of the tree roots in an area. For this reason, keep the trenches as far away from existing tress as possible. Hand-dig any trench placed near a tree or between two trees growing closely together; you may still sever one or two large roots, but hand-digging the trench allows you or the installer to place piping around or beneath most of the tree roots and prevent major injury. If a trencher is allowed to dig a trench close to a tree, it can sever almost one-half of the tree's roots, which severely limits the tree's nutrient and water uptake and results in its decline. Younger, smaller trees may recover from this in time, but older, larger trees may not and may take several years to die. Plan trenches with trees in mind.

Chapter 10
Understanding Insects

Revised and updated by Eric Benson, Ph.D.

Previous version prepared by Bob Polomski, Ph.D. and Eric Benson, Ph.D.

LEARNING OBJECTIVES
- Understand the standard classification system and the precarious use of common names.
- Know the basic morphology of insects.
  - Use morphological characteristics to accurately identify insects.
  - Know the steps to accurately identify insects.
  - Accurately identify common insects in South Carolina landscapes.
  - Understand how insect identification affects management efficacy.
  - Accurately identify pests to effectively manage them using integrated pest management (IPM).
- Define metamorphosis.
  - Understand that insect specimens are submitted in various life stages.
- Be able to identify common insect injuries found in South Carolina landscapes.
- Collect proper and sufficient data and useful specimens to submit to the Plant and Pest Diagnostic Clinic (PPDC) for identification and management recommendations.
- Explain how to collect proper and sufficient data and useful specimens to submit to the Plant and Pest Diagnostic Clinic (PPDC) for identification and management recommendations.
- Accurately refer others to the proper entities for identification, information, and management of insect pests, including professional pest managers or different program teams.
- Know and appreciate the benefits and value of insects.

INTRODUCTION

Insects are among the oldest and most numerous creatures on earth. While insects that cause problems for humans receive the most publicity, the vast majority are either beneficial or harmless. Insects pollinate most fruits and vegetables. They provide food for many animals. Some produce useful products such as honey, wax, shellac, and silk. In addition, some insects feed on other insect pests. Worldwide, less than one percent of known insect species (about 10,000) are economically destructive.

Insects and Their Relatives

Insects belong to the phylum Arthropoda, which means "jointed legs." This large phylum also includes spiders, ticks, crabs, and lobsters. **Arthropods** have segmented bodies and a skeleton outside of the body, called an **exoskeleton**. Many arthropods are mistakenly called insects. These close relatives of insects include mites and spiders (arachnids), centipedes (chilopods), sowbugs and pillbugs (isopods), millipedes (diplopods), and snails and slugs (mollusks). Find illustrations and brief descriptions of these insect relatives in the "Common Non-Insects" section.

INSECT ANATOMY

For an organism to classify as an insect, the adult form must have six legs and three distinct body regions (Figure 10.1). In addition, many adult insects have one or two pairs of wings located on the second and third segment of the thorax.

Three Pairs of Jointed Legs

The most important characteristic of insects is the presence of three pairs of jointed legs. These are almost always present on adult or mature insects and generally present in other stages as well. In addition to walking and jumping, insects often use their legs for digging, grasping, feeling, swimming, carrying, building nests, and cleaning their bodies. The legs of insects vary greatly in size and form, both of which are characteristic used in further classification (Figure 10.2).

Three Distinct Body Regions

An adult insect's body is made up of three parts: head, thorax, and **abdomen** (Figure 10.1). An insect's body is

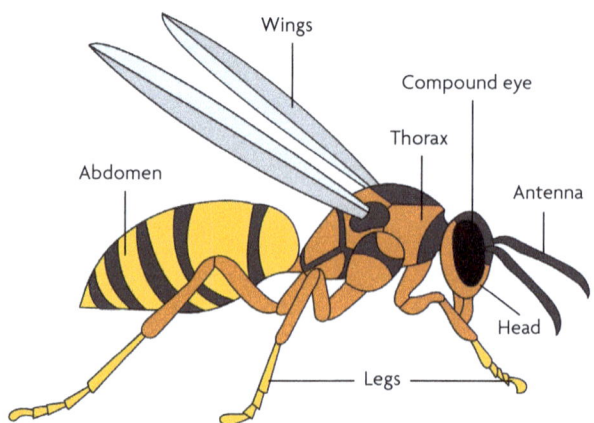

Figure 10.1 Typical body parts of an insect

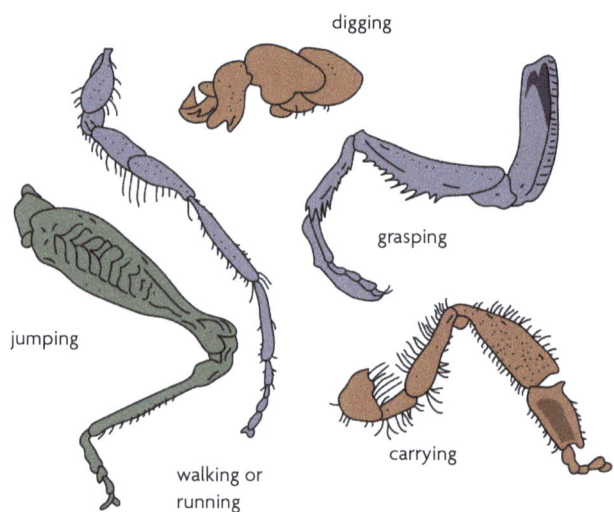

Figure 10.2 Leg adaptations of some insects

not supported by a bony skeleton but by a tough body wall called an exoskeleton. The tough outer covering of the exoskeleton skin is referred to as the cuticle. The cuticle contains a layer of wax that determines its permeability to water (or insecticides) and prevents desiccation (drying). The cuticle of each segment is made of several hardened plates called sclerites that are separated by infolds or sutures that provide both strength and flexibility. The cuticle of the immature or larval stage is not usually as hard as that of the adult.

The main features of an insect's head are the eyes, antennae, and mouthparts. The head serves as an insect's main body region for sensory input and feeding.

The thorax is made up of three segments: prothorax, mesothorax, and metathorax. Each of these segments bears one pair of legs. The wings are attached to the mesothorax and metathorax, never to the prothorax.

The number of segments in the abdomen may vary, but there are usually not more than 11. In most cases, it is difficult to distinguish the exact number of abdominal segments. Some insects have additional appendages at the tip of the abdomen. They may be short, as in grasshoppers, termites, and cockroaches; extremely long, as in mayflies; or curved, as in earwigs.

Many insects respire (breathe) through pores on their thorax or abdomen, called spiracles. Insecticides can also enter the insect's body through the spiracles.

One Pair of Antennae

Antennae are a prominent and distinctive feature of insects. Insects have one pair of antennae located on the adult's head, usually between or in front of the eyes. Antennae are segmented, vary greatly in form and complexity, and are often referred to as horns or "feelers" (Figure 10.3). They are primarily olfactory organs (used to smell), but they serve other functions in some insects, including touch.

Mouthparts

An insect's most remarkable and complicated structural feature is its mouth. The form and function of insect mouthparts vary widely. Although insect mouthparts differ considerably in appearance, all types include the same basic parts.

Most insects fall into one of two broad categories by mouthpart type: those adapted for piercing-sucking, or those adapted for chewing (Figure 10.4). Mouthparts for siphoning and sponging are also common.

Insects with chewing mouthparts have mandibles with teeth and strong jaws. Chewing larvae and adults

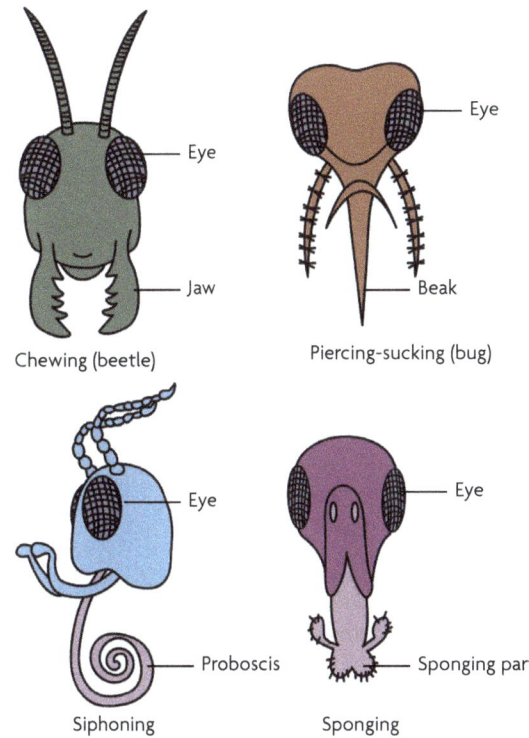

Figure 10.4 Examples of insect mouthparts

bite and chew plant parts and create holes and tunnels in leaves, stems, twigs, and fruits (Figure 10.5). Chewing damage occurs inside stems and branches by borers; inside leaves by miners; in fruits, nuts, and seeds by worms or weevils; and on leaves by defoliators or skeletonizers.

Insects that cause injury by chewing include armyworms, cabbageworms, Colorado potato beetles, grasshoppers, Japanese beetles, and fall webworms.

Insects with sucking mouthparts pierce plants with slender, sharp-pointed mouthparts called stylets. These insects—such as aphids, leafhoppers, true bugs, scale insects, thrips, and whiteflies—feed on photosynthates, the products of photosynthesis (sugars and other complex carbohydrates). The withdrawal of the sap results in minute white, brown, or red spotting on leaves, fruits, or twigs; curling leaves; deformed fruit; or general wilting, browning, and dying of the entire plant. Some of these

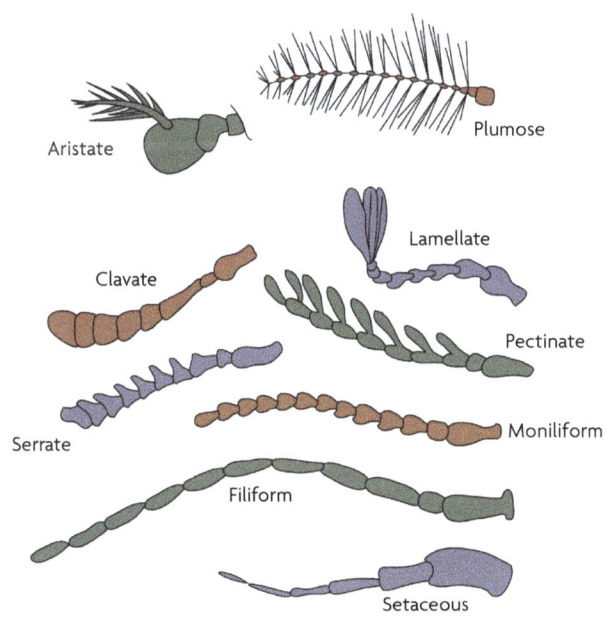

Figure 10.3 Various kinds of antennae

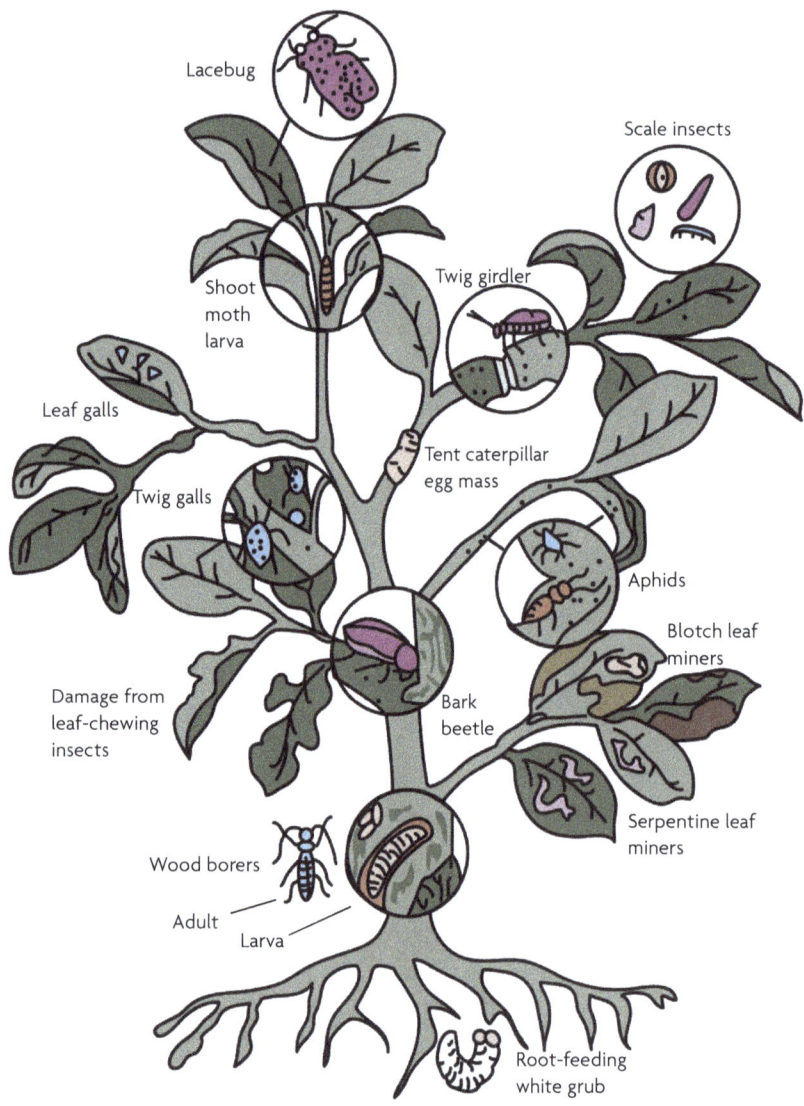

Figure 10.5 Insects and associated feeding damage

remove plant tissue. Knowing the difference in damage caused by chewing or sucking insects is the first step in pest identification.

The mouthparts of larvae tend to be different from the adults of the same species, because they feed on different foods. Caterpillars have chewing mouthparts for consuming leaves and other vegetation; in contrast, adult moths or butterflies feed on liquids such as nectar, so they are equipped with a sucking tube that forms siphoning mouthparts.

Insects that attack plants below the soil surface have chewing or sucking mouthparts. The attacks differ from the above-ground forms only in their position with reference to the soil surface. Some subterranean insects spend their entire life cycle below ground. For example, the woolly apple aphid, as both nymph and adult, sucks sap from the roots of apple trees, causing the development of tumors and subsequent decay of the tree's roots.

Other subterranean insects have at least one life stage above ground. Wireworms, root maggots, strawberry root weevils, blackvine weevils, Japanese beetles, and grape and corn rootworms all fall into this category: their larvae are root feeders while the adults live aboveground.

insects inject toxic salivary products into the plant that results in discolored leaves and dieback of woody plant parts.

Some insects, such as aphids and leafhoppers, are **vector**s or transmitters of diseases (especially viruses). There are more than 200 plant diseases transmitted by insects. Feeding, laying eggs, and boring into plants create entrance points for disease. They may carry disease on or in their bodies or simply create the point of entrance for a disease vectored by another source. Table 10.1 gives some examples of insect-vectored diseases.

The damage done by sucking mouthparts seldom results in loss of plant tissue; rather, they form holes or cause deformed growth. Pests with chewing mouthparts

TABLE 10.1. EXAMPLES OF INSECT-VECTORED PLANT DISEASES

Disease	Vector
Dutch elm disease (fungus)	Elm bark beetle
Fireblight (bacteria)	Pollinating insects
Tomato curly top virus	Beet leafhopper
Cucumber mosaic virus	Aphids
Tomato spotted wilt virus	Thrips
Aster yellows (phytoplasma)	Leafhoppers

Wings

Many insects develop wings as adults; they are the only winged arthropods. The names of some of the insect orders end in "-ptera," which comes from the Greek word meaning "with wings." Thus, each of these names denotes some feature of the wings. Hemiptera (true bugs) means half-winged; Hymenoptera (ants, bees, and wasps) means membrane-winged; and Diptera (flies) means two-winged.

The venation, or the arrangement of veins, in wings is different for each species of insect; thus, it serves as a means of identification (Figure 10.6). There are systems that name different styles of venation for descriptive purposes. Wing surfaces may be bare or covered with fine hairs or scales.

INSECT GROWTH AND DEVELOPMENT

Every insect begins life as an egg; however, the eggs of some harmful pests—such as aphids—hatch within the body of the female parent are born as immatures but living young insects. In some insects, the egg may or may not need to be fertilized by sperm to develop. Females can produce more females (or sometimes, males) by a process called **parthenogenesis**. About 1% of all insects are parthenogenetic. Some bees, ants, wasps, and aphids are notable examples of insects that can reproduce by parthenogenesis. When males are required, sexual mating takes place.

Insects grow by shedding their exoskeleton in a process called molting. Insects increase in size and appearance with each molt. Immature insects may molt many times, often six or more.

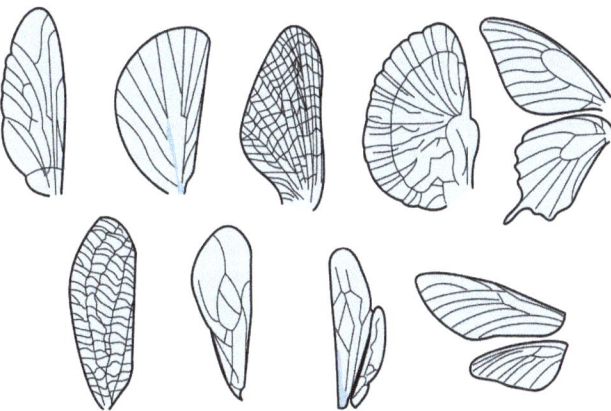

Figure 10.6 Insect wings showing venation

The change in shape and appearance from the juvenile to the adult stage is called **metamorphosis** (Figure 10.7). The term is a combination of two Greek words: "meta," meaning change, and "morphe," meaning form.

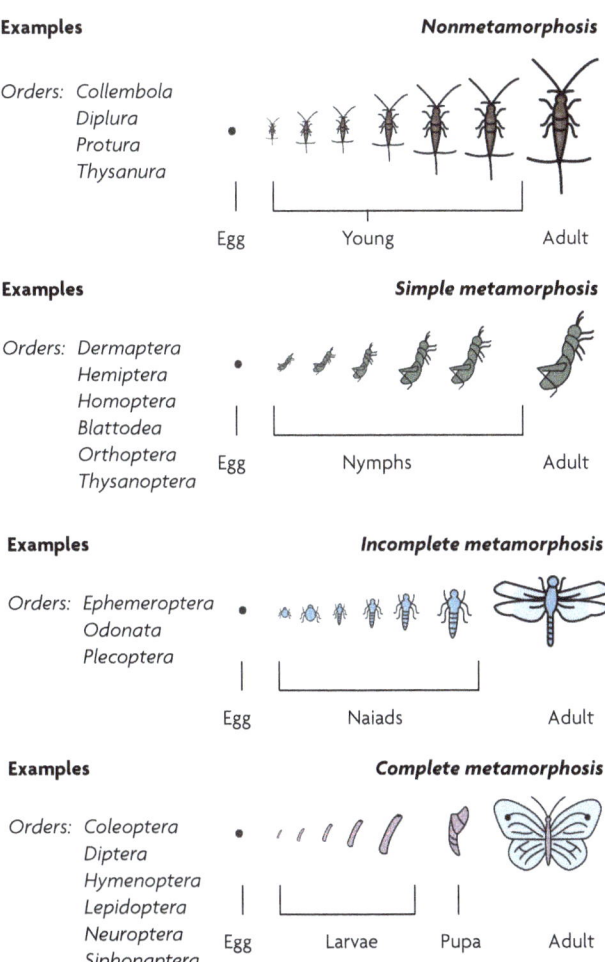

Figure 10.7 Insect development: metamorphosis

It is commonly defined as a marked or abrupt change in form or structure and refers to all stages of development. Related arthropods such as spiders, mites, and centipedes also undergo metamorphosis; however, the changes in shape of spiders and lower insects are much less dramatic than the complete change in shape of more developed insects. This more pronounced change is called complete metamorphosis. Beetles, moths, butterflies, wasps, ants, and flies all go through four markedly different developmental stages: egg, larva, pupa, and adult.

The insects in their larval stage often do the most damage to plants, because insect larvae are basically feeding machines. Over time, the larva or nymph sheds its exoskeleton (molts) at various stages of growth as it outgrows the cuticle. Most insects do not grow gradually, but in stages. When their exoskeleton gets too tight, it splits open and the insect crawls out, protected by a new, soft exoskeleton that formed underneath the old one. The new exoskeleton then hardens larger than the previous exoskeleton and allows new growth and development. The stage of life between each molt is called an instar. Following each molt, the insect increases its feeding. The number of instars, or frequency of molts, varies considerably between species and, to some extent, with food supply, temperature, and moisture.

Feeding by adults may also be destructive. The larval and adult stages of many species feed on different hosts or different parts of a host. The pupa does not feed and appears to be inactive, but in reality, it is in a very active stage of metamorphosis.

Lower insects undergo a slight change of shape that is called simple metamorphosis. True bugs, aphids, grasshoppers, termites, earwigs, and some aquatic insects go through only three developmental stages: egg, nymph, and adult. Nymphs and adults closely resemble each other, but nymphs are smaller and lack wings. In these species, the adults and nymphs usually feed on the same host or host parts.

In some aquatic insect species, such as dragonflies, the nymphs are gill-breathing; this quality makes them look different from and live in different habitats than the adults. Insects in this group are sometimes referred to as having incomplete metamorphosis, and the nymphs are sometimes called naiads.

The most primitive insects go through very little change between stages. The adults lack wings, so they closely resemble the nymphs. Most experts refer to this as non-metamorphosis.

One life cycle lasting from the egg stage to the production of an egg by the adult insect is called a **generation**. Many insect species only have one generation each year, while others have several—especially in the South where warm seasons last longer. A single generation may take many years—such as the 17 years a life cycle lasts for some cicadas, one of the longest-lived insects in North America.

A new generation does not always begin with the egg stage in the spring. However, in any given region, an insect species normally overwinters in the same stage each year. Insects are cold blooded, and their body temperature is influenced by the temperature of their environment. Winter in South Carolina offers gardeners some respite from insects, as most insects are active during the warmer months of the year or during warmer parts of the day.

INSECT CLASSIFICATION

Identifying over one million insect species would be impossible without the organization of a standard classification system. This system of grouping organisms is based on the degrees of similarity between them. It ranges from the broad-based Kingdom to the more specific species level, as shown in order here:

- Kingdom (broadest category)
- Phylum
- Class
- Order
- Family
- Genus
- Species/Specific epithet (narrowest category)

As you learned in Chapter 2: Botany and Plant Physiology, this hierarchical classification system is also used to identify plants. At the highest level, most organisms are divided into two kingdoms: animal and plant. Kingdoms have major divisions known as phyla (phylum is singular). Insects are placed in the phylum Arthropoda and the class Insecta.

Specific Insect Orders

Depending on the authority, the class Insecta is further subdivided into 30 or more categories called orders. Each order may contain dozens, hundreds, or thousands of species that share similar anatomical features (body parts). Insect orders include but are not limited to:

- Blattodea: cockroaches and termites (formerly Isoptera)
- Coleoptera: beetles and weevils
- Dermaptera: earwigs
- Diptera: flies, mosquitos, gnats, and midges
- Hemiptera: true bugs, leafhoppers, aphids, scales, and whiteflies
- Hymenoptera: ants, bees, and wasps
- Lepidoptera: butterflies and moths
- Neuroptera: lacewings and antlions
- Odonata: damselflies and dragonflies
- Orthoptera: crickets, katydids, and grasshoppers
- Thysanoptera: thrips

Table 10.2 lists and elaborates on the most important orders for South Carolina gardeners to be aware of. Not all the insects in this table are plant-feeding pests, even when you find them on a plant. For example, insects in Coleoptera, Diptera, Hymenoptera, and Neuroptera can be found on plants as parasites or predators of plant-feeding insects, pollinators, or scavengers of dead vegetation or materials left behind by other insects.

Insect orders are subdivided into smaller groups known as families, genera, and species. The family is a more finite grouping of very closely related insects. Family names end with "idae." Aphidae (aphids), Aleyrodidae (whiteflies), and Chrysomelidae (leaf beetles) are examples of families of insects.

Families are further subdivided into genera and species. These are usually the most finite levels of the classification system. Consider these examples for classifying two insects:

Japanese Beetle
Order: Coleoptera
Family: Scarabeaidae
Genus: Popillia
Specific epithet: japonica

Euonymus Scale
Order: Hemiptera
Family: Diaspididae
Genus: Unaspis
Specific epithet: euonymi

The majority of insect species have common names, which are often associated at the genus level. The most common insects also acquire common names, and sometimes one species has several common names. For example, when found on corn, *Helicoverpa zea* is called the corn earworm; when it is found on tomatoes, it is called the tomato fruitworm, and on cotton it is called the cotton bollworm.

Common names are often used to refer to large families or orders of insects. For example, the order Lepidoptera refers to butterflies and moths, and the order Coleoptera refers to beetles.

Common Insect Orders in Homes and Gardens

Coleoptera: Beetles and Weevils (Figure 10.8)
Beetles are common insects (about 40% of all insect species), but only a few are garden pests. Flea beetles, wireworms (click beetle larvae), cucumber beetles, vegetable weevils, and green fruit beetles are common in South Carolina home vegetable gardens. Boring beetles infest trunks and branches of fruit and nut trees. Adult pest beetles may feed on the same crop as their larvae, unlike other pest groups such as caterpillars (larvae of butterflies and moths) and maggots (fly larvae) where the adults do little damage.

Ladybird beetles (ladybugs) feed on a wide range of pests, including aphids, scale insects, insect eggs, mites, and other small insects.

Most beetles are characterized by:

- Adults with hardened exoskeletons.
- Adults with two pairs of wings, the outer pair hardened and the inner pair membranous (though a few beetles are practically wingless, and some have only the hard outer pair of wings).

TABLE 10.2 COMMON INSECT ORDERS IN SOUTH CAROLINA GARDENS AND LANDSCAPES

Order	Common Name	Metamorphosis	Mouthparts	Wings
Blattodea	cockroaches, termites	incomplete	chewing	2 pair
Coleoptera	beetles, weevils	complete	chewing	2 pair
Collembola	springtails	none	chewing	none
Dermaptera	earwigs	simple	chewing	2 pair
Diptera	flies	complete	chewing (some larvae), sponging, or piercing-sucking	1 pair
Hemiptera	true bugs, aphids, scale	simple	piercing-sucking	2 pair
Hymenoptera	bees, wasps, ants	complete	chewing-lapping	2 pair
Lepidoptera	butterflies, moths	complete	chewing (larvae), siphoning	2 pair
Neuroptera	lacewings, antlions	complete	chewing	2 pair
Orthoptera	crickets, grasshoppers	incomplete	chewing	2 pair
Siphonaptera	fleas	complete	chewing, piercing-sucking	none

Figure 10.8 June beetle, order Coleoptera
Image Credit: Gerry Carner, Clemson University

- Chewing mouthparts.
- Adults with noticeable antennae.
- Larvae with head capsules, three pairs of legs on the thorax, and no legs on the abdomen (though weevil larvae lack legs on the thorax).
- Complete metamorphosis.

Dermaptera: Earwigs (Figure 10.9)

Members of this order are generally considered harmless creatures. Earwigs are active at night and remain hidden under mulch, boards, rocks, woodpiles, and other cool, damp places. Most earwigs only eat decaying plant material or dead insects. The European earwig is a common species found in South Carolina and can be a nuisance. The striped earwig is another southern species found in agricultural fields and gardens.

Common characteristics of earwigs include:

- Medium-sized, elongated, flattened adults, usually brown to black in color.
- Chewing mouthparts.
- Short, hardened outer wings and folded, membranous, "ear-shaped" inner wings.
- Simple metamorphosis and nymphs that resemble adults but lack wings.
- Adults with strong, movable forceps on the abdomen.
- Curved pinchers located at the end of the abdomen, usually used for protection but sometimes to catch prey.

Diptera: Flies, Mosquitoes, Gnats, and Midges (Figure 10.10)

Dipterans are unusual in that they only have one pair of wings, whereas most insects have two pairs. Size, color, and food sources vary widely; dipterans may be predators or parasites of other insects or feed on nectar or blood. Although not as widely knowns as bees and butterflies, dipterans are also important pollinators. As larvae, many species feed on decaying animal or plant matter, although some feed within living plant tissue.

Members of this order are generally characterized by:

- Adults with one pair of clear, membranous wings.
- Adults with sponging (ex. housefly) or piercing-sucking (ex. mosquito) mouthparts.
- Larvae with mouth hooks or chewing mouthparts.
- Larvae with advanced forms, such as the house fly and its relatives, who have no head capsule, possess mouth hooks, and are called maggots;

Figure 10.9 Earwig, order Dermaptera
Image Credit: Gerry Carner, Clemson University

Figure 10.10 Crane fly, order Diptera
Image Credit: Terasa Lott, Clemson University

lower forms such as mosquito larvae have head capsules.
- Complete metamorphosis.

Hemiptera: Stink Bugs, Plant Bugs, Squash Bugs, Boxelder Bugs, Aphids, Cicadas, Leafhoppers, Mealybugs, Scale Insects, and Whiteflies (Figure 10.11)

Aphids are soft-bodied insects that range in color; they can be green, yellow, red, grey, or black. They suck fluids from leaves and stems, causing stunted or deformed buds and flowers and sometimes curled or puckered leaves.

Mealybugs are oval-shaped and covered with a white, woolly coat. They feed on plant sap and exude honeydew. Look for them in stem crevices and leaf joints.

Scale insects are highly destructive pests because they often remain unnoticed until they've become well-established. They get their name from the protective fish-scale-like covering they produce and are about the size of a pencil tip.

Scale insects anchor to plant parts with their piercing-sucking mouthparts and feed on plant sap. Individual scales may look like oval or rod-shaped bumps, sometimes resembling bark or buds. They range in color between white, yellow, grey, brown, and black. You can spot these insects on leaves, stems, branches, trunks, and occasionally fruit.

There are two types of scale insects.

Soft scales secrete a thin, waxy layer that cannot be separated from their body. When you dislodge a soft scale with a pin or sharp pencil point, look for the telltale shiny spot of honeydew. Legs and antennae attach to the underside of the shell. Because they consume large amounts of plant sap, soft scales excrete a sticky, sugary liquid called "honeydew" as a by-product of their feeding. In humid environments, the shiny, sticky leaves may be colonized by sooty mold fungi that feed on the honeydew and impart a black soot-like coating onto the leaves. Large patches of sooty mold that blacken leaves and stems are often what draws attention to a scale problem.

Armored scales secrete a hard, lacquered covering over their bodies. This cover is not attached and can usually be separated from the scale's body. They are typically smaller than soft scales, about 1/16 –1/8-in. long. Armored scale insects do not excrete honeydew and therefore do not support the growth of sooty mold.

Scale insects produce eggs that hatch into tiny mobile "crawlers," or nymphs. They move around the plant seeking suitable sites to feed, settle down, secrete their scale covering, and mature to adulthood. Some species overwinter as eggs beneath the dead female's cover and hatch in the spring; others overwinter as fertilized females and resume feeding in the spring when they lay eggs and die.

There are 1,200 described species of whiteflies that attack a wide array of agronomic, vegetable, and ornamental crops. Their name is derived from the white, powdery wax they secrete from their abdomens to cover the wings and body of the adult form.

The tiny, white mothlike adults (about 1/12-in. long) usually lay 30–500 tiny, white spindle-shaped eggs, usually on the undersides of the leaves of new growth. The creamy yellow eggs turn dark gray after 24 hours. They hatch within 5–7 days into inconspicuous, translucent white nymphs called "crawlers." The oval, flattened crawlers wander for a short distance before permanently settling down to feed. After the first of their four molting stages, the nymphs lose their legs and antennae and look like tiny scale insects, with a flattened, oval appearance and a waxy secretion covering their bodies. There are three nymphal stages, spaced at 2–4-day intervals, that feed on the plant. The pupal stage lasts about one week.

Both adult and nymph whiteflies, which are usually found on the undersides of the leaves, suck phloem sap with their piercing and sucking mouthparts. Their feeding results in yellowed or mottled leaves and reduced plant vigor. Leaves may shrivel up and drop prematurely. Like aphids, mealybugs, and soft scale insects, whiteflies excrete honeydew as they feed. This sticky, sugary solution collects dust and supports the growth of black sooty mold fungi. Whiteflies produce many generations per year.

Figure 10.11 Southern green stink bug, order Hemiptera
Image Credit: Gerry Carner, Clemson University

Hemipterans are usually characterized by:

- Incomplete metamorphosis via egg, nymph, and adult stages (with the exception of scales and whiteflies).
- Piercing-sucking mouthparts—at all stages—that can injure plants.
- Adults and nymphs that can damage plants.
- Generally small to medium sizes, though cicadas may be large and hard-bodied.
- Adults with two pair of wings.

Hymenoptera: Ants, Bees, Horntails, Sawflies, and Wasps (Figure 10.12)
Some Hymenoptera have modified egg-laying organs that function as stingers, used for defense or to subdue prey. This group of insects are extremely beneficial to humans because of their role as pollinators and their assistance with the control of pest insects through predation and parasitism.

Common characteristics of most Hymenopterans include:

- Adults with two pairs of membranous wings.
- Larvae with no legs (wasps, bees, and ants) or three pairs of legs on the thorax and more than four pairs of legs on the abdomen (some sawflies).
- Chewing mouthparts.
- Rather soft-bodied or slightly hardened-bodied adults.
- Complete metamorphosis.
- Beneficial species that prey on or parasitize

Figure 10.13 Formosan subterranean termites, order Blattodea
Image Credit: Eric Benson, Clemson University

harmful insects.

Blattodea: Cockroaches and Termites (Formerly Isoptera) (Figure 10.13)
This order includes cockroaches and termites. Although not plant pests, we include them in this chapter because it is common to encounter them in the landscape. Cockroaches are scavengers or omnivores, and although some species are commonly found in close association with human dwellings, only a very small percent of cockroach species are considered pests.

Common characteristics of cockroaches include:

- Flattened, elongated bodies.
- Long, filiform antennae.
- Chewing mouthparts.
- Incomplete metamorphosis.

Termites were previously in the order Isoptera. Overall, it is a large and diverse group of insects that fall into one of three categories: subterranean, drywood, and dampwood. This section focuses on subterranean termites.

Subterranean termites feed on cellulose-containing materials such as dead trees. They digest wood with the help of the microorganisms in their digestive

Figure 10.12 Eastern bumble bee, order Hymenoptera
Image Credit: Terasa Lott, Clemson University

tracts. Termites become a problem when wooden structures are built over or near their colonies. They build earthen shelter tubes from the ground into the structure for protection from predators and to maintain a moist environment.

There are two major types of subterranean termites in South Carolina: several species of native subterranean termites and the imported Formosan subterranean termite. Native subterranean termites are common throughout the state. Formosan subterranean termites live mainly in the coastal counties, but have expanded up to Lexington County. A mature Formosan subterranean termite colony may be comprised of millions of workers; in contrast, a native colony may only support several hundred thousand workers. Because of their sheer numbers, Formosan subterranean termites are considered the most destructive termites.

Subterranean termites are characterized by:

- Social structures that produce colonies of hundreds or thousands of individuals comprising a caste system of workers, soldiers, reproductives, and winged forms known as **alates**.
- Chewing mouthparts.
- Simple metamorphosis consisting of an egg stage, an immature stage, and an adult stage and body.

Lepidoptera: Butterflies, Moths, and Skippers (Figure 10.14)
Most people are familiar with this order; Lepidoptera includes butterflies, moths, and skippers. Adults that feed do so on nectar or other liquid sources, such as the juice of rotting fruit. Most larvae feed externally on plant tissue, although some are borers or miners, some make galls, and a few are predatory. In many cases, the damage done to host plants is well tolerated, but some species are quite destructive against agricultural crops and forest trees.

The following are common characteristics of Lepidopterans:

- Soft-bodied adults with two pairs of well-developed membranous wings covered with small scales.
- Larvae (caterpillars) with chewing mouthparts.
- Coiled, sucking tubes called proboscises as adult mouthparts.
- Larvae or caterpillars that are wormlike, variable in color, and voracious feeders.
- Larvae with simple legs on the abdomen as well as the thorax.
- Complete metamorphosis.

Neuroptera: Antlions and Lacewings (Figure 10.15)
This order's name roughly translates to "nerve-wings," which describes the extensive veins in the wings of most adults that, at rest, may fold flat over the abdomen or be held like a roof over the body. Lacewings are generally welcomed by gardeners, since both the larvae and the adults consume aphids.

Most Neuropterans are characterized by:

- Insect predators, both larvae and adults, some with aquatic immatures.

Figure 10.14 Eastern Tiger Swallotail, SC state butterfly, order Lepidoptera
Image Credit: Eddie Lott

Figure 10.15 Ant lion adult, order Neuroptera
Image Credit: Gerry Corner, Clemson University

- Two pair of membranous wings.
- Adults with chewing mouthparts.
- Complete metamorphosis.

Orthoptera: Crickets and Grasshoppers (Figure 10.16)
Orthoptera derives its name from the Greek terms for "straight wing." This group consists of crickets and grasshoppers; there are more than 1,000 species in North America, most of which are herbivores.

Members of this order are often characterized by:

- Moderate to large adults, often with hard bodies.
- Incomplete metamorphosis.
- Adults with two pairs of wings (Elongated, narrow, and hardened forewings; membranous hindwings with extensive folded area).
- Chewing mouthparts.
- Damaging adult and nymph stages.
- Enlarged hind legs for jumping.
- Immature nymph stages that resemble wingless adults.

Thysanoptera: Thrips (Figure 10.17)
Flower thrips are tiny (1/16-in. long) yellowish-brown to amber-colored insects that damage rose flowers by rasping the tissues and sucking up the sap that oozes out. Their feeding causes brown, discolored streaks on flower buds. Often, the buds fail to open or the flowers look distorted. Thrips are especially fond of white or light-colored flowers. To check for thrips, open a flower that you believe is infested over a sheet of white paper and look for tiny scurrying insects that resemble slivers of wood.

Thrips are difficult to control. Fortunately, minute pirate bugs, ladybugs, lacewings, and big-eyed bugs all

Figure 10.17 Thrips, order Thysanoptera
Image Credit: Gerry Carner, Clemson University

eat them. Remove and discard all infested flowers.

Characteristics common to thrips include:

- Small, soft-bodied adult forms.
- Sucking mouthparts.
- Varied metamorphosis (a mixture of complete and incomplete).
- Tendency to stay on the flowers or leaves of plants.
- Two pairs of slender, featherlike wings fringed with hairs.

Common Non-Insect Arthropods

Many insect relatives belong to the phylum Arthropoda. They include spiders, ticks, and mites (class Arachnida); pill bugs (order Isopoda); millipedes (class Diplopoda); and centipedes (class Chilopoda). Snails and slugs in the phylum Mollusca, are also found in gardens and landscapes. Non-insect arthropods lack the characteristic features of insects.

Class Arachnida: Mites, Spiders, and Ticks (Figure 10.18)
Arachnids have no antennae, no wings, and two body regions that aren't clearly distinct from one another. Adults have only four pairs of jointed legs.

Spider mites are tiny, soft-bodied arachnids. They are common pests of many fruit and nut trees, vegetable crops, ornamentals, and houseplants. With their piercing mouthparts, spider mites suck plant sap from the undersides of leaves, causing the upper surfaces to turn bronze or yellow. Eventually, the leaves may turn brown and fall off. They may cover heavily infested leaves with webs.

Common species include: southern red or "cool

Figure 10.16 Grasshopper, order Orthoptera
Image Credit: "xIMG_7739" by David Hill is licensed under CC BY 2.0

Figure 10.18 Wolf spider, class Arachnida
Image Credit: Gerry Carner, Clemson University

weather" mites, which reproduce rapidly in spring and fall; two-spotted spider mites (pale yellow, green, brown or red), which have two spots on their backs and become active during the heat of summer; European red mites, which are red with white spines; and clover mites, which are reddish brown or gray and flat with very long front legs.

Many mites are smaller than the period on this page and are best viewed with a magnifying glass. To inspect for mites, simply tap an affected leaf over a piece of white paper and look through the lens for tiny moving specks.

Eriophyid mites include rust, bud, and blister mites. They have four legs instead of the usual eight that characterize of most arachnids.

Spiders are larger than mites and have two distinct body regions. There are over 3,500 species of spiders in the United States. Most are beneficial predators, and many do not produce webs; instead, they lie in wait for their prey and feed on insects and other small animals by paralyzing them with venom.

Three dangerous spiders are common in South Carolina, all widows. They are all shy and would rather flee than bite a human.

The Southern black widow is found throughout the state. It is easily identifiable by the shiny, black bulbous body and the red hourglass marking on the underside of the abdomen. The Southern black widow is usually found outdoors under stones or logs or in other dark, protected areas in and around buildings.

The Northern black widow is found in the mountains and the Piedmont of South Carolina. The Northern black widow looks like the Southern black widow but lacks the hourglass marking on the underside; it has two red spots instead.

The brown widow, rarer in South Carolina, is widespread in tropical areas. It was introduced into Florida and has expanded its range northward into South Carolina. In the late 1990s, it was first reported in Charleston and Beaufort; now, it is found throughout most of the state. Brown widow spiders are gray to brown in color with white and black markings on the top surface of their bulbous abdomens. The hourglass marking on the underside of the abdomen is yellow to orange, and the legs have dark bands.

Brown recluse spiders, extremely rare in South Carolina, are often confused with harmless southern house spiders, wolf spiders, and other hunting spiders. Brown recluse are light brown or grayish with long, delicate legs. The "fiddle" outline on their backs is not a dependable characteristic for identification, as many brown spiders have similar markings. The mature spider is about the size of a quarter, legs included. The key to identifying brown recluse spiders is to look for three pairs of eyes.

Ticks are external parasites of people and animals. They need a blood meal to survive and reproduce. Ticks can feed on humans and other mammals, reptiles, birds, and even frogs. Ticks feed on blood during all stages of life. Ticks can transmit several diseases—such as Lyme disease, rocky mountain spotted fever, and tick paralysis—but most tick bites do not result in illness.

Class Chilopoda: Centipedes (Figure 10.19)

Centipedes strongly resemble millipedes but have longer antennae, a more flattened cross-section, and only one pair of legs on each body segment. They are beneficial predators of other arthropods. Centipedes are nocturnal and actively seek dark shelter if exposed. The first pair of legs possess venom glands that they use to subdue their prey.

Figure 10.19 Centipede, class Chilopoda
Image Credit: "Centipede" by MattX27 is licensed under CC BY-SA 2.0.

Figure 10.20 Sowbug, order Isopoda
Image Credit: Gerry Carner, Clemson University

Order Isopoda: Sowbugs and Pillbugs (Figure 10.20)
Sowbugs and pillbugs look similar. They are gray, oval-shaped, and about 1/4–5/8-in. long. Their hard, rounded outer shell is composed of several plates. Unlike pillbugs, sowbugs have two tail-like structures. Unlike sowbugs, pillbugs (or "roly-pollies") can roll up into a tight ball when disturbed.

Sowbugs and pillbugs are active at night. They mainly feed on dead plant material and occasionally young plants and their roots, but cause little injury. They breathe with gill-like structures and must be in very moist areas to survive. Look for them during the day in moist areas such as under rocks, boards, mulch, or leaf-litter. They do not bite and are completely harmless to humans.

Class Diplopoda: Millipedes (Figure 10.21)
Millipedes are wormlike and have two visible anatomical regions: a head and body. They generally have round cross-sections, and all but the first four or five body segments include two pairs of legs. Millipedes are generally inoffensive creatures that feed on fungus and decaying plant material. At times, they can cause damage to vegetables or other plants in greenhouses.

INSECT IDENTIFICATION AND MANAGEMENT

Entomologists examine insects under a magnifying lens, dissecting scope, or microscope and use anatomical features to distinguish, classify, and identify insects. Identifying insects to the species level is often difficult and may require a key. There are field keys that help identify insects based on the damage they cause to plants, such as holes chewed or mined into leaves rather than discolored or deformed leaves caused by sap-sucking insects. When an insect specimen is available, keys help identify the insect from orders down to the species level.

Identifying a given insect to the species level is often difficult. It may include counting the number of teeth on the mandibles or the number of segments on the antennae. Sometimes entomologists use the arrangement and length of hairs on the head, thorax, or abdomen or the arrangement of veins in the wings as identifying characteristics.

For home gardeners, knowing the exact species of an insect may not be necessary, especially after you determine whether it's beneficial or harmful. If it's a harmful pest, such as aphids, there's no need to determine the exact species; control measures for most aphid species are the same. The same could be said about mealybugs, most soft scales, spider mites, and many other common pests, provided you have identified the host plant.

Knowing the identity of the host plant is very important; it helps reveal an insect's identity. Although some insect pests are general feeders that feed on a variety of different plants, many are quite specific to their host. For example, the dogwood twig girdler only attacks dogwood; it does not feed on pines, oaks, camellias, or other plants. Knowing the identity of the host and pest is also important when providing recommendations for chemical pesticides, particularly if you plan to apply them to vegetables, fruit, or other edible crops.

Determining the cause of poor plant performance is a difficult task; Master Gardeners and other diagnosticians often have incomplete evidence. The diagnostic begins with gathering facts. Then, draw on your past experiences, published references, and other resources. Ideally, a diagnosis includes a site visit to yield more

Figure 10.21 Millipede, class Diplopoda
Image Credit: Gerry Carner, Clemson University

evidence to contribute to a diagnosis. Unfortunately, visiting the location where a sample was taken is often not possible. So, when confronted by a problem, Master Gardeners should follow these tips for diagnosing insect- and mite-related problems:

- Identity the afflicted plant. Most insects and mites have preferred host plants, while some are general feeders. Many references are organized by host plant, which helps determine potential culprits. Is the problem localized to one or several plants? Is it on a single species or several species of plant? What type of damage is occurring?
- When people notice a pest problem and seek advice, it may be too late to take any corrective action in that particular growing season. In some situations, the pest may be gone, and only the damage remains. Become familiar with pests' life cycles to determine if there are necessary controls against subsequent generations of the pest.
- Exercise caution before making recommendations based on clients' verbal descriptions. Ideally, observe the damage and the insect itself to avoid making an incorrect identification. Incorrect identification results in ineffective control measures, unnecessary expense, and potential harm to beneficial insects.
- Master Gardeners represent Clemson University. All recommendations to the public should be based on and in agreement with published Clemson Cooperative Extension recommendations.
- Be sure to present all appropriate management strategies and allow the client to choose the method or combination that best suits their needs.
- Do not be afraid to say, "I don't know." When in doubt, do not make a diagnosis. Refer to your county agent, specialist, or Plant and Pest Diagnostic Clinic.
- Remember that the problem may not be an insect at all; disease, improper cultural practices, or conditions that include too much or too little water, poor drainage, low or high light levels, physical or chemical injury, poor adaptation to a planting site, too high or too low temperatures, and excessive or deficient levels of nutrients can all cause damage to plants.
- Refer to Chapter 13: Diagnosing and Managing Insects, Diseases, and Weeds, for a broader perspective on diagnosing plant problems. Also, study known samples that have been identified by a county agent, specialist, or Plant and Pest Diagnostic Clinic.
- Your local Extension Office can support you in submitting samples to the Plant and Pest Diagnostic Clinic. Submission guidelines and forms are found on their website (https://www.clemson.edu/public/regulatory/plant-problem/).

Basic Approaches to Successful Insect Pest Management

Identify the Problem

People have different tolerance levels for pest infestations. Some will be indifferent about the number of aphids on their shrub roses, while others who show roses may want to act when aphids first appear. In some cases, when a problem is brought to a Master Gardener's attention, it's too late to take any action; the damage is already done. For example, when orange-striped oakworms have defoliated oak trees in September, it's too late to control the pest. Killing mature or pupating caterpillars to reduce the severity of next year's infestation is not an environmentally sound approach, and besides, the oaks will shed any remaining leaves in the next few months; control is not warranted this late in the season.

Select a Management Strategy

Select one or more appropriate methods that ensure the safety of the people involved as well as the environment. If several methods are appropriate, suggest all that are reasonable and approved by Clemson University. Consider proper timing of the application to coincide with the most vulnerable time in the life cycle of the insect. Then, allow your client to choose the approach that's best for them.

Because of their toxic nature, devote special attention to pesticides to ensure their proper use. Always use pesticides in strict accordance with the instructions on the label. The ornamental or food crop must be listed on the label or referred to under a general heading such as lawns, shrubs, trees, or other ornamentals. Products may have identical ingredients and be sold by different manufacturers, but their formulations, affected pests, and application sites may vary. The user is responsible for finding a product that is appropriate for their pest, plant, and site. See Chapter 13 for information on pesticide formulations, labels and labelling, application equipment, sprayer calibration, storage and disposal, and environmental concerns.

Evaluate Results

Evaluate the results of the pest control method to avoid or effectively manage the pest problem again in the future. For example, future control may necessitate planting squash in early spring to escape squash vine borer or replacing Japanese euonymus (*Euonymus japonicus*) with more resistant species to avoid euonymus scale.

BENEFIT AND VALUE OF INSECTS

Study insects carefully to distinguish the beneficial from the harmful. People often go to great lengths to destroy insects, only to learn later that they were not only harmless but were actually saving crops by eating destructive insects. Insects are beneficial to gardeners for the following reasons:

- Insects are pollinators. Most common fruits, melons, and squash, as well as many other vegetables and many ornamental plants (chrysanthemums, irises, orchids, and yuccas) are pollinated by insects.
- Parasitic predatory insects destroy harmful insects.
- Insects can destroy weeds in the same ways that they injure crop plants.
- Insects improve the physical condition of the soil and promote soil fertility by burrowing throughout the surface layer. The dead bodies and droppings of insects serve as fertilizer.
- Insects perform a valuable service as scavengers by devouring the bodies of dead animals and plants and burying carcasses and dung.

These benefits from insects, although genuine, are insignificant compared with the good that insects do when fighting each other. There is no doubt that the greatest single factor in keeping plant-feeding insects from overwhelming the rest of the world is the predation and parasitism of other insects (Figure 10.22). Insects that eat other insects fall into these two main categories: predators and parasites.

Predators are insects (or other animals) that catch and devour other creatures, called prey; predators usually kill and consume their prey in a single meal. The prey is generally smaller and weaker than the predator. Predatory insect and insect relatives include spiders, praying mantids, lady beetles, and green lacewings.

Parasites are organisms that live on or in the bodies of living organisms (hosts) from which they get their food during at least one stage of their existence. The hosts are usually larger and stronger than the parasites and are not killed promptly but continue to live in close association with the parasite. Braconid wasps and Trichogramma wasps are parasitoids that hatch from eggs inside or on another insect host. They consume and eventually kill the host.

Predators are typically very active and have long life cycles; parasites are often slower and tend to have very short life cycles.

Releasing beneficial insects into your landscape or garden may offer some benefit, but it is better to conserve the beneficial insects already there. Learn to distinguish between pests and beneficial insects in your garden and landscape. Avoid applying broad spectrum insecticides to plants if it could harm beneficial insects, especially if it looks like these beneficial insects are already keeping harmful insects to tolerable levels.

(a) Predaceous stinkbug

(b) Big eyed bug

(c) Lacewing

(d) Carolina mantid

(e) Braconid wasp

Figure 10.22 a, b, c, d, e   Commonly ocurring beneficial insects
Image Credit[a, b, c, d]: Gerry Carner, Clemson University
Image Credit[e]: "Braconid Wasp - Phaenocarpa species, Woodbridge, Virginia" by Judy Gallagher is licensed under CC BY 2.0.

Chapter 11
Plant Diseases and Disorders

Revised and updated by Anthony P. Keinath, Ph.D

Previous version prepared by Anthony P. Keinath, Meg R. Williamson, Robert Polomski, and R. Walker Miller

LEARNING OBJECTIVES

- Know the major disease-causing organisms, how they infect plants, and how they spread.
- Understand the concept of the disease triangle.
- Know the difference between signs and symptoms of disease.
- Understand and give examples of biotic and abiotic diseases and disorders.
- Understand how to prevent or manage plant diseases and disorders according to best practice.

CHAPTER 11 - PLANT DISEASES AND DISORDERS

INTRODUCTION

It is a familiar cry to any gardener: "What is wrong with my plant?"

A variety of agents can harm or cause problems with plants. These problems may be temporary or permanent; a one-time event (an injury) or an ongoing condition (a disease). Plant problems may be negligible or cost millions of dollars in losses and prevention on a national or global scale. For example, sudden oak death has destroyed tens of thousands of native oaks in California and Oregon; nurseries that produce woody ornamentals have lost millions of dollars to the disease.

Plant disease is a process in which living or nonliving entities interfere with a plant's functions over a period of time. This interference may cause changes in the plant's appearance or yield capacity. Indicators of plant disease include:

- smaller leaves,
- fewer leaves,
- smaller root systems,
- shorter internodes,
- fewer or smaller fruit,
- blemished plant parts, and
- death of plant parts or entire plants.

The change in a plant's appearance is relative to a plant of the same age and variety that is not diseased. It's important to know what a healthy plant looks like before determining that a plant does or does not have a disease.

HOW DISEASE AFFECTS PLANT HEALTH

Altering Photosynthesis

If a disease reduces the amount chlorophyll in a leaf, kills part of the leaf, or causes the leaf to fall off prematurely, it reduces photosynthesis. Leaf spots and blights and damage due to air pollution or pesticide toxicity inhibit photosynthesis in these ways.

Damaging Roots

Roots, especially root tips, absorb nutrients and water while structurally supporting the plant. Browning and softening of roots are typical symptoms of root damage or disease. Damage to roots belowground results in yellowing, leaf scorching, stunting, wilt, and dieback of portions of the plant aboveground.

Damaging Vascular Tissue

Vascular tissue is the xylem and/or phloem of a plant. If a disease disrupts water and nutrient transport, leaf tips and margins burn, leaves wilt, and roots die. Stem rots, vascular wilts, cankers, galls, and mechanical injury inhibit the transport of nutrients and water.

Damaging Nutrient Reserves

The roots and stems of perennial plants store nutrients. Root, stem, and crown rots destroy food reserves and can lead to plant death when those reserves run out.

Diverting Food from Plant Growth

Diseases can redirect the nutrients needed for growth towards pathogen growth; this occurs when galls, mildews, nematodes, rusts, and viruses develop on and in the plant. As a result, flower and stem blights, smuts, and many abiotic diseases inhibit plant growth and reproduction.

RECOGNIZING SYMPTOMS AND SIGNS

A **symptom** is a characteristic of a plant indicating that it is diseased. Symptoms may be obvious only if healthy plants are near diseased ones. For example, if all trees appear the same in an area, it gives the impression that all is normal. However, all may be stunted by the same disease. Some symptoms are microscopic and are not visible unless highly magnified.

External symptoms are visible on the outside of a plant and are usually obvious (Figure 11.1). Internal symptoms are inside the plant, like discolored vascular tissue for wilts. To detect these symptoms, you must cut open the plant. Local symptoms are those affecting a small area of the plant. Systemic symptoms affect a large portion of the plant or the entire plant.

Signs are parts of the disease-causing agent present in, on, or near a diseased plant. Fungal spores or mycelium and bacterial ooze from cankers are signs. Signs help identify pathogens.

Seeing symptoms on a diseased plant is like looking at a plant disease from the plant's perspective, while recognizing signs is looking at disease from the pathogen's perspective.

Figure 11.1 Symptoms of anthracnose on pepper fruit.
Image Credit: Anthony Keinath, Clemson University

DISEASE IS AN INTERACTION

Plant disease occurs only through the concurrence of three factors. For a plant disease to occur, all factors must be present—just one or two factors may be a problem but is not disease. This relationship is most easily expressed through the disease triangle (Figure 11.2).

Disease occurs only when a susceptible host plant, a plant pathogen, and a set of environmental conditions favorable to the pathogen all exist at the same time and in the same place. While one factor may be most important in a particular disease and less important in another, no single factor acts alone.

Among the environmental factors most favorable to disease pathogens are moderate to warm temperatures, high relative humidity, wet plant surfaces, saturated soil, and specific periods of exposure to such factors. As you might suspect, the climate of the humid Southeast is a literal breeding ground for disease.

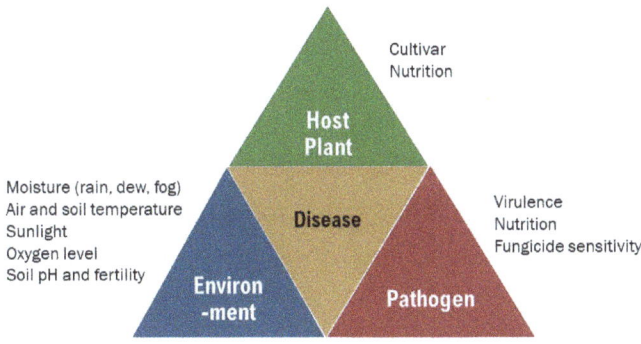

Figure 11.2 The plant disease triangle.
Figure Credit: Anthony Keinath, Clemson University

Plant disease is a dynamic biological process. Once the requirements of the disease triangle are met, the pathogen infects the susceptible host, and the disease begins and continues until the environment becomes unfavorable for the pathogen. Managing the disease requires eliminating any one of these factors. Breeding a resistant host, altering the environment, or spraying chemicals that interfere with pathogen growth are all helpful disease management techniques.

Disease or Disorder?

Biotic, or infectious, diseases are caused by living factors called pathogens. The pathogens that cause biotic diseases reproduce, spread from plant to plant, and grow. If one plant has a biotic infectious disease, it is more likely that a neighboring plant will get the disease. Plant pathogens are classified as fungi, water molds, bacteria, phytoplasmas, viruses, nematodes, and parasitic vascular plants.

Pathogens infect plants and cause disease. Plants infected by pathogens have a disease. Remember: the pathogen is not the disease. The disease does not exist outside or away from the plant, but the pathogen can and often does. Although we often refer to "disease spread," we really mean spread of pathogens from host plant to host plant.

Disorders are caused by nonliving factors. Disorders also are called abiotic diseases or noninfectious diseases. The term "disorder" is more appropriate, however, because the factors that cause disorders do not grow, reproduce, or spread from plant to plant as pathogens do. If one plant has a disorder, it does not increase the likelihood that a neighboring plant will get the same disorder, though disorders often affect groups of plants due to their shared environment.

Disorders occur when plants are exposed to extreme levels of light, moisture, nutrients, temperature, and air pollution. The toxicity of pesticides or plant growth regulators and the disruption of a plant's root environment by soil compaction, excavation, and other human activities can also cause disorders. Diagnosing a disorder is difficult, since many different factors can cause similar symptoms.

Living (Biotic) Factors That Cause Plant Disease

Plant pathogens are organisms that feed on plants and harm them, causing plant diseases. A living organism that obtains its food from another living organism is called a parasite. If it can obtain nutrients only from living tissues, it is an obligate parasite. The living organism that provides the food—willingly or unwillingly—is called the host. If the parasite harms the host while feeding, the parasite is said to be a pathogen. There are six major groups of plant pathogens.

Fungi. Fungi, along with plants and animals, are one of the three main types of living organisms. Commonly, fungi are referred to as molds, mildews, mushrooms, or yeasts. Although there are many types of fungi, this chapter focuses on fungi that attack plants.

Fungi are organisms with threadlike structures called hyphae (Figure 12.3). One of the main components of hyphae is chitin, which is also found in insects. Fungi do not produce their own food through photosynthesis like plants do. They obtain nutrients either from living tissues of plants or from dead organic matter. They secrete enzymes that break down food sources into simple chemicals that are absorbed by hyphae.

An organism that obtains nutrients from dead organic matter is called a **saprophyte**. Many fungi live as saprophytes during part of their yearly life cycles. If a diseased plant dies, these fungi continue to develop on the dead plant. Thus, it is important to remove diseased leaves, branches, and roots to prevent the buildup of pathogens on and in the soil.

Fungi reproduce by forming spores, mycelial fragments, and sclerotia. **Spores** are to fungi what seeds are to plants. A spore is a reproductive unit capable of germination and growth. Spores enable a fungus to reproduce, spread, and survive unfavorable conditions.

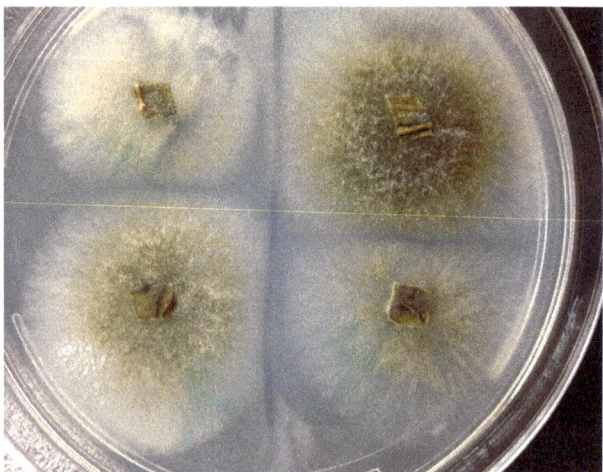

Figure 11.3 Filamentous growth of four fungal cultures on agar medium in a petri dish. A single filamentous thread is called a hypha; the plural is hyphae.

Image Credit: Anthony Keinath, Clemson University

One fungus can produce millions of spores.

Spores can be any shape, a variety of colors, and composed of one or many cells. Many fungi can be recognized by the spores they produce. Scientists use DNA fingerprinting to identify spores, but they can also depend on factors such as the way the spores are formed, their size, their color, and their structure.

Many fungi form spores in characteristic structures called fruiting bodies. Mushrooms are one type of fruiting body. You can see fruiting bodies with the naked eye or with a 10× hand lens. Often, fruiting bodies appear as round or convex swellings on the surface of leaves, branches, or stems. Typically, they are some shade of brown.

After a spore germinates, the fungus can infect a plant through natural openings between plant cells or penetrate directly into the plant cell by digesting the cell wall. The fungus then grows into the plant, sending hyphae into cells to rob them of their nutrients. Some fungi produce chemicals that are toxic to plant cells and kill them.

Some fungi spread from one area to another by pieces of their mycelium, called mycelial fragments. This form of reproduction is similar to vegetative reproduction in plants. Mycelial fragments that remain in previously used greenhouse trays spread Rhizoctonia, a fungus that causes damping-off of young vegetable and bedding plants.

Sclerotia are hard reproductive structures produced by some fungi. Sclerotia remain in the soil for several years or until a susceptible crop is planted. The sclerotia germinate at the soil surface to produce hyphae that grow into the stems of susceptible plants.

One soil fungus, *Agroathelia rolfsii*, produces characteristic sclerotia that cause the disease southern blight on over 1,200 plant species. The fungus grows as a white, fan-shaped mat around plant stems at the soil line. Round sclerotia, about the size of a mustard seed, form on the stem and on the soil surface. The young sclerotia are white but turn tan to dark brown within a few days. When conditions are less favorable for fungal growth, the mycelium disappears, but the sclerotia remain in the soil.

Water Molds. Oomycetes, more commonly called water molds, used to be classified as fungi; now, they are considered very different from fungi. They share a group with brown algae (kelp). Like fungi, water molds form hyphae. Like algae and other plants, the hyphae include cellulose.

In general, it is more difficult to manage diseases caused by water molds than diseases caused by fungi. For example, it is difficult to breed plants that are resistant to water molds, because water molds can adapt and overcome the resistance.

Water mold spores are called **sporangia** (Figure 11.4). They germinate directly, by producing a hypha, or indirectly, by releasing several dozen zoospores (swimming spores). The motile zoospores swim in films of water on leaves or between soil particles to reach host plants.

Many water molds also produce a resistant spore called an **oospore**. Oospores form inside infected fruit or leaves. When the culled fruit or diseased leaves are left in the field or garden, the thick-walled oospores remain there after the plant material decays. Oospores can be dormant for years until another susceptible crop is planted in the same spot. Soilborne water molds cause damping-off, root rots, stem rots, and fruit rots.

Aerial water molds cause foliar diseases such as downy mildew (Figure 11.4) and late blight of potato and tomato. Late blight is arguably the most famous plant disease of all time; it caused the Irish Potato Famine that lasted from 1845-1851. Late blight destroyed the potato crops in Ireland in 1845 and 1846, but the hunger, malnutrition, disease, mass emigrations, and social unrest that resulted lasted several more years. A German plant pathologist, Anton DeBary, later proved that the water mold *Phytophthora infestans* caused late blight. This was the first case study of a plant pathogen. Because of his discovery, DeBary is considered the father of plant pathology.

Bacteria. Bacteria are simple, single-celled microorganisms surrounded by a cell wall. Bacteria lack a true nucleus; this is one way in which they differ from fungi, water molds, nematodes, and parasitic plants. Bacteria absorb nutrients from living or nonliving sources, as fungi and water molds do. Bacteria can reproduce very quickly—in 30 minutes when conditions are favorable.

Bacteria enter plants through natural openings—such as stomata, hydathodes, lenticels, and nectaries—or through wounds made by insect feeding, mechanical injury, pruning, or grafting. Rainfall, insects, and people can all spread bacteria. Most bacterial diseases are more severe or widespread in moist environments.

Some bacterial cells are surrounded by a sticky mucous. A quick way to diagnose bacterial wilt in tomato is to suspend a freshly cut portion from the base of the main stem in water. Look for a white, milky stream of bacteria oozing from the cut stem (Figure 11.5).

Bacterial leaf blight, bacterial spot, fire blight, leaf scorch, and bacterial canker are all bacterial diseases of ornamental and fruit trees (Figure 11.6). In South Carolina, bacterial canker on peach tree trunks leads to a more serious disease called peach tree short life.

Phytoplasmas are specialized bacteria that have no cell wall, so they can survive only inside living plants. They reproduce as bacteria do and are found in the food-conducting vessels (phloem) of an infected plant.

Figure 11.4 Dark-colored masses of sporangia, the spores of cucurbit downy mildew, on the underside of a cucumber leaf.
Image Credit: Zachary Snipes, Clemson University

Figure 11.5 A quick diagnostic test for bacterial wilt of tomato, showing a white, milky stream of bacteria and mucous oozing from an infected tomato stem into water.
Image Credit: Zachary Snipes, Clemson University

Figure 11.6 Symptoms of bacterial canker on the trunk of a peach tree. The bark has been peeled back to reveal the discolored canker underneath.
Image Credit: Guido Schnabel, Clemson University

Symptoms caused by phytoplasmas include abnormal growth, yellowing, very short internodes, and distortion of leaf and flower tissues. Leafhoppers spread phytoplasmas. The most common phytoplasma causes a disease called aster yellows.

Plant-Parasitic Nematodes. Nematodes are microscopic, non-segmented roundworms, generally transparent and colorless. Most are slender, with bodies ranging in size from 1/50—1/8-in. long (Figure 11.7). Nematodes reproduce by eggs and molting, as insects do. Some nematodes deposit eggs in the soil or in plant tissue. Other kinds of nematodes keep their eggs in a jellylike mass attached to or inside the female's body, which becomes a tough protective capsule called a cyst when she completes her life cycle and dies. Each female can produce anywhere from a few dozen to over 500 eggs in her lifetime. Eggs of some species survive for years without hatching but then hatch quickly when a host plant root grows near them.

Rates of nematode growth and reproduction increase as soil temperature rises, from about 50–95°F. Under ideal conditions (when the temperature is between 80°–86°F), nematodes can complete a full life cycle—from newly deposited egg to egg-depositing adult—in as little as 4 weeks.

Some common plant-damaging nematodes are the root-knot, sting, ring, stubby root and lance nematodes. A wide range of vegetable, agronomic, and ornamental plants are host to the Southern root-knot nematode.

How Nematodes Injure Plants. Only about 10% of all known nematode types are parasites on plants. These nematodes are all obligate parasites, meaning they must feed on living tissues. Plant-parasitic nematodes

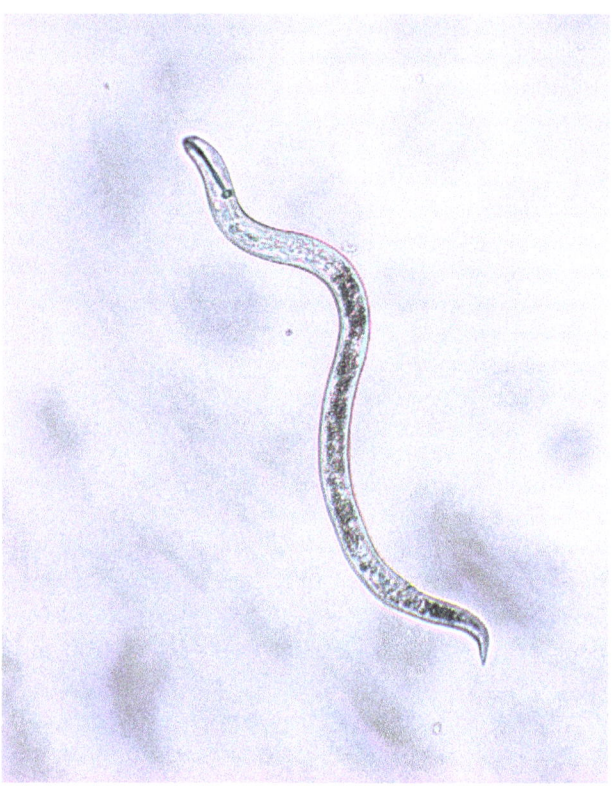

Figure 11.7 Pin nematode larva (highly magnified).
Image Credit: Paula Agudelo, Clemson University

feed with a hollow stylet or oral spear that they use to puncture cell walls, inject digestive juices into cells, and draw liquid contents from cells.

The digestive juices contain enzymes that increase the amount of food the nematode can take in. In some cases, the saliva may also contain:

- toxins that kill the cell and nearby cells, sometimes causing root elongation to stop, root tips to swell, and/or lateral roots to proliferate.
- growth-regulating chemicals that change the way the root tissues develop and grow, which can lead to knotting or galling of roots or other changes in root growth patterns.

As nematodes move through roots, they injure root cells, which may allow root-rotting fungi to invade that may not otherwise have been able to gain entry to a healthy root. Nematode infection sometimes reduces plants' disease resistance, and some nematodes can transmit certain plant viruses.

Viruses. Too small to see even with a light microscope, viruses are very simple organisms consisting of a strand of nucleic acid (either RNA or DNA, the genetic blueprint of all life) surrounded by a protective protein coat. Viruses can multiply only inside living host cells. Viruses replicate by taking over the plant cell's metabolic machinery; during this time, the plant disease develops.

Virus particles spread to all parts of the plant except the few cells at the tips of the growing points. Thus, virus diseases often affect the entire plant. Typical symptoms of viruses include chlorosis or yellowing, mosaic or mottle patterns, deformation, and stunting.

Many viruses depend on a second organism to spread them and inject them into a plant. These other organisms—often insects—are known as vectors. Aphids, whiteflies, thrips, a few mites, fungi, and nematodes all spread viruses. The relationship between a virus and its vector is as specific as the relationship between the virus and its host plant; only certain vectors can spread specific viruses. Viruses can also spread via pruning or grafting, in seed, and in parasitic plants like dodder.

Few viruses persist outside of their host plant. Most viruses, such as cucumber mosaic virus, die quickly if outside a cell or if the cell dies. Tobacco mosaic virus is one of the few viruses that can survive for years after the infected plant dies; it can survive in the tobacco in cigarettes, which is why greenhouse workers are not allowed to smoke. Viruses also survive in their vectors, although for how long—a few hours to the lifetime of the vector—depends on the virus.

Vascular Plants That Parasitize Other Plants. Dodder, mistletoe, witchweed, Indian pipes, and beech drops are seed-bearing plants that gain all or some of their nutrients by parasitizing other seed-bearing plants.

An alga (*Cephaleuros virescens*) causes algal leaf spot that commonly affects evergreen magnolias and camellias (Figure 11.8). These small-to-large leaf spots are slightly raised and grayish-green to dark reddish-brown in color; they can appear velvety. Heavy infections can cause yellowing of leaves and premature defoliation. The algae can also infect wigs and stems. Algal leaf spot is not particularly harmful; established trees can tolerate the infection.

Common Symptoms and Their Causes

Some disease symptoms are distinct; one can identify these diseases reasonably accurately based on symptoms alone. In other cases, several different diseases incited by pathogens in different groups cause similar symptoms. In these cases, you'll need additional information—such as signs or diagnostic tests like biochemical or DNA tests—to identify the pathogen.

Figure 11.8 Algal leaf spot on southern magnolia leaves.
Image Credit: Anthony Keinath, Clemson University

Spots, Blights, and Leaf Scorch.

Spots. Spots are areas of diseased tissue on leaves or fruit. Spots may be yellow at first and then turn tan, brown, or black, sometimes surrounded by a darker border. On leaves, the centers may drop out and leave a shot-hole appearance. When leaf spots merge, they often kill entire leaves. When fruit spots merge, entire fruits may rot.

Blight. Blight is the rapid killing of the leaves, flowers, or branches on a plant. It is usually caused by bacteria, water molds, or fungi (Figure 11.9). Root rots

Figure 11.9 Flower blight on camellia. Note the individual spots that expand to become blight.
Image Credit: Steven Jeffers, Clemson University

and cankers on stems and branches can also result in the rapid death of leaves higher on the plant, so examine affected plants carefully to determine where the initial infection occurred.

Leaf Scorch. Leaf scorch, or marginal leaf burn, refer to dead areas between the veins or along the margin of a leaf.

Rusts. The term "rust" refers to diseases caused by many different species of fungi with dry, powdery, reddish-orange spores. All rusts are obligate parasites. There are leaf rusts, gall rusts, and canker rusts. Some rust fungi require two different species of host plants to be present in an area for the fungus to complete its lifecycle; in the Southeast, these include cedar-apple, cedar-quince, and cedar-hawthorn rusts. Other rusts infect only one host plant. Notable rusts commonly found in the Southeast are hollyhock rust, snapdragon rust, orange rust on blackberry, and bean rust.

Smuts. Fungi related to rust fungi cause smuts. Smuts invade the flowers of grasses and cereals and prevent the seed or grain from forming. Over the centuries, smuts have caused major losses of grain and cereal crops such as barley, corn, oats, and wheat.

One common smut is corn smut. It is characterized by large white swellings of tissue, mostly on ears but also on stalks, leaves, and tassels (Figure 11.10). The galled tissue releases black smut spores late in the season that survive in the soil. Growing resistant corn varieties is the best control for corn smut. Smutted tissue should be destroyed before it can release spores.

Figure 11.10 Smut on corn. The kernels become filled with black smut spores.
Image Credit: Zachary Snipes, Clemson University

Galls. Many different plant problems—including insect feeding, callus tissue from wound-healing, fungi, and bacteria—can cause galls. One important gall-causing organism is the bacterium *Agrobacterium tumefaciens*, which carries a plasmid—a small entity that carries genetic information. The plasmid is transferred from the bacterium to the plant, where it directs the plant to produce an unusual number of cells. Breaking the gall off does not cure the plant; most plants cannot be cured of galls. Galled plants, if particularly unsightly, should be removed.

Cankers. Localized areas of dead bark and underlying wood on twigs, larger branches, and trunks are called cankers (Refer to Figure 11.6). Living organisms (such as fungi and bacteria) and environmental factors (such as extreme temperatures and hail) can cause cankers.

Many fungi that cause tree or shrub cankers inhabit the plant's surface, gain entrance through natural or human-made wounds, and only cause disease when the plant is under stress. Some fungi, however, aggressively attack trees and cause cankers that may considerably shorten a tree's life.

Damping-Off. Damping-off is the infection of young seedlings by any of several different water molds and fungi—most often species of Pythium, Rhizoctonia, and Fusarium. These soil-dwelling microorganisms produce spores that are spread by air, water, soil, and contaminated tools and pots. Excessively wet soil, excessively cool temperatures before germination (or warm ones after), and densely planted seedbeds all contribute to damping-off.

Seedlings affected by pre-emergence damping-off begin to decay before they can reach the soil surface. They become soft and mushy and turn brown or black. Emerged seedlings can be attacked just above or below the soil line. Slightly darkened, water-soaked lesions appear on the stems, and the infected stem tissue may be colorless to dark brown. As the decayed area enlarges, it girdles the stem and causes the seedlings to collapse and fall over. This disease is known as post-emergence damping-off.

Damping-off principally affects young seedlings. As seedlings age, the development of secondary stem tissue creates a protective barrier that thwarts penetration by the fungus.

Root and Crown Rots. Root and crown rots are characterized by discolored areas on a plant's roots and crown (the portion of the plant where the root and stem connect) (Figure 11.11). Diseased root tips are brown and dead and may slough off when plants are pulled from the soil.

Figure 11.11 Crown and root rot on strawberry can be caused by several fungi.
Image Credit: Zachary Snipes, Clemson University

Figure 11.12 Damping-off of Swiss chard seedlings due to extensive root rot.
Image Credit: Anthony Keinath, Clemson University

Root rot can be caused by several different species of fungi, including Rhizoctonia and Fusarium and the water molds Pythium and Phytophthora. In roots infected by Pythium, soft or brown tissue on the outer portion of the root pulls off easily and leaves a bare strand of vascular tissue (Figure 11.12). These pathogens are commonly found in soil and the dead roots of previous crops. Almost all plants are susceptible to root rots at some stage of development.

It is important to remember that anything killing roots will cause similar symptoms above ground. Yellow, wilted, or stunted leaves can be a secondary symptom of root rot. Adequate management of soil drainage and irrigation is important in preventing root rot diseases.

Vascular Wilts. Most fungi and bacteria that attack the food-and water-conducting tissues of plants enter through the roots and grow into the vascular tissue. Other wilt pathogens spread via insects or pass from plant to plant via root grafts. These pathogens survive from year to year, primarily in infected plants; however, some pathogens survive for long periods in the soil. Once inside the plant, the organisms causing vascular wilts are found almost exclusively in the vascular tissue.

How quickly symptoms develop after infection varies with host plant, pathogen, and environmental conditions. Herbaceous plants usually die by the end of the growing season. Vascular diseases may kill a tree in one year or may continuously weaken the tree but never kill it.

The first symptoms of vascular wilts are yellowing, wilting, or defoliation of one or two branches. As the disease progresses, larger and more branches show symptoms. There is often discoloration of vascular tissue in the outer wood.

Some notable types of vascular wilt include Fusarium wilt of tomato and banana; Verticillium wilt of eggplant, tomato, and many deciduous trees and shrubs; Dutch elm disease; and bacterial wilt of tomato. Many hybrid tomato varieties are resistant to Fusarium and Verticillium wilts, but even these varieties are not resistant to bacterial wilt (Figure 11.13).

Symptoms of Viral Diseases

The symptoms of viral diseases vary depending on the virus at fault, the species of plant infected, and environmental conditions. Certain environmental conditions bring out symptoms, while others mask or hide them. Symptoms associated with virus infections include:

- mottle or mosaic pattern of light and dark green or yellow on leaves or fruit (Figure 11.14);
- ring spots or line patterns on leaves;
- yellow spotting or streaking of leaves (especially monocots);
- distortion and malformation of leaves or growing points;

Figure 11.13 Bacterial wilt of tomato causes a rapid wilting of the entire plant.
Image Credit: Zachary Snipes, Clemson University

Figure 11.15 Green spots on yellow summer squash fruit known as "color breaking" caused by Papaya ringspot virus.
Image Credit: Andy Rollins, Clemson University

Figure 11.14 Mosaic symptom characteristic of blackberry yellow vein disease, caused by a virus complex.
Image Credit: Elizabeth Cieniewicz, Clemson University

- uniform yellowing, bronzing, or reddening of foliage;
- reduced growth resulting in stunting; and
- "breaking" or changes in flower or fruit color (Figure 11.15).

High temperatures, phytoplasmas, insect feeding, growth regulators, herbicides, mineral deficiencies, and mineral excesses can also cause some of these symptoms. Viral diseases cannot be diagnosed based on symptoms alone—specialized biochemical tests or DNA fingerprinting are used to identify viruses.

Cases of Mistaken Identity

Some characteristics of barks can be confusing. Certain woody species of elm, sweet gum, and euonymus may exhibit wings of cork around the stem that are easy to mistake for a canker-type disease.

Sooty mold is the name of several black fungi that grow on the surfaces of trees and shrubs during the summer (Figure 11.16). If there is sooty mold, there are also insects. Excrement from aphids, scales, and certain other insects contains sugars and nutrient-rich materials. The excrement, called honeydew, drips onto needles, leaves, and twigs, and the sooty mold grows on this nutrient-rich food source. Eliminate insect activity to wipe out sooty mold; control the insect rather than the fungus.

Perhaps the most distinctive plant in the Lowcountry landscape is the epiphytic plant Spanish moss (*Tillandsia usneoides*). Although it appears to parasitize landscape plants, Spanish moss simply uses them as support structures for growth. Occasionally, Spanish moss becomes dense enough to break twigs when wet or to reduce the amount of sunlight reaching the tree foliage. Neither condition is irreversible or lethal.

Another epiphyte, lichen, is often wrongly identified as a disease-causing agent. In fact, a lichen is composed of a fungus, an alga, and—in some cases—a yeast that have coevolved into a complex, symbiotic lifeform. The fungus contributes support, nutrients, and water, while the alga photosynthesizes foods to support the lichen and the yeast produces toxins and other chemicals.

Figure 11.16 Sooty mold on a citrus leaf on a plant affected with scale. The middle of the sooty mold colony is dissolving after the scale were treated.
Image Credit: Anthony Keinath, Clemson University

Lichens are commonplace on tree trunks, but when they develop on branches and twigs, they are blamed for decline. Lichens can only colonize interior twigs and branches after the leaf canopy has thinned. They follow the sunlight into the plant interior; though they take advantage of declining plants, they do not cause decline. Increased lichen density indicates that a particular plant is under stress and has lost leaf cover. Actual causes of this decline could include nematodes, root diseases, or environmental or cultural stressors.

Slime molds, a group of organisms that are not fungi, were traditionally grouped with fungi. Slime molds appear in South Carolina in the spring on hardwood bark mulch, logs, or turf as a wet, brightly colored mass. "Fried egg slime" is a common bright yellow slime mold. Within a short time, it turns brown and dusty as the body turns into millions of spores. A gray slime mold grows on blades of turf grass in the spring.

Slime molds are saprophytes, not pathogens, even when they cover live plants. You can remove slime molds from plants with a strong stream of water. To prevent slime molds from spreading, remove them while they are still moist—before they form spores.

Fairy rings are found in grasslands, forests, and lawns after rains. Sixty different mushrooms can form fairy rings. Aboveground mushrooms are the fruiting bodies that produce spores. The bulk of the fungus body (**mycelium**) is underground and expands outward from the center of the ring as the fungus consumes organic matter in the soil. Some fairy rings in lawns are associated with cleared trees. Large fairy rings can be over 400 years old.

Disorders

To be healthy, plants require:

- A balance between moisture and air around the roots. All plant cells must have moisture. Root cells need oxygen or they die.
- Friable (not compacted) soil conditions that allow sufficient root growth for water and nutrient uptake.
- Sufficient nutrients in the soil for plant needs but not so many that they become toxic. Plants require a balance of nutrients, since an excess of one nutrient can induce deficiency of another.
- Sufficient light for photosynthesis but not so much that chlorophyll is destroyed.
- Winter site conditions that allow the plant to adapt, survive, and maintain vigor.

If one or more of these requirements are not met, the plant exhibits symptoms of a disorder. These symptoms can include:

- general slowing of growth,
- decline in vigor,
- yellowing of older leaves,
- branch dieback,
- wilt,
- marginal leaf burn or needle tip death,
- premature fall leaf coloration and defoliation, and
- smaller-than-normal leaves.

Diagnosing a disorder is difficult, because many different factors cause similar symptoms. Accurate diagnosis requires observation of all symptoms and when they first appear, a history of growing conditions, careful examination of the site, and examination of neighboring plants—of the same or different species—for similar symptoms (best done by the person maintaining the plants).

Ozone Damage. Ozone, an inorganic atmospheric molecule composed of three oxygen atoms, is normally present at a concentration of 0.6 parts per billion (ppb) in the air. Summertime "inversions," when a mass of warm air traps a mass of cooler air at the earth's surface, increase the concentration of ozone. When concentrations exceed 100 ppb, some plants show symptoms of ozone damage.

Symptoms include stippling, flecking, or bronzing of the upper leaf surface, sometimes followed by necrosis and "shot holing." Symptoms continue to worsen even after the ozone concentration returns to normal. Common ozone-sensitive plants include green bean, cucurbits, petunia, and Irish potato. Different cultivars of the same species, like watermelon, may differ in their sensitivity to ozone.

Excessive Moisture and Poor Soil Aeration. Excessive rainfall or irrigation can cause symptoms of excessive moisture. However, if the soil is poorly drained, even a small amount of moisture can cause symptoms. Soils with high clay content drain poorly even on a slope.

Symptoms of excessive moisture include yellowing of older leaves or needles, defoliation, wilting despite moist soil, and limp roots. Signs include algae or moss growing on the soil surface, soggy soil, and soil that is dark olive green to olive brown in color 6–8 in. below the surface.

Insufficient Moisture. Insufficient moisture results from not watering deeply, insufficient rain, weather that dries the plant faster than the root system can supply moisture, and poor rooting after transplanting. If the planting site is restricted in size (shallow to bedrock or paved around the root system) or if the drainage pattern changes, there may not be sufficient moisture available to the plant. If the size of the root system is reduced by excavation, root rot, nematode feeding, or soil compaction, the plant is not able to take up sufficient moisture. Additionally, if the soil is frozen while air temperatures are mild—a rare occurrence in South Carolina—broad-leaved and needled evergreens continue to lose moisture and are unable to replenish their supply.

Symptoms of insufficient moisture include yellowing, wilting, premature fall leaf coloration, and marginal leaf burn. Soil becomes very dry, dusty, hard, or cracked. The potting mix in containers may pull away from the edge of the pot, or the mix may not be completely moist throughout. Plants in very windy, exposed locations or in containers are very susceptible to problems caused by insufficient moisture.

Nutrient Deficiencies and Imbalances. Symptoms of nutrient deficiencies vary between plant species. When diagnosing nutrient problems, it is best to find a reference book that deals with a specific plant and perform soil and tissue tests.

Symptoms of nutrient toxicities, deficiencies, and imbalances are related to the functions each element has in the plant and the element's mobility in the plant. The mobile elements N, P, K, and magnesium can move from older to younger tissue within the plant. When a deficiency of one of these elements develops, the older tissues show the deficiency because those elements are transported to the younger, developing tissues. The younger tissues appear normal.

Immobile elements (calcium, iron, and manganese) cannot move within the plant. While older tissue may appear normal, new developing tissues lack nutrients and exhibit symptoms (Figure 11.17).

Nutrient deficiencies can be caused by: a lack of nutrients, a soil pH that makes the element unavailable to the plant, and an imbalance between two elements that disrupts intake. Excess calcium leads to magnesium deficiency. Nitrogen deficiency can induce magnesium deficiency. Potassium deficiency can cause excessive uptake of molybdenum.

Excessively High Temperatures or Light Conditions. Heat and light damage occur when a plant is not acclimated to a new location after being moved, a plant is moved from greenhouse or shade house to full sun or a plant is newly exposed to full sun by the removal of overstory trees. In some cases, a building or other structure can reflect heat and light onto a plant and cause damage; in others, heat exhaust from air conditioners, clothes driers, or steam lines damages nearby plants.

Figure 11.17 Blossom end rot on tomato is caused by a calcium deficiency in the expanding fruit.
Image Credit: Joey Williamson, Clemson University

TABLE 11.1 Newsworthy Plant Diseases and Year Discovered in the USA

Disease	Year Discovered
Basil downy mildew	2007
Impatiens downy mildew	2005
Squash vein yellowing (virus)	2005
Citrus greening (bacterium)	2005
Asian soybean rust (fungus)	2004
Laurel wilt (fungus)	2002

Symptoms of heat or light damage include a light-green coloration of leaves, bleaching of leaves or bark, mottling or uneven green coloration on leaves, death of leaf tissue or roots, and dead tissue at the soil line of seedlings. Symptoms may be more severe on one side of a plant than the other.

Protect plants while they acclimate to a new location. Shade or frequently mist the plant with water during the heat of day. Position a lathe or cloth between the plant and any heat-reflecting structures until the plant grows large enough to shade a portion of that structure. Mulch the base of seedlings in hot locations.

Excessively Low Temperatures. Cold damage depends on when low temperatures occur. Continuous cold around hardy, acclimatized plants in the winter causes few problems, but widely fluctuating temperatures can damage plants. Symptoms of excessively low temperatures include the blackening of young tissues, uniform browning of evergreen tips, marginal leaf burn of broad-leaved evergreens, reduced flowering, and death of a plant that was healthy the previous autumn.

Use plant hardiness zone maps to select plants for particular locations. Even within a given hardiness zone, if a site is particularly harsh, consider using plants adapted to a lower number hardiness zone.

Allow plants to harden in autumn by not applying nitrogen. Water plants in late summer and autumn to prevent them from entering winter under drought stress. Drought predisposes plants to winter injury and cankers. Bury pots in soil, and ball and burlap plants to insulate roots. Wrap burlap or build a lathe structure around plants in exposed locations.

Environmental Stress and Plant Disease

Many organisms, especially facultative parasites (those that do not have to be parasitic to live), are not extremely aggressive and attack plants only under certain conditions. Diseases caused by these organisms often only develop when a plant is not vigorous or when conditions are not optimum for the plant to react to the attack. In the landscape, these environmental stress-related diseases are the most common.

The living organisms most often involved in this type of infection are fungi. Some environmental stress is required for them to be able to cause disease; the stress alone does not kill the plant, but weakens it—making it more susceptible to disease.

For example, canker-causing fungi may invade tissue during a plant's dormant season, when the plant's reaction to invasion is slow and the plant is low in vigor. Most canker-causing fungi are not able to cause disease unless the plant is under an environmental stress such as drought. Root pruning that occurs during transplanting causes a drought-like stress and predisposes woody plants to cankers.

Attack by insects can also stress plants and predispose them to fungal attack. For example, repeated defoliation of oaks by orange-striped oakworms and leaf rollers weakens trees and predisposes them to oak root rot.

MANAGING PLANT DISEASES

Successful plant disease management requires a three-pronged approach:

1. Monitoring. The objective of monitoring or examining plants is to avoid introducing a pathogen into an area, to detect and eradicate any disease found, and to detect diseases early so that you can take other appropriate actions.
2. Prevention. Preventive techniques include purchasing and planting pathogen-free or pathogen-resistant material, treating soil before planting to eliminate disease-causing organisms, and—if necessary—applying chemicals before diseases normally appear.
3. Management. When you detect a disease, take actions to manage it by reducing either its severity or its spread.

Many different control measures are used to manage disease; most diseases require more than one type. Integrating several types of controls is usually more successful than relying on only one method.

Exclusion

Regulatory methods of disease control attempt to exclude disease-causing organisms, highly susceptible host plants, or alternate host plants from a growing area. Inspection and quarantine of plant materials prevent the introduction of a pathogen or diseased plant into an area. U.S. Customs provides a list of plant materials that cannot be brought into the United States.

Officials can perform inspections at the point of origin (before the material is packed and shipped) or at the port of entry or receiving site upon arrival. Trained inspectors search for known pests on particular plants, indications of problems due unidentified causes, and unwanted plants. Plants, potting materials, or packing materials may be held for a period of time to allow a disease to develop or a disease-causing organism to grow and be easier to detect if present. However, it is not feasible to inspect all cargo coming into international ports. Wooden pallets from China harboring the red bay ambrosia beetle (*Xyleborus glabratus*), which carries the laurel wilt fungus, brought these pests to Port Wentworth, Georgia, in 2002 (Table 11.1).

The USDA Animal and Plant Health Inspection Service (APHIS) establishes quarantined areas to restrict the movement of pests. Currently, Charleston and Beaufort counties in South Carolina are under quarantine for the citrus greening bacterium. The pathogen was found on April 2, 2009, in downtown Charleston in two mature citrus trees. The plants were removed, but citrus plants cannot be moved out of these counties; this prevent further spread of the bacterium.

Pathogens are also spread by many means that cannot be regulated by quarantines. These include wind, insect vectors, and drainage water.

Eradication

Plant pathogens persist or survive between crops in many different environments. Eradication includes all methods used to eliminate or destroy pathogens. Usually, this means removing the source of a pathogen.

Soil is a common source of pathogens. Fungal pathogens can survive many years in soil and produce sclerotia, oospores, or other resistant spores adapted to survive in a range of environmental conditions. Pathogens are also found in the remnants of diseased plants as long as any tissue remains undecomposed; this period can last more than two years, as is the case with the gummy stem blight fungus in cankered muskmelon crowns. Soilborne water molds such as *Phytophthora capsici* and the tomato bacterial wilt bacterium can survive several months in ponds and drainage ditches.

Pathogens also survive in and are moved with diseased host plants. Vegetatively propagated plant parts, like tubers and bulbs, can harbor pathogens. Seedborne pathogens enter seed through blossoms, while fruit rot pathogens contaminate seed harvested from infected fruit. Weeds can harbor pathogens in seeds or perennial roots; for example, tomato spotted wilt virus survives over winter in dandelion.

Dry Fallow

Dry fallow involves tilling soil to prevent weed growth and keep the upper layers of the soil dry. Nematodes such as the lesion nematode and some bacteria cannot survive these conditions.

Crop Rotation

Crop rotation is a type of eradication as well as avoidance. Plants may be present, but they are not host plants. Thus, the land is still in use, but the crop is not threatened by a certain pathogen.

One suggested rotation for home gardens is tomato followed by corn followed by beans. An example of a poor rotation is tomato followed by eggplant followed by potato; all are members of the same botanical family and therefore susceptible to the same pathogens.

When selecting replacement plants for landscape sites, the gardener should consider the previous plants; the organisms that killed the original plant may still be present in the soil or on surrounding host plants. For example, if Japanese hollies (*Ilex crenata*) are removed because they have black root rot, do not replace them with pansies, which also are susceptible to this disease. The same example applies to root-knot nematodes.

Sanitation

Sanitation is an important method of eradication that involves reducing the amounts of pathogen inoculum present, destroying sites where pathogens overwinter, removing non-crop plants that harbor pathogens, and disinfesting equipment. Raking fallen leaves, removing infected plants, burning debris, pruning infected twigs and branches, and cleaning soil and plant sap from tools are all forms of sanitation (Figure 11.18).

When you use tools to handle infected plants or to prune out infected tissues, they can become contaminated

Figure 11.18 Old, diseased strawberry leaves should be removed to prevent spread of pathogens to new, healthy leaves.
Image Credit: Zachary Snipes, Clemson University

by the pathogen; they may spread the pathogen to the next plant they come in contact with. Disinfest tools by soaking them in a solution of 1 part bleach (sodium hypochlorite 6.0%) to 9 parts water for at least 1 min. Before storing the tools, rinse them in water and lubricate with oil to prevent rusting.

Resistance

One of the most effective ways to prevent disease is to plant varieties that are not susceptible to the pathogen. Plants may be **susceptible**, **tolerant**, **resistant**, or **immune** to various pathogens. The term susceptible indicates that the plant readily becomes diseased if the environment, time, and pathogen are all suitable.

The term tolerant implies that the plant may become diseased, but the yield—of fruit, grain, or other harvested parts—or appearance—of ornamentals—is not severely affected. Some heirloom vegetable cultivars are tolerant of diseases, which is probably why these cultivars were saved over the years.

Resistant plants do not readily become diseased, because they have resistance genes that allow the plant to recognize the pathogen as a threat. Plants that cannot get infected by a particular disease are immune to the disease, and they are not hosts of that particular pathogen.

Resistance and susceptibility are relative terms. There is a continuum among species and cultivars, from extremely susceptible to highly resistant.

Naturally occurring resistance or immunity determines the host range of pathogens. Some diseases, such as Fusarium wilts, only affect one species of crop plant no matter how closely related the crops are—e.g., watermelon but not muskmelon. Other diseases affect several or all members of a plant family, such as downy mildew on cole crops. The third group of diseases affects many different plants, such as damping-off or Southern blight, because few plants are resistant to these diseases.

Plant resistant cultivars when: you desire minimum maintenance (usually in landscapes, in rights of way, and situations with low budgets); the pathogen is always present; environmental conditions are favorable to the disease at some time of year; chemical controls are not available, are not likely to be used in a timely fashion, or are difficult to apply; or plants would be severely disfigured by disease.

Using susceptible cultivars is only advised when the pathogen is rarely present, environmental conditions rarely favor disease development, or you are using intensive management practices. Use nonhost species when no resistant cultivars of another species are available and when the pathogen has a very wide host range and cannot be eliminated from a site.

Grafting a susceptible scion onto a resistant rootstock is another way to use resistance to manage diseases. In South Carolina, the 'Guardian' rootstock is used to manage peach tree short life. You can graft heirloom tomatoes onto rootstocks resistant to Fusarium wilt, Southern blight, and root-knot nematode.

Protection

Protecting plants normally involves applying a substance to plants that acts as a barrier to pathogens. Often the substance is a chemical that is toxic to pathogen spores or to the germ tube emerging from a fungus spore or water mold sporangium.

Biological Controls

A biological control is a beneficial microorganism that attacks or inhibits the activity of a pathogen. For example, the biological fungicide (biofungicide) Serenade® contains a bacterium that produces three antibiotics. Although there are many examples of naturally occurring biological control, results from controlled experiments do not transfer easily to "real-life" disease management situations. Biological control of plant diseases remains much more difficult than biological control of insects.

Biopesticides are plant extracts, microorganisms and

their products, and other biochemical substances (such as potassium bicarbonate) that are not toxic according to the U.S. Environmental Protection Agency definition of toxicity. Organic agriculture uses many biopesticides in place of chemical pesticides.

Chemical Controls

Chemical pesticides may kill pathogens directly or simply inhibit pathogen activity to allow plants to grow relatively unaffected. Many fungicides prevent the germination of fungal spores that land on leaves, but most fungicides become ineffective once the pathogen penetrates the leaf. Some chemicals, such as potassium phosphite, may induce a resistant reaction in an otherwise susceptible plant rather than be toxic to or directly inhibit the organism.

Most pesticides available for disease management are fungicides that target fungi, water molds, or both. Copper hydroxide is the only chemical bactericide available to homeowners. Chemical nematicides, which are normally applied to soil before planting to eradicate nematodes, are restricted-use substances not available to homeowners, due to their toxicity.

Almost all pesticides available to homeowners are protectants and must be applied before or very soon after disease begins. Uniform coverage is essential to protect all aboveground plant parts. In general, you should reapply protectants every 7 days to replace fungicide residues washed off by rain and cover newly emerged foliage.

Contact pesticides must come in direct contact with the pathogen. This requires uniform coverage and frequent application (to protect new tissue). Contact pesticides are usually applied to aboveground plant parts via sprays or dusts, mixed into soil as granules or drenches, or applied directly to seed before sowing.

Systemics are chemicals that enter the plant and redistribute within the plant from the initial point of contact. Uniform coverage is not as important as it is with contact pesticides, although it is helpful. Reapplication is usually less frequent since the chemical is inside the plant; not removed by sun, wind, or rain; and redistributed to newly forming plant parts. Several fungicides available for use on turf grass or roses are systemic.

The most important part of using chemical controls is to apply the appropriate material at the proper time. No single chemical is effective against all pathogens; you must know the cause of the disease, or at least the type of pathogen, to select the proper chemical. Most pathogens have certain stages of development that are extremely resistant to adverse environmental conditions, including the presence of inhibitory chemicals. It's important to know the biology of the pathogen so the chemical can be applied when the pathogen is in a stage of development where treatment can be most effective. If you apply the wrong chemical or apply the right chemical at the wrong time, chemical control fails.

Avoidance

Manipulating the environment to make it less favorable to pathogens can help manage plant diseases. Recall that the environment is one of three factors influencing disease development. If you can manipulate environmental conditions to favor plant vigor and be unfavorable for disease development, you can control certain diseases and, often, enhance the effectiveness of additional management techniques. The shortcoming of avoidance, however, is that the pathogen is still present and if weather conditions change, the pathogen may become active.

Moisture Management

Controlling humidity to reduce the duration of leaf wetness greatly influences the development of foliar disease. Weed control and plant spacing influence air circulation in and around the planting site. The irrigation method used influences the duration of leaf wetness. Drip or trickle irrigation keeps plant surfaces dry and therefore unfavorable for most disease-causing bacteria, water molds, and fungi. Sprinkle irrigation, like rain, wets the foliage and provides the moisture necessary for pathogen activity and splashes pathogens from plant to plant or from the ground onto plants. High tunnels keep rain off the crops growing inside.

Controlling soil moisture strongly influences the development of Pythium and Phytophthora root rots. Both water molds can develop in just 30 min of saturated soil. By draining excessive moisture away from plants, soil conditions become less favorable for these fungi. In South Carolina, it is often necessary to raise planting beds to improve drainage.

Temperature Management

You can use refrigeration to chill plants and fruits and retard the development of pathogens. This technique is most common for plants or plant parts in storage postharvest.

Minimizing Exposure of Plants to Pathogens

If you can time the planting of annual crops to miss the peak periods of pathogen activity, you can prevent or delay disease—perhaps long enough that other control measures are unnecessary. Downy mildew on cole crops and leafy Brassica greens flourishes in cool weather but is much less active when daytime temperatures reach 80°F, so delaying planting reduces the risk of downy mildew. On the other hand, summer plantings of the same crops can be severely affected with Fusarium yellows—a disease that does not occur in fall, winter, or spring, even in infested soil. Root-knot nematodes are dormant in winter and spring, so susceptible plants like snapdragon and parsley can grow safely in infested soil.

Integrated Disease Management

Several common disease problems require an integrated approach that combines several control strategies, simultaneously or in sequence.

Defeating Damping-Off

Damping-off disease is easier to prevent than cure. Once seedlings are infected, little can be done beyond removing them. Prevention starts with good sanitation. Always use clean containers and tools. If necessary, disinfect them with a 10% bleach solution or soak them in hot soapy water (160°F) for at least a half hour. Rather than using sterilized soil, use a soilless growing mixture containing peat, perlite, and vermiculite. While not technically sterile, these media are typically free of pathogen spores.

Some seed is pretreated with fungicide, but rapid seed germination, emergence, and development also reduce the likelihood of damping off. Sow the seeds thinly to avoid overcrowding and ensure sufficient air movement and adequate light. Some growers cover seed flats with a thin layer of milled sphagnum peat moss. The low pH of the peat moss naturally inhibits fungi.

Prior to germination, 70–75°F is the optimal temperature. When the seedlings emerge, remove any plastic covering or lid that was used to increase humidity levels and decrease the air temperature by ten degrees.

Proper watering is also critical. Allow the surface of the potting medium to dry before watering again. When watering seeds by hand, use a watering can or clean nozzle that has not touched the ground.

Finally, avoid over-fertilization. One application of a water-soluble fertilizer applied at half strength is sufficient once the second true leaves appear.

Reducing Root Rot

Root rot disease is difficult to control once it has begun. Direct efforts towards preventing the disease before it begins. Remove and destroy infected plants, including the entire root system. Practice cultural management: avoid planting too deeply, provide excellent drainage, and add organic materials such as compost to the planting area to enhance drainage in clay soils by improving the soil structure.

Managing Viral Diseases

There are no chemicals that cure plants infected by viruses or that protect plants from becoming infected. To guard against viral diseases:

- Purchase virus-free plants.
- Maintain strict control of insect vectors.
- Control weeds, since they may harbor viruses, mites, nematodes, and insects.
- Destroy virus-infected plants.

Promoting Tree Health

Maintaining plant vigor is especially important to prevent declines, diebacks, and canker diseases of trees. Watering, fertilizing, preventing soil compaction, preventing damage from excavation or pedestrian traffic, and other practices that promote plant vigor strengthen a plant's ability to resist disease. For example, take steps to prevent winter injury, retain moisture by mulching, drain excessively wet sites, and avoid root injury by reducing tillage.

Take great care to prevent injury to the trunk and branches. Prune late in the dormant season, close to the trunk, and without damaging surrounding bark (see Chapter 5, Trees and Shrubs, for proper pruning techniques). Prune while unwanted branches are small and wounds can heal quickly. Do not prune during wet weather, and do not prune from mid-August to leaf drop; many canker and wood-decay fungi form and release spores during that period.

Managing Nematodes

If there has been a nematode problem on your growing site in the recent past, it is likely to recur once you plant another susceptible plant or crop on that site. Chemical controls are not available for residential areas, so provide optimum care to plants from the start.

"Optimum" does not mean "maximum." Fertilize as needed to maintain healthy growth, not to produce excessive, succulent growth that invites attack by nematodes and other pests. Water deeply to encourage development of a deep root system that can exploit a large volume of soil for water and nutrients; don't water too frequently or shallowly, as this causes plants to develop a shallow root system. A large root system can better withstand a small amount of nematode damage than a shallow, minimal root system.

Finally, mulch the plant root zone to keep roots cool in hot weather and minimize evaporation of water from the soil surface. Mulches reduce stress on the plant as a whole and the root system specifically, improving the plant's chances to do well despite some nematode damage to roots. Greater organic matter content in soil also stimulates the activity of natural enemies such as certain fungi, bacteria, and predatory nematodes, which may help suppress harmful nematode populations.

SUMMARY

A plant disease occurs when a susceptible host plant, plant pathogen, and set of environmental conditions favorable to the pathogen all exist at the same time and place. Moisture on leaves or in soil is the most important environmental factor that allows pathogens to initiate disease.

Six types of pathogens cause plant diseases: five microorganisms and parasitic plants such as certain algae and mistletoes. The five groups of microorganisms are fungi, water molds, bacteria, nematodes, and viruses. Plant pathogenic members of these broad biological groups have the unique ability to infect plants—and by so doing, harm plants. It is important to realize that many pathogens survive apart from their host plants and may be present in soil or air long before symptoms are visible.

Common disease symptoms include cankers and galls; damping-off and root and stem rots; leaf, flower, and fruit spots and blights; mosaics and color breaking on fruit; rusts and smuts; and wilts. Secondary symptoms of yellowing, wilting, and stunting are often associated with root diseases. Because different types of pathogens can cause similar symptoms, you cannot diagnose all diseases by symptoms alone. Signs are the visible parts of a pathogen on diseased plants. Signs provide key information that makes it easier to diagnose plant diseases.

Disorders are caused by extremes of light, moisture, nutrients, temperature, and air pollution; in essence, the environment is harming the plant without the involvement of a pathogen.

The key to managing plant diseases is prevention because plant diseases cannot be cured like animal and human diseases. Five general control principles are:

1. excluding pathogens from a given area,
2. eradicating pathogens if they become established (but before they spread),
3. growing resistant cultivars of plants,
4. applying biological and synthetic chemical pesticides, and
5. minimizing the exposure of plants to pathogens or modifying the environment to make it less favorable for pathogens.

In general, using multiple strategies is more effective than using only one.

Chapter 12
Dealing with Weeds

Authors: Gary Forrester and Ted Whitwell, Ph.D.

LEARNING OBJECTIVES
- **Understand the growth characteristics of weeds, including life cycles and reproductive characteristics.**
- **Know basic techniques for weed identification.**
- **Understand the application of an integrated weed management plan.**

INTRODUCTION

Weeds are unwanted plants that are not easily eliminated. They compete with desirable plants for essential growth factors: light, nutrients, and water. Weeds may also host other pests such as injurious insects and diseases. Many people are allergic to weedy plant pollen and the oil from leaves and stems of certain species—such as poison ivy. Weeds reproduce from seeds and underground plant parts. They can spread rapidly if control measures are not applied correctly. The most effective way to control weeds is to correctly identify the species and determine its life cycle so that controls are timed according to the weed's growth and reproduction characteristics. Control measures should include physical, cultural, biological, and—if needed—chemical measures. This chapter provides basic information needed to control these unwanted plants.

BASIC WEED ECOLOGY AND MANAGEMENT

According to Ralph Waldo Emerson, "A weed is a plant whose virtues have not yet been discovered." Traditionally, a weed is any plant that was not seeded or planted, requires no cultivation, and comes back despite the gardener's efforts to remove it. But is a weed truly just a plant growing out of place?

According to the Weed Science Society of America, a weed is any plant that is objectionable or interferes with the activities or welfare of people. Weeds also possess certain biological characteristics that make them efficient and successful in their habitats, allowing them to compete with desirable plants for sunlight, water, and nutrients. Of the approximately 250,000 species of plants in the world, about 250 (0.1%) are troublesome enough to be called weeds.

While crop yield loss is a major concern for agricultural produce, our concern with weeds in the garden and landscape is driven by aesthetic and human concern. Weed-infested landscapes lose an aesthetic quality; weeds can also harm people. For instance, weeds with thorns can scratch or puncture skin. Sports fields may become dangerous when large, clumpy weeds cause players to turn ankles and knees. Eating poisonous weeds can cause illness or death, and many weeds produce allergic reactions in sensitive individuals. Weeds may also harbor harmful insects and serve as an alternate host for plant pests.

Some weeds may also be invasive species. An **invasive species** is a species that is nonnative to the ecosystem whose introduction causes or is likely to cause economic or environmental harm. Few nonnative plants escape from cultivation and become naturalized. Even fewer naturalized plants become invasive. Nevertheless, invasive plant species have a profound impact on natural ecosystems; they spread over large areas and displace native species—under certain circumstances, rare and endangered plant species.

Managing invasive species is extremely difficult and expensive. Invasive plants have biological traits that offer them competitive advantages over other species. At the same time, they must be in an environment that is free from the predators, pathogens, and competition that keep their numbers in check in their native habitat. For this reason, no plant is inherently invasive under all circumstances and in all environments. Some species may be highly invasive in some habitats—like along the coast—without persisting or naturalizing in others—like further inland.

As Master Gardeners, you play a critical role in educating others about the problems of invasive plants and offering non-invasive alternatives. The South Carolina Exotic Plant Pest Council maintains a list of invasive species in South Carolina. Some invasive plants are regulated; the State Plant Pest List can be found on the Department of Plant Industry website.

There are also beneficial aspects of weeds. They are considered "guardians of the soil," emerging quickly in disturbed sites and aiding in soil conservation. Weeds also provide food for wildlife. Some weeds take advantage of situations that are not favorable to the growth of desirable plants and grow in areas of compacted soil, soils with nutrient or pH problems, or excessively wet areas. As a result, weeds can indicate soil or management problems that can be rectified to improve the growing conditions for desirable plants (Table 12.1).

This chapter covers the basic principles of weed science, with an emphasis on weed ecology, identification, and management. An effective weed control program integrates nonchemical best gardening practices with specific mechanical, biological, and—if necessary—chemical weed control measures.

Weed Classification

Weeds are divided into three major plant categories and further classified by their life cycle. The major plant categories are grass, broadleaf, and sedge. A weed's life cycle can be annual, biennial, or perennial. Life cycle has a great impact on the selection and success of a given control procedure, so it is important to learn

TABLE 12.1 Weed Indicators of Adverse Soil Conditions

Growing Condition	Indicator Weeds
Acidic soil	Broomsedge, red sorrel, moss
Compacted soil	Annual bluegrass, bermudagrass, common chickweed, mouse-ear chickweed, goosegrass, knotweed, prostrate spurge, rushes, speedwells
Infertile/sandy soil	Bahiagrass, black medic, broomsedge, carpetweed, legumes, red sorrel, sandbur, poorjoe, quackgrass, white clover, yarrow, yellow wood sorrel
High fertility soil	Annual bluegrass, bermudagrass, crabgrass, henbit, purslane, ryegrass, yellow wood sorrel
Low fertility soil	Plantains, red sorrel, white clover
High or infrequent mowing	Chicory, clover, yellow musk thistle
Low mowing height	Annual bluegrass, bermudagrass, chickweeds, crabgrass, pearlwort, white clover
Shade	Annual bluegrass, common chickweed, mouse-ear chickweed, ground ivy, kyllinga, nimblewill, nutsedges, pennywort, rushes, speedwells, violets
Moist or poorly drained soil	Annual bluegrass, common chickweed, mouse-ear chickweed, crabgrass, goosegrass, ground ivy, speedwells, violets, yellow nutsedge

the characteristics of the life cycle of a weed once you identify it.

Weed Types

Grasses. Grassy weeds are monocots. A grass seed germinates and emerges as one single leaf. It develops hollow, rounded stems and hard, closed nodes. The leaf blades alternate on each side of the stem, are much longer than they are wide, and have parallel veins. Common grass weeds are crabgrass, goosegrass, crowfoot grass, dallisgrass, sandbur (sandspur), and annual bluegrass (Figure 12.1a and 12.1b).

Broadleaves. Most broadleaf weeds have leaves with netlike veins, nodes containing one or more leaves, a branched growth habit, and often, showy flowers. As dicots, broadleaf weed seedlings emerge with two leaves. Because of differences in leaf structure and growth habits, they are easy to distinguish from grasses. Broadleaf weeds often have a taproot with a fribrous root system. All broadleaf plants have an exposed growing point at the end of each stem and in each leaf axil. Perennial broadleaf weeds may even have growing points located below ground, on roots and stems, that allow them to reproduce. There is so much diversity in the dicot family that it is extremely important to properly identify a weed before attempting to manage it. Common broadleaf weeds include common chickweed, Florida betony, cudweed, dandelion, Florida pusley, greenbrier, henbit, kudzu, pennywort or dollarweed, spurge, trampweed, Virginia buttonweed, and yellow wood sorrel (Figure 12.2).

Figure 12.1a and 12.1b Crowfootgrass (Dactyloctenium aegyptium) is an example of a grassy weed. Seed heads are needed to accurately identify grassy weeds.

Image Credit: Barbara Smith, Clemson University

Figure 12.2 Floida pusley (Richardia scabra) is a common broadleaf weed.
Image Credit: Terasa Lott, Clemson University

Figure 12.3a and 12.3b A side-by-side comparison of yellow nutsedge (Cyperus esculentas) and purple nutsedge (Cyperus rotundus).
Image Credit: Barbara Smith, Clemson University

Sedges. Sedges are also monocots. Sedges are characterized by solid, triangular stems (making it easy to remember that "sedges have edges") without nodes. Their grass-like leaves appear on the stem in clusters of three, with each one extending in a different direction. Annual sedges are often called "water grasses." Perennial sedges, such as purple and yellow nutsedge, are difficult to control, because they produce underground tubers. Yellow nutsedge produces solitary tubers at the ends of rhizomes. Purple nutsedge is usually smaller than yellow nutsedge; it has reddish-purple seed heads and rhizomatous dark tubers that form "chains" (Figure 12.3).

Green kyllinga is much shorter than nutsedges. It has a finer leaf blade and spreads by rhizomes that do not produce tubers. The seed head of kyllinga is globe- or cylinder-shaped, in contrast to the branched seed heads of the other nutsedges. It is extremely important to be able to distinguish between grasses and sedges and identify which particular sedge you have when developing a control strategy. Globe sedge is common in many areas but overall less widespread than yellow and purple nutsedge; it has spiked seed heads.

Weed Life Cycles

Annuals. Annual weeds germinate, grow, flower, produce seeds, and die in one growing season. They are further categorized by the season in which they germinate and flourish. Winter or cool season annuals germinate in the late fall and die in late spring or early summer; henbit, common chickweed, and annual bluegrass are typical winter annuals. Summer or warm-season annuals—such as crabgrass, goosegrass, and carpetweed—germinate in spring, thrive throughout the summer, and die in early fall.

Biennials. Biennial weeds have a two-year life cycle. They germinate and produce a rosette or crown of leaves from a somewhat fleshy taproot during their first year. In the second year, the overwintered taproot produces new growth, flowers, produces seed, and dies. Wandering cudweed and Carolina false dandelion are biennial weeds. There are only a few species of weedy biennials.

Perennials. Perennial weeds live for more than two years. They reproduce from vegetative parts such as tubers, bulbs, rhizomes, or stolons (Figure 12.4). Many

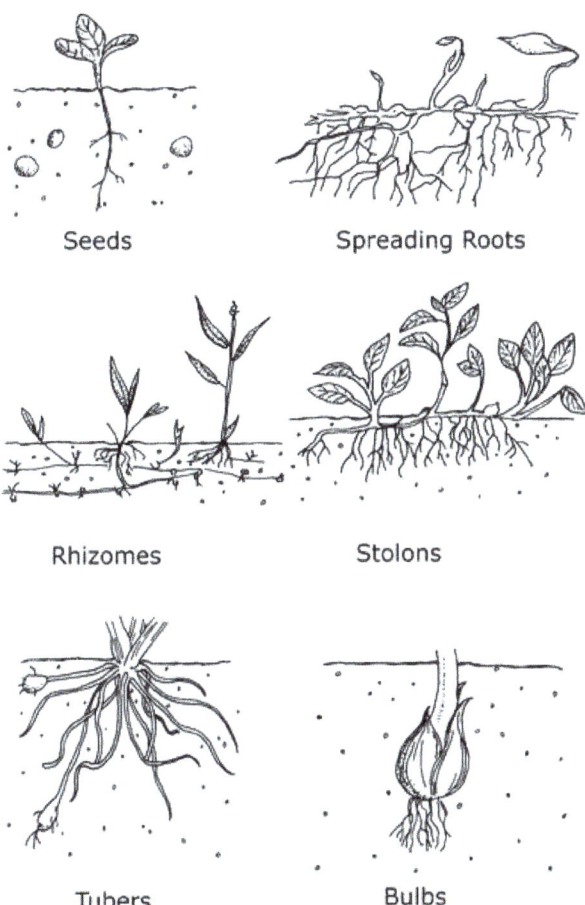

Figure 12.4 The methods by which weeds spread.

Figure 12.5 Florida betony (*Stachys floridana*) is sometimes called rattlesnake weed due to the resemblance of the tubers to a rattlensnkake rattle.
Image Credit: Terasa Lott, Clemson University

also produce seed. Perennial weeds may be herbaceous or woody and are also classified into cool- and warm-season types depending on the time of year in which they grow. During the winter season, most warm season perennial weeds are dormant, and herbaceous perennials lose their aboveground leaves and stems. In the spring, food reserves in the root systems support new growth. Florida betony, a cool-season perennial weed, begins growing in the fall, grows during the winter months, and goes dormant during the heat of the summer. The shape of its edible tubers gives Florida betony the common name "rattlesnake weed" (Figure 12.5).

Perennial weeds may also be categorized by type of root system and reproductive process:

- Simple perennials reproduce primarily by seeds, but root pieces distributed by cultivation or other mechanical means can produce new plants. Dandelion is a simple perennial.
- Bulbous perennials reproduce by seed aboveground or belowground bulbs or corms. Wild garlic produce belowground bulbs and aerial bulbils from its flowering stem.
- Creeping perennials produce seed, but they also produce rhizomes (underground stems), stolons (above-ground horizontal stems), or tubers. Bermudagrass, torpedograss, and purple nutsedge produce rhizomes and stolons that store food. They can produce roots and shoots at each node along a stem. Florida betony reproduces primarily from tubers.

Perennial weeds are the most difficult to control because of their great reproductive potential and persistence. Dallisgrass, docks, nutsedges, and vines such as greenbrier and kudzu belong to this group of weeds.

Weed Ecology

Ecology is the study of relationships between organisms and the environment. Understanding the relationship between weeds, their growth form, their characteristics and species makeup, and their environment is the goal of weed ecology. Four components contribute to a dynamic weed-desirable plant ecosystem: (a) the weed, (b) the desirable plant, (c) humans, and (d) the natural environment.

Weedy plants have a specific type of growth habit and invade under certain conditions; they also possess a remarkable capability to survive. Weedy plant species usually invade bare or open areas that are not conducive to desirable plant growth. Annual grasses usually invade these areas first, followed by annual broadleaf plants, perennial grasses and broadleaves, brambles and vines, and finally, trees.

Growth Habits and Characteristics of Weeds

Weeds are capable of growing under changing conditions. They survive under adverse conditions such as drought and waterlogged or compacted soils, but they can also thrive in conditions favorable to crop growth.

Certain weeds have modified plant parts that allow them to grow in areas not conducive to cultivated plants. Reduced leaf area or fewer aerial parts allow plants to survive dry conditions. Shallow-rooted weeds—such as crabgrass and annual bluegrass—can thrive in compacted, wet soils. A prostrate growth habit allows weeds to survive close mowing.

Many weeds, especially perennials, can regenerate plant parts. For example, a dandelion or plantain with its crown removed can regenerate new shoots, which makes mechanical removal difficult and temporary.

Perennial weeds can regenerate through vegetative means. Rhizomes, stolons, and rootstocks of many plants can spread far and wide during cultivation.

There are certain weeds that produce very small, inconspicuous flowers. Such flowers can produce seeds before the weeds are detected and eliminated.

Many weeds contain a substance that gives off a disagreeable odor or taste. Others are covered with a sticky substance, stiff hairs, or spines. These devices protect the plant against natural enemies or domestic animals. Some weeds develop herbicide resistance, which makes chemical control difficult.

Weed Seeds

Weeds can produce enormous amounts of seed during a growing season. A single plant of some species can produce enough seed in one season to cover an entire acre with new plants if they all germinate. For example, a single common lambsquarters can produce 72,000 seeds in one season (Figure 12.6). Although not as prolific, Clemson University researchers found that a single hairy bittercress plant could produce nearly 5,000 seeds and launch them up to 42 in. away from the mother plant.

Buried weed seeds may remain viable for a few years because of their ability to remain dormant until the experience more favorable conditions—such as the correct sunlight, moisture, and temperature. Recent research indicates that most weed seeds do not survive more than 5 years after being deposited in the soil. Each time the soil is cultivated, dormant weeds are brought up to the soil surface and exposed to sunlight and conditions that favor germination and growth; it can take a few years to exhaust the reserve of weed seeds that exist in the soil.

Many weeds continue to produce seed even after they are removed from the soil. For example, purslane and chickweed may continue to bear flowers and ripen seed for days after being pulled from the soil. The tops of sow thistle and dandelion may ripen seed even after mowing. Because of this, take care when adding weeds to compost piles and mow weedy lawns frequently to avoid seed head production.

Weed seeds disperse in various ways. Many of these are due to special morphological features such as the wind-dispersed achenes of milkweed and the hooks and spines of sandbur.

Figure 12.6 Lambsquarters (*Chenopodium album*) is a prolific seed producer.
Image Credit: "Chenopodium album - leaves, flower bud" by The NYSIPM Image Gallery is licensed under CC BY 2.0.

Spread and Movement of Weeds

Many common weeds were accidentally introduced into the United States alongside crop seed, as is the case with field bindweed. Others were intentionally introduced into the country. Crabgrass was introduced as a forage crop—it was the first grain cultivated during the Stone Age—, and kudzu was introduced as an ornamental vine, forage crop, and soil stabilizer. Other plants have been introduced as landscape plants—such as English ivy, bamboo, and water hyacinth—but have "escaped" and become invasive weeds.

Weed seeds can spread into gardens and landscapes via wind, runoff, animals—and us, if they cling to our pants or shoes or attach to our gardening tools. Gardening activities such as cultivation, mowing, adding topsoil or compost, or planting container-grown plants in weed-infested media can also introduce weed seed and weed parts (Figure 12.7)

Weed seed can also be introduced with the planting of vegetable and landscape plants, because weed seed is difficult to detect or separate from crop seed. Be sure to only purchase and plant weed-free seed in your garden.

Wind Dispersal. The modifications or adaptations of many landscape weeds allow them to be scattered by wind. Seeds that have tufts of hair or small wing-like appendages can be carried by wind over long distances. The achenes (seed) of dandelions and thistles are common in the spring, as they ride on air currents during windy days (especially during periods of heavy shedding).

Figure 12.7 Weeds can be lurking in the containers of purchased plants. Always inspect containers before installing plants.
Image Credit: Sarah White, Clemson University

Water Dispersal. Weeds that depend on water to help them move from site to site often have the ability to float, allowing them to move where water moves. Many of these seeds are washed into streams by surface runoff during heavy rains or are transported from landscape to landscape as stormwater flows to lower areas. Mustards, sedges, eclipta, and ragweeds are a few of the common weeds frequently carried long distances by water. Avoid spreading weeds by limiting the amount of irrigation or stormwater that leaves your landscape, and do not allow runoff into your landscape (as this can deposit seeds).

Animal Dispersal. Many weeds move about on or in animals. Burs on cocklebur and sandspur and fruits or nutlets with hook-like or spiny appendages—such as beggar-ticks or stick-tight—cling to the wool or fur of animals to be carried long distances. Rodents and ants usually accomplish shorter seed transport. Gardeners who enjoy watching and feeding birds may be bringing in weeds. Many birds eat the seeds or fruit of small weeds; the seeds have a hard coating that allows them to pass through the bird's digestive tract, and they are expelled in a viable form. Poison ivy and pokeberries are frequently scattered in this manner.

Cultivation Dispersal. Often, a weedy plant arrives in a local landscape as a single plant or in a small patch. If the location of this small growth is left undisturbed and the plants are prevented from producing seed, the weed spreads little from year to year. However, if the area is cultivated or the soil is dug and moved, the seed, roots, and rhizomes may be scattered over a much larger area. Once an area is tilled or the soil is moved to other areas, one small infestation becomes a field quickly overrun with weeds. To avoid this problem, isolate small areas of weed infestation in your landscape or garden, destroy the growth, and use caution when tilling or moving soil to other areas.

The Spread and Escape of Introduced Plants

There are some weeds in the United States that were originally introduced as landscape plants or for other uses. These plants were well maintained in fields or local landscapes and then escaped into the natural environment. Two examples of this occurring in South Carolina are kudzu and beach vitex.

Kudzu was originally introduced into the United States from Eastern Asia in 1876. Kudzu is found in thickets and thin woods all over Japan. In 1884, kudzu was introduced at the New Orleans Exposition, where people used the plant as a shade vine for arbors. Cattle found the plant tasty, but the stems made it difficult to harvest. The big break came during the Great Depression in the 1930s, when the U.S. Government paid farmers $8.00 per acre to plant kudzu on fallow fields and bare banks to control soil erosion. It has been growing like a weed ever since.

Kudzu vines can grow as much as 1 ft per day during the summer months, climbing trees, power poles, and anything else they can grab hold of. Under ideal conditions, kudzu can grow 60 ft during one growing season. Although kudzu has helped with soil stabilization, the plant can choke out valuable forest areas by reducing sunlight. Because of this, the USDA declared it an invasive species in 1972.

Beach vitex (*Vitex rotundifolia*) is a sprawling, woody shrub native to Hawaii and Korea. It was introduced into South Carolina in the 1980s, when it gained popularity as a salt-tolerant, fast-growing landscape plant. As some fast-growing landscape plants can do, beach vitex has escaped seaside landscapes and invaded the dune system along the coast. The invasion of this plant can be detrimental to native flora and fauna and cause possible difficulties with sea turtle egg laying activities.

WEED MANAGEMENT

A gardener follows a weed management or control program to control unwanted plants from growing and competing with desirable plants. One term often mentioned regarding pests is "eradication". Eradication is the complete elimination of a particular pest. However, eradication is nearly impossible and generally unwanted. For certain weed species with short dormant periods, eradication in a small area may be practical; for most weeds, however, an integrated approach aimed at control—rather than eradication—is most appropriate.

An integrated approach can control most weeds we encounter in a landscape. Integrated weed management combines a variety of methods to achieve maximum weed control with minimum inputs—including minimal use of herbicides. This approach reduces the cost of landscaping and its impact on the surrounding environment.

The components of an integrated weed management plan are: (a) identification, (b) prevention, (c) cultural control, (d) mechanical control, (e) biological control, and (f) chemical control. The very first step in formulating any weed management plan is to correctly identify the problematic weedy species.

Identification

Positive identification of a particular weed and knowledge of its life cycle is the first step in weed management. Comparing a weed to a picture is probably the best way to identify it. Be aware, however, that plants can look different from the seedling stage to the mature or seeding stage. Weeds can also look different under differing cultural practices. Those located in closely mowed lawns or less-than-ideal conditions may not look anything like the same plant allowed to grow naturally.

Weed identification is always easiest once the plant has started to flower. However, once this time has arrived, the weed has already taken a foothold and become competition for other plants. Fortunately, most weed books and web-based resources include vegetative characteristics, photographs, line drawings, and a key to aid in identification. When beginning the process of weed identification, look for some unusual plant characteristic such as thorns or spines, whorled leaves, square stems, or a milky sap. Be sure to include the time of year in your identification process; for example, if the weed is present during the winter, you can rule out summer annuals. Also be aware of the growing conditions; wet soils could lead you to sedges and rule out spurges.

As mentioned earlier, weed identification can be difficult when there are no flowers. You must rely on vegetative characteristics such as growth habit (erect or prostrate), leaf orientation (opposite, alternate, or whorled), simple versus compound leaves, overall leaf shape, and leaf margin. Vegetative identification of grasses relies on unique grass partssuch as the orientation of the leaf bud (rolled or folded), the ligule (absent, hairy, or membranous), the collar (located on the backside of the ligule), the auricle (absent or present), leaf tip shape (boat-shaped or pointed), and the overall growth habit (clumpy or creeping). There are several weed identification phone apps that are helpful in identifying broad leaf weeds, but they are not as effective at identifiying grasses and sedges.

Prevention

The objective of weed prevention is to exclude weeds from entering a site and to prevent their spread to other sites. On-site sanitation is an effective control of weeds in a small landscape. Be sure to clean your equipment before moving from one site to another to avoid spreading weed seed. If you hire a lawn care company to maintain your landscape, be sure they clean their equipment between clients; if a weedy lawn was mowed just before yours and the mowing equipment is not cleaned, your lawn will soon resemble the weedy lawn.

Maintain a clean perimeter around your landscape. Weedy lots, fence rows, drainage ditches, and poorly maintained lawns adjacent to yours can be a source of infestation. Keep vacant lots and ditches mowed and fence rows sprayed with an appropriate herbicide to reduce seed head formation. Start a neighborhood integrated weed management program to help reduce the spread of weeds from yard to yard.

Compost and manures can be a wonderful addition to garden soils. They improve drainage in poorly drained soils, allow sandy soils to hold more nutrients and water, and increase the organic matter content of soil. However, improperly composted yard trimmings can be full of weed seed. Manures that have not been aged can contain numerous weed seeds that have passed through the digestive system of animals but are still capable of germination. To avoid spreading weeds through soil improvement, be sure you follow proper composting procedures. Maintaining a compost pile temperature of 160°F kills most weed seed. Never apply any weedy compost to your landscape. All that does is ensure that you have a weed problem for years to come.

When planting from seed, be sure to use weed-free seed (or at least as weed-free as you can get). State and federal laws regulate the presence of weed seed in crop seed. This information can be found on the crop seed label. If you are planting from containers or using balled and burlapped plants, avoid those with weeds growing in them.

Cultural Weed Control Methods

Gardeners should always strive to provide the best possible growing conditions for their garden and landscape plants. To provide good growing conditions, select the right plant for the site, use adapted plants and cultivars, and maintain adequate soil fertility and pH as recommended by soil test reports. Plant at the proper time of year for the plants that you are growing.

Plant-spacing techniques can also help to reduce weeds. Dense planting of shrubs and annuals can shade out weeds prohibiting growth. You can plant vegetables in wide, multiple rows instead of single rows to shade the soil surface, thus reducing weeds. As a rule, if 80% of the soil is shaded, weeds are seldom a problem. When using dense plantings as a cultural weed control, be careful not to plant too densely; very thick plantings can cause other problems—including insect and disease infestation—due to poor air circulation.

Maintain your turfgrass to promote a healthy, dense sod that naturally reduces weed infestations. Weeds tend to invade thin or bare areas, so the first line of defense is to follow cultural practices that favor the growth and development of a dense, healthy lawn. Start by selecting grass that performs well in your landscape and pay close attention to proper mowing, fertilizing, watering, and pest control.

Mow at the recommended height for the turfgrass and at the right frequency. Mowing at the proper height allows the grass to shade the soil and deprive weed seedlings of sunlight. It encourages the root system to fully develop, which helps the grass tolerate summertime heat and stress.

When cut too low, lawn grass is weakened and less competitive, allowing weeds to establish. Remove no more than one-third of the grass height at a time. Cutting off more than one-third during a single mowing can stop the roots from growing, which invites weeds to take their place.

Fertilize lawn grasses with the right amount of fertilizer based on soil test results and at the proper time of year. Avoid under- or overwatering, which can weaken the lawn and make it susceptible to weed invasions.

In an established landscape, it is important to use proper irrigation techniques. Many weeds thrive in wet or saturated conditions, while landscape plants fail. Use drip or trickle irrigation to apply water only to the plants you want to grow. Do not overwater. Allow your beds and turf to dry thoroughly before irrigating again. This helps eliminate water-loving weeds such as dollarweed and sedges. Also consider planting a low water use landscape and grouping your plants by water requirement. This helps develop and implement a water-conserving strategy that reduces weed growth.

Mechanical Removal and Physical Barriers

An integrated pest management program should always include hand-pulling, hoeing, mowing, and tilling.

Mowing regularly suppresses the development of weeds invading your lawn. Always mow with a sharp mower blade. Sharp blades cut grass blades cleanly, which ensures rapid healing and regrowth; when dull blades tear and bruise the leaves, the wounded grass plants are weakened and less able to ward off marauding weeds.

You can control some winter annuals, such as henbit and common chickweed, by mowing. These weeds mature during the winter, bloom in the spring, and die. Simply removing the flower by hand or with a mower

Figure 12.8 Henbit (*Lamium amplexicaule*) is a winter annual weed.
Image Credit: Barbara Smith, Clemson University

reduces the number of offspring in the fall. (Figure 12.8)

You can hand pull weeds in small areas. Be sure not to disturb the soil too much while hand-weeding, as this can cause more seeds to germinate. Weeds are often easier to pull when the soil is moist, so water lightly before setting out with your gloves and bucket. Hand pulling annual weeds is safe and effective, but time consuming; hand weeding is not effective for the control of most perennial weeds, as reproductive plant parts can break off underground. If you choose to hand pull perennial weeds, such as dandelion, remove as much of the root system as possible; the remaining pieces of rhizomes or roots develop into new plants. Hand pulling a "strange" or "new" weed when it first appears in the lawn helps prevent the spread of that weed. To prevent future invasions, seed, sod, or plug turf areas left bare from weed removal.

Hoe when weeds are small, preferably several days after a rain or irrigation. Turning the soil allows it to dry and stop weed seed germination. A light scratching of the soil accomplishes this without bringing new seed to the surface. Do not use the hoe as a digging tool.

Tilling soil is an excellent way to prepare a seedbed for planting or incorporate organic matter. Use a tiller between vegetable rows to destroy small weeds in row middles. Set the tiller to a depth of 1 in. to eliminate, rather than transplant, weeds. Another option is to till an area several weeks before planting. Allow the weeds to germinate and destroy them with a nonselective herbicide. Once this process is complete, do not disturb the bed again.

Mulch controls weed in plantings by smothering weeds and blocking sunlight from developing weed seedlings. Mulching is by far the best method of preventing annual weed infestations. Many annual weeds are suppressed by the combination of physical interference and obstruction of light. Do not try to make mulches more effective by adding more layers; never apply more than 3 in., and apply less than that on heavy, poorly drained soils. Keep mulches away from the trunks of plants to avoid trunk rots.

Two important notes on mulches:

1. Do not introduce weeds into your landscape by using infested mulch.
2. Mulches do not control creeping perennials and may even enhance their growth.

Mulches can be organic or inorganic. Organic mulches include compost, shredded wood, bark chips, and pine straw. As organic mulches decompose and become humus, they gradually supply valuable nutrients to the soil. Inorganic or synthetic mulches don't break down or decompose. Crushed rock, gravel, seashells, and lava rock are examples of inorganic mulches. The advantage of inorganic mulches is that they don't have to be reapplied often. This may be appealing, but remember that that these mulches won't return organic matter to your soil and may be difficult to move when adding additional plants to the landscape. Rock mulches also trap heat, creating harsh growing conditions. Maintain most organic mulches to a depth of 2-3 in. Maintain inorganic mulches at about 1-3 in. deep.

Landscape fabrics or **geotextiles** are synthetic mulch under liners; they are used to suppress weeds. While they do have applications, they are generally not useful for long-term weed control in residential landscapes. As the fabric degrades, it can become an unattractive maintenance issue. Weeds may grow through the fabric or on top of the fabric as organic material accumulates. There may be reduced water flow through the material and it may restrict gas exchange between the soil and air. (Figure 12.9)

Soil solarization is a natural method that uses the sun's heat to kill weed seeds, disease-causing organisms, and nematodes. Solarizing uses clear plastic or polyethylene to intensify sunlight, which raises soil temperatures and kills soilborne pests. Covering moist soil with clear plastic for at least six weeks solarizes the soil. During this time, light and heat from the sun pass through the plastic and are absorbed by the soil. The plastic traps some of the heat and, over time, the soil temperature rises. The goal is to heat the soil enough to disinfest it and rid it of soilborne pests that cause plant diseases, like nematodes, bacteria, and fungi.

Figure 12.9 Once the landscape fabric was removed, it was eviden it had been restricting the flow of water.
Image Credit: Terasa Lott, Clemson University

The best time to solarize the soil is during the hottest part of summer. In some parts of the state, depending on the weather pattern, June may be a better month for solarization than August.

The degree of control of annual weeds by solarization depends on the weed species. Weeds susceptible to solarization include annual bluegrass (*Poa annua*), chickweed, henbit, lambsquarters, prickly lettuce, pigweed, and shepherd's purse. Partially susceptible weeds include bermudagrass, crabgrass, creeping woodsorrel (*Oxalis corniculata*), field bindweed, purslane, and yellow nutsedge.

Biological Weed Control Methods

Biological approaches to weed control employ natural enemies such as pathogens, predators, and parasites to reduce weed populations below the level of economic injury. Biological controls have been used successfully on perennial weeds on rangelands and in aquatic sites where large infestations of a single weed occur in a new area with no natural enemies. Biological controls are not as effective for rapidly developing annual weeds of annual crops. There aren't many biological weed control options available to home gardeners, though one option is the use of goats to consume weeds such as English ivy and kudzu. Since the plants regrow after the goats are removed, the remaining vegetation must be periodically treated, mowed, or re-grazed.

Chemical Weed Control Methods: The Last Resort

Herbicides are chemicals used to suppress or kill weeds by interrupting a metabolic pathway or normal growth process. One of the biggest challenges with herbicide use is choosing the best chemical. Frequently, two or more herbicides can control the same problem weed. Several factors should affect herbicide selection, including weed and crop species, season, weed growth stage, soil type, proximity of beneficial plants, available application methods, cost, and potential environmental impacts. To determine how effective a particular herbicide is on a weed problem and how safe it is to the crop being treated, be sure to read and follow all directions on the label.

To be effective, herbicides must be applied at the proper time. This time takes into account not only the weed growth stage but also the crop growth stage. Herbicides can damage many plants when applied to young plants or those under moisture or heat stress. Newly transplanted plants are more damaged than well-established plants. The length of time a preemergent herbicide controls weeds depends on soil type, rate of active ingredient, and weather conditions. Many preemergent herbicides, for instance, may need two or three applications during the growing season to effectively control weeds for the whole season.

Types of Herbicides by Mode of Action

Herbicides can be grouped or classified into various categories based on their mode of action and how they are used.

Selective herbicides control the weeds listed on the label but do not harm or seriously affect others. For example, 2,4-D selectively controls broadleaf weeds in grasses such as bermudagrass. Imazaquin controls sedges in certain turfgrasses without any adverse effect to the turf. Many of the herbicides used in landscapes are selective.

Nonselective herbicides damage or kill all green plants regardless of plant species. Since they do not discriminate, always direct nonselective herbicides away from desirable plants.

Nonselective herbicides are often applied along fences, the edges of driveways, and areas that need renovation. A commonly used nonselective herbicide is glyphosate (sold as Roundup®, KleenUp®, and other brand names). Take extreme care when applying these chemicals, as drift can cause problems to non-targeted plants. You may also see some damage from the chemical due to water movement or footprinting. (Figure 12.10)

Figure 12.10 Yellowing at the bases of the leaflets is a symptom of glyphosate damage on tomato.
Image Credit: Justin Ballew, Clemson University

A California jury awarded a grounds keeper millions of dollars in damages against the company Monsanto (now Bayer) in 2018. The decision was based on the claim that the groundskeeper developed non-Hodgkins lymphoma because of his exposure to Roundup®, an herbicide that contains the active ingredient glyphosate—developed by Monsanto. This award was based on the deliberations of 12 jurors, not scientific evidence of the safety of glyphosate or the lack thereof. The World Health Organization classifies glyphosate as a "probable carcinogen," alongside red meat and other products. The US Environmental Protection Agency and the European Union consider glyphosate safe based on scientific studies.

Contact herbicides only control or kill the portion of the plant on which it is sprayed. These herbicides are not translocated within the plant, so good spray coverage is essential. A weed that has been sprayed with a contact herbicide may regrow if coverage was incomplete.

Contact herbicides can be classified as either selective or nonselective. The active ingredient bentazon (Basagran®) is an example of a selective contact herbicide. It is used for selective control of yellow nutsedge in turf and ornamentals. Diquat (Reward®) and pelargonic acid (Scythe®) are examples of nonselective herbicides that damage or kill plants on contact.

Systemic herbicides are those herbicides that move throughout a plant's vascular system. They are typically applied to a plant's leaves and allowed to move and accumulate in the growing points. Unlike the "quick-kill" contact herbicides, systemic herbicides take several days or a few weeks to kill plants. One selective systemic herbicide is 2,4-D, which controls broadleaf weeds without severely injuring most landscape grasses. Glyphosate is a nonselective systemic herbicide. For systemic herbicides to work, apply them to actively-growing weeds.

Types of Herbicides by Application Timing

Preemergent Herbicides. Apply preemergent herbicides to an area prior to weed seed germination. The chemicals form a chemical barrier, and as the weed seeds germinate, the developing shoots and roots contact and absorb the herbicide, resulting in death of the seedlings—usually by inhibition of root growth. It's important to apply the herbicide uniformly. It is also important to identify past weeds to select the proper preemergent herbicide, since the weed is not present when you apply it. Monitor your landscape prior to starting a preemergent weed control program. Since these herbicides stop the emergence of weed seedlings, they control annuals better than perennials. In turf and ornamentals, apply preemergent herbicides in the fall for winter weed control and in early spring for summer weed control.

Apply preemergent herbicides according to the following guidelines:

In fall, when nighttime temperatures drop to 55-60°F, apply preemergence herbicides to control winter annual weeds such as annual bluegrass, henbit, and common chickweed. Annual bluegrass germinates in late summer into early fall, when air temperatures drop consistently into the mid-70s. This is usually around September 15 through October 1 in coastal and central areas and September 1-15 in the Piedmont and Mountain regions. Germination is earliest in weak turf areas such as those that are shaded or wet. Additional annual bluegrass germination also occurs in early winter when there are warm days and cold nights.

In spring, when daytime temperatures reach 65-70°F for 4-5 days, apply preemergence herbicides to control summer annual weeds like crabgrass and goosegrass.

Crabgrass is a troublesome summer annual weed that germinates in the spring, matures and reproduces by seed in the summer, and then dies at the first killing frost in the fall. Crabgrass seed requires sunlight and moisture to germinate, so expect to find it in thin or weak stands of grass or in low, damp areas. Crabgrass is rarely found beneath the shaded canopies of trees or on the north side of buildings.

Crabgrass seed germination often coincides with the flowering of early spring plants such as redbuds, pears, crabapples, and forsythia. Apply preemergence crabgrass controls around the first week of March in the Coastal Plain and Sandhill regions and mid- to late March in the Piedmont and Mountains regions.

Goosegrass germinates about 3-4 weeks later than crabgrass. Apply the preemergent herbicide uniformly across the lawn to establish a chemical barrier about a week before the crabgrass seeds are expected to germinate. Follow label directions, since many preemergent herbicides require at least ½ in. of water after application to ensure that the chemical moves into the thatch and soil layer.

Most preemergent herbicides break down during the summer months, so you may need to reapply 2 months after the initial application to control any late-germinating crabgrass seeds.

Weed 'n Feed. "Weed 'n feed" products are preemergence herbicides formulated with dry fertilizers to create fertilizer-herbicide mixtures. Despite the convenience of controlling weeds and fertilizing the lawn at the same time, consider the kind of turfgrass growing in your lawn and the time of year before taking this approach. It may not be the appropriate time of year for a fertilizer application. For example, you shouldn't fertilize centipedegrass in the spring until it fully greens up; however, waiting until the centipede has fully recovered from winter dormancy is too late to apply a preemergent herbicide, as the weeds may already have emerged.

Weed 'n feed products contain a fertilizer and an herbicide so you can apply them both at once. But timing is critical when applying any herbicide or fertilizer. Whether you apply them separately or in combination, read and follow the manufacturer's instructions. Also be sure you know what the herbicide component is, if it's preemergent or postemergent, how much nitrogen should be applied to the turfgrass at the labeled rate, and if there are any hazards or limitation to the turf you apply it to. Apply preemergent herbicides before weed seeds germinate and postemergent herbicides after weeds emerge or appear in the lawn. The application timing of the weed 'n feed product should coincide with the appropriate growth stage for controlling particular weeds and strengthening the lawn. Ultimately, weed 'n feed products offer convenience but little flexibility in timing.

In most areas of South Carolina, season-long control requires two applications, 10 weeks apart. Alternatively, you can follow a single application of a preemergent herbicide with spot treatments of a selective or nonselective postemergent herbicide (more about those in the following pages) to control escaped weeds.

For adequate weed control, preemergent herbicides must receive water from rainfall or irrigation. Without this step, weed control will be poor. Most preemergent herbicides require ½ in. of water to move the chemical into the upper part of the soil.

A number of factors can reduce the efficacy of a preemergent herbicide treatment. Time of year can cause a loss of weed control, as temperature has a critical effect; some herbicides should only be applied during cool temperatures, as warm weather can speed up the physical breakdown of the chemical. Since preemergent herbicides basically provide a blanket over your landscape, disturbing the soil by tilling or aerification can disrupt weed control. Read and follow directions on all herbicide labels to assure adequate control and be aware of specific restrictions and recommendations.

Follow these general guidelines when using preemergent herbicides on turfgrass:

- Read the label to know how much time must elapse before it is safe to seed.
- Do not use a preemergence herbicide at the time of turfgrass seeding unless that is a labeled procedure. Preemergent herbicides applied after seeding or after sprigging can cause severe injury to turfgrass.
- Mow new turfgrass seedlings at least three times before applying a preemergent herbicide.
- Do not apply a preemergent herbicide to soil before laying sod.
- Return grass clippings to a lawn for 2-3 weeks after applying a preemergent herbicide to ensure that any herbicide absorbed to the leaf blades returns to the soil. Ideally, always return or recycle your clippings.

Postemergent Herbicides. Postemergent herbicides are applied directly to the foliage of actively growing, emerged weeds. As opposed to preemergent herbicides, post-emergent herbicides generally do not provide residual weed control; they only control those weeds that are actively growing. Postemergent herbicides are the best chemical control measure for broadleaf weeds in lawns.

Most of the postemergent herbicides used to control broadleaf weeds are systemic (translocated) and foliar. They must remain on the weed leaves long enough to allow the chemical to penetrate the plant. Rainfall or irrigation within 6 hr of a treatment can wash some chemicals off the weed before it has been absorbed; however, there are some herbicides that are rain-fast after only an hour. Check your label for this information.

Temperature can also reduce postemergent weed control. Herbicide movement within the plant is slower on cool, cloudy days.

Postemergent herbicides are most effective when

weeds are young, actively growing, and able to translocate the chemical within the plant. Adequate soil moisture, high humidity, bright sunshine, and air temperatures between 65 to 85°F benefit weed control. Control of biennial and perennial weeds is generally most effective when herbicides are applied in spring to early summer or in fall. You can control broadleaf weeds during the summer months, but some turfgrasses are very sensitive to broadleaf herbicides, especially when under stress from heat and drought. Spraying during times of higher temperatures increases the chance of nontarget plant damage. Again, read and follow all label direction to minimize or avoid problems.

Herbicides offer reduced control when the weed is under heat, drought, or cold stress. Herbicides also perform poorly when the weed is going to seed or has recently been mowed.

Most postemergent herbicides are systemic. Due to their ability to move throughout the plant, there is no need to apply postemergent herbicides too heavily. Apply the product until runoff begins, then stop. Any herbicide that drips off the plant is wasted and does not increase weed control. When using postemergent herbicides, consider spot-treating problem areas instead of making a blanket application over the entire lawn.

Some herbicides, such as atrazine, have both preemergence and postemergence activity on a variety of annual broadleaf weeds. When these atrazine-fertilizer products are applied to centipedegrass or St. Augustine grass after complete green-up, they can control many annual broadleaf weeds before or after emergence.

Before applying any postemergence herbicide, read and understand the label.

To improve the effectiveness of postemergent herbicides to control emerged annual weeds or when new growth or regrowth occurs on perennial weeds—and to improve the tolerance of turfgrass—follow these guidelines:

- Apply postemergent herbicides in the fall and late spring. The cooler temperatures improve turfgrass tolerance to herbicides. Most postemergent herbicides are more effective in warmer weather and less active on days with temperatures below 60°F, though also be cautious when daytime temperatures soar above 85°F.
- Do not apply postemergent herbicides to turfgrasses that are under stress from high temperatures or drought. Turfgrasses become less tolerant to postemergent herbicides when air temperatures exceed 85-90°F or when they are stressed by drought.
- Do not apply a postemergent herbicide when a warm-season lawn is greening up in the spring. Turfgrass that is coming out of winter dormancy is at greater risk of being injured from a postemergent herbicide than when it is fully dormant or actively growing.
- Summer annual broadleaf weeds such as prostrate spurge, knotweed, and purslane can be very difficult to control, because they germinate over several weeks or months. Also, these weeds develop a thick, waxy leaf as they mature that makes it difficult for the herbicide to enter the plant. For these hard-to-control weeds, consider a nonchemical approach. Mow to the recommended height, water properly, provide adequate fertility aids, and reestablish thin lawn areas by reseeding or sodding.

Turf Weed Management

When developing a turf weed management program, take the following guidelines into consideration:

- Determine what types of turfgrass are present.
- Identify the problem weeds and note what time of year they appear. Past records of weed problems and weedy areas can help you to stay one step ahead of problem weeds.
- Determine the level of lawn quality you desire and can provide. Can you live with a few weeds? Do you have so many weeds that eliminating them would leave you with bare soil? (If so, be prepared to establish a new lawn after you control the weeds.)
- Weeds are usually the result of poorly chosen or mismanaged turf. Plant the right turf species for your site. Determine why the weeds invaded the lawn; some weeds are very specific in their site requirements and can provide clues about a particular site. For example, ground ivy, violets, chickweeds and moss are very shade-tolerant; knotweed and goosegrass grow in compacted soils; and prostrate spurge grows in hot locations with high soil temperatures (that is, along sidewalks and driveways).
- Follow a good turf management program. The most effective long-term solution to minimizing weed problems is a healthy, dense lawn obtained via proper turf management. If herbicides are

not accompanied by basic improvements in a turf management program, weeds can reinfest the area or be replaced by other weeds that are more difficult to control.
- If an herbicide is necessary, select a chemical that is effective for the weeds and safe for the turfgrass. Follow all label directions and apply the herbicide at the proper rate and time. Survey the site for sensitive areas and consider the drift and off-site movement of pesticides.
- Monitor the effectiveness of the weed control program. If you saw poor results from an herbicide application, try to determine why the failure occurred. Always be on the lookout for herbicide damage to desirable plants. In some instances, damage may warrant a change in application rate or herbicide formulation.

Factors Affecting Chemical Control and Selection

There are several different factors of chemical control that complicate weed management. Generally, it is difficult to select an herbicide when the crop and weed share similar physiological traits. When this situation arises, it is important to exploit any differences between the weed and the crop.

Some of these potential differences include:

- Growing points. Plants that shield their growing points from herbicides by encapsulating them in a sheath or placing them underground are protected from contact chemicals.
- Leaf shape. Herbicides tend to run off narrow, upright leaves while broad, flat leaves tend to hold the chemical longer and allow greater absorption and control.
- Waxy leaves or leaves with thick cuticles. These plant features resist herbicide absorption. The waxy surface can also cause the herbicide solution to bead up and roll off the leaf, you can use surfactants to overcome this.
- Leaf hairs. A dense layer of leaf hair prohibits absorption, because the spray solution balls up away from the leaf. A thin layer of hair causes the chemical to stay on the surface longer than normal.
- Plant age. In most cases, young, rapidly growing plants are more susceptible to damage than older, mature plants.

- Special properties. Some plants are very efficient in deactivating the active ingredient in particular herbicides and thus less susceptible to injury.

There is no single herbicide that can control all weeds. There are chemicals that control grass weeds but not broadleaf weeds and vice versa.

Landscape plants, fruit trees, vegetables, flowers, and turfgrass all vary in their ability to tolerate an overspray of an herbicide. Often, a chemical weed control program is complicated by the diversity of plants located within a landscape. To simply use one herbicide without checking the label could lead to major plant damage or death. An herbicide needs to be labeled for both the weed you are wanting to control and the crop you are applying it to. The label lists all of these plants. Be aware that herbicides may be sold under a variety of names; if you cannot identify the trade name, look for a chemical or common name on the label to be sure you know what you are buying. For example, glyphosate is the common name of the active ingredient contained in products such as Roundup®, Eraser®, and Glyphomax®.

Any number of factors may interact to make herbicide weed control successful or a failure. Be sure you follow all label directions to get the maximum benefits out of each application without losing money or harming the environment. Keep in mind, however, that even experienced herbicide users occasionally see poor results.

Factors that Affect Herbicide Performance

- Application rates and uniform coverage. Application errors are probably the number one cause for poor herbicide performance. Be sure to follow application instructions, apply the recommended rate, and use calibrated application equipment.
- Application timing. When choosing an herbicide, take into account the season of application, time of weed germination, weed growth stage, and weed life cycle.
- Weather conditions at the time of application. Preemergent herbicides must be watered in, but too much water can decrease efficacy. Conditions that are too hot, dry, cold or wet can also reduce weed control. Be sure the weed is actively growing and not under stress before applying postemergence herbicides.
- Weed identification. Be sure you have positively identified the weeds and the desirable plants that

you are spraying to select the proper herbicide. Be aware that some tougher or older weeds may require repeat applications.
- Soil type and organic matter content. Organic matter and clay content affect the rate and efficacy of some herbicides and whether they damage nontarget plants.

Application Equipment

Applying herbicides successfully requires that you use the right equipment and application technique. The amount of herbicide that should be applied to a lawn is listed on the label. For home lawns, the recommended rate is often given in an amount (pounds, fluid or dry ounces) of product per 1,000 ft² of lawn. You need to know the square footage of your lawn to apply herbicide at the correct rate. Before application, measure your lawn to determine its square footage so you can then determine how much herbicide would be required to cover that area.

Apply the recommended rate. Avoid falling victim to the adage that "if a little is good, then a lot more is better;" herbicides can severely injure lawn grasses and desirable plants when applied in excess.

Use the right equipment to apply the herbicide evenly and uniformly to the lawn. If you apply too much spray or overlap too much with granular products, the increase in herbicide can also lead to an increased risk of turfgrass injury. On the other hand, if the spray or granule application does not overlap, there are areas of the lawn that won't be treated, which often results in streaks of weeds. Common equipment used with liquid products include hand-held pump-up sprayers and hose-end applicators.

Apply granular herbicides with a drop-type or rotary spreader. To ensure uniform distribution and to help prevent any skips or excessive overlap, divide the required amount in half. Apply one-half the required amount in one direction and the remaining amount at right angles to the first.

Herbicide Safety Precautions. Always read and follow label directions regarding the handling and application of the herbicide. Mix and use only the amount of herbicide that you need to treat your lawn. Store the herbicide in its original container, in a dry area, and protected from freezing temperatures. Finally, always keep herbicides out of the reach of children, pets, and livestock.

For more information about the use, handling, storage, and disposal of pesticides, visit Clemson University's Pesticide Information Program at http://entweb.clemson.edu/pesticid/.

Herbicide Injury

Herbicide injury to nontarget plants can often be traced to improper application or application of an herbicide under inappropriate weather conditions. Herbicides applied on windy days can drift from the target area to plants off site. Some formulations of 2,4-D are very volatile and can drift a great distance; some plants, like tomatoes, are very sensitive to 2,4-D and can be easily damaged. Other factors that can contribute to herbicide drift include the spray droplet size and air temperature. Fine spray mist and hot weather lead to increasing drift and herbicide volatility, providing greater chance of offsite plant damage.

The possibility of root uptake of a soil-applied herbicide is also a factor to consider in chemical weed control. Factors involved with root uptake are the herbicide used, soil type, and soil moisture content. Some herbicides are relatively mobile in the soil and can get into the root zone of plants quickly. Dicamba and atrazine, for example, move rapidly in sandy soils and can get into tree roots. Dogwoods are very sensitive to these chemicals and easily damaged. Atrazine is a common herbicide used in weed 'n feed products. Because of this, be careful where you apply the product and avoid areas where there may be tree roots. Other chemicals, such as glyphosate, do not move in the soil readily and have little or no persistence, lessening the chance for nontarget plant injury.

Herbicide injury symptoms may resemble those created by a variety of other factors, including mites, insects, diseases, drought, root problems, improper soil pH, physical damage, and fertilizer misapplication. Diagnosis of herbicide injury is difficult at best. Plant injury symptoms usually show up within several days after an application. Some plants that are very sensitive to herbicide applications are grapes, tomatoes, roses, dogwoods, and forsythia.

Safe Herbicide Use

Follow these guidelines when using herbicides:

- Identify the desirable plant—that is, turfgrass, shrub, perennials, etc.—and the problem weed.
- Select a labeled herbicide. Remember that information on plants to which the herbicide may be applied, sites where it may be used, and weeds that the herbicide controls are all listed on the label.

- Thoroughly read and understand the entire herbicide label. The label is the best reference on how to use an herbicide effectively and safely.
- Follow all directions on the label for application rate, mixing, time of application, application methods, storage, and disposal of empty herbicide containers.
- Never apply more herbicide than is recommended on the herbicide label. Herbicides are applied at specific amounts (ounces, pounds, pints, etc.) per 1,000 ft^2. Applying more than the recommended amount does not improve weed control but does increase the risk of injury to desirable plants.
- Do not use herbicides that are designed for use on lawns (especially weed 'n feed products) in landscape beds unless the herbicide is also labeled for use on ornamentals in landscape beds. Most landscape plants are very susceptible to damage from the herbicides commonly found in weed 'n feed lawn products, so read labels with great care before application.
- Purchase and maintain proper herbicide application equipment. Apply granular products with a rotary or drop spreader—or in small areas like flower beds, with a shaker-type can (in which the herbicide is packaged) or a gloved hand. Use hand-held pump-up sprayers or hose-end sprayers to apply liquid herbicides.
- Do not be tempted to use an herbicide on a desirable plant that is not listed on the label. The risk of injury to that plant may be very high.

Chapter 13
Pest Management

Revised and updated by Robert G. Bellinger, Ph.D & Terasa Lott.

Previous version prepared by Robert G. Bellinger, Ph.D., Carlin Munnerlyn, and Bob Polomski

LEARNING OBJECTIVES
- Define IPM and outline its important concepts.
- Explain how to scout for pest problems.
- Identify available pest management strategies and evaluate their benefits and limitations.
- Read a pesticide label, identify signal words, and learn pesticide formulations.
- List factors that can cause pest management strategies to fail.
- Calibrate a sprayer, clean pesticide equipment, safely store pesticides, and use safety equipment.
- Recognize pesticide poisoning symptoms and state who you will call in a pesticide emergency.
- Describe how IPM strategies (both chemical and non-chemical) can impact the environment.
- Determine a pest problem, make general recommendations, and develop a basic IPM strategy.

INTRODUCTION

Integrated pest management, or IPM, is an ecologically based decision-making process for managing pests in a way that minimizes adverse effects on the environment. The five steps in IPM are:

- Monitor the garden and landscape for pest activity.
- Accurately identify the pest.
- Assess the damage. Does the damage warrant action?
v Implement a treatment strategy using mechanical, cultural, biological, or chemical controls.
- Evaluate the effectiveness of the treatment strategy.

Monitor Your Garden and Landscape

Inspect your garden and landscape on a regular basis. Examine your plants for signs and symptoms of pests. Generally, most plants have few problems if they are planted in the right location and receive proper care. However, problem-prone species exist, such as plants in the Rosaceae family, which are highly susceptible to an assortment of pests. These "key hosts" are most frequently attacked by "key pests" and must be examined more frequently than other plants. When monitoring your plants, use a hand lens with at least 10x magnification to inspect your plants. Check the key hosts first and record your observations in a gardening journal or other notebook.

Identifying Harmful and Beneficial Organisms

Accurate identification of the pest and host are key to making the right management decision. It's also important to identify beneficial organisms that can help maintain pest populations at tolerable levels. Beneficial organisms consist of predators, parasites, and pathogens. Predators kill and eat their prey. Parasites live in or on their host during at least one stage of their existence; parasitoids are similar to parasites but eventually kill the host. Beneficial pathogens consist of a variety of viruses, fungi, and bacteria that naturally infect and kill harmful pests. Refer back to Chapter 10 for examples of beneficial insects.

Assess The Damage

Before you select appropriate control measures, first consider the **action threshold** for your situation—the "breakpoint," or level at which a plant can sustain no further damage from pests. An action threshold is based on economic, aesthetic, and health considerations. It's a function of the number of pests or the intensity of the pest population that may threaten the health and longevity of plants.

An **economic threshold** is the point at which, if the untreated pest population goes unchecked, the economic losses would exceed the cost of controlling the pest. For example, the economic threshold could be when more than two out of ten leaves are damaged by Mexican bean beetles. Lighter infestations do not warrant control, because they have no appreciable effect on yield. When an economic threshold is exceeded, you need to decide on a course of action; this can range from handpicking pests to applying an insecticide to prevent further injury and loss of the crop.

In landscapes where plants are grown for beauty and not profit, aesthetic injury thresholds are used to make pest management decisions. An **aesthetic injury threshold** is based on appearance and refers to the highest level of pest numbers or damage that would be acceptable to you. This threshold is difficult to establish, because each of us have differing tolerance levels for pests and plant injury. After all, beauty is in the eye of the beholder.

Keep in mind that while it can be difficult to accept any kind of plant damage, some is just cosmetic and poses no real harm to the plant. Fall webworms and gall-forming insects are common pests that produce unsightly webs and galls but do not necessarily threaten the health of the plant.

When left unchecked, there are some pests that will harm or kill plants. For example, orangestriped oakworm (*Anisota senatoria*) may require control when 25% of the tree is defoliated because of the reduced starch reserves.

In summary, healthy plants can usually tolerate some level of insect injury without any adverse effects on growth and development. In fact, low levels of harmful insect pests are an important food source for beneficial insects, so the costs of controlling the pest may far outweigh leaving it alone and letting nature manage it. Try to establish action thresholds for key plant species in your landscape, taking into account the plant's present health, appearance, location, and function in the landscape. When you observe damage, take notes on the time, host, and extent of injury. Your observations help you track potential problems and predict future pest outbreaks.

Choose And Implement a Treatment Strategy

When a pest infestation exceeds an action threshold, use a control strategy that reduces pest numbers to an acceptable level. Ideally, the best approach is to monitor your plants regularly to detect pest problems when they're in the early stages—especially where simple handpicking or judicious pruning can take care of the problem.

In deciding on the best control strategies, consider all treatment options: mechanical, cultural, biological, and chemical. Try to combine strategies that complement one another to provide greater protection from pests.

When you take some kind of action, write it down in your journal. Note the extent of the damage, the action you took, and the effectiveness of that action. In the long run, the time and effort spent on these simple records are an invaluable educational tool for you and the people you counsel in your community.

It's important to be realistic with your expectations. Healthy landscapes contain a wide variety of beneficial insects as well as a tolerable level of damaging pests. A healthy, naturally balanced landscape not only provides you with healthy plants but protects and preserves our environment for future generations.

A balanced landscape works with nature without requiring many outside inputs. As in landscapes that occur naturally, balanced landscapes accommodate an acceptable level of pests. Management is the goal, not elimination. Promoting a natural balance of beneficial organisms and pests in your landscape is not only environmentally sound but also cost efficient. However, there are occasions where harmful pests outnumber beneficial organisms. The IPM program allows for the use of pesticides only when needed. IPM brings together the natural balance of your landscape with targeted management strategies aimed at managing pests while minimizing environmental impacts.

Cultural Controls

Cultural controls alter the environment, the condition of the host plant, or the behavior of the pest to prevent or suppress infections or infestations. Some cultural practices disrupt the normal relationship between the pest and the host plant and make the pest less likely to survive, grow, or reproduce. Examples of cultural controls include:

Soil Management and Preparation. Provide your plants with a solid foundation by adding organic matter, applying mulch, and fertilizing and adjusting soil pH as indicated by a soil test.

Plant Selection. Choose plants suited to the soil and climate of your area. When possible, select resistant species and cultivars. Be thoughtful in selecting a planting location. Research shows that understory plants such as dogwoods are more likely to be attacked by dogwood borers when planted in locations that receive full sun. Similarly, azaleas in full sun are more prone to attack by azalea lace bugs than those in partial shade. Start with healthy plants and, if available, certified disease-free seed.

Planting Time. Determine the appropriate planting dates for each plant species and don't plant out of season. Particularly for vegetables and flowering annuals, planting too early or late results in a stressed plant that is more susceptible to attack.

Watering. Water late at night or early in the morning when dew has formed. Do not water in early evening, as leaves may remain wet for an extended period of time, which favors fungal infections.

Mechanical or Physical Controls

Mechanical or physical barriers include devices, machines, and methods used to control pests or change their environment.

Handpicking. Removing insects or their egg masses by hand is an effective method for managing small populations. Handpick leaf-feeding insects—such as bean beetles, potato beetles, squash bugs, tomato hornworms, and other caterpillars—and snails and discard them in a jar of soapy water. Alternatively, knock them off with a strong spray of water from the hose. Promptly removing diseased leaves and plants may be helpful in reducing some diseases if only a few plants are affected, and the problem is identified early.

Exclusion. Physically block insects from attacking your plants. Use nonwoven, spunbonded polypropylene fabric row covers to prevent pests from infesting small fruit and vegetable crops. Protect transplants from cutworms by placing a collar of stiff paper, cardboard, or aluminum foil around each plant. The barrier should extend 2 in. above and below the surface of the soil.

Handpulling, Cultivating, Mowing, Mulching. These techniques keep unwanted vegetation at bay. Organic and inorganic mulches block sunlight and physically interfere with the emergence of many annual weeds.

Sanitation. Burying or removing crop residues helps to prevent and suppress some pests by directly removing them or their sources of food and shelter. Sanitation pruning is the judicious removal of heavily infested or infected shoots. Remember the 3 Ds of pruning to control pests: remove Dead, Damaged, or Diseased (or insect-infested) leaves, shoots, or branches whenever you spot them.

Biological Controls

Biological control utilizes natural enemies to reduce pest populations. Examples include predators, parasites, and parasitoids, which you learned about in Chapter 10.

One effective biological management strategy for insect pests is to incorporate a diversity of flowering plants in the landscape to attract and sustain beneficial insects. Most of these "good bugs" feed on pollen and nectar as adults. Learn about the specific plant species that attract beneficial insects during spring, summer, and fall and incorporate them into your landscape design. In general, the release of "mail-order" beneficial insects is more effective in greenhouses than in outdoor landscapes or gardens. Releasing beneficial insects into your landscape or garden may offer some benefit, but it is better to conserve the beneficial insects that are already there.

Another biological control method, trap cropping, involves growing plants that are attractive to an insect. For example, growing sunflowers may lure leaf-footed bugs away from tomatoes. Hubbard squash can lure several cucurbit pests, such as squash vine borers and squash bugs.

Chemical Controls

When cultural, physical, or biological controls fail to adequately reduce pest numbers, it may be necessary to use pesticides. According to the action threshold you set, choose the least toxic and most target-specific pesticide. Select a pesticide that disrupts the environment least and has the smallest impact on beneficials and other nontarget organisms.

Any chemical used to kill, attract, alter the behavior of, or repel a pest is a **pesticide** (Table 13.1). The suffix "cide" literally means "kill." Chemicals used to regulate plant growth or function are also classed as pesticides. There are two types of pesticides: biorational and conventional pest control materials.

TABLE 13.1 Types of Common Pesticides

Types of Pesticide	Target Pest
Insecticide	Insects
Miticide	Mites
Nematicide	Nematodes
Fungicide	Fungi
Bactericide	Bacteria
Herbicide	Plants
Rodenticide	Rodents
Molluscicide	Mollusks
Algicide	Algae

Biorational Pesticides

Biorational or "reduced-risk" pesticides are microbial and biochemical products that either occur naturally or are identical to natural products and have pesticidal activity. In general, biorational pesticides have the following characteristics:

- Narrow target range and very specific mode of action
- Slow acting
- Relatively critical application times
- Suppression-focused, rather than elimination-focused
- Limited field persistence and short shelf life
- Safer to humans and the environment than conventional pesticides
- No residue problems

Insecticidal soaps are derived from the salts of fatty acids. These are principal components of fats and oils found in plants and animals. Soaps are strictly contact materials to be used against soft-bodied insects and soft-bodied stages of insects that possess hardened and thickened cuticles as adults. Insecticidal soaps can break down soft cuticular tissues. Internally, soaps destroy cell membranes, which disrupts cellular metabolism. Soaps are only effective against insects that come into direct contact with sprays while they are still wet.

Orchardists have used **dormant oils** for more than a century as an effective way of killing overwintering mites and insects. Traditionally, dormant oils are applied only when the trees are leafless, because the presence of sulfur and other residues tends to injure leaves.

There is now a newer class of **horticultural oils** available that are refined to remove these impurities, thus expanding the use of oils to shade trees, evergreens, and other woody ornamentals during the summer months. These horticultural oils are characterized by a minimum unsulfonated residue (UR) of 92 and a minimum percent paraffin (%Cp) of 60. Final formulations of horticultural oils are normally combined with an emulsifying agent that allows the oil to mix with water.

Research shows that many oils derived from vegetables, such as cottonseed and soybean oil, have insecticidal and miticidal properties. Horticultural oils essentially smother pests by clogging their spiracles, suffocating eggs, or damaging cell membranes. Dormant applications are directed at aphid eggs, caterpillar eggs, overwintering mites, and scale insects. Summer applications control adelgids, aphids, mealybugs, scale insects, spider mites, and whiteflies. The effect of these oils on beneficial insects appears to be minimal, especially if they are applied during the dormant season. Resistance to the horticultural oil is unlikely to develop anytime soon.

No matter the season in which you apply horticultural oil, follow label directions. Generally, this means avoiding temperatures above 90°F or below freezing. The oil, which is mixed with water before application, must dry thoroughly before being exposed to freezing temperatures or precipitation.

Botanical or **plant-derived pesticides** are naturally occurring pesticides derived from plants. Two common botanicals include pyrethrins—insecticidal chemicals extracted from the pyrethrum flower (*Tanacetum cinerariifolium*)—and neem—a botanical insecticide and fungicide extracted from the tropical neem tree (*Azadirachta indica*), which contains the active ingredient azadirachtin.

Pyrethrum is a mixture of four compounds found in the flowers of certain tropical chrysanthemum species. Upon contact, pyrethrum provides a quick reduction of targeted insects. To provide complete control, pyrethrum (marketed as Pyrethrin) is often used in combination with the synergist piperonyl butoxide (pbo); pbo suppresses the detoxification system, which counteracts the effects of pyrethrum.

Pyrethroid insecticides are person-made compounds with chemical structures similar to the pyrethrin components of pyrethrum. Pyrethroids are stable when exposed to sunlight and effective against a wide range of insect pests at very low doses. Various products contain the active ingredients cyfluthrin, esfenvalerate, lambda-cyhalothrin, and permethrin.

Neem is a complex of oil extracts from the seeds of the neem tree. One of the extracts (azadirachtin) acts as an insect growth regulator by inhibiting the metabolism of the ecdysone molting hormone.

There are a number of other botanical insecticides available, some of which—such as limonene and capsaicin—have demonstrated efficacy.

Insect pheromones are naturally occurring chemicals that insects use to locate mates. Manmade pheromones are used to disrupt insect mating by creating confusion during the search for mates or to attract male insects to traps. Pheromone traps are often used to detect or monitor insect populations, but they can also help control them.

Microbial insecticides are another kind of biopesticide that come from naturally occurring or genetically altered bacteria, fungi, algae, viruses, or protozoans. They suppress pests by:

- Producing a toxin specific to the pest
- Causing a disease
- Preventing establishment of other microorganisms through competition
- Other modes of action

Microbial insecticides are sold as sprays, dusts, and granules. Some of these pathogens multiply and spread after application. Others do not. Some become established in the target environment. In some cases, parasitic insects are used to carry the pathogen.

Bacteria. *Bacillus thuringiensis* (*Bt*) is a naturally occurring soil bacteria that is toxic to the larvae of several species of insects but not to nontarget organisms; it is the most widely-known pathogen. *Bt* can be applied to leaves or incorporated into the genetic material of crops. When ingested, it produces toxic crystalline proteins that actively attach to specific receptor sites on the gut wall.

Destruction of the cellular lining causes cell swelling and eventually lysis, which results in death by septicemia (blood poisoning). Different strains and substrains of *Bt* produce species-specific endotoxins that must be matched to the appropriate insect. For example, formulations from *Bacillus thuringiensis var. kurstaki* (*Btk*) help control caterpillars; other strains of *Btk* control fly larvae, such as those of mosquitoes and blackflies.

Fungi. *Beauveria bassiana* spores germinate and produce hyphal strands that penetrate and invade cuticular cells causing rapid water loss and nutrient deprivation resulting in the death of the infected insect.

Actinomycetes. *Saccharopolyspora spinosa* produces substances known as spinosyns. The active ingredient, Spinosad, is a naturally occurring mixture of spinosyn A and spinosyn D. Spinosyns enter the insects via contact and ingestion, eventually causing paralysis and death. Spinosyns are very effective against most caterpillars.

Nematodes. Although not unicellular organisms, entomopathogenic nematodes (multicellular roundworms) are included with microbials due to their small, microscopic size. Infective stage nematodes actively enter pests through natural body openings. Bacterial symbionts within the nematodes are released into the infected pests, which eventually die. Many nematode products are labeled for control of soil-inhabiting pests such as *Steinernema carpocapsae* and *Heterohabditis bacteriphora* to managing root or soil-dwelling weevils.

Conventional Pesticides

Inorganic pesticides are made from minerals such as copper, boron, cryolite, lead, sulfur, tin, and zinc. One example is bordeaux mixture, which is a blend of copper sulfate and hydrated lime.

Synthetic organic pesticides are made by people. They contain carbon, hydrogen, and one or more other elements, such as chlorine, phosphorous, and nitrogen. Some synthetic organic pesticides include carbaryl, glyphosate, imidacloprid, and maneb. These should be your last resort when confronted by damaging pest populations. Use them sparingly to control the targeted pest.

Note that we avoid using specific names of synthetic pesticides in this manual, because products and their labels change rapidly along with the pesticide registration and use process.

Use pesticides only when nonchemical methods fail to provide adequate control of pests and when pest populations reach a level of economic injury.

Because it is virtually impossible to eradicate an entire population of pests, use pesticides as tools to control or manage pest populations to an acceptable level. Understanding the proper use of pesticides is essential to using them effectively and safely.

Use pesticides exactly according to label directions. Be sure to carefully read the label of any pesticide you use and follow the instructions exactly as they are written. Be sure you use all pesticide products only when and where the label says they can be used.

Evaluate Effectiveness

The last step of IPM is to determine if the control efforts you implemented successfully reduced the number of pests in the garden or landscape. If you did not achieve your desired results, try to determine why your efforts weren't effective and adjust your response accordingly.

Remember to monitor your landscape regularly and keep accurate records that can help you make informed pest management decisions in the future.

PESTICIDE CLASSIFICATION

Pesticides can be grouped according to how they work. Many synthetic organic pesticides work in more than one way. They fall into the following major groups:

- Protectants are applied to plants, animals, structures, and products to prevent entry or damage by a pest.
- Contact poisons kill pests when they contact the poison.
- Stomach poisons kill when they are swallowed.
- Systemics are taken into the blood of a host animal or the sap of a host plant.
- Translocated herbicides kill plants by being absorbed by their leaves, stems, or roots and then moving throughout the plant.
- Fumigants are gases that kill pests who inhale or otherwise absorb them.
- Selective kill only certain kinds of plants or animals.
- Nonselective kill many kinds of plants or animals.

USING PESTICIDES

Many terms used in product labeling describe when and how to use pesticides. They also are found in Clemson Extension resources. Understanding these terms helps you understand and follow directions—leading to the best results from pesticides and the least possible risk of harm to you and the environment.

These terms refer to the timing of application:

- Preplant: use before the crop is planted.
- Preemergence: use before crops or weeds emerge (or sometimes, after crops emerge or establish but before weeds emerge).
- Postemergence: use after the crop or weeds emerge.

The following terms describe how to apply pesticides:

- Band: application of a strip over or along each crop row.
- Broadcast: uniform application to an entire

specific area.
- Dip: immersion of a plant in a container of pesticide solution.
- Directed: aimed at a portion of a plant, animal, or structure.
- Drench: saturate the soil with a pesticide.
- Foliar: application to the leaves of plants.
- In-Furrow: application to or in the furrow in which a plant is growing.
- Sidedress: application along the side of a crop row.
- Spot treatment: application of a pesticide to a small section or affected area of a crop or site. Spot treatments conserve populations of beneficial predators and parasites that are present in the garden and landscape.

Factors Affecting Pesticide Activity

The efficacy or activity of pesticides depends on whether we use them correctly but also on a host of environmental factors that we may not even have control over.

For example, soil type affects pesticide efficacy. Organic matter in soils limits pesticide activity. Soils high in organic matter may require higher rates of pesticides for effective pest control.

Climate also impacts the activity of pesticides. Rain and irrigation cause soluble pesticides to leach down through the soil. Rain during or soon after a pesticide application may wash pesticides from the intended target. Sunlight breaks down some pesticides, and wind speeds up the loss of many pesticides and increases the risk of drift.

Another factor of the activity of specific pesticides in specific places is pesticide resistance. The ability of pests to resist poisoning is called pesticide resistance. Rarely does any pesticide kill all the target pests. Each time a pesticide is used, it selectively kills the most sensitive pests. Some pests simply avoid the pesticides, while others can survive its effects. Pests that are not destroyed pass along to their offspring the traits that allowed them to survive.

When we use one pesticide repeatedly in the same place, the pest population can build up resistance. Some pests become almost completely resistant to poisoning by certain pesticides. To delay resistance be sure to: (a) correctly identify the pest; (b) use the correct pesticide; (c) apply the correct dosage (rate); and (d) apply the pesticide correctly.

Pesticide Formulations

The chemical in the pesticide formulation that actually kills the pest is called the **active ingredient**. Active ingredients can rarely be used in their original form. They must be mixed with other substances to make the product easy and safe to formulate or apply. These added substances are called **inert ingredients**. The mixture of active and inert ingredients is called a pesticide formulation. The formulation describes the physical state of a pesticide and dictates how it should be applied. Some products are ready to use when purchased; others must be diluted with water or a petroleum solvent. The product's directions for use will tell how to use a pesticide formulation. Pesticides are rarely applied at full strength, except for fumigants.

The most common types of liquid and dry formulations and their abbreviations are described below. These abbreviations may be found on the product label, sometimes as part of the product name.

Liquid Formulations

Emulsifiable concentrates (EC or E) mean that the active ingredient is mixed with an oil base—often listed as petroleum derivatives—in the product and diluted with water to form an emulsion. Diluted ECs usually need little agitation in the spray tank. ECs can damage some crops. These crops may require a different formulation of the active ingredient, such as a wettable powder or a dust.

Aerosols (A) are liquids that contain the active ingredient in a solution or a solvent. More than one pesticide may be present in these formulations. Most aerosol formulations have a low percentage of active ingredients.

One common type of aerosol comes in a container that also dispenses it. The liquid forms fine droplets when driven through a small nozzle by a pressured gas. Aerosols are used in structures, greenhouses, and barns; few are sold for use on outdoor plants. Most aerosols are insecticides.

Dry Formulations

Dusts (D) formulations are ready to use and contain an active ingredient and a very fine or powdered dry inert carrier. The amount of active ingredients usually ranges from 1-10%. All ingredients are ground into fine, uniform particles. Often, the formulations include inert ingredients that improve storage and handling and dilute the pesticide. These include talc, clay, nut hulls, or volcanic ash. Some active ingredients are prepared as dusts because they are safer for crops in that form. Always use dusts dry. They leave visible residues that may be objectionable. Dusts can easily drift into nontarget areas and irritate the applicator's skin.

Granular (G) formulations are dry. Most products are made of a liquid formulation of the active ingredient mixed with coarse particles or granules of a porous material—often clay, corn cobs, or walnut shells. The granule absorbs the pesticide, or the pesticide coats the outside of the granule; sometimes, both occur. Granule particles are larger than dusts. The amount of active ingredient ranges from 2-40%. Granules are most often used as soil treatments or for aquatic weed control. They may be applied either directly to the soil or over plants. They do not cling to plant foliage, but they may get trapped in the whorls (spiral growth) of some plants.

Like dusts, always use granular formulations dry; never mix them with water. Granular formulations are usually safer to apply than sprays or dusts, as they are less likely to drift than other formulations.

Wettable powder (WP or W) formulations are made by combining the active ingredient with a fine powder. They look like dusts but are made to be mixed with water. These formulations need continuous agitation to maintain a suspension in water and are thus difficult for home gardeners to use. When mixing a WP, first mix the measured quantity with a small amount of water to form a slurry; a paper cup with a craft stick makes a good disposable mixing container. Then add the slurry and the additional water to the spray tank.

Shake the spray tank frequently to maintain the suspension. Most wettable powders are safer for plants and humans than are ECs, but they leave a visible residue that may be objectionable in some situations. They contain 15-95% active ingredient—usually 50% or more.

Soluble powder (SP) formulations are made from an active ingredient in powder form that dissolves in water.

Gardeners sometimes attempt to compare a spray with a dust. Dusts are a type of formulation; sprays are not a formulation. Sprays are a means of applying one of several different formulations that are mixed with water, such as wettable powders or emulsifiable concentrates.

Bait (B) formulations are edible or attractive substances mixed with a pesticide. The bait attracts pests, and the pests die when they eat the pesticide. Baits are usually used to control rodents and insects. They can be used inside or outside. The amount of active ingredient in most bait formulations is low—usually less than 5% and sometimes less than 1%. Almost all baits should be kept dry.

Fertilizer mixtures that contain relatively small concentrations of pesticides are frequently available, often labeled for use on turfgrass. These mixtures are legally classified as pesticides.

PESTICIDE LABELS AND LABELING

The term labeling refers to all information that you receive from a company or its agent about a product. Labeling includes the label on the product but also includes brochures, booklets, flyers, and other supplemental materials that accompany the product.

The label is the information printed on or attached to a container of pesticides. It tells you how to use the product correctly. This section explains some of the items that must be printed on a label. Above all, remember that the label is the law. Always read and follow a pesticide's label exactly as it is written.

Brand Name

Each company has brand names for its products, also called trade names. Brand names are the most prominent words on product labels and are essentially used for marketing purposes. It is important to note that brand names are different from active ingredients; products containing the same active ingredients may be sold under several brand names. Even the same company may use the very similar names for products with completely different active ingredients, as is the case with Sevin® Insect Killer Concentrate and Sevin® Insect Killer Ready-to-Use.

Type of Formulation

Different types of pesticide formulations (explained in more detail in the previous section) require different methods of handling. The label usually indicates what type of formulation a package contains (Figure 13.1). The same active pesticide ingredient may be available in more than one formulation.

Common Name

Most pesticides have complex chemical names. Some have other names to make them easier to identify. These are called common names. For instance, carbaryl is the common name for naphthyl N-methylcarbamate. Chemicals made by more than one company can be

Figure 13.1 This label indicates this pesticide is a dust formulation.
Image Credit: Robert Bellinger, Clemson University

Figure 13.2 From the label, we can tell this pesticide contains castor oil as the active ingredient.
Image Credit: Robert Bellinger, Clemson University

sold under several brand names but may have the same common name or chemical name. When there is a common name, it is usually provided in the active ingredient statement. So 50% Sevin Wettable (brand name) contains carbaryl (common name) as the active ingredient, and the full chemical name of carbaryl is 1-naphthyl N-methylcarbamate. Always check the common chemical name for the active ingredient(s).

Net Contents

The net contents are how much of all ingredients combined are in the container. This can be expressed in gallons, pints, pounds, quarts, or other units of measure.

Name and Address of Manufacturer

The law requires the maker or distributor of a product to print the name and address of the company on the label.

Registration Number

There must be a registration number on every pesticide label; this shows that the product has been registered by the Environmental Protection Agency (EPA) for the uses listed on the label. EPA registers pesticides but does not approve them.

Establishment Number

The establishment number indicates which factory made the chemical.

Ingredient Statement

Every pesticide label must list what is in a product (Figure 13.2). The list is written so that you can quickly identify the active ingredient(s); the label doesn't have to include inert ingredients but does have to include their content in the formulation (given as a percentage).

Signal Words and Symbols

To do their job, most pesticides must kill a target pest; this means that by their nature, pesticides are toxic. Some may be hazardous to people, too. You can tell the relative toxicity of a product by reading the signal word on the label.

Signal Words

One of the most important parts of the label is the signal word. It tells how toxic the material is to people (Table 13.2). Signal words are based on several criteria or standards of toxicity to laboratory animals. These signal words indicate the toxicity of the product, not its potential hazard to the environment. These are the dosages that cause death when swallowed, applied to the skin, or inhaled or that cause irritation or are corrosive to the skin and eyes. The criterion by which the product is graded the most toxic determines the signal word that must appear on the label. See Figure 13.3 for two examples of signal words from pesticide labels.

Figure 13.3 Examples of signal words from pesticide labels
Image Credit: Robert Bellinger, Clemson University

TABLE 13.2 Signal Words and Corresponding Approximate Human Toxicity

Signal Word(s)	Toxicity	Approximate Amount Needed to Kill an Average Adult when Swallowed	Symbol
CAUTION	Low/ relatively non-toxic	1 oz – more than 1 pt	None
WARNING	Moderate	1 tsp – 1 tbsp	None
DANGER	Highly injurious	A taste – 1 tsp	None
DANGER/ POISON	Highly toxic	A taste – 1 tsp	Skull and crossbones

Highly toxic pesticides are generally not sold in the home garden trade. All products must bear the statement "Keep Out of Reach of Children."

Symbol

One of the best ways to catch a person's eye is with symbols. This is why the skull and crossbones symbol is used on all highly toxic materials along with the signal words DANGER/ POISON. Clemson Cooperative Extension should never recommend home use of pesticides with this symbol of toxicity.

Precautionary Statements

Hazards to Humans and Domestic Animals

This section of the label indicates the ways in which the product may be poisonous to humans and animals. It also lists any special steps one should take to avoid getting poisoned, such as using specific protective equipment.

Environmental Hazards

Pesticides are useful tools, but wrong or careless use can cause undesirable effects. To prevent that from occurring, the label contains environmental precautions; always read and follow these instructions.

Physical and Chemical Hazards

This section lists any special fire, explosion, or chemical hazards that the product may pose.

Statement of Practical Treatment (First Aid Statement)

If swallowing or inhaling the product or getting it in the eyes or on skin is harmful, the label describes emergency first aid measures (Figure 13.4). It also tells what kinds of exposure require professional medical attention. If you think someone has been poisoned, the pesticide label is the most important information to take to the physician.

Directions for Use

Instructions for how to use a pesticide are an important part of its label. Reading this is the best way to know the correct way to apply a product. The instructions provide the following information:

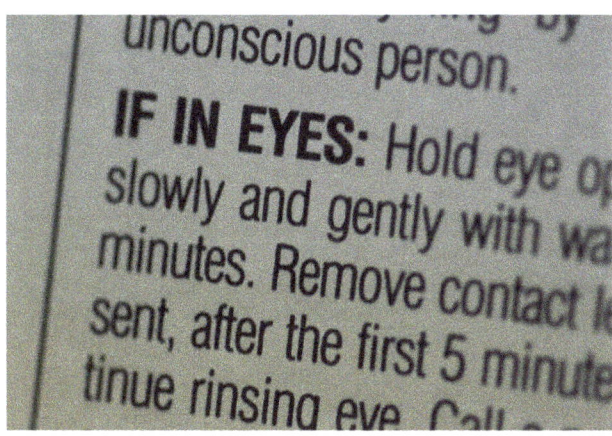

Figure 13.4 The pesticide label will provide first aid measures.
Image Credit: Robert Bellinger, Clemson University

- Crops, animals, or other items or sites on which the product can be used safely.
- Pests the product is registered to control.
- The form in which you should apply the product.
- How much of the product to use (rate.)
- Where to apply the material.
- When to apply the material.
- What kind of equipment you need to apply the material or what equipment not to use to apply it.

Read the pesticide label before buying the product. Be sure to have the proper equipment to apply the pesticide, the proper protective clothing, and a solid understanding of all directions for exact use before purchasing the product.

Misuse Statement

It is a violation of federal and state law to use a product "in a manner inconsistent with its labeling." Do not use a product on a plant, crop, animal, or site not listed on its label. Do not use it at more than the label-recommended rate, nor more often than stated on the label.

Storage and Disposal Directions

Store and dispose of every pesticide correctly. Labels only suggest general disposal instructions, because disposal requirements and options vary between locations. However, always keep pesticides in a secure, locked location inaccessible to children and anyone unable to read the label. Do not store pesticides with or near food or feeds.

APPLICATION EQUIPMENT

The equipment used to apply a pesticide is important to the success of the pest control job. You must first select the right kind of equipment. Then, you must use it correctly to suit your needs and care for it properly.

Using the same sprayer equipment for weed control and insect control is neither safe nor desirable. No matter how well you rinse a tank after using an herbicide, there will be a residue left in the tank, gaskets, hoses, and parts. If the same tank is then used with an insecticide to spray a plant, it is possible to injure or kill the plant with the herbicide residue in the tank. The wisest policy is to maintain separate sprayers for different types of pesticides. Some products have special washing requirements. Do not put rinsate down drains.

Consider the following when choosing, using, and caring for equipment.

Hand Sprayers

Use hand sprayers around the home and garden (Figure 13.5). They may be ideal in restricted areas where a power unit would not work.

Hand sprayers are advantageous in that they are: (a) economical; (b) simple; and (c) easy to use, clean, maintain, and store.

The limitations of hand sprayers include: (a) difficulty in agitation and screening of wettable powders

Figure 13.5 A hand sprayer can be used to apply pesticides around the home and garden.
Image Credit: Robert Bellinger, Clemson University

(always keep WPs in suspension by shaking the sprayer) and (b) difficulty in cleaning.

Hand sprayer tanks should have large openings for easy filling and cleaning. Flush out the tank, pump, lines, and nozzles after each use. If switching to another pesticide where contamination must be prevented, wash out the tank with detergent and water two or three times before flushing with only water. Phenoxy herbicides such as 2,4-D are hard to remove and active in very small amounts. After using them, either follow the special cleaning instructions noted on the pesticide label or avoid using the same sprayer for any other product. Keep the tank clean inside and out. It is best to use separate sprayer tanks for herbicides, insecticides, and other pesticides. Tighten, repair, or replace all leaky tank seals or fittings; keep extra gaskets and seals on hand.

Hand Dusters

Like hand sprayers, hand dusters can be used in gardens. They may consist of a squeeze bulb, bellows, tube, shaker, sliding tube, or hand-crank rotor. These were more common in the past than they are today.

The advantages of hand dusters include: (a) precise and accurate application to target (usually turf); (b) immediate pesticide readiness for application; and (c) good penetration in confined spaces.

The limitations of hand dusters include: (a) high costs for compatible pesticides; (b) difficulty in getting good foliar coverage; (c) significant dust drift; and (d) risk of dust-related irritation to the user during application.

Proportioner or Hose-End Sprayer

These inexpensive small sprayers are designed to attach to garden hoses. A small amount of pesticide is mixed with water—usually no more than a pint—and placed in the receptacle attached to the hose. A tube connects this concentrate to the opening of the hose. When the water is turned on, the suction created by the water passing over the top of the tube pulls the pesticide concentrate up and into the stream of hose water, where it is diluted. The stream can reach into medium-high trees if water pressure is high enough. The most common problems stem from poor spray distribution and nozzle clogs. Equip all hose-end proportioners with an antisiphon device to prevent back-siphoning of toxic chemicals into the water system.

Hose-end sprayers are advantageous in that they are: (a) low in cost and (b) convenient.

Their limitations include: (1) inaccuracy in metering out the concentrate into the stream of hose water (because it is determined by the water pressure) and (b) an excessively high volume of spray for most needs, which uses excessive pesticide.

Compressed Air Sprayer (Knapsack or Tank Sprayer)

Tank sprayers allow the user to mix the spray in a small tank—generally 1-5 gal—and carry it over their shoulders like a backpack. A hand-operated pump supplies pressure during application. These sprayers maintain a uniform concentration of spray, because the pesticide is mixed with a known quantity of water. It is necessary to agitate of the spray mixture frequently when using a wettable powder formulation. These applicators provide excellent control of coverage, making them a good choice for treating dwarf fruit trees, vegetables, and ornamentals. Spray will not reach into tall trees. Because water weighs about 8.3 lbs per gal, small tanks are easier to use than large tanks.

Small Power Sprayers

Small power sprayers are motor driven, so the operator does not have to stop to pump up the tank. They are lightweight, because the spray in the tank is concentrated and diluted with air as it is sprayed. Power sprayers provide uniform pressure, but are generally too expensive for home garden use.

Granular Spreader (Drop Spreader)

Drop spreaders include both hand-carried knapsacks and spinning-disk push types for broadcast coverage.

The advantages of granular spreaders include: (a) precise and accurate application to target, (b) no need to mix, (c) low cost, (d) minimal drift, and (e) user safety.

Limitations include: (a) higher pesticide cost; (b) limited use against some pests, as granules do not stick to most plant surfaces; (c) need to calibrate for each granular formulation; and (d) poor lateral distribution, especially on side slopes. To combat poor lateral distribution when using granular spreaders on inclines, walk up and down slopes rather than across them.

MIXING AND CALIBRATING

Most formulations packaged for home use indicate how many teaspoons, tablespoons, or ounces of pesticide are needed per 1 gal of water. Some labels only tell how many pounds or gallons of formulation are needed per 100 gal of water. We have included some conversion charts and factors below.

When mixing pesticides, wear the recommended personal protective equipment recommended on the label. Calibrate your equipment to provide only the recommended rate—no more, no less.

TABLE 13.3 Liquid Measurement Conversions

Amount per 100 gallons	Amount per gallon
1/4 pt	1/4 tsp
1 pt	1 tsp
1 qt	2 tsp
1 gal	2 1/2 tbsp
2 gal	5 tbsp
4 gal	1/3 pt
11 gal	7/8 pt

TABLE 13.4 Dry Weight Conversions

Amount per 100 gallons	Amount per gallon
1/2 lb	1/12 oz
1 lb	1/6 oz
2 lb	1/3 oz
3 lb	1/2 oz
4 lb	2/3 oz
6 lb	4/5 oz
16 lb	2 3/5 oz
20 lb	3 1/5 oz

TABLE 13.5 Equivalents for Teaspoon, Tablespoon, and Cup

Amount	Equivalent
3 tsp	1 tbsp
2 tbsp	1 fluid oz
16 tbsp	1 cup
8 fluid oz	1 cup
1 fluid oz	29.6 ml
1/2 fluid oz	1 tbsp
15 ml	1 tbsp
1/2 pt	1 cup
1 cup	8 oz
1 cup	237 ml

TABLE 13.6 U.S. Liquid Measure

Amount	Equivalent
16 fluid oz	1 pt
2 pt	1 qt
4 qt	1 gal
1 gal	231 in^3

TABLE 13.7 U.S. Area Measurement System

Area	Equivalent
144 in^2	1 ft^2
9 ft^2	1 yd^2
30 1/4 yd^2	1 rod^2
43,560 ft^2	1 acre
160 rod^2	1 acre
208.71 x 208.71 ft	1 acre
320 rods	1 mi
5,280 ft	1 mi
640 acres	1 section/1 mi^2

TABLE 13.8 Metric Conversions

Metric Amount	U.S. Customary Equivalent
1 meter	1.093 yd = 3.281 ft = 39.37 in
1 km	.621 mi
.91 m	1 yd
1 liter	1.056 U.S. liquid qt
3.785 liters	1 gal

Sprayer Tank Capacity Calculations

Use the following to calculate the capacity of hand power sprayers in gallons:

- For cylindrical tanks, multiply the length (in) by the square of the diameter (in) by 0.0034.
- For rectangular tanks, multiply the length (in) by the width (in) by the depth (in) by 0.004329.
- For tanks with elliptical cross sections, multiply length (in) by short diameter (in) by long diameter (in) by 0.0034.

Circles and Globes

To calculate measurements related to circles and spheres, use the following formulas:

- To find the circumference of a circle, multiply the diameter of the circle by 3.14 (π). This can be written as C=π d
- To calculate the area of a circle, multiply the square of the diameter by 0.7854 OR multiply the square of the radius by 3.14 (π).
- To calculate the surface area of a globe/sphere, multiply the square of the diameter (in) by 3.14 (π).
- To find the volume of a globe/sphere, multiply the cube of the diameter (in) by 3.14 (π) by 1.33.

Calibrating Sprayers and Spray Patterns

Most homeowners apply pesticides over a given area by mixing 1-2 Tbsp of a pesticide and applying it to a problem area. This is acceptable if the label provides recommended rates in teaspoons or tablespoons per gallon. But some pesticides, specifically herbicides and insecticides for lawns, do not list application rates in tablespoons or teaspoons per gallon. Instead, they provide application rates in teaspoons or tablespoons per 100 or 500 ft². Unfortunately, homeowners all too often decide to simply guess how much to use. This can be dangerous; too concentrated may be too toxic—and expensive—, while an extremely diluted concentration does not adequately control the pest. It is irresponsible to apply chemicals at improper rates; it is dangerous to the applicator, the neighbors and others, and the environment. A better approach is to calibrate the sprayer. Calibrating a home sprayer is relatively easy.

Once you calibrate your equipment, record all settings. Because of the wear and tear of parts, recalibrate at the beginning of each season or more frequently. Keep in mind that the rate at which the liquid is applied varies with the pressure and size of the opening in the nozzle. High pressure and a large opening in the nozzle apply more liquid over a given area than low pressure and/or smaller nozzle size. Use the following step-by-step procedure to calibrate a power sprayer:

Step 1. Using only water, fully pressurize the sprayer and determine the delivery time by spraying the water through the sprayer into a pint jar. Mark the delivery time—for example, 60 sec to fill the 1-pt jar—on the tank for future reference.

Step 2. Determine the area of the space you need to treat: measure the length and width of the area. Multiply length times width to determine the area of a rectangle, or multiple length times width and divide by two to determine the area of a triangle. You can calculate the area of most spaces by combining rectangles and triangles or subtracting triangles from rectangles. For round areas, calculate the area of the circle using the formula provided in the previous section. While there may be some error in determining the area of your space, it is still important; get as close of a measurement as you can.

Step 3. Spray an area with water at normal working speed for 30 sec. Measure the area of the space you sprayed. The result shows how much area you can cover in 30 sec; or rather, how much area you can cover with the amount of water sprayed in 30 sec (determined in Step 1). For example, if you determined in Step 1 that 30 sec of spray delivers 4 oz of water and in this step that 30 seconds of spraying covers 100 ft², then you can conclude that 4 oz of spray covers 10 ft². A 1,000-ft² area requires 40 oz. of spray at this same rate (4 oz. x 100/1000). If the label calls for 3 tbsp. (1.5 fl oz) of pesticide per 1,000 ft², then mix 1.5 oz of pesticide with 38.5 oz. of water to achieve proper spray coverage (1.5 oz. of product + 38.5 oz. water = 40 oz.). Many commercial chemical rates are given in pounds per acre or quarts to 100 gal of water. To convert these rates to numbers more useful to residential gardeners, consult the conversion tables in this chapter.

Compressed air sprayers and hose-end sprayers are both options for applying pesticides. Hose-end sprayers do not meter out the pesticide as evenly as compressed air sprayers, but compressed air sprayers do not maintain pressure as evenly as hose-end sprayers (unless frequently pumped). Some hose-end sprayers do not continue to spray pesticide if the thumb hole is not covered. Other hose-end sprayers use a trigger device to control the spraying.

The spray pattern best used to cover an area of ground is one that provides uniform coverage with little spray overlap. Overlap is a problem when it causes certain areas to receive an extra dose of pesticide. The spray pattern used to apply the pesticide should be continuous and uninterrupted. When applying an herbicide, do not slow down or stop at each visible weed. If the herbicide is mixed correctly and the sprayer is properly calibrated, the continuous, uninterrupted flow of chemical is providing sufficient control.

Direct the spray pattern so that you do not walk through it while spraying. The spray pattern should form an arc no more than 3-4 ft on either side of the operator. The sprayed area should have a small amount of overlap to ensure coverage; there are times when overlap can be beneficial. If you question whether you're

Figure 13.6 Obtain good coverage using one-half of the application rate applied in two perpendicular directions

providing adequate spray coverage, such as when using a hose-end sprayer, cut the application rate in half and apply the pesticide first in an east-west pattern, then in a perpendicular north-south direction (Figure 13.6). This technique provides better coverage with devices that don't distribute uniformly.

When the mixture on the label is in teaspoons or tablespoons per gallon and the plants are upright—such as shade trees, fruit trees, shrubs, and vegetables—spray the leaves until the pesticide solution drips from the leaves. Do not forget to spray the undersides of leaves for good coverage.

APPLYING PESTICIDES RESPONSIBLY

When applying pesticides, always wear the protective clothing and equipment stated on the label. You can wear more protection than recommended on the label, but never wear less. To prevent chemical spills, always check application equipment for leaking hoses or connections and plugged, worn, or dripping nozzles before adding pesticide. Before spraying, clear all people, pets, and livestock from the area.

To minimize drift, apply pesticides only on days with no wind or breeze; if moderate winds begin during application, stop immediately. Reduce drift by spraying at a low pressure and using a large nozzle opening. Generally, the safest times of day to spray to reduce the hazard of drift are early morning and late evening.

Vaporization is the evaporation of an active ingredient during or after application. Pesticide vapors can cause injury. High temperatures increase vaporization, so choose pesticide formulations that do not evaporate easily and spray during the cool part of the day to reduce vaporization. Some products, like those containing 2,4-D, are very volatile and can move for miles under certain conditions. Do not use them near highly sensitive plants like grapes and tomatoes, and do not apply pesticides that contain 2,4-D when it is windy or if temperatures following application will exceed 85°F. Read and follow the label for specific precautions.

Cleaning Equipment

Thoroughly clean all equipment immediately after use. Do not let residues dry in tanks. Do not store mixed pesticides. If you mix excess pesticide and have some left over, read the label and spray it on a site that it will not harm. The pesticide label will include a list of safe areas.

Thoroughly clean all spray equipment inside and out with clean water. Do not forget to flush the hoses and nozzles. Be careful that the cleaning water does not damage plants or crops. Do not dump the rinse water in one place, as it will be concentrated and may become a pollutant. Spray the rinse water over a broad area to further dilute the pesticide. Never rinse pesticides down the drain.

To clean 2,4-D-type herbicides from hand-spray equipment such as a 3-gal garden sprayer, use household ammonia. Thoroughly rinse the equipment with fresh water after spraying. Spray the water out. Fill the spray equipment with an ammonia solution of 1/2 cup of ammonia per 3 gal of water. Let the equipment soak for 18-24 hr in a location out of reach of children and animals. Always spray part of this mixture through the pump, hose, and nozzles at the beginning and end of the soaking period.

2,4-D cannot be completely removed from a sprayer once used in it. Do not use this sprayer to apply any other pesticides to desirable plants.

Storage and Disposal

Homeowners and gardeners should store all pesticides and other chemicals in their original containers in a locked cabinet. There are no exceptions; these rules protect children's lives. Protect pesticides from temperature extremes, as freezing temperatures and heat can damage and alter some pesticides. Do not store pesticides in the home. Place empty containers in refuse cans destined for a sanitary landfill. Read and follow the label directions for disposal instructions or wrap containers in newspaper and secure them before disposal. Some states have special disposal sites for pesticides; South Carolina only has disposal sites in some counties.

If the pesticide label states that the container must be rinsed, rinse out the container and pour the rinse water into the spray tank. Again, do not pour rinse water into a household drain, on the ground, or into gutter or storm drains. When possible, use the rinse water to dilute the pesticide in your sprayer or applicator container to the correct concentration or spray it directly on your target site.

When using ready-to-use products that do not have to be diluted, such as some lawn weed-control products or insecticides for indoor use, do not rinse the container. There is no proper way of disposing this rinse water. Some lawn pesticide products come in a single-use hose-end sprayer; do not attempt to pry open these containers. Rinse the container three times, allowing it to drain for 30 sec between each rinse. Never use empty pesticide containers for other uses, and never allow children to play with empty containers. Put holes in the containers before disposing of them.

In South Carolina, it is prohibited to burn or incinerate any pesticide container, including those made of paper or cardboard or bags which contained premixed fertilizer and pesticide products.

USING PESTICIDES SAFELY

There are two good reasons to use pesticides safely:

- to protect yourself and other people—especially children—from poisoning and injury.
- to avoid harm to the environment.

Most pesticides can cause severe illness or death if used incorrectly. Many accidental pesticide poisoning deaths are caused by someone eating or drinking the pesticide or disinfectants; the victims are often young children.

Some people applying pesticides die or are injured when they breathe a pesticide vapor or get a pesticide on their skin. Pesticides can poison you in two ways.

Acute poisoning or toxicity means it can kill or injure you after just one exposure.

Chronic toxins do not produce an effect until you have been exposed to them a certain number of times. However, the number of exposures necessary to produce an effect varies with the kind of pesticide and the health and size of the exposed person. Although chronic toxicity means "not immediately poisoning," it can cause serious damage in the long run.

Always follow safety precautions and treat all pesticides with respect. To prevent accidents with pesticides, use and store them away from children and in their original containers. Always follow label directions.

Safety Precautions

Following labeled safety precautions and using common sense can prevent harm caused by pesticides. At the very minimum, follow the guidelines presented here:

Select the Proper Pesticide

Before buying a pesticide, identify the pest you want to control. If you cannot do this yourself, contact the specialists at the Home & Garden Information Center or submit a sample to the Plant and Pest Diagnostic Clinic.

Then, find out which pesticide will control it. If there is a choice, choose the least hazardous product. The most important step in selecting a pesticide is to read the entire label. Read and understand the product label thoroughly before you select, buy, mix, apply, store, or dispose of a pesticide. Read the label to find out whether the host plant and pest are specifically listed on the label, as the pesticide could be phytotoxic to the plant you want to protect. Understand the safety conditions for proper use of the pesticide, such as special equipment, protective clothing, use restrictions, and environmental precautions.

Buy only the amount of pesticide needed and do not store it for longer then the current season.

Make sure the label of the pesticide you choose contains information that is specific to the site where you plan to apply it, the pest you wish to control, and the equipment you need for application.

Ensure that you have or can get the kinds of application and personal protective equipment and clothing specified on the label. Put on all protective equipment before you open the pesticide container to begin mixing and applying.

Apply Pesticides Safely

Always read and follow label directions. Before opening a pesticide container, read the entire label, understand the signal words and safety precautions, and know what to do in case of an accidental poisoning or pesticide emergency. If you do not understand the instructions, contact the Clemson Extension Home & Garden Information Center. Remember that applying more chemicals than recommended does not increase effectiveness of the pesticide.

Follow all label use directions carefully. Use only the amount directed under the conditions specified and for the purpose(s) listed. Be sure that all application equipment is in working order and properly calibrated to apply the correct amount of mixture.

Never use outdoor-only pesticides indoors.

No one may purchase or use restricted-use pesticides unless they are a certified applicator licensed by the Clemson University Department of Pesticide Regulation.

Open, mix, and dilute the pesticide outdoors or in a well-ventilated area. Always keep children and pets away from the areas where you mix or apply pesticides.

Never apply pesticides outdoors on windy or rainy days or eat, drink, or smoke while using pesticides.

Remove all objects that might be damaged or contaminated by pesticides from the area(s) you plan to treat. Do not replace them or use the area until the spray has dried, the dust has settled, or the waiting time specified on the label has elapsed.

When treating food plants and gardens, be sure the product is labelled for this use and observe the re-entry times and conditions and the waiting period before it is safe to harvest; this period varies with the pesticide used and the food plant treated.

Before applying a pesticide, read the label again to find out the safety measures, including necessary protective clothing and equipment, specific warnings and precautions, with what it can be mixed, mixing instructions, preharvest interval (PHI) for fruit and vegetables, crops to which it can or cannot be applied, and other special instructions such as first aid and container disposal.

Using pesticides in a manner inconsistent with the label can cause secondary pest outbreaks, accelerated pesticide resistance, and increases in environmental hazards due to chemical pollution. Always understand the relative toxicity, mode of action, persistence, and safe and legal use of any pesticide you use.

Properly Store and Dispose of Pesticides

Store pesticides and other household chemicals securely so that children, pets, and others who might not understand the label cannot reach them. Do not store pesticides near wells. Never put pesticides into food or drink containers; never place pesticides in any container other than the original container or the application equipment.

Dispose of waste pesticides and pesticide containers according to the label and local and state laws. In South Carolina it is illegal to burn or bury any pesticide containers.

Clean Up Immediately

If you spill a pesticide, clean it up immediately according to the directions on the label. Clean it, don't wash it away. Cat litter, sawdust, and sand are good cleanup materials. Properly dispose of cleanup materials.

Shower and shampoo thoroughly after using pesticides and wash contaminated clothing separately from the family laundry.

If you cannot or do not want to follow these precautions, call a professional pest control company. Do not use pesticides if you are not willing or able to use them according to labeled and common-sense safety precautions.

Protect Your Body

Pesticides can enter the body in several ways. To prevent this, wear the protective clothing and equipment stated on the label. No safety recommendations can cover all situations, but common sense should tell you to use more protection as the toxicity of the pesticide or the chance of exposure increases. The pesticide label lists the kind of protection you need, but you can always use more protection.

Remember to shower (as bathing does not quickly remove pesticides), using a detergent, when you finish working with pesticides or pesticide-contaminated equipment. Any time you spill a pesticide on yourself, wash immediately.

Body Covering. Anytime you handle pesticides, wear at least long sleeves and long pants or a coverall garment. Your clothes should be made of closely woven or nonwoven fabric. Wear trousers outside of boots to prevent pesticides from getting inside.

Gloves. Always wear waterproof gloves. Do not wear leather or cloth gloves. When you handle concentrated or highly toxic pesticides, wear liquid-proof neoprene gloves. Some pesticide products tell you specifically what kind of material the gloves should or should not be made of; they should be long enough to protect the wrist. Gloves should not be lined with a fabric, as fabric lining is hard to clean if a chemical gets on it. Sleeves should usually be outside of the gloves to keep pesticides from running down the sleeves and into the gloves. If spray is being directed upward by handgun, the sleeves should be inside the gloves.

SYMPTOMS OF PESTICIDE POISONING

It is important to be aware of the early symptoms and signs of pesticide poisoning. Unfortunately, all pesticide poisoning symptoms are not the same, and many symptoms of pesticide poisoning are the same as those of the flu, food poisoning, or other illnesses. Each chemical family—carbamates, pyrethroids, etc.—attacks the human body in a different way. Fumigants and solvents can make a person appear to be drunk. Symptoms include poor coordination, slurring of words, confusion, and sleepiness.

Common pesticides such as carbamates injure the nervous system. The symptoms develop in stages, roughly occurring in this order:

1. Mild poisoning or early symptoms of acute poisoning include fatigue, headache, dizziness, blurred vision, excessive sweating and salivation, nausea and vomiting, and stomach cramps or diarrhea.
2. Moderate poisoning or early symptoms of acute poisoning include the inability to walk, weakness, chest discomfort, muscle twitches, constriction of pupils, and an increase in severity of earlier symptoms.
3. Severe or acute poisoning can cause unconsciousness, severe constriction of the pupils, muscle twitches, convulsions, secretions from the mouth and nose, difficulty breathing, and—if left untreated—death. Illness may occur a few hours after exposure, but if symptoms start more than 12 hr after exposure to a pesticide, they may be due to some other illness. Always check with a physician to be sure.

First Aid Procedures

Read the "Statement of Practical Treatment" (First Aid Statement) on the label before using a pesticide. The directions listed can save lives. If a pesticide gets on your skin, remove the pesticide as quickly as possible and remove all contaminated clothing. Prompt washing may prevent sickness, even when the spill is very large. Detergents work better than soap to remove pesticides. Do not forget to thoroughly wash hair and fingernails. Do not scrub the skin with a brush. Remember, the way to treat pesticide exposures to the skin is to wash, wash, wash.

If someone inhales a pesticide, get them to fresh air right away. Loosen all tight-fitting clothing. If needed, give artificial respiration immediately; do not stop until the victim is either breathing well or medical help arrives. Get the victim professional medical help; do not administer anything to a poison victim unless you are trained in first aid—otherwise, you may compound the injury. Never attempt to give liquids to an unconscious victim.

In case of poisoning, call a physician and provide the following information:

- The victim's name, age, and sex.
- Your name and your relationship to the victim.
- What the victim took or was exposed to and how much was taken (Have the pesticide package in hand).

Keep calm; you have enough time to act, but do not delay unnecessarily. Poisoning information is also available by contacting the local Poison Control Center.

You can reduce accidents with pesticides by: (a) using and storing pesticides away from children and other untrained persons and (b) carefully following directions when using pesticides.

PESTICIDES AND THE ENVIRONMENT

Direct Kill

Fine mists of herbicides can drift to nearby crops or landscape plants and kill them. Bees and other pollinators can die if a crop is treated with an insecticide when they are in the field or if they are nesting nearby. Pesticides can also kill the natural enemies of pests. Life in streams or ponds can be wiped out by accidental spraying of ditches and waterways, runoff from sprayed fields, and careless container disposal. If more than one pesticide can control the pest, choose the one that is the least hazardous to the environment. To protect beneficial insects, do not use insecticides excessively; spray only when warranted by the crop and pest populations.

Protecting Insect Pollinators

Gardeners should give special consideration to protecting insect pollinators such as honeybees from insecticide poisoning. Insecticides highly toxic to bees have restrictions regarding application times to crops frequented by honeybees. Bees are not as active in late evening and very early morning. Do not apply insecticides when temperatures are unusually low, as this extends the period that toxic residues remain on plants.

Persistence and Accumulation

Although most pesticides break down quickly and remain in the environment only a short time, some pesticides may break down slowly and stay in the environment for a long time. These more persistent pesticides may accumulate over time.

Movement in the Environment

Pesticides become problematic when they move off target. This can refer to drifting off the target in the form of dust or mist, moving with eroding soil particles, leaching through the soil, being carried out as residues on crops or livestock, or evaporating (volatilizing) and moving with air currents.

Phytotoxicity

One common result of applying chemicals for disease and insect control is damage to the treated plant. This effect is called phytotoxicity. Phytotoxicity may occur when chemicals are used to protect plants from pests, fertilize plants, or regulate plant growth. Phytotoxicity can occur when:

- Chemicals are properly applied directly to a plant during adverse environmental conditions;
- Chemicals are applied improperly;
- Spray, dust, or vapor drifts from the target plant to a sensitive plant;
- Runoff carries a chemical to a sensitive plant; or
- Persistent residues accumulate in the soil or on a plant.

Symptoms of phytotoxicity include:

- Poor seed germination, especially if a soil drench was used;
- Death of seedlings;
- Death of rapidly growing succulent tissues;
- Stunting or delayed plant development;
- Misshapen or distorted plants, fruits, or leaves;
- Russeting or bronzing of leaves or fruit;
- Dead spots or flecks on leaves;
- Dead leaf tips or margins; and
- Dead areas between the veins of leaves (usually, the injured tissue is sharply defined, with little or no gradation from dead areas to healthy areas; that is, the dead spots are of uniform color and go entirely through the leaf).

The factors involved in phytotoxicity can be:

- **Chemical**. Certain crops are very sensitive to certain chemicals, so always be sure the crop you treat is listed on the container label. Some chemicals are persistent, and repeated applications result in the accumulation at toxic levels.
- **Formulation**. Dusts and wettable powders are generally less phytotoxic than emulsifiable concentrates, which can sometimes dissolve the waxy layer on plant surfaces.
- **Additives**. Additives (adjuvants) such as spreaders, stickers, and wetting agents may cause injury.
- **Concentrations**. Damage to treated plant can occur when concentrations higher than the label recommendations are used.

COMPATIBILITY

Compatibility is when two or more pesticides can be mixed together without reducing their effectiveness or harming the target. For instance, carbaryl (Sevin®) is often combined with a miticide such as dicofol (Kelthane®) to kill both insects and mites in one application. Synergism is the action of two materials that, when used together, produce a greater effect than the sum of the materials when used separately. One of the materials when used alone may not affect the pest, but greatly increases the total effect of the two when used together. For example, Chemical A kills 60% and Chemical B kills 20%; however, mix Chemical A and B together and kill 98% of the pests. Synergism may increase control or require less of each chemical. It may also be more harmful to a nontarget organism. A synergistic effect can also be undesirable, causing death or injury to the organism you want to protect. Never mix chemicals unless the label specifically says they are compatible.

HOME GARDEN VS. COMMERCIAL PESTICIDES

Some pesticides are packaged specifically for use in home gardens. These products are packaged in small quantities. They are seldom highly toxic and usually low-concentrate formulations. The label rate is often given in spoonfuls per gallon or pounds per 1,000 ft². Because of the small label size, home garden products may not list all the plants and/or pests for which the product is registered for use. For example, one manufacturer sells a "Fruit and Vegetable Insect Control" with the same active ingredient found in their "Insect Spray." Basically, both products are the same, but the plants and pests listed on the label vary greatly. This situation causes some confusion in pesticide application, encourages the purchase of excessive amounts of pesticides, and can contribute to misuse.

Products packaged for commercial growers may appear less expensive, but you should not be tempted to use them. They are generally more toxic or formulated at a higher concentration than those meant for home use; thus, they require special protective clothing and equipment for application. These products are more concentrated and sold in larger containers than most homeowners can use or store safely and are much more difficult to calibrate and mix correctly because rates are usually provided per acre.

A few products extremely toxic to humans or the environment are classified by the EPA as Restricted Use Pesticides (RUPS). The labels on these pesticides state that they are "restricted use pesticides for retail sale to and application only by certified applicators or person under their direct supervision." A license from the South Carolina Department of Pesticide Regulation is required by law to purchase and use restricted-use pesticides. This licensing is intended for commercial users and does NOT automatically clear the use of these products by home gardeners.

PESTICIDES AND THE LAW

The registration and use of pesticides are governed by the EPA. Under the amended Federal Insecticide, Fungicide, and Rodenticide Act, often referred to as FIFRA, it is illegal to use a pesticide on a crop or site unless the crop or site is listed on the label. You may not exceed the given rate of application on the label. Fines and other penalties vary according to laws broken.

Under the law, you are liable for misuse of pesticides on your property. Recent court rulings extend your liability to include misuse by commercial applicators you hire. Misuse by gardeners usually results in drift or leaching of a pesticide onto nontarget plants or the direct treatment of plants with the wrong pesticide.

Chapter 14
Diagnosing and Managing Plant Problems

Revised and updated by Juang Chong, Ph. D., Zachary B. Snipes, M. S., Anthony P. Keinath, Ph. D., Gary Forrester, M.S.

Previous version excerpted and modified from Ch. 23, "Diagnosing Ornamental Plant and Turf Problems," Kris Braman, Jean Williams-Woodward, Alfredo Martinez, and Mila Pearce. Georgia Master Gardener Handbook, 6th ed., 2004, The University of Georgia Cooperative Extension Service, CES Handbook 2.

LEARNING OBJECTIVES

- Be familiar with the systematic approach to diagnosing plant problems.
- Use knowledge of common ornamental plant disorders, insects, and diseases to diagnose problems.
- Know how to collect data and plant samples to submit to the Plant and Pest Diagnostic Clinic (PPDC) for identification and management recommendations.
- Understand how to find reputable and research-based resources on the internet.
- Use the HGIC website to gather and disseminate information to clients.

INTRODUCTION

Diagnosing plant problems is like conducting an investigation. An accurate diagnosis requires a combination of knowledge about plant problems, careful observation of the signs and symptoms, and the experience to put all the evidence together to reconstruct the cause of the problem. Once you make an accurate diagnosis, you can take corrective action. In some cases, you can only make a tentative diagnosis—even after consulting fellow Master Gardeners and Extension professionals. A definitive diagnosis may require submitting a sample to the Plant and Pest Diagnostic Clinic for further examination.

Consider diagnosing plant problems a learning experience and an opportunity to educate others. Use these teachable moments to educate your clients about the basic concepts of plant establishment, maintenance, and IPM; you can also teach them how to manage these problems to prevent them from recurring. Your dual role as diagnostician and educator ultimately helps your clients become more successful gardeners.

A SYSTEMATIC APPROACH TO DIAGNOSING PLANT PROBLEMS

To diagnose plant problems, follow a series of deductive steps to gather information from the client and clues about the specimen and site. The following five-step systematic diagnostic process of deduction and elimination will lead you to the issue's most probable cause.

Step 1. Define the problem or abnormality

Identify the plant (genus, species, and cultivar or variety) and know what a "normal" plant should look like at the current time of year. A client may mistake a normal stage of development as a problem. For example, the small, brown, clublike tips that develop on Japanese cryptomeria shoots in midsummer are the male flowers but may be mistaken for deformed shoots.

Look for signs and symptoms to help you assess the problem.

A symptom is a change in the growth or appearance of a plant in response to living (biotic) or nonliving (abiotic) factors. Symptoms can include blights, cankers, galls, rots, necrosis, spots, wilt, and general decline.

A sign is the physical evidence of the actual organism or evidence directly related to it, either of which can serve as clues to identify the specific living organism that caused the damage. Signs can include fungal fruiting bodies such as mushrooms, mycelia, bacterial slime, or—in the case of insects—the presence of entrance holes accompanied by sawdust or frass, insect egg masses, or spider mite webbing. Use a hand lens to look for signs and symptoms. Some county Extension offices are equipped with digital diagnostic equipment to assist in problem diagnosis.

Gather information about the size and age of the plant, site conditions, weather conditions preceding development of the problem, and cultural practices. Compare this information with your general knowledge and understanding of plant growth and development.

Step 2. Look for Patterns

Once you have determined that a problem exists, gather additional clues by evaluating the distribution of symptoms and determining if the problem was caused by living or nonliving factors. If necessary, examine the entire plant and its surroundings. Determine the primary problem and part of the plant where initial damage occurred. Does the problem occur on more than one plant? Does it occur on more than one plant species?

A non-uniform pattern—scattered damage on one or only a few plant species, scattered leaves or shoots on a single plant, or scattered spots on a single leaf—indicates living factors. Biotic factors include pests (like insects, mites, rodents, rabbits, and deer) and pathogens (disease-causing microorganisms including fungi, water molds, bacteria, viruses, and nematodes). However, once the infestation has progressed beyond the initial stage, a biotic factor may affect most of the leaves on a plant or most of the plants in a grouping.

A uniform damage pattern—damage occurring on many plant species in the same area, all the plants in a particular row or bed, or the same aged portion of each leaf or needle—indicates nonliving factors. Abiotic (nonliving) factors include mechanical factors (like breakage, abrasions, and soil compaction), environmental factors (like temperature, light, moisture, oxygen, lightning, and wind), and chemical factors (like fertilizer or pesticide toxicity and nutritional disorders).

Step 3. Determine When the Problem Developed

Knowing the timing of problem development helps distinguish between biotic and abiotic factors.

If the problem spread from plant to plant or to other plant parts over time, suspect a living organism. If the problem does not spread to other plant parts or other plants—or if there is a clear separation between damaged and undamaged tissues—consider abiotic factors. Abiotic factors generally damage a plant at a given point in time; for example, leaf tissue killed by a **phytotoxic** chemical likely came in contact with the chemical on a specific day.

There are exceptions. If a nonliving damaging factor is maintained over time, the damage will continue to intensify with time. For example, a mineral toxicity in soil will continue to damage plants within the contaminated area, but damage will not spread to plants in uncontaminated areas. Cold damage to frost-sensitive plants develops over a period of several days after exposure.

Step 4. Determine Probable Causes

After investigating the distribution and temporal patterns of the problem, gather additional clues from the plant and speak to your client. Use the information to help you decide between biotic and abiotic causes.

Check available resources for common disease and insect pests specific to the plant you identified in Step 1. To distinguish between biotic factors, closely examine the specimen for symptoms and signs. Signs are clues to identify the specific living organism that produced the plant damage; however, a definite conclusion that the damage was caused by a pathogen, insect, mite, or animal requires a combination of clues from both symptoms and signs.

In some cases, you may not be able to make a diagnosis. This may be a new, unique, and unfamiliar problem that requires further examination. Always be prepared to tell a client, "I don't know. Let me investigate further and I'll get back in touch with you." Consult your colleagues and Extension professionals. Submitting a sample to the Plant and Pest Diagnostic Clinic for laboratory examination and analysis will narrow the range of probable causes.

Step 5. Provide Solutions and Recommendations

Once you accurately diagnose a problem, recommend safe, effective, unbiased, research-based, sustainable solutions supported by Clemson Extension. Clemson Extension Master Gardeners must follow specific statewide and local policies for making recommendations. Give your client a range of possible treatments or solutions. Whenever possible, provide the client with written information, such as a link to a fact sheet. In the case of a specific insect or disease, for example, provide information about appropriate cultural practices, mechanical controls, pesticides, and other alternatives that will manage the pest and reduce its damage. Allow the client to choose the course of action that best suits their interests. As part of this step, consider educating your client about IPM.

See Table 14.1 for an easy-to-use summary of these steps to guide diagnosis.

Problems Common to Annuals and Perennials

Table 14.2 provides symptoms, possible causes, and management strategies for a number of general problems common to many annuals and perennials. Table 14.3 provides symptoms, possible causes, and management strategies for common problems in ornamental trees and shrubs.

INSECTS OF ORNAMENTALS

Insects, related arthropods (such as mites), and other invertebrates (such as slugs) are common residents and visitors of gardens and landscapes in South Carolina. However, only a small number of them truly cause damages or nuisance and are considered pests. It is important to accurately identify insects and related arthropods and determine if they are pests, non-pests, or beneficials. Pests may require management, but non-pests and beneficial insects do not.

Nature of Damage

The type and extent of damage done to ornamentals by insect pests depends on the pest and ornamental involved. Several insect pests suck plant juices and cause stippling of foliage, stunting, and leaf drop. Pests with chewing mouthparts chew large holes in leaves or chew through stems and petioles. Other pests bore into plant tissue and tunnel through leaves and stems.

Effective management of insect pests on ornamentals requires proper diagnosis of the problem. Often, we can make tentative but reliable diagnoses based on the damage that insects cause, but the most accurate diagnosis requires identification of the insect or mite itself. Problem diagnoses based on symptoms fall into damage categories:

TABLE 14.1 A Systematic Approach to Diagnosing Plant Problems

Step	Procedure	Question	Answer	Next Step
1	Gather information from the client on the species/cultivar, size, age, site conditions, weather preceding the development of the problem, and maintenance practices. Examine the problem or abnormality carefully for signs or symptoms. Compare the information with your general knowledge and understanding of plant growth and development.	Is the problem or issue normal for this species/cultivar at this time of year?	Yes	*No further examination is needed. Educate client on normal plant growth.*
			Not sure or no	Proceed to **Step 2**
2	Examine the planting and its surroundings. Gather additional information to establish a pattern of problem distribution and severity. Gather additional information to determine when the problem developed.	Does the problem spread from plant to plant, or from one plant part to another over time?	Yes	Biotic or abiotic factor; proceed to next question
			No	Abiotic factor; proceed to **Step 4**
		If the problem becomes worse on one or a group of plants over time, does it spread to nearby plantings of the same species?	Yes	Biotic; proceed to **Step 3**
			No	Abiotic; proceed to **Step 4**
3	Examine sample for signs and symptoms. Refer to available resources to establish probable cause(s). Consult colleagues and Extension professionals.	Can damage by insects and associated invertebrates or other organisms be found?	Yes	Identify the culprit; proceed to **Step 5**
			No	*Suggest contacting HGIC or send a sample to PPDC*
		Can signs of pathogens be seen and identified?	Yes	Identify the culprit; proceed to **Step 5**
			No	*Suggest contacting HGIC or send a sample to PPDC*

- Tattered leaves or flowers
- Stippled, bleached, or bronzed foliage
- Die back of plant parts
- Evidence of insects themselves or their products and wastes such as webs, tents, cases, flocculence (cottony material), frass (fecal material), honeydew, sooty mold, and sawdust.

Different pests are responsible for each category. For example, grasshoppers, caterpillars, slugs, snails, and beetles can cause tattered leaves or flowers. Insects with piercing mouthparts—such as lace bugs, plant bugs, mites, and thrips—may cause stippled, bleached, or bronzed foliage. Scale insects and beetles and moth larvae that bore inside stems are often to blame for die back of plant parts. Specific damage symptoms caused by each pest are described later on in the section, "Pest Damage and Identification."

Pest Management

Although the presence of pests is common, pest infestations do not necessarily require treatment or management. Often, the pest population is not big enough to be noticed or cause significant damage. Part of a client's process in selecting the proper course of action should include considering how much damage the client can tolerate. Management is only necessary when the pests are causing damages to a point that is noticeable or bothersome to the clients or reducing the long-term vigor and health of the plants. In addition to

TABLE 14.1 Continued

Step	Procedure	Question	Answer	Next Step
4	Gather additional information on site characteristics and cultural practices. Check available resources for probable diseases and other pests. Consult your colleagues and Extension professionals.	Is the plant species suitable for this site?	Yes	Proceed to next question
			No	Suspect poor selection of plant species
		Have temperatures, humidity levels, rainfall, or soil moisture levels been outside the normal range?	Yes	Suspect extreme weather conditions
			No	Proceed to next question
		Has a pesticide been applied recently? What pesticide?	Yes, pesticide known to cause phytotoxicity	Suspect phytotoxicity
			No or non-harmful pesticide applied	Proceed to next question
		Is irrigation amount or frequency outside the recommended range?	Yes	Suspect insufficient or excessive irrigation
			No	Proceed to next question
		Has pruning or mowing occurred recently?	Yes	Suspect mechanical damage
			No	Proceed to next question
		Has a soil test been done?	Yes	Suggest contacting HGIC or send a sample to PPDC
			No	Suggest soil test
5	Research solutions and recommendations. Check available resources for appropriate corrective actions. Consult colleagues and Extension professionals as needed.			Provide solutions and recommendations to the client. Be sure to follow all guidelines and policies when making control recommendations; provide a range of management options and let the client choose the most suitable course of action. Include written information whenever possible.

preventive, chemical, biological, and cultural control tactics, management recommendations should include the option to do nothing (when appropriate).

When the reduction of a pest population is necessary, clients should utilize an integrated pest management approach. This process seeks to minimize adverse effects to the environment and non-target organisms.

Prevention

Preventing pest infestation is the most important step in managing their populations and damages. Avoid selecting plant species or cultivars that are not suitable for the site or that are prone to mite or insect problems. Plants grown in unsuitable sites become stressed and are more susceptible to pest infestation. Planting plant species or cultivars that are known to repel pests or are resistant to certain pests can eliminate the need to treat an infestation later.

Pest exclusion is also a part of preventing pests from establishing themselves in gardens. Buying pest or disease-free plants from reputable growers or businesses goes a long way in preventing the introduction of pests into a garden. For those who propagate their own plants, the use of clean stock plants is important in preventing the spread of pests and diseases. Soil sterilization or using clean or sterilized potting medium can exclude

TABLE 14.2 General Problems of Annuals and Perennials

Symptoms	Possible Causes	Management Options and Comments
Wilting and Overall Poor Vigor		
Plants wilt, flowers may drop, and leaves may turn yellow.	Dry soil, waterlogged soil, transplant shock.	If dry, supply water. If too wet, improve drainage and water less frequently. Do not transplant in the heat of the day. Water regularly after transplanting.
Leaves may turn yellow, plant wilts and dies.	Root, stem, or crown rot (fungal or bacterial). Weather injury (drought). Mechanical injury. Improper fertilization. Natural gas injury.	Remove affected plants and surrounding soil. Do not overwater. Use of registered pesticides as soil drench when replanting may be beneficial.
Seedlings wilt. Stems turn brown and soft and may be constricted at the soil line.	Damping-off (fungal disease).	Remove affected plants and surrounding soil. Do not over water. Improve soil drainage. Use of registered pesticides as soil drench when replanting may be beneficial.
Leaf and Flower Problem		
Plant fails to flower, foliage looks healthy.	Wrong season. Cool weather or insufficient light. Too much nitrogen. Immature plants. Undersized bulbs.	Some plants have specific daylength requirements for flowering. Do not plant sun-loving plants in the shade. Do not overfertilize, as this causes excessive vegetative growth. Biennials and perennials often do not flower the first year.
Too many small flowers.	Plants not de-budded.	Some plants such as chrysanthemums need to have some flower buds removed to produce large flowers.
Tall "leggy" plants, stem and foliage pale or yellow.	Insufficient light.	Pay attention to light requirements of plants. Provide more light if possible.
General yellowing of leaves, yellowing may be interveinal, plant may be stunted, no wilting.	Nutrient deficiency. Viral disease.	Soil test. Submit sample to PPDC for diagnosis.
Grayish-white powdery growth on leaves, stems, or flowers.	Powdery mildew (fungal disease).	Usually affects new growth. Remove heavily infested leaves and stems. Use resistant varieties if possible. Rake and remove fallen leaves.
Blister containing orange, yellow, or brown powdery substance on underside of leaves. Yellow areas opposite of pustules seen on upper surface.	Rust (fungal disease).	Remove infected plants. At the very least, remove infected leaves. Avoid prolonged leaf wetness. Do not water late in the day. Rake and remove fallen leaves.
Random brown, dead spots on leaves.	Fungal, bacterial, or leaf nematode disease (any of several).	Submit sample for laboratory diagnosis. Avoid prolonged leaf wetness. Do not water late in the day. Fungicides are ineffective on bacterial or leaf nematode diseases.
Uniform brown, dead areas on margins of leaves.	Scorch due to hot, dry weather. Salt injury due to improper fertilization. Chemical injury. Poor planting site or improper planting depth. Mechanical injury.	Supply water. Fertilizer properly. Do not allow fertilizers or "winter" salt to accumulate in soil. Replant in soil with proper aeration and at proper depth. Avoid mechanical damage to plant during maintenance.
Flowers wilt or fail to open, grayish mold appears on flowers in damp weather.	Gray mold (fungal disease).	Pick off and destroy affected flowers. Avoid prolonged leaf wetness. Remove spent blooms and yellowing leaves.

TABLE 14.2 Continued

Symptoms	Possible Causes	Management Options and Comments
Yellow and green mottling or mosaic pattern on leaves.	Viral disease (any of several).	Plants are seldom killed. Affected plants may need to be removed. Do not touch healthy plants after touching diseased ones. Control insects that spread disease.
Black sooty growth on leaves and stems.	Sooty mold.	Control honeydew-secreting insects.
Tiny white flecks or white interveinal areas on leaves.	Ozone injury. Spider mites.	For spider mites, maintain adequate irrigation. Hose underside of leaves with water sprays. Use registered miticide.
Clusters of insects on stems or undersides of leaves, leaves may be curled or distorted.	Aphids or scale insects.	Remove heavily infested leaves and stems. Use appropriate pesticide.
Leaves chewed or completely eaten.	Various chewing insects, slugs, or sowbugs.	Submit insect for identification. Use commercial slug bait.
Light-colored tunnels or blotches in leaves.	Leafminers.	Remove infested leaves and use registered insecticide.
Leaves stippled with tiny white spots.	Spider mites. Thrips.	After positive identification, use appropriate pesticide if necessary. For spider mites, maintain adequate irrigation. Hose underside of leaves with water sprays. Use registered miticide.
Tiny, white-winged insects on undersides of leaves.	Whiteflies.	Remove infested leaves. Hose with water sprays. Monitor population with yellow sticky cards. Use registered insecticides.
White, cottony masses on leaves or stems.	Mealybugs.	Use registered insecticide if warranted.

soil insect pests from potted house plants. Screens on doors and vents are helpful in preventing the invasion of highly mobile insect pests—such as adult leafminers and moths—into greenhouses. Weed control around and within landscaped areas and hobby greenhouses reduces the opportunity for pests to establish populations on the weeds and spread to ornamentals.

Do not overlook the benefits of good cultural, planting, or maintenance practices in avoiding pest problems. Healthy, vigorous shrubs and flowers can tolerate light infestations of insect pests without becoming unattractive. For example, flushes of new growth on woody shrubs during spring and early summer may mask damages from a previous light infestation; in this case, chemical controls are not needed. Good cultural management, such as maintaining optimum fertility and moisture levels, allows plants to reach maximum tolerance to insect damage. Other chapters within this manual present information on proper cultural management of ornamentals.

Removing infested plants or plant parts can quickly reduce an insect infestation and the chances that the insects spread from one plant to another. When you inspect plants for pests, remove and dispose of infested leaves and old, decaying flowers. Never toss infested plant material on the ground at the base of plants, because pests can move back onto the living plants.

Early Detection is Critical

Since small pest populations or light infestations are easier and cheaper to control, it is important to inspect plants frequently for the presence of pests or pest-related damage so you can create and implement a control plan early on. Often, inspection or scouting every week or every two weeks is sufficient. During spring and summer, some pest species reproduce so rapidly that you should perform close visual inspection of plants every other day. Inspect plants for loss of color, stunting, or holes in leaves. To detect some of the less noticeable pests, examine the undersides of several leaves on each plant.

TABLE 14.3 General Problems of Ornamental Trees and Shrubs

Symptoms	Possible Causes	Management Options and Comments
Damage to Bark		
Large areas of split bark, no decay evident.	Freeze cracks.	Frost can split trunks (especially thin-barked trees), use tree wrap to prevent damage from temperature extremes.
Reduced vigor, scraped or split bark.	Sunscald. Mechanical injury. Lightning injury can cause a tree to explode along the path of the lightning to the ground.	Thin-barked trees split when exposed to intense sunlight. Use tree wrap or block sun with boards on bright winter days. Avoid heavy fertilization in late summer or fall. Remove grass around trunk and replace with mulch to avoid damage from mowers/trimmers. Use lightning rod.
Large areas of split bark, decay evident.	Secondary decay of the wounds described above. Fungal or bacterial canker (any of several).	No adequate controls. Water and fertilize appropriately. Remove if determined to be a hazard.
Sour-smelling sap oozes from cracks in bark.	Slime or alcoholic flux (bacterial disease). Bacterial canker.	No control. Tree may need to be removed.
Damage to Twigs, Branches, and Roots		
Many small twigs broken off.	Squirrel damage. Wind breakage. Twig pruner, twig girdler (insects).	Squirrel damage isn't usually serious. If you suspect insect pests, rake up and destroy fallen twigs.
Large, corky swellings on roots; weak plants.	Crown gall (bacterial disease).	Some galls can be pruned out, but it's best to consult an arborist. Trees may live for years in spite of galls.
Galls on branches.	Fungal disease (any of several). Various insects. Secondary crown gall (bacterial disease).	Submit sample for diagnosis. Prune out galled branches. Most insect-induced galls are harmless.
Proliferation of branches at specific points on plant, forming "witches' broom."	Insect injury. Fungal, viral, or mycoplasma damage.	Submit sample for diagnosis.
Large dead areas in center of trunk or large scaffold limbs.	Heart rot (fungal disease).	Prune out diseased limbs where possible. Fertilize and water appropriately. Reduce stress. If severely affected, especially on the main trunk, the tree may be a hazard and should be removed.
Sunken cankers (lesions) on trunk or branches. Plant may wilt or have poor growth.	Primary fungal disease or sometimes bacterial disease.	Submit sample for diagnosis. Prune out affected branches at least 6 in. below the canker into healthy wood. Disinfect pruning tools between each cut.
Oozing sap on trunk.	Natural causes. Environmental stress. Mechanical injury. Insect borers. Fungal or bacterial disease.	Some trees naturally ooze sap. Drought or waterlogging can cause trees to ooze excessively. Prevent injury from mowers/trimmers. There are no controls for fungal or bacterial diseases affecting this part of the tree.
Large gathering of caterpillars on trunk.	Spring cankerworm.	Handpick and destroy. Use registered insecticide.
Silk webs containing caterpillars in crotches of tree.	Eastern tent caterpillar.	If warranted, use a registered insecticide. Spray surrounding foliage on branch and penetrate web with spray.
Tiny fish-like scales attached to leaves, twigs, or branches.	Scale insects.	Submit sample for diagnosis. Use dormant oil during late winter. Apply appropriate pesticide when scales are in the "crawler" or mobile stage.

TABLE 14.3 Continued

Symptoms	Possible Causes	Management Options and Comments
Brown, gray, green, or yellow crusty, leaf-like growths on trunk and branches.	Lichens.	Lichens do not harm the plant but may indicate poor vigor or health of the tree.
Dense bunchy growth on lower limbs, growth is gray, leaves are narrow.	Ball moss.	Prune out dead wood. Scrape out moss.
Gray growth hanging down from limbs.	Spanish moss.	Seldom becomes dense enough to cause damage.
Leaf Problems		
Grayish-white powdery growth on leaves, leaves may be distorted.	Powdery mildew (fungal disease).	Improve air circulation around plant by selectively pruning branches or increase plant spacing. Use resistant varieties when possible.
Black sooty growth on leaves or stems.	Sooty mold.	Control honeydew-secreting insects. Remove heavily infested leaves or stems.
Uniform brown dead areas on leaf margins.	Leaf scorch caused by insufficient transport of water to leaves. Cold injury. Chemical injury. Salt injury.	Water deeply during dry periods. Scorch is usually caused by hot, dry weather, but root rots and other root damage can play a role. Chemical injury to trees and shrubs is common on home lawns where herbicides are used too close to root zones of trees or shrubs. In regions where salty water is used to irrigate, deep watering is recommended to leach salts out of root zone. Do not use chemically softened water on plants.
Interveinal yellowing of leaves, no wilting.	Yellowing caused by nutrient deficiency or imbalance. Waterlogged soil resulting in poor transport of nutrients to leaves.	Treat leaves with a spray of chelated iron. Improve drainage.
Blister containing yellow, orange, or black powdery substance on leaves, mostly on underside.	Rust (fungal disease).	Avoid prolonged leaf wetness. Avoid late day overhead irrigation. Remove infected leaves. Rake and remove fallen leaves.
Browning of tips of conifers.	Ozone injury.	No controls.
General browning of leaves or needles.	Drought. Salt injury. Gas leak. Root-feeding nematodes. Waterlogged soil. Transplant shock. Girdling roots. Plant is root bound and center of root ball stays dry. Dog urine injury.	Water deeply during drought. Do not use deicing salt on sidewalks or roads near trees or shrubs. Flush soil with water. Check soil roots for gray, crumbly appearance and foul smell indicative of gas leak. Submit nematode sample. Improve drainage. Water regularly after transplanting. Be sure main roots are not wrapped around trunk. Cut root ball in several places before transplanting. Flush away dog urine when possible.
Yellow and green mottling or mosaic pattern on leaves, leaves may be distorted.	Viral disease.	No controls. Removal may be necessary to prevent spread.
Random brown leaf spots, spots seen on both sides of leaf.	Fungal or bacterial disease (any of several).	See section on specific diseases or submit sample to PPDC.

continued

TABLE 14.3 Continued

Symptoms	Possible Causes	Management Options and Comments
Uniform leaf spots, spots on one side of leaf.	Chemical injury.	Avoid using some products under hot, dry, conditions. See pesticide label.
Leaves completely chewed or eaten.	Various caterpillars, sawflies, leaf beetles, etc.	Remove by hand. Identify pest and used registered pesticide if warranted.
Silk webs containing caterpillars covering cluster of leaves at tips of branches.	Fall webworm.	Damage is generally cosmetic. Remove and destroy webs if desired to improve appearance.
Young leaves puckered, curled, or distorted. Clear, sticky substance on leaves. Clusters of small insects on undersides of leaves.	Aphids.	See aphids section in Insects of Ornamentals.
Leaves off-color with tiny white or yellow spots. May appear dirty because of fine webbing and dust that collects on leaves.	Spider mites.	See spider mite information in Insects of Ornamentals.
Leaf galls (abnormal growths on leaves, stems, or other tissues).	Various insects or mites. Various fungal diseases.	Most insect-induced galls are harmless. For fungal disease control, prune affected leaves or pick off galls.

Accurate Identification

Early detection and correct identification of pests are the first two steps to an effective insect management program for ornamentals. Unless you correctly identify an insect, you cannot be certain that the insect you found is the culprit of the damage. Consequently, selecting an appropriate control measure becomes difficult. Homeowners should consult county Extension personnel for assistance in identifying unfamiliar insects. It is not unusual to find an unsuspecting homeowner attempting to control non-pest insects—or worse, beneficial insects! Only after an insect is correctly identified can one determine if, when, and how it should be controlled.

Proper Selection of Control Materials

If chemical control is warranted, it is important to choose the right product. No single pesticide controls all major pests without damaging sensitive plants. As new products and research data become available, experts revise control recommendations. Be sure you reference the most recent research-based recommendations.

Correct Application

Pesticides are applied to ornamentals in every conceivable manner. Growers use aerosols, mists, smokes, fogs, dusts, sprays, drenches, and granules. For control of pests that feed on foliage, most insecticides are applied as sprays; for control of pests that feed in the ground or in plant tissues, granular application may be appropriate. For best performance, an insecticide should be applied at the proper rate and at a time when pests are present and most vulnerable. Use sufficient spray volume to achieve good and thorough coverage of both upper and lower surfaces of leaves. Use appropriate nozzles for uniform coverage and appropriate droplet size.

Common Insect Pests

Aphids

Identification and Biology. Adult aphids may be winged or wingless. For most species, adults vary from 1/16-1/8 in. long. The body is oval or pear shaped with two tubelike cornicles (tailpipes) on the abdomen. Most aphids are green, yellow, orange, red, black, or white.

Aphids have several generations a year and overwinter on plants as eggs. Feeding aphids excrete honeydew, on which sooty mold may grow.

Host Plants. Some aphid species only feed on one plant species, while others are general feeders. Most deciduous trees and shrubs, as well as conifers, are subject to attack by aphids. Many species utilize different plant species as hosts in the cold and warm seasons.

Damage Symptoms. Aphids sucking fluids from buds and leaf veins may cause stunting, deformation, discoloration, and leaf death. They do not cause stippling of green tissue. Aphids rarely cause obvious plant injury, but large populations may cause objectionable levels of honeydew and sooty mold. On indeterminately growing plants, healthy leaves produced later in the season—after the aphid populations declines—usually hide leaves damaged early in the season.

Monitoring Techniques. Aphids can feed on any part of a plant. However, most species prefer to feed on new shoots or leaves. Examine these new growths and the undersides of leaves for distortion, discoloration, and the presence of the aphids or their white shed skins; also look for honeydew and sooty mold. If these are present, but aphids are not on leaves, examine the bark for dark-colored aphids. Also look for the presence and relative numbers of predators and parasitized aphids (mummies).

Management Strategies. Avoid over-fertilizing plant species that are susceptible to aphids because nitrogen fertilization can increase the growth rate of aphid populations. Managing aphids in the landscape is typically unnecessary; usually, aphid disease, predators, and parasites sufficiently suppress or control the population. Distortion of shoots and leaves is permanent; therefore, try to suppress aphid populations on susceptible plants in the spring. To prevent distortion, systemic insecticides may be applied to the soil. To reduce aphid populations and honeydew, oil or soap sprays may be applied whenever you detect an aphid population or the presence of aphid predators and parasites.

Azalea Bark Scale

Identification and Biology. Adult female azalea bark scale insects may be 1/8-in. long. In May, they begin secreting a white, feltlike sac that encloses their bodies and eggs. Overwintering nymphs are about 1/16-in. long, gray, and usually found in twig forks. Males emerge in early spring, mate, and die. There are two generations a year.

Host Plants. This imported scale insect prefers azalea and rhododendron but is also found on other species, including andromeda (*Pieris*), maple, arborvitae, willow, poplar, and hackberry.

Damage Symptoms. Azaleas tolerate low levels of this scale without showing symptoms, though large populations can cause honeydew, sooty mold, leaf yellowing, and dieback. Continuous heavy infestations may kill plants within a few years.

Monitoring Techniques. Look for sooty mold on leaves, yellowing leaves, and twig dieback. This pest does not cause stippling of leaves. Examine twigs for white egg sacs and the presence of reddish crawlers in May and June. Examine egg sacs closely for holes, which indicate the presence of parasites. Look for predators. In light infestations, the scales are found in twig forks. In heavy infestations, they occur anywhere on bark.

Management Strategies. In situations where there are a few egg sacs or scales but no leaf yellowing or sooty mold, no management is necessary; low populations are typically suppressed by beneficial insects. You can use dormant oil to control overwintering nymphs on twigs or summer oil or insecticidal soap to control crawlers.

Azalea Lace Bug

Identification and Biology. Adults are 1/8-in. long. Their lacy, transparent wings have two grayish-brown crossbands connected in the middle and lie flat on their backs. Nymphs are mostly black and spiny. The flask-shaped eggs are partially embedded in leaf tissue and often covered with a black tar-like secretion. There are four generations a year; eggs overwinter in leaf tissue. Lace bug adults and nymphs live and feed on the underside of leaves.

Host Plants. Deciduous and evergreen azaleas, especially those growing in full sun (an unfavorable growing condition for azaleas), are susceptible to infestation.

Damage Symptoms. Nymphs and adults feed on plant juices through leaf tissue, causing white stippling of leaves; they also deposit black excrement spots that stick to the bottom surface of leaves. In heavy infestations, foliage may turn white, and the plant may die back.

Monitoring Techniques. Look for the first signs of damage on plants beginning in March and continuing throughout the summer. Symptoms often first appear and are more noticeable on plants grown in full sun. Look for white stippling on older leaves; turn over stippled leaves to look for lace bugs of all stages and black fecal spots. Examine lace bug eggs with a hand lens for signs of parasitism (a round hole in the top of the egg) and look for predators.

Management Strategies. Management of azalea lace bug begins with growing resistant azalea cultivars such as 'Dawn,' 'Pink Star,' 'Ereka,' 'Cavalier,' 'Pink Fancy,' 'Dram,' 'Seigei,' 'Macrantha,' 'Salmon Pink,' 'Elsie Lee,' 'Red Wing,' 'Sunglow,' and 'Marilee.' Plant azaleas in partial shade to avoid stressful conditions. Apply insecticides at the first presence of first-generation nymphs. Sprays of insecticidal soap or horticultural oil to the underside of leaves provide adequate control. Beneficial insects usually cannot control this pest when azaleas are in sunny locations.

Azalea Leaf Miner

Identification and Biology. Adult moths are about 3/8-in. long with wings folded. They are yellowish brown with purple markings on the wings and when resting, stand at a 60° angle to the leaf with wings folded. Mature larvae are about ½-in. long and yellowish brown. There are two to three generations a year. Pupae overwinter in leaf mines—tunnels the larvae create when they feed on tissue between leaf surfaces.

Host Plants. This pest only attacks azaleas.

Damage Symptoms. Young larvae form elongated blotch mines, usually near the leaf midrib. Older larvae curl the tips of leaves with silk and feed inside the curl. The mined area turns brown after the leaf miner has emerged. Large populations cause leaves to turn brown and drop prematurely.

Monitoring Techniques. Look for leaf mines in April or May. Curled leaf tips in June indicate completion of the first generation. Second-generation leaf mines begin to appear in July. Shake plants in late June and August to make adults fly and estimate their numbers.

Management Strategies. When infestation is low, you can pick the infested leaves and prune more heavily infested branches; discard these tissues. Since azalea leaf miner larvae feed in leaf mines or in curled leaves, systemic insecticides are best. Treat in May if you observe numerous developing leaf mines. Evaluate the size of the second-generation population in July and re-treat if needed. Rake and destroy leaves in fall, as leaf miners may overwinter in the mines on fallen leaves.

Bagworms

Identification and Biology. Adult male moths are about ¾-in. long and black. Adult females retain their larval form and do not develop wings. Females grow, reproduce, and remain inside their bags for their entire life. Males mate with females in their bags. Each female may produce as many as 1,000 eggs. Eggs overwinter before hatching in May or June in South Carolina. Larvae and their bags are 1-2 in. long. Larvae begin construction of their bags soon after hatching; their silken bags are covered with plant parts. There is one generation per year.

Host Plants. This native species seriously damages northern white cedar, red cedar, arborvitae, juniper, and other conifers. Boxelder, sycamore, black locust, willow, elm, poplar, oak, maple, and persimmon may harbor reservoir populations.

Damage Symptoms. Damage is most serious and obvious on conifers such as arborvitae and juniper, where individual branches and even whole plants are completely defoliated. On large deciduous trees and shrubs, defoliation is less evident. Many bagworms hanging on a tree can be unsightly.

Monitoring Techniques. In May and June, begin looking for new bags on host plants, especially where large, old bags are present. Closely examine outer foliage of plants in full sun.

Management Strategies. For light infestations and in the fall and winter, hand pick and destroy bags. For heavy infestations, spray with *Bacillus thuringiensis* (*Bt*) between May and June to target young caterpillars. Use residual insecticides against older caterpillars in June and July.

Bark Beetles (Pine)

Identification and Biology. Adult Ips beetles are brown and vary from 1/8-¼ in. long. Their heads are bent downward, and their wing covers have spines at the end. Larvae feed inside tree trunks and are C-shaped, legless, and white with brown heads. There are three to four generations a year. Larvae overwinter in galleries under bark.

Host Plants. Most pines growing under stressed conditions are susceptible to attack.

Damage Symptoms. Adult beetles bore into trees and cause sticky sap to ooze from the trunk (often called pitch tubes). Brown, sawdust-like material from entrance holes may be evident in severely stressed trees. Weeks or months later, entire tops of infested trees turn yellowish red and die. The tunneling of the beetles causes damage to pine trees, as does a blue-stain fungus introduced by the beetles.

Monitoring Techniques. Look on bark for the first signs of brown dust or white pitch tubes from late March through October. Pay close attention to the crowns of pines grown nearby for early warning of a local bark beetle outbreak. Check under bark of dying trees for signs of galleries, larvae, and blue stain.

Management Strategies. Water trees during drought periods to prevent stress. Prevent beetles from building egg galleries by monitoring trees frequently and treating branches and trunks with a residual insecticide when the first pitch tubes appear. Cut down heavily infested or dying trees and destroy them immediately to prevent emergence of adult beetles.

Boxwood Leaf Miner

Identification and Biology. Adults are orange-yellow mosquito-like flies about 1/8-in. long. They swarm around boxwoods for about two weeks in mid-March through early April after new growth has flushed on the shrubs. The yellow maggots overwinter in leaf mines. There is one generation a year.

Host Plants. This imported gall-forming fly can damage most boxwood species, but *Buxus sempervirens* 'Argenteo-variegata,' 'Pendula,' and 'Suffruticosa' are not usually seriously infested. English boxwoods are less susceptible than American varieties.

Damage Symptoms. Larvae feeding inside the leaves cause blister-like blotch mines to appear on the underside of infested leaves. Heavily mined leaves turn yellow and drop prematurely.

Monitoring Techniques. Beginning in mid-March, periodically monitor boxwood plants to detect flying adults. Examine the underside of the previous year's leaves to detect active mines. Look for the presence of pupal cases sticking out of mines and the orange-colored adults. Mines of the current season do not become obvious until fall.

Management Strategies. Apply a contact insecticide when you detect active adults. If numerous mines are present in the summer or fall, apply a systemic insecticide. Replace susceptible cultivars with resistant cultivars.

Boxwood Psyllid

Identification and Biology. The light green adults are about 1/8-in. long and resemble miniature cicadas. Nymphs are green and flattened, with fluffy white wax protruding from their rear ends. They feed inside distorted or cupped terminal leaves. There is one generation a year; orange eggs overwinter beneath bud scales.

Host Plants. This imported psyllid prefers and most severely damages American boxwood cultivars, except 'Suffruticosa.' They rarely cause significant damage to English boxwoods.

Damage Symptoms. The terminal shoots of infested plants develop cupped, stunted leaves.

Monitoring Techniques. Look inside cupped terminal leaves in early spring for nymphs and white wax. Examine plants in early summer for adults. Shrubs usually outgrow damage by midsummer.

Management Strategies. Use horticultural oil or soap sprays once you detect nymphs in early spring. Use a residual insecticide to control adults discovered later in the growing season if the level of damage is intolerable.

Cottony Maple Scale

Identification and Biology. Adult females are 1/8-1/4 in. long. They are mottled dark brown or black, flat, and oval. The 1/8-in. white, cottony ovisac, or egg sac, is deposited on bark. There is one generation per year, and crawlers appear in June. Nymphs feed through the summer on the underside of leaves and overwinter on the twigs.

Host Plants. This native soft scale may feed on many different shade trees. Preferred hosts include maple, elm, hawthorn, dogwood, sycamore, poplar, and linden.

Damage Symptoms. Heavy infestations that encrust branches may cause leaf yellowing, stunting, and dieback. Moderate to heavy infestation levels deposit objectionable honeydew and sooty mold on structures under trees. Infestations usually do not damage trees.

Monitoring Techniques. Look for white egg sacs on bark and pale yellow-green crawlers on leaves in early spring. During the summer, look on the underside of leaves for flat, yellow nymphs. Examine trees with honeydew and sooty mold for nymphs.

Management Strategies. If infestations are light, honeydew and sooty mold are not objectionable, or beneficials are abundant, it may not be necessary to treat. Reevaluate the situation within two weeks. In the summer, if infestations are heavy and stunting or honeydew and sooty mold are objectionable, spray horticultural oil or insecticidal soap or apply systemic insecticides to the soil to control crawlers and nymphs. Apply dormant oil to the bark to kill overwintering nymphs.

Dogwood Borer

Identification and Biology. Adults are clearwing moths about 3/8 in. long. They have two gold bands on a bluish-black abdomen. The larvae grow to ½ in. long and are white with a brown head and two reddish-brown spots on the back (near the head). There is one generation a year; larvae overwinter in the gallery under bark. Adult emergence peaks around early to mid-May but occurs continually from April to October.

Host Plants. This native clearwing moth primarily attacks stressed or wounded dogwoods but may also attack other landscape trees, such as apple, oak, hickory, cherry, birch, willow, and ash.

Damage Symptoms. Larvae bore under bark, and the gallery may girdle the trees. Repeated multiple infestations may cause dieback on large trees or kill small trees. As the bark and galleries sink, the bark becomes loose and cracks. Brown frass around bark cracks usually indicates active infestation.

Monitoring Techniques. Look for brown frass around wounds and bark cracks. Remove loose bark with a knife. Larvae are often found in short tunnels under the bark.

Management Strategies. Plant trees in proper locations to avoid stressful conditions. Protect tree trunks with mulch bands to prevent wounds from lawn mowers. An early April application of a long-residual insecticide to the bark should prevent infestation. An additional application may be necessary in late May. Systemic insecticides applied to the soil in early spring may provide some protection against infestation and have varying degrees of success in controlling existing infestation. Kousa dogwood appear to be resistant to this borer.

Dogwood Clubgall Midge

Identification and Biology. Adult midges are about 1/16-in. long and resemble mosquitoes. Mature larvae are yellowish-orange maggots. The oval galls are found at branch terminals. There is one generation a year; pupae overwinter in soil under trees.

Host Plants. This native gall-forming fly infests flowering dogwood from New England to Florida.

Damage Symptoms. In spring, newly hatched maggots infest growing tips and form oval or somewhat tubular green galls. In summer, associated terminal leaves slowly wilt and die, and the galls turn brown. Damage and long-term impact on vigor are minimal on well-established mature trees, but heavily infested young trees may be stunted.

Monitoring Techniques. In May, look for green galls on terminal twigs of flowering dogwood. Dead terminals with brown galls from the previous year indicate the possibility of an infestation.

Management Strategies. Prune out and destroy newly formed green galls in spring. There are no insecticides labeled for control of this minor pest.

Eastern Tent Caterpillar

Identification and Biology. Adult moths are about 1 in. long. They are light brown with two white diagonal stripes across each forewing. Mature larvae may reach a length of 2 in. or more and have a white stripe down the back. There is one generation a year; pupae overwinter in cocoons in debris on the ground.

Host Plants. Preferred hosts include wild cherry, crabapple, and apple. In years with heavy infestations, they may also attack ash, birch, black gum, willow, maple, oak, poplar, cherry, and plum.

Damage Symptoms. Silken webs in tree forks appearing during bud break are indicative of this pest. In peak population years, these pests may defoliate preferred hosts.

Monitoring Techniques. Look for the black, 3/4-in.-long egg masses on preferred hosts in the dormant season. Look for silken webs in the branch forks of preferred hosts in early March.

Management Strategies. Prune out egg masses during the dormant season. Mechanically destroy web contents when first discovered. Spray *Bacillus thuringiensis* (*Bt*) onto foliage where larvae are found feeding.

Euonymus Scale

Identification and Biology. Covers of adult females are about 1/8-in. long, brownish-black, and shaped like oyster shells. Male covers are smaller, thinner, white, and ridged. Crawlers are yellowish-orange and most often found on new growth. This species overwinters as fertilized adult females; there are four overlapping generations a year.

Host Plants. This imported armored scale attacks and frequently kills most species of evergreen euonymus.

Damage Symptoms. Light infestations on bark cause no obvious damage. In heavy infestations, the white covers of males are easy to spot on the leaves, and the leaves develop yellow spots. Large shrubs may die after 2-3 years of continuing infestation and no treatment.

Monitoring Techniques. Look for yellow-spotted leaves, branch dieback, and white male covers on the leaves of plants. Always examine Japanese euonymus to discover infestations before they cause damage. Carefully examine the bark on a few stems to detect light infestations. Examine plants for the presence of predators and parasites.

Management Strategies. Replace susceptible euonymus varieties with resistant or tolerant species where possible. Dormant oil sprays should control light bark infestations. For heavy leaf infestations, remove and destroy heavily infested branches and then follow with an application of a systemic insecticide. Horticultural oil, insecticidal soaps, or other contact insecticides should be applied at the time of crawler emergence. Use only oils and soaps if there are numerous predators or parasites.

Fall Webworm

Identification and Biology. Adult moths are about ¾-in. long. Wings are all white or white with black spots. Bases of front legs are orangey yellow. Mature larvae are about 1 in. long and may occur in two color forms: those with black heads are yellowish-white, and those with red heads are brown. Both forms have paired black tubercles running down the back and are covered with long, silky gray hairs. There are four generations a year; pupae overwinter in cocoons in protected places.

Host Plants. This species feeds on more than 100 species of deciduous forest and shade trees. Preferred hosts include mulberry, walnut, hickory, pecan, elm, sweetgum, poplar, willow, oak, linden, ash, apple, persimmon, and other fruit trees.

Damage Symptoms. The caterpillars produce webs of fine silk that cover entire terminals. They feed inside the silken web, which they enlarge to take in more foliage as they grow. The webs are aesthetically distracting, but rarely do the caterpillars consume enough foliage to affect tree growth.

Monitoring Techniques. In early spring, examine the south side of tree crowns for the first signs of webbing over terminals. Continue to monitor host trees throughout the growing season for the presence of webs.

Management Strategies. Prune out webbed terminals as they are detected. Large webs can be disturbed and left open to allow the entrance of predators, parasites, and birds. When large infestations are present, you can use *Bacillus thuringiensis* (*Bt*) to control young caterpillars. Bt will not harm the numerous species of predators and parasites that normally maintain this pest below damaging levels. Insecticides must penetrate the webs to provide good control.

Flatheaded Appletree Borer

Identification and Biology. Adults may reach ½ in. in length. They are oval, flattened beetles, metallic greenish-bronze above and brassy below. Wing covers have wavy, light-colored indentations. The white larvae, commonly called flatheaded borers, have an expanded thorax just behind the small black head. There is one generation per year; larvae overwinter in galleries under the bark.

Host Plants. Preferred hosts include sycamore, red maple, silver maple, willow, oak, tulip tree poplar, elm, beech, hickory, apple, pear, dogwood, and black walnut. Newly planted trees are susceptible to these borers until they establish root systems.

Damage Symptoms. Young trees and trees under stress are particularly attractive to this pest. Larvae bore fairly large, irregular cavities in the phloem tissue of the main trunk and larger branches. Larvae are usually found boring into the base of trees. Tree may ooze sap from the entrance hole in the spring. Affected areas may desiccate and lead to sunken, cracked bark. Small trees are often severely girdled, which leads to crown dieback and death.

Monitoring Techniques. Frequently examine newly transplanted and stressed trees for signs of dieback on branches. Closely examine bark for galleries where cracking and weeping are seen. Adults can sometimes be seen on the sunny sides of tree trunks as they search for egg-laying sites.

Management Strategies. The flatheaded appletree borer prefers to attack stressed trees. Maintain tree vigor by planting trees in appropriate locations and choosing tree species adapted to your specific site and maintaining proper cultural practices. If you note numerous adult beetles on bark, spray the trunk and major branches with an approved residual insecticide. Using systemic insecticides applied to the soil in early spring may prevent infestation and control existing infestation.

Greenstriped Mapleworm

Identification and Biology. Adult moths are about 1 in. long. The front wings are pink with a central yellow band. Mature larvae are about 1 ½ in. long and pale green with a reddish head, two black thoracic horns, and seven longitudinal greenish-black stripes. There are two generations a year; pupae overwinter in soil.

Host Plants. This native giant silkworm moth prefers maples—especially red maple, sugar maple, and silver maple. It also feeds on boxelder and oaks where they grow in mixed stand with maples.

Damage Symptoms. Mature caterpillars are capable of devouring leaves down to the midrib. Feeding usually begins on the lower branches. Heavy infestations may strip small trees.

Monitoring Techniques. Look for damaged foliage on the lower branches of susceptible maples in early summer. Shake lower branches to knock down camouflaged larvae. Larvae feed singly on leaves.

Management Strategies. Treatment of trees is usually impractical, because effective coverage is hard to achieve without special equipment. *Bacillus thuringiensis* (*Bt*) may be effective when caterpillars are young.

Native Holly Leaf Miner

Identification and Biology. Adult flies are about 1/8-in. long and black. The larvae are 1/8-in. long, yellow maggots that tunnel through leaves, creating serpentine mines. Eggs are usually deposited in the midrib or leaf margin. Early mining occurs near midrib. There is one generation a year; larvae overwinter in the mines.

Host Plants. The native holly leaf miner produces mines primarily on American holly. Other holly leaf miner species infest Japanese, Chinese, English, and yaupon hollies.

Damage Symptoms. In summer to fall, mining occurs in the midrib; the obvious, linear, yellowish-green mine in the leaf surface occurs the following spring. Several mines per leaf cause premature leaf drop. Adult females of this fly puncture tender new holly leaves to feed on plant juices, leaving behind yellowish punctures. Parasites often control this pest if they themselves are not eliminated by insecticides.

Monitoring Techniques. Look for short mines in late summer. Look at leaves on the south side of holly for expanding yellowish mines in January and February. Look for adult flies on new terminal leaves in March through April. Look for and count feeding punctures on the underside of new leaves as an indication of fly population size.

Management Strategies. Picking and destroying mined leaves before March may be sufficient to reduce light infestations. For heavy infestations, use systemic insecticides to control larvae in March or late summer. You can use contact insecticides for adults in early April, but their use may disrupt the activities of beneficial parasites, which parasitize 70-85% of the miners.

Japanese Beetle

Identification and Biology. Adults are nearly ½-in. long, broadly oval, thick bodied, with coppery brown wing covers and a metallic green body. Mature larvae are nearly 1 in. long, white, and C-shaped with brown heads. Distinguish Japanese beetle grubs from other species by the two rows of spines that form a "V" on the underside of the last abdominal segment. There is one generation a year; larvae overwinter in soil.

Host Plants. Adults of this imported scarab beetle feed on the flowers and leaves of many plants. Preferred plants include rose, crape myrtle, maples, sycamore, birch, cottonwood, linden, mountain ash, and elms. White grubs feed on roots of turfgrass.

Damage Symptoms. Adults prefer tender young leaves, which they may skeletonize completely. They may defoliate trees in heavily infested areas. Larvae may severely damage lawns and the roots of small plants. Large adult populations may destroy flowers and shrubs such as roses but don't always cause long-term damage to the overall health and vigor of trees such as crape myrtles.

Monitoring Techniques. Look for adults on preferred hosts from early June through August. Japanese beetle trap is a good monitoring tool but not a control device. Examine turfgrass in late summer for the presence of grubs.

Use a spade to cut three sides of a strip of turf, 1 ft^2 and 2-3 in. deep. Force the spade under the sod and lay the flap back, using the uncut side as a hinge. Use a trowel to dislodge soil from the overturned roots. Count the grubs in the exposed soil, then replace the strip of sod. If there are more than eight to ten grubs per square foot, consider treating the turf.

Management Strategies. Milky spore disease is a fungal disease available for controlling Japanese beetle grubs, but results are inconsistent. Application of neonicotinoid (such as imidacloprid) and diamide insecticides (such as chloratranilliprole) to turf in June or July is very effective. Weekly application of residual or contact insecticides to host plants in June and July provide only partial control of adults. Do not use traps for control. Consider replacing highly susceptible plant species such as roses with less susceptible ones such as holly.

Juniper Scale

Identification and Biology. Mature female covers are circular, white, and about 1/16-in. in diameter with a yellow spot (shed skin) at the front. Male covers are smaller, elongated, oval, and white. There is one generation a year, and crawlers emerge in late spring. Adult females overwinter on needles.

Host Plants. This imported armored scale insect prefers juniper but has also been collected from Leyland cypress and cedar.

Damage Symptoms. Light infestations cause no

apparent symptoms. Heavy infestations (ten or more scales per ½ in. of twig) cause foliage to turn yellow. If there is no intervention from beneficial insects or insecticide application, heavy infestation can lead to dieback.

Monitoring Techniques. Examine yellow or off-color needles closely for minute, white, circular scale covers. Examine infested plants closely for evidence of parasite and predator populations and their activities. Scales usually build up first on the south side of shrubs or on the side against a building.

Management Strategies. Dormant oil spray reduces the number of overwintering adults but usually does not provide adequate control. Use horticultural oil or insecticidal soap to control crawlers in late spring. Use systemic insecticides in late summer and fall to reduce heavy populations.

Longtailed Mealybug

Identification and Biology. Adult bodies are about 1/8-in. long. The body is dusted with white waxy powder, and the body margin is ringed with white wax filaments. The last pair of filaments is more than one-half the length of the body. There are two to three generations a year; immatures overwinter on bark. Crawlers may be found at any time of year.

Host Plants. This distinctive, cosmopolitan mealybug is a general feeder. It is usually found in protected locations on pyracantha, holly, yew, cycad, and rhododendron.

Damage Symptoms. Moderate to heavy infestations produce a large amount of sticky honeydew and a dense growth of sooty mold. Terminal leaves may become yellow and distorted.

Monitoring Techniques. Start with dense plants growing in sheltered locations. Examine plants covered with honeydew or sooty mold for active ants and/or the presence of mealybugs on the underside of leaves and stems.

Management Strategies. Horticultural oil sprays suppress growing populations. Systemic insecticides are best if plantings are dense and/or if the pest population is high.

Maple Bladdergall Mite & Maple Spindlegall Mite

Identification and Biology. Adults of these two eriophyid mites are not visible without a hand lens. They live in circular and spindle-shaped galls. They are white to clear in color, 0.15 mm long, and cigar-shaped with only four legs. There are several generations a year; adults overwinter in bark cracks.

Host Plants. The maple bladdergall mite prefers red maple. The maple spindlegall mite prefers silver maple and sugar maple.

Damage Symptoms. Infested leaves develop small circular or spindle-shaped galls in spring that turn from green to red to black over one month. The galls are on the upper side of the leaf, but the opening is on the bottom of the leaf. Most infestations cause no other symptoms and are not a serious threat to the health of the host plant.

Monitoring Techniques. Look at new leaves for gall formation in spring as leaves expand. Look at mature leaves in summer to estimate the abundance of galls. Galls can be a cosmetic concern but do not damage plants.

Management Strategies. Control measures are usually unnecessary.

Oak Lecanium Scale

Identification and Biology. Fully developed adult females are about ¼-in. long. They are oval to almost circular, highly convex, and light to dark brown. Crawlers are pale yellow and active in early to late May. There is one generation a year.; nymphs overwinter on twigs.

Host Plants. This native soft scale is believed to be restricted to the beech family (*Fagaceae*), especially oak and chinquapin.

Damage Symptoms. Heavily infested twigs commonly exhibit stunted leaves and dieback due to the feeding activities of developing females in the spring. They also produce large amounts of honeydew and sooty mold. Crawlers and nymphs spend the summer feeding on leaf veins but usually produce no damage.

Monitoring Techniques. Examine twigs in the dormant season for dead females of the previous season and flat, brown nymphs that begin to enlarge and mature in the spring. Look for crawlers and nymphs feeding on leaf veins from May through the fall.

Management Strategies. Oak lecanium scale populations are especially large and damaging in urban landscapes in which growing conditions are stressful. Practice proper cultural and maintenance practices to maintain tree vigor. Use horticultural oil as a dormant spray or as a crawler spray in mid-June. Using oil reduces impact on parasite activity that peaks with crawler activity. If damage symptoms are evident in July or August and crawlers are present, repeat the oil application to the foliage. You can also apply systemic insecticides to the soil in March to reduce the population of nymphs.

Obscure Scale

Identification and Biology. Fully enlarged adult female covers may reach 1/16-in. in diameter. They are circular, brown to gray, and slightly convex, with central skins that are black when rubbed. Male covers are smaller and broadly oval. This species develops in overlapping clusters; there is one generation a year. They overwinter as nymphs, and crawlers appear in late June and July.

Host Plants. This native armored scale feeds on eastern oak species—especially black oaks—and pecan. In landscapes, this pest often damages pin and willow oaks.

Damage Symptoms. Heavy infestations cause branch dieback on oak trees. Pin oak branches may become gnarled where many scale aggregations depress the bark.

Monitoring Techniques. Look on 3-4-year-old branches for overlapping gray scale covers. Scrape off covers to determine the viability of a population, because covers of dead scales may remain attached to the tree. In mid-summer, live adult female scales are light purple. Scout in mid-July to determine the amount of crawler activity. Look under covers in the dormant season for the small, yellow immatures to see if dormant sprays are needed. Look for holes in covers to estimate the level of parasitism.

Management Strategies. Concentrate dormant oil sprays on 3-4-year-old growth to reduce overwintering populations. Spray summer oil in late July to kill newly settled crawlers. Over-fertilization tends to result in increased scale insect populations. Several parasite species are active when the scale crawlers appear in July. Avoid contact insecticide sprays at this time.

Orangestriped Oakworm

Identification and Biology. Adult moths are about 1¼-in. long; they are reddish brown and translucent with a sub-marginal dark stripe and a white spot on each forewing. Mature larvae are about 1 1/8-in. long and black with eight orange-to-yellow stripes and two black spines behind the head. There are approximately two generations a year. Adults first appear in early summer, and pupae overwinter in soil.

Host Plants. This moth caterpillar prefers to feed on oaks, but it also attacks hickory and birch.

Damage Symptoms. The caterpillars feed in a group. Young caterpillars feed by skeletonizing the leaf surface; older caterpillars are defoliators and may consume all but the midrib. Defoliation usually occurs one branch at a time when populations are small.

Monitoring Techniques. Look for signs of localized skeletonization turning to defoliation on host tree branches. Where this species is a serious problem, use a blacklight trap to determine the first adult appearance and the relative size of each generation.

Management Strategies. Manually destroy aggregations of young larvae when you detect them on small trees. Apply *Bacillus thuringiensis* (*Bt*) or horticultural oil to control young larvae. Controlling large caterpillars often requires contact insecticides.

Pine Needle Scale

Identification and Biology. Adult female covers are about 1/8-in. long. They are white, oyster shell shaped, and found on needles. Male covers are similar but smaller. There are two generations a year, with reddish crawlers in May or June and July. Red eggs overwinter under scales.

Host Plants. This native armored scale feeds on most conifers, including spruce, fir, pine, and hemlock. They prefer white, Mugo, Scots, and Austrian pines.

Damage Symptoms. Conifers are tolerant of light infestations of pine needle scale. Heavy infestations may cause yellowing, stunting, and eventual dieback. Trees along roads and against buildings often suffer severe attacks.

Monitoring Techniques. In May and June, turn over scale covers and examine them with a hand lens to determine if eggs or crawlers are present. Look for holes in covers that indicate the presence of parasites or predators. Look for active, reddish crawlers and translucent, yellow, settled and feeding crawlers.

Management Strategies. Many predators and parasites attack this pest. Apply a dormant oil to reduce overwintering populations. Spray a horticultural oil or insecticidal soap when crawlers are present. Application of a long residual insecticide is warranted if infestation is heavy enough to cause needle yellowing and if no beneficial insects are found.

Pine Spittlebug

Identification and Biology. Adults are about ¼-in. long and tan with two irregular whitish bands on each wing. Nymphs are mostly black except for their whitish abdomens, and they are covered with frothy honeydew called spittle. There is one generation a year, and eggs overwinter on bark.

Host Plants. This native spittlebug prefers Scots pine, but also attacks eastern white, Virginia, jack, slash, loblolly, Japanese, and Mugo pines as well as Norway, white, and red spruces, balsam fir, larch, eastern hemlock, and Douglas fir.

Damage Symptoms. Both adults and nymphs suck sap from twigs. This feeding activity may cause twig and branch dieback and even tree death. Some flagging injury is due to the fungus *Diplodia pini*, which can enter pines through spittlebug feeding punctures in hot spring weather.

Monitoring Techniques. Look for nymphs under spittle on twigs in early spring; look for adults feeding in the same locations in early summer without a covering of spittle. Nymphs are slow-moving and may be collected by hand; adults are active and may be swept from twigs with an insect net.

Management Strategies. You can remove light spittlebug infestations from small pines manually. Light infestations have little effect on trees and usually do not warrant chemical control.

Redhumped Caterpillar

Identification and Biology. Adult moths are about 1 in. long. They are grayish brown with black markings. Fully grown caterpillars are about 1¼-in. long and spiny, with many black and yellow longitudinal stripes, a reddish head, and reddish humps on abdominal segments 1 and 8. There is one generation a year; pupae overwinter in cocoons in leaf litter.

Host Plants. This native moth is a general feeder that attacks plants in the rose family and many shade trees—such as poplar, elm, willow, hickory, walnut, sweetgum, persimmon, birch, redbud, and dogwood.

Damage Symptoms. Caterpillars feed in groups. Young caterpillars skeletonize the underside of leaves. Older larvae consume leaves to the midrib. On large trees, individual branches may be defoliated; small trees may suffer complete defoliation.

Monitoring Techniques. Look for the distinctive caterpillars feeding in groups when skeletonization begins to appear on leaves in June. Later in the summer, defoliation becomes obvious as larger larvae consume leaves.

Management Strategies. On small trees and the low branches on large trees, prune out clusters of larvae when they first appear. For heavy infestations, spray young caterpillars with *Bacillus thuringiensis* (*Bt*) or horticultural oil. Use contact insecticides for older larvae.

Rhododendron Borer

Identification and Biology. Adult moths are about ¼-in. long. Their wings are mostly clear, and the body is black with three gold abdominal bands. Mature larvae are about ½-in. long and white, with a brown head and five pairs of short ventral prolegs. There is one generation a year; larvae overwinter in tunnels in branches.

Host Plants. This native clearwing moth prefers to feed on rhododendron but occasionally attacks deciduous azalea and mountain laurel.

Damage Symptoms. The boring activities of larvae in branches may cause the bark to crack, revealing tunnels and frass inside. Heavy infestations girdle branches, causing wilting and eventual branch dieback.

Monitoring Techniques. Look for wilting rhododendron leaves and dieback. Prune off suspect branches and dissect them longitudinally to see if larvae are present.

Management Strategies. Prune out and destroy wilting branches in late summer or early spring. Treat infested host plants with a systemic insecticide when the first males are active (usually in early summer).

Rhododendron Lace Bug

Identification and Biology. Adults are about 1/8-in. long. The body is pale yellow. The lacy, transparent wings have two dark spots and are held flat on the back. Nymphs are black and spiny. Eggs are partially buried in leaf tissue along the midvein and overwinter in leaves. There are four generations a year.

Host Plants. This native pest prefers rhododendron species but occasionally attacks andromeda and mountain laurel.

Damage Symptoms. Nymphs and adults suck chlorophyll from leaves, causing a course, yellowish stippling. Both stages deposit black excrement spots that stick to the underside of leaves. In severe infestations, most leaves turn yellowish brown.

Monitoring Techniques. Look for first signs of stippling damage on plants grown in full sun. Beginning in early spring and continuing throughout the summer, examine plants closely for signs of stippling on older leaves. Examine the underside of stippled leaves for the presence of lace bugs and black fecal spots.

Management Strategies. Horticultural oil and insecticidal soap provide control if sprayed carefully on the underside of leaves. Make application in early spring, when the first generation of the insect appears. It may be necessary to apply a contact or systemic insecticide to control heavy infestations that are present late spring through the fall.

Sawflies

Identification and Biology. Several sawfly species are pests of ornamental plants. Adults are wasps. Larvae resemble caterpillars but have more than five pairs of abdominal prolegs. Most species have one to two generations a year and overwinter as pupae in soil. Most sawfly larvae are ½-1 in. long; most are external feeders on foliage. Some eat needles, some eat entire leaves, and others only skeletonize the leaves of shrubs and trees. Cocoons may form on foliage, twigs, or the ground.

Host Plants. As a group, sawflies have a wide range of hosts. They feed on conifers and various oaks, roses, black locust, azaleas, ash, black walnut, elm, and other woody ornamentals.

Damage Symptoms. Most sawflies are gregarious feeders. In light infestations, damage may appear as skeletonization or defoliation on leaves or needles of individual branches or shoots. Heavy infestations may cause complete defoliation.

Monitoring Techniques. Look for symptoms of localized defoliation or skeletonized leaves on exposed branches and shoots of coniferous and deciduous trees and shrubs. Look for clusters of spotted or striped larvae in the vicinity of damage symptoms.

Management Strategies. Hand-pick or prune small infestations and destroy them. Spray large infestations of young larvae with horticultural oil; spray early mature larvae with a contact insecticide. Sawfly larvae are not caterpillars; *Bacillus thuringiensis* only works on caterpillars and does not affect sawfly larvae.

Southern Red Mite

Identification and Biology. Adults are 0.5 mm long, oval, and purplish or reddish, with eight legs. The red eggs overwinter on the undersides of leaves. There are several generations each year. Most activity occurs in spring and fall, so they are considered cool-season mites.

Host Plants. This imported spider mite has a wide range of hosts but prefers broad-leaved evergreens. It is common on azalea, rhododendron, mountain laurel, holly, rose, viburnum, firethorn, and yew.

Damage Symptoms. In light infestations, mites remove contents from leaf cells, resulting in white stippling usually concentrated along the midrib on the lower leaf surface. In heavy infestations, stippling is produced on upper and lower leaf surfaces, and leaves turn gray or brown and die. Lower leaf surfaces often appear dusty because of the numerous eggshells and shed skins.

Monitoring Techniques. Examine plants closely for signs of stippling and the various mite stages on the lower and upper leaf surfaces of broadleaved evergreens in early spring and fall. When you do notice stippling, tap leaves over white paper to dislodge and count mites, beneficial insects, and predaceous mites. Predaceous mites have longer legs than the southern red mite and move much faster. Look for red overwintering eggs on the lower surface of leaves from November through early spring.

Management Strategies. In light infestations, the use of a horticultural oil or insecticidal soap controls these mites with minimal impact on beneficial organisms. The application of miticides is often necessary against heavy infestations.

Spruce Spider Mite

Identification and Biology. This is another cool-season mite. Adults are about 0.5 mm long and have eight legs; they are yellowish-green when young and grayish black with a tan area behind the mouthparts when mature. Eggs are oval and reddish brown and overwinter on bark and needles. There are several generations per year.

Host Plants. This cosmopolitan pest prefers spruce, pine, hemlock, and arborvitae but may also attack cedar, yew, larch, cryptomeria, dawn redwood, and false cypress.

Damage Symptoms. These spider mites suck chlorophyll from needles, leaving minute yellowish stipples or flecks at the feeding sites. In heavy infestations, the stipples coalesce, and needles turn yellow, then brown. Small trees may die, and large trees may suffer dieback. Most damage occurs during the cooler temperatures in the spring and fall.

Monitoring Techniques. At the first sign of stippling on the needles, tap branches over white paper and count the dark, slow-moving spider mites. Note the presence of white, fast-moving predatory mites and the minute, black lady beetle. Concentrate monitoring activities from March through June and September through November.

Management Strategies. Spraying is not best practice for control of spruce spider mites unless: (a) there is stippling damage on more than 10% of green foliage, (b) more than about ten spider mites are tapped from a tree's branches, and (c) beneficial mites and beetles are not found in all branch samples. In the growing season, use summer oil or insecticidal soap sprays if predator populations are present.

Thrips

Identification and Biology. Adult thrips are tiny—1/20 in. long—slender insects with long fringes on the margins of their wings. Adults are commonly yellowish or black and shiny. Nymphs are clear to yellowish and smaller than adults. Females lay eggs within leaf tissue or in curled, distorted foliage caused by feeding nymphs and adults. Several generations of thrips hatch each year.

Host Plants. Thrips attack a wide range of herbaceous and woody landscape plants.

Damage Symptoms. Damage from feeding may result in discoloration, distortion, and premature shedding of leaves, flowers, and buds. There may be silver- or bronze-colored speckles as well as small black specks of waste materials.

Monitoring Techniques. Monitor for thrips by beating branches or shaking foliage or flowers onto a sheet of paper. Monitor adult populations using bright yellow or blue sticky traps.

Management Strategies. Healthy woody plants can usually tolerate damage from thrips. Provide appropriate cultural care to keep plants vigorous. Prune and destroy infested terminals, flowers, and buds when possible. For heavy infestations of thrips, the application of contact or residual insecticides is often necessary.

Two-Lined Spittlebug

Identification and Biology. Adults are about ¼-½ in. long, smoky brown to black in color, broadly oval, and convex with prominent eyes. They have two bright orange stripes across their wings. Nymphs are smaller, usually pale greenish yellow, and covered by frothy bubbles called spittle. Two generations occur per year.

Host Plants. Spittlebigs in immature stages are found in turfgrass; adults are found on numerous woody ornamentals, especially hollies.

Damage Symptoms. Both nymphs and adults feed on plant sap. Their feeding destroys plant tissue, causing stunting, distortion, and death of tissues. The frothy masses they produce can be unsightly.

Monitoring Techniques. Look for the frothy spittle masses in turf, particularly centipedegrass, beginning in early spring. The second generation of nymphs usually appears in late summer. Look for active adults beginning in early summer. The second generation of adults usually appears in September.

Management Strategies. Don't allow heavy thatch layers to accumulate on lawns. Avoid planting host plants that attract adults, especially Japanese holly, near susceptible turfgrasses. Apply insecticides to heavily infested turf in July: mow and irrigate the grass several hours before applying treatment late in the day.

Twospotted Spider Mite

Identification and Biology. In the growing season, adults are about 0.7 mm long. They have one oval body segment and eight legs and are greenish yellow with a black spot on each side of the body. Eggs are white to yellow. Reddish-orange adult females overwinter in bark cracks. The twospotted spider mite is a warm-season mite, meaning that the population and damage are more noticeable in the warmer months of spring and summer.

Host Plants. Twospotted spider mites have a very broad range of hosts. They feed on deciduous trees and shrubs and herbaceous plants.

Damage Symptoms. Spider mites remove cell content and chlorophyll from the underside of leaves, causing minute white-to-yellow stipples to appear on leaf surface. When large spider mite populations feed, the stipples coalesce, and leaves may turn white to yellow to grayish-brown and then die.

Monitoring Techniques. Look for early signs of stippling when hot summer weather begins. Examine the underside of damaged leaves or tap them over white paper and look for spider mites with two spots on the body. Also look for predators such as phytoseiid mites and lady beetles and note their relative abundance in relation to the mites.

Management Strategies. In dry, hot, sunny locations, there may be one generation of twospotted spider mites per week. Use horticultural oil or insecticidal soap sprays to control low mite populations and conserve any beneficials. When damage becomes objectionable, mite populations are high, and there are no beneficials, consider using a miticide spray. Reevaluate in one week.

Wax Scales

Identification and Biology. Two wax scale species are common in South Carolina: Florida wax scale and Indian wax scale. Adult female Florida wax scale is about 1/8-in. in diameter, semi-hemispherical, and pink. Adult female Indian wax scale is ¼-in. in diameter, semi-hemispherical, and white. They are covered with a thick layer of gummy wax. Immatures resemble cameos with the developing areas of white wax not yet completely covering the reddish body. There is one generation a year of Indian wax scale and two generations per year of Florida wax scale. Adult females overwinter on bark.

Host Plants. Wax scales feed on many shrubs and trees but prefer Japanese holly, Chinese holly, euonymus, boxwood, firethorn, spirea, barberry, and flowering quince.

Damage Symptoms. Light to moderate infestations may produce nuisance levels of honeydew and sooty mold. Heavy infestations may cause early leaf yellowing and premature leaf drop. Eventually dieback occurs.

Monitoring Techniques. Large numbers of foraging bees, wasps, hornets, and ants on dense shrubs may indicate wax scale. Look for honeydew and sooty mold. Look on twigs and small branches for all wax scale stages. Crawlers of Indian wax scale begin hatching in early summer; crawlers of Florida wax scale are most abundant in May and August.

Management Strategies. Beginning in May, examine female wax scales on leaves and branches every 1-2 weeks and determine when the eggs begin to hatch. Remove heavily infested twigs or branches. Thoroughly spray infested twigs and branches with horticultural oil. For effective control, use a contact or systemic insecticide after egg hatch and when crawlers are present on the plant.

Whiteflies

Identification and Biology. Several species of whiteflies are common on ornamentals. Adult whiteflies range from 1/16-1/8 in. long. Most species resemble tiny white moths. Identification is easiest when they are in the scale insect-like pupal stages.

Host Plants. Whiteflies have numerous hosts, including rhododendron and azalea, ash, dogwood, sycamore, sweetgum, honeylocust, black locust, barberries, redbud, roses, and herbaceous plants like hibiscus and verbena.

Damage Symptoms. Medium infestations may produce objectionable levels of honeydew and sooty mold. Heavy infestations may cause leaves to turn yellow and drop prematurely. All stages feed on the underside of leaves.

Monitoring Techniques. When you first see honeydew, sooty mold, or leaf yellowing, examine the underside of leaves for feeding adults and nymphs. Ants foraging on leaves may also indicate the presence of whiteflies.

Management Strategies. Rake up and destroy fallen leaves. If honeydew or damage is objectionable, spray the underside of leaves with soap or oil to conserve beneficials. Remove heavily infested leaves. Predators and parasites usually keep these pests at low levels in the landscape.

White Pine Weevil

Identification and Biology. Adults are about ¼ in. long. They are oval and brown with a long snout and two white spots that often run together on the back of the hardened front wings. Larvae are about 1/8 in. long, C-shaped, legless, and white with brown heads. There is one generation a year; adults overwinter in duff under trees.

Host Plants. This native bark weevil may feed and breed in many native and exotic pine and spruce species.

Damage Symptoms. Adults chew holes to feed on leaders near terminal buds, causing pitch flow. They lay eggs in holes, and the larvae bore in the leader and cause it to stunt, flag, and die. Small trees may die, while large trees develop irregular forms. Look for adults feeding and laying eggs within 12 in. of terminal buds on pines and spruces from March through May.

Monitoring Techniques. Look for infested terminals beginning in June. These flagging terminals form a characteristic shepherd's crook. Remove and split terminals to be certain weevil larvae, and not disease, are the problem.

Management Strategies. Prune out and destroy flagging terminals on small trees in June. For heavy infestations, spray terminals with a residual insecticide in March or April when adults are feeding but before they begin laying eggs. Once inside plant tissues, the larvae are difficult to control.

DISEASES OF ORNAMENTALS

Plant disease is defined as any deviation from normal plant functions. Disease, therefore, can be caused by biotic or abiotic agents. However, traditionally, plant diseases are caused by biotic agents called pathogens, whereas disorders are caused by abiotic agents. Abiotic disorders are those problems not caused by a biological organism and often result from poor site preparation and soil drainage, poor or excessive fertilization or irrigation, or chemical damage such as misapplied pesticides or excessive salt uptake. Diseases, on the other hand, are biotic and the result of biological agents called pathogens—including fungi, water molds, bacteria, phytoplasmas, nematodes, and viruses.

As you learned in Plant Diseases and Disorders, disease occurs only when a susceptible host plant, a plant pathogen, and a set of environmental conditions favorable to the pathogen all exist in the same time and place. For example, for leaf-spotting fungi to infect susceptible leaves, water must be present on the leaf surface for several hours. If water is not present for the required time, infection does not take place.

When diagnosing plant diseases, act like a detective. Don't limit yourself to looking only at blighted or discolored leaves. Look at the plant's surroundings. Ask yourself questions like: does the soil feel very wet or dry? When did it last rain or when was the last watering? Is the problem affecting the whole plant or just a few leaves? Is the problem affecting both sides of the leaf? Is there a pattern to the problem? Does it affect all plants equally or only a few? Answers to questions like these give you clues to the problem and help you formulate disease control recommendations.

In general, abiotic disorders cause uniform symptoms. They affect the whole plant or discolor the entire leaf margin. Diseases typically show random symptoms, at least in the early stages of development. Spots are randomly distributed on the surface of the leaf, or only a few leaves or branches are affected.

This chapter addresses the effect of host, environment, and pathogen on common disease problems and describes symptoms associated with specific pathogens; we also give general control recommendations for common diseases affecting woody and herbaceous ornamentals.

Disease Factors

Host Plant

A happy plant is a healthy plant. A plant growing under ideal conditions that meet its specific growth requirements is less likely to have a disease or disorder. Plants that are stressed, such as those planted out of their USDA hardiness zone or planted in the wrong location with too little or too much light or water—as well as injured plants from improper pruning or mowing—are more susceptible to diseases, because the plant's defenses are weakened (and injuries provide a direct entry point for a pathogen into the plant).

A general decline of a plant, such as yellowing leaves, thinning foliage, reduced flowering, or reduced growth growth (stunting) may result from improper site location or root problems, including root rots and nematodes. Often, you can't correctly diagnose the problem without digging the plant. Sometimes sacrificing one plant may save many, and if the plant is not diseased, it can be replanted.

Some plants are more susceptible to infection than others. When selecting vegetables, many seed catalogs list whether a particular cultivar is resistant to a disease. Unfortunately, the selection and breeding of ornamental cultivars is often based on flower color, flower size, or other aesthetic qualities rather than disease resistance, but this is changing. For example, there are many crapemyrtle and phlox cultivars that are resistant to powdery mildew disease, the primary disease problem on these two hosts. Look for disease resistance information on plant tags and labels when shopping for new plants. Planting a disease-resistant plant is the easiest ways to avoid or lessen disease problems in the landscape.

Environment

Again, a happy plant is a healthy plant. The environmental factors mentioned in the host section apply to this section as well. In addition, providing plants with proper horticultural needs such as fertilization, water, and pruning reduces the risk of disease. See specific sections on plant care throughout this book.

Most pathogens require moisture to infect plant tissues. Therefore, anything that reduces the length of time water is present on leaves or roots reduces disease. Improving ventilation around ornamental plants by selectively pruning or thinning branches of woody ornamentals and increasing plant spacing of herbaceous ornamentals enables wet plant tissue to dry rapidly. Also, manipulating the environment by watering early in the day so that plants have plenty of time to dry before nightfall reduces the length of time the leaves may be wet and reduces disease.

For root diseases, improving drainage reduces the risk of developing root rot and nematode damage. Improve drainage in heavy clay soils by placing drainage tile under gardens to redirect and remove water or by incorporating pine bark mulch into the soil. The ratio of pine bark to soil should not exceed 25-30% (1 part pine bark to 2-3 parts soil). You can also use other organic amendments, such as compost and peat moss; however, their beneficial effects on soil porosity and drainage are short-lived, and they require incorporation on a yearly basis.

Be aware that plants often show the same symptoms when facing opposing environmental conditions. For instance, a plant may wilt if it receives too little or too much water. Root rot disease develops when soils are overly wet. The disease collapses the root, so the roots cannot absorb and translocate water through the plant. Therefore, the plant wilts. If you water the wilting plant thinking that it is wilting because it is dry, you would actually be increasing the spread and development of the root rot. Be aware of the plant's environment. Don't just treat the symptom, treat the cause of the symptom.

Pathogens

Fungi, water molds, bacteria, phytoplasmas, nematodes, and viruses are all pathogens that can infect ornamentals. Many are ubiquitous and found naturally in soil, vectored by insects, or carried in the wind. If environmental conditions favor the pathogen on a susceptible host, disease develops. Other pathogens are introduced via planting of infected plants or re-use of contaminated soil.

Fungi. The most common pathogens that affect ornamentals are fungi. Symptoms caused by fungal infections include leaf spots and blights, petal blights, cankers, vascular wilts, and root and crown rots.

Fungal leaf spots and blights favor wet leaves and humid conditions. A variety of fungi can cause leaf spots, including Alternaria, Septoria, and Cercospora. Black spot of rose (caused by *Diplocarpon rosae*) and spot anthracnose on dogwood (caused by *Elsinoe corni*) are both common leaf spot diseases on ornamentals. Typically, fungal leaf spots have a tan to gray center surrounded by a darker reddish, brown, or black border. These spots may be concentrated along the leaf margin and veins. Often, the spots grow together, sometimes forming concentric rings of dead, brown tissue. Within the dead tissue, there are sometimes black, pimple-like fungal fruiting bodies. Leaf spots are termed "blights" when the entire leaf or stem is affected. Often, infected leaves drop prematurely. Leaf-spotting pathogens survive on fallen leaf litter and on dead branches or cankers. Leaf spot diseases rarely kill infected plants; however, they can be aesthetically displeasing.

Powdery mildew is another type of fungal leaf blight; it is probably one of the most troublesome diseases of ornamentals. Powdery mildew rarely kills plants, but it can cause premature defoliation under high disease pressure. Powdery mildew diseases look the same regardless of host, but the fungi are host specific, meaning that a powdery mildew pathogen on rose is specific to rose and will not infect crape myrtle, and vice versa. Leaves develop patches of frosty, white fungal growth, primarily on the upper leaf surface and stem. The infected leaf tissue may yellow. Unlike other fungal leaf pathogens, powdery mildew does not proliferate under wet conditions; instead, symptoms develop under dry conditions in mid to late summer and when humidity is high with warmer daytime and cooler nighttime temperatures.

Rust fungi also cause leaf spots and blights. Pale yellow spots appear on the upper leaf surface, while pustules containing rusty, reddish-brown powdery spores break through the lower—and sometimes upper—leaf surfaces. You can easily rub the spores off with your fingers or paper. Pustules develop as individual spots or as concentric rings in a bullseye pattern, with an inner pustule surrounded by an outer ring. Rust fungi are host specific. Common ornamental plants affected by rusts include daylily, snapdragon, mealy-cup sage, and hollyhock.

Petal blights are primarily caused by the fungus Botrytis. The gray, fuzzy fungus often found covering old strawberries is Botrytis—the same fungus that infects the leaves, stems, and flowers of numerous ornamentals. This fungus favors wet, humid conditions, and under these conditions, the fungus produces an abundance of grayish, fuzzy spores that are easily seen and spread by water, wind, and human activity in the garden. Blighted flowers have darkly colored spots that appear water soaked. Eventually, the flowers disintegrate.

Other petal blights are common on landscape azaleas and older plantings of camellia. These blights cause the flowers to brown and disintegrate shortly after blooming; they cause hard, black fungal structures called sclerotia that are easy to see embedded in the blighted petals.

Cankers are dead portions of plant stem tissue. When the canker is at the end of a branch or shoot, it is referred to as dieback. Cankers are brown or blackened areas that become shrunken with time as the healthy adjacent tissue grows around it. As the canker grows, it girdles the stem, which causes wilting and death of the tissue above the canker.

When inspecting branches and young trees for cankers, look for:

- Localized areas of roughened or cracked bark, especially around wounds and branch stubs
- Callus formation in multiple layers or ridges
- Small, pimple-like, fungal-spore-forming structures either in the centers or around the edges of either symptom described above. These may be red, dark brown, or black.

If these three things occur on branches, prune them off well back from the canker. Symptoms on the main trunk of saplings indicate that the entire tree should be removed.

Both bacteria and fungi cause cankers. These pathogens enter the stem through wounds made by hail, insects, or humans (via mechanical damage from pruning and lawnmowers). One common fungal canker is "Bot" canker, caused by the fungus Botryosphaeria that infects numerous hosts, in particular Leyland cypress and rhododendron. Within old, cankered tissue, there are often black, pimple-like fruiting bodies.

Vascular wilts occur when vascular (water- and nutrient-conducting) tissues are infected by fungi—and sometimes bacteria. One obvious symptom of these diseases is wilting due to water stress, which is caused by the pathogen or its by-products blocking the water-conducting vessels of infected plants; another is death of plant sections. Other foliar symptoms include yellow or scorched leaves and stunting.

Sometimes, as with the fungus *Verticillium spp.*, wilt pathogens infect the root and move upward to the leaves, producing symptoms that appear on only one side of the plant or on one half of a leaf. A lengthwise cut across infected stems reveals dark streaks within the vascular tissue. These pathogens are often introduced into gardens from infected plants. Symptom expression is more likely when a plant is stressed by high temperatures and drought.

Root and crown rots are caused by numerous soil fungi, including Pythium, Phytophthora, Rhizoctonia, and Sclerotium. These fungi infect a wide variety of herbaceous and woody ornamentals. Most of these pathogens favor cool, wet soil conditions.

Pythium and Phytophthora are classified as water molds. These pathogens produce a motile spore (called a zoospore) that can swim in water. The fungi inhabit soil naturally, and under stressful conditions for plant growth—such as over watering and poor soil drainage—they infect the feeder roots.

Diseased roots are discolored and brown or black. Often, small feeder roots are sloughed-off, greatly reducing the plant's ability to absorb water and nutrients. Above-ground foliar symptoms are similar to those produced by an unhealthy root system, such as yellowing of older leaves, stunting, and general decline. In the early stages of decline, diseased plants wilt at midday and recover at night. Often, root rot symptoms mimic nutritional deficiencies. Stems rot at the soil line and have a dry, shredded appearance; stem or crown rot is not always accompanied by root rot. Stem rot also may affect cuttings taken for propagation.

Bacteria. Bacteria are single-celled microscopic organisms. Bacterial pathogens include symptoms such as leaf spots and blights, cankers, and soft rots. Bacterial leaf spots are not easy to distinguish visually from fungal leaf spots. Bacterial infections are characterized as "water-soaked" spots. Often, brown, dead leaf spots are surrounded by darker water-soaked tissue. Yellow halos sometimes border the spot margin. Spots, tan to black in color, can be irregular in shape along leaf margins or angular and contained within leaf veins. Some of the most common bacterial pathogens are (a) *Xanthomonas campestris,* which causes leaf spots on zinnia, begonia, oak-leaf hydrangea, and geranium and (b) *Pseudomonas spp.*, which causes leaf spots on delphinium, poinsettia, and impatiens.

Bacterial cankers occur on woody landscape plants. The most common bacterial canker is fire blight, caused by *Erwinia amylovora*. This disease commonly affects flowering pear, crabapple, quince, cotoneaster, Photinia, Indian hawthorne, and pyracantha during warm, wet conditions in the spring. Wetwood or slime flux is also a bacterial disease; it is characterized by sweet-smelling, sometimes bubbly, ooze from older tree trunks. The disease develops as a result of internal heart rot. Secondary organisms such as yeasts and bacteria colonize the internal cavity and their metabolic activity creates gas pressure that releases through a wound or crack in the tree. Sap then flows from the crack, often staining the tree trunk as it runs down the tree over time.

Bacterial soft rot is another common disease on rhizomatous or bulbous herbaceous ornamentals including iris, hosta, and daylily. Soft rot is caused by the bacterium *Erwinia carotovora*. The bacterium quickly dissolves the rhizome, bulb, or corm under warm, wet conditions. The infected, soft tissues often produce a diagnostic foul odor.

Nematodes. Nematodes are microscopic, non-segmented roundworms. Plant-parasitic nematodes usually feed on plant roots. Symptoms of nematode infestation in the roots are like those of root rots and include stunting, wilting, yellowing of leaves, and nutritional deficiencies. The most easily diagnosed symptom of nematode infestation is galls or knots on the roots caused by the root-knot nematode, *Meloidogyne spp*. Another major nematode pathogen of ornamentals, especially boxwoods, is the root lesion nematode *Pratylenchus*; the feeding of this nematode causes dark brown to black lesions on the secondary roots, often killing the root system. Severe nematode damage is more common in coarse-textured sandy soils than fine-textured clay soils.

Symptoms only indicate nematodes as one possible cause of damage. A laboratory analysis of soil and/or plant tissues is the only way to determine the kinds of plant-parasitic nematodes present, their approximate population levels, and the relative risk that nematodes pose to the plants on site or to be planted. Visit Clemson University's Nematode Assay Lab website for more information.

The foliar nematode (*Aphelenchoides spp.*) burrows through and feeds on leaf and stem tissue. Leaf symptoms of foliar nematode infestations include wedge-shaped dead areas bordered by the leaf veins that initially appear reddish or yellowish but turn brown as the tissue dies. Although symptoms of foliar nematode damage resemble leaf spots caused by downy mildews, no spores are produced on or by nematode lesions. Removal of infected leaves reduces the spread of the nematode within the plant and to adjacent plants.

Nematode control is difficult, since infestations often go unnoticed until symptoms are severe. There are no chemical (nematicide or fumigant) control alternatives for landscape garden beds; these products are highly toxic, and it is illegal to use them in residential areas. The best control is to avoid the problem by purchasing healthy, vigorous plants and providing good horticultural conditions that meet the plants' needs. Some plant cultivars are less susceptible to nematodes and should be used if nematodes, particularly root-knot nematodes, are established in a landscape. Dwarf yaupon and inkberry hollies (*Ilex vomitoria* and *Ilex glabra*, respectively) can be used as a replacement for the very root-knot-nematode-susceptible boxwood or Japanese holly (*I. crenata*).

When to Suspect Nematodes. Aboveground (secondary) symptoms of nematode infestation include:

- Premature wilting or other evidence of unusual sensitivity to heat or moisture stress.
- Stunting or abnormally slow growth.
- Chlorosis (yellowing) of leaves.
- Premature loss of leaves (older first) and fruit, especially during periods of stress.
- Thinning out of turf and its failure to compete with weeds.
- Irregular shape and distribution of the affected areas (that is, not all plants are equally affected).

The belowground (primary) symptoms of nematode infestations are:

- Galls or "knots" anywhere along a root.
- Abbreviated roots, often with swollen tips or lateral root proliferation near the tips.
- Dark-colored roots.
- Very small, round bodies produced by cyst nematodes and attached to the roots, ranging in color from white to yellowish or golden to brown, about the size of a period on this page, and possibly visible to a careful observer (especially with the help of a hand lens or low-power microscope).
- General stunting of roots which otherwise appear normal.

Viruses. Some viruses have a wide range of hosts, whereas others may only infect one or two species. Some of the more common viruses in ornamentals are tobacco mosaic virus (TMV), tomato spotted wilt virus (TSWV), impatiens necrotic spot virus (INSV), and cucumber mosaic virus (CMV). Symptoms of virus infection are easy to distinguish from other biotic diseases but are often confused with abiotic disorders such as herbicide injury or nutrient imbalance. Typical foliar symptoms include mosaic, mottle, or ring spot patterns on the leaf, where bright yellow or white areas within the leaf are bordered by darker-than-normal green areas. Leaf and stem distortions, such as cupping and twisting of leaves and thickening of leaf veins, are also common symptoms of virus infection that can be confused with 2,4-D or other growth-regulating herbicide damage.

Once a plant is infected with a virus, any new plants vegetatively propagated from it carry the same virus. Additionally, a virus-infected plant in a garden is the source of inoculum for future spread of the virus by insect vectors. Removing infected plants and controlling insect pests are the only ways to control the spread of viral pathogens.

Controlling Disease

Cultural Disease Control

The first step to controlling diseases in ornamental plants is to prevent the disease from developing. Prevention is key. Purchase only healthy plants from reputable dealers, practice the good horticultural methods discussed elsewhere in this manual, and avoid environmental conditions that foster the development of disease.

Pathogens like bacteria and fungi favor wet leaves and high humidity. Reduce the amount of time water is present on leaf surfaces by avoiding overhead sprinkler irrigation and directing water to the base of the plant. Watering in the early morning allows plant surfaces to dry quickly and reduces the likelihood of plants having wet leaves in the evening or overnight. Reduce humidity by increasing air circulation around plants through increased plant spacing, thinning of overgrown areas, and trellising; selectively pruning lower branches to allow air circulation within the plant canopy can greatly reduce leaf spot diseases.

Improve soil drainage by installing French drains (tiling) or incorporating organic material to reduce the risk of developing root and crown rots and nematode problems. Avoid replanting in areas where these diseases have been a problem. Redesigning the garden and replanting these areas with grass may reduce disease and alleviate frustration on the part of the homeowner.

Rotating plants—such as different flowering annuals—from year to year can reduce the buildup of host-specific pathogens. Use resistant plant varieties when possible; some plants are bred to be resistant to powdery mildew, rust, and viruses. Reduce fire blight by planting resistant crabapple and pear varieties. Control insects and weeds; insects are vectors for many diseases, and weeds can be infected by the same pathogens that ornamentals can and serve as a reservoir of inoculum for future infections.

Good care of ornamental plants prevents many growth difficulties. Remember that perennials (vines, shrubs, and trees) live for many years, and their susceptibility to disease is influenced by climatic and environmental conditions, both past and present. Improper management; abuse from lawnmowers, compaction, or construction injury; and lack of appropriate watering and fertilization are the most important factors that contribute to plant decline and disease development. Many problems can be traced back to earlier abuses, such as improper site location and preparation, planting too deep (plants should be planted no deeper than what they are growing in the root ball or container), or natural or man-made wounds to the stem or roots.

Sanitation

Sanitation is another key component in disease control. Prompt removal and destruction of infected plant material—either infected leaves and roots or whole plants—reduces the spread of disease. Collection and removal of fallen leaf litter in the fall also reduces disease potential for the following year. DO not compost severely infected material at home unless the compost pile reaches temperatures in excess of 140°F and maintains these temperatures for 3 weeks.

Prune out dead or cankered branches. Make cuts at least 3-4 in. below the extent of the canker into healthy tissue for fungal cankers and at least 8 in. below the canker for bacterial cankers like fire blight. Disinfest pruning tools between each cut by dipping the tool in 70% rubbing alcohol, dipping the tool in a solution of 1 part household bleach to 9 parts water for 10 seconds, or spraying liberally with Lysol® disinfectant spray. Immediately wash metal tools after use when using bleach, as it can damage and discolor the tools.

When propagating or dividing plant material, take cuttings from healthy, noninfected plants. Cut and remove any diseased or discolored portions. Inspect tubers, corms, rhizomes, and bulbs for signs of infection before planting or storing. Discard rotted and diseased corms and bulbs. Rotted sections of rhizomes and tubers can be cut away, and wounded areas should be treated with a fungicide dust. Store bulbs, tubers, corms, and rhizomes in a cool, dry place.

Always use fresh potting mixes when repotting plants. Never reuse old mixes, since they may be contaminated by soil pathogens. Packaged, soilless potting mixes cause the least amount of disease problems. Natural soils contain numerous fungi and bacteria that, under the right environmental conditions, initiate disease. Wash or spray all old pots, flats, and other supplies to remove soil and disinfest with a bleach solution (1 part bleach in 9 parts water) before reuse. Change the solution every 30 min if disinfesting many pots, because the chlorine in the bleach volatilizes and the solution loses its effectiveness over time.

Chemical Disease Control

Prevention and sanitation are the most practical approaches against disease. Chemicals are not available for controlling most bacterial, nematode, viral, and phytoplasma diseases. Fungicides for controlling fungal pathogens are the most widely available chemicals, but note that several fungicides marketed to control rose diseases should not be used on other plants. Copper-containing fungicides (copper hydroxide, copper sulfate or Bordeaux mixture) have some activity against bacterial pathogens. In some cases, fungicide application may be worthwhile; but for the home gardener, generally the cost of application exceeds the plant's value. If you use fungicides or any other pesticide, be sure to read and follow the pesticide label precisely. Do not apply more chemical than recommended. Over-application of some chemicals can injure or kill plants. Visit the Home & Garden Information Center website for chemical disease control recommendations.

Diseases of Woody Ornamentals

Ornamental plants in the landscape are subject to many diseases and disorders. Five groups of pathogens cause disease: fungi, bacteria, nematodes, viruses, and phytoplasmas. By far, fungi cause the greatest number of diseases in ornamental plants, and most disease control practices or products are directed at controlling fungi.

Three main components must be present for a disease to occur:

- Susceptible plant (host)
- Pathogen
- Environment favoring disease development

Disease control relies on breaking this disease triangle in some way. Removing the plant is not always possible or desirable. Choosing and growing disease-resistant varieties or not stressing non-disease-resistant varieties can greatly reduce the occurrence of disease and the need to use pesticides. The levels of the pathogen can be reduced by removing infected plant parts that could spread the disease. Changing the environment—such as watering less, protecting plants from extended periods of wetness, and increasing air circulation around plants—can reduce disease.

Disease management relies on an integrated use of cultural and chemical controls. Relying on chemicals alone to control disease is not be sufficient. In this section, we provide a list of diseases commonly found on numerous plants, descriptions of their symptoms, and control practices (including both cultural and chemical suggestions). The fungicides listed are provided for reference only, and it is up to the user of the product to read and follow all label directions for use on a particular plant. Seasonal occurrence information is based on "average" years for USDA Zone 7 and may need to be adjusted forward or backward for use in other hardiness zones.

Table 14.5 provides general information on diseases common to most plants and diseases specific to certain plants.

Submitting Samples to the Plant and Pest Diagnostic Clinic (PPDC)

The Clemson University Plant and Pest Diagnostic Clinic (PPDC) is a multi-disciplinary program that provides diagnoses and management recommendations for plant and turf problems including diseases, nematodes, weeds, environmental issues, nutritional deficiencies, and insect pests of plants. The PPDC also identifies insects infesting structures, humans, pets, and livestock.

As a South Carolina Master Gardener, you may need to assist a client in the submission of a sample. Sample submission guidelines and forms are located on the PPDC website.

TABLE 14.4 General Diseases Common to Many Plants

Disease	Symptom Description	Suggested Practices for Control
General Diseases		
A. Fungal leaf spots (Septoria, Cercospora, Alternaria)	Randomly distributed definitive spots on leaf surfaces. Spots have a tan to gray center with a darker border. Fungal fruiting structures seen in center of spot.	Promptly remove and discard leaves. Discard severely diseased plants. Keep leaf surfaces dry, especially at night.
B. Root and stem rot (Pythium, Thelaviopsis, Rhizoctonia, Phytophthora)	Plants wilt. Blackish discoloration of lower stems. Roots are soft and appear light to dark brown. Stems may pull easily from the crown.	Improve soil structure and drainage by incorporating compost, pine bark, or other organic material. Avoid setting transplants too deeply. Do not over-water or over-fertilize.
C. Vascular wilts (Fusarium, Verticillium)	Sudden wilting or slow stunting of plants. Vascular tissue is usually discolored (brown), which can be seen by cutting across the stem.	Follow proper sanitation practices. Use either sterile soil or soilless media. Avoid splashing water. Select resistant cultivars if possible.
D. Powdery Mildew	White to gray powdery patches on leaves, flowers, and new growth.	Lower humidity by increasing air circulation around plants. Increase spacing.
E. Botrytis blight or "gray mold" of leaves, stems, and flowers	Dark, water-soaked blight of leaves, petioles, and flowers. Gray to buff colored powdery fungal growth may occur on diseased tissue.	Remove and destroy dead plant parts promptly. Increase air circulation. Keep foliage dry, especially at night. Fungicides are generally unnecessary.

TABLE 14.4 Continued

Disease	Symptom Description	Suggested Practices for Control
Specific Hosts and Diseases		
African Violet – See A, B, D, and E in General Diseases		
Ring spot (Physiological)	White, yellow, or brown rings on leaves.	Use tepid water when watering. Avoid wetting leaves.
Amaryllis – See B in General Diseases		
Red blotch or Stagnospora leaf spot (fungus)	Red, sunken spots develop on leaves, often in a bullseye (zonate) pattern and especially in the spring.	Remove affected leaves. Keep foliage as dry as possible, especially at night. Apply fungicides to protect new growth and reduce disease spread.
Begonia – See A, B, C, D, and E in General Diseases		
Bacterial leaf spot (Xanthomonas)	Small translucent spots enlarge and coalesce to form irregular brownish areas on leaves.	Remove infected leaves. Avoid wetting leaves when irrigating.
Foliar nematodes (Aphelenchoides)	Bronzing of upper leaf surface followed by death of tissue, often in wedge-shaped pattern.	Remove infested leaves. Keep foliage dry. Avoid overhead watering. Discard heavily infested plants.
Crysanthemum – See A, B, C, D, and E in General Diseases		
Ascochyta stem and ray blight	Flowers have brown, deformed petals, usually just on one side. Brown lesions on stem.	Apply fungicides on a regular schedule. Avoid wet leaves at night.
Coneflower (Echinacea) – See A, B, C, and D in General Diseases		
Aster Yellows (Phytoplasma)	Flower parts remain green and may develop additional flowers, leaves, or stems from floral parts.	Discard infected plants to reduce disease spread. Disease spread is slow via insect vector (leafhoppers). Do not propagate from infected plants.
Coreopsis – See B and D in General Diseases		
Downy mildew (water mold)	Lower leaves are purplish or yellow. Whitish fuzzy growth can be seen on underside of leaves during wet, humid, cool weather of spring and fall.	Do not purchase infected plants. Remove affected foliage and discard away from the garden. Keep foliage as dry as possible, especially at night. Avoid overhead watering.
Cyclamen – See A, B, and E in General Diseases		
Stunt (*Ramularia cyclaminicola*)	Stunted plants. Extreme dwarfing of flower stems. Blooms below leaves.	Discard infected plants.
Dahlia – See B, D, and E in General Diseases		
Mosaic virus	Mottled leaf color. Pale green bands of color along midribs. Veins are larger than ordinary, and plant may be stunted with many shortened lateral shoots.	Dig up and dispose of diseased plant. Plant only tubers from healthy plants. Control aphids with approved pesticides.
Ringspot virus	Scattered areas of yellow or light green tissue in leaves. Ring pattern develops.	Control thrips with approved pesticides.
Daylily (Hemorocallis) – See A, B, and E in General Diseases		
Rust (fungus)	Yellow, raised spots to streaks in leaves in the spring and fall. Bright orange spores erupt from pustules on the underside of the leaf.	Remove affected foliage (typically affects weakened foliage). Keep foliage as dry as possible. Avoid overhead watering.

continued

TABLE 14.4 Continued

Disease	Symptom Description	Suggested Practices for Control
Delphinium or Larkspur – See A, B, and D in General Diseases		
Black leaf spot (Pseudomonas)	Black irregular spots on upper leaf surface, stems, petioles, and flowers. Lower leaves infected first. Disease progresses upward until the entire stalk is killed.	Remove and destroy infected plants and old residue.
Bud and crown rot (*Erwinia carotovora*)	Rapid wilting of the whole plant. Plant dies. Softened tissues have strong, offensive odor.	Avoid planting in low, poorly drained sites. Avoid overhead watering.
Foliage House Plants – See A, B, C, D, and E in General Diseases		
Oedema (physiological)	Leaf cells swell, burst, and become scab-like on the underside of the leaf.	Too much water and high fertility cause this problem. Reduce humidity, watering, and fertilizer.
Foliar nematode	Tan and black wedge-shaped lesions bordered by leaf veins develop on infected leaves.	Promptly remove and discard affected leaves. Keep foliage as dry as possible.
Soft rot (bacteria: Erwinia)	Tissue is soft, water-soaked, mushy, and may have a foul odor.	Discard plants. Avoid splashing water. Keep stems and foliage dry. Use clean potting mix.
Root knot nematode	Roots are galled. Plants are stunted and often show nutrient deficiencies.	Discard plants.
Geranium – See A, B, C, D, and E in General Diseases		
Oedema (physiological)	Same as foliage house plants above. Too much water and high fertility cause this problem.	Reduce humidity, watering, and fertilizer.
Rust	Brown to rust-colored powdery pustules appear on underside of leaf in clusters or bullseye patterns. May be on stems or petals.	Remove and discard infected leaves. Spray with fungicides at weekly intervals until rust spots are no longer evident.
Gladiolus – See E in General Diseases		
Corm rots (fungi)	Brown, sunken lesions on the corms. Leaf spots or rotted stems may develop later.	Avoid injury when digging. Store at 35-40°F in a dry location. Treat corm with fungicide prior to planting.
Cucumber mosaic virus (CMV)	Mottling of leaves. Whitish streaks and color break in flowers.	Destroy diseased plants. Control insects, especially aphids.
Rust	Small, brown pustules on leaf underside. Bright yellow or orange spots with reddish centers on upper surface.	Remove affected foliage and discard. Spray new growth with a protective fungicide.
Bacterial leaf spot (Xanthomonas)	Brown to black angular spots with yellow margins on lower section of leaves.	Remove and destroy infected foliage. Keep foliage dry. Avoid overhead watering.
Gloxinia – See A, B, C, D, and E in General Diseases		
Bud rot (*Botrytis cinerea*)	Buds brown to black, fail to open. Gray fungal growth may be present.	Provide good air circulation and low humidity. Remove dead buds and leaves promptly.
Crown rot (Pythium, Rhizoctonia, and Phytophthora)	Leaves, petioles, and roots blackened and water soaked.	Avoid use of natural soil in pots. Use soilless potting mixes. Fungicide drenches after proper diagnosis.
Ring spot		See African violets above

TABLE 14.4 Continued

Disease	Symptom Description	Suggested Practices for Control
Hosta – See A, B, and E in General Diseases		
Anthracnose (fungus)	Large, irregularly shaped tan spots with brown borders. Leaves may appear yellow to tan in color. Leaf edges are tattered.	Keep foliage dry.
Sun scorch (physiological)	Leaf margins are brown or yellow, associated with dieback of plants.	Avoid direct, full sun exposure. Provide adequate water during dry periods.
Foliar nematode	Yellow to tan lesions bordered by the veins. Looks like tan streaks on the leaf.	Remove affected foliage and discard away from the garden.
Crown and stem rot (fungus: Sclerotium rolfsii)	Petioles wilt and collapse in mid-summer. Petioles pull easily from the crown. White fungal threads (hyphae) visible on the rotting petiole end. Mustard-seed-sized tan, round, hard sclerotia (survival structures visible on tissues and in soil surrounding affected plant.	Dig and remove infected plants. Discard immediately away from garden. Turn at least top 8 in. of soil to bury sclerotia and reduce disease development in the same area. Don't purchase infected plants.
Impatiens – See A, B, D, and E in General Diseases		
Impatiens necrotic spot virus (INSV)	Black to tan colored ring spots in bullseye pattern on leaf surface. Can cause color breaks, distortion, and leaf puckering on New Guinea impatiens.	Discard severely infected plants.
Crown rot (Rhizoctonia)	Causes collapse of entire plant. Lower stem and crown tissue discolored. Stem lesions.	Remove infected plans and soil around them. Fungus may survive in the soil for many years.
Bacterial leaf spot (Pseudomonas)	Discrete, small, tan circular spots on leaves with purple margins.	Remove and destroy infected leaves. Keep foliage dry. Avoid overhead watering.
Iris – See A, B, and E in General Diseases		
Crown rot (fungus: Sclerotium rolfsii)	Tips of outer leaves die, moving downward until entire leaf is dead. As rot progresses, leaves collapse inward at the base of the plant. White fungal growth (later brown) is visible between leaves near soil line. Rhizomes are not destroyed but weakened. Light tan to brown bodies, the size of a mustard seed, may be found on rhizomes.	Do not overcrowd plants. Thin and discard infected plants. Turn soil at least 8 in. to bury sclerotia (survival structures) and reduce disease in the same location. Fungus is capable of surviving in the location for 7 years in the absence of a host plant.
Leaf spot (Didymellina)	Small brown leaf spots surrounded by water-soaked margins. The spots enlarge, killing the entire leaf. Center of older spots turn gray, dotted with small black spore clusters.	Cut off old leaves at the soil line in the fall and discard. Spray with a fungicide in the spring to protect new growth. Keep foliage as dry as possible.
Soft rot (Erwinia carotovora)	Leaves wilt slightly at first, later becoming limp and dying. Rhizome shows a soft, slimy rot and later turns dry and granular, finally decaying entirely. Often associated with wounds or injuries caused by insects, freezing, or plant division.	Do not overcrowd plants. Dig out infected rhizomes and cut out rotted areas.
Rust	Reddish-brown rust pustules generally appear on lower leaf surface.	Plant resistant varieties. Thin to improve air circulation. Avoid wetting foliage. Spray with preventive fungicide.

continued

TABLE 14.4 Continued

Disease	Symptom Description	Suggested Practices for Control
Lily – See A in General Diseases		
Botrytis blight or fire blight	Orange to red leaf spots. Brown spots on flowers.	See E in General Diseases
Root and Bulb rots	Soft, brown decay of roots and bulb scales. Plants stunted.	Discard severely affected bulbs.
Marigold – See A, B, C, D, and E in General Diseases		
Aster yellows (phytoplasma)	Infected plants develop distorted witches' broom growth. Leaf color yellows. Abnormal flower color and growth.	Remove and destroy infected plants.
Pachysandra – See A and B in General Diseases		
Leaf and stem blight (fungus: Volutella)	Circular brown blotches on leaves that progress to blight. The rest of the leaf turns yellow. A brown stem rot with orange-brown spore pustules is visible.	Remove diseased plants. Improve air circulation by thinning plants. Apply protective fungicide.
Dieback	Terminal buds and leaves turn brown, roll up, and droop. Cankers found on small branches.	Prune out infected twigs.
Pansy – See A, B, D, and E in General Diseases		
Downy mildew (water mold)	Grayish growth on leaf undersides. Upper leaf surface discolored (yellow).	Keep foliage dry. Increase air circulation. Remove infected plants or plant parts.
Peony – See B and E in General Diseases		
Leaf blotch	Glossy, dark purple spots on top of leaf. Dull brown color below. Problem during moist weather.	Spray with fungicide. Destroy old, infected foliage at the end of the season.
Phytophthora blight	Blossoms and succulent growing tips are blighted and become dark brown to black and somewhat leathery. Usually more severe in wet springs or where plants are shaded or crowded. May invade crown, causing root rot.	Remove and destroy all infected parts as soon as they are detected. Cut off tops at the ground line in the fall and burn. Spray foliage with a fungicide. Remove infected plants and soil. Improve drainage of planting site and plant in mounds.
Petunia – See A and E in General Diseases		
Impatiens necrotic spot virus (INSV)	Circular black spots. May be in a ring pattern on lower leaves.	Remove and destroy infected plants. Control insects, especially thrips.
Poinsettia – See A, B, and D in General Diseases		
Bract and leaf spots (fungus: Corynespora)	Brown spots on leaves and bracts.	Keep foliage dry. Remove and destroy infected tissue.
Root and stem rots	Plants wilt. Blackish-brown discoloration of lower stem. Roots rot.	Improve soil structure and drainage. Avoid setting transplants too deep.
Rudbeckia – See A, B, and D in General Diseases		
Foliar nematode	Purplish angular leaf spots, often concentrated along the veins.	Promptly remove and discard affected leaves away from the garden.
Downy mildew (water mold: Plasmopora)	Purplish discoloration acrossleaf. Grayish to white fuzzy growth on leaf underside in humid, wet, cool weather.	Do not purchase infected plants. Remove infected tissue. Keep foliage dry, especially at night. Avoid overhead watering.

TABLE 14.4 Continued

Disease	Symptom Description	Suggested Practices for Control
Salvia – See A, B, and D in General Diseases		
Downy mildew (water mold)	Angular purple to black spots develop on leaves during cool, humid, wet weather.	Do not purchase infected plants. Remove and discard affected foliage and/or plants. Avoid overhead watering and keep foliage as dry as possible.
Snapdragon – See A, B, and C in General Diseases		
Downy mildew (water mold)	Grayish patches appear on lower leaf surface. Upper leaf surface has yellowish discolored patches.	Remove infected tissues. Keep foliage dry, especially at night. Avoid overhead watering.
Rust (fungus)	Yellow blotches appear on upper leaf surface. Dark brown, dusty pustules on leaf undersides.	Remove infected tissue. Keep foliage dry. Improve air circulation. Apply protective fungicide spray.
Impatiens necrotic spot virus (INSV)	Round tan necrotic ring spots on leaves in bullseye pattern.	Remove and destroy infected plants. Control insects, especially thrips.
Tulip – See A in General Diseases		
Botrytis blight or fire blight	Black, pin-head-sized sclerotia on brown bulb husks. Yellow to brown lesions on bulb. Small, yellowish water-soaked spots on leaves. These may enlarge, turn gray, and become covered with gray mold. White to light brown spots on some blossoms. Others may blight before or after emergence.	Remove outer husks. Sort bulbs carefully and discard diseased ones before planting. Remove infected plants soon after they come up. Remove and destroy all plant debris after blooming. If bulbs are to remain in the soil, cut yellowed tops below ground and burn them. Dust bulbs with fungicide prior to storage or planting. Practice sanitation.
Verbena – See A, B, and D in General Diseases		
Powdery mildew (fungus)	The most common disease on verbena. Whitish growth occurs on leaves, stems, and flowers. Leaves may have a purplish appearance.	Remove affected foliage from the plants. Increase air circulation by thinning foliage.
Veronica (Speedwell) – See B and D in General Diseases		
Downy mildew (water mold)	Angular yellow to purplish lesions develop during cool, wet, humid weather. Entire leaves may turn purple. Disease can become systemic, causing whole plants to be distorted or stunted with abnormally small new growth in the spring.	Do not purchase infected plants. Remove infected foliage and/or plants if the disease has become systemic. Keep foliage as dry as possible. Avoid overhead irrigation.
Foliar nematode	Angular purplish to black spots develop on leaves, especially along veins. Spot color shades range from very light to very dark on leaf underside.	Remove infected leaves and discard away from the garden. Keep foliage as dry as possible. Avoid overhead watering.
Vinca (Catharanthus) – See A, B, and D in General Diseases		
Phytophthora aerial blight (fungus)	Stems brown or blacken, wilt, and collapse. Typically occurs mid-summer.	Remove infected plants. Avoid over-watering and overhead irrigation. Do not replant for one year.

TABLE 14.4 Continued

Disease	Symptom Description	Suggested Practices for Control
Zinnia – See A, B, and E in General Diseases		
Bacterial leaf spot (Xanthomonas)	Angular to irregularly circular brown spots are produced on leaves. Spots are surrounded by a prominent yellow halo.	Avoid water splash. Change seed source. Treat seed with a 1:5 dilute solution of household bleach for 10 mins.
Aster yellows (phytoplasma)	Flowers are greenish and distorted, with excessive petal formation. Witches' broom growth habit.	Remove and destroy infected plants.

TABLE 14.5 Common Diseases of Woody Ornamentals

Disease	Seasonal Occurrence	Symptoms	Management Options
Arborvitae (Thuja)			
Bot canker (*Botryosphaeria obtusa, B. dothiodea*)	March-October	Poor growth on some branches. Always associated with a wound on a plant from pruning, mechanical damage, freeze cracks, etc. or natural openings (lenticels) following a stress event such as drought. Wounds sometimes ooze sap, a possible indicator of canker development. Foliage above canker dies. Black, pimple-like fruiting bodies develop on branches.	Prune infected branches at least 4-6 in. below the infected tissue. Avoid plant stress and promote healthy plant growth. Avoid wounding plants. No fungicides are effective once this occurs. A protective fungicide application at the time of injury can reduce possible infection.
Ash			
Anthracnose (*Apiognomonia errabunda,* syn. *Discula sp.*)	April-June, peak in May	Irregularly shaped light-colored spots, often with a dark border or chlorotic halo. Spots concentrated along leaf margins and veins. Blotching and distortion of young leaves and shoots. Excess defoliation can occur. Cool, wet weather fosters infection.	Fungus survives on infected leaves and in dead twigs and branches. Collect and remove fallen leaf litter before new growth appears in the spring. Fungicide application is rarely warranted on large landscape trees; if used, apply to completely cover tree beginning at bud break and continuing through cool, wet weather.
Azalea and Rhododendron			
Leaf gall (*Exobasidium vaccinii*)	April-June, peak in May	Leaves become distorted with pale green, thickened, flesh-like galls. As galls mature, they turn white, then brown, dry, and fall to the ground. Spores are released while the gall is white. Disease only affects new growth. Older leaves are resistant to infection. The pathogen favors cool, moist spring weather. Under dry conditions and sunny location, this disease is seldom seen.	Pick off or prune affected leaves from the plant before they turn white. Applications of fungicides once galls are present have no effect on controlling the disease. Applying fungicides before and as the leaf buds open and expand in early spring can reduce infection, but timing is critical, and sprays aren't usually necessary.

TABLE 14.5 Continued

Disease	Seasonal Occurrence	Symptoms	Management Options
Petal blight (*Ovulinia azaleae*)	March-May, peak in April	Mostly a problem on azalea. Tiny, round pale spots that rapidly enlarge to irregular blotches appear on infected flowers. Flowers quickly turn brown, limp, and mushy. Under humid conditions, affected flowers are covered in a white mold growth. Affected blooms hang on plants for weeks or months. Hard, black survival and fruiting bodies (sclerotia) are produced on affected blooms. Blossoms eventually drop from the plant.	Rake and remove flower debris from underneath bushes. Remove old flowers from plants. Mulch around base of plants. Fungicides can be applied to the base of plants to prevent sporulation from sclerotia, but this is only marginally effective. On large azalea plantings, apply fungicide just before bloom and repeat weekly or more frequently during the entire bloom period.
Phomopsis canker and dieback (*Phomopsis spp.*)	April-October, peak in July-August	Mostly a problem on Southern Indica type azaleas. Death of leaves and stems. Reddish-brown discoloration of wood on diseased stems. Enters plants through wounds, especially pruning wounds. Stressed plants are most susceptible.	Prune out wounded/damaged branches. Prevent moisture stress and stem splitting from cold. Mulch plants.
Web blight (*Rhizoctonia solani*)	May-September, peak in July-August	Symptoms develop rapidly under humid, wet conditions. Small necrotic leaf spots rapidly enlarge, become dark brown to black, and advance along the leaf margin and midrib. Affected leaves abscise but remain attached to the plant due to the fungus. Leaves are matter or clumped together. In the fall, infected leaves drop as the fungus dies and plants look defoliated.	Crowded, close-growing azaleas are most susceptible (e.g. 'Gumpo' azaleas). Avoid prolonged plant wetness. Do not water late in the day. Increase plant spacing to prevent plant-to-plant infection. Apply protective fungicide beginning in mid-June when temperatures warm to 80°F.
Phytophthora dieback (*Phytophthora cactorum, P. nicotianae var. parasitica, P. citricola*)	June-September, peak in July-August	Brown, irregularly shaped lesions on leaf margins that progress along midrib through the petiole to the stem. Brown discoloration extending up and down the stem. Infection only on current season's growth, but slowly moves through the plant.	Avoid prolonged plant wetness. Do not water late in the day or evening. Prune affected shoots. Excess shade and nitrogen fertilization increase susceptibility. Susceptibility varies from cultivar to cultivar. Fungicides can reduce disease incidence.

continued

TABLE 14.5 Continued

Disease	Seasonal Occurrence	Symptoms	Management Options
Botryosphaeria dieback (*Botryosphaeria dothidea, B. ribis*)	April–October	Mostly affects rhododendron. Leaves on affected stem droop and roll inward. Reddish-black sunken canker girdles affected stem. Infection develops at pruning wounds, leaf scars, and flower cluster attachment.	Prune stems below the cankered, discolored area. Disinfect pruning tools. Avoid drought stress or freeze injury which predisposes plants to infection. No resistant cultivars or fungicide treatments are known.
Birch			
Anthracnose (*Discula betulina*, syn. *Gleosporium botulinum*)	May–September, peak June–July	Large tan spots or blotches with brown to dark black margins and yellow halos. Affected leaves fall prematurely, often when much of the leaf is still green.	Collect and remove fallen leaf litter before new growth appears in spring. If small or newly transplanted tree, apply fungicide spray when leaves begin expansion and repeat twice, 10–14 days apart.
Cylindrosporium leaf spot (*Cylindrosporium betulae*)	June–October, peak in August–September	Small tan, brown, or purple spots with no definite margin.	Collect and remove fallen leaf litter before new growth appears in the spring. Fungicides are not usually necessary. Disease is worse in wet weather.
Boxwood			
Volutella blight (*Volutella buxi*)	June–October, peak August–September	Pinkish sporulation on leaves and twigs, especially dead or dying tissues. Discoloration and death of current year's growth.	Prune affected stems below diseased tissue; heavy pruning of plants promotes infection. Dieback of branches is often due to root rot or other factors that affect good root growth (poor soils, compaction, over-watering, poor nutrition, etc.).
Root-knot nematode (*Meloidogyne spp.*)	March–November	Chlorosis and bronzing of foliage. Reduced leaf size and eventual defoliation. Root galling and decay. Plants are stunted and slowly decline, often one branch at a time.	Improve drainage. Promote good plant growth through proper horticultural practices. No post-plant chemical treatment is available.
Camellia			
Canker and stem dieback (*Glomerella cinulata*)	April–September, peak in May–July	Sudden wilting of leaves. Leaves turn brown and remain attached to young twigs. Elliptical and sunken cankers form on infected branches. The bark and wood of infected branches turns brown. Pinkish orange spore masses may be seen around the cankers during extended periods of wet weather.	Prune infected branches 4 in. below the infected area into healthy tissue and discard diseased branches. Disinfect pruning tools in 10% bleach solution or wipe blades with rubbing alcohol between cuts. Fungicides provide limited control but can be applied to pruning wounds and cuts.

TABLE 14.5 Continued

Disease	Seasonal Occurrence	Symptoms	Management Options
Leaf gall (*Exobasidium camelliae*)	April-June, peak in May	New expanding leaves are larger, thickened, and pinkish-green in color on the upper surface; underside eventually turns white when the fungus releases spores. Infected leaves dry and turn brown to black in late spring. Infection is most severe in cool, moist weather as the leaves expand in the spring.	Remove and destroy diseased leaves as they appear in early spring, before the lower leaf surface turns white. This reduces the inoculum source for next year's infection. Do not leave infected leaves or branches on the ground after pruning, as spores can still release from infected clippings. Fungicide applications are seldom necessary and only provide limited control. Applications must be made as the leaf buds swell in the spring. Spraying after seeing the galls has no effect on this or next year's infection.
Petal blight (*Ciborinia camelliae*, syn. *Sclerotinia camelliae*)	February-April, peak in March	Small brown, irregularly shaped spots appear on expanding petals. Spots rapidly enlarge toward the center of the flower until the entire flower is dead and brown. Venation is pronounced, giving flower a netted appearance in early stages of disease development. This distinguishes petal blight from frost or wind injury. Blighted flowers drop and the fungus produces dark, hard, survival structures (sclerotia) within the tissue, which then releases spores and infect flowers the following year.	Remove and destroy infected flowers as they appear. Rake and remove fallen blossoms and other plant debris underneath bushes. Apply a fungicide prior to flowers blooming, both to the soil beneath the plants and in an area 10 ft beyond each bush.
Algal leaf spot (*Cephaleuros virescens*)	April-November, peak in July-August	Velvety green, brown, or reddish spots develop on the upper leaf surface under wet conditions. Older infections become greenish-gray and lichen-like in appearance.	Doesn't usually harm plant. Fungicides can reduce incidence.
Yellow mottle or ring spot virus	April-September	Irregular yellow or white spots (mottling) or ring spots appear on infected leaves. This is often seen on older, winter-injured leaves. Affected leaves may drop, but plants are rarely killed.	There is no control for viral diseases except for removal of the affected plant. Pruning and removing symptomatic branches does not control viruses.
Oedema (physiological)	November-June	Tannish-brown corky or scabby appearance to leaves.	No control is necessary. The problem develops in high humidity, cloudy weather, poor drainage, and excess moisture.

continued

TABLE 14.5 Continued

Disease	Seasonal Occurrence	Symptoms	Management Options
Cherry (Flowering)			
Black knot (*Plowrightia morbusa*)	January-December	Hard, dark brown to black swellings form on twigs and branches. At first, galls are small, but they enlarge each year. In spring, galls are covered with dark olive-green felt-like growth. Galls may girdle and kill branches. Affects numerous Prunus species.	Prune and destroy galls, cutting several inches below the gall during plant dormancy. Usually not necessary to apply fungicides.
Crabapple (Flowering)			
Fire blight (*Erwinia amylovora*)	April-June, peak May-June	Young twigs and branches die from the terminal end and appear burned or deep rust colored. Branch may be bent, resembling shepherd's crook. Dead leaves and fruit generally remain on the branch. Infection occurs during blooming and favors wet conditions.	Prune out branches 6 in. below damage. Disinfect pruning tools in 70% isopropyl alcohol (rubbing alcohol) or 10% bleach solution between cuts. Avoid heavy nitrogen fertilization, especially in summer. Avoid splashing water. Plant resistant varieties.
Apple scab (*Venturia inaequalis*)	April-October, peak April-June	Dull, olive-green, velvety fungal growth develops on upper leaf surface in spring. Leaves yellow and fall prematurely. Trees bare by mid-season. Infected fruit have circular rough spots on surface. Infection favors cooler temperatures and prolonged leaf wetness.	Plant resistant cultivars. Rake and remove fallen leaves and fruit. Beginning at bud break, apply fungicides at 7-10-day intervals. Make 5-8 applications through early to mid-June.
Cedar-apple rust (*Gymnosporangium juniperi-virginiae*)	May-August, peak in July	Bright yellow-orange spots form on leaves. On upper surface of spot, small, dark fungal fruiting structures form. Later, on underside of infected leaves, clusters of cap shaped structures with fringed edges are visible.	Remove unwanted junipers/cedars from the area. Remove galls from junipers during dormancy. If disease is frequent and severe, apply a fungicide when crabapple flower bud tissue can be seen and again at petal fall.
Crape Myrtle			
Powdery mildew (*Erysiphe lagerstroemiae*)	May-October, peak in June-July	White powdery spots appear on leaves, stems, and flowers. May cause distortion of new growth and suckers.	Plant resistant varieties. Prune infected sprouts and new growth from plant. Apply fungicides at first sign of disease if plants are small.

TABLE 14.5 Continued

Disease	Seasonal Occurrence	Symptoms	Management Options
Dogwood			
Spot anthracnose (*Elsinoe cornii*)	March-September, peak in May	Small reddish spots first appear on flower bracts. Reddish spots on leaves distorted from infection in bud stage. May cause leaves to drop.	Rake and remove fallen leaves. Disease does not cause significant damage to the tree. Fungicides applied at swollen bud state for flowers and leaves can reduce infection, but are only recommended for young, newly transplanted trees. Kousa variety is moderately resistant.
Dogwood anthracnose (*Discula destructiva*)	March-September, peak in June	Medium to large, purple-bordered leaf spots develop into large, scorched, tan blotches that enlarge and may kill the entire leaf. Infected leaves cling to stems after normal leaf drop in fall. Symptoms start in the lower crown and progress up the tree. Numerous shoots form along the main stem and on major branches. The shoots frequently become infected and die. Cankers form on main trunk at junction of dead twig or shoot. Trees may die within 2-3 years following infection. Disease is less severe on trees planted in open, sunny sites.	Prune and destroy any dead wood from tree before it reaches the main trunk. Avoid plant stress. Remove severely infected trees and fallen leaf litter and destroy them. Fungicides are often ineffective. In some cases, they may provide some control if applied as buds break in the spring and at least twice thereafter as leaves expand.
Septoria and Cercospora leaf spots (*Septoria cornicola, Cercospora cornicola*)	June-October, peak August-September	Uniform, medium purplish spots on leaves. Spots may be angular. Centers of spots turn gray but retain deep purple border. May cause leaf drop. Mostly seen in late summer/early fall prior to leaf drop.	Chemical control not usually recommended. Disease causes little damage to the tree. Stressed trees more susceptible to the disease. Avoid plant stress.
Algae/lichen	January-December	Greenish-gray spots or crusty to feathery growths on stems and branches. Not a disease—indicates slow growth which may indicate the tree is stressed.	No control is necessary for algae/lichen. If tree is stressed, improve conditions causing stress.

continued

TABLE 14.5 Continued

Disease	Seasonal Occurrence	Symptoms	Management Options
Euonymus			
Powdery mildew (*Microsphaera euonymi-japonici*)	May-October, peak in May-June	Small patches of white-to-gray powdery growth on leaves and stems. Mostly seen on new growth. Infection favors high humidity, poor air circulation, and cool night temperatures. Most common in early summer and late to early fall.	Remove affected stems or leaves from the plant. Improve air circulation around plants by increasing plant spacing or thinning branches. Apply a fungicide at the first sign of infection. Do not wait until the entire leaf is covered with mildew. Repeat 10-14 days later.
Crown gall (*Agrobacterium tumefaciens*)	March-October	Roots and base of stems infected with golf-ball-sized, knobby galls. Secondary galls sometimes visible on branches. Mostly introduced into the landscape through infected nursery stock. May spread via cutting tools. Infection favors wounded plants and wet conditions.	Destroy heavily infected plants. Prune out galls if few are present on some branches and lower stems. Disinfect pruning tools with 70% isopropyl (rubbing) alcohol or 10% bleach solution between cuts. *E. elatus* not susceptible to infection.
Gardenia			
Canker or galling (*Phomopsis gardeniae*, syn. *Diaporthe gardeniae*)	January-December, peak April-June	Perennial cankers or cankerous rough-surfaced galls that enlarge and girdle stems. Commonly found near the soil line. Diseased branches lose vigor and may wilt, drop leaves, and die back. Enters plants through wounds.	Prune affected branches from plant.
Algal leaf spot (*Cephaleuros viresens*)	April-November, peak July-August	Velvety green, brown, or reddish spots develop on the upper leaf surface and stems under wet conditions.	Doesn't usually harm the plant. Fungicides can reduce disease incidence.
Holly			
Web or thread blight (*Rhizoctonia solani*, *R. ramicola*)	March-September, peak in July-August	Very rapid development under humid, wet conditions. Small, necrotic leaf spots rapidly enlarge, become dark brown to black, and advance along leaf margin and midrib. Affected leaves abscise but remain attached to the plants, matted together due to the fungus.	Crowded, close-growing hollies are most susceptible (Compacta, Helleri, Dwarf Yaupon, etc.). Avoid prolonged plant wetness. Do not water late in the day. Increase plant spacing to prevent plant-to-plant infection. Apply protective fungicide mid-June when temperatures warm to about 80°F.
Sphaeropsis gall or knot (*Sphaeropsis tumafaciens*)	Uncertain	Affects American and dahoon hollies in the South. Young twigs swell, forming galls with witches' brooms of new, leafless shoots from galled tissue. Infects primary wounds and can spread on pruning tools.	Disinfect pruning tools between cuts. Prune affected branches 4-6 in. below galls.

TABLE 14.5 Continued

Disease	Seasonal Occurrence	Symptoms	Management Options
Black root rot (*Thielaviopsis basicola, Chalara elegans*)	January-December, peak in April-July	Chloritic, stunted foliage. Death of feeder roots. Black lesions visible on washed roots. Dieback of individual branches.	Remove affected plants. Improve soil drainage. Fungicide drenches marginally effective.
Anthracnose (*Glomerella cingulata*, syn. *Colletotrichum gloesporioides*)	March-November, peak in May-June	Irregular leaf spots. Scorching along leaf margin. Sunken stem cankers. Dieback of branches. Most serious on stressed or weaken plants.	Avoid prolonged plant wetness. Do not water late in the day. Avoid plant stress. Prune affected branches from plant if cankers are evident. Fungicides are of little benefit and need to be applied as the leaf buds swell and begin expansion. Repeat applications at 7-10-day intervals until leaf fully expands.
Spine spot (not a disease)	January-December	Small gray spots with purple halos caused by puncturing of leaves by spines of adjacent leaves or insects.	Prune plants to thin growth and prevent injury. Control insects.
Hydrangea			
Cercospora leaf spot (*Cercospora hydrangea*)	May-October	Randomly distributed leaf spots with a tan center and a dark purplish red border. Infection favors cooler temperatures and extended periods of leaf wetness, usually in late spring.	Avoid prolonged periods of leaf wetness. Remove heavily infected leaves. Remove leaf litter under plants. Apply fungicide sprays beginning in early spring as leaves emerge. Repeat applications every 10-14 days.
Bacterial leaf spot (*Xanthomonas campestris, Pseudomonas spp.*)	March-September, peak in April-June	Irregularly shaped spots bordered by leaf veins. May cause leave to pucker. Infection develops during extended periods of leaf wetness, poor air circulation, and warmer temperatures, usually in early summer.	Doesn't usually cause significant damage. Remove heavily infected leaves. Avoid wetting foliage when watering. Mulch under plants. Chemical control is usually ineffective.
Clitocybe root rot (*Armillaria tabescens*, syn. *Clitocybe tabescens*)	April-November, peak in August-October	Plants decline over time. Leaves scorch or wilt. Bark sloughs at trunk base at soil line. White, fungal mycelium visible under sloughing bark. Root rot is usually associated with older plants under root stress and poor site conditions (poor drainage, over-watering, etc.)	Remove affected plants; they will not recover. No fungicides are effective against this disease. Improve site conditions.
Indian Hawthorne (*Raphiolepsis spp.*)			
Entomosporium leaf spot (*Entomosporium mespili*, syn. *Fabraea maculata*)	January-December, peak in February-April and August-October	Small reddish spots on leaves. Older spots have a tannish center with a purple-red border. In some cultivars, defoliation can occur.	Plant resistant varieties. Fungicide application may reduce disease but must be reapplied at 10-14-day intervals from spring to late summer.

continued

TABLE 14.5 Continued

Disease	Seasonal Occurrence	Symptoms	Management Options
Ivy			
Anthracnose (*Colletotrichum trichellum*)	April–October, peak in August–September	Round, large, irregularly shaped tan to brown spots with numerous tiny, dark brown, pimple-like fungal fruiting structures within spots appear. Spots often have zonate appearance and may coalesce to cause leaf blight.	Remove infected plant material. Avoid splashing water and overhead irrigation. Keep foliage dry. Apply protective fungicide in early summer and reapply at 10-14-day intervals.
Bacterial leaf spot (*Xanthomonas campestris pv. hederae*)	April–October, peak in June	Leaf spots are brown to black with yellow halos. Spots look greasy when viewed from underneath. Spots may coalesce, causing extensive blighted areas. Leaf stems blacken and shrivel. Cankers may form in woody portion of vine.	Remove infected plant material. Avoid planting in areas that stress plants (full sun, poor soil conditions, excess water). Avoid splashing water and overhead irrigation. Keep foliage dry. Apply copper-based fungicides in warm, wet weather.
Juniper and Eastern Red Cedar (*Juniperus*)			
Tip blight (*Phomopsis juniperovora*)	April–September, peak in May	New branch tips turn brown and die. Older, mature growth is resistant to infection. Infections occur in late spring and early summer following growth flushes. Infected tissue turns gray and black fungal fruiting bodies are visible on the infected tips.	Prune affected branches when plants are dry. Remove clippings from the area. Avoid wetting plants late in the day or evening hours. Fungicide applications when new growth is present in spring or after pruning can reduce infection. Plant resistant or tolerant juniper varieties.
Cercosporidium needle blight (*Cercosporidium sequoinea var. juniperi*)	April–September, peak in June	Progressive browning and loss of foliage beginning on lower branches close to the stem and moving upward and outward until plant dies or only tufts of green shoots remain on topmost branches.	Avoid plant stress. Application of fungicides in early to mid-summer can help reduce disease. Remove severely affected plants.
Seridium canker (*Seridium unicome*)	February–December, peak in April–May	Yellowing and browning of old foliage precedes fading and death of twigs and branches. Long, sunken cankers develop at wounds or bark openings. Bark is darkened and resin exudes from the margins of cankers. Needles on affected branches fall off easily when rubbed with your hands.	Avoid plant stress and wounding. Irrigate during periods of drought to avoid drought injury. Fungicides are ineffective once infection takes place.

TABLE 14.5 Continued

Disease	Seasonal Occurrence	Symptoms	Management Options
Cedar-apple rust (*Gymnosporangium juniperi-virginianae*), Cedar-hawthorn rust (*Gymnosporangium globosum*)	March-May, peak in April-May	Hard, dark brown galls form in winter. In spring, galls exude reddish, jelly-like "tentacles" of spores (called telial horns) that infect apple and crabapple. Infects mostly eastern red cedars and horizontal junipers. Hawthorn rust is similar, causing short, blunt telial horns.	Doesn't usually harm junipers. Prune out galls when noticed, see control on crabapple if necessary.
Cedar-quince rust (*Gymnosporangium clavipes*)	March-May, peak in April-May	Young shoots are infected and devlop spindle-shaped swellings that encircle twigs and small branches. Bright orange pustules expand from diseased bark in early spring. Diseased twigs and branches often die.	Prune affected branches and twigs from cedar trees. Fungicides have limited effectiveness reducing rust on cedar. Apply fungicides to hawthorn, flowering quince, and pear when leaf buds swell and expand.
Leyland Cypress (x *Cupressocyparis leylandii*)			
Bot canker (*Botryosphaeria dothidea, B. obtusa, Sphaeropsis, Macrophoma*)	February-November, peak in April-May	Bright, rust-colored branches most often visible in spring and fall. Infection always associated with wound from pruning, mechanical damage, freeze cracks, etc., or natural openings (lenticels) following a stress event such as drought. A canker develops at the infection site and may ooze sap. Canker darkly discolors cambial tissues. All foliage above canker will die. Prune affected branches 6 in. below the infected tissue.	Avoid plant stress. Promote healthy plant growth. Avoid wounding plants. Avoid planting too close together. Planted on at least 8-ft centers. No fungicides are effective once infection has occurred. A protective fungicide application at the time of injury may reduce possible infection.
Passalora needle blight (*Passalora sequoiae*)	June-November, peak in August-September	Foliage in the lower one-third of tree thins from the inside outward and the bottom upward. Individual needles progress from yellow to brown to gray and eventually fall from the tree. Typically infects growth that is at least 1 year old, but new season's growth can be infected. Branches often look bare, with tufts of green growth at tips.	Avoid planting Leylands too close together to allow for air circulation around trees. Fungicides can help reduce infection and disease spread; begin applications in late spring and continue until the cooler, less humid months of fall. Keep foliage as dry as possible. Avoid overhead irrigation.

continued

TABLE 14.5 Continued

Disease	Seasonal Occurrence	Symptoms	Management Options
Seridium canker (*Seridium unicorne*)	February-November, peak in April-May	Yellowing and browning of old foliage precedes fading and death of twigs and branches. Long, sunken cankers with reddish tinge develop at wounds or bark openings. Bark is darkened and resin exudes from margins of cankers. Infection seems to occur from the lower branches up and from the inside out. Infected trees look thinly branched.	Avoid plant stress and wounding. Keep plants well irrigated during drought. If possible, prune affected branches 6 in. below the canker before the infection reaches the main stem. No fungicides are effective in controlling the disease once infection takes place.
Maple			
Tar spot (*Rhytisma acerinum*)	April-October, peak in June-July	Raised, black tar-like spots develop on the upper side of mature leaves in mid to late summer. Infected leaves may drop prematurely.	Rake and remove fallen leaves. Disease does not cause significant damage. No chemical control is recommended.
Phyllosticta leaf spot (*Phyllosticta minima*)	April-October, peak in May-June	Small, round, light-colored leaf spots with purple borders. Pycnidia (fungal fruiting bodies) form a circular pattern within the spots. Infected leaves may drop prematurely.	Control is often not necessary. Disease causes little damage to trees. Rake and remove fallen leaves.
Anthracnose (*Apiognomonia errabunda* or *Kabatiella apocrypta*)	April-October, peak in May-June	Necrotic, irregular, tannish to reddish-brown spots concentrated along leaf veins. Fungal fruiting bodies (acervuli) prominent on upper surface of spots. Scorching pattern along leaf margin (Japanese maples).	Control usually unnecessary except in wet years, when severe defoliation can occur. Apply fungicides as leaves swell and expand from the buds. Repeat applications every 7-10 days until leaves fully expand. Rake and remove fallen leaves.
Oak			
Oak leaf blister (*Taphrina caerulasence*)	May-June	Bulging, blister-like spots on leaves. May cause leaf distortion. Underside of leaves turn brown following spore production. Can be confused with eriophyid mite or midge damage. Affected leaves drop prematurely.	Disease seldom causes significant damage. Apply fungicide when leaf buds swell in the spring and reapply at 7-10-day intervals until the leaves fully expand to reduce disease.
Anthracnose (*Apiognomonia quercina*, syn. *Discula quercina*)	April-September, peak in May-June	Young leaves brown and shrivel. Large necrotic areas develop on expanding leaves. Infection of fully mature leaves develops small, necrotic spots. Twigs die back. Infected leaves drop prematurely.	Rake and remove fallen leaf litter. Fungicides may be beneficial to small, newly transplanted trees. Apply as buds swell in spring and reapply at 7-10-day intervals until leaves fully expand.

TABLE 14.5 Continued

Disease	Seasonal Occurrence	Symptoms	Management Options
Hypoxylon canker or oak decline (*Hypoxylon spp.*)	May-October, peak in July-August	Slow growth. Chlorotic leaves or leaf scorch. Wilting of foliage. "Flagging" of brown foliage. Dieback of branches and major limbs. Corky outer bark sloughs, exposing smooth, tan to silver-gray stromata. Old stromata loses its silvery surface and appears black. Only infects stressed trees.	Remove infected trees because it can spread via spores and root grafts with adjacent trees.
Rust (*Cronartium quercum* causes pine-oak gall rust, *C. quercum f. sp. fusiforme* causes fusiform rust on pines)	May-July, peak in June-July	Small yellow spots with brown centers on the upper leaf surface. Hair-like brown telia (spore tendrils) on the leaf underside.	Disease is insignificant on oaks. Damage is primarily on the alternate host (two- or three-needled pines).
Oak wilt (*Ceratocystis fagacearum*)	May-October, peak in June	Leaves become chlorotic or bronze along leaf veins, often with leaf tip necrosis. Diseased trees defoliate and show progressive dieback of twigs and branches. Affected trees may wilt in late spring to late summer. Disease spreads primarily through roots grafts and secondly by beetles.	Remove wilting or recently wilted trees. Mechanical barriers using a vibratory plow can break up root grafts. Avoid wounding or pruning trees when beetles are active, typically April-June. Fungicide injections may reduce disease.
Pear (Flowering)			
Fire blight (*Erwinia amylovora*)	April-June, peak in May-June	Young twigs and branches die from the terminal end and appear burned or deep rust colored. Branch may be bent, resembling a shepherd's crook. Dead leaves and fruit remain on branch. Infection occurs in early spring during flowering and is favored by wet conditions.	Prune out dead branches 6 in. below signs of damage. Dip pruning tool in 70% isopropyl (rubbing) alcohol or 10% bleach solution between cuts. Avoid heavy nitrogen fertilization, especially in summer. Avoid splashing water. Plant resistant varieties.
Alternaria leaf spot (*Alternaria alternata*)	May-October, peak in July-August	Small, round, tan to brown spots develop on leaves about mid-summer. Spots often have zonate appearance. Spots may coalesce and blight leaf. Severely infected leaves drop prematurely. Infection favors prolonged leaf wetness, warm temperatures, high humidity, and poor air circulation.	Avoid prolonged leaf wetness and overhead watering. Rake and remove fallen leaf litter. Apply protective fungicide applications in early summer and continue through fall.

continued

TABLE 14.5 Continued

Disease	Seasonal Occurrence	Symptoms	Management Options
Photinia (Red Tip)			
Entomosporium leaf spot (*Entomosporium mespilli*, syn. *Fabrea maculata*)	February-November, peak in March-April	Small reddish leaf spots. As spots age, center is grayish with a dark purple border. Leaf spots may coalesce to cause severe leaf blight. Severely infected leaves drop prematurely. Over time, severely infected plants die. Infection favors poor air circulation and prolonged leaf wetness.	Rake and remove fallen leaf litter. Avoid wetting foliage. Increase plant spacing or selectively prune plants to improve air circulation through the plant canopy. Apply protective fungicides in spring and reapply at 10-14-day intervals.
Pine			
Needle rust (*Coleosporium* spp.)	March-May, peak in April	White shelf-like projections from the needles. Orange rust spores produced within rupture through white covering. Affected needles may drop.	Rarely causes significant decline. Eliminate alternate host (*Asteracea* family; goldenrod). Fungicides not recommended.
Pitch canker (*Fusarium circinatum*)	January-December, peak in August-October	Resin-soaked twigs and cankers on larger branches and trunk. Diseased bark turns dark reddish-brown. Shoot or limb dieback. Needles yellow then brown and remain on tree, glued with crystalline residue.	If canker can be completely removed, this may stop the disease. If it is too extensive, the tree should be removed.
Fusiform rust (*Cronartium quercuum* f.sp. *fusiforme*)	April-May, peak in April	Stem swellings and spindle-shaped galls on branches. Multiple shoots causing witches'-broom growth from galls. Yellow, blister-like protrusions from bark in spring. Pine bark dies, resulting in cankers.	Remove affected branches or trees. Usually causes minor damage to landscape trees. Fungicides generally not recommended.
Needle cast (*Lophodermium pinastri*)	March-May, peak in April-May	Yellowing and shedding of older needles. Do not confuse with fall needle drop.	Weak pathogen. Rarely causes damage in landscape trees. Fungicides generally not recommended.
Pyracantha (Firethorn)			
Fire blight (*Erwinia amylovora*)	April-June, peak in May-June	Young twigs and branches die from the terminal end and appear burned or deep rust colored. Branch may be bent, resembling a shepherd's crook. Dead leaves and fruit remain on the branch. Infection occurs in early spring during flowering and favors wet conditions.	Prune out branches 6 in. below signs of damage. Dip pruning tool in 70% isopropyl (rubbing) alcohol or 10% bleach solution between cuts. Avoid heavy nitrogen fertilization, especially in summer. Avoid splashing water. Plant resistant varieties.

TABLE 14.5 Continued

Disease	Seasonal Occurrence	Symptoms	Management Options
Scab (*Spilocaea pyracanthae*)	April-June	Fruits covered with scabby lesions that turn black. Velvety, olive-green sooty spots form on leaves. Infected leaves turn yellow and fruit and leaves drop prematurely.	Plant scab-resistant varieties. Avoid wetting foliage when watering. Apply fungicide in the spring as leaves emerge.

Rose

Disease	Seasonal Occurrence	Symptoms	Management Options
Black spot (*Diplocarpon rosae*, syn. *Marsonnina rosae*)	January-December, peak in March-June and August-November	Two stages of disease may be present: (a) Black, round to irregular spots with fringed margins mainly on upper leaf surface. Tissue around spots turns yellow. Causes premature defoliation. Infection favors prolonged leaf wetness, poor air circulation, and high humidity. It occurs throughout the growing season. (b) Reddish sunken lesions develop on the young canes or on canes overwintering from the fall. These lesions are the primary source of the spores that initiate leaf infection in the spring.	Use sanitary measures by destroying infected leaves and canes from the previous year. Mulch under plants. Avoid wetting leaves. Prune canes to allow for better air circulation. Begin a fungicide spray program before the disease appears in early spring and continue at 7-10-day intervals throughout the growing season. Plant resistant varieties.
Powdery mildew (*Spaerotheca pannosa* var. *rosae*)	January-December, peak in April-July and November	White to grayish patches appear on the leaves, flowers, and stems. Patches enlarge rapidly and may cover the entire leaf. Affected leaves dry and droop prematurely.	Apply protective fungicides at the first sign of infection and reapply at 10-14-day intervals. Mulch under plants. Remove fallen leaf litter. Increase air circulation around plants.
Downy mildew (*Peronospora sparsa*)	April-June, peak in May	Purple, irregularly shaped lesions develop on the upper leaf surface. Spots often concentrated along veins and midrib. Grayish, fuzzy growth visible on the leaf underside opposite purple leaf spots in wet weather. Infection favors cooler, wet weather. Mostly seen in late spring and sometimes early fall.	Remove affected leaves. Mulch plants and remove fallen leaf litter. Avoid wetting foliage. Apply protective fungicide at first sign of disease and repeat 10-14 days later as label directs.
Rose mosaic virus	May-October	Yellow or white mosaic pattern or patches on the green leaf. Affected leaves may scorch or drop prematurely.	Does not significantly harm plants. No control is necessary. Pruning does not remove the virus from the plant. Symptoms may appear when the plant is stressed.

continued

TABLE 14.5 Continued

Disease	Seasonal Occurrence	Symptoms	Management Options
Stem canker and dieback (*Botryosphaeria, Leptosphaeria, Coniothyrium,* and *Cryptosporella*)	March–October, peak in June–July	Often occurs on the canes at the pruning wound. Young cankers are yellowish or reddish. With age, cankers turn brown, sunken, and cracked. Center turns light gray-brown with dark border. Numerous pucnidia (fruiting structures) develop beneath the upper surface.	There are no fungicides specifically to control stem canker. Keeping plants healthy can help minimize disease development. Avoid wounding plants.
Rust (*Phragmidium spp.*)	April–July, peak in June	Bright orange to rust-colored pustules develop on the underside of leaves. Yellow spots develop on upper side of leaves. Severely infected leaves drop prematurely. Infection most common in early summer during periods of prolonged leaf wetness with warmer day and cooler night temperatures.	Remove fallen leaf litter. Mulch plants. Apply fungicide at first sign of disease and reapply at 10-14-day intervals.
Crown gall (*Agrobacterium tumefaciens*)	March–October	Galls form at the soil line but can also form on branches or roots. Galls are initially white, spherical, and soft but darken with age as the outer cells die.	Purchase and propagate gall-free plants. Avoid wounding plants, especially at the soil line. Disinfect tools with 70% isopropyl (rubbing) alcohol or 10% bleach solution. Remove severely infected plants.

Sycamore

Disease	Seasonal Occurrence	Symptoms	Management Options
Anthracnose (*Apiognomonia veneta*)	April–June, peak in May	Dead twigs and branches have sunken cankers. Bud death followed by new bud formation and death causes witches' broom proliferation of branch ends. Black fungal fruiting structures visible in spring on bark and newly killed twigs. Leaves, especially in lower and inner branches, are blighted in spring, and tan dead areas expand along leaf veins. Large and irregularly shaped areas are killed along the leaf margins and between the veins.	Prune and destroy dead twigs and branches during dormancy, cutting 3-4 in. below the canker. Plant resistant cultivars. Tree injection in the fall before leaf drop can provide some protection.

Glossary

Abdomen – An insect's largest and final body segment, which contains the majority of its organs.

Absorption – The process by which plants take in water and dissolved minerals through their roots. It can also refer to the process of plant pigments taking in light energy.

Accessory bud – A bud that occurs at the base of terminal buds or at the side of axillary buds.

Accessory pigment – A pigment that captures light energy outside of the normal range of chlorophyll and transfers that energy to chlorophyll.

Achene – A small, dry one-seeded fruit that does not open to release the seed.

Acid (reaction of soil) – Soil with a pH of less than 7. Most vegetables grow well at 6.0 to 6.5, which is slightly acidic; some, however, prefer more or less acidity in the soil. The soil pH is lowered by adding sulfur or raised by adding lime.

Action threshold – The number of pests or level of damage that triggers management action.

Active ingredient – The chemical in a pesticide formulation that kills the pest.

Adsorption – The adhesion of gas, liquid, or dissolved solid particles to a surface, leading to an increased concentration of nutrients as ions on a soil surface, including exchangeable cations and anions onto various soils and organic matter.

Adventitious bud – A plant structure arising from an unexpected location, such as a bud in a site other than the apical or axillary position arising from a stem or a leaf.

Aesthetic injury threshold – The highest level of plant damage to appearance due to pests that is acceptable to the grower.

Aggregate fruit – A fruit that develops from a single flower with many pistils on a common receptacle.

Alate – Something, especially an insect, that has wings or winglike structures.

Alkaline (reaction of soil) – Soil with a pH above 7. Soil will become more alkaline by adding lime in significant quantities. Soil will become less alkaline by adding sulfur in significant quantities.

Angiosperm – (Greek for "vessel seed") A plant whose seeds are born within a mature ovary (fruit). Flowering plants belong to this group.

Anion – a negatively charged ion, such as sulfate, phosphate, borate, or nitrate anions.

Annual – A plant whose entire lifecycle is completed in a single growing season. It germinates, grows, flowers, releases seed and dies in less than one year.

Antennae – Sensory organs found on the heads of arthropods such as insects and myriapods.

Anther – The pollen-bearing portion of a stamen.

Antitranspirants – Substances applied to the leaves of plants to slow water loss.

Apex – The tip of a shoot or root.

Apical meristem – The meristem at the tip of a shoot or root. Referred to as the apical or terminal bud in shoots.

Arthropod – An animal with a segmented body, jointed legs, and an exoskeleton.

Axil – The upper angle created where a leaf joins a stem or where a stem joins a branch.

Axillary bud – A lateral bud located in the axil of a leaf.

Bacteria – Simple, single-celled microorganisms surrounded by a cell wall.

Balanced fertilizer – A fertilizer that has the same proportion of nitrogen (N), phosphate (P_2O_5), and potash (K_2O), such as a 10-10-10 or a 20-20-20.

Bark – All of the tissues produced outside of the vascular cambium in a woody stem. Inner bark consists of living phloem that conducts photosynthates. The outer bark consists of dead phloem and serves mostly a protective role.

Basal plate – A compact, fleshy stem at the bottom of a bulb.

Basal rosette – A growth habit where many leaves are closely clustered on a stem with very short internodes near the soil surface

Biennial – A plant which requires two growing seasons to complete its lifecycle. It germinates and grows in the first season and flowers, releases seed, and dies in the second season. Typically overwintering as a basal rosette.

Binomial nomenclature – The international scientific plant naming system using two Latinized names, the genus and the specific epithet, to make a binomial species name.

Biological control – A pest management strategy that relies on using natural enemies, such as predators, parasites, and parasitoids to reduce pest populations.

Biotic disease – A disease caused by living organisms known as pathogens.

Blight – Describes plant diseases whose symptoms include sudden and severe symptoms such as yellowing, browning, spotting, withering, or dying of portions of or an entire plant.

Bolt – The production of a flowering stem on an agricultural or horticultural crop before the crop has been harvested.

Botanical/Plant-derived pesticide – A naturally occurring pesticide derived from plants.

Botany – The study of plants.

Bract – A modified leaf at the base of a flower or inflorescence.

Branch – A stem arising from an axillary bud of another stem.

Broadleaf weed – A type of weed with netlike veins, nodes containing one or more leaves, a branched growth habit, and often showy flowers.

Bud – An undeveloped collection of shoot and/or flower parts comprised of meristematic tissue.

Bud leaf – The arrangement of an emerging new leaf or leaves in a budshoot.

Bulb – An underground storage organ comprised of a highly compressed stem surrounded by fleshy, storage leaves called scales.

Bulblet – An aerial deciduous bud capable of producing a new plant when separated from the original plant.

Calyx – The sepals of a flower collectively.

Cambium – A thick layer of meristematic cells that is responsible for the increase in stem and diameter.

Cane – A woody stem containing pith.

Canker – A localized area of dead bark and underlying wood on twigs, larger branches, and trunks.

Carpel – The female reproductive organ of a flower.

Cation – An ion carrying a positive charge, such as calcium, potassium, magnesium, or ammonium cations.

Cation exchange capacity (CEC) – Soil's capacity to hold onto cations as a storehouse of reserve nutrients. Clays and organic matter have mostly negative charges which can hold onto the nutrient cations and make these available for absorption by plant roots.

Chlorophyll – Green pigment in leaves that is responsible for absorbing light energy needed for photosynthesis.

Chloroplast – A specialized component of certain cells; contains chlorophyll and is responsible for photosynthesis.

Clay – Soil particles <0.002 mm in diameter. The smallest type of soil particles. Clays are a textural class of soils.

Cold stratification – The process of exposing seeds to cold, moist conditions to aid in germination.

Colloid – A mixture in which one substance consisting of microscopically dispersed insoluble particles is dispersed in another. Soil colloids are the smallest particles in soil. Made of clay and organic matter, they are responsible for the soil's chemical and physical properties.

Complete fertilizer – A fertilizer that contains nitrogen, phosphorus, and potassium.

Composite inflorescence – A tight cluster of many small flowers typically devoted to attracting pollinators.

Compost – The useable end product of the decomposition process of organic matter. It has an earthy smell, and when added to soils, acts as a soil builder to improve the structure and fertility of soils.

Compound leaf – A single leaf in which the blade is divided into multiple, distinct leaflets arising from the same petiole.

Contact pesticide – Pesticides that must come into direct contact with pests to be effective.

Contractile root – A specialized root that extends and contracts to keep a bulb, corm, or rhizome at a certain level in the ground.

Cool-season turfgrass – A turfgrass best adapted for growth in cooler regions; ryegrasses, fescues, bluegrasses.

Core aeration/aerification – The practice of physically removing cores of soil and leaving holes or cavities in a lawn.

Corm – An underground storage organ comprised of a solid, thickened, compressed stem.

Cortex – The primary tissue of a stem or root immediately to the inside of the epidermis.

Corymb – An inflorescence of individual florets whose stalks are arranged at random along the peduncle.

Cotyledon – The first leaf that appears on a seedling and differs from the characteristic leaves of the plant. Also known as a "seed leaf".

Cover crop – A crop grown to help prevent weeds and erosion and to add organic matter to the soil. They are often called green manure crops.

Crown (herbaceous plants) – A collection of short stems that have leaves and flowers on short internodes.

Crown (woody plants) – The above ground portion of a tree or shrub.

Cultivar (cultivated variety) – A taxonomic group of plants, originally developed and now maintained under cultivation, that are horticulturally significant and are clearly distinguished by a characteristic that is retained when plants are propagated.

Cuticle – A thin waxy or varnish-like layer that covers the epidermis of above-ground parts (e.g. stems and leaves) formed of cutin and wax.

Cyme – A broad, flat-topped inflorescence.

Day-neutral plants – Plants that produce flowers regardless of day length.

Deciduous – Plants that shed all of their leaves in one season.

Dehiscent fruit – A fruit that splits open along a defined suture or seam at maturity.

Dicot – An angiosperm containing two cotyledons, a continuous vascular system, net-veined leaves, and sepals/petals numbering four, five, or multiples thereof in a single flower.

Dioecious – (Greek for "two houses") Plants with staminate and pistillate flowers on separate plants.

Disc flowers – The central flowers in a composite inflorescence.

Disorder – Occurrences that prohibit a plant from thriving that are caused by nonliving factors.

Dormant oil – A type of biorational pesticide consisting of an oil applied to woody plants during dormant stages of growth.

Drip irrigation – A type of irrigation that routes water through tubing with emitters that are placed on the ground alongside plants.

Drip line – The outermost circumference of a tree's canopy, from which water drips on the ground.

Drop-type spreader – A tool that acts by dropping fertilizer through a series of small openings at the base of a hopper. Best used to fertilize small areas or for precise applications.

Drupe – A fleshy fruit containing a stony endocarp.

Ecology – The study of the relationship between living organisms and their environments.

Economic threshold – The level at which the monetary losses of damage from pests, if untreated, would exceed the cost of controlling the pest.

Embryo – The part of a seed or bud that contains the earliest forms of a plant's roots, stem, and leaves.

Endodermis – A layer of cells that regulate the flow of water and nutrients entering a root.

Endosperm – The part of a seed which stores food for a developing plant embryo.

Epicotyl – The region of an embryo stem above the cotyledon.

Epidermis – The outermost layer of cells on all the primary parts of a plant: stem, roots, leaves, flower, fruit, and seeds.

Evergreen – A woody perennial plant that does not lose all of its leaves at one time but sheds older leaves periodically.

Exoskeleton – A hard outer covering that protects and supports the body of some animals.

Fairy ring – A naturally occurring ring or arc of mushrooms.

Fertilizer analysis – Numbers representing the percentages of nitrogen (N), phosphate (P2O5), and potash (K2O) that are available from the bag of fertilizer.

Fertilizer filler – The additional material added to a bag of fertilizer besides the N, P2O5, K2O, and micronutrients. Typically, this material is either clay or dolomitic limestone.

Fibrous root system – A system characterized by long, branching roots growing from a stem.

Field-grown – A tree or plant that is grown in open soil, rather than in a nursery container.

Filament – The stalk of a stamen that holds up the anther.

Flower – The seed-bearing part of a plant, consisting of reproductive organs that are typically surrounded by a brightly colored corolla (petals) and a green calyx (sepals).

Friction loss – The loss of energy or pressure due to the resistance created by pipe walls as water flows through them.

Fruit – A mature, ripened ovary.

Generation – One life cycle lasting from the egg stage to the production of an egg by an adult insect.

Genetics – The study of genes and their expression and inheritance.

Genus (pl. genera) – A biological classification unit representing a group of closely related organisms. It is the first term used in an organism's two-part scientific name.

Germination – The start or resumption of growth of a seed, embryo, or spore including the pollen grain on a stigma.

Grassy weeds – True grasses with hollow, rounded stems and hard, closed nodes.

Ground cover – Vigorous, low-growing, ground-hugging herbaceous and woody plants.

Guard cells – Specialized cells that surround a stoma and control its opening and closing.

Gymnosperm – (Greek for "naked seed") Plant with seeds not enclosed in an ovary. Conifers, cycads, and ginkgo belong to this group.

Gypsum – The common name for calcium sulfate, also called landplaster, and is used as a source of calcium and sulfur. Gypsum does not lower or raise the soil pH.

Half-hardy/cool-season annual – Annuals that can tolerate freezing temperatures above 26°F and that grow best in cool weather.

Hardy – A plant able to withstand cold temperatures. Usually categorized in accordance with USDA Plant Hardiness Zones.

Herbaceous – A non-woody plant.

Herbicide – A chemical agent used to kill or inhibit the growth of unwanted plants.

Hesperidium – A fruit with sectioned pulp inside a separable rind (such as a citrus fruit).

Horticultural oil – A type of biorational pesticide consisting of oils that are applied to plants to smother pests.

Horticulture – The art and science of the intensive cultivation and use of fruits, vegetables, ornamentals, herbs and other high value, often perishable specialty crops.

Humus – Organic matter that is completely decomposed and is brown or black. It is a complex colloid, which has a very high cation exchange capacity (CEC) and holds relatively large amounts of water. It gives soil a dark color.

Hybrid – A plant that is the result of cross-pollinating two different plant species or varieties.

Hypha (pl., **Hyphae**) – A single threadlike structure that makes up the body of a fungus.

Hypocotyl – The part of a stem of an embryo plant beneath the cotyledons and directly above the root.

Immobilization – The process by which soil microorganisms use any available nitrogen as they break down materials with a high C:N ratio, such as dried leaves or straw. They then absorb the nitrogen for their growth and reproduction, and thus reduce the amount of nitrogen available to plants.

Immune – A term designating that a plant cannot be infected by a particular disease.

Included bark – A branch defect that occurs when two or more tree stems grow closely together in a V-shape.

Incomplete fertilizer – A fertilizer formulation lacking one or more of the primary nutrients: N, P or K, eg., calcium nitrate (15.5-0-0), triple super phosphate (0-46-0), or a centipedegrass fertilizer (15-0-15).

Indehiscent fruit – A fruit that does not split open when ripe.

Inert ingredient – A substance added to a product that does not actively contribute to that product's function, but instead helps to make the product easier or safer to formulate or apply.

Infiltration capacity – The maximum rate at which a particular soil can accept water.

Infiltration rate – The rate at which soil accepts water during a particular irrigation or rainfall event.

Inflorescence – A cluster of flowers arising from a single shoot.

Inorganic nitrogen – Nitrate (NO_3^-) and ammonium nitrogen (NH_4^+) are the predominant forms of inorganic nitrogen found in fertilizers. These forms are found in calcium nitrate, ammonium sulfate, ammonium nitrate, and are present in most commercial fertilizers.

Inorganic pesticide – A pesticide comprised of minerals such as copper, boron, cryolite, lead, sulfur, tin, and zinc.

Insecticidal soap – A type of biorational pesticide derived from the salts of fatty acids and used to control soft-bodied insects.

Intercalary meristem – An additional meristem found in grasses that supports regeneration of leafy growth.

Internode – The space between nodes on a stem.

Interstem – A length of shoot that is grafted between scion and rootstock.

Invasive species – A species that is nonnative to the ecosystem whose introduction causes or is likely to cause economic or environmental harm.

Iron chlorosis – The symptom of insufficient iron taken up by a plant, which appears as interveinal chlorosis of newer foliage. This means that the leaf blades become yellow, yet the veins remain green. A higher pH often makes soil iron become less available to the plant.

Landscape fabrics/geotextiles – Synthetic mulch sheeting used to suppress weeds.

Latent bud – A dormant bud that is capable of growth and development.

Lateral bud – A smaller bud on the side of a stem that is responsible for the growth of leaves, flowers and side branches. Also called axillary buds.

Lateral meristem – A region of cell division located along the length of a stem or root. Examples included the vascular and cork cambiums.

Layering – A type of vegetative propagation that involves manipulating a stem or branch to encourage new root development while it remains attached to the parent plant.

Leaching – The loss of water-soluble plant nutrients from the soil due to rain and irrigation.

Leaf blade – The broad, sheet-like region of a leaf that intercepts and absorbs light energy.

Leaf mold – A compost made primarily of partially decomposed or decayed deciduous tree leaves.

Leaf scorch/marginal leaf burn – The browning of plant tissues, including leaf margins and tips.

Legume – A plant of the Leguminosae (or bean family), with a pea-like fruit pod, and with a root system that is a host to nitrogen-fixing bacteria. These bacteria form nitrogen-fixing nodules on the legume plant roots, and in these nodules, nitrogen gas from the soil air is converted forms that are available to the plant.

Lichen – Plant-like organisms composed of an alga or cyanobacterium and a fungus growing in symbiosis. Not a plant disease.

Ligule – A narrow, strap-shaped membranous scale found on the inner side of a leaf sheath; common to most grasses.

Limestone – A mineral substance that can be added to the soil to increase soil pH. Calcitic limestone contains calcium carbonate, and dolomitic limestone contains both calcium and magnesium carbonates. Limestone is available as pulverized or pelletized.

Long-day plants – Plants that must be exposed to long days (short nights) for flowering to occur. Typically spring- or summer-flowering plants.

Macronutrients – The nutrients needed in large amounts by plants: nitrogen, phosphorous, potassium, magnesium, calcium, and sulfur.

Magnoliid – An angiosperm with primitive features of both monocots and dicots.

Mat – A fine, dense, peat-like layer of soil that provides a poor growth climate for turf roots.

Meristem – Plant tissue in the process of formation; vegetative cells in a state of active division and growth, e.g., those at the apex of growing-stems and roots.

Mesophyll – (Latin for "middle of leaf") Leaf tissue in between the upper and lower epidermis. Responsible for much of the photosynthesis in plant leaves.

Mesophyte – A plant that requires conditions that are neither too wet nor too dry.

Metamorphosis – The change in shape and appearance of an insect from the juvenile to the adult stage.

Microbial insecticide – A type of biopesticide formulated from naturally occurring or genetically altered bacteria, fungi, algae, viruses, or protozoans.

Micronutrients – The essential trace elements or nutrients that are needed in small amounts by plants: iron, manganese, zinc, copper, molybdenum, boron, chlorine, and nickel.

Mineralization – The conversion of an essential elements or nutrients from organic compounds (such as, from plant or animal proteins or amino acids), which are unavailable to plants, to ionic forms (such as, NO_3^- or NH_4^+), which are available to plants.

Mixed fertilizer – A fertilizer that contains two or more of the elements of phosphorous, nitrogen, and potassium.

Monocot – An angiosperm containing one cotyledon, a diffuse vascular system, net-veined leaves, and sepals/petals typically numbering three or multiples of three in a single flower.

Monoecious – (Greek for "one house") Plants with separate staminate and pistillate flowers on the same plant.

Morphology – The study of biological forms and the relationships between their structures.

Mulching mower – A grass-cutting tool designed to cut leaf blades into very small pieces that can fall onto a lawn rather than remaining on top of the grass.

Multiple fruit – A fruit formed by the merging of many independent flowers in a single inflorescence.

Mycelium – A root-like network of thread-like fungal strands that make up the body of a fungus.

Mycorrhizae – The association of plant roots with beneficial fungi that colonize and infect plant roots, and then enhance the uptake of nutrients from the soil.

Nematodes – Microscopic, non-segmented roundworms that can infect and damage plants.

Nonhardy – A plant unable to withstand cold temperatures. Tender.

Node – An area on a stem where a leaf, stem, or flower bud is located.

Nonselective herbicide – A chemical plant control agent that damages or kills all green plants regardless of species.

Oospore – A type of resistant spore produced by water molds.

Organic fertilizer – A natural fertilizer material that has undergone little or no processing. It can include plant, animal, and/or mineral materials. Examples are blood meal, bone meal, cottonseed meal, feather meal, and fish emulsion.

Organic nitrogen – Nitrogen sourced from the decomposition of plant and animal material. It is initially in complex organic forms, such as proteins and amino acids.

Ovary – The swollen basal portion of a pistil; the flower part containing the ovule(s) or seed.

Ovule – The part of the ovary containing one female egg. Following fertilization, the ovule develops into the seed.

Oxidation – The process by which carbohydrates (sugars and starches) are converted into energy.

Panicle – A loose branching cluster of flowers.

Parasite – An organism that lives on or in the body of another living organism and feeds on the host organism during at least one stage of its existence.

Parthenogenesis – A form of asexual reproduction in which an embryo develops from an unfertilized egg.

Pathogen – Living factors that infect plants and cause disease.

Pedicel – The stalk of an individual flower in an inflorescence.

Peduncle – The stalk of a flower.

Pepo – The characteristic fruit of plants in the gourd family, which have a fleshy, many-seeded interior and a hard or firm rind.

Perennial – A plant that lives for two or more growing seasons. May be herbaceous or woody.

Perianth – A collective term for the sepals and petals in a flower.

Pericycle – The meristematic region which gives rise to lateral roots during maturation.

Pesticide – A chemical used to kill, attract, alter the behavior of, or repel a pest.

Petals – The typically highly colored flower parts often used to attract pollinators.

Petiole – The stalk that attaches a leaf to a stem.

Phloem – Photosynthate-conducting tissue.

Phosphorus – One of three major elements necessary for plant growth. It is typically associated with the transformation of energy within a plant.

Photomorphogenesis – The effect of light on plant shape or form. Example: Larger leaves in shade than sun.

Photoperiodism – The effect of day length on plant development.

Photosynthates – The products of photosynthesis; sugars.

Photosynthesis – The conversion of light energy into chemical energy within green plant cells. The production of carbohydrates from water and carbon dioxide in the presence of chlorophyll and sunlight; oxygen is released as a byproduct.

Physiology – The study of plant growth and development.

Phytoplasmas – Specialized bacteria that have no cell wall and can only survive inside plants.

Phytotoxic – Poisonous to plants.

Pistil - The female flower part; consists of a stigma, style, and ovary.

Pistillate – A flower having pistils and no functional stamens; a female flower.

Pith – The center of a stem or root. May be hollow, spongy or chambered.

Plugging – A method of sodding that involves arranging small squares, circles, or blocks of sod at regular intervals.

Plumule – The rudimentary shoot or stem of an embryo plant.

Pollination – The transfer of pollen from an anther to a stigma.

Pome – A fleshy fruit with a tough central core containing seeds.

Postemergence herbicide – A chemical plant control agent that controls only weeds that have emerged from the soil and are actively growing at the time of application.

Potassium – One of three major elements necessary for plant growth. It contributes to a plant's ability to withstand environmental and mechanical stresses.

Pot-bound – A descriptor for a plant that has a root structure featuring many large-diameter woody roots circling the outside of the root ball.

Pot-in-pot – A nursery production system in which plants are grown inside production pots that are themselves placed in permanent in-ground containers.

Power rake – A tool featuring flexible spring steel tines that is used to strip through turf and loosen debris for removal.

Preemergence herbicide – A chemical plant control agent that forms a barrier in the soil to kill weeds shortly after germination, but before emergence.

Primary growth – Growth originating from the apical meristems of shoots and roots resulting in the elongation of stems and roots.

Primary root – The first root of a plant to develop after germination.

Quick-release fertilizer – A fertilizer that includes water soluble nitrogen that is readily available to plants after a short response period. The most common quick-release nitrogen sources are ammonium nitrate, urea, ammonium sulfate, and calcium nitrate.

Quiescent seed – A seed that has entered a resting phase where the embryo stops growing and cell division slows.

Raceme – An indeterminate inflorescence featuring florets with short stalks attached to the main stem.

Radicle – The first root to arise from a seed. The "seed root."

Rain sensor – A device, activated by rainfall, that deactivates irrigation systems during rainfall events to conserve water.

Receptacle – The enlarged tip of a pedicel where floral structures are attached.

Reel mower – A grass-cutting tool featuring scissor-like blades that produces a clean, even cut.

Renovation – The process of improving a turfgrass stand without removing previous turfgrass and starting from scratch.

Resistant – A term designating that a plant does not readily become diseased by a particular pathogen.

Respiration – Controlled oxidation of carbohydrates within a living cell. It releases energy that is used for growth and other processes. Respiration occurs in all living cells.

Rhizome – A specialized stem, usually horizontal in position at or just below the soil surface which differs from a root by the presence of nodes and internodes and sometimes buds.

Rhizoplane – The region composed primarily of the plant root surface, along with very closely adjacent soil. Many microorganisms attach themselves to the surface of the roots to gain nutrients.

Rhizosphere – The thin layer of soil immediately surrounding plant roots. Typically possesses large numbers of microorganisms because of nutrients that are secreted or leak from plant roots.

Root flare – The point at which a tree's main roots attach to its trunk.

Root zone – A roughly circular area extending approximately 1.5x as far as a tree's branch spread that encompasses the soil in which most of its roots are found.

Rooting hormone – A chemical used in propagation that stimulates root growth on plant cuttings.

Rotary mower – A grass-cutting tool featuring a spinning blade that cuts quickly, but less precisely than other mowing tools.

Rotary/cyclone spreader – A tool that acts by using a rotating disc to distribute fertilizer or pesticide in a semi-circular pattern over a set area.

Runoff – Water that leaves a landscape due to exceeding the infiltration capacity of soil.

Sand – A loose granular material that results from the disintegration of rocks. Consists of particles smaller than gravel, but coarser than silt. The diameter of the particles ranges from 0.0625 to 2 mm.

Saprophyte – An organism that obtains nutrients the decomposition of dead or decaying organic material.

Scale (insect) – Small herbivorous insects covered by a protective waxy shell.

Scale (bulb) – Modified leaves that form the outer covering of certain bulbs.

Scion – A portion of a plant graft consisting of a shoot with wood, bark, and dormant buds. The scion will become the top of the grafted plant.

Sclerotia – Hard reproductive structures produced by some fungi.

Secondary growth – Growth originating from the lateral meristems of shoots and roots resulting in increased girth of stems and roots.

Sedges – Monocots characterized by solid, triangular stems without nodes.

Seed – A mature ovule containing an embryo and stored food.

Seed coat – A dry outer covering that protects a seed from disease and insects.

Seed stratification – A process by which seeds are pre-treated to simulate natural soil conditions over-winter and initiate germination.

Selective herbicide – A chemical plant control agent that targets specific plants without harming or seriously affecting others.

Self-cleaning plants – Cultivars that drop dead leaves on their own without additional assistance.

Semievergreen – A plant that carries leaves for most of the year.

Sepals – The outer, often green flower parts that usually surround the petals of flowers. Collectively, the sepals are known as the calyx.

Sexual propagation – A plant reproduction method that involves the combining of genetic material of two parent plants via pollination and fertilization; reproduction of plants by seeds.

Shoots – Collective term for stems and their leaves.

Short-day plants – Plants that flower in response to short days (long nights). Typically bloom in autumn.

Shrub – A woody perennial plant typically with many stems emerging from a single point or crown.

Sign – Part or product of a disease-causing agent or insect present in, on, or near an affected plant.

Slime mold – A simple saprophyte that spreads via spores.

Slow-release fertilizer – A fertilizer that includes a source of nitrogen that releases into soil over an extended period of time. The most common slow-release nitrogen sources are urea formaldehyde, methylene ureas, sulfur-coated urea, isobutylidene diurea, natural organics, and activated sewer sludge.

Soil solarization – A natural method of soil control that uses the sun's heat to kill unwanted plants, disease-causing organisms, and nematodes.

Sooty mold – A fungal organism that appears as a black, sooty coating on plants, fruit, and other surfaces.

Spadix – A densely flowered structure surrounded by a spathe.

Species (pl. species) – Closely related plants of the same genus that freely interbreed. The genus and specific epithet together comprise the species name.

Specific epithet – The second term in a scientific name, which identifies the species within a genus.

Spike – An inflorescence in which many individual flowers or stemless florets are attached to an elongated flower stem.

Sporangia – A structure in which spores are produced.

Spores – A reproductive unit common to fungi and saprophytes that is capable of germination and growth.

Spray head – A device that sprays a pattern of water over an area.

Spurs – Short, stubby stems, such as the branches of trees.

Stamen – The male flower part; consists of an anther and a supporting filament.

Staminate – A flower having stamens and no functional pistils; a male flower.

Stigma – The top of a flower's pistil that receives pollen.

Stipule – A leaf-like appendage at the base of a petiole, often encircling the stem.

Stolon – Also called a runner, this horizontal or trailing stem that gives rise to new shoots.

Stolonizing – A type of turfgrass planting that involves broadcasting stolons over a soil surface and covering the stolons by topdressing or pressing them into the soil.

Stoma (pl. stomates, stomata) – Tiny openings in the epidermis that allow water, oxygen, and carbon dioxide to pass into and out of a plant.

String mower – A grass-cutting tool featuring a monofilament line that rotates at a high speed to cut cleanly through turfgrass; most often used for trimming, edging, and cutting hard-to-mow areas.

Style – The part of the female flower that connects the stigma to the ovary. Pollen travels down the style to reach the ovary, where fertilization occurs.

Subsurface injection – The process of injecting fertilizer 4-8 inches below a soil surface to more directly access fibrous root systems.

Sucker – An adventitious shoot arising from the roots of some plants.

Summer/warm-season annual – Annuals that cannot tolerate freezing temperatures and typically grow best in warm weather.

Susceptible – A term designating that a plant readily becomes diseased by a particular pathogen.

Symptom – A characteristic of a plant that indicates that it is diseased.

Synthetic organic pesticide – A pesticide comprised of organic material that is engineered and formulated by humans.

Systemic herbicide – A chemical plant control agent that moves throughout a plant's vascular system to thoroughly weaken or kill unwanted plants.

Taproot system – A system characterized by a single, thick primary root with short secondary roots.

Taxonomy – The branch of science concerned with the classification and naming of things.

Tensiometer – A device used to measure the level of moisture in soil.

Tepals – Perianth parts when sepals and petals are not clearly distinguishable.

Texture – A term used to describe the leaf or blade width of turfgrasses.

Thatch – A layer of partially decomposed plant material in turfgrass that builds up on the surface of the soil.

Thermoperiod – Daily change in temperature; difference in day and night temperatures.

Tolerant – A term designating that a plant may become diseased by a particular pathogen, but that its yield is not severely affected.

Topdressing – The application of a thin layer of sand, compost, or another media to an area of turfgrass.

Topworking – A grafting method used to change cultivars on established trees.

Transpiration – The evaporative loss of water from a plant. Typically occurs through stomata. Drives water and nutrient uptake and transport from the soil up to the plant leaves.

Tree – A large, woody perennial plant with a definite trunk and distinct crown.

Trifoliate – Having three leaves. May also be used to describe a compound leaf with three leaflets.

True bulb – A bulb comprised of a basal plate and scales. Corms, tubers, and rhizomes are often called "bulbs" but are not botanically a true bulb.

Trunk – The main stem of a woody plant.

Tuber – An underground storage organ comprised of an enlarged, fleshy underground stem, such as a potato.

Tuberous root – A root consisting of enlarged, fleshy tissue that has been modified to store food, such as a sweet potato.

Tunicate – A type of bulb covered in a papery skin that protects underlying fleshy scales.

Twig – Woody stem in the current or previous year's growth.

Umbel – A flower cluster in which stalks of nearly equal length spring from a common center.

Variety – A naturally occurring population of individuals comprising a subdivision of a species. Although technically different, *variety* and *cultivar* are often used interchangeably.

Vascular tissues – Conductive tissue (xylem and phloem) for transporting water, minerals, and the products of photosynthesis.

Vector – Insects or other organisms that transmit infectious diseases to plants, animals, and humans.

Vegetative (Asexual) Propagation – A plant reproduction method that uses parts of a parent plant to create a genetically identical new plant.

Venation – The arrangement of veins in a leaf blade.

Vertical mower – A lawn care tool with vertical blades that cuts into the thatch on a lawn to remove it.

Virus – Simple organisms consisting of a strand of nucleic acid surrounded by a protein coat.

Warm-season turfgrass – A turfgrass best adapted for growth in warmer regions; St. Augustinegrass, bermudagrass, centipedegrass, zoysiagrass.

Wavelength – The length of light waves measured in nanometers (nm). The smaller the wavelength the higher the light energy. Visible light falls within the range of 400 to 700 nm.

"Weed 'n feed" – A descriptor for a subset of preemergence herbicides formulated with dry fertilizers to both control unwanted plants and fertilize those that remain.

Woody – A perennial plant that has undergone secondary growth and typically has permanent aboveground stems.

Woundwood – Response tissue that grows quickly to seal a pruning cut on a tree.

Xylem – Vascular tissue primarily responsible for transporting water and mineral nutrients from the roots to the shoots; the primary component of wood in trees.

Zygote – A single cell resulting from the fertilization of an egg by a sperm and capable of developing into an embryo.

www.ingramcontent.com/pod-product-compliance
Lightning Source LLC
Chambersburg PA
CBHW042225010526
44111CB00046B/2966